Zondervan Illustrated Bible Backgrounds Commentary

ABOUT THE AUTHORS

General Editor, Ephesians; Colossians:

Clinton E. Arnold (Ph.D., University of Aberdeen), professor and chairman, department of New Testament, Talbot School of Theology, Biola University, Los Angeles, California

Romans:

Douglas J. Moo (Ph.D., University of St. Andrews), Blanchard professor of New Testament, Wheaton College Graduate School, Wheaton, Illinois

1 Corinthians:

David W. J. Gill (D.Phil., University of Oxford), Sub-dean of the faculty of arts and social studies and senior lecturer, Department of classics and ancient history, University of Wales Swansea, United Kingdom

2 Corinthians

Moyer V. Hubbard (D.Phil., University of Oxford), assistant professor of New Testament, Talbot School of Theology, Biola University, Los Angeles, California

Galatians:

Ralph P. Martin (Ph.D. University of London, King's College), distinguished scholar in residence, Fuller Theological Seminary, Haggard School of Theology, Azusa Pacific University, Logos Evangelical Seminary, El Monte, California; *Julie L. Wu* (Ph.D. Fuller Theological Seminary), vice president and professor of New Testament, China Bible Seminary, Hong Kong, China.

Philippians:

Frank Thielman (Ph.D., Duke University), Presbyterian professor of divinity, Beeson Divinity School, Samford University, Birmingham, Alabama

1 & 2 Thessalonians:

Jeffrey A. D. Weima (Ph.D., University of Toronto), professor of New Testament, Calvin Theological Seminary, Grand Rapids, Michigan

1 & 2 Timothy; Titus; Philemon:

S. M. Baugh (Ph.D., University of California, Irvine), associate professor of New Testament, Westminster Theological Seminary in California, Escondido, California

Volume **3**

Romans to Philemon

Zondervan Illustrated Bible Backgrounds Commentary

Clinton E. Arnold
GENERAL EDITOR

ZONDERVAN™

GRAND RAPIDS, MICHIGAN 49530

ZONDERVAN™

Zondervan Illustrated Bible Backgrounds Commentary: Volume 3, *Romans to Philemon*
Romans—Copyright © 2002 by Douglas J. Moo
1 Corinthians—Copyright © 2002 by David Gill
2 Corinthians—Copyright © 2002 by Moyer Hubbard
Galatians—Copyright © 2002 by Ralph P. Martin and Julie Wu
Ephesians and Colossians—Copyright © 2002 by Clinton E. Arnold
Philippians—Copyright © 2002 by Frank S. Thielman
1 and 2 Thessalonians—Copyright © 2002 by Jeffrey A. D. Weima
1 and 2 Timothy, Titus, and Philemon—Copyright © 2002 by Stephen M. Baugh

Requests for information should be addressed to:

Zondervan, *Grand Rapids, Michigan 49530*

Library of Congress Cataloging-in-Publication Data
Zondervan illustrated Bible backgrounds commentary / Clinton E. Arnold, general editor.
p.cm.
Includes bibliographical references.
Contents: v. 1. Matthew, Mark, Luke—2. John, Acts—v. 3. Romans to Philemon—
v. 4. Hebrews to Revelation.
ISBN 0-310-21806-3 (v. 1)—ISBN 0-310-21807-1 (v. 2)—ISBN 0-310-21808-X (v. 3)—
ISBN 0-310-21809-8 (v. 4)
1. Bible. N.T.—Commentaries.   I. Arnold, Clinton E.
BS2341.52.Z66 2001
225.7—dc21   2001046801
                                                                                CIP

Printed in China

Interior design by Sherri L. Hoffman

02 03 04 05 06 07 08 /❖ HK/ 10 9 8 7 6 5 4 3 2 1

CONTENTS

INTRODUCTION

All readers of the Bible have a tendency to view what it says it through their own culture and life circumstances. This can happen almost subconsiously as we read the pages of the text.

When most people in the church read about the thief on the cross, for instance, they immediately think of a burglar that held up a store or broke into a home. They may be rather shocked to find out that the guy was actually a Jewish revolutionary figure who was part of a growing movement in Palestine eager to throw off Roman rule.

It also comes as something of a surprise to contemporary Christians that "cursing" in the New Testament era had little or nothing to do with cussing somebody out. It had far more to do with the invocation of spirits to cause someone harm.

No doubt there is a need in the church for learning more about the world of the New Testament to avoid erroneous interpretations of the text of Scripture. But relevant historical and cultural insights also provide an added dimension of perspective to the words of the Bible. This kind of information often functions in the same way as watching a movie in color rather than in black and white. Finding out, for instance, how Paul compared Christ's victory on the cross to a joyous celebration parade in honor of a Roman general after winning an extraordinary battle brings does indeed magnify the profundity and implications of Jesus' work on the cross. Discovering that the factions at Corinth ("I follow Paul . . . I follow Apollos . . .") had plenty of precedent in the local cults ("I follow Aphrodite; I follow Apollo . . .") helps us understand the "why" of a particular problem. Learning about the water supply from the springs of Hierapolis that flowed into Laodicea as "lukewarm" water enables us to appreciate the relevance of the metaphor Jesus used when he addressed the spiritual laxity of this church.

My sense is that most Christians are eager to learn more about the real life setting of the New Testament. In the preaching and teaching of the Bible in the church, congregants are always grateful when they learn something of the background and historical context of the text. It not only helps them understand the text more accurately, but often enables them to identify with the people and circumstances of the Bible. I have been asked on countless occasions by Christians, "Where can I get access to good historical background information about this passage?" Earnest Christians are hungry for information that makes their Bibles come alive.

The stimulus for this commentary came from the church and the aim is to serve the church. The contributors to this series have sought to provide illuminating and interesting historical/cultural background information. The intent was to draw upon relevant papyri, inscriptions, archaeological discoveries, and the numerous studies of Judaism, Roman culture, Hellenism, and other features of the world of the New Testament and to make the results accessible to people in the church. We recognize that some readers of the commentary will want to go further, and so the sources of the information have been carefully documented in endnotes.

The written information has been supplemented with hundreds of photographs, maps, charts, artwork, and other graphics that help the reader better understand the world of the New Testament. Each of the writers was given an opportunity to dream up a "wish list" of illustrations that he thought would help to illustrate the passages in the New Testament book for which he was writing commentary. Although we were not able to obtain everything they were looking for, we came close.

The team of commentators are writing for the benefit of the broad array of Christians who simply want to better understand their Bibles from the vantage point of the historical context. This is an installment in a new genre of "Bible background" commentaries that was kicked off by Craig Keener's fine volume. Consequently, this is not an "exegetical" commentary that provides linguistic insight and background into Greek constructions and verb tenses. Neither is this work an "expository" commentary that provides a verse-by-verse exposition of the text; for in-depth philological or theological insight, readers will need to have other more specialized or comprehensive commentaries available. Nor is this an "historical-critical" commentary, although the contributors are all scholars and have already made substantial academic contributions on the New Testament books they are writing on for this set. The team intentionally does not engage all of the issues that are discussed in the scholarly guild.

Rather, our goal is to offer a reading and interpretation of the text informed by what we regard as the most relevant historical information. For many in the church, this commentary will serve as an important entry point into the interpretation and appreciation of the text. For other more serious students of the Word, these volumes will provide an important supplement to many of the fine exegetical, expository, and critical available.

The contributors represent a group of scholars who embrace the Bible as the Word of God and believe that the message of its pages has life-changing relevance for faith and practice today. Accordingly, we offer "Reflections" on the relevance of the Scripture to life for every chapter of the New Testament.

I pray that this commentary brings you both delight and insight in digging deeper into the Word of God.

Clinton E. Arnold
General Editor

LIST OF SIDEBARS

Romans

1 Corinthians

2 Corinthians

Galatians

Ephesians

Philippians

Titus

Philemon

LIST OF CHARTS

INDEX OF PHOTOS AND MAPS

ABBREVIATIONS

1. Books of the Bible and Apocrypha

1 Chron.	1 Chronicles	Hab.	Habakkuk
2 Chron.	2 Chronicles	Hag.	Haggai
1 Cor.	1 Corinthians	Heb.	Hebrews
2 Cor.	2 Corinthians	Hos.	Hosea
1 Esd.	1 Esdras	Isa.	Isaiah
2 Esd.	2 Esdras	James	James
1 John	1 John	Jer.	Jeremiah
2 John	2 John	Job	Job
3 John	3 John	Joel	Joel
1 Kings	1 Kings	John	John
2 Kings	2 Kings	Jonah	Jonah
1 Macc.	1 Maccabees	Josh.	Joshua
2 Macc.	2 Maccabees	Jude	Jude
1 Peter	1 Peter	Judg.	Judges
2 Peter	2 Peter	Judith	Judith
1 Sam.	1 Samuel	Lam.	Lamentations
2 Sam.	2 Samuel	Lev.	Leviticus
1 Thess.	1 Thessalonians	Luke	Luke
2 Thess.	2 Thessalonians	Mal.	Malachi
1 Tim.	1 Timothy	Mark	Mark
2 Tim.	2 Timothy	Matt.	Matthew
Acts	Acts	Mic.	Micah
Amos	Amos	Nah.	Nahum
Bar.	Baruch	Neh.	Nehemiah
Bel	Bel and the Dragon	Num.	Numbers
Col.	Colossians	Obad.	Obadiah
Dan.	Daniel	Phil.	Philippians
Deut.	Deuteronomy	Philem.	Philemon
Eccl.	Ecclesiastes	Pr. Man.	Prayer of Manassah
Ep. Jer.	Epistle of Jeremiah	Prov.	Proverbs
Eph.	Ephesians	Ps.	Psalm
Est.	Esther	Rest. of Est.	The Rest of Esther
Ezek.	Ezekiel	Rev.	Revelation
Ex.	Exodus	Rom.	Romans
Ezra	Ezra	Ruth	Ruth
Gal.	Galatians	S. of III Ch.	The Song of the Three Holy Children
Gen.	Genesis	Sir.	Sirach/Ecclesiasticus
		Song	Song of Songs

Sus.	Susanna
Titus	Titus
Tobit	Tobit
Wisd. Sol.	The Wisdom of Solomon
Zech.	Zechariah
Zeph.	Zephaniah

2. Old and New Testament Pseudepigrapha and Rabbinic Literature

Individual tractates of rabbinic literature follow the abbreviations of the *SBL Handbook of Style*, pp. 79–80. Qumran documents follow standard Dead Sea Scroll conventions.

2 Bar.	2 Baruch
3 Bar.	3 Baruch
4 Bar.	4 Baruch
1 En.	1 Enoch
2 En.	2 Enoch
3 En.	3 Enoch
4 Ezra	4 Ezra
3 Macc.	3 Maccabees
4 Macc.	4 Maccabees
5 Macc.	5 Maccabees
Acts Phil.	Acts of Philip
Acts Pet.	Acts of Peter and the 12 Apostles
Apoc. Elijah	Apocalypse of Elijah
As. Mos.	Assumption of Moses
b.	Babylonian Talmud (+ tractate)
Gos. Thom.	Gospel of Thomas
Jos. Asen.	Joseph and Aseneth
Jub.	Jubilees
Let. Aris.	Letter of Aristeas
m.	Mishnah (+ tractate)
Mek.	Mekilta
Midr.	Midrash I (+ biblical book)
Odes Sol.	Odes of Solomon
Pesiq. Rab.	Pesiqta Rabbati
Pirqe. R. El.	Pirqe Rabbi Eliezer
Pss. Sol.	Psalms of Solomon
Rab.	Rabbah (+biblical book); (e.g., Gen. Rab.=Genesis Rabbah)

S. ᶜOlam Rab.	Seder ᶜOlam Rabbah
Sem.	Semahot
Sib. Or.	Sibylline Oracles
T. Ab.	Testament of Abraham
T. Adam	Testament of Adam
T. Ash.	Testament of Asher
T. Benj.	Testament of Benjamin
T. Dan	Testament of Dan
T. Gad	Testament of Gad
T. Hez.	Testament of Hezekiah
T. Isaac	Testament of Isaac
T. Iss.	Testament of Issachar
T. Jac.	Testament of Jacob
T. Job	Testament of Job
T. Jos.	Testament of Joseph
T. Jud.	Testament of Judah
T. Levi	Testament of Levi
T. Mos.	Testament of Moses
T. Naph.	Testament of Naphtali
T. Reu.	Testament of Reuben
T. Sim.	Testament of Simeon
T. Sol.	Testament of Solomon
T. Zeb.	Testament of Zebulum
Tanh.	Tanhuma
Tg. Isa.	Targum of Isaiah
Tg. Lam.	Targum of Lamentations
Tg. Neof.	Targum Neofiti
Tg. Onq.	Targum Onqelos
Tg. Ps.-J.	Targum Pseudo-Jonathan
y.	Jerusalem Talmud (+ tractate)

3. Classical Historians

For an extended list of classical historians and church fathers, see *SBL Handbook of Style*, pp. 84–87. For many works of classical antiquity, the abbreviations have been subjected to the author's discretion; the names of these works should be obvious upon consulting entries of the classical writers in classical dictionaries or encyclopedias.

Eusebius

Eccl. Hist.	Ecclesiastical History

Josephus

Ag. Ap.	Against Apion
Ant.	Jewish Antiquities
J.W.	Jewish War
Life	The Life

Philo

Abraham	On the Life of Abraham
Agriculture	On Agriculture
Alleg. Interp	Allegorical Interpretation
Animals	Whether Animals Have Reason
Cherubim	On the Cherubim
Confusion	On the Confusion of Thomas
Contempl. Life	On the Contemplative Life
Creation	On the Creation of the World
Curses	On Curses
Decalogue	On the Decalogue
Dreams	On Dreams
Drunkenness	On Drunkenness
Embassy	On the Embassy to Gaius
Eternity	On the Eternity of the World
Flaccus	Against Flaccus
Flight	On Flight and Finding
Giants	On Giants
God	On God
Heir	Who Is the Heir?
Hypothetica	Hypothetica
Joseph	On the Life of Joseph
Migration	On the Migration of Abraham
Moses	On the Life of Moses
Names	On the Change of Names
Person	That Every Good Person Is Free
Planting	On Planting
Posterity	On the Posterity of Cain
Prelim. Studies	On the Preliminary Studies
Providence	On Providence
QE	Questions and Answers on Exodus
QG	Questions and Answers on Genesis
Rewards	On Rewards and Punishments
Sacrifices	On the Sacrifices of Cain and Abel
Sobriety	On Sobriety
Spec. Laws	On the Special Laws
Unchangeable	That God Is Unchangeable
Virtues	On the Virtues
Worse	That the Worse Attacks the Better

Apostolic Fathers

1 Clem.	First Letter of Clement
Barn.	Epistle of Barnabas
Clem. Hom.	Ancient Homily of Clement (also called 2 Clement)
Did.	Didache
Herm. Vis.; Sim.	Shepherd of Hermas, Visions; Similitudes
Ignatius	Epistles of Ignatius (followed by the letter's name)
Mart. Pol.	Martyrdom of Polycarp

4. Modern Abbreviations

AASOR	Annual of the American Schools of Oriental Research
AB	Anchor Bible
ABD	Anchor Bible Dictionary
ABRL	Anchor Bible Reference Library
AGJU	Arbeiten zur Geschichte des antiken Judentums und des Urchristentums
AH	Agricultural History
ALGHJ	Arbeiten zur Literatur und Geschichte des Hellenistischen Judentums
AnBib	Analecta biblica
ANRW	Aufstieg und Niedergang der römischen Welt

ANTC	Abingdon New Testament Commentaries	BSV	Biblical Social Values
		BT	*The Bible Translator*
BAGD	Bauer, W., W. F. Arndt, F. W. Gingrich, and F. W. Danker. *Greek-English Lexicon of the New Testament and Other Early Christina Literature* (2d. ed.)	BTB	*Biblical Theology Bulletin*
		BZ	*Biblische Zeitschrift*
		CBQ	*Catholic Biblical Quarterly*
		CBTJ	*Calvary Baptist Theological Journal*
		CGTC	Cambridge Greek Testament Commentary
BA	*Biblical Archaeologist*	CH	*Church History*
BAFCS	Book of Acts in Its First Century Setting	CIL	*Corpus inscriptionum latinarum*
BAR	*Biblical Archaeology Review*	CPJ	*Corpus papyrorum judaicorum*
BASOR	*Bulletin of the American Schools of Oriental Research*	CRINT	*Compendia rerum iudaicarum ad Novum Testamentum*
BBC	*Bible Background Commentary*	CTJ	*Calvin Theological Journal*
BBR	*Bulletin for Biblical Research*	CTM	*Concordia Theological Monthly*
BDB	Brown, F., S. R. Driver, and C. A. Briggs. *A Hebrew and English Lexicon of the Old Testament*	CTT	Contours of Christian Theology
		DBI	*Dictionary of Biblical Imagery*
		DCM	*Dictionary of Classical Mythology.*
BDF	Blass, F., A. Debrunner, and R. W. Funk. *A Greek Grammar of the New Testament and Other Early Christian Literature*	DDD	*Dictionary of Deities and Demons in the Bible*
		DJBP	*Dictionary of Judaism in the Biblical Period*
		DJG	*Dictionary of Jesus and the Gospels*
BECNT	Baker Exegetical Commentary on the New Testament	DLNT	*Dictionary of the Later New Testament and Its Developments*
BI	*Biblical Illustrator*	DNTB	*Dictionary of New Testament Background*
Bib	*Biblica*		
BibSac	*Bibliotheca Sacra*	DPL	*Dictionary of Paul and His Letters*
BLT	Brethren Life and Thought	EBC	*Expositor's Bible Commentary*
BNTC	Black's New Testament Commentary	EDBT	*Evangelical Dictionary of Biblical Theology*
BRev	*Bible Review*		
BSHJ	Baltimore Studies in the History of Judaism	EDNT	*Exegetical Dictionary of the New Testament*
BST	The Bible Speaks Today		

EJR	Encyclopedia of the Jewish Religion	JAC	Jahrbuch fur Antike und Christentum
EPRO	Études préliminaires aux religions orientales dans l'empire romain	JBL	Journal of Biblical Literature
EvQ	Evangelical Quarterly	JETS	Journal of the Evangelical Theological Society
ExpTim	Expository Times	JHS	Journal of Hellenic Studies
FRLANT	Forsuchungen zur Religion und Literatur des Alten und Neuen Testament	JJS	Journal of Jewish Studies
		JOAIW	Jahreshefte des Osterreeichischen Archaologischen Instites in Wien
GNC	Good News Commentary		
GNS	Good News Studies	JSJ	Journal for the Study of Judaism in the Persian, Hellenistic, and Roman Periods
HCNT	Hellenistic Commentary to the New Testament		
HDB	Hastings Dictionary of the Bible		
		JRS	Journal of Roman Studies
HJP	History of the Jewish People in the Age of Jesus Christ, by E. Schürer	JSNT	Journal for the Study of the New Testament
		JSNTSup	Journal for the Study of the New Testament: Supplement Series
HTR	Harvard Theological Review		
HTS	Harvard Theological Studies	JSOT	Journal for the Study of the Old Testament
HUCA	Hebrew Union College Annual	JSOTSup	Journal for the Study of the Old Testament: Supplement Series
IBD	Illustrated Bible Dictionary		
IBS	Irish Biblical Studies	JTS	Journal of Theological Studies
ICC	International Critical Commentary		
		KTR	Kings Theological Review
IDB	The Interpreter's Dictionary of the Bible	LCL	Loeb Classical Library
		LEC	Library of Early Christianity
IEJ	Israel Exploration Journal		
IG	Inscriptiones graecae	LSJ	Liddell, H. G., R. Scott, H. S. Jones. A Greek-English Lexicon
IGRR	Inscriptiones graecae ad res romanas pertinentes		
ILS	Inscriptiones Latinae Selectae	MM	Moulton, J. H., and G. Milligan. The Vocabulary of the Greek Testament
Imm	Immanuel		
ISBE	International Standard Bible Encyclopedia	MNTC	Moffatt New Testament Commentary
Int	Interpretation	NBD	New Bible Dictionary
IvE	Inschriften von Ephesos	NC	Narrative Commentaries
IVPNTC	InterVarsity Press New Testament Commentary	NCBC	New Century Bible Commentary Eerdmans

NEAE   *New Encyclopedia of Archaeological Excavations in the Holy Land*

NEASB   *Near East Archaeological Society Bulletin*

New Docs   *New Documents Illustrating Early Christianity*

NIBC   New International Biblical Commentary

NICNT   New International Commentary on the New Testament

NIDNTT   *New International Dictionary of New Testament Theology*

NIGTC   New International Greek Testament Commentary

NIVAC   NIV Application Commentary

NorTT   *Norsk Teologisk Tidsskrift*

NoT   *Notes on Translation*

NovT   *Novum Testamentum*

NovTSup   Novum Testamentum Supplements

NTAbh   Neutestamentliche Abhandlungen

NTS   *New Testament Studies*

NTT   New Testament Theology

NTTS   New Testament Tools and Studies

OAG   *Oxford Archaeological Guides*

OCCC   *Oxford Companion to Classical Civilization*

OCD   *Oxford Classical Dictionary*

ODCC   *The Oxford Dictionary of the Christian Church*

OGIS   *Orientis graeci inscriptiones selectae*

OHCW   *The Oxford History of the Classical World*

OHRW   *Oxford History of the Roman World*

OTP   *Old Testament Pseudepigrapha*, ed. by J. H. Charlesworth

PEQ   *Palestine Exploration Quarterly*

PG   *Patrologia graeca*

PGM   *Papyri graecae magicae: Die griechischen Zauberpapyri*

PL   *Patrologia latina*

PNTC   Pelican New Testament Commentaries

Rb   *Revista biblica*

RB   *Revue biblique*

RivB   *Rivista biblica italiana*

RTR   *Reformed Theological Review*

SB   Sources bibliques

SBL   Society of Biblical Literature

SBLDS   Society of Biblical Literature Dissertation Series

SBLMS   Society of Biblical Literature Monograph Series

SBLSP   *Society of Biblical Literature Seminar Papers*

SBS   Stuttgarter Bibelstudien

SBT   Studies in Biblical Theology

SCJ   *Stone-Campbell Journal*

Scr   *Scripture*

SE   *Studia Evangelica*

SEG   *Supplementum epigraphicum graecum*

SJLA   Studies in Judaism in Late Antiquity

SJT   *Scottish Journal of Theology*

SNTSMS   Society for New Testament Studies Monograph Series

SSC   Social Science Commentary

SSCSSG	Social-Science Commentary on the Synoptic Gospels
Str-B	Strack, H. L., and P. Billerbeck. *Kommentar zum Neuen Testament aus Talmud und Midrasch*
TC	Thornapple Commentaries
TDNT	*Theological Dictionary of the New Testament*
TDOT	*Theological Dictionary of the Old Testament*
TLNT	*Theological Lexicon of the New Testament*
TLZ	*Theologische Literaturzeitung*
TNTC	Tyndale New Testament Commentary
TrinJ	*Trinity Journal*
TS	*Theological Studies*
TSAJ	Texte und Studien zum antiken Judentum
TWNT	*Theologische Wörterbuch zum Neuen Testament*
TynBul	*Tyndale Bulletin*
WBC	Word Biblical Commentary Waco: Word, 1982
WMANT	Wissenschaftliche Monographien zum Alten und Neuen Testament
WUNT	Wissenschaftliche Untersuchungen zum Neuen Testament

YJS	Yale Judaica Series
ZNW	*Zeitschrift fur die neutestamentliche Wissenschaft und die Junde der alteren Kirche*
ZPE	*Zeischrift der Papyrolgie und Epigraphkik*
ZPEB	*Zondervan Pictorial Encyclopedia of the Bible*

5. General Abbreviations

ad. loc.	in the place cited
b.	born
c., ca.	circa
cf.	compare
d.	died
ed(s).	editors(s), edited by
e.g.	for example
ET	English translation
frg.	fragment
i.e.	that is
ibid.	in the same place
idem	the same (author)
lit.	literally
l(1)	line(s)
MSS	manuscripts
n.d.	no date
NS	New Series
par.	parallel
passim	here and there
repr.	reprint
ser.	series
s.v.	*sub verbo*, under the word
trans.	translator, translated by; transitive

Zondervan Illustrated Bible Backgrounds Commentary

ROMANS

by Douglas J. Moo

All kinds of issues would need to be tackled in a full-scale introduction to Paul's letter to the Romans: not least the questions about the letter's purpose and theme. But the introductory remarks that follow will concentrate on the background issues that are the focus of this commentary. Other issues will be ignored or touched on only briefly.

Events Leading up to Paul's Writing of Romans

Understanding Paul's own situation as he writes Romans helps us appreciate the purpose and theme of the letter. In 15:14–22, he looks back at a period of ministry just concluded. "From Jerusalem all the way around to Illyricum," Paul tells us, "I have fully proclaimed the gospel of

TIBER RIVER

▶ **Romans**
IMPORTANT FACTS:

■ **AUTHOR:** Paul the apostle.

■ **DATE:** A.D. 57.

■ **OCCASION:** Paul writes toward the end of the third missionary journey to a church that is divided between Jewish and Gentile Christians.

■ **PURPOSE:** To help the Roman Christians understand the gospel, especially in its implications for the relationship of Jew and Gentile in the church.

show how the gospel spread from the Jews to the Gentiles. Second, the city stands at one geographic extremity in his missionary travels. At the other extremity is Illyricum, the Roman province occupying what is today Albania and parts of Yugoslavia and Bosnia-Herzegovina. Only here does Paul refer to missionary work in this province, although such a ministry can be fit easily into the movements of Paul on his third missionary journey (see comments on Rom. 15:19). An "arc" drawn from Jersualem to Illyricum, therefore, passes over, or nearby, the important churches that Paul has planted in south Galatia (Pisidian Antioch, Lystra, Iconium, Derbe), Asia (Ephesus), Macedonia (Philippi, Thessalonica, Berea), and Achaia (Corinth).

But what does Paul mean when he claims that he has "fully proclaimed" the gospel in these areas? The Greek has simply the equivalent of our verb "fulfill" (*peplērōkenai*). To "fulfill" the gospel, therefore, probably means to preach it sufficiently such that viable churches are established. These churches can then carry on the task of evangelism in their own territories while Paul moves on to plant new churches in virgin gospel territory (cf. 15:20–21).

Christ" (15:19). This verse indicates that Paul's ministry has reached a significant geographical turning point. As Luke tells us in Acts, Paul first preached Christ in Damascus (and perhaps Arabia) after his conversion (Acts 9:19–22; cf. Gal. 1:17). Only after three years did he go to Jerusalem to preach, and then only briefly (Gal. 1:18; cf. Acts 9:28–29). Why, then, mention Jerusalem as the starting point for his ministry? For two reasons. First, the city represents the center of Judaism, and Paul is concerned to

In pursuit of this calling, Paul is moving on to Spain (15:24). On the way, he hopes to stop off in Rome, evidently to enlist the Roman Christians' support for his new gospel outreach (see comments on 15:24). But before he can begin his trip to the western Mediterranean, he must first return to Jerusalem (15:25). Throughout the third missionary journey, Paul has collected money from the Gentile churches he planted to bring back to the impoverished Jerusalem believers. Now he is ready to embark on this trip, and he earnestly asks the Roman Christians to pray for it (15:30–33). The collection represents for Paul a key step in what he hopes will be the reconciliation of Jewish and Gentile Christians in the early church.

The Life-Situation of Paul and Why He Wrote

Four pieces of information from 15:23–33 are especially helpful in understanding the situation of Paul as he writes Romans. First, he is almost certainly writing the letter during his winter stay in Corinth at the end of the third missionary journey

(Acts 20:2–3; cf. 2 Cor. 13:1). Not only does this place and time best fit the movements Paul describes in chapter 15; it also explains why he commends to the Romans' attention a prominent woman from the church in Cenchrea, the seaport of Corinth (16:1–2).

Second, Paul is conscious of having reached a significant turning point in his missionary career. He has "fulfilled" the gospel task in the eastern Mediterranean and is now ready for new, fresh fields, "white for the harvest." Such a turning point is a natural time for Paul to reflect

◄

ROMAN CATACOMB

The "Priscilla Catacomb" dates to the second or third century A.D. and contains hundreds of burial niches.

THE MEDITERRANEAN WORLD

Judea to Spain.

▼

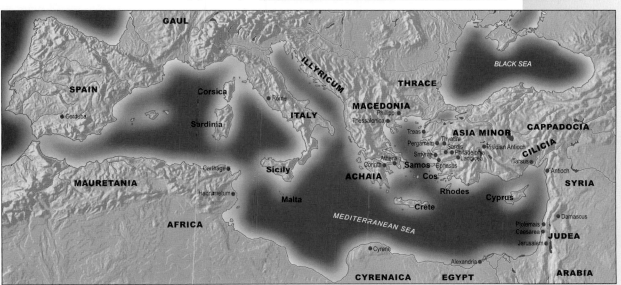

on the gospel he has preached and the controversies he has come through.

Third, Paul is deeply concerned about the results of his impending trip to Jerusalem with all its implications for what is to him, and to many others, a central theological issue in the early church: the integration of Gentiles into the people of God. We should not be sur-

prised, then, that this issue plays such a large role in Romans.

Finally, Paul is seeking the support of the Roman Christians for his new ministry in Spain. Perhaps one of the reasons Paul writes this letter to the church in Rome is to introduce himself and explain his theology so that the church will feel comfortable in supporting him.

ROME

(top) The Forum.

(bottom right) The Arch of Titus, built by Domitian to celebrate his brother's military victory over Jerusalem and Judea.

(bottom left) The Via Appia.

▼ ▶

Rome and Its Church

Some scholars surmise that Paul's own circumstances suffice to explain why he writes Romans. At a key transition point in his ministry, the apostle sets forth the gospel he preaches to the Roman Christians so that they can pray intelligently for his visit to Jerusalem and so that they will be willing to support his new evangelistic effort in Spain. But left out in all this is the Roman church itself. And what we know about that church provides further critical information about the nature and purpose of Romans.

We have no direct evidence about the origins of Christianity in Rome. The tradition that Peter (or Peter and Paul together) founded the church is almost certainly erroneous.[1] Not only is it difficult to place Peter in Rome at such an early date, but it is difficult to imagine Paul writing to a church founded by Peter in the way he does, considering his expressed principle not to build "on someone else's foundation" (15:20). No other tradition from the ancient church associates any other apostle with the founding of the church.

Thus, the assessment of the fourth-century Ambrosiaster is probably accurate: the Romans "embraced the faith of Christ, albeit according to the Jewish rite, without seeing any sign of mighty works

---

▶ The Disturbance of "Chrestus" and the Roman Church

One circumstance in the life of the Jews in Rome probably played a significant role in explaining why Paul writes Romans the way he does. The ancient historian Suetonius tells us that Emperor Claudius "expelled all the Jews from Rome because they were constantly rioting at the instigation of Chrestus" (*Life of Claudius* 25.2).

Most scholars are convinced that "Chrestus" is a corruption of the term "Christ" and that Suetonius is thereby hinting at disputes within the Jewish community over Jesus' claim to be the Christ. Modern historians are less certain over the date of this expulsion. But a fifth-century Christian writer, Orosius, puts the event in A.D. 49; and this date fits nicely with Acts 18:2, which tells us that Priscilla and Aquila ended up in Corinth during Paul's second missionary journey, "because Claudius had ordered all the Jews to leave Rome."[A-1]

One can imagine the catastrophic effect this would have had on the fledging Christian community in Rome. Originating from the synagogue, the bulk of Christians would probably have been Jewish. Suddenly they are forced to leave (Claudius would not have distinguished Jews and Jewish-Christians). Left behind are Gentiles who had been converted over the years. Many, if not most, were probably from the class of "God-fearers," Gentiles who had an interest in Judaism and heard the message of Jesus in the synagogue. These Gentiles are the only Christians left in Rome, so the church naturally becomes less and less Jewish in orientation.

But by A.D. 54, the date of Claudius's death, Jews are beginning to return. As Jewish-Christians (like Priscilla and Aquila; cf. Rom. 16:3–5) filter back into the church, they find that they are now in a minority. The social tensions created by this history go a long way in explaining the tensions between Jews and Gentiles that the letter to the Romans abundantly attests (cf. 11:13, 25; 14:1–15:13).[A-2]

◀

CLAUDIUS
Roman emperor
A.D. 41–54.

or any of the apostles."[2] Luke tells us that "visitors from Rome" were present on the day of Pentecost (Acts 2:10). Some of them were probably converted as a result of Peter's powerful speech. They would have returned to their home city and begun preaching Jesus as the Messiah. We know that enough Jews had emigrated to Rome by the first century B.C. to make up a significant portion of the population.[3] The Jewish community was not apparently unified, with many synagogues independent of one another.[4] This circumstance may help explain why the Christians in Rome are also divided.

The Letter and Ancient Genre Considerations

Romans is, of course, a letter—but what kind of letter? Ancient authors used letters for many different purposes. Scholars have been eager to identify the particular persuasive, or "rhetorical," model that Romans belongs in. It has been labeled an "epideictic" letter,[5] an ambassadorial letter,[6] a "protreptic" letter,[7] and a "letter essay,"[8] to name just a few of the more prominent suggestions.

A good case can be made for several of these identifications. But, in the last analysis, Romans does not fit neatly into any specific genre. As James Dunn concludes, "the distinctiveness of the letter far outweighs the significance of its conformity with current literary or rhetorical custom."[9]

Other scholars have noted the similarities between sections of Romans and the diatribe. The diatribe was a style of argument popular with Cynic-Stoic philosophers (the best example being Epictetus's *Discourses* [1st–2d c. A.D.]). The diatribe features dialogues with fictional characters, rhetorical questions, and the use of the emphatic negation *mē genoito* ("may it never be!") to advance a line of argument. These are just the features Paul uses in passages such as 2:1–3:9; 3:27–31; 6:1–7:25; 9:14–23. Earlier scholars thought the diatribe had a polemical purpose and therefore tended to read Romans as a debate with an opponent (perhaps Jewish).[10] But scholars have recently come to realize that the diatribe was used more often as a means of clarifying truth for converts and disciples.[11] The dialogical "arguments" of Romans therefore have the purpose of helping the Christians in Rome better understand the gospel and its implications.

Address and Greeting (1:1–7)

People in Paul's day usually began their letters by identifying themselves and their addressee(s) and then adding a greeting. Acts 23:26 is a good example: "Claudius Lysias, To His Excellency, Governor Felix: Greetings." Paul follows this conventional structure but elaborates each element. He spends six verses identifying himself, probably because he needs to establish his credentials in a church that he did not found and has not visited. Paul claims to be an apostle, dedicated to the "gospel," the good news about Jesus, God's Son. This Jesus, a descendant of David in his earthly life, has now been invested with new power through his resurrection. It is this Jesus whom Paul serves by calling on Gentiles everywhere to trust God and to obey him. And since the Roman Christians are mainly Gentile, Paul has a perfect right to proclaim God's good news to them.

Servant of Christ Jesus (1:1). Great leaders in the Old Testament were also called "servants" of the Lord (see, e.g., Josh. 14:7: "I was forty years old when Moses the servant of the LORD sent me from Kadesh Barnea to explore the land"). The phrase therefore hints at Paul's own status and authority. "Christ" comes from the Greek word for "anointed" and is equivalent to the Hebrew-derived "Messiah." Placing "Christ" first focuses attention on the word as a title.

The gospel of God (1:1). "Gospel," or "good news," has backgrounds in both the Old Testament and the Roman world. The prophets used the word to depict God's saving intervention on behalf of his people: "You who bring good tidings to Zion, go up on a high mountain. You who bring good tidings to Jerusalem, lift up your voice with a shout, lift it up, do not be afraid; say to the towns of Judah, 'Here is your God!'" (Isa. 40:9). But the word was also applied by the Romans to the emperor, whose birth, life, and great deeds were "good news" for the world. A decree

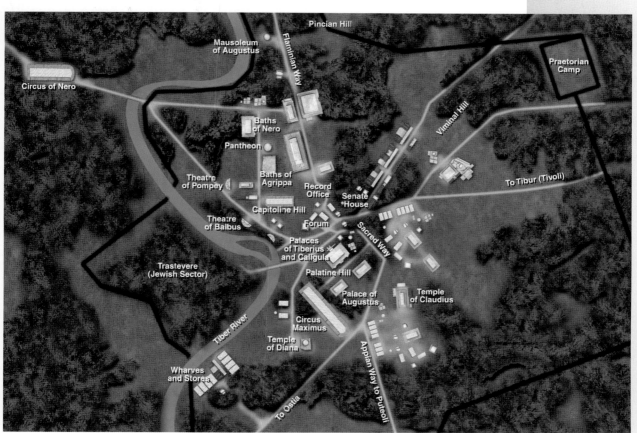

issued in 9 B.C. marking the birthday of Emperor Augustus, for instance, claims that his birth was "the beginning for the world of glad tidings."[12] The salvation and happiness that many Romans looked to the emperor to provide are available only, claims Paul, in Jesus Christ, the essence of the "good news of God."

A descendant of David (1:3). In the Old Testament, God promises that a descendant of David will have an eternal reign. Perhaps the most famous of such prophecies is found in 2 Samuel 7:12–14a, as the prophet Nathan addresses David: "When your days are over and you rest with your fathers, I will raise up your offspring to succeed you, who will come from your own body, and I will establish his kingdom. He is the one who will build a house for my Name, and I will establish the throne of his kingdom forever. I will be his father, and he will be my son." Paul is identifying Jesus as the one in whom the ultimate significance of this prophecy is fulfilled.

Declared with power to be the Son of God (1:4). The NIV suggests that the resurrection marked the time when God, as it were, "announced" to the world that Jesus was Son of God. But the verb Paul uses suggests rather that Jesus was appointed to a new role at the time of the resurrection. Since Jesus has always been Son of God (see 1:3), this new role must be "Son of God in power." Paul may again be alluding to Old Testament messianic passages—in this case, to ones that use language about the installment of a king to predict the coming of Messiah. Note, for instance, Psalm 2:7: "I will proclaim the decree of the LORD: He said to me, 'You are my Son; today I have become your Father.'"

And you also are among those who are called to belong to Jesus Christ (1:6). Or, better: "you also, called to belong to Jesus Christ, are among those [e.g., the Gentiles of 1:5]." Paul wants to claim the Roman Christians as Gentiles who belong within his sphere of ministry.

Thanksgiving and Occasion (1:8–15)

Paul continues to adapt the typical Greco-Roman letter form, which often had an expression of thanks at the beginning.[13] Paul is grateful to the Lord for the evidence of the Spirit's work in the Roman church and is hopeful that he will finally be able to pay them a visit and share his gospel with them.

That is, that you and I may be mutually encouraged by each other's faith (1:12). After expressing his desire to "impart . . . some spiritual gift" to the Romans, Paul immediately corrects himself by emphasizing the mutual spiritual benefit that he hopes will follow from his visit. We need not doubt Paul's sincerity; but Paul is also using an ancient rhetorical convention, the *captatio benevolentiae*, to "capture the good will" of his audience. He does not want to come across as dictatorial or arrogant.

I planned many times to come to you (but have been prevented from doing so until now) (1:13). We cannot be certain what it was that kept Paul from visiting Rome earlier. But it was probably the need to minister to the churches that he had founded in the eastern Mediterranean. Paul is writing the letter from Corinth, a church that demanded a lot of his pastoral time and attention (see 1 and 2 Corinthians).

Greeks and non-Greeks (1:14). "Non-Greeks" translates the word *barbaros*, from which we get "barbarian." Greeks applied the word to people who could not speak Greek and who therefore used uncouth languages that sounded like nonsense ("bar-bar").

The Theme of the Letter (1:16–17)

These verses are the transition between the letter's introduction and its body. In them Paul announces the theme of the letter: the gospel. Paul proudly proclaims the gospel because he knows it unleashes God's power to rescue human beings— both Jews and Gentiles—from sin and death. The gospel has this power because God reveals his righteousness in it, which can only be experienced through faith.

First for the Jew, then for the Gentile (1:16). Running like a golden thread through Romans is the insistence that the gospel has overcome the distinction between Jew and Gentile. We find it difficult to appreciate just how deep the divide between Jew and Gentile was for first-century Jews. Jews believed that God had chosen them, from among all the nations of the earth, to be his very own people.

Two developments during the two centuries before Christ made it more important than ever for Jews to insist on their distinctiveness. First, the Seleucid ruler Antiochus Epiphanes tried to eradicate the Jewish religion. Pious Jews rose up in revolt and prevented the Seleucids from carrying out their intention (see the apocryphal books 1 and 2 Maccabees). But the experience strengthened Jewish resolve to maintain their distinctive culture. The second development leading to this same emphasis was the diaspora. By Jesus' time, many more Jews were living outside of Palestine than in it. Jews living as a minority in a hostile culture naturally focused on those lifestyle issues that maintained their separateness from the surrounding culture.

A righteousness from God (1:17). The NIV translation is interpretive; a more literal rendering would be simply "righteousness of God." The NIV assumes that Paul is speaking about righteousness as the "right status" that God gives to the sinner who believes. But the Old Testament background suggests a different way of understanding the phrase. Occurring over fifty times in the Old Testament, the phrase "his [e.g., God's] righteousness" sometimes refers to God's activity of "making things right" in the last days. Isaiah 46:13 is an excellent example: "I am bringing my righteousness near, it is not far away; and my salvation will not be delayed. I will grant salvation to Zion, my splendor to Israel." As a parallel to "salvation," God's "righteousness" is his activity of establishing "right" in a world that has gone terribly wrong. But it is important to note that this "rightness" is not moral but legal. Paul is not referring to God's activity of turning sinners into people who live "right" but to his act of proclaiming that sinners are "right" before him—innocent in the divine court of justice.[14]

"The righteous will live by faith" (1:17). We can also translate this, "the one who is righteous by faith will live" (see RSV; TEV). The words come from Habakkuk 2:4, which enjoin God's people, the "righteous," to look at the strange and perplexing work of God in Habakkuk's day with the eyes of faith. Paul finds in the language a key Old Testament insistence that faith is essential to establish true righteousness and life (see also Gal. 3:11; Heb. 10:38).

Gentiles Justly Stand Under God's Wrath (1:18–32)

Paul has introduced the theme of the letter: In the preaching of the gospel, God acts to put people in right relationship with himself. Any person, Gentile as well as Jew, who exercises trust in God can therefore be saved. But Paul postpones further explanation of this "good news" until 3:21 and following. First must come the "bad news." Paul knows that we will not appreciate the solution until we understand the problem. So, in 1:18–3:20 he explains that all human beings are locked up under sin's power and justly stand under the sentence of God's wrath. Both Gentiles (1:18–32) and Jews (2:1–29) have been given knowledge about God's will for human beings. But

they have all turned away from that knowledge and are therefore "without excuse" (1:20; cf. 2:1) before the righteous judgment of God.

In 1:18–32, Paul focuses on the way that human beings have turned from God's revelation in nature and fallen into idolatry (1:22–23, 25), illegitimate sexual behavior (1:24, 26–27), and all kinds of other sins (1:28–31). The passage is structured around the threefold repetition of human "exchange"/divine "giving over" (1:23–24, 25–26a, 26b–28). God has sentenced people to the consequences of the sin they have chosen for themselves.

The wrath of God (1:18). The "wrath of the gods" is a common theme in Greco-Roman literature. When other gods offend them, or human beings fail to give a god his or her due (e.g., by failing to offer sacrifices), the god reacts with "wrath." In keeping with the human qualities of the traditional Greek pantheon, this wrath could be selfish in its motivation and capricious in its effects. For this reason, some of the Greek philosophers urged people to avoid "wrath," since it manifested a lack of self-control. Some modern theologians echo this critique, claiming that the biblical teaching about God's wrath must be understood as a kind of mechanistic process within history.

But the God of the Bible is a personal God, and his wrath, while just and measured, is no impersonal force. The Old Testament frequently refers to God's wrath in precisely this way, as he inflicts punishment on human sin (e.g., Ex. 32:10–12; Num. 11:1; Jer. 21:3–7). But it also predicts a climactic outpouring of God's wrath in the last day (e.g., Isa. 63:3–6; Zeph. 1:15). Since Paul speaks similarly in this very context (Rom. 2:5), he may also think of the "revealing" of God's wrath in this verse as taking place on the Day of Judgment. But the present tense of the verb "being revealed" suggests rather that he is alluding to the many ways in which God manifests his wrath against sin in history.

Exchanged the glory of the immortal God for images made to look like mortal man and birds and animals and reptiles (1:23). Once people turned from knowledge of the true God (1:20–21), they "became fools" (1:22) and worshiped gods of their own making. Idolatry is the basic sin, and it was almost universal in the ancient world. Israel fell into the worship of false gods again and again, and God eventually sent the people into exile for their misplaced worship. But the Exile and various crises of the intertestamental period cured Israel of idolatry. In fact, Jewish writings from this period frequently mock the Gentiles for their foolish worship of gods fashioned by their own hands. One of the most important of these texts is found in the apocryphal book Wisdom of Solomon. Note, for instance 13:1–2:

For all people who were ignorant of God were foolish by nature; and they were unable from the good things that are seen to know the one who exists, nor did they recognize the artisan while paying heed to his works; but they supposed that either fire or wind or swift air, or the circle of the stars, or turbulent water, or the luminaries of heaven were the gods that rule the world.

Paul also alludes to two Old Testament texts. The threefold description of the animal world is reminiscent of the creation account: "And God said, 'Let the land produce living creatures according to their kinds: livestock, creatures that

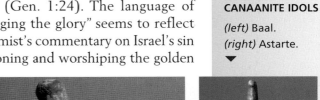

REFLECTIONS

FEW OF US HAVE A STONE STATUE in our house that we worship. But we are far from escaping the sin of idolatry. At root, idolatry is giving something the priority that God alone deserves to have. We can idolize another human being by making a spouse more important to us than God. We can idolize money by making its accumulation more important than God. And we can idolize pleasure by spending more time and energy on sex, or golf, or mountain-biking than we do on God and his service.

move along the ground, and wild animals, each according to its kind.' And it was so" (Gen. 1:24). The language of "exchanging the glory" seems to reflect the psalmist's commentary on Israel's sin in fashioning and worshiping the golden

CANAANITE IDOLS
(left) Baal.
(right) Astarte.
▼

calf (Ex. 32): "They exchanged their Glory for an image of a bull, which eats grass" (Ps. 106:20). By his choice of words, therefore, Paul brands idolatry as a tragic departure from the intention of God in creation, a departure that Israel herself has not escaped.

Because of this, God gave them over to shameful lusts (1:26). The move from idolatry to sexual sin again echoes typical Jewish diatribes against the Gentiles. Jews were relatively free from this sin, but it was rampant in the ancient Greco-Roman world.

They not only continue to do these very things but also approve of those who practice them (1:32). The suggestion that approval of the sin of others can be worse than one's own sin echoes Jewish teaching: "The two-faced are doubly punished because they both practice evil and approve of others who practice it; they imitate the spirits of error and join in the struggle against mankind" (*T. Asher* 6:2).

Jews Justly Stand Under God's Wrath (2:1–16)

After condemning Gentiles for turning from the knowledge of God that they were given in the created world, Paul now castigates Jews for failing to live up to the knowledge of God that they were given in the law. As a seasoned preacher of the gospel, Paul knows how Jews will react to his condemnation of the Gentiles in 1:18–32: They will be quite willing to join him in his denunciation. Thus, Paul denies that they have any right to assume they are superior to the Gentiles, for Jews do "the same things" as the Gentiles (2:1). They may not worship idols or engage in homosexuality; but they put their own law in the place of God and are just as guilty as Gentiles of "greed," "envy," "strife," and so on (see 1:29–31). As a result, Jews also "have no excuse" (2:1), storing up wrath for the day of wrath (2:5).

Paul justifies his critique of the Jews by arguing in the two following paragraphs that Jew and Gentile stand on the same footing before the judgment seat of God. God impartially judges every person—Jew and Gentile alike—on the basis of their works (2:6–11). The law, though a precious possession of the Jew, will make no difference in the outcome (2:12–16), for it is doing the law, not possessing it, that matters. Moreover, Gentiles, though not given the Mosaic law, also have some knowledge of God's law.

▶ Homosexuality

The Jewish viewpoint on sexual sin is well summarized in *Sybilline Oracles* 3.594–600: "Surpassing, indeed, all humans, they [Jewish men] are mindful of holy wedlock and do not engage in evil intercourse with male children, as do Phoenicians, Egyptians, and Romans, spacious Greece and many other nations, Persians, Galatians, and all Asia, transgressing the holy law of the immortal God." The Jews' condemnation of homosexuality is rooted, of course, in the Old Testament, which plainly and repeatedly denounces the practice (see, e.g., Gen. 19:1–28; Lev. 18:22; 20:13; Deut. 23:17–18). Many Greeks, however, not only tolerated homosexuality, but considered consensual sex between men to be a higher form of love than heterosexual relations. Contrary to revisionist interpretations, Paul follows the Old Testament and Jewish teaching in condemning homosexual practice as sinful.

▶ Paul and Rhetoric

When we use the word "rhetorical," we usually mean elaborate speech. But in the ancient world "rhetoric" was the art of persuasion and a prime subject of study.[A-3] The Greeks and Romans were fond of public speaking and developed sophisticated techniques to help a speaker to dazzle or persuade his audience. Paul occasionally uses some of the styles popular in the rhetorical schools (such as "diatribe"). But, as 1 Corinthians 2:1–5 reveals, he renounces many of the rhetorical "tricks" of his day, wanting his converts to be convinced by logic and the power of the Spirit rather than by superficial arguments. Preachers today would do well to follow Paul in turning their backs on any means of persuasion that do not rely on God's power and the working of the Spirit.

You, therefore, have no excuse (2:1). The "you" in Greek is singular. In 2:17 Paul identifies this person whom he is addressing as a Jew. Why does Paul point to a single Jew for his discussion? He is adopting an ancient literary style called the diatribe. Ancient Greeks used this style as a teaching device, letting their audience "listen in" to a discussion between two different viewpoints. Here Paul teaches the Roman church about his view of Judaism by describing for them the kind of argument he would make to the typical Jew about sin and salvation.

Do you show contempt for the riches of his kindness . . . not realizing that God's kindness leads you toward repentance? (2:4). With this question, Paul gets to the heart of the issue. Because of their covenant relationship with God, Jews frequently fell into the habit of thinking that they were immune from the judgment of God. The Old Testament prophets often critiqued this presumptuous attitude. But it remained as a basic attitude among the Jews in Paul's day.

Particularly informative of Paul's rhetorical move in this part of Romans is the sequence of thought in Wisdom of Solomon 11–15. As we noted in our comments on Romans 1:23, this book of the Apocrypha contains a long description of Gentile folly and sin (Wisd. Sol. 11–14). Paul echoes many of its points in Romans 1:18–32. Then, in Wisdom of Solomon 15, the author reflects on the situation of himself and other Jewish people: "But you, our God, are kind and true, patient, and ruling all things in mercy. For even if we sin we are yours, knowing your power; but we will not sin, because we know that you acknowledge us as yours. For to know you is complete righteousness, and to know your power is the root of immortality." The writer does just what Paul condemns: assumes that God's kindness guarantees escape from judgment for Jews.

God "will give to each person according to what he has done.". . . For God does not show favoritism (2:6–11). This paragraph is one of the clearest examples within the Bible of a popular way of arranging material in the ancient world that we call "chiasm." The word comes from the name of a Greek letter of the alphabet, chi, that looks like our "x." The literary form in question takes this name because it arranges material in an A-B-B'-A' pattern, as if each element were at the apex of the two lines of the "x." Romans 2:6–11 is a bit more complicated, following an A-B-C-C'-B'-A' arrangement:

A God "will give to each person according to what he has done." (v. 6)

  B To those who by persistence in doing good seek glory, honor and immortality, he will give eternal life. (v. 7)

    C But for those who are self-seeking and who reject the truth and follow evil, there will be wrath and anger. (v. 8)

    C' There will be trouble and distress for every human being who does evil: first for the Jew, then for the Gentile; (v. 9)

  B' but glory, honor and peace for everyone who does good: first for the Jew, then for the Gentile. (v. 10)

A' For God does not show favoritism. (v. 11)

The main point of a chiasm sometimes comes at its center, but in this case it comes at the "extremes" (point A/A'): God does not show favoritism in dispensing salvation and judgment to people.

All who sin apart from the law will also perish apart from the law, and all who sin under the law will be judged by the law (2:12). This is the first occurrence in Romans of the word "law" (*nomos*). The word occurs almost eighty times in the letter, and Paul's teaching on "law" runs right through all the topics he discusses. Yet the modern English reader can easily get the wrong impression about what Paul is talking about. We think of secular law or, if we are familiar with some theological traditions, of the commands of God for his people that are found throughout the Bible. But Paul's teaching

is rooted in a more historical reading of the Bible. For him as a Jew, *nomos* is preeminently the law of Moses: the body of commands that God gave to his people Israel through his servant Moses.

Modern scholars often use the transliterated Hebrew word *torah* to denote this body of laws. In this verse, therefore, those "under the law" are Jews, placed under the jurisdiction of the Mosaic law by God himself. Those who sin "apart from the law" are then Gentiles. Not being Jews, they have not been made subject to the law of Moses. But Paul's point in this verse is that knowledge of that law makes no difference in the judgment: All people stand condemned. For, as Paul explains in 2:13, people can escape God's judgment only by doing the law—and the universal power of sin (see 3:9, 20) prevents people from ever fulfilling that law.

When Gentiles, who do not have the law, do by nature things required by the law, they are a law for themselves (2:14). Some commentators think that Paul is referring to Gentile Christians, who were not by "nature" or "birth" recipients of the law of Moses, but who now have that law "written on the heart," in accordance with the new covenant prophecy of Jeremiah 31:31–34.[15] But Paul's language appears rather to allude to a widespread Greco-Roman tradition about the "unwritten law." Stoic philosophers especially developed the notion of a universal moral standard rooted in nature. Hellenistic Jews, like the Alexandrian philosopher Philo, applied this notion to the Mosaic law: "All right reason is infallible law engraved not by this mortal or that, and thus perishable, nor on lifeless parchment or slabs, and therefore soulless as they, but immortal nature on the immortal mind, never to perish" (*Every Good Man Is Free* 46; see also *Special Laws* 1.36–54; *Abraham* 276).

Following this tradition, Paul claims that non-Christian Gentiles, even though they may never have heard of the law of Moses, have in their very natures, created by God, knowledge of the "rights and wrongs" that the law of Moses ultimately points to. They will therefore do things that the law of Moses itself demands, such as refraining from murder and adultery, honoring their parents, and so on. These universal moral absolutes reveal that all people have access to knowledge of God's moral will. Thus, he is just in condemning both Jew and Gentile (Rom. 2:15–16).

Judgment Despite the Law and Circumcision (2:17–29)

Now you, if you call yourself a Jew; if you rely on the law and brag about your relationship to God (2:17). With this verse Paul begins a long sentence in which he piles up description after description of the Jews' privileges and claims (2:17–20), only to show that these blessings mean little because Jews have not lived up to their privileges (2:21–24). As his address of a single Jew makes clear, Paul is again using the style of the diatribe (see 2:1–4). Ancient writers who used this style often criticized opponents for failing to "practice what they preached."[16] So Paul also claims that Jews, who take pride in their name because it means that they have been given the law with all its blessings, fail to do the law. As Paul has argued in 2:12–13, possession of the law without actually doing it does not count before God.

A guide for the blind, a light for those who are in the dark, an instructor of the foolish (2:19–20). These three descrip-

tions of Israel's role as witness of God's power and grace to the world reflect both Old Testament and Jewish texts. According to Isaiah 42:6–7, God had destined Israel, his "servant," to be "a light for the Gentiles, to open eyes that are blind, to free captives from prison and to release from the dungeon those who sit in darkness" (see also 49:6). *Sibylline Oracles* 3.194–95 echoes this language: "The people of the great God will again be strong who will be guides in life for all mortals." Note also *1 Enoch* 105:1: "In those days, he says, 'The Lord will be patient and cause the children of the earth to hear. Reveal it to them with your wisdom, for you are their guides.'" This "evangelistic" mission to the world is one, however, that Israel has failed to accomplish. The Jews' preoccupation with the law and their failure to recognize Jesus as Messiah turned them, as Jesus himself claimed, into "blind guides" (Matt. 15:14). The servant's mission as "light to the Gentiles" has now been taken over by the church (see, e.g., Acts 26:18).

You who abhor idols, do you rob temples? (2:22). This is one of three specific examples of Jewish disobedience of the

law that Paul cites to prove that Jews do not "do" the law that they possess. The other two—stealing and committing adultery—are straightforward. But what does Paul mean by accusing the Jews of "robbing temples"? (1) If the word Paul uses here (*hierosyleō*) is given its literal meaning, than the reference is probably to Jews who robbed pagan temples of their idolatrous statues in order to melt them down and profit from their precious metals. The Old Testament specifically prohibits the practice (e.g., Deut. 7:26).

(2) Paul may be using the word metaphorically, referring to Jews who did not pay the required "temple tax." This tax, levied on all Jews wherever they lived, was designed to support the Jerusalem temple and its ministries. Jewish texts suggest that failure to pay this tax was widespread.[17]

(3) We have some evidence that the word could refer in a vague way to sacrilege.[18] Paul could, then, be accusing the Jews of elevating the law to such a place that it infringed on the rights and honor of God himself.[19] While this third alternative is attractive, the first should probably be accepted, for this view best accounts for the relationship between the first part of the statement and the second. Robbing pagan temples is a natural contrast to "abhorring idols."

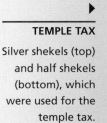

TEMPLE TAX
Silver shekels (top) and half shekels (bottom), which were used for the temple tax.

As it is written, "God's name is blasphemed among the Gentiles because of you" (2:24). Paul concludes his indictment of the Jews for failing to obey the law they take so much pride in with a quotation from the Old Testament. Two different prophetic passages contain language like this: Isaiah 52:5 and Ezekiel 36:20. The latter verse comes from the

▶ Circumcision As a "Boundary Marker"

God first instituted circumcision as a "sign of the covenant" that God entered into with Abraham and his descendants (Gen. 17:10–14). All males descended from Abraham were to be circumcised on the eighth day as a mark of their identity as the people of God.

Jews, of course, practiced the rite throughout the Old Testament period, but it became especially significant when Jews, because of the Exile, lived as a minority group in the midst of a pagan environment. To preserve their identity and to prevent intermingling with the Gentiles, they put great emphasis on "boundary marker" rituals such as circumcision, food laws, and the observance of Sabbath. This emphasis explains why, for instance in Galatians, it is just these rites that become the focus of debate with the Judaizers. Indeed, these external rituals became so important that some Jews fell into the habit of thinking that simply being born into the people of the Jews (marked for males by circumcision) and following these kinds of rituals would guarantee their salvation.

The rabbinic claim that "no person who is circumcised will go down to Gehenna" (*Exod. Rab.* 19 [81c]), while dating from the post-New Testament period, undoubtedly reflects the opinion of many Jews in Paul's day.

famous "new heart" and "new spirit" prophecy, which Paul uses elsewhere, including a possible allusion later in Romans. But the text of Paul's quotation is closer to the Isaiah passage. Since the sense of the two Old Testament passages is the same, the issue is not of major importance; but the allusion to Isaiah is more likely. Not only is Isaiah Paul's favorite Old Testament book, but he also quotes from this very section (Isa. 52:7) in Romans 10:15 to sketch the course of evangelistic preaching.

What makes Paul's quotation of this text interesting is that Isaiah (and Ezekiel also) ascribe the blasphemy of God's name not to Israel's sin but to her condition of exile, which has led the nations to question God's existence and faithfulness. Paul shifts the application of the text slightly to suit his larger theme in this part of Romans, "leveling the playing field" between Israel and the Gentiles.

Circumcision has value if you observe the law (2:25). In 2:25–29, Paul challenges a widespread Jewish notion that if a man was circumcised, he would ultimately be saved. The apostle attacks this attitude head-on by claiming that the outward rite of circumcision helps a person in the judgment of God only if it is accompanied by heartfelt (see 2:29) obedience to the law. Again, Paul insists, it is what the Jew *does*, not what the Jew *has*, that matters for God.

The one who is not circumcised physically and yet obeys the law will condemn you (2:27). Paul's claim is a radical one. (1) Jews in Paul's day insisted that Gentiles had to be circumcised if they wanted to become members of the people of God. Indeed, a few more "Hellenized" Jews, such as Philo of Alexandria, spiritualized circumcision, along with most Jewish rituals. But they still insisted that the physical rite was essential (*Special Laws* 1.1–11, 304–6; *Abraham* 92). An intriguing story about the conversion of a Gentile king in Josephus suggests that some Jews may not have insisted on circumcision for converts.[20] But the prevailing opinion was that only circumcised Gentiles could be considered true "proselytes," that is, converts to Judaism.[21] When Paul therefore suggests that a Gentile who is not circumcised may stand in judgment over Jews, he is breaking with a basic Jewish tradition. (2) For Jews, circumcision was an indispensable part of keeping the law. Yet Paul suggests that uncircumcised Gentiles may be "obeying the law." Paul begins hinting here at a redefinition of what it means to "keep the law" that he will develop further in Romans (see esp. 3:31; 8:4; 13:8–10).

Circumcision is circumcision of the heart, by the Spirit, not by the written code (2:29). "Written code" translates a Greek

---

REFLECTIONS

WHAT PAUL SAYS IN THESE VERSES ABOUT CIRCUMCISION is in some ways limited because of the unique status of circumcision and of the Jewish faith. For only Judaism and its institutions are rooted in God's revelation in the Old Testament. But one important point about circumcision does apply broadly to any religious ritual: Any such ritual only has value if it is accompanied by heartfelt obedience. In the Christian church, we can apply the principle to such rites as baptism and the celebration of the Lord's Supper. These are rituals instituted by Christ himself and appointed for our benefit. Yet they will only have value in our lives when they are met by faith and a commitment to make Christ the Lord of our lives. The temptation to substitute the outward form for the inward reality is always present.

word that means "letter" (*gramma*). In later Christian theology, Paul's contrast between "letter" and "spirit" was applied to the interpretation of the Old Testament. Christians, it was argued, needed to penetrate behind the "letter" of the words of the Old Testament in order to be able to understand its true, "spiritual," meaning. We preserve this same metaphor when we speak of obeying the "spirit" of the law.

But Paul has no such application of this language in view. In the three places where he uses the contrast (see also Rom. 7:6; 2 Cor. 3:3–5), "spirit" refers to the Holy Spirit, poured out by God as part of the new covenant blessing, while "letter" refers to the Old Testament law. In Romans 2:29, therefore, Paul hints again at the argument that will follow in the book, where he makes clear that only God's Spirit, empowered by God's new covenant grace, can change the heart of a person and make it acceptable to God.

God's Faithfulness and the Judgment of Jews (3:1–8)

The dialogical style of Romans, reminiscent of the ancient diatribe (see comments on 2:1ff.), is revealed in Paul's frequent pauses to respond to objections of misunderstandings of what he has just taught. Paul knows that some of his readers might draw the wrong conclusion about what he has taught in Romans 2. He seems to have eliminated any special privileges for Jews, accusing them of being just as guilty as the Gentiles of breaking God's law. But, while Gentile and Jew are equally condemned for failing to live up to God's demands of them, it is not the case that Jews have no advantage at all. It is this point that Paul briefly makes in this short paragraph. But he does not stop there. He also suggests that God's judgment of the Jews is

entirely in keeping with his covenant promises and person.

First of all, they have been entrusted with the very words of God (3:2). Paul does not follow up his "first of all" with a "second" or "third." Perhaps "first of all" means something like "most important." Or perhaps Paul started a list but was sidetracked before finishing it. But we can guess what that list would have looked like from the similar context in 9:4–5. Having access to "the very words of God" is the greatest blessing the Jews enjoy. The Greek word here (*logia*) has the connotation of "spoken words," or "oracles"; it draws attention to the fact that God himself has spoken to the Jews in his Old Testament word to them. The enormous advantage this gives to the Jews is brought out in many passages. Note, for instance: "What other nation is so great as to have such righteous decrees and laws as this body of laws I am setting before you today?" (Deut 4:8); "He has revealed his word to Jacob, his laws and decrees to Israel. He has done this for no other nation; they do not know his laws. Praise the LORD" (Ps. 147:19–20).

So that you may be proved right when you speak and prevail when you judge (3:4). Paul quotes from Psalm 51:4, part of David's acknowledgment to God that he was perfectly justified in judging David for his sin with Bathsheba. What is telling in this quotation is its emphasis on God's justice *in judgment*. Paul conceives of God's "faithfulness" (3:3), truth (3:4a), and "righteousness" (3:5) quite broadly. Many first-century Jews (and modern interpreters) think that these words all contain promises of blessing only for Israel. God will be faithful and true to his covenant with Israel, rescuing them from their enemies and saving them. But, as Paul hints in this verse, God's faithfulness has ultimately a much wider reference than to his promises of blessing to Israel. God is faithful to *all* his words—the ones that threaten judgment for disobedience as well as to the ones that promise blessing. If, then, Paul implies, God judges Israel for her sins, he is still faithful, true, and just.

The theme of God's justice in punishing his people is one found in many Jewish books of Paul's time, as the Jews tried to interpret the disasters they had suffered in light of God's word and promises. This motif is especially prominent in the first-century B.C. book *Psalms of Solomon*. See, for instance, 8:7–8: "I thought about the judgments of God since the creation of heaven and earth; I proved God right in his judgments in ages past. God exposed their sins in the full light of day; the whole earth knew the righteous judgments of God" (see also 2:18; 3:5; 4:8).

God's righteousness (3:5). In 1:17, we argued that "righteousness of God" refers to God's activity of putting sinners into right relationship with himself. This is the dominant meaning of the phrase in Romans, and Paul will use the phrase with this sense later in this chapter (3:21–22). But, as we hinted in our comments on 3:4, God's "righteousness" here is not his "saving" righteousness but his "personal" righteousness. "Righteousness," or "being in the right," implies a standard of measurement. But there can be no standard above God; God is his own standard of measurement. Therefore God's "righteousness" ultimately includes his always acting in accordance with his own nature. Paul's point is that human sin can never cancel God's faithfulness to his own standard of behavior. Israel's sin has

given God the opportunity of manifesting his righteousness in his judgment. Several Old Testament passages also use the language of "righteousness" or "justice" to make a similar point (see esp. Neh. 9:32–33):

> Now therefore, O our God, the great, mighty and awesome God, who keeps his covenant of love, do not let all this hardship seem trifling in your eyes—the hardship that has come upon us, upon our kings and leaders, upon our priests and prophets, upon our fathers and all your people, from the days of the kings of Assyria until today. In all that has happened to us, you have been just; you have acted faithfully, while we did wrong.

How could God judge the world? (3:6). Paul probably alludes to Genesis 18:25, where Abraham is pleading with God to spare the lives of people in Sodom and Gomorrah: "Far be it from you to do such a thing—to kill the righteous with the wicked, treating the righteous and the wicked alike. Far be it from you! Will not the Judge of all the earth do right?"

The Guilt of All Humanity (3:9–20)

Paul brings the threads of his indictment together in a grand conclusion. All people, Jews as well as Gentiles, are under sin's power (3:9), incapable of rescuing themselves from their plight by anything that they might do (3:20). In this way, he paves the way for his exposition of the good news of redemption through Jesus (3:21ff.).

Under sin (3:9). In a way similar to non-Western cultures today, ancient people tended to view the world in terms of dominating "powers": astral forces, general and local deities, magical spells, and so on. This worldview surfaces at many points in the Bible; and we need to appreciate it if we are to understand its message. In this text, for instance, it is not by chance that Paul claims the human dilemma consists not in the fact that people commit sins, but that they are "under sin." Paul pictures sin as a ruthless taskmaster and human beings as sin's helpless slaves. Clearly, then, what is required if people are to be rescued from this plight is not a teacher or a moral example, but a liberator. Jesus Christ, Paul will announce in 3:24, is just that liberator.

As it is written (3:10–18). In 3:10–18, Paul quotes from as many as six different Old Testament passages to buttress his claim that all people are under sin's power. Such a series of quotations is similar to the later rabbinic practice of "pearl-stringing." But we have evidence from the Dead Sea Scrolls that Jews even before the time of Christ were already collecting Old Testament "proof texts" for various key doctrinal ideas. One of the scrolls, for instance (4QTestimonia), consists entirely of quotations, with interspersed comments, about a messianic prophet. Scholars have long speculated that the early Christians put together such series of texts as an apologetic device in their witness to the truth of their faith. Some think that the quotations in 3:10–18 may come from just such a document.[22] Whether that is true or not (and proof is, in the nature of the case, not forthcoming), the series of quotations fits Paul's purpose very well. He here uses the literary device of inclusio, with the phrase "there is no" occurring in

the opening and closing lines as a frame around the whole.

Therefore no one will be declared righteous in his sight by observing the law (3:20). The phrase "observing the law" is the NIV rendering of a Greek phrase literally translated "works of the law." Paul uses this phrase seven other times (3:28; Gal. 2:16 [3x]; 3:2, 5, 10), and in each case he denies that justification (or a related concept) can be attained by these "works of the law." The NIV rendering reflects the traditional interpretation of the phrase: anything a person does in obedience to the law. No "work" that a person does, even when that work is one demanded by God himself in his holy law, is capable of putting that person in a right relationship with the God of the universe. But, noting the prominence of what we have above called "boundary markers" in first-century Judaism (see comments on Rom. 2:25), some recent interpreters think the phrase may have a more nuanced reference. Paul may be referring to the Jewish tendency to obey the law as means of establishing their own superiority over the Gentiles. The focus within this interpretation shifts from the *performance* of the law (as in the traditional interpretation) to the *possession* of the law.[23]

We think the traditional interpretation has much in its favor. The Hebrew phrase equivalent to the Greek expression that Paul uses here is found several times in the Dead Sea Scrolls (4QFlor 1:7; 1QS 5:21; 6:18; 4QMMT 3:29). It also seems similar to the rabbis' common reference to "works" or "commandments" (see also *2 Apoc. Bar.* 57:2, "the works of the commandments"). Each of these Jewish expressions has the general sense of "obeying the law." Any other nuance has to be read into the phrases from a particular reading of the broader Jewish context; and that broader reading is not convincing.

Justification and the Righteousness of God (3:21–26)

In one of the greatest paragraphs of the Bible, Paul rehearses some of the reasons why the coming of Jesus Christ is, indeed, good news. In Christ, God has acted to manifest his saving righteousness, making it possible for any person who believes to be "justified"—pronounced innocent before the judgment seat of God himself (3:21–23). This verdict of justification is possible because Christ has redeemed us from our enslavement to sin (3:24), giving himself as a sacrifice that provides atonement for all people (3:25a). But what gives this paragraph its unparalleled significance is its claim that God did all this while preserving his own righteousness (3:25b–26a). In Christ—God become man and sacrificed for us—God found a way both to "justify" undeserving sinners *and* to remain "just" as he did so (3:26b).

Apart from law . . . to which the Law and the Prophets testify (3:21). "Law" in the first phrase refers to the Mosaic law, and thus should probably be made definite: *the* law. "The Law and the Prophets," on the other hand, is a way by which Jews referred to the Old Testament as a whole (see, e.g., Matt. 5:17; 7:12).[24]

Through the redemption that came by Christ Jesus (3:24). The word "redemption" (*apolytrōsis*) means "liberation through payment of a price." Some interpreters think that this word, and its cognates, "redeem" (Gal. 3:13–14; 4:5; Titus 2:14; 1 Peter 1:18; Rev. 14:3) and "ransom" (Matt. 20:28//Mark 10:45; 1 Tim. 2:6; Heb. 9:15), have, through their use in the Old Testament, lost any sense of a "price paid." The terms simply mean "deliverance" or "deliver."[25] But this is probably not the case. Several New Testament texts keep alive the idea of a "price." The terms were widely used in the ancient world to refer to the process by which prisoners of war or slaves could be bought out of their bondage.[26] Paul, then, presents Christ's death as a price that has been paid to release human beings from their slavery to sin (see comments on Rom. 3:9). Theologians and laypeople alike have asked the question: "To whom, then, was the price paid?" But Paul gives no answer; and perhaps even asking the question pushes Paul's metaphor further than he intended.

God presented him as a sacrifice of atonement (3:25). Another significant theological term with a debated background lies behind the NIV's "sacrifice of atonement" (*hilastērion*). This word was used widely in the Greek world to refer to altars, monuments, etc., that would have the power to "propitiate" the wrath of gods. Many interpreters think this is the context from which Paul takes the term, and thus prefer to translate "propitiation."[27] But the word is also used in the

Old Testament in a more specific sense, where it refers to the "mercy seat" (KJV language), the place on the altar where blood was placed and atonement took place. In fact, so often does the term have this meaning in Leviticus 16, in the description of the Day of Atonement ritual, that it virtually takes on the meaning "place of atonement" (see Lev. 3:1, 13, 14, 15). Since the only other occurrence of the word in the New Testament has this same reference (Heb. 9:5), we should probably accept this as the reference Paul intended.

There is some reason to think Paul may here be taking over an early Christian tradition that portrayed Christ's death against the background of the Old Testament sacrificial system. The allusion would have been striking and extremely significant for believers acquainted with the Old Testament. The cross of Christ, Paul asserts, is now the place, in this new covenant age, where God deals with the

MERCY SEAT

(left) A model of the Most Holy Place with a priest sprinkling blood on the mercy seat in the Day of Atonement ritual.

(right) The mercy seat, which also serves as the lid to the ark of the covenant.

THE TABERNACLE

A model of the tabernacle showing a sacrificial scene.

sins of his people. No longer behind a veil, God's atoning work is now displayed for all to see. Since this atoning work includes (in both the Old Testament sacrificial system and in the New Testament portrayal of Christ's death) the turning away of God's wrath, we are also justified in concluding that his atoning work includes the notion of propitiation.

Because in his forbearance he had left the sins committed beforehand unpunished (3:25). "Left . . . unpunished" captures well the interesting word that Paul uses here (*paresis*), which means "postponement of punishment" or "neglect of prosecution." God did not prosecute Old Testament sinners with the full vigor of the law, but allowed them to go unpunished. Now, however, that debt must be paid; and Christ, the "sacrifice of atonement," has paid it.

"By Faith Alone" (3:27–31)

Paul now elaborates one crucial point from 3:21–26: God makes his righteousness available to people by faith alone.

Is God the God of Jews only? Is he not the God of Gentiles too? Yes, of Gentiles too, since there is only one God (3:29–30a). Perhaps the most basic of all Jewish beliefs was the confession: "Hear, O Israel: The LORD our God, the LORD is one" (Deut. 6:4). Pious Jews uttered this confession, called the *Shema* (from the opening word in Hebrew), every day. Paul here turns this confession on the Jews. For if there is only one God, then he must be God of Gentiles as well as Jews, for it would be inconceivable in the ancient mind for a people to have no god. But, Paul goes on to argue, if God is God of

both Jews and Gentiles, then he must justify them in the same way (Rom. 3:30b).

"By Faith Alone": The Case of Abraham (4:1–25)

In 3:27–31 Paul establishes the point that a person can be put right with God only by faith. Now, in chapter 4, he elaborates this "faith alone" viewpoint with respect to one of the most important figures in the history of Israel: the patriarch Abraham. Despite his reputation among Jews as a strict adherent of the law, Abraham, Paul explains, has nothing to boast about. For he, too, was justified by faith alone (4:1–8). Neither his circumcision (4:9–12) nor the law (4:13–17) had anything to do with his acceptance before God. It was his faith, a faith that remained firm despite much evidence to the contrary, that enabled him to experience what God had promised (4:18–21). It is by that same faith that Christians inherit the

---

REFLECTIONS

UNDERSTANDING AND APPLYING THE GOOD NEWS of Jesus Christ means not only understanding the first-century context but also understanding ours. We live in an age that is not comfortable with the notion of sin. The idea that God might actually be angry with people for their sin is uncongenial indeed. But we will not appreciate just why Jesus Christ is such good news for the world until we adjust our thinking to match that of the biblical authors. They knew the reality of sin; and they knew the reality of a holy God who could not tolerate sin. Only through the sacrifice of Christ, paying the debt incurred by our sin that we could never pay, could God make a way of accepting people who are by nature unacceptable to him. Those people in our day who ignore or minimize the problem of human sin in the face of a holy God do well to heed the warning of the great medieval theologian Anselm: "You have not yet considered the weight of sin."

righteousness made available in Jesus Christ (4:22–25).

Abraham, our forefather. . . . If, in fact, Abraham was justified by works (4:1–2). The Old Testament itself calls Abraham the "father" of Israel (Isa. 51:2), recognizing the role that the book of Genesis gives him as the founder of the people of promise (see Gen. 12:1–3). But Jewish tradition made Abraham even more significant and tended to attribute his unique salvation-historical status to his obedience. According to the apocryphal book Prayer of Manasseh, Abraham "did not sin" against God (v. 8); Sirach claims that "no one has been found like him in glory" (Sir. 44:19). *Jubilees* 23:10 lauds Abraham for being "perfect in all his deeds with the Lord, and well-pleasing in righteousness all the days of his life." He was even said to have perfectly obeyed the law before it had been given (*m. Qidd.* 4.14; cf. *2 Apoc. Bar.* 57:2). Paul therefore discusses Abraham not only because he is a foundational figure within the Old Testament, but also because he must combat tendencies in Judaism to attribute Abraham's righteousness and salvation-historical significance to his works.

Abraham believed God, and it was credited to him for righteousness (4:3). In order to capture Abraham for his own teaching about the righteousness of faith, Paul seizes on the crucial text of Genesis 15:6 (see also Gal. 3:6). In the Genesis story, Abraham's faith is specifically his conviction that God would send him a natural descendant (Gen. 15:4–5). But this promise of a son born to him and Sarah represents the whole promise of God to Abraham. Critical to Paul's citation of the passage is the idea of "crediting" (Gk. *logizomai + eis*). The Hebrew construction does not indicate that Abraham's faith was itself a righteous deed (as some Jews interpreted the text), but that his faith was the means by which God graciously gave Abraham the status of righteousness. Paul seizes on this notion and plays on it throughout Romans 4. This "crediting" was on the basis of faith, not works—a matter of pure grace on God's part (4:4–8). The "crediting" was, moreover, not based on circumcision (4:9–12) or the law (4:13–17). This recurring reference to Genesis 15:6 is somewhat similar to the Jewish interpretational technique called *midrash*, in which a Scripture text becomes the basis for an extended discussion.

God who justifies the wicked (4:5). This famous assertion is particularly striking because it seems to fly in the face of explicit Old Testament teaching. God condemns human judges who "justify" the guilty (see Prov. 17:15; Isa. 5:23) and himself declares that "I will not acquit the wicked" (Ex. 23:7). But Paul is using the word "justify" (Gk. *dikaioō*) in a new way, to describe the creative act by which God, on the basis of Christ's own righteousness, gives to sinful people a status they do not have and could not earn.

David says the same thing (4:6). One feature of the midrashic technique (see comments on 4:3) is the use of texts from the Prophets or the Psalms to illuminate an original text from the law (the Pentateuch). A single word common to both texts was often enough to bring them together. Paul falls into this standard Jewish interpretational technique when he illustrates the meaning of the key word "credit" from Genesis 15:6 by citing Psalm 35:1–2 in Romans 4:7–8. The word "count" in the quotation translates the same Greek word (*logizomai*) that is translated "credit" in the Genesis text.

Under what circumstances was it credited? Was it after he was circumcised, or before? It was not after, but before! (4:10). As we made clear in our notes on 2:25, circumcision became for Jews, facing the threat of persecution and assimilation into larger Gentile populations, a key sign of Jewish identity. Paul reminds his readers that the righteous status Abraham gained with God was not based on his circumcision. The Genesis account makes this clear, for God's pronouncement of Abraham's righteousness comes in Genesis 15, while circumcision is not even introduced until chapter 17. The rabbis speculated that twenty-nine years went by between the two events.

The sign of circumcision, a seal of the righteousness that he had by faith (4:11). The Old Testament calls circumcision a "sign of the covenant" (Gen. 17:11), and Jewish texts dating from after the New Testament period also characterize circumcision as a "seal" (*b. Šabb.* 137b; *Exod. Rab.* 19 [81c]; *Tg. Ket. Cant.* 3:8). Some scholars think this language may have been current in Paul's day,[28] but others are not so sure.[29] What is clear is that Paul, against tendencies in Judaism to connect circumcision to the Mosaic covenant and to the law, insists that it was significant only as an identifying marker for the righteous status Abraham had already gained through his faith.

That he would be heir of the world (4:13). The Old Testament does not use this same language when referring to God's promise to Abraham. But Paul's language seems to be chosen to summarize the three key provisions of God's promise: that Abraham would have innumerable descendants, making a "great nation" (Gen. 12:2; cf. 13:16; 15:5; 17:4–6, 16–20; 22:17); that he would possess the "land" (13:15–17; 15:12–21; 17:8); and that he would be the means of blessing to "all the peoples of the earth" (12:3; 18:18; 22:18). Note especially the promise of 22:17, that Abraham's descendants would "take possession of the cities of their enemies." The prophet Isaiah expands the promise of the land to include the entire world (Isa. 55:3–5), and some Jewish texts use similar universal language to describe God's promise to his people. For instance, the *Book of Jubilees* presents Abraham as blessing Jacob with these words: "May he strengthen and bless you, and may you inherit all of the earth" (*Jub.* 22:14).[30]

Where there is no law there is no transgression (4:15). The key to the interpretation of this difficult assertion is the restricted meaning of the word "transgression" (*parabasis*). It refers to a "stepping over" of a specific law or custom.[31] Paul's point, then, is definitional: Only

CIRCUMCISION

An ancient Egyptian tomb relief depicting the circumcision of a boy.

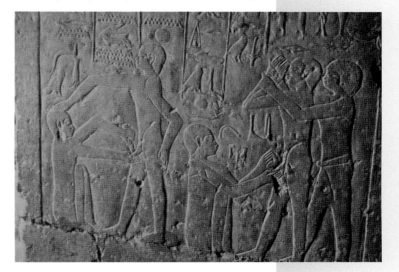

where a specific law exists can sin take the specific form of a "transgression." In the case of Israel, the coming of the Mosaic law brought "wrath" by turning the peoples' sin into the more serious and blameworthy category of *parabasis*.

The God who gives life to the dead and calls things that are not as though they were (4:17). This description of the God in whom Abraham believed is difficult grammatically; but our concern is with some interesting parallels to the language in Jewish literature. God's power to give life is featured in the Old Testament (Deut. 32:39; 1 Sam. 2:6) and was even enshrined in one of the most common Jewish liturgies, the "Eighteen Benedictions." In light of the context, Paul probably applies the language specifically to God's creating of life in the dead womb of Sarah.

The second description of God may reflect a widespread Jewish teaching that God created the world out of nothing (*creatio ex nihilo*). The verb "call" often refers to God's creative work (see, e.g., Isa. 41:4; 48:13), and Philo often used the verb in statements about God's creative work (see, e.g., *Special Laws* 4.187: "for he called things that are not into being"). But the language of "giving life" was sometimes combined with God's call to describe conversion. Especially important is *Joseph and Aseneth* 8:9: "Lord, God of my father Israel, highest and most powerful God, who gives life to all things and calls from darkness into light, and from error into truth, and from death into life." Paul may be picking up this language to emphasize that God has the power to create new spiritual life in the midst of the deadness of human sin and alienation.[32]

Abraham in hope believed and so became the father of many nations (4:18). Paul's use of the story of the miraculous birth of Isaac in 4:18–20 to stress the strength of Abraham's faith is similar to Hebrews 11:11–12; these two texts, in turn, resemble Philo's description of Abraham and an early Christian text, *1 Clement* 10. This raises the possibility that Paul is here quoting a widespread tradition about Abraham's faith.

Without weakening in his faith, he faced the fact that his body was as good as dead (4:19). This description of Abraham's faith appears to clash with two elements in the Genesis narrative about Abraham. (1) According to Genesis 17:17, when told that Sarah would bear him a son, Abraham "fell facedown; he laughed and said to himself, 'Will a son be born to a man a hundred years old? Will Sarah bear a child at the age of ninety?'" Philo suggests that Abraham's laughter may have been an expression of joy rather than of disbelief (*Questions and Answers on Genesis* 3.55); and some of the rabbis followed suit. But the parallel reaction of Sarah in 18:12–15 and

R E F L E C T I O N S

ABRAHAM'S FAITH IS A MODEL FOR THE KIND OF FAITH that God is still looking for in his people. He believed "against hope," yet "in hope." His faith was "against hope" because it flew in the face of material evidence and common sense. He was too old to have children; his wife was barren. How could they possibly conceive a child? Yet Abraham did not let this evidence detract from the promise that God had given him. It was "in [the] hope" created by God's word to him that he believed God would give him and Sarah a child, even though it made no rational sense. Are we willing and able to believe God's promises when all the evidence points in the other direction?

the context make this solution unlikely. Probably Paul is making a generalization about the whole course of Abraham's life. (2) A second problem with Paul's description is the fact that Genesis 25:1–2 indicates that Abraham later produced children through another wife, Keturah. The best solution is to assume that God's gift of procreative power to Abraham remained after the birth of Isaac.

He was delivered over to death for our sins and was raised to life for our justification (4:25). This brief description of Christ's work on our behalf is carefully worded, with the parts of the statement parallel to one another. Many scholars therefore think it is likely that Paul is quoting an early Christian confession. The confession may have been modeled partly on the prophet Isaiah's description of the work of the Suffering Servant, who would be "handed over because of their sins" (Isa. 53:12 in LXX).

The Hope of Glory (5:1–11)

Paul shifts gears in this chapter. In chapters 1–4, he has outlined the heart of his gospel: that sinful people can be put right with God through their faith in Jesus Christ. Now he goes on to show (in chs. 5–8) that the person who has been justified is assured of being saved from God's wrath and delivered from the ravages of sin and death in the last day. Paul announces this theme in 5:1–11, arguing that those who are justified, though still subject to life's trials, have a secure hope for future deliverance from wrath.

We have peace with God (5:1). "Peace" is, of course, a common word in the ancient world and can have many different nuances. It generally referred, negatively, to a cessation of hostility. But Paul's use of the word is more in keeping with the positive concept of the word found in the Old Testament: the well-being, prosperity, or salvation of the godly person. The prophets predicted a day when God would establish a new era of peace (see, e.g., Isa. 52:7, quoted in Rom. 10:15): "How beautiful on the mountains are the feet of those who bring good news, who proclaim peace, who bring good tidings, who proclaim salvation, who say to Zion, 'Your God reigns!'"

Through whom we have gained access by faith into this grace in which we now stand (5:2). The word "access" (*prosagōgē*) was used in the ancient world to refer to a person's being conducted into the presence of royalty (see LSJ, who cite Xenophon, *Cyr.* 7.5.45). Whether the word was used often enough for this situation to lead Paul's first readers to make this association is not clear. But the image is one that would have struck a note with the Christians in Rome, aware of court protocol that restricted "access" to the emperor to certain highly placed individuals. Through Jesus Christ, every believer has this kind of access to the grace of the King of heaven.

We also rejoice in our sufferings ... knowing ... (5:3–4). In these verses, Paul lists a series of virtues that Christians who respond to suffering in the right way can experience. Such a list, with the most important items coming at the end, resembles the ancient literary form called *sorites*. Similar claims about the beneficial effects of suffering for the Lord's sake are found elsewhere in the New Testament:

> Consider it pure joy, my brothers, whenever you face trials of many

kinds, because you know that the testing of your faith develops perseverance. Perseverance must finish its work so that you may be mature and complete, not lacking anything. (James 1:2–4)

In this you greatly rejoice, though now for a little while you may have had to suffer grief in all kinds of trials. These have come so that your faith—of greater worth than gold, which perishes even though refined by fire—may be proved genuine and may result in praise, glory and honor when Jesus Christ is revealed. (1 Peter 1:6–7)

The teaching was probably a widespread tradition in the early church that Paul here quotes to establish contact with Christians in Rome who do not know him.

And hope does not disappoint us (5:5). The word "disappoint" could be more literally translated "put to shame" (*kataischynō*). This verb is used in the Old Testament to mean "suffer judgment." Typical is Isaiah 28:16 (quoted by Paul in Rom. 9:33 and 10:11): "So this is what the Sovereign LORD says: 'See, I lay a stone in Zion, a tested stone, a precious cornerstone for a sure foundation; the one who trusts will never be dismayed [or ashamed; *kataischynthē*]" (see also Ps. 22:5: "They cried to you and were saved; in you they trusted and were not disappointed [or ashamed; *kateschynthēsan*]"). Believers have a secure hope, based in the love and activity of God in Christ, so we need have no fear of being "ashamed" in the time of judgment.

God has poured out his love into our hearts by the Holy Spirit (5:5). The language of "pouring out" reminds us of Joel's famous prophecy about God's "pouring out" his Spirit in the last days (Joel 2:28–32, quoted by Peter on the Day of Pentecost; Acts 2:17–21).

Very rarely will anyone die for a righteous man, though for a good man someone might possibly dare to die (5:7). The difference between these two assertions probably lies in a distinction between "righteous" and "good," illustrated by the gnostics, who contrasted the "righteous" god of the Old Testament with the "good" god of the New (see Irenaeus, *Haer.* 1.27.1). In order to underscore the magnitude of God's love for us, Paul reminds his readers that it is extremely rare for a human being to give his or her life for a person who is upright and moral, though one can find examples of people giving their lives for people they love. Yet God has given Christ to die for people who were hostile to him.

Since we have now been justified by his blood, how much more shall we be saved from God's wrath through him! (5:9). We can understand better why Paul so emphasizes the unbreakable connection between justification and final salvation when we appreciate the general Jewish view of justification. Jews generally believed that a person would only be justified in the last day, when God evaluated a person's life in the judgment. See, as a typical example, *Psalms of Solomon* 17:26–29:

He will gather a holy people whom he will lead in righteousness; and he will judge the tribes of the people that have been made holy by the Lord their God. He will not tolerate unrighteousness (even) to pause among them, and any person who knows wickedness shall not live with them. For he shall know them that they are children of their God. He will distribute them upon the land according to their tribes; the alien and the foreigner will no longer live near them. He will judge peoples and nations in the wisdom of his righteousness.

Jesus' own use of "justify" language is in keeping with this Jewish perspective. Note, for instance, the contrast in Matthew 12:37: "For by your words you will be acquitted [or "justified"; the verb is *dikaioō*], and by your words you will be condemned." Paul proclaims that a person can experience this end-time justifying verdict in this life, the moment he or she puts faith in the Lord Jesus. A Jewish objector might well wonder what value that verdict would have for the time of judgment. Paul affirms that justification leads infallibly to a positive verdict in the judgment. For the judgment of that last day simply ratifies the escha-tological verdict God has already pronounced in favor of the believer.

The Reign of Grace and Life (5:12–21)

Paul reinforces the security of Christian hope by grounding it in the work of Jesus Christ, whose "act of righteousness" brings life to those who belong to him just as certainly as Adam brought death to all who belong to him. Throughout this text, Paul assumes that both Adam and Christ have representative significance, as he adopts popular ancient Jewish ideas of the solidarity among individuals.

Just as sin entered the world through one man (5:12). Important for our appreciation of this famous theological text is the fact that the word "man" in Hebrew (*ʾādām*) is also the name "Adam." The very name of Adam, therefore, suggests his representative significance: Adam *is* "man."

▶Corporate Solidarity and Adam's Sin

Modern readers are often disturbed or even offended at the idea that Adam, millennia ago, might have done something to affect all people who have lived since him. The Christian philosopher Pascal called this idea—"original sin"—an "offense to reason." However, while it does not necessarily remove all the offense, it is helpful to remember that ancient people—and Jews in particular—had a strong notion of "corporate solidarity." Jews believed that people were bound to one another in various relationships and that the actions of one person could have a determinative influence on all those to whom they were related.

The classic Old Testament example is Achan, whose sin in keeping for himself some of the plunder from the battle of Jericho is also said to be "Israel's sin" (Josh. 7:1, 11) and the reason why God's anger burns against Israel as a whole (5:1). Some scholars have taken the notion too far, suggesting that Hebrew thinking merged individuals into a corporate personality. But the importance of corporate thinking for ancient Jews is generally acknowledged and should correct the tendency in the modern West to look at such texts from too "individualistic" a perspective.

Death came to all men, because all sinned (5:12). The exact relationship between the sin of Adam and the death and condemnation of all people is a matter of long-standing debate among theologians. Paul is not explicit about the relationship, and so it is appropriate to ask what he might have assumed from his Jewish background.

Unfortunately, Jewish literature does not manifest a consistent view. A few Jewish texts attribute sin and death to the devil (see, e.g., Wisd. Sol. 2:24: "through the devil's envy death entered the world, and those who belong to his company experience it"). A very few even put the blame on Eve: "From a woman sin had its beginning, and because of her we all die" (Sir. 25:24). But more typical of the Jewish perspective is the tension exhibited on this matter in the Syriac *Apocalypse of Baruch*. The writer of this second-century A.D. book can assert, on the one hand, that Adam brought death to all his descendants: "When Adam sinned a death was decreed against those who were to be born" (*Apoc. Bar.* 23:4); "What did you [Adam] do to all who were born after you?" (48:42; see also *4 Ezra* 7:118). On the other hand, he also makes every person responsible for his or her own death: "Adam is, therefore, not the cause, except only for himself, but each of us has become our own Adam" (*Apoc. Bar.* 54:19); "Although Adam sinned first and has brought death upon all who were not in his own time, yet each of them who has been born from him has prepared for himself the coming torments" (54:15; see also *Bib. Ant.* 13:8–9).

The interpreter of Romans cannot, therefore, attribute to Paul any specific view on the relationship of Adam to humankind based on Jewish literature. A few interpreters have suggested that Paul may have taken over a deterministic tra-

---

▶ Paul and Jewish Apocalyptic

Jewish apocalyptic tended to divide the world into two "ages," separated by the coming of the Messiah. The "old age" of Israel's sin and degradation would give way to a new age in which God would bless and vindicate his people. A good representative text is *4 Ezra* 7:112–15:

He [an angel sent to instruct Ezra] answered me and said, "This present world is not the end; the full glory does not remain in it; therefore those who were strong prayed for the weak. But the day of judgment will be the end of this age and the beginning of the immortal age to come, in which corruption has passed away, sinful indulgence has come to an end, unbelief has been cut off, and righteousness has increased and truth has appeared. Therefore no one will then be able to have mercy on someone who has been condemned in the judgment, or to harm him who is victorious."

Paul adapted this basic scheme, modifying it to suit the Christian understanding that Messiah would come not once, but twice. Accordingly, the early Christians believed that the "new age" had been inaugurated with Christ's first coming but would only be consummated at his second. So the present time was a period of "overlap" between the two ages: by faith in Christ believers belonged to the new age of salvation but still lived and were influenced by the old age of sin and death. In Romans 5–8, Paul uses this two-age scheme to explain why Christians can have joy and confidence in their salvation even as they continue to struggle against sin (ch. 6), death (chs. 5, 8), and the law (ch. 7). Paul therefore contrasts the evil powers that "reign" in the present age (sin and death) with the powers of the age that has already dawned in Christ (grace, life, and righteousness).

dition about Adam's sin popular in gnostic-oriented circles.[33] But the gnostic myths to which scholars appeal cannot be traced definitely to Paul's time.

Sin is not taken into account when there is no law (5:13). Paul reflects here the same perspective on the law that we observed in our notes on 4:15: The coming of the Mosaic law enabled God for the first time to record sin as a violation of specific commands and prohibitions. The verb "take into account" (*ellogeō*) perfectly captures this nuance, since it was used to describe the careful, precise recording of accounts necessary in bookkeeping. A second-century papyrus document has two women writing to their steward: "Put down to our account everything you expend on the cultivation of the holding."[34]

A pattern of the one to come (5:14). "Pattern" translates *typos*, from which we get the word "typology." A *typos* was the impression left by the blow of a hammer or similar implement, and therefore came to have the meaning of form, pattern, or example. Old Testament people, events, and institutions, under God's sovereign direction, can become patterns for their New Testament counterparts. So, Paul affirms, Adam, in his representative significance, is a *typos* of Christ. "The one to come" is similar to other New Testament descriptions of the Messiah as the "coming one" (cf. Matt. 11:3; 21:9; 23:39; John 4:25; 6:14; 11:27; Heb. 10:37). We have little evidence from intertestamental literature that this title was being widely used to denote the Messiah.

The many (5:15, 19). Many scholars think that Paul's use of the word "many" in this passage reflects certain occurrences of the same word in Hebrew, where the word was a stylistic equivalent of "all." Reference is especially made to Isaiah 53:11–12: ". . . by his knowledge my righteous servant will justify many. . . . For he bore the sin of many, and made intercession for the transgressors."[35] "Many" may be equivalent to "all" in this passage. But the claim that it regularly *means* "all" is exaggerated.

How much more will those who receive God's abundant provision of grace and of the gift of righteousness reign in life through the one man, Jesus Christ (5:17). Verses 18–19 could give the impression that the scope of salvation is as wide as the scope of sin and death. But what Paul says in 5:17 corrects this possible misapprehension. For by insisting that only those who "receive" God's gift will reign in life, he makes clear that one can enjoy life in Christ only by responding to the offer of grace.

Just as sin reigned in death, so also grace might reign through righteousness (5:21). The contrast between two "reigns"

R E F L E C T I O N S

WHEN WE THINK OF ROMANS 5:12–21, WE NORMALLY think "original sin." It is certainly true that this passage is the most important in the Bible on this topic. But a careful reading of the paragraph reveals that sin is not Paul's main point. He argues *from* the fact that Adam brought sin and death to all people *to* the corresponding truth that Jesus Christ has brought righteousness and life to all who belong to him. Our plight as sinners is assumed. What Paul wants us to understand is that God in Christ has more than cancelled that plight. Christ, the second Adam, has reversed the disastrous effects of Adam's sin, providing for all who belong to him by faith the assurance that they will "reign in life."

in this verse reflects a fundamental structure that Paul uses throughout his letters, but especially in chapters 5–8, to interpret and explain the significance of Christ. The structure has its roots in Jewish apocalyptic, a popular and diverse approach to understanding history and the future in Paul's day. Attempts to define the essence of Jewish apocalyptic vary considerably, and any attempt to survey the movement would require considerable space.

"Dead to Sin" and "Alive to God" (6:1–14)

What Paul has said in 5:20 about grace increasing all the more where sin increased might lead readers to the wrong conclusion. They might think that God's promise to meet sin with his grace means that sin does not matter—that Christians, because they are ruled by grace, need no longer concern themselves with sin. Like the seasoned preacher that he is, Paul anticipates this incorrect inference and heads it off immediately in chapter 6.

What shall we say, then? (6:1). As we noted in our comments on chapter 2, the question and answer style of writing that Paul frequently uses in Romans is similar to the ancient style of diatribe. In this case, however, he uses the style to teach Christians, not to debate with opponents of the faith. Scholars have shown that the diatribe style was often used in the ancient world in just this educational kind of setting.[36]

All of us who were baptized into Christ Jesus were baptized into his death (6:3). Paul's teaching that baptized believers become participants in Jesus' death and resurrection (cf. 6:5) has led to a long and contentious search for the background that might have led him to this idea. In the late 1800s and early 1900s, many scholars, persuaded that Paul's interpretation of Christ was deeply indebted to Greco-Roman influences, thought his conception of baptism into Christ's death came from the so-called mystery religions. These religions, which adherents joined by undergoing a secret rite of ini-

▶

"BAPTISMAL" POOL

A traditional Jewish purification bath (*miqveh*) discovered near Herod's palace in Jericho.

tiation, or *mystērion*, sometimes offered people the opportunity to be mystically joined to a dying and rising god. Paul, it was thought, adopted this idea and applied it to the Christian's union with Jesus in his death and resurrection through baptism. However, most scholars today don't think that the mystery religions had much influence on the early Christians' conception of Christ and his benefits. As A. J. M. Wedderburn has argued, it is improbable that Paul's presentation of the Christian's identification with Christ in his death and resurrection through baptism in Romans 6 has much to do with the mystery religions.[37]

What does inform Paul's notion of the believer's identification with Christ is his "second Adam Christology." As we have seen, Romans 5 presents Adam as representative head of the human race. Because all people are represented in Adam, his sin can at the same time be the sin of all people. Now Paul, of course, presents Christ as a representative figure similar to Adam. He can, then, portray Christians dying *with* Christ and being buried *with* him because he thinks of believers participating in Christ's acts of redemption. Baptism, as we will see, is Pauline shorthand in this text for the conversion experience.

Also debated is what Paul means by claiming that baptism is "*into* Christ Jesus." Paul may simply be abbreviating the common formula "in the name of Christ/Jesus," used several times in the New Testament in relationship to baptism (see Matt. 28:19; Acts 8:16; 19:5; cf. 1 Cor. 1:13, 15). But the "name" in the culture of that day represented the person himself or herself. Thus, this concept inevitably shades into the other idea, that Paul views believers as incorporated into Christ through baptism. At least one rab-binic text (*b. Yebam.* 45b) suggests that "wash in the name of" signifies being bound to the person in whose name one is washed.

We were therefore buried with him through baptism (6:4). An important concept in 6:4–8 is the notion that Christians were "with" Christ in his death/crucifixion (6:5, 6, 8), burial (6:4), and resurrection (6:5, 8). How are we to understand this "withness"? Many scholars appeal to the general religious notion of "mysticism" to explain the idea. The identification with a god who died and rose to new life each year (imitating the cycle of nature) in the mystery religions (see above) would be one example of such a mystical concept. But the notion of some kind of merging of personality between a person and a god was found in many ancient Near-Eastern religions as well.

The basic concept that informs Paul's language here, however, should not be labeled "mysticism." As we noted in our comments on 5:12–21, Paul's teaching grows out of the Old Testament/Jewish notion of corporate solidarity. This notion is not properly "mystical," since it does not posit any merging of personalities. The solidarity is judicial or forensic. This is particularly clear with respect to Adam, who is, of course, not a god but an individual human being, whose significance for others is as their representative. This notion carries over into Romans 6 and explains how Paul can claim that believers were "with" Christ in his death, burial, and resurrection. As Adam in his sin represents all people, so Christ in his redemptive work represents people. Death, burial, and resurrection are singled out here because these three events were part of the core early Christian tradition about Christ's redemptive work. Note, for example, 1 Corinthians 15:3–4: "For what I received I passed on to you as of first importance: that Christ died for our sins according to the Scriptures, that he was buried, that he was raised on the third day according to the Scriptures."

In order that . . . we too may live a new life (6:4). A literal translation would be: "in order that . . . we too may walk in newness of life." Paul's use of the word "walk" to describe a person's lifestyle reflects a widespread Jewish metaphor (using the Hebrew word *hlk*). See, for example, Deuteronomy 26:17: "You have declared this day that the LORD is your God and that you will walk in his ways, that you will keep his decrees, commands and laws, and that you will obey him."

If we have been united with him like this in his death, we will certainly also be united with him in his resurrection (6:5). "United with" comes from a verb that means "grow together" (*symphyō*) and is often used in horticulture. Many interpreters, therefore, conclude that Paul may be alluding to Jesus' famous illustration of the vine and the branches (John 15). However, the word is used in many contexts, most of them not horticultural. We have no reason to think that this particular connotation of the word would have been in Paul's mind at this point.

Our old self was crucified with him (6:6). Paul uses the language of the "old self" or "old man" also in Ephesians 4:22–24 and Colossians 3:9–11. In both of these, the "old self," which Christians "put off," is contrasted with the "new self," which they have put on (Col. 3) or are to put on (Eph. 4). Modern interpreters often give the imagery an individualistic interpretation, as if the "old self" were the believer's sinful "nature" and the "new self" the renewed nature given at conversion. But Paul's idea is probably more corporate than this. We must again remember what he said about Adam's representative significance in chapter 5. With this notion present in the context, we are probably right to think of the "old self" as essentially Adam himself. Christ is then the "new self" (see Eph. 2:15; 4:13). What is crucified with Christ, then, is not some part, or nature, of us, but, as J. R. W. Stott puts it, "the whole of me as I was before I was converted."[38] When a person comes to Christ, that person is no longer under the domination of (though still influenced by) the nexus of sin and death brought into the world by Adam.

REFLECTIONS

SOME POPULAR EXPLANATIONS OF THE CHRISTIAN life use Paul's language of "old self" and "new self" to conceptualize the biblical teaching. One view, for instance, holds that when a person is converted, they lose the "old self" and become entirely a "new self." Another maintains that the "new self" is simply added to the "old self" when a person comes to Christ. Neither explanation does justice to all the biblical data or to our own experience. The former view cannot explain why Paul calls on Christians to "put off your old self" (Eph. 4:22–24) and has a hard time explaining the reality of continuing sinfulness in the believer. The latter, by contrast, does not do justice to the decisive change in our status that verses like Romans 6:6 teach. A better approach, then, is to think of the "old self" as Adam (cf. Rom. 5) and the "new self" as Christ. When we come to Christ, our servitude to the "old self" (or, better, "old man"), Adam, is broken, and we are tied inextricably to the "new self," Jesus Christ. So a decisive change occurs, but a change that does not make us immune from the continuing influence of our old Adamic self.

Anyone who has died has been freed from sin (6:7). "Freed [from]" actually translates the verb that is regularly translated "justify" (*dikaioō*). Many commentators think this translation should be preserved here. If so, then this verse is claiming that the believer's freedom from sin's power (6:6) is based on (note the "because" at the beginning of 6:7) the believer's justification (from sin's penalty). This idea may be theologically quite acceptable. But the NIV rendering has a lot to be said for it. Only here in his writings does Paul use the preposition "from" (*apo*) after the verb "justify" (though cf. Acts 13:38). More important, Paul may well be reflecting here a Jewish tradition, preserved in *b. Šabb.* 151b: "When a man is dead he is freed from fulfilling the law."[39]

The death he died, he died to sin once for all (6:10). The believer's death "to sin" is the ruling idea of this paragraph (see 6:2). It is a metaphor Paul uses to indicate the believer's complete break with the domination or mastery of sin. Being "dead to sin" means that Christians are no longer "slaves to sin" (6:6); sin is no longer our master (6:14). But why would Christ have had to "die to sin," as 6:10 claims? Some commentators think Paul may be using the metaphor in a different way here, to depict the redemptive benefits of Christ's death on our behalf. But we can maintain the same basic significance of the metaphor when we remember that Paul is writing in the context of his ruling "two-age" salvation-historical scheme (see comments on 5:21). In his incarnation, Christ took on our humanity and entered into the present evil age. Sin rules this age, and so Christ was subject to its power throughout his earthly life. To be sure, he never succumbed to

that power and actually sinned. But he did need to be released from its power; and his death was that release. The main line of Paul's argument in these verses thus becomes clear:

- Christ died to sin (6:10).
- We died with Christ (6:5, 6, 8).
- Therefore, we have died to sin (6:2).

In Christ Jesus (6:11). Paul's salvation-historical conception, rooted in Jewish apocalyptic, can again explain his claim that believers are "in" Christ. This idea, widespread in his letters, is again often thought to reflect ancient religious mystical notions. A. Deissmann, who popularized the notion in the early 1900s, argued that Paul viewed Christ as the "medium" or "ether" in which the Christian lives. But such a conception tends to depersonalize Christ and therefore runs counter to New Testament views of Jesus. A better explanation is to refer again to Paul's belief that Christ is the representative head of the new age of salvation. He incorporates within himself all who belong to him by faith. To be "in Christ," then, means to be identified with Christ as our representative and to have all the benefits he has won in his redemptive work applied to us.[40]

You are not under law, but under grace (6:14). Failure to appreciate the background of Paul's teaching can lead casual readers of Romans to misunderstand this assertion badly. Some might think that Paul proclaims believers to be free from any code of ethics at all. Those who have some knowledge of the history of theology might conclude that Paul proclaims the freedom of the believer from any divine commands—"law" in the sense the word is used in Lutheran theology, as the contrast to the gospel.

But, as we have seen earlier (see comments on 2:12), "law" (*nomos*) in Paul, a first-century Jew, almost always refers to the Mosaic law, the Torah. Paul is not claiming that believers are free from any divine commands (such as those we find in the teaching of Jesus or the New Testament letters). What he means is that believers are no longer bound to the Mosaic law. A new era in God's plan of salvation has dawned, an era in which God's eschatological grace is being poured out. With the coming of this new era, the old era has ceased to be the one to which we belong. The law of Moses was part of that old era. (Paul develops this argument in great detail in Gal. 3:15–4:7.) Paul's statement here is similar, then, to John's claim: "The law was given through Moses; grace and truth came through Jesus Christ" (John 1:17).

Freed from Sin's Power to Serve Righteousness (6:15–23)

Paul's focus in 6:1–14 has been on the negative: Believers are no longer slaves of sin (6:6). In 6:15–23, he broadens the perspective by including the positive side as well: Set free from sin, believers are now slaves of righteousness and of God.

Don't you know that when you offer yourselves to someone to obey him as slaves, you are slaves to the one you obey (6:16). Slavery was one of the best-known institutions in the ancient world. Almost 35–40 percent of the inhabitants of Rome and the peninsula of Italy in the first century were slaves; and the situation in the provinces may have been comparable.[41] So Paul's analogy would have been one that all his readers could

immediately have identified with. Making the analogy even more exact is the fact that people in the ancient world could sell themselves into slavery (e.g., to avoid a ruinous debt).[42] Similarly, Paul suggests, believers who constantly obey sin rather than God might find themselves to be slaves of sin again, doomed to eternal death.

You have been set free from sin and have become slaves to righteousness (6:18). Modern people, especially in the West, prize their autonomy. As heirs of the humanism of the Enlightenment, they assume that the noblest human being is the one who is subject to nothing but his or her own rational considerations. Ancient people, however, had a much stronger belief in the degree to which all human beings were under the control of outside powers—whether they be gods, the stars, or fate in general. The biblical writers certainly share this conviction. Nowhere in this paragraph does Paul suggest a person might not be a slave of something. Either he or she is dominated by sin or by righteousness and God—there is no middle ground. Jesus reflects the same perspective when he claims that "no one can serve two masters. Either he will hate the one and love the

other, or he will be devoted to the one and despise the other. You cannot serve both God and Money" (Matt. 6:24).

Offer them in slavery to righteousness leading to holiness (6:19). "Holiness" (which suggests the state of being holy) can also be translated "sanctification" (which suggests the process of becoming holy). In either case, Paul picks up the imagery from the Old Testament, where the root *qds* is widely used to denote the idea of being "set apart" from the world for the service of the Lord. As Christians give themselves in slavery to righteousness, they will progress further and further on the path of becoming different from the world and closer to the Lord's own holiness.

The wages of sin is death (6:23). "Wages" translates *opsōnia*, a word that means "provisions," but which is often used of money paid for services rendered. It was particularly applied to the pay given to soldiers (all three uses in the LXX have this sense [1 Esd. 4:56; 1 Macc. 3:28; 14:32]). The specific imagery in this verse, therefore, might be sin, as a commanding officer, paying a wage to his soldiers.

Released from the Law, Joined to Christ (7:1–6)

As Paul has suggested in 6:14 (see comments), the law of Moses belongs to the old age. In order to belong to the new age, therefore, believers must be released from the domination of the Mosaic law. In this paragraph Paul asserts that release and explains its consequences.

I am speaking to men who know the law (7:1). The "law" here, as throughout chapter 7, is probably the Mosaic law. We might therefore conclude that "[those] who know the law" must be Jews. But this is not necessarily the case. A substantial number of Gentiles in the ancient world were attracted to the Jewish religion. They regularly attended synagogue meetings, knew the Old Testament, and endeavored to follow the law as much as possible. But they were not considered Jews because they stopped short of becoming circumcised. These Gentile sympathizers, called "God-fearers" (see, e.g., Acts 13:26), were probably numerous in the early Christian churches, and many of the Gentiles Paul addresses in Rome were probably drawn from their number.

The law has authority over a man only as long as he lives (7:1). Paul refers to what may have been a well-known maxim in his day. See, for instance, *b. Šabb.* 30a: "If a person is dead, he is free from the Torah and the fulfilling of the commandments."[43]

If she marries another man (7:3). The Greek phrase means, literally, "become to a man" (*ginomai andri*). It is a colloquialism for "marry," as the LXX reveals, so the NIV rendering is accurate.[44] But Paul may use this particular wording so that he can create a better parallel with the believer's being "joined to" Christ (7:4, the Greek there is the same).

When we were controlled by the sinful nature (7:5). "Sinful nature" is the NIV rendering of the Greek word *sarx*, whose literal meaning is "flesh." The word has this literal meaning in the New Testament (e.g., 1 Cor. 15:39), but Paul particularly often uses *sarx* as a metaphor to denote the sinful tendency that governs people apart from Christ. As in this verse, the NIV generally chooses to translate this word with the phrase "sinful nature" when it has this metaphorical connotation.

Paul's use of this particular word in this way is striking and has created considerable controversy. A few scholars have thought that Paul might be influenced by certain Greek traditions that tended to view the physical body as evil. But a more likely background is the Old Testament use of the Hebrew word *bāsār* ("flesh") to denote the human being, and particularly the human being in his or her weakness, frailty, and proneness to sin (see Gen. 6:3, 12; Ps. 78:39). This background makes it clear that "flesh" is not a *part* of the human being (as the NIV translation may suggest), but the whole person looked upon as tied to this world, with its sin and corruption. Paul extends this basic sense a bit further, conceiving of *sarx* as virtually a power that exercises control over people outside of Christ. This, in turn, fits nicely into his two-age salvation-historical scheme. *Sarx* becomes another one of those ruling powers of the old age, from which believers are released through conversion to Christ. This is why Paul can in this verse describe our pre-Christian past as, literally, the time when we were "in the flesh."

The Coming of the Law (7:7–12)

The beginning of Romans 7 is the climax in Paul's negative assessment of the Mosaic law in Romans (see also 3:20, 28; 4:15; 5:20; 6:14, 15). Like sin, the law is something that people must "die to" if they are to enjoy the benefits of incorporation into Christ. As a seasoned preacher and teacher, Paul well knows the conclusion that people might draw

from this negative assessment. So he himself brings this faulty inference out into the open at the beginning of this paragraph: "What shall we say, then? Is the law sin?" He then shows why the inference is a faulty one, arguing that sin, not the law, is at fault in bringing about the human plight of death.

I would not have known what sin was except through the law (7:7). The Hebrew verb for "know" (*yd*ᶜ) often has the sense "experience, be in relationship with." The NIV obscures this sense of "know" by choosing other English renderings where the verb has this sense. But a more literal translation quickly reveals this usage. See, for instance, Jeremiah 9:6: "'You live in the midst of deception; in their deceit they refuse to *know* [NIV acknowledge] me,' declares the LORD." What the Lord is rebuking the people for is their failure to maintain their relationship with him. This same meaning occurs frequently in the New Testament with the comparable Greek verbs for "know." Second Corinthians 5:21, which claims that Christ did not "know" sin, is a good example.

Some interpreters apply this meaning to the verbs in this verse. Paul is then claiming that Israel did not "experience" sin until the law came. But this experien-

tial sense of the verbs is by no means common in the New Testament. Nevertheless, Paul seems to be claiming more than that the law simply "defined" what sin was. What he probably means is that the law gave to Israel a sense for what sin really is, in all its heinousness (see Rom. 7:13).

"Do not covet" (7:7). A few scholars, thinking that Paul refers to the experience of Adam and Eve throughout this paragraph, argue that Paul here refers to the prohibition that the Lord gave to the first human pair in the Garden of Eden. They note that the Aramaic targum *Neofiti I* uses a word that could be translated "desire" in Genesis 3:6 and that a rabbinic text claims that "desire" was injected into Eve by the serpent.[45] But these connections are tenuous at best. The words are

---

▶ The Use of "I" in Light of Paul's Corporate Solidarity With Israel

Throughout 7:7–25, Paul writes in the first person singular: "I," "me," "my," etc. The modern reader would naturally conclude that Paul does so because he is describing his own experience in these verses. Perhaps the modern reader is right. But the ancient world also furnishes some rhetorical models that suggest a different conclusion. Some scholars have drawn attention to texts in which the "I" is "fictive"; that is, an author writes in the first-person singular to describe a situation or experience without including himself or herself at all. A familiar example comes from Paul himself: "If I speak in the tongues of men and of angels, but have not love, I am only a resounding gong or a clanging cymbal. If I have the gift of prophecy and can fathom all mysteries and all knowledge, and if I have a faith that can move mountains, but have not love, I am nothing. If I give all I possess to the poor and surrender my body to the flames, but have not love, I gain nothing" (1 Cor. 13:1–3).[A-4] However, these texts are not close in nature to Romans 7. They are almost always cast in a hypothetical mold (as is the Corinthians text cited above) or include the author.

Closer in nature to Romans 7 and more relevant to Paul's own background and the context of Romans are Old Testament and Jewish texts that use "I" to depict the people of Israel. Note, for example, Micah 7:8–10, in which "I" is the nation of Israel, lamenting its judgment and expressing its hope:

> Do not gloat over me, my enemy!
> Though I have fallen, I will rise.
> Though I sit in darkness,
> the LORD will be my light.
> Because I have sinned against him,
> I will bear the LORD's wrath,
> until he pleads my case
> and establishes my right.
> He will bring me out into the light;
> I will see his righteousness.
> Then my enemy will see it
> and will be covered with shame,
> she who said to me,
> "Where is the LORD your God?"
> My eyes will see her downfall;
> even now she will be trampled underfoot
> like mire in the streets.[A-5]

Since Paul is writing in these verses about the coming of the Mosaic law (not "law" in general), a reference to the people of Israel makes good sense here. But this is not to exclude Paul himself. In the kind of solidarity viewpoint typical of these chapters, he identifies himself with the history of his own people Israel. Their experience is, in a real sense, his also. What happened when God gave the law to Israel at Sinai has also affected Paul. Such a close identification with the history of Israel is also typical of first-century Jews. In the yearly Passover ritual, every Jew confessed that he or she was a slave in Egypt and experienced the Lord's deliverance from bondage (see, e.g., *m. Pesaḥ* 10).

almost certainly an abbreviated citation of the tenth commandment of the Decalogue (Ex. 20:17; Deut. 5:21). There is Jewish precedent for such an abbreviation.[46] Paul probably quotes this commandment because some Jews viewed "coveting," or illicit desire, as the root evil.[47] The prohibition could then become a representative summation of the Mosaic law as a whole.[48] Paul uses the commandment in just this sense. He is writing about Israel's experience with the Mosaic law as a whole—not one person's experience (the "I") with one commandment.

Produced in me every kind of covetous desire (7:8). This language has been taken to refer to Paul's own sexual awakening at the time of his puberty.[49] But the word "desire" (*epithymeō*) generally has a broader meaning in Paul; moreover, as we have seen, a reference to Paul's individual experience in this paragraph is unlikely. Several other interpreters have suggested that Paul may be thinking of his *bar mitzvah*. But the ceremony was unknown in Paul's day; it was a medieval creation.[50]

The very commandment that was intended to bring life actually brought death (7:10). Interpreters who think Paul is describing the experience of Adam (as a representative person) in this paragraph argue that this language can only properly be applied to Adam and Eve. For only they actually experienced death when "the commandment came" and they sinned against the Lord. All other human beings since them were born in sin, condemned to death already.

But the commandment, in light of the context, must refer to a representative commandment from the Mosaic law (see 7:7). To be sure, Jewish tradition sometimes claimed that Adam and Eve were subject to the law itself. One of the Aramaic paraphrases of the Old Testament, *Neofiti I*, translates Genesis 2:15–16: "And the Lord God took man and caused him to dwell in the Garden of Eden, in order to keep the Law and to follow his commandments." But it is vital to Paul's understanding of salvation history to claim that the law came only with Moses, introduced 430 years after Abraham (Gal. 3:17). He would hardly give up such a vital point here.

What we must understand is that Paul is writing to counteract a certain Jewish tradition about the Mosaic law. That tradition, rooted in the Old Testament itself (Lev. 18:5; Ps. 19:7–10; Ezek. 20:11), ascribed virtual salvific power to the law (see, e.g., *t. Šabb.* 15.17: "The commands were given only that men should live through them, not that men should die through them"[51]). Paul turns this tradition on its head: The law brought not life, but death. Paul does not mean that the people of Israel experienced spiritual death for the first time when the law came. But what he does mean is that they were driven more deeply into spiritual helplessness because of the way the law so clearly spelled out the divine demands. When failure to meet these demands inevitably ensued, Israel's penalty for its sin was simply made all the greater (see also Rom. 4:15; 5:13–14).

Sin . . . deceived me (7:11). Advocates of the "Adamic" interpretation of these verses view this assertion as an allusion to Genesis 3:13, in which Eve claims that "the serpent deceived me, and I ate" (note that Paul uses this same verb to describe Eve's deception in 2 Cor. 11:13; 1 Tim. 2:14). Paul puts sin in the role of the serpent. But Paul uses the verb elsewhere with no allusion to the Fall.[52] That some allusion to the experience of Adam might be present in these verses need not be denied. In fact, Jewish tradition sometimes paralleled Adam and Israel. But Paul's main focus is on the Mosaic law and therefore on Israel, not Adam.

Life Under the Law (7:13–25)

Scholars and laypeople have debated for centuries over the interpretation of this passage. This commentary is not the place to discuss the matter. Suffice it to say that we think Paul is referring to the experience of the Jewish people (before Christ) under the law.[53] In 7:7–12, he describes what happened when the law "came" to the people of Israel. Now he turns to the nature of their experience living under that law.

Sold as a slave to sin (7:14). The NIV "as a slave" is an inference from one common application of the verb that Paul uses here. The verb itself means simply "sell," but it refers specifically to the selling of slaves in eleven of its twenty-four LXX occurrences and in one of its nine New Testament uses (Matt. 18:25). The slave imagery is further suggested by Paul's use of a preposition (*hypo*) that means "under" (see 3:9).

What I want to do I do not do, but what I hate I do (7:15). This confession of frustration at not being able to put into practice what one knows to be the right thing to do is similar to many found in the ancient world. Certainly the most famous comes from the Latin writer Ovid: "I see and approve the better course, but I follow the worse."[54]

That is, in my sinful nature (7:18). Or "flesh" (*sarx*); see comments on 7:5.

I see another law at work in the members of my body (7:23). Paul's introduction of a second "law," alongside "God's law" (7:22), is problematic. What is this "another law"? Since Paul has consistently used the word "law" to refer to the Mosaic law throughout this passage, this other law may simply be the Mosaic law in another guise. As a revelation of God's righteous will for his people, this law is "holy, righteous and good" (7:12). But when perverted by sin, that same law brings frustration and death (7:7–11). However, the word "another" makes it difficult to think that this second law has any relationship to the Mosaic law. Paul seems to be talking about a different law altogether. Ancient writers could sometimes use the word "law" (*nomos*) to refer to a general authority, norm, or power (see comments on 2:12). A contrast between God's law and an evil "law" is found elsewhere in Jewish literature, as in *T. Naph.* 2.6: "As a person's strength, so also is his work . . . as is his soul, so also

REFLECTIONS

IF ROMANS 7 IS ABOUT THE EXPERIENCE OF ISRAEL with the Mosaic law, what value does the chapter have for the Gentile Christian? For Gentiles have never been "under" the law of Moses. But Paul regards Israel's experience with the Mosaic law as typical of the experience of all people with "law" of any kind. Even God's own good and righteous commandments could not rescue Israel from her sin; how much less will other laws, be they moral codes or private resolutions, deliver us from our human plight. For law, in its very nature, tells us what to do but does not give us the power to do it. As long as we are held captive by sin, law will only reveal more clearly our problem and frustrate our efforts to live up to its standards. Deliverance from this dilemma, as Paul makes clear in 7:25, comes only through "Jesus Christ our Lord."

is this thought, whether on the Law of the Lord or on the law of Beliar."

What a wretched man I am! (7:24). "Wretched" (*talaipōros*) is a strong word. This word and its cognates are used several times in the Old Testament to refer to the "misery" or "distress" that come on the wicked in God's judgment (e.g., Isa. 47:11; Jer. 6:7).[55]

The Spirit of Life (8:1–13)

In chapters 6 and 7, Paul has answered possible objections to his teaching in chapter 5 that Christians who have been justified by faith have full assurance of being saved in the last day. Neither sin (ch. 6) nor the law (ch. 7) can stand in the way of our ultimate vindication. In chapter 8, Paul takes up the theme of assurance once again. "No condemnation" is the great claim that stands over all of the chapter. Especially important is the introduction of a new "power" on the scene: the Holy Spirit. Mentioned in passing in 7:6, the Spirit's work is the focal point of the chapter. It is because of the Spirit's powerful influence that the believer can experience the blessings of salvation both now and into the future.

In Christ Jesus (8:1). The language of incorporation into Christ reminds us of the teaching of 5:12–21. As all human beings are "in Adam" and so suffer the death that his sin introduced into the world, so believers are "in Christ" and enjoy the benefits of the righteousness and life that his work on the cross secured.

The law of the Spirit of life (8:2). As Paul has done twice earlier in the letter (3:27; 7:23), he contrasts one "law" with

another "law." The "law of the Spirit" could be a reference to the Mosaic law as it is used and actuated by the Holy Spirit. Appeal can be made here to a prophecy that was influential on the early Christian understanding of the new age: Jeremiah 31:31–34 and its close parallel, Ezekiel 36:24–32. These texts predict that God will one day write his law on the hearts of his people and put his Spirit in their hearts in such a way that they will be able to obey that law. "The law of the Spirit" may be Paul's way of referring to that internalized, Spirit-influenced law.

However, while the prophets looked for a day when God's people would be able to follow his law, they do not present that law as the liberating power (as Paul here presents "the law of the Spirit"). Nor does Paul ever suggest that the law would have such a role. It is better, then, to think that the word "law" in the phrase "law of the Spirit" has the meaning of "authority" or "power" (see comments on 2:12 and 7:23). The second "law" in this verse, "the law of sin and death," may be the Mosaic law, since Paul in chapter 7 has shown how that law was used by sin to bring death. But "law of sin" in 7:23 is not the Mosaic law, but a rhetorical counterpart to God's law. So here also "the law of sin and death" is probably the power of sin, leading to death, that holds people in its sway.

Sinful nature . . . sinful man (8:3). In both cases (as the NIV note indicates), these phrases translate a single Greek word, *sarx* ("flesh"). As we have seen (see comments on 7:5), Paul picks up the Old Testament use of this word to refer to human weakness and bondage to sin. What he is affirming, then, is that God has won the victory over the "flesh" in the "flesh" itself. By sending his Son to become fully human, God entered the arena of "flesh" and overcame its power to prevent people from obeying God and his law.

Sin offering (8:3). The Greek words here (*peri hamartias*) could be translated simply "concerning sin." But in the LXX, the phrase usually refers to a sacrificial offering; and three of the eight New Testament occurrences also have this meaning (Heb. 10:6, 8; 13:11). Christ is himself the sin offering that effects forgiveness and the turning away of God's wrath. God condemned sin in Christ, our substitute, so that we could escape condemnation.

The righteous requirements of the law (8:4). The NIV plural "requirements" is interpretive; the Greek word (*dikaiōma*) is singular. The plural of this word is common in the Old Testament to refer to the "statutes" of the law, a usage continued in the New Testament.[56] In the light of this usage, Paul's use of the word in the singular here must be deliberate. He is thinking not of the way Spirit-led Christians obey the detailed requirements of the law, but of the way believers, because they are in Christ, fulfill the overall demand of the law.

Who do not live according to the sinful nature but according to the Spirit (8:4). Dominating 8:4–11 is the contrast between the Spirit and the "flesh" (*sarx*, rendered "sinful nature" or "sinful mind" or simply "sinful" in the NIV). The Greek way of conceptualizing the human being has exerted a strong influence on those of us who live in the West. We naturally bring that conception into our Christian faith. The Greeks tended to take a dualistic view of human beings. That is, they divided, often quite sharply, the "material part" of the human being—the body or the flesh—from the "immaterial part"—the soul or the spirit. Under this influence, we can easily read 8:4–11 as if Paul were calling on believers to live according to their immaterial spirit and not according to their material body.

But such a reading badly misrepresents Paul's argument. (1) While some dualism is apparent in the New Testament view of the human being (for the soul can be separated from the body at death), the early Christians generally adopted the Old Testament/mainstream Jewish view of the human being as a fundamental unity. Indeed, it is this essentially unitary way of looking at people that requires resurrection: The body and soul cannot be separated forever.

(2) *Sarx*, when used to describe human proneness to sin in Paul, is not a part of the human being, but a perspective from which the whole human being is viewed. It is not that one part of us is sinful; we are, apart from Christ, sinful throughout—in mind, body, and soul.

SIN OFFERING

A model of a Jewish sacrificial scene at the tabernacle.

(3) The "spirit" in this passage is the Holy Spirit, not the human spirit. Note that the NIV capitalizes every occurrence of "spirit" (*pneuma*) in these verses except one (8:10). Even this one probably should be capitalized, for the text is best translated "the Spirit is life." Reading these verses against their appropriate Old Testament/mainstream Jewish/early Christian background, then, makes clear that Paul is working throughout with a contrast between God's Spirit, the power of the new age that he sends into the lives of his people, and the human propensity to sin and evil. God's Spirit inevitably wins this battle. In this life he plants within us a new way of thinking (8:5–7) that must infallibly lead to a new way of living (8:4). Ultimately, that same Spirit will raise and transform our bodies themselves (8:11).

Have their minds set ... the mind (8:5–6). The Greek words behind these translations (*phroneō* and *phronēma*) refer not just to the mental process of thinking, but to the general direction of the will.

The mind controlled by the Spirit is life and peace (8:6). The peace Paul refers to here is not the subjective "peace of mind," but the objective state of peace between God and his people and the general well-being that this relationship brings. Informing this concept is the Old Testament use of *shalom* to denote the eschatological blessing that God promises to his people (see comments on 5:1).

You, however, are controlled not by the sinful nature but by the Spirit (8:9). The NIV rendering is accurate enough. But a literal translation reveals the "two-age" salvation-historical conception that again informs Paul's teaching: "You are not in

the flesh but in the Spirit." To be "in" the flesh is to belong to the sphere or realm of sinful, depraved humanity. All people, because of Adam's sin, begin life trapped in this realm, destined to spiritual death. But in his grace, God removes us from that realm and puts us in another realm, ruled by Christ, righteousness, life, and the Spirit. All Christians, by definition, are therefore "in" the Spirit—living in the realm dominated by God's Holy Spirit.

If the Spirit ... lives in you (8:9). Paul's shift from the idea of believers being "in the Spirit" to the Spirit being "in" believers reveals that both are figures of speech, metaphors used to convey the truth that believers are ruled over and empowered by the Spirit.

He who raised Christ from the dead will also give life to your mortal bodies (8:11). Paul here reflects a key underlying tension in his celebration of the believer's blessings in Christ. Through the sacrifice of his son and the work of his Spirit, God has given his people "life" in the present: freedom from condemnation (8:1–9). But that "life" is not complete. The blessing of the new age has begun, but it is not yet here in its fullness. Believers must still face the reality of physical death, in that our bodies are still "mortal." Therefore, God's life-giving work is not finished until the body has been raised.

We have an obligation (8:12). Here Paul reflects the important "correction" that he makes to the simple Jewish idea of the "two ages." No longer is the transition from the one to the other a sharp, one-time event. The new age has dawned with the coming of Christ, and believers enjoy the benefits of that age, or realm, even now. But the old age has not disappeared. It has been judged and defeated, but will not be finally vanquished until the return of Christ in glory. With all the blessings we have received, therefore, believers still have a battle to fight. Sin and the flesh can still exert a powerful influence on us, an influence that must be resisted.

The Spirit of Adoption (8:14–17)

The Spirit gives life (8:1–13); he also confers on believers the status of God's own children. That new status is a source of joy in the present; but also a source of confidence for the future.

Sons of God (8:14). In the Old Testament and Judaism, "son of God" was used to depict Israel as the people whom God has called to be his own. See, for instance, Hosea 11:1 (quoted in Matt. 2:15): "When Israel was a child, I loved him, and out of Egypt I called my son."[57] The plural "sons of God" is less often used of the people of Israel, but it occurs often enough to justify our thinking that this background has influenced Paul's use of the phrase here (see Deut. 14:1; Isa. 43:6).[58] Paul therefore implies that Christians now take on the status and privileges of the people of Israel. This attribution to Christians of blessings once held by the people of Israel becomes an important theme in Romans 8 and sets up the problem Paul begins to deal with in chapter 9: Has God simply disenfranchised Israel?

The Spirit of sonship (8:15). The Greek word behind "sonship" can also be translated "adoption" (*huiothesia*). "Sonship" denotes the state of being God's own children; "adoption" refers to the process that leads to that state. Since almost all of the uses of the word outside the New Testament mean "adoption," that is probably the best rendering here.[59]

The process of adoption was unknown among Jews, but was common in the Greek, and especially the Roman, world. It was a legal institution by which a person could adopt a child and confer on that child all the legal rights and privileges that would accrue to a natural child.[60] One of the most famous "adoptions" in the Roman world was Julius Caesar's adoption of Octavian, who became Emperor Augustus. Paul's readers in Rome would naturally have thought immediately of this institution when they read these verses. The language would have conveyed to them the amazing grace of God in taking sinful human beings, making them his own children, and conferring on them all the rights and privileges of heaven itself (see also 8:23; Gal. 4:5; Eph. 1:5). But, while the language Paul uses here undoubtedly points to this Roman

ADOPTION

Octavian (Caesar Augustus), who is pictured here, was adopted by Julius Caesar.

institution, the word also indirectly conjures up the Old Testament and Jewish background we sketched above. Israel herself, Paul affirms in Romans 9:4, experienced this same "adoption." Here again is a blessing given to Israel that is now "transferred" to Christians.

And by him we cry, "*Abba*, Father" (8:15). "Cry" or "cry out" (*krazō*) is used in the Gospels of people who "cry out" under the influence of demons (e.g., Mark 3:11; 5:5, 7). We find the same usage in some ancient magical texts, in which a demon, or someone possessed, is said to "cry out." Since Paul has been describing the believer as a person, in a sense, "possessed" by the Spirit, we may view this "crying out" here as "ecstatic" in nature. If so, however, we must carefully qualify the idea to make clear that this exclamation is the product not of mindless possession but of conscious understanding. Note the emphasis in Romans 8:16 on the "testifying" work of the Spirit. Another background is suggested in the Psalms, where worshipers are frequently portrayed as crying out to God in praise or in supplication (see, e.g., Ps. 55:16: "But I call to God, and the LORD saves me"). Nevertheless, properly nuanced, the former option makes better sense in this context.

The Spirit himself testifies with our spirit that we are God's children (8:16). This is the only place in chapter 8 where the word "spirit" refers to the human spirit rather than to the Holy Spirit of God ("spirit" in 8:15 is not the human spirit, but a rhetorical counterpart to the Holy Spirit). The translation "testifies with" is not certain. The verb Paul uses (*symmartyreō*) can also mean simply "testify to." But the "with" idea is preserved in a second-century A.D. papyrus, where each person who adds his signature to attest the truth of the document claims to be "joining in witness."[61] This idea makes good sense here. God's own Spirit adds his voice to our own inner conviction that we are God's own dear children. Paul may even want to follow the biblical legal requirement of at least two witnesses (see Deut. 19:15: "One witness is not enough to convict a man accused of any crime or offense he may have committed. A matter must be established by the testimony of two or three witnesses").

Now if we are children, then we are heirs (8:17). The move from being "children" to being "heirs" is a most appropriate way to introduce the idea of Christian hope. As Paul argues elsewhere (see esp. Gal. 4:1–3), a child is by definition not yet at

---

▶ "*Abba*" as "Daddy"?

Many Christians know that the word *Abba* is an Aramaic word that means "father, daddy." Jesus himself must have used this word in addressing God, for the New Testament authors, writing in Greek, nevertheless preserved this word in their text (see Mark 14:36). The word generally connotes an intimate relationship and suggests the close familial union of believers with their God. However, the claim that Jews never used this word for God or that it always has the informal sense conveyed by a word like our "Daddy" is exaggerated. Jews could use *Abba* in prayers to God, and it is not always used by little children.[A-6]

the legal age to come into all the rights and privileges of family membership. So also, he suggests, the Christian, while adopted into God's family, does not yet experience all the blessings of that relationship. Only when Christ returns in glory will the final transformation into the image of Christ, God's Son, be complete.

Paul's readers would be familiar with the rules of inheritance from the Roman law of their time.[62] But, in addition to this "everyday" background to the inheritance idea, another background may also figure into Paul's imagery here. The Old Testament regularly depicts God's promise to his people as an "inheritance." In the early stages of the Old Testament, this inheritance was identified particularly with the land of Israel. See, for example, Numbers 34:2: "Command the Israelites and say to them: 'When you enter Canaan, the land that will be allotted to you as an inheritance will have these boundaries.'"[63] In later Judaism, however, "inheritance" could also describe the life that God will give his people in these last days: "But the devout of the Lord will inherit life in happiness" (*Pss. Sol.* 14:10).[64]

The Spirit of Glory (8:18–30)

The "glory" that the believer will experience as his or her inheritance on the last day is the theme of this section. The text begins on this note—"the glory that will be revealed in us"—and ends on it—"those he justified, he also glorified." In between, Paul shows how the glory of God's children is the goal of all creation (8:18–25) and how God is working during this life to give the believer confidence for that last day (8:26–30).

The glory that will be revealed in us (8:18). The sequence of present suffer-

ing leading to future glory is common in Jewish literature. See, for example, *2 Apoc. Bar.* 15:8: "For this world is to them [the righteous] a struggle and an effort and much trouble. And that accordingly which will come, a crown with great glory." However, because Paul looked back at the realization of God's promises in Christ, he put more stress than Jewish writers did on the participation of the believer in that eventual glory. We will not only be ushered into a state of glory; we will share in Christ's own glory.

The creation waits in eager expectation (8:19). Paul's reference to "creation" in this context is debated. Since he claims that creation "waits" (8:19), "was subjected to frustration" (8:20), and has been "groaning" (8:22), many interpreters think that he must have in mind human beings. But Paul seems to contrast creation with believers (see 8:23); and he never portrays unbelievers as having hope for the future. Probably, then, "creation" in these verses denotes the subhuman world. Sufficient precedent for Paul's vivid personification of creation here is found in the Old Testament, which depicts the hills, meadows, and valleys as shouting for joy and singing (Ps. 65:12–13), and the earth itself as mourning (Isa. 24:4; Jer. 4:28; 12:4).

The creation was subjected to frustration, not by its own choice, but by the will of the one who subjected it (8:20). When Adam and Eve fell into sin, Genesis 3 tells us, the earth itself was "cursed" (Gen. 3:17–18). It is this curse to which Paul refers when he claims that creation has been "subjected to frustration": that is, it has not attained the ends for which God first made it. Since God is the One who uttered the curse, it is his will that so subjected it. But human sin was the immediate occasion for the curse, and Jewish literature frequently alludes to the connection between sin and the earth's fallen condition. See, for example, *4 Ezra* 7:11–12:

> For I made the world for their sake, and when Adam transgressed my statutes, what had been made was judged. And so the entrances of this world were made narrow and sorrowful and toilsome; they are few and evil, full of dangers and involved in great hardships.

The creation itself will be liberated from its bondage to decay (8:21). Along with the fall of the earth through human sin, Jewish writers also celebrated the earth's eventual renewal. This theme is especially prominent in Jewish apocalyptic, and Paul seems to derive some of his ideas in this section from that influential strand of Jewish thinking. As a typical example, sharing also the personification

of creation that we find in Romans 8, see *1 Enoch* 51:4–5:

> In those days, mountains shall dance like rams; and the hills shall leap like kids satiated with milk. And the faces of all the angels in heaven shall glow with joy, because on that day the Elect One has arisen. And the earth shall rejoice; and the righteous ones shall dwell upon her and the elect ones shall walk upon her.[65]

While human beings are the focus of God's attention in his plan of salvation, the earth itself will also be rescued from the effects of the Fall. If one adopts a premillennial eschatology, then the Millennium may be regarded as that period when the earth is restored to its original "good" condition.

The whole creation has been groaning as in the pains of childbirth (8:22). The pain of labor is a natural metaphor for Christian hope. In each case the suffering is momentary, leading to joy at the end. See especially John 16:20b–22:

> You will grieve, but your grief will turn to joy. A woman giving birth to a child has pain because her time has come; but when her baby is born she forgets the anguish because of her joy that a child is born into the world. So with you: Now is your time of grief, but I will see you again and you will rejoice, and no one will take away your joy. (Note also Matt. 24:8; Mark 13:8).

We ourselves, who have the firstfruits of the Spirit, groan inwardly (8:23). "Firstfruits" is used repeatedly in the Old Testament to describe the initial part of the harvest offered to the Lord and to his priests.[66] It is hard to know whether this background plays a significant role in the New Testament use of the term, where it refers to the first stage of a series—the

REFLECTIONS

AN ISSUE THAT LOOMS EVER LARGER AS DEBATES about the extent of "global warming" heat up is the Christian attitude toward the environment. Horrified by the excesses of radical environmentalists, who often deny the special nature of human beings as created in the image of God, many Christians have taken a strong anti-environmental position. It is true that the New Testament says little about the world of nature. It focuses mainly on the redemption and growth in grace of people. But passages such as Romans 8 remind us that God has a concern for the world of nature in itself. He created it, and he plans to redeem it one day. The environment, therefore, has value in itself, and Christians need to practice good stewardship of that environment. We are called under God to resist the materialism that makes our own comfort the standard by which we make decisions and to give God's creation the protection it deserves.

first converts in an area (Rom. 16:5; 1 Cor. 16:15), the first steps in God's redemptive plan, and Christ himself, the first to be raised from the dead.[67] In each case, however, the idea of "firstfruits" implies the certainty of more to come.

"Groan" is a keyword in these verses. Creation groans (8:22), Christians groan (8:23), and the Holy Spirit groans (8:26). Paul may use the word in this context where hope is so prominent because righteous sufferers in the Old Testament frequently describe themselves as "groaning" in their present sufferings as they call out to God for deliverance (see Ex. 2:24; 6:5).[68] The word, therefore, nicely captures the combination of frustrated longing for final deliverance that characterizes this passage.

The Spirit helps us in our weakness (8:26). As long as we are in this life, we are "weak," incapable of finally overcoming sin and destined to die. But God sends help for us during this time of waiting for our hope to reach its fruition. The Spirit's ministry is one of the most important sources of help and support. The word "help" in the NIV translates a verb that can be rendered "bear a burden along with" (*synantilambanomai*).[69] A few interpreters have suggested that Paul may have derived his idea of the intercession of the Spirit from Hellenistic religions or even Gnosticism. But a more likely source is the Old Testament and especially apocalyptic Judaism, which emphasized the importance of angelic and other mediators.[70]

He who searches our hearts knows the mind of the Spirit (8:27). Paul's language picks up Old Testament descriptions of God as the One who "knows" or "judges" the hearts of his people (e.g., 1 Sam. 16:7; 1 Kings 8:39).[71]

God works for the good (8:28). Many Christians misinterpret this verse, thinking that God here promises to give us all kinds of "good" things: jobs, money, health, and so on. But, as the context makes clear, "good" is primarily the glory God will one day enable us to share with Christ, our Lord. In the Old Testament, "good" sometimes has a similar focus, denoting the blessings of the age to come.[72]

Those God foreknew he predestined (8:29). Theologians have debated for many years just what Paul means by "foreknow." In Greek generally, the verb means "know something ahead of time." Some scholars thus think that Paul is teaching that God knew ahead of time about the faith people would have and predestined those who would believe. But a characteristic biblical use of the verb "know" raises another possibility. This verb often connotes not mental "knowledge" but an intimate relationship. See, for instance, Genesis 18:19, where the NIV translates "for I have chosen him [Abraham]," although the verb is the usual Hebrew word for "know" (*yd^c*; see also, e.g., Jer. 1:5; Amos 3:2). Most of the other New Testament occurrences of "foreknow" have this sense.[73] Since Paul here does not say that God knew anything about us but rather that he knew *us*, the idea "choose ahead of time" makes the best sense.

The firstborn among many brothers (8:29). "Firstborn" is similar to the idea of "firstfruits" (see comments on 8:23). As the first to be raised from the dead and enter into the state of glory, Christ paves the way for his brothers and sisters to follow. Also possibly contributing to the imagery of this verse is the use of "firstborn" in the Old Testament to refer to the Messiah (Ps. 89:27).

Celebration of the Believer's Security (8:31–39)

Paul now reflects on the wonder of the confidence believers have, as he has outlined this assurance in chapters 5–8. The series of questions in 8:31–35 invite the reader to join in with the celebration.

He who did not spare his own Son, but gave him up for us all (8:32). The wording of this sentence is similar to that found in the famous story about Abraham's offering of Isaac. God commends Abraham for not "sparing" his own son (Gen. 22:12, 16; the NIV translates "withhold" in these verses, but the Greek verb in the LXX is the same verb Paul uses). In later rabbinic tradition, Abraham's offering of Isaac grew into an elaborate tradition, called the *Aqedah* ("binding"; the name derives from the fact that Abraham "bound" Isaac with ropes [Gen. 22:9]). But the tradition does not seem to have existed in Paul's day; the earliest evidence for it comes from the Amoraic (post A.D. 200) period.

As it is written, "For your sake we face death all day long; we are considered as sheep to be slaughtered" (8:36). Paul quotes Psalm 44:22 to show that God's people have always had to face opposition from the ungodly. Paul writes before the great persecution of Christians in Rome under Nero, but the terrible trial these Roman Christians were destined to experience illustrates the degree of opposition that God's people may sometimes face in this fallen world. The appropriateness of this citation is suggested by the

▶

THE ROMAN COLOSSEUM

Outside and inside view. The bottom photo shows the hallways and rooms under the Colosseum floor (no longer visible).

▶

fact that the later rabbis applied this text to the death of the martyrs.[74]

Neither height nor depth (8:39). These words, and other words like them, were used in the ancient world to denote the celestial space above and below the horizon.[75] Since spiritual beings were thought to reside in the heavens, these terms could also be applied to spiritual beings. But there is little lexical evidence that these terms have such a denotation. Probably, as in Ephesians 3:18, the imagery is simply spatial: Nothing in the heavens above or on the earth below can separate believers from God's love for them in Christ.

God's Promises and Israel's Plight (9:1–5)

In chapter 9, Paul's argument enters a new phase. He has shown that the gospel of Jesus Christ provides justification for anyone who believes (chs. 1–4) and that this divine verdict will hold good at the judgment of God (chs. 5–8). Throughout this argument, a key subtheme has been that Gentiles have equal access with Jews to this new work of God. The blessings God promised to his people in the Old Testament are now available for any Christian. Believers, whether Jew or Gentile, are children of Abraham (ch. 4), children and heirs of God (8:14–17), destined for glory (8:18–30).

But all this raises an insistent question: What about God's promises to Israel? Paul seems to be affirming that what God first promised Israel he has given to the church. Israel, as a whole, remains in her sin (9:1–3); what, then, of all her privileges (9:4–5)? The gospel Paul preaches, therefore, creates an apparent problem for the faithfulness of God to his word. This issue, enunciated in 9:6, is the driving issue of chapters 9–11. Paul must show that his interpretation of the gospel is consistent with the Old Testament promises to Israel. Not surprisingly, he turns to the Old Testament itself to make his case. Almost one-third of Paul's quotations from the Old Testament occur in these three chapters of Romans.

Conscience (9:1). This word is one of the few that Paul takes from the Hellenistic world.[76] The Greek word used here (*syneidēsis*) appears only once in the canonical books of the Old Testament (Eccl. 10:20 LXX). "Conscience" played an important role in Stoic philosophy, but Paul shows no dependence on the technical use of the word. He seems instead to use it in its more "everyday" meaning, to denote the faculty within us that monitors our agreement with moral norms.

I have great sorrow and unceasing anguish in my heart (9:2). Paul's grief over the spiritual state of his fellow Israelites reminds us of the Old Testament prophets, who lamented the sin and resulting judgment of God on the people of Israel in their own day. See, for example, Jeremiah 4:19–22:

Oh, my anguish, my anguish!
I writhe in pain.
Oh, the agony of my heart!
My heart pounds within me,
I cannot keep silent.
For I have heard the sound of the trumpet;
I have heard the battle cry.
Disaster follows disaster;
the whole land lies in ruins.
In an instant my tents are destroyed,
my shelter in a moment.
How long must I see the battle standard
and hear the sound of the trumpet?

My people are fools;
    they do not know me.
They are senseless children;
    they have no understanding.
They are skilled in doing evil;
    they know not how to do good.

Cursed (9:3). The Greek word is *anathema*, which has been taken into English as a way of denoting something or someone rejected and denied status. The Greek word itself translates the Hebrew *ḥerem*, "something set apart for God." What is set apart for God may have a positive purpose, as when sacrifices are called "anathema."[77] But the word usually has a negative sense, referring to something or someone set aside by God for destruction. For instance, the city of Jericho and the Canaanite cities conquered by Israel are said to be "anathema."[78] The rabbis later used the same word to refer to those who were excommunicated from the faith.[79]

I could wish that I myself were . . . cut off from Christ for the sake of my brothers (9:3). Paul takes on a role here similar to that of Moses with respect to the people of Israel after their sin in worshiping the golden calf. Moses asks that God would blot his name out of "the book" if he would not forgive the people (Ex. 32:30–32). So also Paul is ready to sacrifice his own salvation for the sake of his "brothers," the people of Israel who have not responded to the gospel.

The people of Israel (9:4). Paul's use here of the word "Israelites" (NASB; Gk. *Israēlitai*) marks a significant shift from his use of "Jew" or "Jews" in chapters 1–8 (1:16; 2:9, 10, 17, 28, 29; 3:1, 9, 29). "Jew" (*Ioudaios*), deriving from the territory of Judea, is a politically and nationally oriented term. It is the word that most people in the Roman Empire used to denote people who lived in the land of Israel. But "Israelite" often has a more theological connotation. This word, of course, goes back to the name that God bestowed on Jacob (Gen. 32:28; 35:10) and passed down to his offspring (32:32; 46:8). It therefore hints at the favored status of the people of Israel in the eyes of God.

Several intertestamental books preserve this distinction between the words. In 1 Maccabees, for instance, "Jew" is used in letters to foreign nations or when the focus is on politics. But "Israel" is used when the focus is on the people's religious status in relationship to other nations. Simply by shifting from "Jew" to "Israelites," then, Paul signals his intent to consider seriously the special position and promises enjoyed by that people.

Adoption as sons (9:4). In 8:15 and 23, Paul used the word "adoption" or "sonship" (*huiothesia*) to describe Christians' special blessing as God's own children. In applying that same word here to unbelieving Israel, Paul shifts the meaning a bit. God "adopted" Israel as a nation in the sense that he selected that nation to be the recipient of his old covenant blessing and to act as the conduit of his blessing to the rest of the world (see Ex. 4:22–23; Deut. 14:1–2).[80]

The divine glory (9:4). In chapter 8, Paul has also attributed "glory" to Christians (e.g., 8:18, 30). We must again assume that the "glory" ascribed here to Israel is different from the eschatological glory Christians are destined for. The Old Testament repeatedly speaks of the appearance of "the glory of the LORD" on special occasions and in the temple (e.g.,

Ex. 16:7, 10).[81] Thus, what Paul probably refers to here is the divine presence of the Lord with his people.

The covenants (9:4). The plural form of the word is unusual. We generally think of one "old" covenant and one "new." Paul could be referring to both of these here, but he seems to be describing the privileges of Israel apart from their fulfillment in Christ. In other words, Paul is probably thinking of the several covenants that God made with various Old Testament people (e.g., Noah, Abraham, Israel at Sinai, and David [cf. 2 Sam. 23:5]).

The temple worship (9:4). The regular offering of sacrifices in the temple in Jerusalem was a central focus of Jewish religious life. As a famous text from the Mishnah proclaims, "By three things is the world sustained: by the Law, by the [Temple-]service, and by deeds of loving-kindness."[82] Jews who lived close enough were expected to travel to Jerusalem for the great pilgrimage festivals every year, and Jews in the Diaspora were to contribute yearly to a fund to maintain the temple service.

The patriarchs (9:5). The promises that God gave Abraham, Isaac, and Jacob became the focal point of Israel's identity as a nation and her blessings before the Lord. Reference to the "patriarchs" (lit., "fathers") brackets Paul's argument in these chapters (see also 11:28), focusing attention on Israel's special status.

Defining the Promise (1): God's Sovereign Election (9:6–29)

As the first step in Paul's defense of God's faithfulness to his promises to Israel, he uses the Old Testament itself to show just what God has promised Israel. His key point is that God never promised salvation to every individual Jew. All along, Paul demonstrates, God's own sovereign act of "calling" was what brought the Jew to salvation. Throughout this section, Paul is responding to the popular Jewish view of election, which held that God's covenant with Abraham, renewed through Moses, guaranteed salvation to every Jew who did not separate himself or herself (e.g., by renouncing the law) from Israel. Paul's response, to quote the phrase of N. T. Wright, is that "what counts is grace, not race."[83]

Paul's extensive use of the Old Testament throughout this section is similar in some ways to the Jewish practice of

REFLECTIONS

WE HAVE NOT COMMENTED ON THE VERY END OF Romans 9:5 because the text does not have significant "background" issues. But we should not pass by the verse without noting the significance of the text for Christology. The NIV renders the end of the verse "and from them is traced the human ancestry of Christ, who is God over all, forever praised." With the comma after "Christ," this translation attributed the title "God" to Jesus—an explicit statement of his deity.

But note the RSV rendering of the same text: "and of their race, according to the flesh, is the Christ. God who is over all be blessed forever. Amen!" Here we find a period after "Christ," making the last blessing one that applies to God the Father. The problem here is that our earliest Greek manuscripts (for the most part) had no punctuation at all. The Greek letters run continuously without breaks between words. So modern editors, commentators, and translators have to decide where to put punctuation marks and what marks to use. A good case can be made here for either the comma or the period after "Christ." But the evidence leans toward the comma, suggested by the fact that the NRSV has gone that direction. On the most probable interpretation, therefore, Romans 9:5 is an important New Testament testimony to the deity of Christ.

scriptural commentary called *midrash*. To be sure, Paul uses certain techniques found among Jewish *midrashim*, such as bringing together texts on the basis of common words ("descendants"/"offspring" in Gen. 21:12 [9:7] and Isa. 1:9 [9:29]). But, the overall integration of Scripture into Paul's own argument is quite different than the more strictly "commentary" format of the Jewish midrashic writers.

Not all who are descended from Israel are Israel (9:6). The first occurrence of "Israel" refers to "physical" Israel: All the people descended from Jacob, whose name, we might recall, was changed to "Israel" (Gen. 32:28). The second "Israel" in the verse must, however, have a spiritual significance, referring to people who truly have a relationship with the Lord. But how broadly does Paul intend the word to apply? While it is debated, Galatians 6:16 seems to suggest that Paul could use the word "Israel" to refer to everyone who belonged to the Lord, Gentile or Jew. But this "transfer" of the term from physical Israel to the church is rare; we have no other example until the second century. Because of this, and because of the nature of the argument in these chapters, then, it is better to think of this spiritual Israel here as an Israel *within* Israel: those Jews truly saved within the larger nation.

Abraham's children (9:7). Paul's defense of the proposition that only some Jews are truly Jews in the spiritual sense begins, naturally enough, with Abraham. For, as we noted in our comments on chapter 4, the Old Testament makes God's call and promise to Abraham the starting point of the people of Israel (Gen. 12:1–3; 15:1–5, 18–21).[84] The

true, spiritual "descendants" (or "offspring," *sperma*) of Abraham are those who are "reckoned" to be so through Isaac. For the Old Testament teaches that Abraham had other natural children, through the slave woman, Hagar. Yet they do not participate in the promise of God. Genesis 21:12, the verse that Paul quotes here, was God's assurance to Abraham that he would have children through Isaac and that these children would inherit the promise.

In other words (9:8). The NIV rendering paraphrases the Greek, which, literally translated, is "that is." This phrase is similar to the one used by the sectarians at Qumran to introduce a contemporary application of the Old Testament. The Hebrew phrase is *pesharo*, from which is derived the name given to the method of Old Testament interpretation in the Dead Sea Scrolls, *pesher*. Paul therefore signals that 9:8 is his "interpretation" of the passage he has quoted in 9:7.

At the appointed time I will return, and Sarah will have a son (9:9). This quotation is a mixture of Genesis 18:10 and 14, in which God insists that he will take the initiative in bringing a son to Abraham through Sarah.

Rebekah's children had one and the same father (9:10). An objector to Paul's argument might point out that the distinction between Isaac and Ishmael did have a physical component to it, in that they had different mothers. Thus, to make his point crystal clear, Paul moves down a generation, reminding his readers that both Jacob and Esau were born to the same mother, Rebekah, and father, Isaac. Indeed, Paul goes even further. While not clear from the NIV, the Greek

Paul uses here (*koitē*, from which we get the word "coitus") probably means "semen."[85] In other words, Paul reminds us that Jacob and Esau were conceived in one act of sexual intercourse. How much less basis, physically, could there be for a distinction between them?

Paul's argument picks up certain emphases within Judaism itself, as *4 Ezra* 3:13–16 makes clear:

> And when they were committing iniquity in your sight, you chose for yourself one of them, whose name was Abraham; you loved him, and to him alone you revealed the end of the times, secretly by night. You made an everlasting covenant with him, and promised him that you would never forsake his descendants; and you gave him Isaac, and to Isaac you gave Jacob and Esau. You set apart Jacob for yourself, but Esau you rejected; and Jacob became a great multitude.

God's purpose in election (9:11). "Purpose" translates a word (*prothesis*) that emphasizes God's plan as predetermined (see 8:28). The Dead Sea Scrolls use a parallel Hebrew word (*mahahsabâ*) in a similar way. See, for example, 1QS 3:15–16a:

> From the God of knowledge stems all there is and all there shall be. Before they existed he made all their plans and when they came into being they will execute all their works in compliance with his instructions, according to his glorious design without altering anything.

Not by works but by him who calls (9:12). Modern scholars are not agreed about just what the Jewish view of election may have been. But there is a grow-ing consensus that there was not a single doctrine, but a variety of views. At least one strand of Judaism linked God's election to human works. A particularly interesting text from Philo comments on the distinction between Jacob and Esau and attributes it, at least in part, to their works, which God had foreseen:

> Once again, of Jacob and Esau, when still in the womb, God declares that the one is a ruler and leader and master, but that Esau is a subject and slave. For God the Maker of living beings knows well the different pieces of his own handwork, even before he has thoroughly chiseled and consummated them, and the faculties which they are to display at a later time, in a word their deeds and experiences. And so when Rebecca, the soul that waits on God, goes to inquire of God, he tells her in reply, "Two nations are in your womb, and two peoples shall be separated from your belly, and one people shall be above the other people, and the elder shall serve the younger."[86]

Jacob I loved, but Esau I hated (9:13). This famous—and difficult!—quotation is from Malachi 1:2–3. A quick glance at Malachi reveals that the prophet is not talking about the individuals Jacob and Esau. He is using these names to refer to the nations founded by these individuals: Israel and Edom, respectively. The words that come immediately before the text that Paul quotes in Romans 9:12 (Gen. 25:23) move in the same direction: "Two nations are in your womb, and two peoples from within you will be separated; one people will be stronger than the other, and the older will serve the younger."

With this Old Testament background in view, many scholars think Paul is speaking throughout this chapter about

God's calling of nations and their place in his plan of salvation. He is not—as so many interpreters have thought—teaching anything about the salvation of individuals. The Old Testament context of Paul's quotations forces us to reckon seriously with the possibility that Paul's focus is corporate and not individual. But many features from within Romans 9 are difficult to reconcile with the corporate interpretation: the focus on the identity of God's children (9:7–9, 29); the contrast between wrath and glory in 9:22–23; and the whole point of the discussion, which is to demonstrate which people from within the single nation of Israel are really chosen by God. Probably, then, Paul is choosing Old Testament texts about God's sovereign and gracious election to illustrate the point about the salvation of individuals that is the heart of Romans 9.[87]

The verbs "love" and "hate" in Malachi are covenantal terms. They do not express God's emotions about Israel and Edom but his actions with respect to them. We might paraphrase, "Jacob I have chosen, but Esau I have rejected."

Is God unjust? (9:14). The modern reader immediately assumes the issue here is about God's "fairness": his justice in acting as he has toward Jacob and Esau. But the Greek word used here (*adikia*) comes from a root that is used throughout the Old and New Testaments to designate God's "righteousness," a term that often refers to God's faithfulness to his covenant with Israel or, more basically, to his commitment to his own person and name. Rather than raising the notion of God's "fairness" here, then, Paul may be asking whether God's actions in regard to Jacob and Esau contradict his own nature. And, of course, it is ultimately only by the standard of God's own nature that his "fairness" can be properly measured.

It does not, therefore, depend on man's desire or effort (9:16). "Effort" translates the verb *trechō*, "to run." Paul's metaphor may come from Greco-Roman athletics, since he elsewhere uses language drawn from that sphere.[88] But the Jews also spoke of "walking" or "running" in the way of the law (cf. Ps. 119:32).

The Scripture says to Pharaoh: "I raised you up for this very purpose" (9:17). "I raised you up" has the connotation "appoint to a significant role in salvation history" (cf. Jer. 50:41 [LXX 27:41]; Hab. 1:6; Zech. 11:16).

He hardens whom he wants to harden (9:18). In secular Greek, the verb "harden" (*sklērynō*) usually occurs in medical contexts, with reference to the hardness of bones. But the specific background for Paul's use of the word is Exodus 4–14, where the verb occurs fourteen times to denote the spiritual insensitivity that God brought on Pharaoh (e.g. Ex. 4:21; 7:22).[89] Paul expects us to understand the general

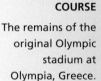

method of God's hardening in light of the Exodus story.

But what does the Exodus story teach us about God's hardening? Some scholars insist that God's hardening of Pharaoh is a response to Pharaoh's previous decision to harden himself. They note that reference to God's hardening of Pharaoh's heart (9:12) occurs only after references to Pharaoh's hardening of his own heart (8:15, 32). Thus, it can be concluded, God only hardens people who have already made themselves insensitive to his will. However, the Exodus narrative is not so clear on this matter. Before Pharaoh hardens his own heart, five times we read that Pharaoh's heart "was hardened" (Ex. 7:13, 14, 22; 8:15, 32). The subject of these passive verbs may be God, since the narrative opens with predictions that God would himself harden Pharaoh (4:21 and 7:3). The upshot is that the Exodus story does not tip the scales decisively one way or the other about how we should integrate God's hardening with peoples' own sinful obstinacy.

One of you will say to me (9:19). The diatribe style of question and answer becomes more pronounced at this point, as Paul deals with objections to his strong emphasis on God's sovereignty in 9:14–18. As we have seen (see comments in introduction and on 2:1), this style need not have a specific objector in view. But Paul may well be reflecting in these verses his own "take" on a current debate within Judaism about God's sovereignty and human free will.

Shall what is formed say to him who formed it, "Why did you make me like this?" Does not the potter have the right . . . ? (9:20–21). Few household items were as common as the pottery jar. So

POTTER

▶ The Debate on Sovereignty and Free Will in First-Century Judaism

Though Josephus may be trying to "dress up" Jewish views in philosophical terms more appealing to his Greek audience, what he says about the differences among the Jewish groups of his day is still likely to reflect a genuine debate:

Now at this time there were three schools of thought among the Jews, which held different opinions concerning human affairs; the first being that of the Pharisees, the second that of the Sadducees, and the third that of the Essenes. As for the Pharisees, they say that certain events are the work of Fate, but not all; as to other events, it depends upon ourselves whether they shall take place or not. The sect of the Essenes, however, declares that Fate is mistress of all things, and that nothing befalls men unless it be in accordance with her decree. But the Sadducees do away with Fate, holding that there is no such thing and that human actions are not achieved in accordance with her decree, but that all things lie within our own power, so that we ourselves are responsible for our well-being, while we suffer misfortune through our own thoughtlessness.[A-7] the imagery of potter and clay would have been immediately accessible to all Paul's readers. The Old Testament frequently applies this imagery to God's control over his creation.[90] Jewish writers followed suit. See, for example, Sirach 33:13: "Like clay in the hand of the potter, to be molded as he pleases, so all are in the hand of their Maker, to be given whatever he decides." In Romans 9:20, Paul quotes from Isaiah 29:16, with probable allusion also to Isaiah 45:9. But the imagery was familiar enough that no single text can be identified as the one Paul definitively had in mind here.

What if God . . . bore with great patience his objects of wrath . . . to make the riches of his glory known to the objects of his mercy (9:22–23). Verses 22–23 are difficult to understand. The syntax is complicated and the theology debated. But one strand of Jewish thinking may illuminate Paul's purpose. According to some Jewish authors, God's decision to wait until the end to judge the nations of the world was for the purpose that they might fill up the full measure of their sins and so receive the full force of his wrath. See, for instance, 2 Maccabees 6:12–14, where the author seeks to comfort the people of Israel as they go through severe persecution:

> Now I urge those who read this book not to be depressed by such calamities, but to recognize that these punishments were designed not to destroy but to discipline our people. In fact, it is a sign of great kindness not to let the impious alone for long, but to punish them immediately. For in the case of the other nations the Lord waits patiently to punish them until they have reached the full measure of their sins; but he does not deal in this way with us.[91]

As he says in Hosea (9:25–26). Paul quotes two verses from Hosea (2:23 in 9:25; 1:10 [LXX 2:1] in 9:26) to buttress his claim that Gentiles are now among those being "called" (9:24) as "objects of his mercy" (9:23). Note, however, that Hosea is not predicting the conversion of Gentiles but the return of the "lost" ten northern tribes to the people of Israel. Paul reflects here a hermeneutical axiom that he assumes throughout his interpretation of the Old Testament: Predictions about a renewed Israel can be fulfilled in God's new "Israel," the church.

▶

SODOM AND GOMORRAH

Bab edh-Dhra and the Lisan peninsula—the possible site of Sodom.

Isaiah cries out concerning Israel: "Though the number of the Israelites be like the sand by the sea, only the remnant will be saved" (9:27). The "remnant" concept develops in the Prophets, who pronounce doom on Israel as a whole because of her sin but promise blessing for a smaller number on whom God would have mercy in the end. The concept fits perfectly Paul's overall purpose of proving that the relatively small number of Jews being saved in his day does not contradict God's promise to Israel. Paul's attention may have been drawn to this text especially because it uses a phrase—"the number of the Israelites"—that occurs in the verse that Paul has just cited in 9:26 (Hos. 1:10).

We would have become like Sodom, we would have been like Gomorrah (9:29). The prophet Isaiah, from whom Paul is quoting (Isa. 1:9), uses the fate of the cities of Sodom and Gomorrah (see Gen. 19) as a striking example of God's judgment on sin. The imagery is natural and common in Scripture (e.g. Isa. 3:9; 13:19).[92]

Christ, the Climax of Salvation History (9:30–10:21)

In this section Paul deviates a bit from his main argument. He will continue to outline his understanding of God's election of Israel and its consequences for the present in chapter 11. But before he does so, he pauses to analyze in more detail the somewhat unexpected turn that salvation history has taken. Most Jews, the ones to whom the promises were made, have rejected their Messiah and the salvation he offers; many Gentiles, by contrast, are streaming into God's new covenant people. Why has this happened? Because, Paul claims, Israel stubbornly refused to recognize God's offer of righteousness in Christ, the climax of salvation history.

Israel, who pursued a law of righteousness, has not attained it (9:31). Behind the pair of verbs "pursue" and "attain" may lie the imagery of the runner who seeks the prize at the end of the race. In the Old Testament, this pair of verbs usually refers to people who pursue others in order to overtake them, especially in battle (e.g., Gen. 31:23; Ex. 15:9).[93] Israel, Paul suggests, earnestly and sincerely pursued the law as a means of attaining righteousness. But she has not been able to achieve this status, for the power of sin prevents people from finding salvation through the law or the works it demands (cf. 9:32).

They stumbled over the "stumbling stone." As it is written . . . (9:32–33). Paul takes language from two different verses in Isaiah (28:16 and 8:14) to characterize Christ as a "roadblock" in Israel's pursuit of the law of righteousness. He begins with language from Isaiah 28:16—"See, I lay a stone in Zion"—but quickly turns to the negative portrayal of the "stumbling stone" in Isaiah 8:14 to complete the idea. He then returns to Isaiah 28:16 at the end, promising that the person who trusts in Christ, the stone, will "never be put to shame." What is especially interesting about this combination is that Peter also juxtaposes these same two verses, along with another "stone" verse, Psalm 118:22 (cf. Matt. 21:42). This combination of texts probably existed in the early church as a way of viewing Christ in light of the Old Testament. Some scholars, indeed, postulate that the church might have put together "testimony books" containing Old Testament texts especially relevant to the church's interpretation of Jesus and his significance.[94]

They are zealous for God (10:2). "Zeal" emerged as an especially commendable virtue among Jews in the intertestamental period, when the existence of the Jewish faith was threatened by both external enemies and (more seriously) by internal compromise. Mattathias, the first leader of the most famous Jewish resistance movement, the Maccabees, called followers in these words: "Let every one who is zealous for the law and supports the covenant come out with me!" (1 Macc. 2:27). Phinehas, who killed a Jewish woman and her pagan lover for their flaunting of the law (Num. 25), was the prototypical "zealot." The New Testament therefore uniformly praises "zeal," and this verse is no exception. Paul is thankful for Israel's zeal; the problem is that it is misdirected.[95]

Since they did not know the righteousness that comes from God and sought to establish their own (10:3). "Their own" righteousness can have two different meanings. It may refer to what some contemporary scholars call "national righteousness"—the tendency of Jews to keep their covenant relationship with God very much to themselves, to focus exclusively on their own privileges, and to ignore their mission to the world at large. That this was a problem among Jews in Paul's day is clear. But Paul's use of this same kind of language in Philippians 3:6–9 points in a different direction. When Paul contrasts "a righteousness of my own that comes from the law" with "that which is through faith in Christ—the righteousness that comes

from God and is by faith," he seems to imply that "his own" righteousness was a standing before God that he thought he could maintain by his obedience to the law. So Israel, Paul here suggests, was seeking to make the law into a "law of righteousness" (Rom. 9:31), a means of marking out those whom God would save in the last day. They were therefore ignoring the Lord's warning to the people of Israel when they entered the Promised Land:

> After the LORD your God has driven them out before you, do not say to yourself, "The LORD has brought me here to take possession of this land because of my righteousness." No, it is on account of the wickedness of these nations that the LORD is going to drive them out before you. It is not because of your righteousness or your integrity that you are going in to take possession of their land; but on account of the wickedness of these nations, the LORD your God will drive them out before you, to accomplish what he swore to your fathers, to Abraham, Isaac and Jacob. Understand, then, that it is not because of your righteousness that the LORD your God is giving you this good land to possess, for you are a stiff-necked people (Deut. 9:4–6).

They did not submit to God's righteousness (10:3). Paul's use of "submit" in this sense here is similar to the use we find in *2 Apoc. Bar.* 54:5: "[You] reveal the secrets to those who are spotless, to those who subjected themselves to you and your Law in faith."

Christ is the end of the law (10:4). The English word "end" is ambiguous; but it can be taken to mean "termination," as in "The end of class finally came!" The Greek word here, *telos*, however, has the added nuance of "goal." Paul presents Christ as both end and goal of the law, much like the finish line of a race course. When the runner reaches that finish line, the race is ended; but crossing the finish line is also the goal. So God intended all along that the law would find its end and goal—its climax or culmination—in Christ. He ends the era of the law's rule even as he ushers in the times of fulfillment to which the law itself always pointed.

The man who does these things will live by them (10:5). Paul quotes Leviticus 18:5 to describe "the righteousness that is by the law." This Old Testament verse comes in a series of commands from the Lord through Moses to the people of Israel. In its original context, the "life" that the Lord promises in response to obedience is not eternal life, but the enjoyment of blessing in the Promised Land (for this use of "life" see also Deut. 30:15, 19). Paul is probably not, then, suggesting that Moses offered people salvation by means of obedience to the law. His point simply is that what the law promises can be had only through obedience to that law. Thus, any righteousness that the law promises (see Rom. 9:31) can come only through works. But our always imperfect and inconsistent works can never bring us into relationship with a perfect and holy God.

The connection between obedience and life established in Leviticus 18:5 becomes almost proverbial in the Old Testament and Judaism. See, for instance, Ezekiel 20:13:

> Yet the people of Israel rebelled against me in the desert. They did not follow my decrees but rejected my laws—although the man who obeys

them will live by them—and they utterly desecrated my Sabbaths. So I said I would pour out my wrath on them and destroy them in the desert.[96]

But the righteousness that is by faith says (10:6–8). In contrast to the righteousness that is by the law (10:5) is "the righteousness that is by faith." In a striking personification, Paul puts language from two passages in Deuteronomy on the lips of this personified righteousness. The opening words, "Do not say in your heart," come from Deuteronomy 9:4, the text we cited above to illustrate the idea of "their own righteousness" (see 10:3). Paul then goes on to use phrases from Deuteronomy 30:11–14. His application of this language to the righteousness of faith is puzzling, because in the Deuteronomy passage, Moses is encouraging the Israelites to obey the law:

> Now what I am commanding you today is not too difficult for you or beyond your reach. It is not up in heaven, so that you have to ask, "Who will ascend into heaven to get it and proclaim it to us so we may obey it?" Nor is it beyond the sea, so that you have to ask, "Who will cross the sea to get it and proclaim it to us so we may obey it?" No, the word is very near you; it is in your mouth and in your heart so you may obey it.

How could Paul take this language and apply it to the righteousness by faith in contrast to the law? Some commentators think that Paul may merely be using the language of the text with no intent to "quote" it—as we will sometimes lift words from a Shakespeare play without regard to their original context.[97] But the repeated "that is" formula points to an intention to quote this text. Others think

Paul might have been influenced by the early Christian identification of Christ with the Old Testament figure of "wisdom."[98] Baruch 3:29–30 uses language from Deuteronomy 30 to describe wisdom: "Who has gone up into heaven, and taken her, and brought her down from the clouds? Who has gone over the sea, and found her, and will buy her for pure gold?" But little in the context prepares us for a Christ-wisdom connection. Probably, then, Paul wants to claim that the new covenant offer of righteousness is now that "word" that is near to the people: accessible and available for all who respond in faith.

Two further notes on the details of the quotation. (1) The language of "ascending into heaven" (10:6) is proverbial for a humanly impossible task.[99] (2) Paul's quotation of this Deuteronomy text differs from the original at one point. Where Deuteronomy 30:13 asks "who will cross the sea to get it?" Paul asks "Who will descend into the deep?" Paul may be influenced by the wording of

Psalm 107:26: "They mounted up to the heavens and went down to the depths; in their peril their courage melted away." "Sea" and the "depths" (or "abyss") were often interchanged in the Old Testament and Judaism. An early Aramaic paraphrase of Deuteronomy 30:13 combined both images: "Neither is the Law beyond the Great Sea that one may say: Would that we had one like the prophet Jonah who would descend into the depths of the Great Sea and bring it up for us."[100] The reference to Jonah reminds us also of Christ's appeal to Jonah's experience in the belly of the great fish to illuminate his own death and resurrection (Matt. 12:40). Jonah 2:3–10 parallels "sea" and "abyss" in describing Jonah's experience.

Anyone who trusts in [me] will never be put to shame (10:11). Paul quotes again from Isaiah 28:16 (see 9:33). "Put to shame" refers to a negative verdict at the judgment. Note the contrasting parallelism in Isaiah 50:7b–8a: "I know I will not be put to shame. He who vindicates me is near."

Everyone who calls on the name of the Lord will be saved (10:13). To call on someone in secular Greek referred to an appeal (especially to a god) for assistance and favor. But the language was also common in the LXX and Jewish literature.[101] The early Christians "called on" both God and Christ for mercy and favor.[102]

Paul is again here quoting the Old Testament: Joel 2:32 (3:5 in the LXX). The "Lord" in Joel is, of course, Yahweh. But Paul applies the text to believers who call on the name of Jesus (see "Jesus is Lord" in 10:9 and the context of 10:10–12). The way the early Christians applied language from the Old Testament about Jehovah God to Jesus conveys an impor-

REFLECTIONS

IN THE OLD COVENANT, GOD GRACIOUSLY BRINGS his word "near" to his people. He informs them about who he is, enters into relationship with them, and requires them to keep his law in order to maintain their status as his people. But the Old Testament is one long description of the people's failure to keep God's law. It becomes clear that human beings are not capable of obeying God apart from a special work of his grace. It is that special work that the new covenant promises. God comes "near" to us in a new way, sending his Spirit to enable obedience to him. Jesus himself has done what seemed to be impossible: risen from the dead to provide the basis for a new life. It is the good news we preach that mediates this new experience of grace. Throughout this passage, therefore, Paul highlights the importance of preaching as an indispensable stage in God's gracious plan of redemption.

Isaiah 52:7 to support the need for preachers of the good news and implicitly suggests that God has himself sent these preachers. Crucial to Paul's application is the use in the Isaiah text of the critical "good news" language (*euangelizomai*).

Their voice has gone out into all the earth, their words to the ends of the world (10:18). Paul cites Psalm 19:4 to prove that the Israelites have indeed heard the good news about Christ. But the application is by no means an obvious one. For Psalm 19 is about the revelation of God in nature and history. Does Paul really think that this psalm refers to the preaching of the good news? Probably not. He may be using the words from the psalm verse to create an analogy: As the message about God went out everywhere in nature, so now the message about God's work in Christ has been broadcast worldwide—or at least empire-wide. The Greek word behind "world" (*oikoumenē*) may refer to the Roman empire rather than to the entire inhabited world.

I will make you envious by those who are not a nation; I will make you angry by a nation that has no understanding (10:19). Israel should have understood what God was doing in Christ, for he had predicted it in the Old Testament. This quotation comes from the Song of Moses in Deuteronomy 32, a passage Paul uses a lot in this part of Romans. What probably draws his attention to this particular verse was the language of "not a nation," or "no people" (*laos*), which is identical to the language of Hosea 1:10 and 2:23 (which Paul quotes in Rom. 9:25–26). "Not a nation" refers, then, to the Gentiles, for God had not called them and

tant clue about the divine status they implicitly accorded to Jesus. To be sure, pre-Christian manuscripts of the Greek Old Testament almost universally avoided the Greek work *kyrios* ("Lord") in translating the tetragrammaton (the four Hebrew consonants that constitute the biblical name for God); they simply transliterated the Hebrew. So we do not have much written evidence that the Greek word *kyrios* was being applied to Yahweh. But we do have evidence that Greek-speaking Jews supplied the word *kyrios* when passages with the transliterated tetragrammaton were read aloud.[103] On the whole, then, the application of *kyrios* language from the Old Testament to Jesus does suggest his deity.

How beautiful are the feet of those who bring good news (10:15). In 10:14–21, Paul is showing that Israel's ignorance about God's righteousness in Christ (10:2) is inexcusable. God has sent preachers to Israel, and they have had ample opportunity to come to know the essence of God's plan. Here he quotes

formed them into a people as he had formed Israel.

A Summary: Israel, the "Elect," and the "Hardened" (11:1–10)

Having explored in more detail in 9:30–10:21 the reasons why so many Jews have not responded to Christ and so many Gentiles have, Paul now returns to the theme of 9:6–29, summarizing the situation in salvation history of his day. He begins with the theme that will sound throughout chapter 11: Despite Israel's disobedience (10:21), God has not rejected his people (11:2). Israel as a whole has not experienced the messianic salvation; most of them have been "hardened." But the "elect," chosen by grace, are enjoying the fulfillment of God's promise to be faithful to his people Israel.

From the tribe of Benjamin (11:1). Paul cites himself as an example of a believing Jew, illustrating the truth that God has not rejected his people. It is obvious why he would call himself an "Israelite" and "a descendant of Abraham." But why would he claim to be from the tribe of Benjamin? Rabbinic tradition claims that the tribe of Benjamin was the first to cross the "Sea of Reeds" at the time of the Exodus and that its restoration would be the sign of the renewal of all Israel.[104] But it is not clear that either of these traditions dates to the time of Paul. Perhaps he mentions his tribal derivation simply to reinforce his Jewish identity (see Phil. 3:5).

God did not reject his people, whom he foreknew (11:2). The wording of this key assertion reflects the language of Psalm 94:14 ("For the LORD will not reject his people; he will never forsake his inheritance") and 1 Samuel 12:22 ("For the

sake of his great name the LORD will not reject his people, because the LORD was pleased to make you his own"). Particularly significant for the direction of Paul's argument is his emphasis on God's concern for his own name in the latter text. Israel, despite her sin, remains the object of God's concern and blessing because of his great grace. As in Romans 8:29, "foreknew" means "chose ahead of time" (see comments on that verse).

The passage about Elijah (11:2). The Greek has simply "in Elijah." Identifying a text of Scripture by reference to a key figure within the narrative is a standard Jewish practice. The rabbis, for instance, introduce a reference to 1 Chronicles 29:14 with the words "It is written in David" (b. ʾAbot 3:7; in the New Testament see also Mark 12:26 [Luke 20:37], which lit. translates "in the bush," i.e., "in the passage about the burning bush").

The passage to which Paul refers is 1 Kings 19:1–8, which relates King Ahab's attack on the prophets of the Lord. The king's wife, the infamous Jezebel, threatens Elijah with the same death suffered by the other prophets. Elijah flees into the desert, where the Lord comforts him by assuring him that, against all the evidence, God is working out his plan for Israel and the surrounding nations (Rom. 11:15–18). Paul quotes Elijah's lament about being left alone (11:3), with the prophets of Baal apparently in control of matters, and the Lord's concluding reassurance to Elijah about the "seven thousand" whom he had "reserved for [himself]" (11:4; see 1 Kings 19:18). This Old Testament passage introduces the concept of the "remnant," a body of true believers whom the Lord preserves in the midst of an apostate nation. Paul goes on to affirm that God

As it is written (11:8). Paul here uses quotations from the Old Testament to show that God himself is responsible for the hardening of so many Jews. He has given them "a spirit of stupor" (11:8), and it is he who has responded to the imprecatory prayers of the psalmist (11:9–10). Paul follows the rabbinic *haraz* method in choosing citations from every major part of the Old Testament: the "Law" (Deut. 29:4 in Rom. 11:8a); the "Prophets" (Isa. 29:10 in Rom. 11:8b); and the "Writings" (Ps. 69:22–23 in Rom. 11:9–10).

Defining the Promise (2): The Future of Israel (11:11–36)

Paul began his defense of God's faithfulness to his word of promise in chapters 9–11 by explaining how a correct understanding of God's promise made sense of the present situation of Israel. Since God had from the beginning chosen only some from within Israel to be his true, spiritual people, the small number of Jewish believers in Paul's day did not contradict God's Word (9:6–29). Now Paul returns to that word of promise, showing what it means for the future of Israel. He argues that the great incursion of Gentiles into the people of God will ultimately have a positive effect on Israel itself.

Salvation has come to the Gentiles to make Israel envious (11:11). Paul's idea is drawn from Deuteronomy 32:21, which he quotes in Romans 10:19: "I will make you envious by those who are not a nation; I will make you angry by a nation that has no understanding." "Make you envious" translates a word (*parazē-loō*) that denotes God's jealousy for his people or a human being's jealousy of

has graciously preserved such a remnant of true believers within Israel right up to his own day (Rom. 11:5–6).

What Israel sought so earnestly it did not obtain, but the elect did. The others were hardened (11:7). Paul neatly summarizes the situation of the Jewish people in his own time. The nation as a whole, though seeking righteousness (see 9:31), has not attained it. Yet, as Paul has just argued, God has preserved a remnant, chosen by grace, who have reached this goal. But most of Israel is "hardened." The verb Paul uses here (*pōroō*) is rare in biblical Greek (see Job 17:7; Prov. 10:20).[105] In secular Greek the word occurs especially often in medical contexts, where it refers to the forming of a "hard sphere" in the body (e.g., a stone in the bladder) or to the "hardening" of a bone after it is broken. So also do people become "hard" with respect to things of the Lord, stubbornly rejecting his grace in Christ. Paul uses a different Greek word to denote this spiritual "hardening" in Romans 9:18, but the idea is the same.[106]

another human being.[107] Paul finds in these words of Moses in Deuteronomy hope for Israel. For, as Romans 11:14 makes clear, Paul hopes that the envy of Israel will lead ultimately to her salvation. While he is not explicit about the matter, Paul evidently thinks that the Gentiles' enjoyment of the blessings of salvation will lead Jews to desire those same blessings and so accept Jesus as their Messiah and Savior.

How much greater riches will their fullness bring! (11:12). The word "fullness" (Gk. *plērōma*) is sometimes given a quantitative meaning, as in TEV: "the complete number of Jews." But the word almost never has such a meaning. It usually (and always in biblical Greek) has a qualitative sense: "completeness" (cf. NASB). Paul is apparently referring to the full restoration to Israel of her kingdom blessings. Israel's "loss"—that is, her refusal to acknowledge Jesus as Messiah—has meant "riches for the Gentiles." Her "fullness" should bring an even greater blessing to the world.

What will their acceptance be but life from the dead? (11:15). What is this "life from the dead" that Israel's acceptance into God's kingdom will effect? Paul, of course, often pictures Christian experience in terms of new life; and he even uses language similar to this earlier in Romans to depict conversion: "Offer yourselves to God, as those who have been brought from death to life" (6:13). However, Paul more often uses this kind of language to denote the bodily resurrection of the dead. A consideration of the background of Paul's thinking in this passage also points to this meaning. One of the most influential streams in Jewish theology during this era was apocalyptic.

Apocalyptic is not easy to define; but for our purposes, we can characterize it as an attempt to make sense of history by appealing to "revelation" (the meaning of the Gk. *apokalypsis*) of heavenly mysteries. Many of the books that take an apocalyptic approach to Israel's situation focus on the events of the end. They often look for a restoration of Israel at the end of history, when the resurrection of the dead takes place.[108]

If the part of the dough offered as firstfruits is holy, then the whole batch is holy (11:16). Paul alludes to Numbers 15:17–21, where the Lord commands the people to offer to the Lord "a cake from the first of your ground meal." The word "firstfruits" (*aparchē*) is common in both secular Greek and the Old Testament to denote the initial or representative portion of a commodity to be offered in sacrifice (e.g., Lev. 2:12; 23:10; Deut. 18:4). Paul applies the imagery to the situation of Israel. Some part within Israel (the "firstfruits") is still holy; and the holiness of that initial portion makes holy the rest of Israel as well. This holy part within Israel might be the remnant of Jewish believers in Paul's day (see Rom. 11:5–7). But the following image makes it more likely that Paul is referring to the patriarchs.

If the root is holy, so are the branches (11:16). Jewish writers sometimes referred to the patriarchs as the "root." See, for example, Philo, *Who Is the Heir?* 279: "Surely he [Abraham] is indeed the founder of the nation and the race, since from him as root sprang the young plant called Israel."[109] Paul explicitly rests his hope for Israel's future on God's promise to the patriarchs (Rom. 11:28; cf. 9:5). Since he suggests that the holiness of the patriarchs makes the rest of Israel holy, one might conclude that the text teaches that all Jews will be saved. But Paul is using the word "holy" here in the way it is used in Old Testament sacrificial texts. It does not mean "set apart for salvation" (as usually in the New Testament), but "set apart" for God's special attention (see also 1 Cor. 7:14).

Branches . . . wild olive shoot . . . olive root (11:17). In 11:17–24, Paul uses different parts of an olive tree to represent key figures in the salvation history that he sketches in this chapter. The "root," as we have seen (11:16), stands for the patriarchs. The (natural) branches are the Jewish people, descended physically from the patriarchs. The wild olive shoots are Gentile Christians, grafted into the

olive tree "contrary to nature" (11:24) by God's grace. Paul perhaps chooses to use the olive tree for his comparison because it was the most widely cultivated fruit tree in the Mediterranean basin. But the olive tree also symbolizes Israel in the Old Testament and in Jewish literature (Jer. 11:16; Hos. 14:5–6).[110]

The imagery of wild olive shoots being grafted into a cultivated olive tree is not, however, realistic. Farmers, in fact, do just the reverse; they graft branches from cultivated trees into wild ones in order to improve their production. Some scholars claim that Paul, an urban man from Tarsus, simply did not understand the usual technique. Others cite evidence that farmers might occasionally graft a wild olive shoot into a cultivated tree.[111] Still others think that Paul is deliberately reversing the usual procedure in order to highlight the role of God's grace in the process. But none of these suggestions is necessary. Writers will choose illustrations that represent the reality they are trying to depict—but rarely will the analogy match the reality in every respect. So

OLIVE TREE

elements that stretch or do not exactly correspond to the reality of the analogy are often introduced.

Consider therefore the kindness and sternness of God (11:22). Paul may be influenced in his use of the word "sternness" (*apotomos*) here by Wisdom of Solomon, which uses this word and its cognates to describe the nature of God's judgment. See, for example, Wisdom of Solomon 6:5: "He will come upon you terribly and swiftly, because severe judgment falls on those in high places" (see also 5:20, 22; 11:10; 12:9; 18:15).

I do not want you to be ignorant of this mystery (11:25). Paul uses the word "mystery" (*mystērion*) with a technical theological meaning derived from Jewish apocalyptic. Books that reflect this perspective use "mystery" to refer to events of the end times that have already been determined by God—and so, in that

DEAD SEA SCROLLS MANUSCRIPT

A copy of the Temple Scroll from Qumran.

sense already exist in heaven—and which are finally revealed by God to his people for their encouragement and understanding.

This general usage of *mystērion* appears first in Daniel, with reference to the dreams of King Nebuchadnezzar. It is "God in heaven" who reveals the mysteries of these dreams through Daniel to the king (cf. 2:28). A good example from Jewish apocalyptic is *T. Levi* 2:10: "And when you [Levi, being addressed by an angel] have mounted up there [to another heaven], you shall stand near the Lord. You shall be his priest and you shall tell forth his mysteries to men. You shall announce the one who is about to redeem Israel."[112] This concept was especially prominent in the Dead Sea Scrolls.[113] The sequence by which God planned to bring salvation to both Jews and Gentiles had not been revealed to God's people before this time. Paul is now the instrument through whom the Lord discloses the details of his plan.

Until the full number of the Gentiles has come in (11:25). "Full number" translates the same Greek word (*plērōma*) translated "fullness" in 11:12 (see comments). As we noted in commenting on that verse, the word almost always has a qualitative meaning. Is the quantitative rendering of the NIV here therefore wrong? Probably not. For the "fullness" or "completeness" that Paul ascribes to the Gentiles has in this context probably a strong numerical component. "Come in" is likely shorthand for "come into the kingdom of God" (see Matt. 7:13; 23:13; Luke 13:24). Paul is perhaps reflecting certain Jewish traditions about a fixed number of people who would enter the kingdom before the end. *Fourth Ezra* 4:35–37 is a representative text:

Did not the souls of the righteous in their chambers ask about these matters, saying, "How long are we to remain here? And when will the harvest of our reward come?" And the archangel Jeremiel answered them and said, "When the number of those like yourselves is completed; for he has weighed the age in the balance, and measured the times by measure, and numbered the times by number; and he will not move or arouse them until that measure is fulfilled."

And so all Israel will be saved (11:26). In the context, which so carefully distinguishes Gentiles and Jews, "Israel" probably refers here to national Israel. The apocalyptic background against which he writes suggests that the salvation of "all Israel" will occur in the end time (see esp. 11:15 and comments there). But how many Jews are included in the "all Israel" to be saved? Here it is important to note that this phrase in the Old Testament frequently has a collective sense, referring not to every single Israelite but to a significant or even simply representative number.

Two examples might be cited: Joshua 7:25: "Joshua said, 'Why have you brought this trouble on us? The LORD will bring trouble on you today.' Then all Israel stoned [Achan], and after they had stoned the rest, they burned them"; 2 Samuel 16:22: "So they pitched a tent for Absalom on the roof, and he lay with his father's concubines in the sight of all Israel." It is unlikely that every single Israelite alive in Joshua's day cast a stone at Achan; or that all the Jews in David's day saw the sexual dalliances of Absalom. "All Israel" in each text is representative, in that enough Jews were involved so as to give the events national significance. Thus Romans 11:26 does not promise salvation for every Jew alive at the time of Christ's return. What it promises is that a significant number, representative of the nation as a whole, will find salvation in Jesus their Messiah.[114]

The deliverer will come from Zion (11:26). To buttress his claim that "all Israel will be saved," Paul offers a quotation made up of phrases from two or three Old Testament texts. The initial

◀

MOUNT ZION

A view of Old Jerusalem in the direction of Mount Zion from the Mount of Olives.

words come from Isaiah 59:20, which was given a messianic interpretation in the targum, though the late date of that Aramaic paraphrase renders it uncertain whether the tradition was alive in Paul's day. A comparison between Isaiah 59:20 and Paul's version of the text reveals an interesting change. Whereas Isaiah predicts that the deliverer will come "to" Zion, Paul quotes him as saying that the deliverer will come "from" Zion. Paul may be depending on a form of the LXX that had the equivalent to the word "from" in it. But it is more likely that Paul, as he does elsewhere, changes the text slightly to make a theological point. What is that point? We cannot be certain, but Hebrews 12:22 associates "Zion" with the heavenly Jerusalem, the site of Jesus' high-priestly ministry. Perhaps, then, Paul changes the text to bring out a bit more clearly a reference to the Parousia.

How unsearchable his judgments, and his paths beyond tracing out! (11:33). In response to his sketch of the plan of sal-vation for both Jews and Gentiles, Paul celebrates the wisdom and power of God. "Judgments" refer not to God's role as judge but to his role as the executor of salvation history; they are the decrees he has issued in order to bring about his plan for the world.[115] Paul's attempt to explain the plight of Israel in his own day is rooted in his desire to demonstrate the agreement between God's Old Testament promise and the gospel.

Other Jewish writers in Paul's day struggled in similar ways with the plan of God in relation to the plight of Israel. The author of the book we call *2 Baruch* was one of those, and he expresses his awe at God's plan in terms similar to Paul's: "O Lord, my Lord, who can understand your judgment? Or who can explore the depth of your way? Or who can discern the majesty of your path? Or who can discern the beginning and the end of your wisdom?"[116]

From him and through him and to him are all things (11:36). The idea of God as

▶

ST. PETER'S SQUARE IN MODERN ROME

the source, sustainer, and goal of all things was especially common among Greco-Roman Stoic philosophers. See, for example, the words of the second-century Roman emperor Marcus Aurelius: "From you are all things, in you are all things, for you are all things."[117] Hellenistic Jews picked up this language and applied it to their God.[118] Paul, therefore, probably knew the language from the synagogue. By the time it reaches him, of course, it has left behind the metaphysical baggage of its Stoic origin. When placed into a Christian worldview, the language appropriately emphasizes the ultimacy of God.

The Transforming Power of the Gospel (12:1–2)

The gospel has the power of rescuing any human being—Jew or Gentile—from sin's power and establishing that person in a new "right" relationship with God. But the gospel is also intended to transform the way people live. In 12:3–15:13, Paul sketches a few of the characteristics of the transformed believer. But, first, in 12:1–2, he issues a general call for believers to respond to that transforming power of God.

I urge you (12:1). The Greek behind the NIV "urge" is *parakaleō*. The word is stronger than "ask" and weaker than "command." It is the perfect word to express the moral imperative of the gospel. This word was widely used in ancient Greek moral treatises, where it often signaled a shift from one topic to another.[119]

Living sacrifices (12:1). The sacrifice of animals was central to most ancient religions, including, of course, Judaism. In call-

ing for Christians to present themselves to God as "living sacrifices," therefore, Paul is employing a metaphor that is universally understood in his day. Nor is Paul the first to use the language of sacrifice in a metaphorical way. Such metaphors are common in both the Old Testament and Judaism.[120] But Paul takes the metaphor a step further. Old Testament or Jewish use of the sacrificial metaphor implies, of course, that literal sacrifices will continue to be offered. But for Paul and the other early Christians, Jesus' once-for-all death on the cross puts an end to any further sacrifice (cf. Heb. 10:1–14).

This is your spiritual act of worship (12:1). The NIV "spiritual" translates a Greek word (*logikēn*) that is difficult to render in English (note the NIV footnote, "reasonable"). The word itself is rare in the New Testament, occurring elsewhere only in 1 Peter 2:2 (where its meaning is also debated). But the word does have a rich background in Greek and Hellenistic Jewish philosophy and religion. Arguing that God and human beings share *logos*, some Greek philosophers argued that only *logikos* worship could be pleasing to God. They contrasted this "rational" worship with what they considered to be the silly superstitions of many Greek and Near Eastern religions. Two texts can serve to demonstrate this idea:

> If I were a nightingale, I should be singing as a nightingale; if a swan, as a swan. But as it is I am a rational [*logikos*] being, therefore I must be singing hymns of praise to God.[121]

> That which is precious in the sight of God is not the number of victims immolated but the true purity of a rational [*logikon*] spirit in him who makes the sacrifice.[122]

The word "spiritual" can bring out this sense, but perhaps better is the rendering "rational." The worship God seeks from us in our everyday lives is a worship offered with a full understanding of the gospel and its implications. It flows from a renewed heart *and* mind.

Humility and Mutual Service (12:3–8)

One way in which believers reveal their transformed way of thinking is in an attitude of realistic humility toward themselves and of dedicated service to the community.

Think of yourself with sober judgment (12:3). "Think" translates a verb (*phroneō*)

that indicates the basic orientation of a person (in Romans, see also 8:5; 11:20; the cognate noun occurs in 8:6, 7, 27, and a cognate adjective in 11:25). It indicates not just one's mental state, but one's "mind-set" or attitude. Paul wants believers to form an accurate picture of themselves in their own minds. They should not consider themselves more important than they are; but neither should they think too little of themselves. Sincere and unreserved service of God and the church begins with a realistic appraisal of one's own strengths and weaknesses.

In Christ we who are many form one body (12:5). Paul's comparison of the church to the human body is well known. But the source of this comparison is not clear. The significance of Christ's own body, given in sacrifice on the cross and memorialized frequently in the celebration of the Lord's Supper, must have been a key factor. But the use of the human body to illustrate the unity and diversity of a group of people was known from other sources in the ancient world. The Roman historian Livy cites a parable of Menenius Agrippa that compares the body politic of his day with a human body.[123]

In proportion to his faith (12:6). Paul cites the different gifts God has given the church to illustrate the diversity of the Christian church. He urges those who have been given such gifts to use them effectively to serve the community. The prophet is to use his gift "in proportion to his faith." "Proportion" translates *analogia*, a word drawn from the world of mathematics and logic, where it denoted the correct proportion or right relationship. Josephus, for instance, claims that the porticos of the temple in Jerusalem were in

---

REFLECTIONS

THE "WORSHIP" PAUL IS TALKING ABOUT IN ROMANS 12:2 applies to the whole of life. His point is that we are to consider every part of our existence as an opportunity to serve God by living out the principles of the new age to which we belong. The division with which we sometimes operate between the sphere of the "secular" and the "religious" is one Paul would simply not have recognized. Nevertheless, what Paul says here about the life of worship certainly applies to the corporate gathering for weekly praise that we call the worship "service."

The modern church is convulsed over what this service should be like, some churches insisting on organs, choirs, and hymnals and others on guitars, worship teams, and overhead transparencies. But the Bible itself says nothing about the kind of music we use or the instruments that accompany it. What texts like Romans 12:2 insist on, however, is that true worship of God must always flow from minds that have grasped and been impressed by the truth of God. Whether we sing to the accompaniment of guitars or organs, then, the *words* we sing should be carefully chosen to present an aspect of God's character to us so that we can respond with thoughtful, sincere worship.

"right proportion" to the temple as a whole.[124] The language of this text has furnished theology with its slogan "the analogy of faith," the principle that Scripture must always be interpreted in light of other Scripture. But Paul simply means that the prophet should exercise his or her gift in "right proportion" to the faith about the prophecy that God has given the prophet. Prophets should say no more and no less than what God has given them.

Let him give generously (12:8). The person with the gift of giving should exercise that gift by giving "with *haplotēs*." This word is usually translated "generously" (see NIV); but its root meaning is simply "singleness."[125] Some intertestamental Jewish texts hold up this quality of "singleness" as a key moral virtue (the entire *T. Iss.* is about this virtue). Those who give, suggests Paul, should do so with a single, undivided intent. No ulterior motives or secondary concerns should be involved.

Love and Its Manifestations (12:9–21)

This section of Paul's exhortations to the Roman Christians appears to unfold rather haphazardly. No clear theme dominates the section. Paul seems to move back and forth between admonitions about believers' relationships to other believers (12:9–13, 15–16) and to unbelievers (12:14, 17–21). The lack of clear organization may reflect Paul's use of a popular ancient style, called *paraenesis*. Found in both Greek and Jewish sources, paraenesis "strings together admonitions of a general ethical content."[126] The writer moves quickly through a variety of themes and issues, not always relating them to one another.

Paraenesis is characterized by another feature that is prominent in 12:9–21: eclecticism, or borrowing from a variety of sources. Paul quotes the Old Testament in this passage (12:19, 20), and much of what he says has parallels in Jewish and Greek ethical and wisdom sayings. But particularly striking are the parallels between 12:9–21 and the teaching of Jesus (see esp. 12:14, 17, 18, and 21). Paul absorbs some of the key ethical emphases into his own instruction and passes them on to the Romans.

Love must be sincere (12:9). The NIV, along with most English versions, supplies a verb where, in fact, none appears in the Greek text. The addition may be justified; but it is also possible that Paul views the simple "Sincere Love" as the heading for the exhortations that follow. "Love" translates the well-known Greek word *agapē*. One sometimes hears that this word is a distinctive term for the Christian conception of love. But that claim must be carefully nuanced. The word was certainly not invented by the early Christians; it occurs twenty times in the LXX, while the cognate verb is found over 250 times. But it may be true that the early Christians used this word in preference to other Greek words for "love" because it lacked some of the "baggage" (sexual and other) that other terms carried.

"Sincere" translates *anypokritos*, which is more literally translated "without hypocrisy" or "without playing a role" (such as an actor does on stage).

Be devoted to one another in brotherly love (12:10). "Brotherly love" reflects another basic Greek word for love: *philia*, here in a compound form, *philadephia*. No difference between the concept of love denoted by *philia* and that denoted by *agapē* is evident here. But the word does remind readers that the church is to be characterized by the tender love evident in the best of human families. The word "devoted" (*philostorgoi*) conveys the same nuance. See *4 Maccabees* 15:13: "O sacred nature and affection of parental love, *yearning of parents* toward offspring, nurture and indomitable suffering by mothers!"

Practice hospitality (12:13). Hospitality was especially important in the first-century world, where motels and hotels were virtually unknown. Christians traveling on ordinary business and in the service of the church depended on fellow Christians for lodging and food. Paul not only commands believers to exercise hospitality; he urges them to "pursue" it.

Bless those who persecute you; bless and do not curse (12:14). Paul's admonition echoes the teaching of Jesus, combining versions found in Matthew and Luke:

> "But I tell you: Love your enemies and pray for *those who persecute you*" (Matt. 5:44).

> "But I tell you who hear me: Love your enemies, do good to those who hate you, *bless* those who curse you, pray for those who mistreat you" (Luke 6:27–28).

Jesus' command that his followers respond to persecution and hatred with love and blessing was unprecedented in the ancient world, so Paul's dependence on Jesus is almost certain. Paul has no need to introduce the words as a quotation since they would have been well known in the early church.

Rejoice with those who rejoice; mourn with those who mourn (12:15). After

instructing Christians to respond to outsiders with love and forgiveness, Paul now turns back to the Christian community, enjoining a sincere identification with others whatever their state might be. Note how Paul's commands here echo what he says about relations within the body of Christ in 1 Corinthians 12:26: "If one part suffers, every part suffers with it; if one part is honored, every part rejoices with it." But the need for such mutual identification is found in Jewish sources as well. See, for instance, Sirach 7:34: "Do not avoid those who weep, but mourn with those who mourn."[127]

Be willing to associate with people of low position (12:16). "People of low position" can also be translated "humble activities" (the Gk. word can be either masculine or neuter). If Paul's reference is to people who rank low on the world's socioeconomic scale, he is urging Christians to imitate their Father in heaven, who frequently stresses his own concern for the "down and out" (e.g., Judg. 6:15; Ps. 10:18).[128]

Do not repay anyone evil for evil (12:17). Prohibitions of retaliation are found widely in Judaism; see, for instance, *Joseph and Aseneth* 23:9: "And we are men who worship God, and it does not befit us to repay evil with evil." But other references to Jesus' teaching in this same context argue that Paul depends directly here on Jesus' prohibition of retaliation from the Sermon on the Mount (Matt. 5:38–42).

You will heap burning coals on his head (12:20). These words come from Proverbs 25:21–22a, which Paul quotes as the response that believers are to make to their enemies. The words "coals" and "fire" in the Old Testament are usually used metaphorically to refer to God's awesome presence and especially to his judgment.[129] A few scholars, therefore, think that the Proverbs text refers to God's judgment and that Paul views the believers' kindness to enemies as ultimately increasing the degree of judgment that they will receive.[130] But the context seems to require that "heap[ing] burning coals" has a positive rather than a negative impact on the unbeliever. Thus, some scholars have theorized that the imagery in Proverbs may go back to an Egyptian ritual, in which a penitent carried coals of fire on the head as a sign of repentance.[131]

The Christian and Secular Rulers (13:1–7)

Paul interrupts his outline of the various workings of "sincere love," continued in 13:8–10, with this paragraph requiring submission to the governmental rulers.

Everyone must submit himself to the governing authorities (13:1). When Paul uses the word "authority" (*exousia*) in the plural, he elsewhere refers to spiritual "authorities"—angelic beings, whether good or evil.[132] In this text, it is clear that the word refers to human beings who have been placed—ultimately by God—in positions of authority in the government (cf. "rulers" in 13:3). But a few scholars have thought that some allusion to spiritual authorities may nevertheless be intended; that is, that Paul is referring at the same time both to human rulers and to the spiritual powers that stand behind them. Paul would thus be assuming the widespread worldview of his day, according to which spiritual beings influenced

---

▶ The Social-Political Setting of Paul's Appeal to Obey the Government

What motivates Paul to address the topic of the Christian's attitude toward the government? One reason may be theological: Paul is worried that Christians will take his demand not to "conform . . . to the pattern of this world" (12:2) too far, lumping government into the category of "this world" and therefore refusing to respect its legitimate, divinely ordained position and function. But three other specific historical movements may have contributed to "anti-government" thinking among the Roman Christians.

(1) The Jewish Christians in Rome had experienced a severe disruption in their lives when Emperor Claudius expelled all the Jews (including Jewish Christians) from the city in A.D. 49 (see the introduction). This event may well have led to resentment against the government in Rome.

(2) The decade of the 50s saw a spectacular increase in Jewish Zealot activity and popularity. The Zealots were the political terrorists of their day.

They preached insurrection against the Roman government, insisting that Israel's subjection under foreign domination was contrary to her calling to be a theocracy. The Zealots eventually won enough people to their side to incite a violent four-year insurrection against Rome (A.D. 66–70; in fact, the last holdouts, at Masada, were not defeated until A.D. 73). We do not have much evidence of Zealot sympathy among Roman Jews in these years,[A-8] but it is possible that the movement indirectly influenced attitudes of the Roman Christians.

(3) The Roman historian Tacitus mentions resistance against the payment of indirect taxes in the middle 50s in Rome.[A-9] The resistance culminated in a tax revolt against the government in A.D. 58, a year or two after Paul wrote Romans. Some of the Roman Christians may well have shared these sentiments; note how Paul climaxes his call to submit to the authorities with commands to pay taxes (13:7).

the course of human affairs, especially the affairs of nations.[133]

But this suggestion is unlikely. The word *exousia* was a normal way of referring to human rulers in Paul's day; it translated the Latin *potestates*, which was used to refer to a broad range of Roman government officials. Moreover, in all the places except one where Paul uses the plural *exousiai* to refer to spiritual authorities it is coupled with *archai*, "rulers." There is nothing in this passage to suggest a dual reference.

"Submit" translates the Gk. *hypotassō*, a verb Paul uses to denote the appropriate response of people who recognize their place in a hierarchical order. Thus, Christians are urged to "submit" to governing authorities, to their spiritual leaders, and to one another.[134] Similarly, slaves are to submit to their masters, Christian prophets to other prophets, and wives to husbands.[135] Assumed in each hierarchy is that the highest authority is always God, whose claims must always take precedence.

There is no authority except that which God has established (13:1). Paul's teaching about the divine ordination of government in general and of individual rulers in particular echoes a consistent biblical theme. Daniel, for instance, tells the arrogant King Nebuchadnezzar that God was teaching him that "the Most High is sovereign over the kingdoms of men and gives them to anyone he wishes and sets over them the lowliest of men" (Dan. 4:17).[136] Despite the disasters Israel suffered at the hands of foreign powers, this teaching remained basic throughout the intertestamental period. Note Wisdom of Solomon 6:1–3: "Listen, therefore, O kings, and understand; learn, O judges of the ends of the earth. Give ear, you that rule over multitudes, and boast of many nations. For your dominion was given you from the Lord, and your sovereignty from the Most High; he will search out your works and inquire into your plans."

Do what is right and he will commend you (13:3). Paul may be thinking here specifically of the practice of Roman authorities to publish in inscriptions the names of "benefactors" of society. "Do what is right" may then refer in turn to the activities of Christians as "good citizens" in their own society.[137]

He is God's servant to do you good (13:4). "Servant" translates *diakonos*, a word that Paul usually uses to refer to Christians as "servants" of God and of the gospel. But the word in secular Greek was used to denote a secular official of various kinds.[138] The idea that secular rulers dispense divine justice is, of course, deeply rooted in Scripture; but it is also found in secular sources of the time. See, for instance, Plutarch: "Rulers are ministers of God for the care and safety of mankind, that they may distribute or hold in safe keeping the blessings and benefits which God gives to man."[139]

He does not bear the sword for nothing (13:4). Scholars have advanced several specific suggestions for Paul's reference here. Several point to the Roman *ius gladii*, the authority possessed of all higher magistrates of inflicting the sentence of death.[140] But the authority seems to have been confined to Roman provincial governors and restricted to their power to condemn to death Roman citizens serving in the military.[141] Others note Philo's use of the term "sword-bearers" to refer to Egyptian police officials; and still others to Roman mili-

▶ Paul and Government

One of the striking elements of this passage is Paul's rosy view of government. According to him, civil authorities "hold no terror for those who do right, but for those who do wrong" (13:3). Paul may be reflecting to some extent his own experience with Roman authorities, which, on the whole, was quite positive. He used his Roman citizenship to his advantage; and when brought before the Roman governor of Achaia, his right to preach the gospel was vindicated (Acts 18:12–17).

But Paul could hardly be naive about the potential for governments to be unjust. He would have known that his people's history was littered with persecution from foreign governments. He was proclaiming as Lord of the universe One who was unjustly executed by the Roman authorities. Paul well knew that some governmental officials rewarded evildoers and punished those who did good. Probably, then, what Paul is doing in Romans 13:3–4 is describing how governments *are supposed to function* under their divine mandate. Perhaps he also implies that the submission of Christians to rulers need not take the form of obedience when governments do not implement divine justice.

---

tary power (to put down insurrection).[142] But Paul's rather vague wording does not enable us to pinpoint any of these situations as that to which he is referring. The most that can be said is that he refers generally to the right of governments to punish those who violate its laws.

Because of conscience (13:5). "Conscience" (*syneidēsis*) is a word that Paul takes from the world of Greco-Roman philosophy and religion (see comments on 9:1). In its original sense, *syneidēsis* referred to the painful knowledge that came after breaking a law or custom. Some scholars argue that Paul always uses it with this meaning. If that were the case here, he would be urging believers to submit to government so that they can avoid that sense of wrongdoing. But New Testament writers frequently "extend" the meanings of words that they borrow from another sphere. In the case of *syneidēsis*, there is good evidence that this has happened—that the word can also denote "consciousness" of God and his demands (cf. 2:15). This meaning fits well in the present context. It is because the believer is conscious of God's ordaining of governmental authorities that he or she will willingly submit to them.

The authorities are God's servants (13:6). In 13:4, Paul called the ruler a *diakonos* ("servant"; see comments on 13:4). But the word for "servant" here is a different one—*leitourgos*. It and its cognates occur frequently in the LXX to denote people who served in the temple, and in the New Testament the word group always refers to religious service or servants of some kind.[143] A strong case can therefore be made here that Paul views secular authorities as having religious significance. However, *leitourgos* was used in secular Greek to denote public officials of various kinds (cf. our "public servant"), and the word occurs with this meaning in the LXX as well.[144]

If you owe taxes, pay taxes; if revenue, then revenue (13:7). "Taxes" (Gk. *phoros*;

Lat. *tributa*) denotes direct taxes (cf. also Luke 20:22; 23:2), while "revenue" (Gk. *telos*; Lat. *portoria*) refers to "indirect" governmental taxes, such as fees for various services and customs duties (cf. Matt. 17:25, where the NIV translates "duty").

Love and the Law (13:8–10)

After his "excursus" about the Christian's responsibility to the government, Paul returns to the subject that has dominated 12:9–21: love. He now highlights love as the virtue that brings all the commandments of the Mosaic law to their ultimate fulfillment.

The commandments, "Do not commit adultery," "Do not murder," "Do not steal," "Do not covet" (13:9). In both Exodus 20:1–17 and Deuteronomy 5:6–21, the prohibition of murder comes before the prohibition of adultery. However, at least one important LXX manuscript of Deuteronomy (Vaticanus) has them in the same order as Paul, and this order is attested also in the Nash Papyrus (a first or second-century B.C. scrap of text with the Ten Commandments) and in several Jewish and early Christian texts.[145] This may, therefore, have been the order of commandments popular in certain circles of Diaspora Judaism.

Are summed up in the one rule, "Love your neighbor as yourself" (13:9). The Greek word for "rule" is simply *logos*, "word." There is precedent in Judaism to use this word to refer to commandments, and especially the Ten Commandments, which were often called the "Ten Words."[146]

The love command of Leviticus 19:18 had been singled out by some Jews as central to the demands of the law; Paul

is, of course, borrowing here again from the teaching of Jesus, who claimed that "all the Law and the Prophets" hung on this command and the command to love the Lord God.[147] Some Jews interpreted "neighbor" (*ra'*) in the command to refer to fellow Israelites only[148]; others gave a broader interpretation.[149] Jesus and Paul assume the broader interpretation.

Living in Light of "the Day" (13:11–14)

Paul wraps up this general section of his ethical exhortations by returning to the theme of salvation history with which he began. Believers are to avoid conformity to "this age" (cf. 12:2), because it is an age of darkness that is passing away, to be replaced by a new age of light and salvation (13:11–14).

The hour has come for you to wake up from your slumber (13:11). Sleep is

right ▶

ROMAN SOLDIERS IN ARMOR

Authentic reconstruction of Roman armor by a reenactment group.

often a metaphor for spiritual insensitivity in the ancient world.[150]

The night is nearly over; the day is almost here. So let us put aside the deeds of darkness and put on the armor of light (13:12). Darkness veils the activities of criminals and is also the time for drinking bouts, carousing, and sexual dalliance. It is therefore almost universally associated with evil. To that extent, Paul's imagery communicates rather clearly to any audience. But the Old Testament and Judaism supply a further, theological

---

▶ The "Weak" and the "Strong" in Rome

Applying Paul's plea for tolerance in these chapters requires that we understand something about just what the underlying issue in all these divisions may have been. What particular set of values or beliefs led to the dissensions over food, wine, and holy days that Paul mentions in these verses? Scholars suggest several scenarios, but two deserve consideration.

1. The "weak" may have been Gentile Christians who brought into their practice of Christianity certain ascetic practices from their pagan background. A popular philosophical/religious group of the time, for instance, were the neo-Pythagoreans, who avoided eating anything that had a "soul" (including, in their view, animals).[A-10] Some of the later gnostics also avoided eating "flesh," and certain ideas that later became part of the system of "Gnosticism" were already circulating in the first century. Pagans also had superstitions about "lucky" and "unlucky" days, and several Greco-Roman religious cults also observed special days. However, specific language within 14:1–15:13 as well as the tenor of Romans as a whole make it much more likely that the specific problems Paul treats in these chapters had their roots in debates about the continuing relevance of the Torah.

2. This leads us to the second alternative: that the "weak in faith" abstained from meat, observed special days, and avoided wine out of a concern to maintain Jewish "purity." The Torah itself did not require Jews to refrain from eating all meat or from wine. But Jews who lived in dominantly pagan cultures often refrained from such food out of concern that it was not "kosher." The notable biblical example, of course, is Daniel, who "resolved not to defile himself with the royal food and wine, and he asked the chief official for permission not to defile himself this way" (Dan. 1:8).[A-11] Pious Jews often abstained from wine out of fear that it had been contaminated by the pagan practice of offering wine as a libation to the gods.[A-12] We know from many Jewish sources that matters such as the food laws and the observance of Sabbath and other festivals took on a heightened importance in the intertestamental period, as Jews sought to hold on to their distinct identity in the midst of persecution and an often hostile Gentile environment.

Ascetic tendencies found in other ancient religions may have encouraged such decisions on the part of Jews. Note, for instance, Philo's description of the Therapeutae, a Jewish sect of the pre-Christian era:

> For as nature has set hunger and thirst as mistresses over mortal kind they propitiate them without using anything to curry favour but only such things as are actually needed and without which life cannot be maintained. Therefore they eat enough to keep from hunger and drink enough to keep from thirst but abhor surfeiting as a malignant enemy both to soul and body.[A-13]

Reflections of the influence of this ascetic tendency surface elsewhere in the New Testament.[A-14] Early church historians report that some Jewish Christians at a later day abstained from eating flesh.[A-15] On this hypothesis, the "days" that the weak were observing probably included the Sabbath and the annual Jewish festivals.

dimension to the night/day imagery used here. The Old Testament prophets frequently used the expression "the day of the LORD" to denote the time when God would intervene decisively to save his people and judge their enemies.[151] This phrase is taken over and adapted by the New Testament writers, who spoke of the "day of Christ," and so on. Since, therefore, the era of salvation and blessing can be called "the day," "the night" may represent this present evil age. Note, for instance, *1 Enoch* 58:

> The righteous ones shall be in the light of the sun and the elect ones in the light of eternal life which has no end [v. 2]. . . . The sun has shined upon the earth and the darkness is over. There shall be a light that has no end. . . . For already darkness has been destroyed, light shall be permanent before the Lord of the Spirits, and the light of uprightness shall stand firm

forever and ever before the Lord of the Spirits [v. 6].

The Qumran covenanters called themselves "the children of light" and their enemies, the unspiritual, the "children of darkness." In light of this background, Paul must be seen to be urging believers to live in accordance with the new age of salvation that has already been inaugurated by Christ but remains to be consummated in the future.

A Plea for Tolerance (14:1–12)

In 14:1–15:13, Paul rebukes the Roman Christians for standing in judgment over one another. They have divided into two "camps" over certain issues. Those whom Paul labels "weak in faith" (cf. 14:1) hold that believers should not eat meat (14:2), that they should regard certain days as more "holy" than others (cf. 14:5), and, perhaps, that they should not drink wine (cf. 14:21). The "strong" (cf. 15:1), by contrast, feel free to eat meat, to drink wine, and to treat every day alike. Paul comes down on the side of the strong (14:14, 20; 15:1), but his main concern is the disunity that these issues are creating within the Christian community. He wants both weak and strong to respect the views of the others and to cease the mutual recriminations that are tearing apart the community.

Accept him whose faith is weak (14:1). At both the beginning and end of chapter 14 (see 14:22–23), Paul characterizes the "weak" with respect to their "faith." Paul's use of the word throughout Romans requires that it refers to that "trust in Christ" that is fundamental to the gospel. Yet, as 14:2 makes clear, this faith is being looked at here from a spe-

R E F L E C T I O N S

IF OUR IDENTIFICATION OF THE ROOT PROBLEM IN Rome is correct, then the source of division between the "weak" and "strong" had to do with certain Jewish customs that the "weak" thought important to retain in living out their new life in Christ. What is especially significant for contemporary application is the recognition that such practices are neither required nor condemned in the New Testament. Jewish Christians who wanted to continue to observe the foods laws and Sabbath were entirely free to do so; but they could not insist that other Jewish Christians or Gentile Christians follow suit. The issue that Paul deals with in Romans 14–15, therefore, falls into the category we call *adiaphora*: things neither required nor prohibited. Paul's plea for tolerance, therefore, cannot be extended to other kinds of issues. The apostle could be very intolerant when the truth of the gospel was at stake (see, e.g., Galatians).

cific angle: what one thinks one's faith in Christ allows one to do. The person "weak in faith," therefore, is not necessarily one who is immature in his or her faith. It is, rather, a person who has not yet come to the conviction—because of the "pull" of a life spent in Judaism—that the Christian faith allows him or her to eat meat, drink wine, and ignore Jewish holy days.

One man considers one day more sacred than another (14:5). As we argued above, the "sacred" days are probably Jewish holy days, which the weak insisted carried over into the Christian era. Just what these holy days may have included is not clear. Jews, of course, celebrated annually several great festivals inaugurated in both the Old Testament (e.g., the Day of Atonement, Passover) and in the intertestamental period (e.g., Purim, Hanukkah). Many Jews observed regular days of fasting; the Pharisees fasted twice a week. And, of course, the weekly Sabbath was central to Jewish life.

That the Sabbath was one of the days in dispute is probable from two circumstances. (1) Sabbath observance became a key identification marker for Jews in Paul's day and was therefore likely a point of contention between Jewish and Gentile Christians. (2) Colossians 2:16, where Paul deals with a somewhat similar issue, specifically mentions the Sabbath as one of the holy days at issue.

He who eats meat, eats to the Lord, for he gives thanks to God; and he who abstains, does so to the Lord and gives thanks to God (14:6). This is the earliest mention in Christian literature of the practice of giving thanks at mealtime.[152] It is, of course, a continuation of the Jewish practice.[153] The "Lord" in this verse

may be God the Father. But the fact that the "Lord" in Romans 14:9 is Christ suggests that Paul is thinking of Christ as the Lord throughout these verses.

Christ died and returned to life (14:9). Paul cites bedrock Christian tradition: "For what I received I passed on to you as of first importance: that Christ died for our sins according to the Scriptures, that he was buried, that he was raised on the third day according to the Scriptures."[154] Only here, however, do we have in this tradition the language of "come to life" rather than "raised." Paul tailors the wording to suit his context, in which he will note that Christ is the Lord of both "the dead and the living."

We will all stand before God's judgment seat (14:10). Paul is the only New Testament author to put a theological twist on the well-known *bēma*, the scene of secular judgment.[155] In 2 Corinthians 5:10, he refers to the "judgment seat of Christ," but the variant in divine name should not suggest that he thinks of a different setting, or time, of judgment.

"As surely as I live," says the Lord, "every knee shall bow before me; every tongue will confess to God" (14:11). The bulk of this quotation is from Isaiah 45:23, a text apropos to the issue Paul is discussing here, since the verse is surrounded with claims of the Lord's unique sovereignty: "I am God, and there is no other" (45:22); "In the LORD alone are righteousness and strength" (45:24). The opening words of the quotation, "As surely as I live," do not come from Isaiah 45. This phrase, however, does occur twenty-two times in the Old Testament, including Isaiah 49:18, which may be Paul's specific reference. Why does he add these words? Perhaps to suggest that the "Lord" of the quotation from Isaiah 45:23 is none other than the Lord Christ, who died and was raised.

Limiting Liberty by Love (14:13–23)

Most of 14:13–23 is directed to the "strong," as Paul is urging them not to insist on the exercise of their own rights at the expense of the spiritual health of the "weak."

Let us stop passing judgment on one another (14:13). Paul may be alluding to Jesus' teaching: "Do not judge, or you too will be judged" (Matt. 7:1). Absolute prohibitions of judging are rare in Judaism, and Paul consistently alludes to Jesus' teaching in this part of Romans.

Stumbling block (14:13). The Greek word *proskomma* refers to any obstacle that might cause a person to trip or stumble. It is therefore a perfect metaphor for a practice or word that might cause a believer to "stumble" in his or her walk with the Lord. This is its significance throughout the New Testament.[156]

Obstacle (14:13). The Greek word here is *skandalon*, which originally denoted a "trap." But the word also became a metaphor for the idea of "occasion of misfortune" or "cause of ruin." All fourteen New Testament occurrences of this word have this significance. Leviticus 19:14 ("Do not curse the deaf or put a stumbling block in front of the blind, but fear your God. I am the LORD") may have been the seminal text for this metaphorical significance in the Scripture.

No food is unclean in itself (14:14). "Unclean" translates *koinos*, which means "common"; it is the word used to describe the Greek of the New Testament period: *koinē*, or "common" (i.e., widespread) Greek. The Jews began to use this word to denote food that was "common," that is, secular and therefore to be avoided by the zealous Jew.[157]

Approved by men (14:18). "Approved" (*dokimos*) can also be translated here "esteemed." The word normally denotes the quality of having been approved through a test.[158] But there is some evidence that the word could also mean "esteemed" or "respected."[159]

REFLECTIONS

NEW TESTAMENT CLAIMS SUCH AS PAUL'S IN 14:20, that "all food is clean," are sometimes taken by Christians to mean that they do not need to observe any limitations of any kind on their food or activities. If an activity is not expressly forbidden in Scripture, they claim, they have a complete right to do it.

But such Christians miss two important counterpoints in Scripture. (1) The essence of New Testament ethics is to encourage God's people to embody certain key moral principles that will direct their activity. Thus, many practices not forbidden in Scripture might be forbidden because of an extension of these principles. Most believers, for instance, are convinced that the recreational use of drugs is wrong, not because it is prohibited in Scripture, but because it violates the principle that we are to honor God with our bodies.

(2) Each of us comes to our Christianity with different backgrounds and make-ups, and therefore with different weaknesses. We are called on by God to exercise wisdom in identifying activities that may be without harm in themselves but which could become a temptation to ourselves. The principle that Paul enunciates in 1 Corinthians 6:12 is an important one to set alongside of Romans 14:20: " 'Everything is permissible for me'—but not everything is beneficial. 'Everything is permissible for me'—but I will not be mastered by anything."

All food is clean (14:20). The Old Testament uses the word "clean" to denote food that was uncontaminated and therefore acceptable for Jews to eat (see, e.g., Gen. 7:2–3, 8; 8:20).[160]

Or drink wine (14:21). Since Paul introduces the drinking of wine as an example of his own behavior, it is not clear whether it was one of the points dividing the weak and the strong. We do know that many Jews abstained from wine in pagan contexts out of fear that it had been involved in ritual libations to the gods.

Unity Through Mutual Respect (15:1–13)

Paul now calls on the strong to imitate Christ in pleasing other people rather than themselves (15:1–6). He then climaxes his appeal for tolerance and mutual respect in the Roman Christian community by calling on each group to "accept" the other and so fulfill the plan of God, set forth in the Old Testament, to bring Jews and Gentiles together in one people of God (15:7–13).

We who are strong ought to bear with the failings of the weak (15:1). The word "strong" here comes from a Greek word that means "powerful" or "capable" (*dynatos*), while "weak" translates *adynaton*, "incapable." The *dynatoi* are those Christians, like Paul himself, who are "capable" of understanding that their faith in Christ frees them from requirements of observing ritual aspects of the law of Moses. But others, with strong emotional ties perhaps to their Jewish upbringing, are not "capable" of living out this freedom. While Paul therefore shifts vocabulary here, he is continuing to address the same issue as he did in chapter 14.

Each of us should please his neighbor for his good (15:2). The unexpected use of the word "neighbor" reveals that Paul has the "love command" of Leviticus 19:18 in mind: "Love your neighbor as yourself." Following the lead of Jesus (e.g., Matt. 22:34–40), Paul finds in this command the essence of new covenant ethics (see Rom. 13:8–10). An allusion to the command is especially appropriate in a context dealing with tolerance toward fellow Christians, for the love command is preceded in Leviticus 19:18 by a prohibition of negative attitudes toward other Israelites: "Do not seek revenge or bear a grudge against one of your people."

For even Christ did not please himself but, as it is written, "The insults of those who insult you have fallen on me" (Rom. 15:3). Paul puts words from Psalm 69:9b on the lips of Jesus. The "you" in the quotation is therefore God, while the "me" is Christ himself. Language from Psalm 69 is often applied in the New Testament to the suffering of Christ on the cross.[161] Paul thus makes two points via this quotation. (1) If Jesus could endure the insults of others, his followers should certainly be willing to put up with the minor irritations occasioned by Christians with different viewpoints. (2) Jesus'

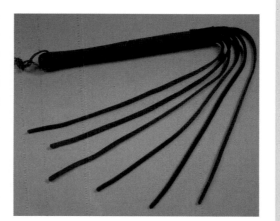

own suffering on the cross serves as the preeminent example of pleasing others rather than oneself.

So that through endurance and the encouragement of the Scriptures we might have hope (15:4). A perhaps preferable rendering is "through endurance and the comfort that comes from the Scriptures." This alternative takes the Greek word *paraklēsis* to mean "comfort" rather than "encouragement" and attaches the genitive *tōn graphōn* (as a genitive of source) to that word only rather than to both nouns. One argument for this rendering is the possible influence of Jewish texts on Paul's wording here. Note 1 Maccabees 12:9: "since we have as encouragement [*paraklēsin*] the holy books that are in our hands." Paul seems to stray from his main point a bit here, writing more generally about the sufferings that believers, following their Lord, are destined to experience. In their midst, Paul reminds us, the Scriptures comfort us as we read about God's sovereign control of the world and his promises to his people.

Christ has become a servant of the Jews on behalf of God's truth, to confirm the promises made to the patriarchs so that the Gentiles may glorify God for his mercy (15:8b–9a). While the structure of this sentence is debated, the NIV has probably accurately captured its basic sense. The ministry of Messiah ("Christ") Jesus to Israel fulfills God's promises to his people and at the same time opens the way for Gentiles to be admitted into the people of God. Paul succinctly summarizes a key motif of the letter to the Romans.

Throughout the letter, the apostle has labored to show that the Abrahamic promise includes Gentiles (cf. ch. 4) without canceling Israel's own privileges and blessings (cf. chs. 9–11). The "truth" (*alētheia*) of God in 15:8 can perhaps more accurately be translated the "faithfulness" of God. The translators of the LXX frequently used this Greek word to render Hebrew words meaning "faithfulness." A good example is Psalm 36:5: "Your love, O LORD, reaches to the heavens, your faithfulness [LXX *alētheia*] to the skies" (cf. also Rom. 3:7). In light of the argument of Romans 4, "the promise made to the patriarchs" might include faithful Gentiles. But Paul has brought the language of "promise" and "fathers" together in Romans 9–11 (cf. 9:5 and 11:28) to refer to the things promised by God to the Jewish people specifically. This is probably his intention here also.

As it is written (15:9). The four quotations from the Old Testament in 15:9b–12 all contain the key word "Gentiles." Paul's purpose is to confirm from Scripture that Gentiles were all along included in God's gracious promise to create and bless a people for his own name. Paul follows Jewish custom in quoting from every part of the Old Testament canon: the Law, the Prophets, and the Writings.[162]

I will praise you among the Gentiles (15:9b). These words come from Psalm 18:49 (or possibly 2 Sam. 22:50, which has these identical words). In this psalm, the speaker is David, who praises God for the victory that the Lord has given him over the Gentile nations. As he did in quoting Psalm 69 in Romans 15:3, Paul again puts these words of David on the lips of Jesus. It is Messiah Jesus who has finally subdued the nations and brought them under the benefits of his kingdom reign.

Rejoice, O Gentiles, with his people (15:10). The careful student of Scripture, who compares Paul's quotations with their Old Testament originals, will be perplexed here. For the Hebrew text of Deuteronomy 32:43, which Paul is quoting, is translated, "Make his people rejoice, O nations." Paul's wording is found in the LXX version. This is not in itself surprising; Paul usually quotes the Old Testament according to the LXX. But in this case, by following the Greek translation, Paul may be misquoting the text and thereby making an incorrect application of the text.

This problem is a difficult one in some New Testament texts. But it might not be so difficult here. Note how most English versions (including the NIV) follow the LXX reading in translating Deuteronomy 32:43. They do so partly because a Hebrew manuscript containing this verse has been found at Qumran (4QDeut[a]) that agrees with the LXX rendering. In this case, therefore, there is good reason to think that the LXX has preserved the original Hebrew text.

Praise the Lord, all you Gentiles, and sing praises to him, all you peoples (15:11). Paying careful attention to the Old Testament context of the words that Paul quotes often sheds light on his purpose. In this case, Paul is probably drawn to these opening words from Psalm 117 because verse 2 (the only other verse in this psalm) goes on to cite God's "mercy" (*eleos*) and "truth" (*alētheia*) as reasons for the psalmist's praise. God's "truth," or "faithfulness," demonstrated to Israel and his "mercy" revealed to the Gentiles are the lead ideas that govern these quotations (15:8–9).

The Root of Jesse will spring up (15:12). "Root" is a common messianic designation, usually found in conjunction with the name David (see, e.g., Jer. 23:5; 33:15).[163]

Paul's Ministry and Travel Plans (15:14–33)

Paul typically closes his letters with some personal notes, referring to his own plans

MEDITERRANEAN WORLD

Jerusalem, Illyricum, and Spain were part of Paul's ministry goals.
▼

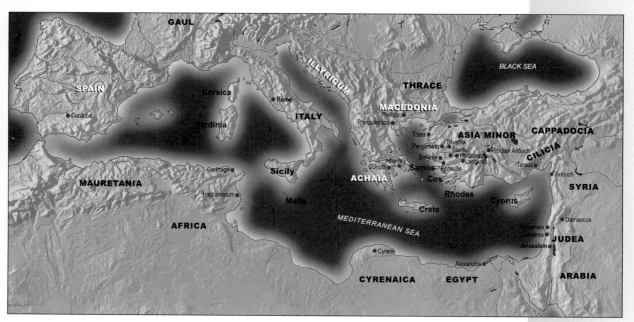

and asking prayer for them. Typical of Romans is the long elaboration of these points that we find in these verses. Paul rehearses his past travels in 15:14–21, focusing on his ministry among the Gentiles. In 15:22–29, he announces his future travel plans: to go to Spain via Jerusalem and Rome. He then requests prayer for the collection he is bringing to the Jewish Christians in Jerusalem in 15:30–33.

You yourselves are full of goodness, complete in knowledge and competent to instruct one another (15:14). Without suggesting that Paul indulges in insincere flattery, he may here be using a popular ancient literary device, the *captatio benevolentiae*, an expression of confidence in his readers. Ancient writers frequently used such flattery of their readers to gain adherence for their ideas.[164]

A minister of Christ Jesus . . . with the priestly duty of proclaiming the gospel of God, so that the Gentiles might become an offering acceptable to God, sanctified by the Holy Spirit (15:16). Paul's description of his ministry in this verse

is remarkable for its extended use of priestly metaphors. It is important to note that they are metaphors. Paul does not consider himself a "priest" but compares his gospel ministry of proclamation in word and deed to the ministry of a priest. The word "minister" itself, at the beginning of the verse, probably has priestly connotations. The Greek word is *leitourgos*. While it can mean simply "servant" (see comments on 13:6), the other cultic terms in the verse suggest that it has the meaning of "priest," as it often does in the Old Testament and Jewish writings.[165]

"The priestly duty of proclaiming the gospel of God" renders a difficult Greek phrase, with "gospel" as the object of the verb "offer sacrifice." But a parallel is found in *4 Maccabees* 7:8, which speaks of "administrators of the law" (lit., "those who serve the law as priests"). The sacrifice Paul offers in his priestly ministry is the Gentiles themselves. Paul is probably reflecting here Isaiah's prediction of an influx of Gentiles into God's kingdom on the Day of the Lord in Isaiah 66:19–20:

"I will set a sign among them, and I will send some of those who survive to the nations—to Tarshish, to the Libyans and Lydians (famous as archers), to Tubal and Greece, and to the distant islands that have not heard of my fame or seen my glory. They will proclaim my glory among the nations. And they will bring all your brothers, from all the nations, to my holy mountain in Jerusalem as an offering to the LORD—on horses, in chariots and wagons, and on mules and camels," says the LORD. "They will bring them, as the Israelites bring their grain offerings, to the temple of the LORD in ceremonially clean vessels."

Paul reflects here the typical New Testament eschatological transformation

REFLECTIONS

PAUL IDENTIFIES THE GENTILES themselves as the offering he hopes to make to God (15:16). He reminds us that people are what ministry is all about. We can easily become preoccupied with the programs we administer, the subject matter that we are teaching, the books we are writing. We can forget that the purpose of programs, classes, and books is the formation of strong Christians, sanctified, and therefore an acceptable offering to God.

of the sacrificial system of the Old Testament: Animal sacrifices are replaced by obedient Christians (cf. 12:1 and comments) and the praise they offer God (cf. Heb. 13:15), and the priest is replaced by Christian ministers.

By the power of signs and miracles (15:19). "Signs and miracles" (or the more usual rendering "signs and wonders"; *sēmeia kai terata*) is standard biblical terminology for miracles. The phrase occurs particularly often in the account of the Exodus (15 of the 29 occurrences of the phrase refer to the Exodus events); see, for example, Deuteronomy 4:34: "Has any god ever tried to take for himself one nation out of another nation, by testings, by miraculous signs and wonders, by war, by a mighty hand and an outstretched arm, or by great and awesome deeds, like all the things the LORD your God did for you in Egypt before your very eyes?" Some scholars think Paul deliberately uses this language in order implicitly to put himself on a par with Moses in his salvation-historical significance.

From Jerusalem all the way around to Illyricum (15:19). Paul probably chooses Jerusalem as the starting point for his ministry because it was the center of Judaism. Both Paul (Gal. 1:18–19, 22) and Luke (Acts 9:26–30; cf. 26:20) affirm Paul's ministry in Jerusalem. Why Paul chooses Illyricum is harder to say, since neither he nor Luke ever explicitly indicate that Paul ministered there. But Illyricum, the Roman province covering the area today known as northern Albania and much of Yugoslavia and Bosnia-Herzegovina, was located on the Egnatian Way, a road that Paul traveled as he preached the gospel in Phillipi and Thessalonica.[166] Considering, then, Paul's preference of sticking to well-traveled Roman roads, he may well have preached in Illyricum during the movements mentioned in Acts 20:1–2.

When I go to Spain (15:24). Parts of Spain (which in ancient times included all of the Iberian Peninsula) had been occupied by Roman troops since about 200 B.C. But Rome fully organized Spain as a province only in Paul's lifetime. Scholars used to think that there was a significant Jewish presence in Spain at this time, but this is now doubted.[167] Why did Paul choose Spain as the next target of his pioneer church-planting ministry? It may be simply because it was a relatively new "Romanized" area. But it may also be that Paul thought of Spain as identical to the Old Testament "Tarshish," the "ends of the earth" that Isaiah predicted would be the culmination of God's eschatological work among the Gentiles (see Isa. 66:19, quoted above).[168]

Whether Paul ever got to Spain is not clear. If, as we think, the Pastoral Letters were written after Paul's release from his first Roman imprisonment (Acts 28), it is perhaps unlikely; for these letters reveal Paul back in the eastern Mediterranean. Yet one early Christian text, *1 Clement* 5:7, seems to suggest that Paul did eventually reach Spain.

To have you assist me on my journey (15:24). The NIV pretty well captures the nuance of the verb *propempō* that Paul uses here, for it became almost a technical early Christian word for missionary support.[169] Paul makes clear that he expects the Romans to offer him material assistance for his plans to evangelize Spain.

In the service of the saints there (15:25). Here and in the following verses Paul refers to his famous "collection" for the impoverished Jerusalem Christians. During his third missionary journey, Paul gathered money from his Gentile churches to be sent as an offering to Jerusalem.[170] Paul saw this collection not only as a practical demonstration of Christian charity, but also as an opportunity to close the growing rift between Gentile and Jewish Christians.

Macedonia and Achaia were pleased to make a contribution (15:26). Paul refers to the churches he planted in Philippi, Thessalonica, and Berea (all in the Roman province of Macedonia) and in Corinth (in Achaia).

The poor among the saints (15:26). This phrase can also be translated "the poor who are the saints" (taking *tōn hagiōn* as an epexegetic genitive). In this case the word "poor" is a technical description of the righteous ones. Such a designation is possible, since "poor" becomes almost a technical way of denoting God's people in some Old Testament and Jewish texts. But it is probably not called for here. The NIV rendering makes better sense.

After I . . . have made sure that they have received this fruit (15:28). A literal rendering of the Greek is "having sealed for them this fruit." The idea of sealing suggests an official proclamation of authenticity (e.g., Est. 8:8, 10; John 3:33); a papyrus text speaks of "sealing [sacks] of grain" in order to guarantee their contents.[171] Paul, the apostle to the Gentiles, will accompany the collection to Jerusalem to ensure its integrity and interpret its significance.

Join me in my struggle (15:30). Paul probably reflects the Jewish use of the word "struggle" to depict the spiritual striving of the righteous in this world.[172]

Greetings and Epistolary Conclusion (16:1–23)

In this section Paul continues with the items typical of the closing parts of his letters: a commendation of a fellow Christian (16:1–2), greetings (16:3–15, 16b, 21–23), a promise of spiritual victory (16:20a), and a benediction (16:20b). But somewhat unexpected is his sudden condemnation of false teachers (16:17–19), as well as the number of people he greets (since Paul has never visited Rome before).

I commend to you our sister Phoebe (16:1). Letters of commendation were common in the ancient world.[173] Travelers could not count on public facilities for food or lodging, so they had to rely on networks of personal relationships. Phoebe is a fellow Christian whom Paul has gotten to know during his ministry in Corinth. She is traveling to Rome, perhaps on business, so Paul wants to introduce her and to give her his stamp of approval.

A servant of the church in Cenchrea (16:1). The city of Corinth, where Paul spent considerable time on both his second and third missionary journeys, was situated about one and a half miles inland from its closest seaport (Lechaeum). The Gulf of Corinth lies to the northwest and the Saronic Gulf to the northeast. Cenchrea is located roughly five miles due east of Corinth on the Saronic Gulf and served as the main seaport for Corinth. In Paul's day the cities were linked by a series of forts.[174] We can presume that Phoebe, frequently in Corinth on business, had become converted through the ministry of the church there and was well known to Paul.

But what does Paul intend in calling her a "servant"? The Greek word (*diakonos*) is often used in the New Testament to denote any Christian, called to serve the Lord and minister to his people. Note especially 1 Peter 4:10, where the cognate verb is used: "Each one should use whatever gift he has received to serve [*diakoneō*] others, faithfully administering God's grace in its various forms."[175] Thus, Paul may here mean no more than that Phoebe is a fellow Christian.

But the phrase "*diakonos* of the church" suggests a more official role. This word is also used to refer to a specific position of ministry in the early church: the "deacon" (in Paul, see Phil. 1:1; 1 Tim. 3:8, 12). Probably Paul identifies Phoebe as one of the deacons in the Cenchrean church. In later centuries, the office of "deaconess" was officially recognized.[176] But the masculine *diakonos* was also applied to female office-holders in the early church.[177] The New Testament reveals little about the role of deacons in the church, but many scholars suspect that they are particularly involved in visiting the sick, providing for the needy, and caring for the financial and material needs of the church in general. Such a function would suit well Phoebe's apparent secular position (see below).

She has been a great help to many people, including me (16:2). The NIV paraphrases here, since the Greek simply calls Phoebe a *prostatis* to many. This word is found only here in biblical Greek, but it comes from a verb that can mean either to care for, give aid to, or to direct, preside over. The NIV assumes the former meaning; some advocates of expanded roles for women in ministry argue for the latter, claiming that

Phoebe is a "leader" of the church. But it is unlikely that Paul would acknowledge Phoebe as a leader or director of himself. A better alternative is to adopt the meaning this word sometimes has in the Greco-Roman world: "patron." The patron played an important role in society, using his or her influence and financial resources to sponsor people for various positions and promotions. We can envisage Phoebe as a prominent and wealthy woman, who used her resources and influence to assist Christians like Paul.[178]

Greet (16:3–15). Before noting some points of significance with regard to individual names, it is worth commenting on the cumulative force of the names. These names may not make interesting reading for the modern Christian or obvious material for the preacher. But for the historian of ancient Christianity, they are a gold mine. Names in the ancient world were rarely simply nice-sounding tags; they almost always carried meaning. Sometimes that meaning provides to the student of the ancient church a window into that church's socioeconomic composition. Two particular points emerge from careful study of the names in Romans 16.[179] (1) A majority of the names are Gentile, confirming the evidence from elsewhere of the mainly Gentile makeup of the Roman church. (2) Most of the names are ones usually

ROMAN APARTMENT BUILDING

The remains of a multi-storied *insula* in Ostia, the port city of Rome.

given to slaves or "freemen" (persons who had been set free from slavery).

Priscilla and Aquila (16:3). The Greek actually has "Prisca [*Priska*] and Aquila"; the NIV has the practice of "normalizing" variants of the same name. "Priscilla," the form that Luke prefers, is the diminutive form of the name "Prisca." Priscilla and Aquila were from the Roman province of Pontus, in northern Asia Minor. They lived for a time in Rome but were forced to leave when Emperor Claudius banned all Jews from the city in A.D. 49 (cf. Acts 18:1–2). They ministered with Paul during his eighteen-month stay in Corinth and then left to establish a church in Ephesus (Acts 18:18), where Paul eventually rejoined them (cf. 1 Cor. 16:19). We do not know when they returned to Rome, but we do know that the ban of Jews was allowed to lapse after the death of Claudius in A.D. 54. Paul notes that they "risked their lives" for him (Rom. 16:4); perhaps at the time of the riot in Ephesus (Acts 19).

The church that meets at their house (16:5). The early Christians could not afford their own meeting places, so they met in private homes. Here Paul mentions the Christians who gathered for worship in the home of Priscilla and Aquila; and he mentions two others later (16:11, 14). The Roman "church," then, in effect, is made up of several separate "house churches"— accounting perhaps for the disunity that Paul must rebuke in chapters 14–15. The size of the ancient Roman home would also have meant that the largest congregation would have numbered no more than twenty to thirty Christians.

Andronicus and Junias . . . outstanding among the apostles (16:7). Andronicus is a male name; and so is Junias. But the latter is only one of the possible readings of the Greek name. The word is *Iounia* (found here in the accusative singular form, *Iounian*). *Iounia* can either be a female name, "Junia" (cf. KJV; NRSV; REB), or a contracted form of the male name Junianus, "Junias" (cf. NIV; RSV; NASB; TEV; NJB). A contracted form of a name would be in order, since Paul uses several others in this context. But we do not have evidence from ancient sources that Junianus was ever contracted to Junias. The feminine Latin name "Junia," by contrast, was common. Probably, then, Andronicus and Junia are another husband-and-wife ministry team (along with Priscilla and Aquila).

In calling them "apostles," Paul is almost certainly not putting them on a

---

R E F L E C T I O N S

PAUL'S REFERENCES TO PHOEBE (16:1–2) AND JUNIA[S] in 16:7 have become a storm center in the recent debates about the roles of women in ministry. Both are clearly prominent women in the early church, but just what roles they actually played is debated. This debate reveals strikingly the tendency for this issue to polarize opinion and run roughshod over careful, balanced interpretation. On the one hand are many egalitarians, who insist Phoebe was "president" or "head pastor" of the church in Cenchrea and that Junia was a female "apostle," equal in rank and authority to Peter, John, and Paul. On the other are certain complementarians, who insist that Phoebe was no more than an ordinary Christian "servant" with a ministry of helps and that Junia[s] was a man (or, if a woman, was not esteemed "*among* the apostles" but esteemed "*by* the apostles").

Neither extreme does justice to the text, as we have briefly suggested in the notes above. But the extremes of opinion remind us that, especially when issues are explosive and emotions run high, we must make doubly sure that we approach the text to see what it says, not to insist on making it say what we want.

par with Peter, John, James, himself, and so on. "Apostle" (*apostolos*) also refers in the New Testament to a commissioned missionary and this usage was carried over into the early church.[180]

Those who belong to the household of Aristobulus (16:10). The ancient Greco-Roman "household" (the word does not occur in the Greek but is implied) consisted both of the immediate and perhaps extended family living in the home as well as the household servants. While we cannot be certain, the Aristobulus mentioned here may have been the brother of King Herod Agrippa I, ruler of Palestine under Roman auspices from A.D. 41–44 (his death is described in Acts 12:19b–23). Aristobulus went with Agrippa as a hostage to Rome and died in A.D. 48 or 49.[181] But servants in his household may still have been identified with their famous deceased master.

Narcissus (16:11). Narcissus was a well-known freedman who served Emperor Claudius and who committed suicide just before Paul wrote Romans.[182]

Rufus (16:13). Rufus may be the son of Simon of Cyrene, who carried the crossbar of Christ's cross part of the way to Golgotha (cf. Mark 15:21: "A certain man from Cyrene, Simon, the father of Alexander and Rufus, was passing by on his way in from the country, and they forced him to carry the cross"). Mark was

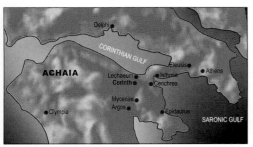

probably written from Rome, and he may therefore mention Alexander and Rufus because he has come to know them during his stay there. Yet Rufus was a common name, so we cannot be certain of the identification.

Greet one another with a holy kiss (16:16). The kiss was a common form of greeting in the ancient world generally and in Judaism in particular.[183] It is referred to often in the New Testament, and by the second century, the Christian liturgy contained a "kiss of peace" as a standard feature.[184] We don't know that this kiss was a part of worship services in Paul's day. But if so, Paul probably envisages his letter being read aloud in a worship service, concluded with such a kiss.

Watch out for those who cause divisions (16:17). The identity of the false teachers about whom Paul warns the Romans cannot be determined. He speaks of them generally, we have no evidence elsewhere in Romans of specific false teachers, and we have insufficient evidence about first-century Roman Christianity.

Such people are not serving our Lord Christ, but their own appetites (16:18). "Appetites" translates the Greek word *koilia*, "belly." The NIV, along with most commentators, take the word by metonymy to refer to the sensual urges generally. But the word may refer to the preoccupation with food laws typical of many Jews in the first century (the same issue arises in Philippians 3:19, where Paul talks of false teachers whose "god is their stomach").

The God of peace will soon crush Satan under your feet (16:20). This promise of eschatological victory may echo the famous "proto-evangelium" of Genesis 3:15: "And I will put enmity between you and the woman, and between your offspring and hers; he will crush your [the Serpent] head, and you will strike his heel." Some Jewish texts also seem to echo this promise.[185]

Lucius (16:21). This Lucius has sometimes been identified with Lucius of Cyrene, a prophet/teacher in the church at Syrian Antioch (Acts 13:1), or with Luke the Evangelist ("Luke" can be a variant of "Lucius"). But the name was common, and neither identification is likely.

Jason (16:21). This Jason is likely the same person who gave Paul shelter during the tumult in Thessalonica (Acts 17:5–9).

Sosipater (16:21). Sosipater is a variant of "Sopater," the name of a man from Berea who accompanied Paul when he left Greece at the end of his third missionary journey (Acts 20:4).

I, Tertius, who wrote down this letter (16:22). Tertius is otherwise unknown to us, but he here identifies himself as the "amanuensis," the trained scribe who physically copied down Paul's dictation to the Roman Christians. Amanuenses, trained to write small and neatly, were often employed in a day when paper was both scarce and expensive.

Gaius (16:23). "Gaius" is a common name, and at least three different New Testament Christians bore it: Gaius of Derbe (Acts 20:4; cf. 19:29); a Gaius from Corinth (1 Cor. 1:14); and a Gaius who was a church leader in Asia Minor (3 John 1). Since Paul writes from Corinth, the Gaius who sends greetings is probably the Corinthian Gaius.

Erastus (16:23). This Erastus may be the same Erastus whom Paul sent from Ephesus to Macedonia on an errand during the third missionary journey (Acts 19:21–22; cf. 2 Tim. 4:20). But the name of Erastus has also been discovered on an inscription from Corinth, identifying him as an *aedile* of the city. The term Paul uses to describe Erastus, *oikonomos* ("director of public works"), may be roughly equivalent.[186]

The Doxology (16:25–27)

Because this doxology appears in several different places in manuscripts of Romans, many scholars are convinced that it was added to Romans after Paul wrote the letter. But there is good reason to think that Paul himself wrote it as a fitting conclusion to his great theological treatise.

Prophetic writings (16:26). Since Paul claims the mystery is "made known" in these writings, some have identified them with the New Testament. But Paul has also shown that the Old Testament, properly interpreted, testifies to the mystery. Moreover, the phrase seems to echo the opening words of Romans: "the gospel he promised beforehand through his prophets in the Holy Scriptures."

ANNOTATED BIBLIOGRAPHY

Cranfield, C. E. B. *A Critical and Exegetical Commentary on the Epistle to the Romans.* 2 vols. ICC. Edinburgh: T. & T. Clark, 1975, 1979.

Academic-level commentary especially strong on grammar, history of interpretation, and theology.

Dunn, James D. G. *Romans 1–8, Romans 9–16.* WBC. Waco, Tex.: Word, 1988.

Academic-level commentary representing the "new perspective" on Paul.

Edwards, James. *Romans.* NIBC. Peabody, Mass.: Hendrickson, 1992.

A readable exposition that does a good job of presenting current scholarly options.

Fitzmyer, Joseph. *Romans: A New Translation with Introduction and Commentary.* AB. Garden City: Doubleday, 1993.

Especially strong on introductory issues and history of interpretation.

Käsemann, Ernst. *Commentary on Romans.* Eerdmans, 1980.

A dense but important commentary emphasizing Paul's apocalyptic theology.

Moo, Douglas J. *The Epistle to the Romans.* NICNT. Grand Rapids: Eerdmans, 1996.

English-text based exposition with focus on theological meaning and application.

_____. *Romans.* NIVAC. Grand Rapids: Zondervan, 2000.

English-text based exposition with focus on application of the text to today's world.

CHAPTER NOTES

Main Text Notes

1. The *Catalogus Liberianus* (A.D. 354) claims Peter as the founder and first bishop of the Roman church, but earlier tradition associates both Peter and Paul with the founding of the church (Irenaeus, *Haer.* 3.1.2; 3.3.1).
2. See the text in *PL*, col. 46.
3. Philo (*Embassy to Gaius* 23.155) claims that the nucleus of the Roman Jewish community was made up of enslaved prisoners of war. But H. J. Leon is not disposed to accept this claim (*The Jews of Ancient Rome* [Philadelphia: Jewish Publication Society, 1960; updated edition by C. Osiek, Peabody, Mass.: Hendrickson, 1996], 4–5).
4. Leon, *Jews*, 135–70; cf. Romano Penna, "Les Juifs à Rome au temps de l'apôtre Paul," *NTS* 28 (1982): 327–28.
5. W. Wuellner, "Paul's Rhetoric of Argumentation," in *The Romans Debate*, ed. K. Donfried (2d ed.: Peabody, Mass.: Hendrickson, 1991), 128–46.
6. R. Jewett, "Romans as an Ambassadorial Letter," *Int* 36 (1982): 5–20.
7. D. Aune, "Romans as a *Logos Protreptikos* in the Context of Ancient Religions and Philosophical Propaganda," in *Paulus und das antike Judentum* (WUNT 58; eds. M. Hengel and U. Heckel; Tubingen: Mohr, 1991), 91–121.
8. M. L. Stirewalt Jr., "The Form and Function of the Greek Letter-Essay," in *The Romans Debate*, 147–71.
9. James D. G. Dunn, *Romans 1–8* (WBC; Waco, Tex.: Word, 1988), lix.
10. See esp. R. Bultmann, *Der Stil der paulinischen Predigt und die kynisch-stoische Diatribe* (FRLANT 13; Gottingen: Vandenhoeck & Ruprecht, 1910).
11. S. K. Stowers, *The Diatribe and Paul's Letter to the Romans* (SBLDS 57; Chico, Calif.: Scholars, 1981).
12. The language comes from the Priene inscription; see W. Dittenberger, *Orientis Graeci Inscriptiones*, II, no. 458.
13. See Peter T. O'Brien, *Introductory Thanksgivings in the Letters of Paul* (NovTSup 49; Leiden: Brill, 1977).
14. See Douglas J. Moo, *The Epistle to the Romans* (NICNT; Grand Rapids: Eerdmans, 1996), 70–76, 79–90.
15. See, e.g., C. E. B. Cranfield, *A Critical and Exegetical Commentary on the Epistle to the Romans* (2 vols.; ICC; Edinburgh: T. & T. Clark, 1975, 1979), 1.155–57.

16. See, e.g., Epictetus, *Diss.* 2.19–20; 3:7, 17. On the diatribe style, see esp. Stowers, *Diatribe.*

17. See *Pss. Sol.* 8:11–13; *T. Levi* 14:5.

18. See 2 Macc. 13:6; Acts 19:37; Philo, *Decalogue* 133.

19. See esp. D. B. Garlington, "ΙΕΡΟΣΥΛΕΙΝ and the Idolatry of Israel (Romans 2.22)," *NTS* 36 (1990): 142–51.

20. Josephus, *Ant.* 20.2.1–4 §§17–48.

21. George Foot Moore, *Judaism in the First Centuries of the Christian Era* (repr.; 2 vols.; New York: Schocken, 1971), 1.323–35.

22. See, e.g., L. E. Keck, "The Function of Rom. 3, 10–18: Observations and Suggestions," in *God's Christ and His People: Studies in Honor of Nils Alstrup Dahl,* eds. J. Jervell and W. A. Meeks (Oslo: Universitetsforleget, 1977), 141–57.

23. For this view, see esp. J. D. G. Dunn, *Romans 1–8* (WBC; Waco, Tex.: Word, 1988), 153–55; also his essay "Echoes of Intra-Jewish Polemic in Paul's Letter to the Galatians," *JBL* 112 (1993): 465–67.

24. See also *4 Macc.* 18:10; Matt. 11:13; Luke 16:16; John 1:45; Acts 13:15; 24:14; 28:23.

25. See David Hill, *Greek Words with Hebrew Meanings* (SNTSMS 5; Cambridge: Cambridge Univ. Press, 1967), 58–80.

26. See Leon Morris, *The Apostolic Preaching of the Cross* (Grand Rapids: Eerdmans, 1955), 9–26.

27. See ibid., 136–56.

28. D. Flusser and S. Safira, "Who Sanctified the Beloved in the Womb," *Immanuel* 11 (1980): 46–55.

29. G. Fitzer, "σφραγίς," *TDNT,* 7.949.

30. See also *Jub.* 32:19; Sir. 44:21; *2 Apoc. Bar.* 14:13; 51:3.

31. See, e.g., Philo, *Spec. Laws* 2.242; *Dreams* 2.123; Josephus, *Ant.* 3.8.9 §218; 8.4.6 §129; 18.8.2 §263; 18.8.8 §304; 19.6.3 §302.

32. For this interpretation, see esp. H. Moxnes, *Theology in Conflict: Studies in Paul's Understanding of God in Romans* (NovTSup 53; Leiden: Brill, 1980), 241–50.

33. See, e.g., E. Brandenburger, *Adam und Christus: Exegetisch-religionsgeschichtliche Untersuchungen zu Röm. 5:12–21 (1 Kor 15)* (WMANT 7; Neukirchen/Vluyn: Neukirchener, 1962), esp. 157, 175–78.

34. P. Ryl. 2.243, as cited in MM, 204.

35. See esp. J. Jeremias, "πολλοί," *TDNT,* 6:536–41.

36. See esp. Stowers, *Diatribe.*

37. A. J. M. Wedderburn, *Baptism and Resurrection: Studies in Pauline Theology Against Its Graeco-Roman Background* (WUNT 44; Tübingen: Mohr, 1987). Note also G. Wagner, *Pauline Baptism and the Pagan Mysteries* (London: Oliver & Boyd, 1967).

38. J. R. W. Stott, *Men Made New: An Exposition of Romans 5–8* (London: InterVarsity, 1966), 45.

39. Cf. Str-B, 3:232.

40. See esp. H. N. Ridderbos, *Paul: An Outline of His Theology* (Grand Rapids: Eerdmans, 1974), 57–62.

41. Keith Bradley, *Slavery and Society at Rome* (Key Themes in Ancient History; Cambridge: Cambridge Univ. Press, 1994), 29–30. See also A. Rupprecht, "Slave, Slavery," in *DPL,* 880.

42. See, e.g., W. A. Meeks, *The First Urban Christians: The Social World of the Apostle Paul* (New Haven: Yale Univ. Press, 1983), 20–23.

43. See also *b. Šabb.* 151b.

44. Cf. Lev. 22:12; Deut. 24:2; Hos. 3:3.

45. *b. Šabb.* 145b–146a.

46. *Pesiq. Rab.* 21 (107a).

47. See *Life of Adam and Eve* 19; Philo, *Spec. Laws* 4.84–94.

48. Philo, *Decalogue* 142–43, 173; *4 Macc.* 2:6.

49. See, e.g., R. H. Gundry, "The Moral Frustration of Paul Before His Conversion: Sexual Lust in Romans 7:7–25," in *Pauline Studies: Essays Presented to Professor F. F. Bruce on His 70th Birthday,* eds. D. A. Hagner and M. J. Harris (Grand Rapids: Eerdmans, 1980), 80–94.

50. S. Safrai, "Home and Family," in *The Jewish People in the First Century,* eds. S. Safrai and M. Stern (CRINT 1; Philadelphia: Fortress, 1976), 2:771.

51. See also Sir. 17:11; *m. ʾAbot* 6:7; *Pss. Sol.* 14:2; Bar. 3:9. See the discussion in E. E. Urbach, *The Sages: Their Concepts and Beliefs* (Jerusalem: Magnes, 1979), 1:424–26.

52. Rom. 16:18; 1 Cor. 3:18; 2 Thess. 2:3.

53. For elaboration, see Moo, *The Epistle to the Romans,* 442–51.

54. Ovid, *Metamorphoses* 7.21; see also Epictetus, *Diss.* 2.26.4.

55. See also Jer. 15:8; 20:8; 51:56; Joel 1:15; Amos 5:9; Mic. 2:4; Zeph. 1:15.

56. E.g., Deut. 4:1; 5:1; Ps. 119 (29x); Luke 1:6; Rom. 2:26; Heb. 9:1, 10.

57. See also Ex. 4:22; Jer. 3:19; 31:9; *4 Ezra* 6:58.

58. See also Hos. 2:1 [LXX]; Wisd. Sol. 5:5; *T. Mos.* 10:3; *2 Apoc. Bar.* 13:9.

59. See especially J. M. Scott, *Adoption as Sons of God: An Exegetical Investigation into the Background of ΥΙΟΘΕΣΙΑ in the Pauline Corpus* (WUNT 2.48; Tübingen: Mohr, 1992), 3–57.

60. On this institution, see esp. F. Lyall, *Slaves, Citizens, Sons: Legal Metaphors in the Epistles* (Grand Rapids: Zondervan, 1984), 67–99.

61. See MM, 610.

62. See, e.g., Lyall, *Slaves, Citizens, Sons,* 102–3.

63. See also Gen. 15:7; 17:8; Deut. 30:5; Isa. 60:21; Ezek. 36:8–12 (the verbs in these verses mean "to inherit").

64. See also *1 En.* 40:9; *4 Macc.* 18:3.

65. See also *1 En.* 45:5; 72:1; *2 Apoc. Bar.* 29; 32:6; 44:12; 57:2; *Jub.* 1:29; 4:26.

66. E.g., Num. 5:9; Deut. 18:4; 2 Chron. 31:5–6.

67. 2 Thess. 2:13; James 1:18; Rev. 14:4; 1 Cor. 15:20, 23; cf. Rom. 11:16.

68. See also Judg. 2:18; Ps. 6:6; 12:5; 31:10; 38:9; 79:11; 102:20.

69. See Ex. 18:22; Num. 11:17; Ps. 89:21; Luke 10:40.

70. See esp. E. A. Obeng, "The Origins of the Spirit Intercession Motif in Romans 8:26," *NTS* 32 (1986): 621–32.

71. See also Ps. 7:9; 17:3; cf. Acts 1:24; 15:8; Rev. 2:23.

72. Isa. 32:15, 20; 52:7; Jer. 8:15; cf. Sir. 39:25, 27.

73. Clearly in Acts 2:23; Rom. 11:2; 1 Peter 1:20; debated is 1 Peter 1:2; in Acts 26:5, it refers to mental knowledge.

74. Str-B, 3.259–60.

75. For "height" in this sense, see, e.g., Plutarch, *Moralia* 149a; Vettius Valens 241.26. "Depth" (*bathos*) less frequently has such a connotation; but BAGD cite a magical papyrus, *PGM* 4.575.

76. On the Greek view of "conscience," see C. Maurer, "συνείδησις," *TDNT*, 9:902–4; H.-J. Eckstein, *Der Begriff Syneidesis bei Paulus: Ein neutestamentlich-exegetische Untersuchung zum Gewissenbegriff* (Tübingen: Mohr-Siebeck, 1983).

77. E.g., Lev. 27:28; Judg. 16:19; cf. Luke 21:5; Acts 23:14.

78. Josh. 6:17, 18; 7:1, 11–13; 22:20; 1 Chron. 2:7.

79. Str-B, 3.260.

80. See also Isa. 63:16; 64:8; Jer. 31:9; Hos. 11:1; Mal. 1:6; 2:10.

81. See also Ex. 24:16; 40:34–35; Lev. 9:6; 1 Kings 8:11; Ezek. 1:28.

82. *m. ʾAbot* 1:2.

83. N. T. Wright, *The Climax of the Covenant* (Minneapolis: Fortress, 1992), 238.

84. See also Gen. 17:1–8, 15–16, 19–21; 18:18–19; 22:17–18.

85. See Lev. 15:16–17, 32; 18:20; 22:4; Num. 5:20.

86. Philo, *Alleg. Interp.* 3.88.

87. See esp. John Piper, *The Justification of God: An Exegetical and Theological Study of Romans 9:1–23* (Grand Rapids: Baker, 1983).

88. 1 Cor. 9:24, 26; cf. Gal. 2:2; 5:7; Phil. 2:16; 2 Tim. 2:5.

89. See also Ex. 8:15; 9:12, 35; 10:1, 20, 27; 11:10; 14:4, 8, 17; other verbs for the same idea occur in 7:13, 14; 8:15, 32; 9:7, 34.

90. E.g., Job 10:9; 38:14; Isa. 29:16; 45:9–10; Jer. 18:1–6.

91. See also *4 Ezra* 7:72–74; *Pss. Sol.* 13; 1QH 15:14–20.

92. See also Jer. 23:14; 49:18; 50:40; Lam. 4:6; Ezek. 16:46–56; Amos 4:11; Zeph. 2:9; Matt. 10:15; 11:23, 24; Luke 10:12; 17:29; 2 Peter 2:6; Jude 7; Rev. 11:8.

93. See also Deut. 19:6; Josh. 2:5; 1 Sam. 30:8; 2 Kings 25:5; Ps. 7:5; Lam. 1:3.

94. The classic case for the "testimony book" hypothesis was made by J. Rendell Harris, *Testimonies* (2 vols.; Cambridge: Cambridge Univ. Press, 1916, 1920).

95. Cf. John 2:17; Acts 22:3; 2 Cor. 11:2; Phil. 3:6.

96. See also Neh. 9:29; CD 3:14–16; *b. Sanh.* 59b; note also Paul's quotation of Lev. 18:5 in Gal. 3:12.

97. E.g., Joseph Fitzmyer, *Romans* (AB; Garden City, N.Y.: Doubleday, 1993), 591.

98. E.g., M. J. Suggs, "'The Word Is Near You': Romans 10:6–10 Within the Purpose of the Letter," in *Christian History and Interpretation: Studies Presented to John Knox* (ed. W. R. Farmer, et al.; Cambridge: Cambridge Univ. Press, 1967), 289–312.

99. See Ps. 139:8; Prov. 30:4; Isa. 14:13; Amos 9:2.

100. The translation is from M. McNamara, *The New Testament and the Palestinian Targum to the Pentateuch* (AnBib 27; Rome: Pontifical Biblical Institute, 1966), 370–78.

101. E.g., Deut. 33:29; Isa. 45:22; 2 Macc. 3:22; Judith 16:2.

102. Acts 9:14, 21; 22:16; 1 Cor. 1:2; 2 Tim. 2:22; 1 Peter 1:17.

103. See esp. J. Fitzmyer, "The Semitic Background of the New Testament *kyrios* Title," in *A Wandering Aramean: Collected Aramaic Essays* (SBLDS 25; Missoula, Mont.: Scholars, 1979), 115–42.

104. *Mek. Exod.* 14:22 (37b).

105. See also Mark 6:52; 8:17; John 12:40; 2 Cor. 3:14; the noun form, *pōrōsis*, occurs in Mark 3:5; Rom. 11:25; Eph. 4:18.

106. See, e.g., Aristotle, *History of Animals* 3.19; Marcus Aurelius, *Meditations* 9.36.

107. 1 Kings 14:22; Ps. 78:58; 1 Cor. 10:22; Ps. 37:1, 7, 8; Sir. 30:3.

108. See, e.g., *T. Sim.* 6:2–7; *2 Apoc. Bar.* 78:6–7; *4 Ezra* 4:38–43; cf. also Acts 3:19–20.

109. Cf. also *1 En.* 93:5, 8; *Jub.* 21:24.

110. See also *1 En.* 10:16; 93:2, 5, 8, 10; *Jub.* 16:26; 21:4; *Pss. Sol.* 14:3–4; 1QS 8:5; 11:8; 1QH 6:15–16; 8:5–7, 9–10.

111. W. M. Ramsay, "The Olive-Tree and the Wild Olive," in *Paul and Other Studies in Early Christian History* (London: Hodder and Stoughton, 1908), 219–50. Ramsay cites Columella, *De re rustica* 5.9.16, and Palladius, *De insitione* 53–54.

112. See also *4 Ezra* 10:38; 12:36–38; 14:5; *1 Enoch* 9:6; 103:2; *2 Apoc. Bar.* 48:3; 81:4.

113. See, e.g., 1QS 3:23; 4:18; 9:18; 11:3, 5, 19; 1QH 1:21; 2:13; 4:27–28; 7:27; 11:10; 12:13; 1QpHab 7:5, 8, 14.

114. An oft-quoted parallel to Rom. 11:26 is *m. Sanh.* 10:1: "All Israelites have a share in the world to come," since the text goes on to list several kinds of exceptions to this promise. But (1) this text uses the plural "all Israelites" rather than the singular "all Israel," and (2) there are no explicit exceptions in Romans 11.

115. See Ps. 19:9; 36:6; 119:75; Sir. 17:12.

116. *2 Apoc. Bar.* 14:8–9.

117. Marcus Aurelius, *Meditations* 4.23.

118. See, e.g., Philo, *Spec. Laws* 1.208.

119. See esp. C. J. Bjerkelund, *Parakalo: Form, Function und Sinn der parakalo-Sätze in den paulinischen Briefen* (Bibliotheca Theologica Norvegica 1; Oslo: Universitetsforlaget, 1967).

120. E.g., Ps. 50:14, 23; 51:16–17; 141:2; Sir. 35:1; Tobit 4:10–11; 12:12; 2 Macc. 12:43–44.

121. Epictetus, *Disc.* 1.16.20–21.

122. Philo, *Spec. Laws* 1.277.

123. Livy, 2.32; cf. Epictetus, *Disc.* 2.10.4–5.

124. Josephus, *Ant.* 15.11.3 §396; cf. also Philo, *Virtues* 95.

125. See 2 Cor. 11:3; Eph. 6:5; Col. 3:22.

126. Martin Dibelius, *James*, ed. by H. Greeven (Hermeneia; Philadelphia: Fortress, 1976), 3.

127. See also *T. Iss.* 7:5; *T. Zeb.* 7:4; *T. Jos.* 17:7.

128. See also Ps. 34:18; Isa. 14:32; 49:13; Zeph. 2:3; cf. James 4:6.

129. See 2 Sam. 22:9, 13; Ps. 18:8, 12; 140:10; Isa. 5:24.

130. See esp. John Piper, *Love Your Enemies: Jesus' Love Command in the Synoptic Gospels and in the Early Christian Paraenesis* (SNTSMS 38; Cambridge: Cambridge Univ. Press, 1979), 115–18.

131. See S. Morenz, "Feurige Kohlen auf dem Haupt," in *Religion und Geschichte der alter Agypten. Gesammelte Aufsätze* (Weimar: Hermann Böhlaus, 1975), 433–44.

132. Eph. 3:10; 6:12; Col. 1:16; 2:15; cf. 1 Peter 3:22; see also the singular in Eph. 1:21; Col. 2:10.

133. See esp. Karl Barth, *Church and State* (London: SCM, 1939), 23–36; Oscar Cullmann, *The State in the New Testament* (New York: Harper & Row, 1956), 55–70.

134. See also Titus 3:1; 1 Cor. 16:16; Eph. 5:21.

135. Titus 2:9; 1 Cor. 14:32, 34; Eph. 5:24; Col. 3:18; Titus 2:5.

136. See also 1 Sam. 12:8; Prov. 8:15–16; Isa. 41:2–4; 45:1–7; Jer. 2:7, 10; 27:5–6; Dan. 4:25, 32; 5:21.

137. See esp. Bruce W. Winter, "The Public Honouring of Christian Benefactors: Romans 13.3–4 and 1 Peter 2.14–15," *JSNT* 34 (1988): 87–103.

138. See, e.g., in the LXX, Est. 1:10; 2:2; 6:3; Jer. 25:9; cf. also Wis. So. 6:4.

139. Plutarch, *Princip. inerud.* 5.13.22–14.2.

140. Cf. Tacitus, *Histories* 3.68.

141. A. N. Sherwin-White, *Roman Society and Roman Law in the New Testament* (Oxford: Clarendon, 1963), 8–11.

142. Philo, *Spec. Laws* 2.92–95; 3.159–63.

143. See also Acts 13:2; 2 Cor. 9:12; Phil. 2:17, 25; Heb. 1:7, 14; 8:2, 6; 9:21; 10:11; Num. 4:37, 41; 1 Sam. 2:18; Luke 1:23; Rom. 15:16, 27.

144. Cf. 2 Sam. 13:18; 1 Kings 10:5; 2 Chron. 9:4.

145. See, e.g., Luke 18:20; James 2:11; Philo, *Decalogue* 24, 36, 51, 121–37, 167–71; Clement of Alexandria, *Stromateis* 6.16.

146. See Deut. 10:4; Philo, *Heir* 168; *Decalogue* 32; Josephus *Ant.* 3.6.5 §138.

147. Matt. 22:34–40; cf. Mark 12:28–34; Luke 10:25–28; John 13:34–35.

148. See the Targum and *Sifra* on Lev. 19:18.

149. See *T. Zeb.* 5:1; *T. Ash.* 5:7; *T. Naph.* 5:2.

150. See, e.g., Philo, *Migration* 222; *Dreams* 1.117.

151. E.g., Isa. 27; Jer. 30:8–9; Joel 2:32; 3:18; Obad. 15–17.

152. See also Acts 27:35; 1 Cor. 11:24; 1 Tim. 4:3; *Did.* 10:1–6.

153. See esp. Deut. 8:10; cf. Mark 8:6; 14:23; John 6:11, 23.

154. 1 Cor. 15:3–4; cf. also Rom. 8:34; 1 Thess. 4:14.

155. See Matt. 27:19; John 19:13; Acts 12:21; 18:12, 16, 17; 25:6, 10, 17.

156. See Rom. 9:32, 33; 1 Cor. 8:9; 1 Peter 2:8.

157. See 1 Macc. 1:47, 62; Josephus, *Ant.* 12.2.14 §112; 131.1.1 §4.

158. See Rom. 16:10; 1 Cor. 11:19; 2 Cor. 10:18; 13:7; 2 Tim. 2:15; James 1:12.

159. See Philo, *Creation* 128; *Joseph* 201; Josephus, *Ag. Ap.* 1.3 §18.

160. See also Lev. 4:12; 6:11; 7:19; Ezra 6:20; Mal. 1:11; in the New Testament see also Luke 11:41; John 13:10, 11; Acts 18:6; 20:26.

161. Matt. 27:34, 48; Mark 15:35–36; Luke 23:36; John 15:25; 19:28–29; cf. also John 2:17; Acts 1:20; Rom. 11:9.

162. Deut. 32:43 in 15:10; Isa. 11:10 in 15:12; Ps. 18:49 in 15:9b; 117:1 in 15:11.

163. See also Sir. 47:22; 4QFlor 1:11; 4QPat 3–4; Rev. 5:5; 22:16.

164. See S. N. Olson, "Pauline Expressions of Confidence in his Addressees," *CBQ* 47 (1985): 282–95.

165. See Isa. 61:6; 2 Esd. 20:36 (=Neh. 10:39); Sir. 7:30; *Let. Aris.* 95; *T. Levi* 2:10; 4:2; 8:3–10; 9:3; Philo, *Moses* 2.94, 149; *Spec. Laws* 1.249; 4.191; *Alleg. Interp.* 3.175; *Posterity* 184.

166. Cf. Strabo 7.7.4.

167. See esp. W. P. Bowers, "Jewish Communities in Spain at the Time of Paul the Apostle," *JTS* 26 (1975): 395–402.

168. See Roger Aus, "Paul's Travel Plans to Spain and the 'Full Number of the Gentiles,' Romans XI 25," *NovT* 21 (1979): 242–46.

169. Cf. Acts 15:3; 20:38; 21:5; 1 Cor. 16:6, 11; 2 Cor. 1:16; Titus 3:13; 3 John 6.

170. See also 1 Cor. 16:1–2; 2 Cor. 8–9.

171. See MM.

172. E.g., Philo, *Husbandry* 112, 119; in *4 Macc.*, the word describes the struggles of the martyrs.

173. See esp. C.-H. Kim, *Form and Structure of the Familiar Greek Letter of Recommendation* (SBLDS 4; Missoula, Mont.: Scholars, 1972).

174. See D. Madvig, "Corinth," *ISBE*, 1:772.

175. Cf. also 1 Cor. 3:5; 2 Cor. 3:6; 6:4; Eph. 3:7; 6:21; Col. 1:7, 23, 25; 4:7; 1 Tim. 4:6.

176. Cf. *Apost. Const.* 8.19, 20, 28; the feminine *diakonissa* is used.

177. See *New Docs.*, 2:193–94; 4:239–41.

178. See esp. E. Judge, "Cultural Conformity and Innovation in Paul: Some Clues from Contemporary Documents," *TynBul* 35 (1984): 20–21.

179. See esp. Peter Lampe, "The Roman Christians of Romans 16," in *The Romans Debate*, 218; building on his major work, *Die Stadtrömischen Christen in den ersten beiden Jahrhunderten: Untersuchungen zur Socialgeschicthe* (2d ed.; WUNT 2.18; Tubingen: Mohr, 1989).

180. See esp. E. E. Elis, "Paul and His Co-Workers," in *DPL*, 186; cf. Acts 14:4; 1 Cor. 9:5–6; 15:7; Gal. 2:9; *Did.* 11:4; *Herm. Vis.* 3.5.1; *Sim.* 9.15.4; 16.5; 25:2.

181. Josephus, *Ant.* 18.8.4 §§273–76; *J.W.* 2.11.6 §221.

182. Tacitus, *Ann.* 31.1; Cassius Dio, *Rom. Hist.* 60.34.

183. S. Benko, *Pagan Rome and the Early Christians* (Bloomington, Ind.: Indiana Univ. Press, 1984), 79–102.

184. 1 Cor. 16:20; 2 Cor. 13:12; 1 Thess. 5:26; 1 Peter 5:14; cf. Justin, *Apol.* 1.65.

185. *Jub.* 23:29; *T. Mos.* 10:1; *T. Levi* 18:37; *T. Sim.* 6:6.

186. See the discussion in A. D. Clarke, "Another Corinthian Erastus Inscription," *TynBul* 42 (1991):146–51.

Sidebar and Chart Notes

A-1. On the date, see esp. E. M. Smallwood, *The Jews Under Roman Rule* (SJLA 20; Leiden: Brill, 1976), 210–16.

A-2. See esp. W. Wiefel, "The Jewish Community in Ancient Rome and the Origins of Roman Christianity," in *The Romans Debate*, 92–101.

A-3. On rhetoric, see esp. Michael Bullmore, *Saint Paul's Theology of Rhetorical Style: An Examination of I Corinthians 2:1–5 in Light of First-Century Greco-Roman Rhetorical Culture* (New York: International Scholars Press, 1995); Duane Litfin, *Saint Paul's Theology of Proclamation: 1 Corinthians 1–4 and Greco-Roman Rhetoric* (Cambridge: Cambridge Univ. Press, 1994).

A-4. For other examples, see Demosthenes, *Kata Philippou* 3.9.17; Ps.-Xenophon, *Re Publica Athen.* 1.11 and 2.11; Epictetus, *Diss.* 1.10.7; 1.29.9–10; 3.26.29; 4.7.26–31.

A-5. See also Jer. 10:19–20; Lam. 1:9–22; 2:20–22; *Pss. of Sol.* 1:1–2, 6.

A-6. See, e.g., J. Barr, "'Abba, Father' and the Familiarity of Jesus' Speech," *Theology* 91 (1988): 173–79.

A-7. Josephus, *Ant.* 13.5.9 §§171–73; see also *J.W.* 2.8.2–14 §§119–66.

A-8. See E. Käsemann, *Romans* (Grand Rapids: Eerdmans, 1980), 350.

A-9. Tacitus, *Ann.* 13.50ff.

A-10. See, e.g., Diogenes Laertius 8.38; Philostratus, *Vita Apollonii* 1.8. See J. Behm, "ἐσθίω," *TDNT*, 2:690.

A-11. See also Dan. 10:3; Tobit 1:10–12; Judith 12:2; Rest of Est. 14:17; *Jos. Asen.* 7:1; 8:5; Josephus, *Life* 3 §14; *m.* ʾ*Abot* 3:3.

A-12. See Dan. 1:3–16; *T. Reu.* 1:10; *T. Jud.* 15:4; *m.* ᶜ*Abod. Zar.* 2:3.

A-13. Philo, *Contempl. Life* 37.

A-14. See esp. Col. 2:16, 21; 1 Tim. 4:3; 5:23.

A-15. Eusebius, *Eccl. Hist.* 2.23.5.

1 CORINTHIANS

by David W. J. Gill

orinth was a major city in the eastern Peloponnese of Greece.[1] It lay near the narrow isthmus that joined the Peloponnese to the mainland. The city lay at the foot of a mountain, Akrocorinth (elevation 1883 feet), which also served as a location for some of the cults of the city.

The City of Corinth

The history of the city of Corinth can be traced back to the earliest periods of Greek history. In the archaic period (6th cent. B.C.) it was ruled by the Kypselid family. During the Peloponnesian War (late 5th cent. B.C.) Corinth fought against Athens. During the second century B.C. Corinth joined other Greek states to fight against the domination of Rome, and in 146 B.C. the city was captured and razed to the ground by the Roman general Mummius. As a result, the city was left derelict for over a hundred years until Julius Caesar decided to found a colony, with the full Latin title of *Colonia Laus Iulia Corinthienses*,

CORINTH

◀

▶ 1 Corinthians
IMPORTANT FACTS:

- **AUTHOR:** The apostle Paul and Sosthenes.
- **DATE:** c. A.D. 55 (Paul writing from Ephesus).
- **OCCASION:**
  - To respond to information that there had been quarrels in the church.
  - To prepare for a visit from Timothy and Paul himself.
- **KEY THEMES:**
  1. The impact of the Christian gospel on the life of the Christian.
  2. The ordering of the local church.

in 44 B.C. As Caesar was assassinated in March of that year, it seems likely that Mark Antony, Caesar's co-consul, may have been responsible for implementing the legislation. Some of the Roman sources suggest that the colony was established with Italian freedmen, that is, former slaves, though they probably only formed a small part of the overall population. The geographer Strabo records some of the details of the colony at this time:

Now after Corinth had remained deserted for a long time, it was restored again, because of its favourable position, by the deified Caesar, who colonised it with people that belonged for the most part to the freedman class. And when these were removing the ruins and at the same time digging open the graves, they found numbers of terracotta reliefs, and also many bronze vessels. And since they admired the worksmanship they left no grave unransacked.[2]

It is important to stress the lack of continuity between the Greek and Roman city. A number of buildings were demolished and the archaic temple in the heart of the town may have had its roof timbers removed. One of the famous descriptions of the ruined city occurs in a letter from Ser. Sulpicius to the Roman orator Cicero in 45 B.C.[3] There are other references to individuals living among the ruins[4], but the key point is that Corinth no longer existed as a political entity.

Corinth was one of a number of city-states (Gk. *polis*) in the Greek world. Her territory, the Corinthia, bordered on that of a number of other city-states. To the east along the isthmus that joined the Peloponnese to the Greek mainland was Megara. Northwards, along the coast of the Corinthian Gulf, was Sikyon. Along the southern side of the Corinthia was the Argolid, with cities such as Argos and Epidauros (where there was a major sanctuary for the healing-god Asklepios). Within the Corinthia were two main harbors, Lechaeum and Cenchreae, giving access respectively to the Corinthian Gulf (and Italy) and the Saronic Gulf and the eastern Mediterranean. These were some of the major harbors of the Mediterranean, rivaling those of Ostia (the port of Rome), Alexandria in Egypt, and Caesarea (the major port that gave access to Judea).

CORINTH AND ITS ENVIRONS

▶ The City of Corinth
IMPORTANT FACTS:

- Population: Approximately 100,000 (80,000 colony, 20,000 *territorium*).
- Religion: Patron deity Aphrodite; major sanctuary of Poseidon at nearby Isthmia; numerous other deities worshiped.
- Port city.
- Seat of the Roman governor for the province of Achaia.

▶Strabo in Corinth

One of the earliest accounts of the Roman colony at Corinth was by the geographer Strabo (c. 64 B.C.–A.D. 21), who came from Amaseia in Pontus (northwest Asia Minor). The account is based on a personal autopsy "from what I myself saw after the recent restoration of the city by the Romans."[A-1] Strabo may have been visiting the colony when Octavian—the future emperor Augustus—was on his way back to Italy after the battle of Actium (Sept. 2, 31 B.C.) and the capture of Alexandria (Aug. 1, 30 B.C.) for his triple triumph (held Aug. 13–15, 29 B.C.). Octavian is known to have stopped at

Corinth at this time. One of Strabo's vantage points was the Acrocorinth: "I myself have looked down at the settlement from Acrocorinth."[A-2] From the mountain he could look across the Corinthian Gulf to the mountains of Parnassos and Helikon on the Greek mainland. Strabo apparently made use of earlier accounts of the colony, including Apollodoros's commentary on the Homeric *Catalogue of the Ships* (written in the second century B.C. on the eve of the Roman destruction of the colony), Hieronymos of Cardia (300 B.C.), and the fourth-century B.C. geographer Eudoxos of Knidos.

CORINTH

▼

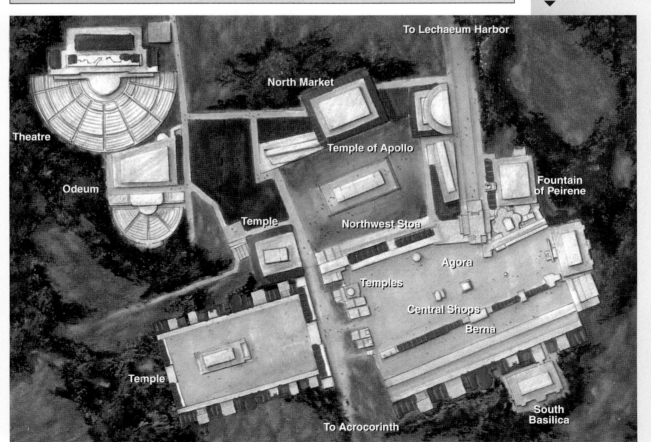

To Lechaeum Harbor
North Market
Theatre
Temple of Apollo
Odeum
Fountain of Peirene
Temple
Northwest Stoa
Agora
Temples
Central Shops
Berna
Temple
South Basilica
To Acrocorinth

(clockwise from top)

CORINTH

Aerial view of the remains of the ancient city.

A Corinthian inscription with a list of victors in the Isthmian games.

The *diolkos*—a rock road that the Romans built enabling them to drag boats across the narrowest point of the isthmus.

The Acrocorinth with some of the ruins of ancient Corinth in the foreground.

View from the Lechaeum, Corinth's western port, toward Corinth and the Acrocorinth.

Corinth became the residence for the Roman governor of the senatorial province of Achaia, which was reestablished by Claudius in A.D. 44. Prior to that, the province had been combined with Macedonia as one of the military "imperial" provinces (see comments on 16:15). This administrative function allowed Corinth to become the leading city in the province. It seems to have attracted members of elite families to reside there, such as the Euryclids from Sparta. It also meant that individual cities would need to consult the governor at Corinth; thus, members of the Corinthian elite allowed themselves to be used as intermediaries or *proxenoi*. One of these *proxenoi*, L. Licinnius Anteros, was honored by the city of Methana near Troezen in A.D. 1/2.[5]

The Spiritual Climate of the Area

The second-century A.D. Roman orator Favorinus of Arles (in the south of France) praised Corinth as a city "favoured by Aphrodite."[6] Certainly in the Hellenistic period before the sack of the city, the sanctuary of Aphrodite on the Acrocorinth had been a complex affair. Strabo, probably drawing on classical or Hellenistic historians of the city, noted that at this earlier time, "the temple of Aphrodite was so rich that it owned more than a thousand temple-slaves, courtesans, whom both men and women had dedicated to the goddess."[7] However, Strabo's own visit to the Acrocorinth showed that the Roman temple was far more modest: "The summit has a small temple of Aphrodite."[8] Aphrodite or Venus (her Roman name) was seen as the ancestor of Julius Caesar, the founder of the Roman colony. Indeed in the Julian

Forum at Rome, completed by Caesar's adopted son Augustus, there was a temple to Venus Genetrix. A further temple of Aphrodite at Corinth appears to have been located on a terrace at the west end of the forum, as part of an inscription has been found that links the structure to Venus.[9] The second-century A.D. travel writer Pausanias also noted that this part of the forum contained a statue of Aphrodite made by the sculptor Hermogenes of Kythera (an island off the south coast of the Peloponnese).[10]

The forum of Corinth today is dominated by the columns of a Greek temple of the Doric order of architecture, probably erected in the sixth century B.C. It survived the sack of the city and was adapted in the Roman period for a new type of cult. Some of the earlier cults of the Greek city may have been reestablished, though it is not clear how much continuity there was with cult practice of the second century B.C. The sanctuary of Demeter and Kore (Persephone) on the slopes of the Acrocorinth may not have been revived until the second century A.D.

The colony also housed the cult to the Roman emperors. This may have been focused on the temple that coins of the colony show was dedicated to the Gens Iulia (the Julian family); Julius Caesar was deified after his assassination in March 44 B.C. and his adopted son Augustus was able to enjoy the associated benefits of divinity.[11]

One of the most important cults of the Corinthia was that of Poseidon (Lat. Neptune), a god associated with the sea and earthquakes. His cult was located at Isthmia at the neck of the Corinthian isthmus. This sanctuary, with a temple to the god, was associated with one of the sets of Panhellenic games that attracted people to attend from all over the Greek world. Such games, like those at Olympia, Delphi, and Nemea, continued in the Roman period and became the model for the establishment of festivals in the cities of the Greek east. While the emperor Nero was taking part in the Isthmian games in November 67, he declared Greece to be free from taxes—a right later removed by the emperor Vespasian.[12] The responsibility of the games had been transferred to nearby Sikyon after Corinth was sacked, but was restored to the colony some time after its foundation.

Eastern deities are known from Corinth, though it is not always easy to decide when in the Roman period they were introduced. Often the main source for information is Pausanias, writing some 120 years after the establishment of the church at Corinth. One of the most colorful accounts of the Egyptian deity Isis in the Corinthia is contained in the work of Lucius Apuleius, in his visions of the goddess at Cenchreae described in his work, *The Golden Ass*.[13] Certainly the worship of Isis and Serapis can be traced back to the Hellenistic period, and Corinth, as a major port, would have been in contact with Egypt. A similar phenomenon for these Egyptian deities can be found on the island of Crete.[14]

The Introduction of Christianity to Corinth

The church had been established at Corinth after Paul's visit to Macedonia and Athens (Acts 18). Paul possibly arrived at Corinth by sea, in which case he would have sailed from the Piraeus, the port of Athens, and arrived at Cenchrea, the eastern port of Corinth. The land route along the isthmus of Corinth was not an easy one. The date can be fixed by the mention of the presence of the Roman governor of the province of Achaia, L. Junius Gallio. An

TEMPLE OF APHRODITE

The scant remains of this famous temple on top of the Acrocorinth. ▼

▶ Pausanias in Corinth

Pausanias probably came from Lydia in modern Turkey, in the region of Mount Sipylus, as it is a feature regularly mentioned in the text.[A-3] A likely city for his upbringing is Magnesia on the Sipylus.[A-4] Pausanias's discussion of the refoundation of Corinth, 217 years before his day, provides a date of A.D. 174 for the writing of this part of the work.[A-5] Scholars think he completed his writing by around 180. The colony of Corinth is discussed in Book 2 of his travel guide to the Greek world. As in many places, he notes "things worthy of mention"—the "starred" sites still common in modern travel accounts, including "the extant remains of antiquity," that is, the pre-Roman city. Pausanias qualifies his recommendation by noting that "the greater number of them belong to the period of its second ascendancy."[A-6] Like Strabo he likely ascended Acrocorinth and commented on the sanctuary of Aphrodite found there. He left Corinth by traveling up the coast of the Corinthian Gulf toward neighboring Sikyon.

inscription from the sanctuary of Apollo at Delphi shows that he was governor in Greece when Claudius had obtained "tribunician power" twelve times and had been acclaimed emperor twenty-six times. From other inscriptions, these events place the Delphi inscription between the end of 51 and August 52 (when he was acclaimed emperor for the twenty-seventh time). An undated statue base, originally no doubt bearing a portrait of the governor, was erected in honor of Gallio at Plataia in Boiotia (central Greece). Paul stayed in the city for some eighteen months. Early members of the church included Priscilla and Aquila, who had been expelled from Rome by Emperor Claudius.

Issues in the Church at Corinth

It was perhaps at Corinth that Christianity came into contact with a city that was mainly Italian in culture and with a population that, officially at least, was Latin-speaking. It was to Corinth that those who had aspirations in the province of Achaia moved, and it had become fashionable to adopt Roman culture. Perhaps this accounts for the personal rivalry that becomes such an issue in 1 Corinthians. The ambitions and emphasis on status so clear in the colony were being transferred to the church community. Thus we also find issues of dress being used to make statements about positions in society. Even Paul's

▶ Archaeological Prospects at Corinth

Since 1895 Corinth has been explored by the American School of Classical Studies at Athens, in conjunction with the Archaeological Institute of America, though excavations have focused on the area of the forum.[A-7] Changes in sea levels have taken place since antiquity, which has hindered the exploration of the two harbors of Corinth. Cenchrea, the eastern port of Corinth, is now partly submerged, but it has been the focus of excavations by an American team, including staff of Chicago and Indiana Universities.[A-8] Lechaeum, on the Gulf of Corinth, has been the subject of limited excavation by a team from the Greek archaeological service.[A-9] The Panhellenic sanctuary of Poseidon at Isthmia has been excavated by an American team from the University of Chicago.[A-10]

ARCHAEOLOGICAL SITES

(left) The remains of the harbor at Cenchrae. The partially submerged foundations are the remnants of a temple of Isis.

(right) The forum at Corinth.

role as preacher and apostle were questioned in the light of the expectation from the educated elite of what a good public orator should be like.[15]

The letter is a response to specific issues raised by the church as well as to more informal information that has reached Paul in the province of Asia. In chapter 7 Paul mentions "the matters you wrote about" (7:1), which perhaps include marriage (7:1), single people (7:25), food sacrificed to pagan gods (8:1), spiritual gifts (12:1), and a collection for God's people (16:1). Paul writes to a dynamic church that is trying to find its feet in an alien culture.

Introduction to the Letter (1:1–3)

Paul . . . and our brother Sosthenes (1:1). The opening sentence of the letter shows that it was jointly written by Paul and Sosthenes. Paul emphasizes his authoritative position by drawing attention to his role as an apostle of Jesus Christ; the central role of Jesus Christ is underscored throughout this opening chapter. Sosthenes is designated not as an apostle but as "our brother." A possible candidate for this individual is the Corinthian synagogue ruler, Sosthenes, who was beaten during Paul's time in Corinth (Acts 18:17). Other individuals of this name are known from Corinth, including a magistrate possibly during the reign of Emperor Trajan.[16] Paul, however, is the main correspondent, for later he instructs them "to imitate me" (4:16).

To the church of God in Corinth (1:2). This letter is addressed to the church at Corinth in contrast to the second letter, which was also to "the saints" throughout the Roman province of Achaia. Paul uses a Greek political word for the church, *ekklēsia*; it implies the whole body of Christ's people in the city. Paul provides a list of reasons why individuals could call themselves members of the church in the same way that citizens of Corinth would be able to point to certain criteria by which they could call themselves Corinthians.

Grace and peace to you from God our Father and the Lord Jesus Christ (1:3). The combination of grace and peace is a common formula in New Testament letters. The more usual Greek greeting, *chaire*, has been transformed to the Christian word for grace, *charis*, and linked to the Greek word for the Hebrew *shalom*.

Thanksgiving (1:4–9)

I always thank God . . . because of his grace given you (1:4). Paul follows a standard pattern in his thanksgiving for the church at Corinth. He gives particular thanks for the grace they have received undeservedly from God. In a church characterized by boasting, the members need to be reminded of what they have already received.

You have been enriched in every way (1:5). In a church that contained every shade of society (1:26), all have been enriched, not in a worldly way, but with two specific characteristics, speaking (*logos*) and knowledge (*gnōsis*). *Logos* and *gnōsis* were both characteristics valued by the elite in the Roman colony; within the church such gifts are open to all, regardless of status. The Roman orator Favorinus visited Corinth in the first part of the second century A.D. and recorded a love of public-speaking in the city.[17] Paul may be placing an emphasis on speaking with meetings of the church.

Our testimony . . . was confirmed in you (1:6). The Greek word for "confirmed" suggests that Paul is using a legal metaphor to illustrate that God has completed a contract with the church at Corinth, marked by the evidence of the gifts of "speaking" and "knowledge."

As you eagerly wait for our Lord Jesus Christ to be revealed (1:7). The view that the present world will come to an end with the appearing of Jesus Christ is in marked contrast to the Roman worldview, which expected an unchecked continuation of its empire's domination and authority.

That you will be blameless on the day of our Lord Jesus Christ (1:8). Paul continues the legal metaphor by using the word "blameless." The "day of the Lord" is an expression drawn from the Old Testament prophets (Amos 5:18–20; Joel 2:31), which suggests that part of the readership of Paul's letter is Jewish.

God, who has called you into fellowship with his Son Jesus Christ our Lord, is faithful (1:9). This verse draws on the imagery of the Mosaic law: "Know therefore that the LORD your God is God; he is the faithful God" (Deut. 7:9). Paul is reminding individual members of the Corinthian church that whatever their social status, a faithful God will equip them for service.

Loyalties and Divisions (1:10–17)

Paul now starts a section in the letter where he responds to issues in the church brought to his attention both by a report from "Chloe's household" (1:12) and from the personal report of Stephanas, Fortunatus, and Achaicus (16:15–17).

I appeal . . . that . . . you agree with one another so that there may be no divisions among you and that you may be perfectly united in mind and thought (1:10). This issue of divisions in the church was clearly known by the early Christian writer Clement (c. A.D. 95). Paul uses the verb "appeal," which usually had the meaning of writing with authority; this is no empty rhetoric, but an appeal coming from an apostle of Jesus Christ. The Corinthian church needs to take note. Paul uses two metaphors in his appeal. The word "divisions" recalls the furrows created by ploughing, whereas the vision of being "perfectly united" recalls the mending of nets (Mark 1:19).

CORINTH

(left) Corinthian columns on a temple dedicated to Octavia, the sister of Caesar Augustus.

(right) The well-preserved structure of the Fountain of Peirene.

▼

Some from Chloe's household have informed me that there are quarrels among you (1:11). The members of Chloe's household are likely domestic servants—either slaves or former slaves (so-called freedmen). Insofar as Paul writes the letter from Asia (16:19)—which probably means the city of Ephesus—the movement of slaves or freedmen between Corinth and western Turkey has been plausibly interpreted as indicating that Chloe was in fact from Asia but had settled in Corinth. A first-century example of such an individual is presented by the case of Junia Theodora, originally from Lycia (in southwestern Turkey), but who had settled in the colony and proudly called herself "resident of Corinth."[18] The word *eris* ("quarrels") is often linked to divisions and strife, frequently within the political sphere. Such quarrels were characteristics of pupils in the intellectual world of the first century, where great emphasis was placed on loyalty to the master or teacher. Paul urges the Corinthians to look away from their spiritual teachers and rather to Jesus Christ.

I follow Paul . . . Apollos . . . Cephas . . . Christ (1:12). Paul lists the different named leaders within the Corinthian church. Apollos was a Jew from Alexandria (in Egypt), who is described as "learned" or "eloquent" (Acts 18:24). He had come under the influence of Priscilla and Aquila at Ephesus and from there had moved to Corinth. Cephas is the Aramaic name for Peter. The Greek phrase translated as "I follow" (or equally well as "I belong to") is sometimes found inscribed on objects dedicated to the pagan gods of the Greek world. For example, an archaic column-krater (a two-handled bowl) found on the site of the later Asklepieion carries the inscription "I belong to Apollo."[19] Thus, there may be different groups within the church at Corinth who are more keen to support their own theological position than to be united in Jesus Christ. These divisions or parties are of the same sort as found in contemporary political bodies.

Is Christ divided? (1:13). Paul uses a series of rhetorical questions to confront the church with the foolishness of their position. Thus Paul uses a means of communication that was familiar to the well educated.

Crispus and Gaius (1:14). Crispus is almost certainly to be identified with the synagogue ruler at Corinth, who with "his entire household believed in the

APHRODITE
Statue of the goddess, also known as Venus to the Romans.
▼

▶ "I Belong to Aphrodite"

The series of slogans found at the beginning of 1 Corinthians showing allegiance to individuals ("I follow Paul"; "I follow Apollos"; etc.) use the same Greek phrase found on objects dedicated in sanctuaries in Corinth. A bronze dedication found in the excavations carries the statement "I belong to Aphrodite," thereby signifying that an individual had offered it to the goddess in her sanctuary at Corinth. Although this came from the archaic city, it is possible that individuals at Corinth have adopted slogans ultimately derived from the religious language of the colony.

REFLECTIONS

IT IS EASY TO FALL INTO THE TRAP of preferring the leadership style of one person over the other. Perhaps one individual's preaching speaks more directly to us, or his or her pastoral concern is more relevant. Such split allegiances can divide a church community. We need to ensure that our main commitment is to Jesus Christ.

Lord" during Paul's first visit to the city (Acts 18:8). A synagogue ruler at Corinth is likely to have been a wealthy individual, for he was responsible for the upkeep of the building. Gaius was not only a common Roman name (note the Macedonian Gaius who accompanied Paul; Acts 19:29; 20:4), but inscriptions from Corinth show that it was a relatively common name in first-century Corinth. This Gaius is likely the same person "whose hospitality I [Paul] and the whole church here enjoy" (Rom. 16:23, a letter written from Corinth). Gaius almost certainly holds Roman citizenship; it is undoubtedly the praenomen of those freedmen who received their citizenship from Gaius Julius Caesar.

The household of Stephanas (1:16). In addition to Crispus and Gaius Paul has also baptized "the household of Stephanas" while at Corinth. The term "household" (*oikos*) is likely to have included not only Stephanas's immediate family, but also those attached to the household, perhaps including slaves. This same household is mentioned later in the letter, when Paul records the delegation sent to him (16:15, 17). Stephanas, along with Crispus and Gaius, are likely to have

been among the "wise," "influential," and those of "noble birth" (1:26) of the colony.

Not with words of human wisdom (1:17). Paul makes a distinction between using sophisticated rhetorical techniques and the preaching of the Christian gospel. He challenges the Corinthian church not to use the techniques of contemporary oratory unless they retain the cross as a central feature of their message. Paul's worry is that if he uses special rhetorical techniques, members of the church might admire him rather than heed his message.

Wisdom and Rhetoric (1:18–31)

Paul now develops the contrast between the wisdom of the age and the message of the cross. The background to this section is perhaps the way that itinerant speakers of his day, so-called sophists, used rhetorical techniques to influence their audiences. Such oratory was widely valued, and Paul has to remind the Corinthian church that the content matters more than the presentation.

The message of the cross (1:18). The word "message" translates the Greek

ROMAN CROSS

A model of a typical Roman cross with a nameplate on the top and two wooden beams for the arms and legs.

▼

word *logos*. As such, it allows a distinction to be drawn between the "words of human wisdom" (1:17) and the "word" or "message" of the cross. Indeed, it is the "oratory" of the cross itself that becomes central in communication.

Those who are perishing, but to us who are being saved (1:18). Paul presents the church with a new vision of world order. A Roman colony like Corinth has certain social distinctions: Roman citizen and noncitizen, slave and free, male and female. For Paul the Jew (and at the same time Roman citizen) there is the distinction between Jews and Gentiles. The Greeks made a distinction between themselves and those who do not speak Greek, whom they called by the word *barbaros* (see comments on 14:11). However, the new way of perceiving the world must ignore these worldly distinctions. Society consisted of two groups: those like Paul and the members of the Corinthian church ("but to us") who can be described as "being saved," and those outside the church "who are perishing." Note too that those in the colony who have power but are outside the church view the cross as "foolishness"; in contrast, those considered to be foolish have experienced the power of God.

I will destroy the wisdom of the wise; the intelligence of the intelligent I will frustrate (1:19). Paul appeals to Isaiah 29:14 to support his argument. He quotes the Greek Septuagint version of the prophecy, although he changes the last word; the LXX reads "I will hide" rather than "I will frustrate." The "wise" was a recognized Greek term for members of the social elite; thus, Paul is applying Old Testament Scripture to the Corinthian situation. Such an appeal would suggest that mem-

bers of the Corinthian church were conversant with the Jewish Scriptures.

The wise man ... the scholar ... the philosopher of this age (1:20). Paul uses four rhetorical questions, which may be a deliberate allusion to another passage of Isaiah (33:18): "Where is that chief officer? Where is the one who took the revenue? Where is the officer in charge of the towers?" However, there are key differences. Paul chooses three figures representative of education in the Greek provinces of the eastern Mediterranean. The "wise man" (*sophos*) can be understood as a Greek philosopher. The "scholar" (*grammateus*) can have two meanings. In a Jewish setting, the *grammateus* was an expert in the Mosaic law; in the Gospels the word is translated as "the teachers of the law" (e.g., Matt. 5:20). A *grammateus* in the Greek world

was the normal term for a "city clerk"; such a figure features in the riot in Ephesus (Acts 19:35). As Paul goes on to make a distinction between Jews and Greeks (1:22), it is likely that he has in mind Jewish "teachers of the law." "The philosopher [*syzētētēs*] of this age" means "the disputer of this age"; it seems likely that Paul is alluding to the emergence of itinerant orators or sophists.[20]

The world through its wisdom (1:21). The "wisdom of the world," alluded to in the previous verse, may refer to the intellectual climate of the Roman empire. The "world" (*kosmos*) was a way of defining the limit of Roman rule. For example, in a decree passed by the provincial council of Asia c. A.D. 15 and found at Halikarnassos (in western Turkey), the emperor Augustus was described as "father of his country and of the whole world."[21]

Jews demand miraculous signs and Greeks look for wisdom (1:22). Paul identifies two main cultural groups, "Jews" and "Greeks," while ignoring the Romans; both Jews and Greeks could hold Roman citizenship. Paul characterizes the Jews as looking for "miraculous signs" that authenticate the coming of their Messiah. Such an interest is reflected in the Gospel of Mark, where the Pharisees, in order to test Jesus, "asked him for a sign from heaven"; Jesus replied, "Why does this generation ask for a miraculous sign? I tell you the truth, no sign will be given to it" (Mark 8:11–12). The Greeks had a reputation, which can be traced back to the Greek historian Herodotus, of a love for wisdom (*sophia*). Herodotus tells the story that the king of Scythia (an area adjoining the Black Sea) once sent to find out what the Greeks were like; it was reported, "all Greeks were keen for every kind of learning, except the Lacedaemonians."[22] Particular groups of Greek philosophers, such as the Stoics and Epicureans, gave discourses on "the nature of the gods" as part of their search for wisdom.

We preach Christ crucified: a stumbling block to Jews and foolishness to Gentiles (1:23). "Stumbling block" (*skandalon*) in fact implies that for the Jews the cross was a literal scandal or an offensive action. Since the Jews believed that "anyone who is hung on a tree is under God's curse" (Deut. 21:23), the thought of the promised Messiah being crucified on a wooden cross was scandalous. For the Gentiles (i.e., non-Jews), the preaching of the crucified Christ seemed ridiculous. Jesus had been convicted by the Roman governor of a province of the empire and had been crucified according to Roman law. The idea that a criminal could be the

▶ Coins at Corinth

Corinth, in common with other Roman colonies, issued coinage with the names of the two chief magistrates, the *duovirs*. Such coinage helps to provide a list of the names of wealthy individuals who dominated the political life of the colony, and as such help to date some of the buildings they helped build. The coins sometimes carried images of new buildings in the colony, such as the temple of the Divine Julius Caesar. Such local coinage emphasizes the identity and status of the colony within the province of Achaia and the wider Roman empire.

Christ was regarded as foolish. Such views about Christianity can be detected in the correspondence between Pliny the Younger, governor of the province of Bithynia (in northwest Turkey), and the Roman emperor Trajan.[23]

Not many of you were wise by human standards; not many were influential; not many were of noble birth (1:26). Paul makes an important statement here about the status of members of the Corinthian church. In a Roman colony organized in terms of citizenship, birth, and wealth, membership of the church was purely on the basis of calling (a theme first developed at 1:24). Paul identifies three groups here: the "wise" (*sophoi*), the "influential" or those who held power (*dynatoi*) in the colony, and those of "noble birth" (lit., "well born"). These three terms describe the social elite of the Roman colony and may have been used as marks of pride. The fact that "not many" were called does imply that a few members of the Corinthian church were drawn from the elite of Corinthian society. In other words, the message of Jesus Christ was reaching the full range of social strata at Corinth (and presumably elsewhere).

The foolish things of the world . . . the weak things of the world . . . the lowly things of this world and the despised things—and the things that are not (1:27–28). The elite of Corinthian society may well have despised the lower members who perhaps did not hold Roman citizenship. Certainly the orators or sophists of the day would have ridiculed the foolish, the weak, the lowly, the despised, and the nobodies. Yet it was this latter group who had been chosen by God. Paul is using a recognized rhetorical technique of constructing arguments from opposites. The Greek uses the neuter—conveyed by the translation "things"—to outline the attributes of the individuals called by God.[24]

No one may boast before him (1:29). "To boast" regularly features in the Corinthian letters. The sophists regularly boasted of their status. If educated members of the social elite were taking positions of leadership in the Corinthian church, they may have being using oratorical skills to "boast" of their own social position, emphasizing that they were "wise," "influential," or of "noble birth." Paul makes it clear that such boasting has no place in the church.

Let him who boasts boast in the Lord (1:31). Paul supports his argument with Jeremiah 9:24, but replaces "about this" with "in the Lord." Those familiar with the Old Testament would be able to complete

▶ Jews at Corinth

According to Acts 18:4, Corinth had a Jewish synagogue. Among the early converts was the *archisynagōgos* (the "ruler of the synagogue"), Crispus, who has a suggestively Roman name. Philo also mentions Corinth as one of the cities of the province of Achaia that had a synagogue.[A-11] A synagogue inscription, almost certainly dating to several hundred years after Paul's time, has been found at Corinth. The location of Corinth, with its contacts with both the eastern Mediterranean and Italy, make it a likely place for a Jewish community. Paul's frequent reference and allusion to the Old Testament suggest that the Christian community there included members who were Jewish by background.

the quotation that resonates with the issues of the preceding verses: "Let not the wise man boast of his wisdom or the strong man boast of his strength but let him who boasts boast about this: that he understands and knows me, that I am the LORD, who exercises kindness, justice and righteousness on earth, for in these I delight" (Jer. 9:23–24).

Paul's Arrival at Corinth (2:1–5)

Paul turns from considering the way in which the Corinthians have considered wisdom and rhetoric and instead focuses on the content of his own ministry. He presents a preaching style that may have become less familiar to the Corinthian Christians.

I did not come with eloquence or superior wisdom (2:1). Paul refers here to his original arrival in the colony, probably in the fall of A.D. 50 (Acts 18). He had "reasoned in the synagogue, trying to persuade Jews and Greeks" (18:4), trying to draw attention to Jesus Christ. He is drawing a contrast with the way that public speakers in the ancient world—sophists and orators—would arrive in a city and follow a set (and expected) protocol of heaping praise on the city and its achievements; in using such "eloquence" and "superior wisdom", these sophists tried both to win an audience and to draw attention to themselves.[25] So, for example, Favorinus, who visited Corinth probably in the early second century A.D., observed, "When I first visited your city [polis] the first time . . . and gave your people [dēmos] and magistrates a sample of my eloquence [lit., words], I seemed to be on friendly, yes intimate, terms with you."[26] Dio Chrysostom, addressing the assembly of his own city Prusa in Bithynia (northwestern

Turkey), observed that in his travels he could visit "the greatest cities"—including Rome—and his arrival was "escorted with much enthusiasm and éclat [philotimia], the recipients of my visits being grateful for my presence and begging me to address them and advise them and flocking about my doors from early dawn, all without my having incurred any expense or having made any contribution, with the result that all would admire me."[27]

Paul followed a different strategy, for his oratory proclaimed "the testimony about God." The Greek words translated as "superior" are better translated as "according to excellence" and apply both to the "oratory" ("eloquence") and to the "wisdom."[28] The stress on excellence was familiar to an elite group at Corinth.

For I resolved to know nothing while I was with you except Jesus Christ and him crucified (2:2). Paul had made his mind up that his arrival at Corinth would be marked by a presentation of Jesus Christ. He did not want his preaching to be confused with the oratory of a sophist, which would be done merely for its own sake. An orator might, for example, have included praise of the colony at Corinth, but Paul's emphasis was on the cross.

I came to you in weakness and fear, and with much trembling (2:3). In contrast to the sophists and orators, who arrived in Corinth with what might be termed "presence," Paul describes himself in some negative terms. "Weakness" is probably better translated "hardships," reflecting the difficulties he faced through his traveling ministry. "With much trembling" is not found in the Greek, which rather links "fear" and "trembling"—words that in the Old Testament reflect the presence of God. Such words contrast with the first-century speaker Scopelian, who used an "extremely melodious voice" and certainly could not be seen as a "timid speaker."[29] Thus, Paul was a man in whose message his hearers could detect the word of God.

My message and my preaching were not with wise and persuasive words, but with a demonstration of the Spirit's power (2:4).

Paul's message (or "oratory") led to his preaching; by contrast, the Corinthians were familiar with the sophists of their day, who used "wise and persuasive words" to bring their hearers to wisdom.[30] "Demonstration" (*apodeixis*) is a word Paul has borrowed from oratory itself. Cicero defines this term as "a process of reasoning that leads from

WISDOM AND RHETORIC

(left) A statue of Sophia in the Celsus library façade in Ephesus.

(right) Aristotle (384–322 B.C.), the father of rhetoric.

▶ Oratory in Corinth

Public speaking or oratory is one of the issues lying behind the letter. A speech by the orator Favorinus (c. A.D. 80–150), who came from Arles in the south of France, is preserved in the corpus of speeches by his teacher Dio Chrysostom.[A-12] Although the speech was delivered some time after Paul's day and in a period when the colony was becoming more Greek, it provides detail about the way in which orators addressed their audiences. After talking about the colorful and eminent visitors who had visited the city—including Arion, who was saved by a dolphin, Solon, the great lawgiver of the city of Athens, and the historian Herodotus—Favorinus recalled this about his second visit to the city:

You were so glad to see me that you did your best to get me to stay with you, but seeing that to be impossible, you did have a likeness made of me, and you took this and set it up in your Library, a front row seat as it were, where you felt it would most effectively stimulate the youth to persevere in the same pursuits as myself.[A-13]

Favorinus was himself a great rival of another orator, Polemo of Laodicea,[A-14] and through this speech it is possible to detect the way that Favorinus used his speech to promote himself—and in this case to have the Corinthians reinstate his statue.

things perceived to something not previously perceived."[31] In Quintilian's study of oratory the "demonstration" or "proof" is seen as "a method of proving what is not certain by means of what is certain."[32] Paul's technique is essentially a "proof" of the Spirit's power.

So that your faith might not rest on men's wisdom, but on God's power (2:5). Paul warns the Corinthians about allowing their faith to be based on the hearing of fine oratory; faith comes as a result of hearing the message and by God's intervention. The word "power" (*dynamis*) was used by ancient rhetoricians, such as Dio Chrysostom, for eloquence in oratory.[33] Christian preachers are not in the business of using persuasive techniques; rather, they persuade people by relying on God's, not their own, power.

God's Wisdom and Human Wisdom (2:6–16)

Paul has refuted the wisdom being presented to the Corinthians by contemporary orators. He has demonstrated that he is different from such speakers. Paul now picks on a word much loved by the Corinthians, "wisdom," but uses it to point them to God.

We do . . . speak a message of wisdom among the mature, but not the wisdom of this age or of the rulers of this age (2:6). "Mature" (*teleios*) was a word the public orators of Paul's day used about themselves; as they gathered followers— or disciples—around them, they progressed into maturity. Such "mature" people, no doubt from elite families, would go on to hold magistracies in the colony. For Paul, however, the "mature" are those who hear and respond to his

message about "Jesus Christ and him crucified" (2:2). "Rulers of this age" also occurs a few lines later (2:8), which suggests he has in mind the Jewish and Roman authorities responsible for Jesus' death. Corinth, as the seat of the provincial governor of Achaia, was one of the centers for "rulers" of the Roman empire.

A wisdom . . . hidden (2:7). There is a sense of irony here, for as the Corinthian elite seek wisdom by listening to the sophists and orators and thus grow into maturity, they have failed to understand the nature of true "wisdom."

None of the rulers of this age understood it, for if they had, they would not have crucified the Lord of glory (2:8). The Roman governor Pontius Pilate and the educated Jewish elite had put Jesus to death; in spite of their "wisdom" they did not recognize the "Lord of glory." Paul demonstrates that members of the Corinthian church who wish to follow the type of wisdom recommended by their secular society are no different from those who crucified the Christ. Wise Corinthian Christians will not be uncritical followers of the "rulers of the age." Interestingly, Paul used a similar argument about rulers failing to recognize Christ in his sermon preached at Pisidian Antioch (Acts 13:27).

No eye has seen, no ear has heard, no mind has conceived what God has prepared for those who love him (2:9). Paul alludes to Isaiah 64:4, which, although not a precise quotation, makes the point that God's grace will be given to those who love him.

God has revealed it to us by his Spirit (2:10). God's grace has been revealed to the Corinthian Christians. In other words, Paul's poor oratorical style has nevertheless conveyed the message about "Jesus Christ and him crucified" that was endorsed by "the Spirit's power." There is no point for seeking more mature "wisdom."

Not in words taught us by human wisdom (2:13). The "words" to which Paul alludes are those presented by the secular orators; it is interchangeable with "speech." They must be cautious about adopting the techniques devised by orators, which were intended to generate admiration among the listeners. The contrast is made with the words taught by the Holy Spirit.

For who has known the mind of the Lord that he may instruct him? (2:16). Paul quotes here from Isaiah 40:13, though in an adapted form, "Who has understood the mind of the LORD, or instructed him as his counselor?" Such a change allows Paul to turn the quotation into a rhetorical device that requires the Corinthians to answer that nobody is in that position.

Spiritual or Worldly Members of the Church (3:1–4)

I could not address you as spiritual but as worldly (3:1). Paul is describing the time when he was originally with the

Corinthian Christians. He describes them at that time as "worldly"—more accurately "fleshly" or even "those composed of flesh." The Corinthian Christians may have described themselves as "the spiritual ones" (*pneumatikoi*). Paul's implication is that the Corinthian Christians are un-spiritual, by which he means that their lives are unworthy of the Spirit who has made them believers in Christ. The "infants" contrast with the "mature" (2:6). Paul uses imagery found in both Hellenistic[34] and Jewish philosophy[35] to show the growth of maturity. His argument is that whereas the Corinthians would describe themselves as "spiritual" and "mature," Paul would describe them as "fleshly" and "immature."

Not solid food (3:2). Would the Corinthians have accused Paul of not offering them wisdom, which they considered to be "solid food"? Yet if this section develops Paul's preceding arguments (2:6–16), then the milk is the good news that allowed the Corinthians to become Christians, and the solid food is a developed understanding of the Cross. Paul's concern is that the Corinthians consume the "solid food" of the gospel (even if in the form of milk!), not the "solid food" of wisdom that inhibits Christian or spiritual growth.

You are still worldly (3:3). "Worldly" contrasts with the Greek word used at 3:1 and here effectively means, "You are still characteristic of flesh." The Corinthian Christians have not taken on the characteristics of the Spirit but rather of the world.

There is jealousy and quarreling among you (3:3). Paul introduces a new word, "jealousy," alongside that of "quarreling"

R E F L E C T I O N S

NOTICE THAT THREE TIMES IN 1 CORINTHIANS 2, PAUL uses the phrase "we speak" (2:6, 7, 13). This reflects the authority with which Paul, "an apostle of Christ Jesus by the will of God" (1:1), speaks. Those who teach with authority in the church today need to take the teaching of the apostles—revealed in the New Testament—seriously. Teachers are accountable to the One who authorizes their role.

(see 1:11). This combination is found elsewhere in Paul (2 Cor. 12:20; Gal. 5:20). Such jealousy is akin to "rivalry," a characteristic of those who follow the sophists; such behavior can be described as "worldly" (or "fleshly") or of "men" (i.e., a common human trait). Christian maturity leads men and women to reject the partisanship found in secular society. Faith rests on the power of the Spirit; human values rest on wisdom (1 Cor. 2:4–5). Paul's imagery sees life as a walk (NIV "acting"), a process informed by sophists or by the Spirit.

"I follow Paul," and another, "I follow Apollos" (3:4). Paul returns to his earlier argument (1:12) and shows that those who seek to follow specific Christian leaders or teachers (as opposed to Christ or the Spirit) are adopting secular values. Paul's concern is for all Christian people to be recognized and characterized by a spiritual (i.e., Spirit-led) life.

Images of Christian Ministry and the Church (3:5–17)

Paul is concerned that the Corinthian church realizes the meaning of Christian ministry and the church.

What, after all, is Apollos? And what is Paul? (3:5). At the beginning of the letter Paul introduced himself as "an apostle of Christ Jesus" (1:1). Now he brackets himself with Apollos—who is not described in the New Testament as an apostle and here is deliberately given primacy before Paul—as one of the "servants" (*diakonos*, the equivalent of "deacon"). All Christian ministers are primarily subject to God's authority: God allocates the tasks in his fields (3:9). As a "servant" of the Lord, both Paul and Apollos, indeed all Christian ministers, have a duty to present the Christian gospel so that individuals come to believe in Jesus Christ. Paul emphasizes that Christian belief is not in the minister who brings the good news, but rather through the minister.

I planted the seed, Apollos watered it, but God made it grow (3:6). Christian ministers have different functions or ministries; Paul shows the differences between himself and Apollos by using an agricultural metaphor. The territory of ancient Corinth was rich in agriculture. Yet it still needed individuals to plant and irrigate the crop. Without watering, the crop would fail; without planting, there would be nothing to water. Thus both Paul and Apollos have valid and mutually dependent ministries, and both are subject to God, who in fact brings the growth. Christian ministers need to be obedient to the task that the Lord has allocated to them (3:5) in the same way as those working in the fields need to obey the owner if there is to be a crop.

So neither he who plants nor he who waters is anything, but only God, who makes things grow (3:7). Individuals at Corinth may say they follow a specific individual, but Paul insists that true Christian ministers are in fact "nobodies" because it is Christ who brings the growth. When we eat a loaf of bread, the name of the man or woman who planted the seed is unimportant. So in the church, the personality who brings the good news is unimportant compared to the God whose Son died on the cross for us.

Each will be rewarded according to his own labor (3:8). Those working in the fields around Corinth have a united purpose: to ensure there is a crop to provide themselves with food and a livelihood; that is their reward (or "pay"). Those ministering in the church likewise have a single purpose; thus, it is foolish to be partisan because all ministers are working—or should be working—toward a common goal.

You are God's field, God's building (3:9). Once again Paul emphasizes that all who work in God's field must have a sense of working together with others who seek to present the same gospel of Jesus Christ. Note too that those who work in the field have no claim to it; that right belongs to God alone—Christian ministers can hold no claim on the church in which they serve. Paul places an emphasis on "we," not just the minister, but all who are involved in the life of the church. Paul then switches the imagery from the fields of Corinth to a city with God's building.

I laid a foundation as an expert builder (3:10). Paul uses an image taken from the urban landscape of the Roman colony. Since the creation of the colony in 44 B.C. wealthy benefactors had been giving new buildings, which had decorated the space around the forum at the heart of the colony (see "Buildings at Corinth"). Paul is

alluding to such building projects. Like the agricultural metaphor, two people are involved in the construction of the building: the first lays a foundation, the second builds up the walls. As in the previous metaphor, Paul is addressing the issue of how to build up the church at Corinth. The grace of God has been given to Paul specifically to found the church. He describes himself as an "expert" builder, using the Greek word *sophos*, which resonates and contrasts with the way that the elite members of the church have described themselves (1:20). The word "builder" literally means "chief builder" (i.e., architect), which suggests that Paul has been given specific responsibility for the building project. "Someone else" probably refers to various teachers in Corinth who are moving away from what Paul originally taught.

No one can lay any foundation other than the one already laid (3:11). Foundations are prepared for specific buildings anticipated by the chief builder; any other construction would be inappropriate. For example, if the architects of Corinth had prepared foundations for a substantial Roman temple and somebody built a house instead, there would have been a scandal. Likewise, Paul has prepared foundations based on Jesus Christ, and those seeking to develop the church must continue to encourage the church to focus on the crucified Jesus (1:23).

Using gold, silver, costly stones, wood, hay or straw (3:12). All buildings need a foundation, but once that has been established the superstructure can be built from a range of materials. At the bottom end is the simple house of mud-brick, which used hay or straw as a binding agent; the house would be equipped with

THE FORUM

A portion of the forum with the Apollo temple in the background.

▼

wooden doors and lintels (which were often removed when the house was abandoned). At the other end of the scale are the major public buildings, which could have gilded features or other metallic attachments. These buildings were made of stone. A particularly wealthy benefactor might bring in marble over some distance to enhance a building; this may be hinted at by the "costly stones." For example, the temple of Apollo at Delphi had stone brought from near Corinth when it was rebuilt in the fourth century B.C.[36] In the Roman period the colored marble *laconia* was particularly valued and quarried extensively. "Costly stones" may also refer to gemstones used to decorate parts of the building. The range of such materials—gold, silver, and precious stones—may also be a deliberate allusion to the materials used for the temple at Jerusalem (e.g., 1 Chron. 29:2).

The Day will bring it to light (3:13). The "Day" refers to the "day of our Lord Jesus Christ" (1:8), that is, the Day of Judgment. The fire, which is a Jewish image for what will happen on that day, will reveal whether the superstructure of the building—that is, the body of the believing Christians at Corinth—has been built with gospel or worldly wisdom material.

If what he has built survives, he will receive his reward (3:14). The architect or chief builder on a project would receive his payment ("reward") on its completion. Some of the most detailed building accounts from the ancient world relate to the classical period, in particular to projects at Athens like the building of the Parthenon, but also to work at the sanctuary of Asclepius at Epidauros.[37] Paul's comment resonates with the situation at Rome under Tiberius, who "restored all

▶ Buildings at Corinth

One of the ways that individuals could express their position in Roman society was to become benefactors of the city in which they lived and where they might also serve as magistrates. The American excavations at Corinth have concentrated on the main public area of the colony, the forum, where a large number of inscriptions have been found. Many of these come from buildings around the forum and record the details of the benefaction. According to one inscription from the mid-first century A.D., a benefactor whose name is lost paid for the revetment of the *bēma*, the public platform in the forum, and "paid personally the expense of making all its marble."[A-15] One of the chief magistrates of the colony, an *aedile* by name of Gnaeus Babbius Philinus, seems to have made a major building dedication in the forum in the early first century A.D.[A-16] These include basilicas for legal hearings as well as temples. What is clear from the archaeological record as well as the building inscriptions is that by the middle of the first century the colony had been endowed with a number of significant buildings, largely paid for by private individuals.[A-17]

the buildings which had suffered damage (he himself built no completely new building, except the temple of Augustus), he claimed none of them as his own, but rather he bestowed the names of the original builders on all of them."[38] Although the names of architects are rare in the Roman world, it is likely that those involved in major building projects at Corinth would be celebrated by the local community for enhancing their city.

If it is burned up, he will suffer loss; he himself will be saved, but only as one escaping through the flames (3:15). In contrast to the architect who completes his project and is paid, if the builder who follows on from Paul uses inappropriate materials, such as wisdom, the day of reckoning will find him out. Certainly the builder has not been saved by his works, but by the grace of God.

Don't you know that you yourselves are God's temple and that God's Spirit lives in you? (3:16). This third image tries to explain to the Corinthian churches what is meant by the "temple of God." Jewish members of the church will identify "temple" (*naos*) with the temple at Jerusalem, whereas Gentile members would associate that word with the religious structures that dotted their city, such as the archaic temple dominating the forum. In both cases, it is the place where God or a god dwelt. This new temple is something very different, however, as it is a temple made of living stones, that is, the Christian community at Corinth. The definition of members of the church is that God's Spirit dwells in them; in other words, they are "spiritual." "Fleshly" or "worldly" individuals (3:1, 3) need to think whether their lives are suitable for this holy building. There is also the implication that as there can only be one temple of God at Jerusalem or one temple for a particular god in Corinth, so there can only be one church at Corinth.[39]

If anyone destroys God's temple, God will destroy him (3:17). The jealousy and quarrelling in the Corinthian church (3:3) is damaging God's holy temple, the body of believers. If there is only one church, partisanship can only be damaging and unworthy of something that is holy. There is a great emphasis on individual members seeking to maintain the unity of the church.

"You Are of Christ" (3:18–23)

This paragraph concludes the argument about those who allow jealousy and quarrelling to divide the church. The section divides into two, introduced by parallel constructions in the Greek that can be translated, "Let no one deceive himself" (3:18 RSV) and "Let no one boast of men (3:21 RSV).

If any one of you thinks he is wise by the standards of this age, he should become a "fool" so that he may become wise (3:18). The deception of the church comes not

APOLLO TEMPLE

▼

from outside, but from within the Christian community. Paul returns to the theme he started in 2:8, where wisdom was a sign of Christian maturity, not a mark of the spirit of the age. The foolishness refers back to 1:25, where "the foolishness of God is wiser than man's wisdom."

The wisdom of this world is foolishness in God's sight. As it is written: "He catches the wise in their craftiness" (3:19). Paul reverses the argument of 1:25. The Corinthian Christians are now forced to see their position and quarrelling from God's perspective. Paul quotes, perhaps using his own Greek translation from the Hebrew, from the words of Eliphaz in Job 5:13; the verse continues "and the schemes of the wily are swept away," reminding the Corinthians of the foolishness of the position of those who wish to follow human wisdom.

"The Lord knows that the thoughts of the wise are futile." (3:20). Paul quotes from the LXX of Psalm 94:1, except that he replaces "the thoughts of men" with "the thoughts of the wise," thereby applying this verse to his specific situation.

From God's perspective a love of the wisdom of the age is foolish or futile.

So then, no more boasting about men! (3:21). Paul returns the Corinthians' attention to Jeremiah 9:24 (cf. 1 Cor. 1:31), showing that boasting should only be in the Lord. The partisanship of 1:12 with different groups following Paul, Apollos, or Cephas is now obsolete, for Christians are "of Christ." It is Jesus Christ, the Son of God, who gives the Corinthian believers their identity.

All are yours (3:22). Paul stresses that allegiance to Christ is universal (lit., the *kosmos*); it is for all time, even in death, and is as relevant now as it will be in the future without the need for development along the lines of human wisdom.

Fools for Christ (4:1–13)

Men ought to regard us as servants of Christ and as those entrusted with the secret things of God (4:1). In 3:5 Paul used the Greek word *diakonos* ("servant") to describe his ministry. Now he emphasizes that he is one of several people working for Christ among the Corinthian Christians. The word translated "servants" here is *hyperetes*. The word literally means an "under rower," but came to mean a servant. In a many-oared ship it was important to have everyone pulling in time; no doubt Paul is here thinking of a team of Christian ministers working in cooperation and collaboration. The word "entrusted" (*oikonomos*) was commonly used in the Hellenistic period of the person in charge of an estate belonging to an absentee landlord. For example, on the Saronic Gulf, not far from Corinth, the Methana peninsula was under the care of an *oikonomos* who looked after the city for the Ptolemies of Egypt. The term *mystēria* ("secret things") picks up on 2:7. In the ancient world so-called mystery cults from the eastern Mediterranean became popular at Rome. Though much of the evidence is after this time, the Anatolian deity Cybele seems to have been particularly popular. She was worshiped not in human form but as a rock or *baetyl*, which was moved to Rome in 204 B.C.[40]

Those who have been given a trust must prove faithful (4:2). The *oikonomos* looking after estates was in a position of great trust, especially if the absentee landlord was far removed. Paul is highlighting the characteristic of those entrusted with Christian responsibility to be "faithful." This characteristic is very different from the eloquence and wisdom expected by some in the church at Corinth.

I care very little if I am judged by you or by any human court; indeed, I do not even judge myself (4:3). The Greek idiom translated "by any human court" refers to having one's day in court. Such a "day" resonates with the Day of Judgment (3:13; 4:5). In a city dominated by the law of Rome, Paul reminds the Corinthians that there is a judge above human magistrates and that his actions are ones he wants to be judged in this higher court.

My conscience is clear, but that does not make me innocent. It is the Lord who judges me (4:4). "The Lord" here clearly means Christ, but in the secular world, the *oikonomos* would be looking after the estate for his absent "lord" or *kyrios*. In legal terms only the "lord" has the right to judge his servants. Christians must

remember that their actions will be judged by God, not by their peers within the church.

So that you may learn from us the meaning of the saying, "Do not go beyond what is written." Then you will not take pride in one man over against another (4:6). The Corinthians have been emphasizing "pride." Part of this was extended to comparing Paul and Apollos, debating who was the most effective servant of Christ. Indeed, later in the letter it appears as if the Corinthian church may have requested a return visit from Apollos (16:12). "Do not go beyond what is written" is an allusion to the Old Testament writings. Scripture is meant to form the boundary for the conduct of the Christian life.

You have become rich! You have become kings (4:8). Professional orators were able to command large sums where they presented their speeches. Philo commented that such wealth "exist[s] not only for our security, but also for our happiness."[41] In other words, oratory could give an individual high status. The Corinthians placed so much emphasis on this skill that Paul comments they had become as rich as kings. Perhaps he has in mind the legendary riches of the now dead Hellenistic rulers or the riches of the Roman emperor. Though the concept of kingship was abhorrent to Romans after the expulsion of the Tarquins as kings of Rome at the end of the sixth century B.C., more recently *basileus* ("king") was being applied to the emperor.

Like men condemned to die in the arena (4:9). Paul takes as his imagery the spectacle of the Roman arena, where criminals or captives of war were paraded in triumph by the conquering commander — at this date only the emperor had that privilege—before fighting each other to death to entertain the people. Such gladiatorial shows were uncommon in the Greek east, but would, perhaps, have appealed to the people of a Roman colony. It is ironic that the Roman emperor, sometimes designated as "master of the universe,"[42] had his show viewed by a different "universe" or *kosmos*. The spectacle resonates with the word *theatron* ("arena"), the place where the spectacle takes place (more accurately the amphitheater, of which Corinth was in fact equipped). This lay to the northeast of the city, outside the line of the later city wall.[43] Roman testimony makes reference to "the Corinthians watch[ing] these combats outside the city in a ravine, a place that is able to hold a large crowd, but otherwise is sordid and such that no one would even bury there a freeborn citizen."[44] The earliest structure may have been temporary, but as Corinth became the focus for games associated with the imperial cult, a more permanent structure would have been needed.[45]

We are fools for Christ, but you are so wise in Christ! We are weak, but you are strong! You are honored, we are dishonored! (4:10). Paul uses a series of contrasts that indicates that the Corinthian Christians are using words of high status about themselves—"wise," "strong," "honored"—whereas Paul uses low status terms for himself and those who maintain an apostolic ministry—"fools," "weak," "dishonored" (cf. also 1:26).

We go hungry and thirsty, we are in rags, we are brutally treated, we are homeless (4:11). This image is one that picks up on the theme that these are men condemned to die. The contrast would be to the emperor leading the procession.

We work hard with our own hands (4:12). The social elite were scornful of those who worked for a living. Roman social hierarchy in fact precluded some groups—notably those at the top of the social scale—from handling money or conducting business, which was the preserve of members of the equestrian order. The believers in Corinthians are unlikely to have been wealthy enough to be patricians, but they would have adopted wider Roman values towards wealth.

When we are cursed, we bless (4:12b). The first of these three pairs of contrasting actions reflects the teaching of Jesus in Luke: "Bless those who curse you" (Luke 4:28). Paul is presenting a model for the church at Corinth.

The scum of the earth, the refuse of the world (4:13). Paul alludes to Lamentations 3:45: "You have made us scum and refuse among the nations," though his words differ from the LXX.

Paul as Founder and Father (4:14–17)

I am not writing this to shame you (4:14). Shame was to be avoided in Roman society, so Paul makes it clear that he was only writing as a warning.

Ten thousand guardians in Christ . . . in Christ Jesus I became your father through the gospel (4:15). "Guardians" translates a word for the person who accompanied the children of wealthy families to school. Paul describes himself as the *patēr* ("father") of the Christian community. In the same way, members of the colony looked to Julius Caesar as the founding father of the colony at Corinth, or to the emperor himself, who carried the honorific title "father of the country."

Therefore I urge you to imitate me (4:16). There was considerable pressure in Roman society to aspire to a set career and to follow set patterns of behavior; Paul is urging the Corinthians to set themselves free by following his pattern of example. Unfortunately, already some of the Christians had become imitators of the orators.

I am sending to you Timothy (4:17). This is one of two mentions of Timothy in this letter. Paul, writing from Ephesus, dispatched Timothy and Erastus to Macedonia while he himself stayed in the province of Asia (Acts 19:22). Although Erastus is not mentioned here, he set out from Ephesus with Timothy; a man of the same name is also mentioned in Romans 16:23 (see "Paul Quotes an Athenian Playwright" at 15:33).

A Kingdom of Power (4:18–21)

As if I were not coming to you (4:18). The Corinthian Christians presumably expected Paul, now in Ephesus, to have returned, just as one of the orators on the circuit of the great cities of the Greek east might return to Corinth.

I will come to you very soon (4:19). Paul provides the details of his plans and those of Timothy later (16:5–9).

I will find out not only how these arrogant people are talking, but what power they have (4:19). A contrast is made between the "talk" (*logos*) of the arrogant and their "power." Paul's preaching (*logos*) at Corinth may not have had the eloquence of traveling orators, but the result of the preaching was that a Corinthian Christian's faith rested on God's power (1:17–18).

For the kingdom of God is not a matter of talk but of power (4:20). The "kingdom of God" is a major theme of Jesus' teaching in the Gospels. The linking of the kingdom with power recalls Jesus' words: "I tell you the truth, some who are standing here will not taste death before they see the kingdom of God come with power" (Mark 9:1).

Shall I come to you with a whip (4:21). The Greek word translated "whip" (*rhabdos*) is the same used as the "rod" used for

---

▶Timothy in Corinth

Timothy came from Lystra in the province of Galatia. He was the son of a Greek father and a Jewish mother, Eunice (Acts 16:1; 2 Tim. 1:5). He had accompanied Paul in his travels through Macedonia (Acts 17:14). Timothy arrived at Corinth along with Silas when Paul first came to the colony (18:5) and so was known to the congregation. Timothy is also mentioned in other Corinthian contexts. He is one of the people who sends greetings in the concluding section of the letter to the Romans (Rom. 16:21), written from Corinth, and he is the cowriter of the second letter to the Corinthians (2 Cor. 1:1).

WHAT IS OUR ATTITUDE TOWARD those who minister to us in our churches? How do we treat those who have been given charge of our church "flock"? It is all too easy to view them in secular eyes as "employees" rather than as "servants of Christ" who have come to minister among us.

correction; for example, "I will punish their sin with the rod, their iniquity with flogging" (Ps. 89:32). In ancient Greece, the *rhabdos* was the stick that was struck rhythmically during the recitation of poetic works by a rhapsode.

Immorality and the Church's Response (5:1–8)

It is actually reported that there is sexual immorality among you, and of a kind that does not occur even among pagans (5:1). A situation of sexual immorality (*porneia*) seems to be common knowledge within the Corinthian church. The Jewish world considered *porneia* as a regular feature of the surrounding pagan cultures. Thus the council of Jerusalem asked the Gentile Christians "to abstain from food sacrificed to idols, from blood, from the meat of strangled animals and from sexual immorality [*porneia*]" (Acts 15:29; cf. 15:20; 21:25). Although this word is associated with "prostitution," it could also be extended to homosexual acts (Jude 7). It is ironic that within the Corinthian church, such a hallmark of pagan society is in fact of a type not found among the pagans.

A man has his father's wife (5:1). Paul now spells out the nature of this *porneia*: A man

has an ongoing sexual relationship—implied by the Greek word translated as "has"—with his father's wife—that is, undoubtedly this man's stepmother. This would be shocking to Jewish society as such a relationship was forbidden: "Do not have sexual relations with your father's wife; that would dishonor your father" (Lev. 18:8). But such a liaison was also banned under Roman law—in particular, the *lex Iulia de adulteriis* introduced by Augustus between 18 and 16 B.C. The punishment for such activity was exile to an island. The incentive for such a relationship may have been in the hope of retaining the woman's marriage dowry to her family when perhaps her husband died. It may have been hoped that the son and stepmother might have had children, thereby increasing the claim for retaining the dowry within the present family.[46]

You are proud! (5:2). Paul describes the Corinthian Christians as "proud" or "puffed up with pride"; the term used here is translated "arrogant" earlier in 4:18–19. Paul would prefer a response of grief. Such pride may be explained if the man in the incestuous relationship has high status within the colony, perhaps a Roman citizen of high standing. Indeed, he may well have been the patron of the church. Such patron-client relationships were important mechanisms of control within Roman society, and members of the church may have felt it inappropriate to question the sexual morals of such a high-standing individual. But rather than being proud that such a high-profile individual was a member of their Christian community, Paul insists they should be ashamed at tolerating such activity. If this is the scenario, Paul's criticism is aimed as much at the attitude of the Corinthian Christians toward status as it is toward sexual immorality. The word translated as "filled with grief" conveys the meaning of "mourning." It was as if this individual in the colony has died and the church—and indeed the wider colony—should be grieving.

Even though I am not physically present, I am with you in spirit. And I have already passed judgment on the one who did this, just as if I were present (5:3). Paul reacts to the Corinthian response by his own personal comment (emphasized in the Greek by introducing this sentence with *egō men*, "And I for my part"). Paul, the apostle who established the Corinthian church, may not be present in person, but he has the right and authority to intervene in the situation. Paul then uses legal language. A case has been reported to him and the hearing has started. In Roman society one could only bring lawsuits against one's peers. Thus, if the man involved in the incestuous relationship was of high status, the Corinthian Christians, especially if they were in a client-patron relationship with him, would not wish to initiate proceedings. But the case has been reported (5:1) to the apostle.

When you are assembled in the name of our Lord Jesus and I am with you in spirit, and the power of our Lord Jesus is present (5:4). Paul in effect is calling the Christian community together to make a corporate act. What characterizes the members of the gathering is that each one bears the name of the Lord Jesus; status in the wider community does not matter. Paul the apostle of Jesus Christ (1:1) is with them "in spirit," a phrase that on the one hand may mean he identifies with them in the decision they have to make, and on the other endorses the fact that each one has been empowered by the Spirit of God. The "power of our Lord Jesus" contrasts with the wider perception of power in the Roman colony that normally went with high status.

Hand this man over to Satan (5:5). A similar expression of handing individuals over to Satan occurs in 1 Timothy 1:20, where Hymenaeus and Alexander are cited. "That the sinful nature may be destroyed" is a translation of the Greek equivalent of "the destruction of the flesh." A physical death may be expected, and a parallel can be drawn with the deaths of Ananias and Sapphira in Acts 5:1–11 or the incorrect use of the Lord's Supper in 1 Corinthians 11:30–32. Clearly the intention is that this man must be excluded from the fellowship with the goal of putting to death that part of his sinful nature so that on the Day of Judgment he will be saved. The loss of status as a Christian is not implied.

Your boasting is not good. Don't you know that a little yeast works through the whole batch of dough? (5:6). Paul draws attention to one of the unacceptable characteristics of the Christian community at Corinth: their boasting especially about human beings (see also 3:21). Such a feature is similar to their arrogance or the way in which they are puffed up with pride (5:2). "Don't you know that" is a rhetorical device Paul uses twice more in the letter (3:16; 9:13). The expression "a little yeast works through the whole batch of dough" may have been a well-known saying, perhaps Jewish in origin. The word *zymē* is best translated as "leaven" rather than yeast. In other words, a piece of fermented dough is kept back from the baking so that it can be used to "leaven" the next batch of dough. Paul here is using the image of baking to show that even a small amount of evil will permeate the whole church.

Get rid of the old yeast that you may be a new batch without yeast—as you really are. For Christ, our Passover lamb, has been sacrificed (5:7). The reference to being rid of old "yeast" or (better) "leaven" is an allusion to the Feast of Unleavened Bread, when God's people left Egypt: "For seven days you are to eat bread made without yeast. On the first day remove the yeast from your houses, for whoever eats anything with yeast in it from the first day through the seventh must be cut off from Israel" (Ex. 12:15). "Leaven" was not to be added to grain offerings (cited throughout Leviticus), no doubt because it detracted from the purity, and therefore holiness, of the offering. Paul's powerful image, which in fact makes the Corinthian Christians the new batch of dough (without the impurity of the incestuous man), develops into the full Passover image with Christ as the lamb. It was the slaying of the Passover lamb (cf. Ex. 12:21) that gave the purity to the people of God as they left Egypt; in effect, they were unleavened.

Therefore let us keep the Festival, not with the old yeast, the yeast of malice and wickedness, but with bread without yeast, the bread of sincerity and truth (5:8). Paul contrasts the leavened bread with the unleavened. The former contains all types of bad things ("malice") and iniquities ("wickedness"), whereas the latter contains pure things ("sincerity and truth"). By using the present tense, Paul urges the Corinthian Christians to celebrate "the Festival," that is, to lead a life that day by day is unpermeated by "malice and wickedness" and is characterized by "sincerity and truth."

Limiting Associations (5:9–13)

I have written you in my letter not to associate with sexually immoral people (5:9). Paul continues on the theme of the incestuous man who has already been described as "sexually immoral." Clearly this issue has been raised by Paul beforehand in an earlier letter that has not survived. The key issue is that the Corinthian churches should not get mixed up with sexually immoral people; just as leaven should not be added to pure dough.

The people of this world who are immoral, or the greedy and swindlers, or idolaters (5:10). The Corinthian Christians should not take on the secular values

PASSOVER SACRIFICE

A model of the altar of sacrifice in the Court of the Priests in the Jerusalem temple.

of the world around them; at the same time, they must be an integrated part of society as a witness to it. Apparently the Corinthians have misunderstood Paul's earlier letter. Their response to his desire for them not to associate with sexually immoral people was to ask, "But how can we do that, when we rub shoulders with such people in the forum and other public spaces?" Paul's intention was not for them to cut themselves off from the world. Notice his characterization of pagan Roman society as people who are "[sexually] immoral ... greedy ... swindlers, or idolaters." Such issues were as prevalent in mid-first-century Corinth as they are in our own societies. The issue of idolatry will be picked up later in the letter (chs. 8–10). The Jewish world was familiar with groups such as the Essenes, who took themselves into the desert to remove themselves from the pressures and iniquities of society.

You must not associate with anyone who calls himself a brother but is sexually immoral or greedy, an idolater or a slanderer, a drunkard or a swindler (5:11). The list of "vices" in pagan society is repeated and expanded to include drunkards and slanderers; this list will be augmented even further in 6:9–10. Such lists are common in Jewish characterizations of the society around them, such as Philo,[47] as well as in other Pauline letters. Such individuals are to be excluded from common meals, which presumably include the Lord's Supper. Drinking was an integral part of the ancient banquet, and drunkenness could allow such functions to degenerate into orgies. In a thriving commercial center like Corinth, with its active shipping interest, swindling is perhaps linked to business interests of members of the church.

"Expel the wicked man from among you" (5:13). The Mosaic law insisted that God's people "must purge the evil from among you" (or "from Israel"); this included worshiping other gods (Deut. 17:7), giving false testimony or witness in a court of law (19:19), premarital sexual relations (22:21), adultery (22:22, 24), and abduction (24:7). Paul quotes from the Mosaic law here to suggest that the wicked man should be expelled from the Christian community. As such it picks up and concludes earlier remarks throughout this chapter (5:2, 5, 7). Notice the way that the Christian community is first to deal with sin within itself.

Civil Litigation in Corinth (6:1–11)

If any of you has a dispute with another, dare he take it before the ungodly for judgment instead of before the saints? (6:1). The Roman legal system prevented those of inferior status from prosecuting their "superiors," such as patrons and magistrates.[48] Thus these disputes are likely to have been between those of

---

REFLECTIONS

IT IS EASY TO BE SHOCKED ABOUT the latest revelation of sexual impropriety in the church community when we see it on TV. Yet there is nothing new; it was there in Corinth. What is important is our attitude towards immorality that we encounter among fellow Christians. We need to ask ourselves how we can become God's holy people in our communities, unpermeated by the wickedness that surrounds us.

the same social status within the Roman colony; no doubt they are drawn from those who would consider themselves as "powerful" (*dynatoi*, 1:26). Alternatively they could be cases brought by an individual with high social status against someone with a lower social status—for example, a magistrate against a freedman. The case would be initiated by taking the matter before one of the two main magistrates in the colony, one of the *duovirs*. The case would be heard before a judge or a jury of one's peers.[49] Jurors were selected from wealthier social groups; in Cyrenaica (North Africa) jurors had to have a property value of 7,500 *denarii*.[50] The Cyrene edict of Augustus dating to 7/6 B.C. suggests that juries could sometimes act in an unjust way, constituting some form of cliques.[51] Later sources show that Corinth itself suffered from such legal corruption.[52] The word "ungodly" can also be translated "unrighteous" (or perhaps "corrupt"). Since Paul himself used the Roman legal system from time to time, it is unlikely that he is recommending a distancing from it; he is more likely drawing attention to the potentially corrupt nature of the system.

Do you not know that the saints will judge the world? (6:2). Paul asks a rhetorical question that seems to draw on the LXX of Daniel 7:22, which provides the context of the Day of Judgment. This implies that some of the readers of this letter are familiar with Jewish writings and theology surrounding the end of the world.

If you are to judge the world, are you not competent to judge trivial cases? (6:2). "Trivial cases" indicates that the disputes between the Corinthian Christians come under the aegis of civil law rather than criminal law (which would cover things such as acts of treason and murder[53]). Civil law included areas such as "legal possession, breach of contract, damages, fraud and injury."[54] Young men drawn from the social elite might bring "trivial cases" to demonstrate their forensic skills. Perhaps some of the social elite from the church at Corinth are bringing "trivial" civil cases against fellow Christians in order to establish their own position (and harm their opponents), and this has caused tensions within the church.

Appoint as judges even men of little account in the church! (6:4). The "men of little account" or of "small esteem" contrast with the social elite who are in fact bringing such cases and who are indeed able to judge them. The Greek word translated here as church, *ekklēsia*, is the same word used for the secular gathering of the citizen body. Thus, there is irony that those unable to participate in the public *ekklēsia* are nevertheless suitable judges in the Christian *ekklēsia*.

I say this to shame you (6:5). Shame was something that members of the Corinthian elite would want to avoid. It contrasts with Paul's earlier comment that he is not writing to shame them (4:14). Shame continues to be an important aspect of Paul's instruction to the Corinthian church (15:34).

Is it possible that there is nobody among you wise enough to judge a dispute between believers? (6:5). Since the Corinthian church contains members of the social elite—the powerful and well-born (1:26)—they have been educated to judge such legal cases. Among this group should be some "capable"[55] enough to have become arbitrators in the

▶ Roman Civil Law in Corinth

Roman legal arrangements in the Augustan period—for the province of Crete and Cyrene—can be detected in a decree of 7/6 B.C. preserved at Cyrene, where Augustus stated:

Regarding disputes which occur . . . excluding indictments for capital crimes, where the governor must himself conduct the inquiry and render a decision or else set up a panel of jurors—for all other cases it is my pleasure that Greek jurors shall be assigned unless some defendant or accused desires to have Roman citizens as jurors.[A-18]

Although Corinth was a Roman colony, it seems likely that such civil cases would be heard before judges and juries rather than before the governor. In the Greek east it seems to have been common for personal enmity to have been continued through bringing civil actions, thus damaging an opponent's reputation; such actions were described by the Latin terms *reprehension vitae* or *vituperatio*.

disagreements among Christians, thereby diffusing the situation before divisions occur. Those who are educated, however, would consider themselves to be wise (*sophos*) or sophisticated, a danger Paul earlier pointed out in the life of the church (1:27; 3:18).

One brother goes to law against another—and this in front of unbelievers! (6:6). The unbelievers refer to the civic magistrates of the Roman colony who are not part of the Christian community. This means that cases brought by Christians against fellow Christians are being heard in a public court.

The very fact that you have lawsuits among you means you have been completely defeated already (6:7). These words are aimed at the plaintiff, who has not seen that by taking action against the defendant, members of the Christian community are being presented as lawbreakers in the colony. Such a publicly held view is detrimental to the church.

You yourselves cheat and do wrong, and you do this to your brothers (6:8). "Do wrong" carries the meaning of "defraud." These words are clearly aimed at the defendant and imply that there may have been some wrong-doing. Christians have an ethical imperative laid on them to abide by the law.

Do you not know that the wicked will not inherit the kingdom of God? Do not be deceived: Neither the sexually immoral nor idolaters nor adulterers nor male prostitutes nor homosexual offenders (6:9). Paul introduces a range of people whose lifestyles may have been accepted in wider Roman and Greek society, but which was defined as "wicked" by God's standards. The "sexually immoral" (*pornoi*) include Christians who are sexually active before marriage; this contrasts with "adulterers" (*moichoi*), who have sexual partners outside marriage. In Roman elite society it was acceptable for the husband to have sexual relations outside marriage, but such standards were not to be tolerated within the Christian community.

Paul uses specialized terminology here.[56] Roman law, in particular the *lex Scantinia* of the mid-second century B.C., legislated about homosexual behavior.[57] Such laws protected Roman citizens against homosexual acts. Corinth as a Roman colony would thus consider homosexual acts with fellow citizens as illegal, but not with noncitizens (i.e., non-Romans) and slaves.

Male prostitutes (6:9). This expression translates *malakoi*. The Greek word *malakos* transferred to the Latin *malacus*. It means in effect "a soft person" and took on the meaning of somebody effeminate. The fact that Latin has no indigenous word for such a person may suggest that a passive participant in a homosexual relationship was not condemned by Roman law so long as he was not a Roman citizen.

Homosexual offenders (6:9). This expression translates the Greek word *arsenokoitai*. This may be a word derived from the LXX of Leviticus 18:22: "Do not lie with a man as one lies with a woman; that is detestable." The *malakos* (see previous comment) is probably the passive participant, whereas the *arsenokoitēs* is the active participant. Thus, both stand criticized by Paul within the Christian community. Note, however, that these are but two areas of life that Paul highlights, and the church has not always had the right balance.

Nor thieves nor the greedy nor drunkards nor slanderers nor swindlers will inherit the kingdom of God (6:10). The "greedy" are literally those "who wish to have more"; in other words they are covetous. In spite of what God has given to them, they want more. "Drunkards" probably implies those people who regularly attend the drinking parties of the colony, whether in private homes or at public festivals. "Swindlers" are those who snatch things

from others and perhaps reflects on the fact that those involved in the trading life of this busy city with its two ports were less than honest.

That is what some of you were (6:11). At the beginning of the letter Paul characterized the church as having few who "were wise by human standards; not many were influential; not many were of noble birth" (1:26). Now it becomes clear that although a few members of the church came from elite backgrounds, a cross-section of the members of the church had morally questionable backgrounds.

But you were washed (6:11). This is clearly a reference to baptism after repentance (cf. Paul's use of this same verb in one of his accounts of his conversion on the road to Damascus, Acts 22:16). This is a reminder that whatever our backgrounds, we are new creations in Christ.

Immorality (6:12–20)

"Everything is permissible for me" (6:12). Paul seems to be quoting a phrase used by the Corinthian church, which he repeats later in the letter (10:23).

"Food for the stomach and the stomach for food"—but God will destroy them both. The body is not meant for sexual immorality, but for the Lord, and the Lord for the body (6:13). The Roman love of food is reflected in the cookbooks that have survived from antiquity, such as that attributed to Apicius. His recipes include, "Numidian chicken," "rabbit with fruit sauce," "liver sausage," "anchovy delight without the anchovies," and "sweet and sour pork."[58] By reminding the Corinthian Christians that their bodies belonged to

God, Paul counters the claim that if sexual liberty was acceptable in the colony, it could also be acceptable in the Christian community. Believers are not free to do as they please. Paul may be quoting one of the sayings of the Corinthian church.

By his power God raised the Lord from the dead, and he will raise us also (6:14). Corinthian Christians, drawing on Platonic philosophy, may have tried to separate the soul from the body so that they could partake in sexual immorality without feeling that it mattered to their soul. Paul stresses the importance of the human body by referring them to the idea of the bodily resurrection of Jesus Christ from the grave and our own bodily resurrection at the last day.

Never! (6:15). Paul uses the Greek words translated as "Never!" (*mē genoito*) in other letters (e.g., Romans, Galatians). It may be a rhetorical device, as it is a phrase used in diatribe.

Do you not know that he who unites himself with a prostitute is one with her in body? For it is said, "The two will become one flesh." (6:16). It has been suggested that prostitutes would have been made available at the banquet when young men came of age.[59] Paul uses the LXX of Genesis 2:24 to make the theological point that sexual intercourse institutes a bond between the two people. Sexual activity outside marriage cannot be justified.

Your body is a temple of the Holy Spirit (6:19). In the pagan urban landscape of the Roman colony, the temples on their high podia were the places where the gods—in the form of their cult-statues—were thought to dwell. In contrast, the

REFLECTIONS

WHAT IMPACT DOES THE KNOWL-edge of what Christ achieved on the cross have on us? Our past wrongdoings have been forgiven; the slate has been wiped clean. Yet sometimes we find it hard to show the same level of forgiveness to our brothers and sisters in Christ. How hard do we try to resolve conflict within the Christian community?

bodies of Christians are the temple of the Holy Spirit.

You were bought at a price. Therefore honor God with your body (6:20). Christ's death on the cross has "bought" the lives of Christians as it removed them from the ownership of "sin." The Greek verb "honor" can also be translated "glorify"; earlier Paul talked about Jesus as the "Lord of glory" (2:8).

Sexual Abstinence, Singleness, and Marriage (7:1–16)

Now for the matters you wrote about (7:1). Paul turns to issues raised in a letter ("you wrote about") by the Corinthian church. In the remaining chapters there are five distinct issues he addresses:

1. "It is good for a man not to marry" (7:1).
2. "Now about virgins" (7:25).
3. "Now about food sacrificed to idols" (8:1).
4. "Now about spiritual gifts" (12:1).
5. "Now about the collection for God's people" (16:1).

A sixth issue may concern Apollos (16:12). It is important to understand the issues raised with Paul against the background of "the present crisis" (7:26).

It is good for a man not to marry (7:1). The Greek in this sentence ("to marry," lit. trans., is "to touch a woman") is at first sight ambiguous in that there is no distinction in the Greek word *gynē* between "a wife" or "a woman"; the NIV takes the noun with the verb as "to marry." However the Greek can be taken to mean, "It is a fine thing/good for a man not to touch a woman/(his) wife." The Greek verb (*haptomai*) in this clause means to touch or grasp and was used in Greek athletics when two wrestlers came together in the ring. The sense here implies a sexual relationship.

Since there is so much immorality, each man should have his own wife, and each woman her own husband (7:2). The Greek verb translated as "have" implies a sexual relationship. Because of the sexual immorality (*porneia*) in Corinthian society, husbands and wives should be faithful to their partner in sexual matters. This sentence picks up the language of Paul's earlier argument about the sexual immorality concerning the man having an incestuous relationship with his stepmother (5:1). Roman epitaphs often speak of the relationship between husband and wife. For example, in a first century B.C. example from Rome, the husband talks of his wife Aurelia Philematium, who died aged forty, as "chaste in body, with a loving spirit, she lived faithful to her faithful husband, always optimistic, even in bitter times, she never shirked her duties."[60]

The husband should fulfill his marital duty to his wife, and likewise the wife to her husband (7:3). Paul is moving away from the usual Roman norm, in which the husband dominated the wife; in Christian marriage there is to be a mutuality of relations.

The wife's body does not belong to her alone but also to her husband. In the same way, the husband's body does not belong to him alone but also to his wife (7:4). This teaching is radical for a Roman audience. Men felt free to have sexual intercourse with slaves or other women. Sexual fulfillment was seen as an end in itself. According to ancient marriage contracts, of which a number have survived on papyri from Egypt, male promiscuity was acceptable.[61] Paul is reminding husbands and wives of the exclusivity of their relationship. Extramarital activity is not acceptable for Christians.

Do not deprive each other except by mutual consent and for a time, so that you may devote yourselves to prayer. Then come together again (7:5). Paul may be addressing the issue of married couples abstaining from sexual intercourse in the light of the "present crisis" (7:26). In the ancient world the only effective form of contraception was not to engage in sexual activity. Soranus, writing in the second century A.D., noted that "it is safer to prevent conception from occurring than to destroy the fetus through abortion."[62] Yet Paul reminds such couples that sexual relations ("come together") are part of marriage.

I say this as a concession, not as a command (7:6). The "concession" refers to Paul's own singleness (7:7). The "command" refers to the issues in the preceding verses, especially indicated by the word "should" (7:2, 3).

I wish that all men were as I am. But each man has his own gift from God (7:7). Paul recognizes that singleness can be a gift from God. Roman citizens were encouraged to marry (and by implication have children) through Roman legislation. Emperor Augustus had initiated such laws partly to increase the citizen body in the face of depletions during the civil wars of the first century B.C., notably the great struggle against Antony and Cleopatra that culminated in the battle of Actium in 31 B.C. and the fall of Alexandria in 30 B.C. The church needs to recognize the gift of singleness even if the social norm is for individuals to marry.

Now to the unmarried and the widows I say: It is good for them to stay unmarried, as I am (7:8). Paul turns from issues for those who are already married to those who have yet to marry or who have been widowed. Paul's advice is the same as that given to the virgins, namely, to stay in the state of singlehood in which Paul himself is. It has been suggested that the Greek word for "the unmarried" (*agamoi*) may refer to (male) widowers, for "virgins" (i.e., those never married) are dealt with in 7:25–26.[63] Given "the pre-

sent crisis" Paul is advocating that this group not marry because if they have children, they will have to live through troubled times. Paul's language reflects that of the disciples when they responded to Jesus' teaching on divorce: "If this is the situation between a husband and a wife, it is better not to marry" (Matt. 19:10). Marriage should not be undertaken lightly, as it has personal and social consequences.

But if they cannot control themselves, they should marry, for it is better to marry than to burn with passion (7:9). Women tended to marry in their teens, though their husbands were often older.

To the married I give this command (not I, but the Lord): A wife must not separate from her husband (7:10). Paul turns to the sensitive issue of separation in marriage and divorce. His teaching is clear, and the authority he takes is not ultimately his own but that of Jesus Christ ("the Lord"; see also 9:14; 11:23). Subsequent verses make it clear that both husband and wife referred to in this verse are Christians. The "command" does not appear elsewhere in the New Testament as a quotation of Jesus, but it is a summary of teaching found in the Gospels. In Mark 10:1–12 (see also Matt. 19:1–12) Jesus is confronted by the Pharisees, who asked him, "Is it lawful for a man to divorce his wife?" (Mark 10:2). Jesus then clarified his teaching with the disciples: "Anyone who divorces his wife and marries another woman commits adultery against her. And if she divorces her husband and marries another man, she commits adultery" (10:11–12; see also Luke 16:18). This command, given originally in the context of Jewish marriage, is applicable to Christians. Roman law might allow divorce, but not Jesus' teaching. Still, some Roman marriages were long-lasting. Pliny the Younger, governor of the province of Bithynia under the emperor Trajan, wrote about his friend Macrinus, whose wife had died after thirty-nine years of marriage "without a single quarrel or bitter word."[64]

If she does, she must remain unmarried or else be reconciled to her husband. And a husband must not divorce his wife (7:11). Paul lays out the two options available to Christians if they separate from their spouses: either remain unmarried or seek reconciliation. Remarriage of a Christian divorcee comes under Jesus' specific teaching (e.g., Luke 16:18). This is in contrast with the Roman legal situation. A divorce settlement from Egypt dated 13 B.C. (after it became a Roman province) declared, "From this day it will be lawful for Zois to marry another man and for Antipater to marry another woman, with neither party being liable to prosecution."[65]

If any brother has a wife who is not a believer and she is willing to live with him, he must not divorce her. And if a woman has a husband who is not a believer and he is willing to live with her, she must not divorce him (7:12–13). Within the Christian community at Corinth, and almost certainly elsewhere, Paul faces the issue of men and women converted to Jesus Christ but the spouse remains an unbeliever. Clearly this may cause tensions within the marriage. If the unbelieving partner is willing to remain married, there should be no move to seek a divorce. The Christians at Corinth may have pointed to Old Testament examples where Jews married non-Jews and brought God's displeasure (e.g., 2 Chron.

21:6) and therefore thought it appropriate for a Christian to seek a divorce.

If the unbeliever leaves, let him do so. . . . God has called us to live in peace (7:15). In a divorce the husband was expected to hand back the dowry he had received over from the bride's family at the time of marriage. For example in a divorce settlement of 13 B.C., the husband had to hand back "the items he received as her dowry, namely, clothing valued at 120 silver drachmas and a pair of gold earrings."[66] A (Christian) husband might try to be difficult and retain such a dowry, but Paul reminds the Christian to live in peace and to let the (unbelieving) wife go.

How do you know, wife, whether you will save your husband? Or, how do you know, husband, whether you will save your wife? (7:16). Paul can give no guarantees about the future destiny of an unbelieving marriage partner, but the hope of conversion is there.

Status and Calling in the Secular World (7:17–24)

Each one should retain the place in life that the Lord assigned to him and to which God has called him. This is the rule I lay down in all the churches (7:17). Paul the apostle presented standard guidelines or rules in each of the churches, not just the ones he founded.[67] In the Roman east there were aspirations for upward social mobility, with the main goal to gain Roman citizenship that was relatively rare in the eastern Mediterranean outside Roman colonies. It may be that some of the Corinthian Christians had been drawn to live in the colony from other cities of the province of Achaia, but that did not make them

Roman citizens. The calling (*klēsis*) can also take the meaning of social class.[68]

Was a man already circumcised when he was called? He should not become uncircumcised. Was a man uncircumcised when he was called? He should not be circumcised (7:18). Within the Corinthian church there were Christian Jews who bore the marks of circumcision. They may have been tempted to undergo surgery—epispasm—to disguise their circumcision. This operation is discussed in a medical treatise, *De Medicina*, by Celsus, written during the Julio-Claudian period.[69]

Each one should remain in the situation which he was in when God called him (7:20). The Christian should be satisfied with the position or status he or she held prior to conversion. There is no advantage of trying to appear a former Jew.

Were you a slave when you were called? Don't let it trouble you—although if you can gain your freedom, do so (7:21). The second group within the church who have aspirations are slaves. They might hope to be manumitted by their owners

and gain the status of being a freedman. The cost of receiving their freedom would allow their owner to buy a replacement slave. Slaves were able to earn money and amass money, which could be used to pay for their freedom. Paul is merely describing a common practice in the ancient world.

For he who was a slave when he was called by the Lord is the Lord's freedman; similarly, he who was a free man when he was called is Christ's slave (7:22). Paul uses the Greek technical word for a "freedman," the status to which a slave might aspire. Paul makes the point that those who have been called by Christ are already freedmen (and women). On receiving their freedom, former slaves became clients of their former masters, who were then considered their patron and who could expect support from them. Paul stresses that the Christian's patron is the Lord; thus, there is a duty to put oneself in his service. A number of individuals at Corinth with the status of "freedman" can be identified in surviving inscriptions, for they have the three Roman names. Former slaves tended to take on the *praenomen* and *nomen* of their former master.

▶ Jewish Circumcision and the Gymnasium

Circumcision was viewed with suspicion by Roman citizens, in part because it identified Jews (and Egyptians) as having separate ethnic origins. Ancient authors such as Martial[A-19] and the Jewish Philo[A-20] record Jews taking part in the gymnasium of their communities. This establishment was more than an exercise area and often included lecture rooms and other educational and cultural facilities. If Jews wished to take part in civic institutions such as the gymnasium or adopt the Roman cultural habit of taking hot baths, they would be easily identified when stripped naked.[A-21] Young men were usually enrolled as *ephēboi* in the gymnasium if they were entitled, whether or not they were Jews, and thus it may be that the reversal of the circumcision would be undertaken before the age of puberty; certainly Celsus indicates that this was the preferable age for such an operation. Such enrollment would give the young men opportunities, and some Jews did gain important positions of authority, such as Tiberius Claudius Alexander, who became governor of Judea.

You were bought at a price; do not become slaves of men (7:23). Some free-born Christians seemed to be willing to sell themselves into slavery. Such individuals, usually from poorer backgrounds, could then join the household of high-status individuals and, on paying for their freedom, could gain a higher status as a freedman; certainly their sons would be full, free-born Roman citizens if their patron was one. Some freedmen had considerable status and money. One of the best caricatures of a free-born man selling himself into slavery and then gaining his freedom appears in Petronius' *Satyricon*, written about the same time as 1 Corinthians.[70] The man would also be expected to worship his new master as a god, something that may have given concern to Paul.[71] The phrase "bought at a price" repeats that of 6:20.

Each man, as responsible to God, should remain in the situation God called him to (7:24). Paul has been discussing those who might wish to hide the fact that they were Jews so that they could progress in Gentile society (7:18), or slaves who aspired to have the status of "freedman" or "freedwoman" in Roman law (7:22). His concern is that ambition for promotion and elevation in the wider society should not interfere with one's Christian service.

Between Betrothal and Consummation (7:25–40)

Now about virgins: I have no command from the Lord, but I give a judgment (7:25). A group has raised the issue of "virgins" and marriage with Paul and he is responding. It seems that the group asking the question does not consist of the girls' fathers, but rather of young men within the church seeking to marry (7:28, 36–37). Girls were usually given in marriage at a young age.[72]

Because of the present crisis, I think that it is good for you to remain as you are (7:26). The "present crisis" or "dislocation" may refer to a period of food shortages in the Mediterranean.[73] At this time a certain Tiberius Claudius Dinippus was honored by elements within Corinth for acting as *curator* of the grain supply on three different occasions.[74] The Roman historian Tacitus has also recorded food shortages at this time.[75] Food shortages could induce social unrest and even riots. Such food shortages as well as earthquakes were seen by Christians as indicators that Christ would return (Matt. 24:7; Mark 13:8; Luke 21:11).

Are you married? Do not seek a divorce. Are you unmarried? Do not look for a wife (7:27). In Roman elite society men were encouraged to marry. Tacitus records that "towards the end of his life, Augustus passed the Papia-Poppaean Law, which supplemented the earlier Julian Laws, to encourage the enforcement of penalties for celibacy and to enrich the Treasury."[76]

But if you do marry, you have not sinned; and if a virgin marries, she has not sinned. But those who marry will face many troubles in this life (7:28). Paul's advice stems from his understanding of "the present crisis" (7:26), which he thinks will bring food shortages and other traumas. Marriage is not sinful, but Paul recognizes that if Corinthian Christians marry in the face of the present crisis, their children may suffer.

The time is short (7:29). The rise of Augustus created a new starting point for

▶ The Dinippus Inscriptions

During excavations in the central part of Corinth at least ten inscriptions have been found that serve as the bases for honorific statues to Tiberius Claudius Dinippus.[A-22] This individual, who originally served as a military tribune in the Legion VI Hispanensis ("Spanish") as well as *agōnothetēs* ("official in charge of the games") in the city, appears to have been honored by each of the tribes of which the citizen body of the colony of Corinth was composed. The inscriptions record that he had held the post of *curator annonae* three times. This post involved the supervision of the grain supply and implies that there had been a period of grain shortage. Since Dinippus apparently held the post of quinquennial *duovir* in A.D. 52/53, it is reasonable to suppose that he held the curatorship in the 50s, a period known to have been one of famines or food shortages.[A-23] His generosity led the different tribes of the colony to show their appreciation of his role.

time; note the inscriptions from the province of Achaia, such as the honorific inscription of the Corinthian citizen L. Licinnius Anteros from Methana on the Saronic Gulf, dated (using the new calendar initiated after the battle of Actium) to A.D. 1/2.[77] Paul emphasizes here that the time "has been shortened" (not as in NIV, "the time is short"). He encourages Christians to move away from the worries of the "present crisis" (7:26) to a Christian perspective on time.

Those who have wives should live as if they had none; those who mourn, as if they did not; those who are happy, as if they were not (7:29–30). Paul refers to the "seasons" in life, derived from Ecclesiastes 3:1–8:[78]

> *There is a time for everything,*
> *and a season for every activity under*
>   *heaven:*
> *a time to be born and a time to die,*
> *a time to plant and a time to uproot,*
> *a time to kill and a time to heal,*
> *a time to tear down and a time to*
>   *build,*
> *a time to weep and a time to laugh,*
> *a time to mourn and a time to dance,*
> *a time to scatter stones and a time to*
>   *gather them,*
> *a time to embrace and a time to*
>   *refrain,*
> *a time to search and a time to give up,*
> *a time to keep and a time to throw*
>   *away,*
> *a time to tear and a time to mend,*
> *a time to be silent and a time to*
>   *speak,*
> *a time to love and a time to hate,*
> *a time for war and a time for peace.*

This world in its present form is passing away (7:31). The social consequences of the "present crisis" (7:26) mean changes in the world order. In one sense Roman rule has brought order, at least to the Mediterranean world, but that too will be thrown into crisis as military commanders seek to wrestle power from the dynastic emperor, as was the case with the fall of Nero in A.D. 69, the year of the four emperors.

An unmarried man is concerned about the Lord's affairs—how he can please the Lord (7:32). Paul reminds unmarried men that without the responsibility of wife and family, they will be free to concentrate on Christian work. In a world where travel was difficult, single men were best equipped to move from city to city, province to province.

A married man is concerned about the affairs of this world—how he can please his wife—and his interests are divided (7:33–34a). Paul does not want the Christian husband to neglect his wife and family because of Christian ministry and work. He recognizes there will be a division of interests and time, and it is up to the Christian to find the right balance of commitments. An unmarried man can be more single-minded in his work for the kingdom of God.

Undivided devotion to the Lord (7:35). Christian devotion is expressed through honoring marriage commitments made before conversion.

If anyone thinks he is acting improperly toward the virgin he is engaged to, and if she is getting along in years and he feels he ought to marry, he should do as he wants (7:36). The term "improperly" can also be translated "in an unseemly way."[79] First-century use suggests it includes acts of immodesty as well as fornication, but may also include acts considered unacceptable in wider society.[80] In the Roman world it was acceptable for some sort of sexual contact between a betrothed couple, although there was protection for women from those who might be trying to seduce them.[81] However, it seems that in this context there has been no contact of a sexual nature, for Paul has already condemned fornication (6:9).

The term "virgin" (*parthenos*) refers to the unmarried status of a woman. "Getting along in years" (*hyperakmos*) can also be translated as "past the bloom of youth."[82] The term was used by the Ephesian medical writer Soranus in his work on gynecology dating to the late first century A.D.[83] He uses the term to refer to women after the onset of menstruation, around age fourteen. A later source suggests that the term could also have the meaning of passion.[84]

REFLECTIONS

MARRIAGE BRINGS WITH IT RESPONSIBILITIES TOWARD both spouse and children. Moreover, there are numerous pressures on marriage and relationships. In Paul's day there may have been the fear of starvation. Today there are still responsibilities. If I take this job away from home, what will it mean for my wife and children? Paul reminds us that Christian couples need to share their hopes and aspirations, weighing them up realistically before making the decision to marry. Marriage is a partnership—strengthened for the Christian by a common faith in Jesus Christ.

But the man . . . who has made up his mind not to marry the virgin . . . also does the right thing (7:37). Given the present crisis, the man who had been planning to marry is under no obligation as long as all parties, especially the fiancée's family, understand his reason for the decision.

So then, he who marries the virgin does right, but he who does not marry her does even better (7:38). If after consideration it is thought appropriate to marry, Paul is happy for the marriage to proceed. The central issue is that the decision is taken after weighing the options.

A woman is bound to her husband as long as he lives. But if her husband dies, she is free to marry anyone she wishes, but he must belong to the Lord (7:39). Christians are not free to marry whomever they would choose, but only other Christians. The context here is for those who have been widowed, but it is equally true for those who have never married. The Julian Law of 18 B.C. (*Lex Iulia de maritandis ordinibus*) allowed a widow to be exempt from marriage for one year after her husband's death, and the Papia-Poppaean Law of A.D. 9 two years.[85]

In my judgment, she is happier if she stays as she is—and I think that I too have the Spirit of God (7:40). Paul is contrasting himself with those in the Corinthian church who claimed to be "spiritual" (cf. 1 Cor. 2:15). Paul is "spiritual" in the sense that he is filled with the Spirit of God. This may be compared with his claim to have "the mind of Christ" (1 Cor. 2:16).

Food Sacrificed to Idols (8:1–13)

This is another issue raised by the Corinthians in a letter to Paul (see 7:1). Parts of this letter may be quoted (e.g., 8:5–6). The issue in this section relates to food eaten in the precinct of the temple (8:10), rather than the issue discussed later (10:25–11:1) about eating food offered to an idol in a private home.

Now about food sacrificed to idols (8:1). The food offered to idols may be linked to major civic festivals. Meat was not a common item in the ancient diet and was usually only consumed as part of a religious ceremony. At Corinth some of the wealthy magistrates were known to give such banquets. Lucius Castricius Regu-

lus, probably dating to the early first century A.D., who was the first president (*agōnothetēs*) of the Panhellenic Games within the territory of Corinth, once gave a banquet for all the "inhabitants of the colony"[86]; those who were not Roman citizens and who were merely considered residents would have been excluded. A similar banquet was given by Sospis, president of the Isthmian Games and friend of Plutarch.[87]

We know that we all possess knowledge (8:1). This may be a quotation from the letter written by the Corinthians to Paul. The "knowledge" (*gnōsis*) of the Christian is ultimately derived from Jesus Christ, as Paul emphasized at the beginning of the letter (1:5). This word was common in philosophical language, ultimately deriving from individuals like Plato. The members of the elite within the church at Corinth are likely to have been instructed in philosophy as part of their general education. The knowledge the

Corinthian Christians display is developed later in the chapter (8:4).

We know that an idol is nothing at all in the world and that there is no God but one (8:4). The Corinthians have boasted about their knowledge, and this is clearly a quotation from their letter. No doubt Paul had to address this issue when he was at Corinth, as many converts would have been involved with pagan deities. The same was true in the Macedonian city of Thessalonica, where the Christians there had "turned to God from idols to serve the living and true God" (1 Thess. 1:9). Some Christians may have believed that it meant nothing if they entered a pagan sanctuary and consumed meat that was explicitly linked to sacrifice. Paul quotes from the law of Moses: "Hear, O Israel: The Lord our God, the Lord is one" (Deut. 6:4).

For even if there are so-called gods, whether in heaven or on earth (as indeed there are many "gods" and many "lords") (8:5). Paul is making the point that *even though* there are so-called gods, their claim is false.[88] The gods "in heaven" would include deities such as Jupiter, the

chief of the pagan gods, and Aphrodite, the patron deity of the colony. The gods "on earth" may be an allusion to the way the Roman imperial family was worshiped and considered to be divine. At Corinth there was a temple of Octavia, dedicated to the sister of the emperor Augustus. The focus for a provincial imperial cult, based at Corinth, was established about A.D. 54.[89] There was a regular festival celebrating the imperial family; thus a Christian attending a banquet in honor of the deified emperor might be compromised.[90]

One God, the Father, from whom all things came and for whom we live; and ... one Lord, Jesus Christ, through whom all things came and through whom we live (8:6). Paul turns the language widespread in the ancient world to show that there is only one God and one Lord. Before Paul was shipwrecked on the way to Rome, he addressed his fellows with the statement about "God whose I am and whom I serve" (Acts 27:23).

Some people are still so accustomed to idols that when they eat such food they think of it as having been sacrificed to an

idol, and since their conscience is weak, it is defiled (8:7). When people in the ancient world described a cult statue to be displayed in a temple, they would drop the word "statue." Thus at Olympia in the Peloponnese, the seated figure in the temple was Zeus; Strabo, writing during the reign of Augustus, made the comment that if the god were to stand up, "he would take the roof off the temple"![91] Those believers who had been brought up to believe in the presence of a god within pagan sanctuaries would feel defiled if they continued to participate in such ritual meals.

Food does not bring us near to God (8:8). The partaking of food offered to idols makes no material difference to the standing of a Christian before God. It is the attitude with which a Corinthian believer is involved with such meals that is significant.

Be careful, however, that the exercise of your freedom does not become a stumbling block to the weak (8:9). The phrase translated as "the exercise of your freedom" can in fact mean "this right of yours." One's right (*exousia*) can be equated with civic privilege held by leading citizens within the colony.[92] This can be compared with the rights of an apostle in the next chapter (which uses the same Greek word). As citizens and Greeks, the leading members of the city may have had the right to participate in the festivals and associated athletic events, such as at Isthmia.

For if anyone with a weak conscience sees you who have this knowledge eating in an idol's temple, won't he be emboldened to eat what has been sacrificed to idols? (8:10). Some of the Corinthian

Christians were clearly attending feasts within the precincts of the cult centers of Corinth and its territory. A number of dining rooms linked to sanctuaries are known in the Corinthia, though not all date to the first century.[93] Dining rooms formed part of the complex of the Asklepieion at Corinth. Dining rooms were usually small, sometimes for only seven reclining individuals; thus, banquets were intimate occasions. The Greek word translated "eating" means reclining; the picture is of an individual reclining on a couch, arranged around the outer wall of a small room, to eat.

Not all such feasts were eaten in sanctuaries. A mass of animal bones were found near the theater, and it seems possible that the meat was distributed to the people and consumed within the theater itself. But note that the issue being discussed is about eating food within the pagan sanctuary, not eating food that has been sacrificed (this is dealt with separately at 10:14–22). The result of one Christian eating within the sanctuary is that a weaker Christian may see him and

be, literally, "built up" to go and do the
same.

**So this weak brother, for whom Christ
died, is destroyed by your knowledge
(8:11).** The destruction for the "weak
brother" is that he reverts to his old pagan
ways.

**When you sin against your brothers in
this way and wound their weak conscience, you sin against Christ (8:12).**
When Paul was confronted by Jesus on
the road to Damascus, Jesus asked him,
"Saul, Saul, why do you persecute me?"
(Acts 9:4). Actions against our brothers
and sisters in Christ are actions against
the person of Jesus Christ.

Paul the Apostle (9:1–27)

Have I not seen Jesus our Lord? (9:1).
Paul considered the events on the Damascus road not as a vision but as a real
encounter with the risen Lord Jesus.

**For you are the seal of my apostleship in
the Lord (9:2).** To deny Paul's apostleship,
as some at Corinth clearly did, is to deny
the validity of the church at Corinth.

**This is my defense to those who sit in
judgment on me (9:3).** This verse introduces a series of questions intended to
defend Paul from criticisms being made
against him.

**Don't we have the right to food and
drink? (9:4).** As the Corinthian Christians considered themselves to have

ASCLEPIUS

(left) The theater at
Epidaurus, the cen-
ter for the worship
of Asclepius.

(right) Statue of
Asclepius at the
Epidaurus museum.

▼

rights (8:9), so Paul as an apostle considers he has rights.

Don't we have the right to take a believing wife along with us, as do the other apostles and the Lord's brothers and Cephas? (9:5). Notice that the wife of an apostle comes from the community of Christians. Jesus' brothers appear as a distinct group within the early church (Acts 1:14).

Barnabas (9:6). Barnabas, originally from the island of Cyprus, was a Levite (Acts 4:36). He accompanied Paul on his first missionary journey until they had a disagreement over John Mark (Acts 15:37).

Who serves as a soldier (9:7). Achaia was a senatorial province and had no legionary garrison. However, soldiers from neighboring provinces were seconded to the provincial administration at Corinth. A first-century example of this is the tombstone of Caius Valerius Valens, found at Kranion.[94] The text reads:

> C[aius] Valerius Valens, son of C[aius], Quirinan tribe, from the Cam[unni] people, a soldier [*miles*] of the 8th Augustan legion, century of Senucius [or Senucus], he lived 35 years, he was a soldier for 14 years. *Heres ex testamento.*

The abbreviation "Cam" on the tombstone may indicate that he came from the Alpine tribe of the Camunni, who had been incorporated into the empire in 16 B.C.; members of the tribe were enrolled in the Roman Quirinan tribe when they became Roman citizens. Valens's legion is known to have served in Moesia (the lower Danube) from A.D. 45 to 69, and it is possible that Valens

was seconded to the governor's staff of Achaia. Although he is described as a soldier, Valens is shown in the grave relief as an officer, perhaps holding the rank of *optio*.[95]

Who plants a vineyard and does not eat of its grapes? Who tends a flock and does not drink of the milk? (9:7). Archaeological field survey in Greece has done much to throw light on ancient agricultural practice. The situation is likely to be with absentee landlords and tenant farmers. In other words, the social elite at Corinth may have owned land in different parts of the province, such as Laconia, and had tenants to plant their vineyards. Others, such as L. Licinnius Anteros in the Augustan period, resided at Corinth and were given the privilege of grazing their flocks elsewhere (e.g., on the Methana peninsula near Troezen).[96] It would be unreasonable for the landlord to expect his tenants not to eat some of the grapes or to drink some of the milk.

Doesn't the Law say the same thing? (9:8). Paul turns from secular illustrations that could be observed in contemporary Corinth to examples from the Old Testament.

Do not muzzle an ox while it is treading out the grain (9:9). Paul quotes from Deuteronomy 25:4. The ox is representative of those who work to bring in the harvest.

This was written for us, because when the plowman plows and the thresher threshes, they ought to do so in the hope of sharing in the harvest (9:10). Paul goes from the text to the application of the law to the people in Corinth. The Christian community needs to recognize that those who minister to them deserve material and financial support.

We did not use this right. On the contrary, we put up with anything rather than hinder the gospel of Christ (9:12). When Paul bade farewell to the elders at Ephesus, he reminded them of the words of Jesus, "It is more blessed to give than to receive" (Acts 20:35). This was one principle for his apostolic ministry—in sharp contrast with the roving professional speakers, the sophists, who expected honors and financial gain from their public speaking.

Those who work in the temple get their food from the temple, and those who serve at the altar share in what is offered on the altar (9:13). It is not clear if the intended background is Jewish or Gentile. Jews knew that the priests in the temple at Jerusalem were allowed to share in a proportion of what was offered (e.g., Num. 1:8–19). Those involved with the pagan temples of the Roman colony knew that any engaged in the sacrifices received a share of the sacrifice; it was, of course, going to be a specific issue in the church about "food offered to idols" (8:1–13).

The Lord has commanded that those who preach the gospel should receive their living from the gospel (9:14). When Jesus sent out his disciples to preach the gospel, he commanded them, "Do not take along any gold or silver or copper in your belts; take no bag for the journey, or extra tunic, or sandals or a staff; for the worker is worth his keep" (Matt. 10:10).

I have not used any of these rights. And I am not writing this in the hope that you will do such things for me. I would rather die than have anyone deprive me of this boast (9:15). In the ancient world a discussion of money led to the feeling that money was being sought. Paul distances

◄

ALTAR OF SACRIFICE

A model of the altar in the Court of Priests in the Jerusalem temple.

himself from such expectation. The Greek sentence is left hanging to emphasize Paul's unwillingness to accept money in response to this teaching: "For it is good for me rather to die than. . . ."[97] In Paul's mind, the integrity of the gospel is at stake here.

I am compelled to preach. Woe to me if I do not preach the gospel! (9:16). Paul refers to this compulsion to preach in 2 Corinthians 5:14: "For Christ's love compels us, because we are convinced that one died for all, and therefore all died."

What then is my reward? Just this: that in preaching the gospel I may offer it free of charge (9:18). Travelling orators or sophists might come to Corinth and make a fine speech in the hope of being honored by the colony or receiving some financial reward. Paul's preaching stands in marked contrast because it is done with no expectation of human reward.

Though I am free and belong to no man, I make myself a slave to everyone, to win as many as possible (9:19). Tutors might be engaged by a wealthy family for the education of children. Although Paul has links with some of the wealthy households of Corinth, such as that of Stephanas (1:16; 16:15), he can state unequivocally that he is independent.

To the Jews I became like a Jew, to win the Jews. To those under the law I became like one under the law . . . so as to win those under the law (9:20). Paul is sensitive to Jewish culture so as to present the gospel of Jesus Christ to the Jews.

To those not having the law I became like one not having the law . . . so as to win those not having the law (9:21). Paul rec-

ognizes that the Christian gospel is relevant to the Gentiles (i.e., non-Jews), and so he seeks to find points of contact with their culture.

To the weak I became weak, to win the weak. I have become all things to all men so that by all possible means I might save some (9:22). Although "the weak" may refer to the "weak brother" of 8:9–13, this group are among those who have yet to respond to the gospel. A possible third group might be those who hold to various ancient superstitions.

I do all this for the sake of the gospel, that I may share in its blessings (9:23). Paul's life has been committed to sharing the good news of Jesus Christ with the different groups he has encountered in

his journeys through the provinces of the eastern Roman empire.

All the runners run, but only one gets the prize? Run in such a way as to get the prize (9:24). Track events were the key element in any set of Greek games. The original event was the *stadion*, which was the length of the track, about 630 feet (the equivalent of 192 meters). The prestige of winning the event was such that the winner's name was often attached to the set of games; Greek historians refer to the year in which "x" won the *stadion* at the Olympic Games. Other foot-races were developed, including the *diaulos*, consisting of two lengths of the running track, as well as the *dolichos*, or long-distance race. In A.D. 69 Polites won all three of these running events at Olympia.

Everyone who competes in the games goes into strict training (9:25). The "games" to which Paul alludes are probably those of the Isthmian Festival, held in the nearby sanctuary of Poseidon at Isthmia.[98] This was one of a number of so-called Panhellenic games—others were held at Olympia, Delphi ("Pythian Games"), and Nemea—where competitors from all over the Greek world competed. Training was taken seriously. Philostratos the Elder (2d century A.D.) comments, "If you have worked hard enough to render yourself worthy of going to Olympia, if you have not been idle or ill-disciplined, then go with confidence; but those who have not trained in this fashion, let them go where they will."[99] Olympic athletes had to reside at Elis (the town that controlled Olympia) for a month before the games.

A crown that will not last (9:25). The crowns for the Panhellenic games were often no more than wreaths. At Olympia

149

1 Corinthians

▶ Athletics at Corinth

The sanctuary of Poseidon at Isthmia was located within the territory of the city of Corinth. This was located at the Isthmus of Corinth, some 8 miles (12 km) away. Attached to the sanctuary were athletic games held every two years. These were one of the Panhellenic festivals, which drew competitors from all over the Greek world; other similar festivals were held at Delphi and in the Peloponnese at Olympia and Nemea. The games continued into the Roman period, and in A.D. 67 the emperor Nero used the games as the moment to proclaim the freedom of Greece, a privilege repealed by the subsequent emperor Vespasian.

Excavations at Isthmia have revealed remains of the sanctuary as well as parts of the stadium. One of the most important discoveries, though dating from the classical city rather than the Roman period, was a specially designed starting gate for the runners.

Inscriptions from Corinth give the names of the magistrates or *agonothetai* responsible for holding the games. Monuments recording specific victors as well as victor lists are also known.[A-24] These show that there were three main groups of events at the Isthmian festival: cultural, including music, equestrian, and athletic. There were separate events for boys and men. The winning victors had originally been given a garland of celery, which was replaced by one of pine.[A-25]

In the Roman period the games were expanded to include events linked to the imperial cult. The Caesarean games were established under Tiberius and held every four years. When these Caesarean games coincided with the Isthmian festival, they were known as the Great Isthmia; in the intervening years the local games were known as the Lesser Isthmia.

it was an olive wreath, at Isthmia one of pine.[100] The individual was often honored with a statue at Olympia as well as in his own city.

No, I beat my body and make it my slave so that after I have preached to others, I myself will not be disqualified for the prize (9:27). The integrity of the gospel is at stake if Paul does not follow his own advice. It might be possible for Paul to

offer encouraging teaching to the Christian community at Corinth but then succumb to the same temptations they faced.

Eating Food Offered to Idols in the Idol Temple (10:1–22)

Paul finished the last section looking at the way in which a competitor in an athletic event might be disqualified as an illustration for Christian ministry. The next section, linked with "for" (10:1), develops the argument. It addresses the key issue in a Roman colony of how the Christian can take part in civic life, yet remain untainted by the pagan beliefs of his or her fellow-citizens.

For I do not want you to be ignorant of the fact, brothers, that our forefathers were all under the cloud and that they all passed through the sea (10:1). Any members of the Corinthian church from a Gentile background would be ignorant about Jewish history. Thus, Paul takes the trouble to explain that the God of the Jews leaving Egypt is the same as the God of the church of Corinth. Therefore, the Old Testament provides lessons for them. The "cloud" refers to the pillar of cloud that led the Jews out from Egypt (e.g., Ex. 13:21), and the "sea" refers to the parting of the waters (14:21–22). Notice how our Christian heritage lies in our Jewish past by the way Paul presents the Jews of the Exodus as "our forefathers." The condensed story of the Exodus that Paul relates is similar to that found in Psalm 78:13–16, which in its original context reminded God's people of the dangers of disobedience. The emphasis on "all" in this and subsequent verses contrasts with the "some" within the Christian community at Corinth (4:18; 6:11).

COMPETING IN THE GAMES

The starting grid for the runners in the games held at Isthmia.

They were all baptized into Moses in the cloud and in the sea (10:2). The "cloud" led the people (Ex. 13:21; 14:19–20) and the "sea" parted to allow them to leave Egypt (14:21–31), but it was placing their trust in Moses that was important.

They all ate the same spiritual food (10:3). In the desert of Zin—the great desert of the Negev—the people of Israel started to grumble about the food they had been able to eat in Egypt (Ex. 16:3). In response God provided first quail and then manna (16:13–15). This manna was to be their sustenance for the duration of the forty years in the desert (16:35).

They drank from the spiritual rock that accompanied them, and that rock was Christ (10:4). There are two incidents in the wandering in the desert that refer to rocks being struck. The first was at Rephidim before the people of Israel reached Mount Sinai (Ex. 17:1–7). The second was in the Desert of Zin, a place that became known as the waters of Meribah (or quarrelling) (Num. 20:2–13). The people grumbled about the lack of water and their departure from the "benefits" of Egypt, and the Lord commanded Moses to strike the rock with his staff.

Their bodies were scattered over the desert (10:5). The language evokes the prayer used by Moses to God where he anticipates what the nations will say if God punishes the people for their disobedience: "The LORD was not able to bring these people into the land he promised them on oath; so he slaughtered them in the desert" (Num. 14:16). Although all had passed through the waters of the Red Sea and all had been sustained by the bread, God's displeasure

fell on "most of them" because they had not followed his commands.

Now these things occurred as examples to keep us from setting our hearts on evil things as they did (10:6). The events of Jewish history may seem irrelevant to those brought up in a Roman (or Greek) culture. Yet the issues of idolatry, sexual immorality, putting God to the test, and grumbling are all issues that the Corinthians are facing.

Do not be idolaters, as some of them were; as it is written: "The people sat down to eat and drink and got up to indulge in pagan revelry" (10:7). Paul quotes here from Exodus 32:6. While the people were camped at the foot of Mount Sinai, they became disenchanted, created a golden calf, and made offerings before it. As a result Moses, when he had come down from the mountain, instructed certain Levites to kill those who had rebelled against the Lord (32:25–29). The application for this lesson from history is for those Corinthian Christians who feel that they can still attend festivals in the sanctuaries and precincts of the colony, including the sanctuary of Poseidon at Isthmia, and yet be loyal to the Lord. In Corinth, pagan festivals included the sacrifice of animals, and parts of the offerings were consumed by the participants.

We should not commit sexual immorality, as some of them did—and in one day twenty-three thousand of them died (10:8). The allusion here is to the incident when the people of Israel were staying at Shittim (Num. 25:1–9). The Moabite women seduced the Israelite men and then encouraged them to worship Baal of Peor. Moses dealt with this

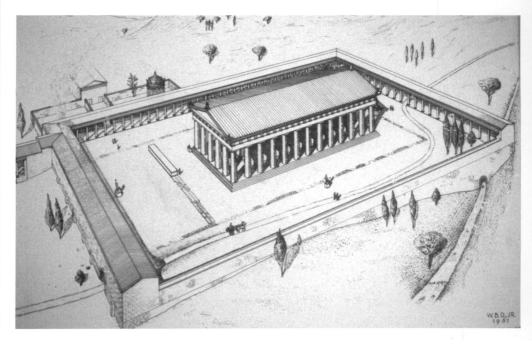

immorality, and the plague that deci-mated the Israelites was brought to a halt. In the Roman world, prostitutes were frequently present at banquets. Dio Chrysostom mentions prostitutes being taken from festival to festival to satisfy the sexual needs of the participants and those attending.[101] Paul was no doubt concerned that indulgence with prosti-tutes might lead people into engagement with the pagan festivals of the colony.

We should not test the Lord, as some of them did—and were killed by snakes (10:9). This refers to another incident during Israel's desert wandering. When the people "spoke against God and against Moses" (Num. 21:5), God sent poisonous snakes, which killed a number of the Israelites. People were only saved when a bronze snake was erected in their midst for them to look upon (21:6–9). Some of the Corinthian Christians may have felt that since nothing seemed to have happened to them as they contin-ued to attend festivals in pagan sanctu-aries, they might as well continue. Paul views such an attitude as tempting God.

And do not grumble, as some of them did—and were killed by the destroying angel (10:10). When the spies returned from exploring Canaan, the Promised Land, the people were frightened at the report the majority of them brought (Num. 13); this led to grumbling against Moses and Aaron and an attempt to choose a new leader (14:1–4). Conse-quently, God promised that not one of the adults who left Egypt would enter the Promised Land (except Caleb and Joshua, 14:30). The men who had spread the depressing reports about Canaan were "struck down and died of a plague before the Lord" (14:37).

Examples and . . . warnings for us, on whom the fulfillment of the ages has come (10:11). These lessons from Jewish history are applicable to Gentiles because of God's promise to Abram, "All peoples on earth will be blessed through you" (Gen. 12:3).

If you think you are standing firm, be careful that you don't fall! (10:12). Some in the church seem to be using the argument, "We know that an idol is nothing at all in the world and that there is no God but one" (8:4). Some may even be "eating in an idol's temple" (8:10). The lesson from Israel's history is that such people may be in for a fall.

No temptation has seized you except what is common to man. And God is faithful (10:13). The Corinthian Christians may be faced by the general temptations Paul has been rehearsing. They would be foolish to pretend that such temptations do not face them. They also are presented with specific temptations or possible compromises because of the nature of their involvement in the life of the ancient city, with its emphasis on religious cults and activities.

Flee from idolatry (10:14). Corinthian Christians can flee from idolatry by making sure they take no part in the pagan life of the colony. This would create tensions for those perhaps holding civic magistracies, who are expected to attend festivals and make sacrifices.

I speak to sensible people (10:15). Paul has used the same Greek word for "sensible" (*phronimos*) in an ironic way earlier in the letter (4:10). Here he recognizes that the Corinthian Christians have obtained wisdom in the way they relate to their pagan world.

Is not the cup of thanksgiving for which we give thanks a participation in the blood of Christ? (10:16). At the Passover meal, celebrating the Exodus from Egypt and thus picking up on the thrust of Paul's earlier illustrations, four cups of wine were drunk during the course of the meal. The cup of thanksgiving was the third cup.

Is not the bread that we break a participation in the body of Christ? (10:16). When animals were sacrificed in pagan sanctuaries, meat was offered to the participants, something that did not form part of a regular diet in the ancient world. Yet the use of bread reminded the Christians of the sacrifice Jesus Christ had made on the cross on their behalf.

People of Israel (10:18). The Greek phrase here (lit., "Israel according to the flesh") refers to the Jews of Paul's day who continued to offer sacrifices in the temple at Jerusalem.

Participate in the altar (10:18). The Jewish writer Philo saw that those who took part in the sacrifice were "partners in the altar."[102] The imagery goes back to the days of Moses when the priests were required to eat the food together by the altar, "for it is most holy" (Lev. 10:12). The parts of the offerings that were not consumed by fire on the altar of God could be consumed by the priests and Levites (Num. 17:8–10; Deut. 18:1–5). However others could also consume by the altar part of what had been offered to God (e.g., Deut. 12:4–7).

Do I mean then that a sacrifice offered to an idol is anything, or that an idol is anything? (10:19). Paul clarifies the three strands of his argument: those who take part in the Lord's Supper, those who participate in Jewish sacrifices, and those who have engaged with pagan practices. Paul has already reminded them that "an idol is nothing at all and that there is no God but one" (8:4). The language used for the idol meat (*eidōlothyton*) is derived from the Jewish background.

The sacrifices of pagans are offered to demons, not to God, and I do not want you to be participants with demons (10:20). This theme of sacrificing to demons picks up on the Song of Moses in Deuteronomy (32:17): "They sacrificed to demons, which are not God." This picks up on the themes from the desert wandering earlier in the chapter.

You cannot drink the cup of the Lord and the cup of demons too; you cannot have a part in both the Lord's table and the table of demons (10:21). Paul makes it clear that participation in any form of pagan worship, whether festivals or the imperial cult, is prohibited to the Christian. Metal and ceramic vessels were often inscribed in antiquity with the name of a deity to which they had been dedicated.

Are we trying to arouse the Lord's jealousy? Are we stronger than he? (10:22). The Jews remembered that when in the desert they had worshiped other gods, "they made [God] jealous by what is no god and angered [God] with their worthless idols" (Deut. 32:21).

Eating Food Offered to Idols in Private Gatherings (10:23–11:1)

"Everything is permissible "—but not everything is beneficial. "Everything is permissible "—but not everything is constructive (10:23). The slogan "everything is permissible" has a link with the rights asserted by the Corinthian Christians (8:9). Thus this phrase can be translated "Everything is lawful" or "Everything is allowed."[103] But Paul's main point is to urge the Corinthian Christians to seek what is "beneficial" for their city and society[104] and what "is constructive"; this latter phrase can also be translated as "builds up" or "edifies," indicating the way that the Christian life develops like a building.

Nobody should seek his own good, but the good of others (10:24). The colony of Corinth, like virtually any other city in the Roman world, gave opportunity for the social elite to display their status. Buildings prominently displayed details of their benefactors; portrait statues were erected in public places. For example, the dedication by the city magistrate Erastus of a piazza next to the theater at Corinth had bronze letters (see "Paul Quotes an Athenian Playwright" at 15:33). By contrast, the Christian is to serve others rather than promote himself or herself.

Eat anything sold in the meat market without raising questions of conscience (10:25). The meat market (*makellon*) lay

near to the forum in Corinth and has been partially excavated.[105] Similar markets of roughly the same date have been recognized at Pompeii and in North Africa. Food for sale in a *makellon* may have been initially sacrificed in a temple or sanctuary.

"The earth is the Lord's, and everything in it" (10:26). The quotation from Psalm 24:1 was used in Jewish society as a means of giving thanks for food.[106]

If some unbeliever invites you to a meal and you want to go, eat whatever is put before you (10:27). The context for this meal is clearly in the private home rather than in the temple. The Christian community does not have to separate itself from fellow Corinthians. The word used for "invites" is found in papyri from Egypt relating to both secular and religious meals.

If anyone says to you, "This has been offered in sacrifice," then do not eat it (10:28). The "anyone" need not be another Christian. It may be the non-Christian host at the meal or a fellow diner who is puzzled how a Christian can eat something offered to a pagan god. The phrase in quotation marks can be translated, "This is sacred meat" (*hierothyton*), using language that might be more appropriate for somebody from a non-Jewish background; it contrasts with the Jewish expression "idol meat" used earlier in 10:19.

The other man's conscience (10:29). If the person who pointed out the origin of the meat was a pagan, then "conscience" may be better translated as "moral consciousness."[107] Thus the person who has made the statement at the dinner was

concerned that the Christian might follow Jewish dietary regulations.

If I take part in the meal with thankfulness, why am I denounced because of something I thank God for? (10:30). The thanksgiving at the Jewish meal would be Psalm 24:1 (quoted in 10:26), endorsing that God is the origin of all things.

So whether you eat or drink or whatever you do, do it all for the glory of God (10:31). God touches every corner of the Christian life, even aspects not regularly thought of as "sacred" in the ancient world.

Do not cause anyone to stumble, whether Jews, Greeks or the church of God (10:32). The Jews and the Greeks reflect the cultural composition of the church at Corinth. Consideration must be given to the backgrounds and perceptions of the members of the church.

I am not seeking my own good but the good of many, so that they may be saved (10:33). The good mentioned here is the "welfare" or "benefit" mentioned in 10:23 (see comments).

Follow my example (11:1). "Follow" is better translated as "imitate." The Corinthian Christians are urged to follow Paul's model as he has had to work out his response to the pagan backdrop of civic life in the Greek East.

Veiling the Head (11:2–16)

After talking about the way Christians relate to the pagan festivals and cult practices of the Roman colony, Paul now turns to how Christian fellowship operates; in particular, he emphasizes points that will make it distinctive as a community.

I praise you for remembering me in everything and for holding to the teachings, just as I passed them on to you (11:2). Praise was a feature of elite society, and so Paul is using language to which the Corinthians can respond. He refers to teachings that have been "passed . . . on" (lit., "handed down"), that is to say, "traditions." They are, of course, tra-ditions that carry the weight of an apostle. Presumably some of the issues Paul goes on to address in chapter 11 are ones that had not arisen during his time in the colony.

The head of every man is Christ, and the head of the woman is man, and the head of Christ is God (11:3). The words "man" and "woman" can also be translated as "husband" and "wife." The choice of the word "head" (*kephalē*) seems to indicate that Paul has a hierarchical structure in mind. Although the Liddell, Scott, and Jones' *Greek Lexicon* allows the possibility of the translation "source," this has been disputed.[108] The thinking behind Paul's metaphor is not obvious.

Every man who prays or prophesies with his head covered dishonors his head (11:4). The covering of the man's head—called the *capite velato*—was commonplace in a Roman religious cult. One explanation was that it helped to reduce the noise of the animals being sacrificed (see "Roman Portraits"). The statue of Augustus displayed at Corinth showed the emperor with his head covered; similar iconography is found on the frieze of the Ara Pacis ("Altar of Peace") that he dedicated at Rome. The social elite took an active part in the religious cults of the city by serving as priests, and thus those who had joined the church may have introduced this Roman cultural norm into Christian worship. Thus, Christian worship was expressing not that all were one in Christ but the social divisions of secular society. Praying with a covered head drew attention to the man's place in Roman society, whereas in Christian worship the focus should be on Christ.

REFLECTIONS

IN CORINTH, SOME CHRISTIANS were offended when they saw other members of their church community eating meat that had been offered as a sacrifice to the pagan gods. Those eating could come up with a theological argument to allow them to enjoy the festivities—but they may not have thought through the practical pastoral considerations. What sort of things do we do that might become stumbling blocks to other Christians?

ARA PACIS IN ROME
▼

Every woman who prays or prophesies with her head uncovered dishonors her head (11:5). Notice that Paul clearly envisages that women should be involved in prayer and prophecy in the fellowship. The hairstyles of the women in the imperial family at Rome tended to set the trends for women in the rest of the empire. It is clear from portraits on coins and in sculpture that women's hair in the middle of the first century A.D. tended to be worn longer than under Augustus. Agrippina the Younger, the wife of the emperor Claudius, and the mother of the future emperor Nero (from a previous marriage), adopted a hairstyle where "the hair is braided and gathered into a long loop; two long strands of curled hair fall at either side of the neck."[109] The covering of the head is an emblem found in sculptural representation in the late republic and under Augustus, where the palla is pulled up over the top of the head. This became an emblem for modesty and chastity.[110] Presumably women who felt able to uncover their heads were considered immodest, unchaste, and therefore by definition un-Roman.

It is just as though her head were shaved (11:5). A shaved head could be equated with shame for a women. There is some evidence that shaving was a punishment for adultery.[111]

If a woman does not cover her head, she should have her hair cut off; and if it is a disgrace for a woman to have her hair cut or shaved off, she should cover her head (11:6). Failing to cover a woman's

▶ Roman Portraits

The covering and uncovering of heads, which is a feature of this letter, needs to be considered against the norms of Roman dress. A major insight is provided by the discovery of a number of imperial and private portrait statues in Corinth.[A-26] For example, the statue of Augustus from the Julian basilica at Corinth (though probably originally displayed elsewhere as it is earlier than that particular building) shows the emperor dressed in a toga.[A-27] A fold of the cloth is pulled over his head in the so-called *capite velato*. Plutarch tells us that a priest pulled the cloth over his head in this way to exclude the noise of the animal being sacrificed.[A-28] This portrait was a standard image of the emperor and of a type found elsewhere in the empire. In contrast, portrait statues of Augustus' adopted heirs, Gaius and Lucius, found in the same basilica were shown naked like athletes. Because they died young, they could be presented unclothed as athletes. In the Julian basilica other imperial statues were also displayed, such as that of the emperor Nero, also shown with his toga pulled over his head.[A-29]

Coin portraits of the emperor's wife (e.g., Livia) could show her either with her head covered or bare. These coin portraits show how hairstyles developed during the first century into elaborate creations; no doubt the women of the imperial elite in colonies such as Corinth followed the fashion of the imperial court. An early first century A.D. portrait of a woman found at Corinth shows her with her head uncovered and with the hair braided and brought together above the forehead.[A-30]

◀ BRAIDED HAIR

REFLECTIONS

IN THE ROMAN WORLD THE TYPE of dress worn by women could indicate status. A toga, for example, would indicate coveted Roman citizenship. In the church in Corinth there was tension. Some men were adopting a dress code that tried to make a statement about their "high" status in the church community. Some women were dressed in a way that might have led to critical comment from outside the church. How does the dress we adopt for worship reflect Christian values to those outside the church? Do we dress up? Or dress down?

head was dishonoring to her husband. A woman would cover her head when she was married.[112] Thus if "woman" is translated as "wife" (see comments on 11:3), immodest dress would reflect badly on her marriage and therefore her husband.

A man ought not to cover his head, since he is the image and glory of God; but the woman is the glory of man (11:7). Paul uses an illustration from creation to discuss the role of the man (or husband): "So God created man in his own image, in the image of God he created him" (Gen. 1:27a). The woman's role is seen in relation to her husband: "A wife of noble character is her husband's crown" (Prov. 12:4a).

For man did not come from woman, but woman from man; neither was man created for woman, but woman for man (11:8–9). Paul follows the order of creation in Genesis 2:23b: "She shall be called 'woman,' for she was taken out of man." Paul has moved away from social conven-

tions to a theological reason for the wife to reflect respect for her husband.

Because of the angels (11:10). It is not immediately clear what Paul means here. He may be developing an idea, noted at Qumran, that angels participated in worship. Perhaps Paul has in mind that Christians, men and women, will one day "judge angels" (6:3).

The woman ought to have a sign of authority on her head (11:10). The sign of authority may be an allusion to the veil a Roman woman might use to cover her head.

In the Lord, however, woman is not independent of man, nor is man independent of woman (11:11). This develops the idea in Christian marriage that there is mutual respect (see comments on 7:4). This is in contrast with the status of a Roman wife, whose identity was entirely bound up with that of her husband.

As woman came from man, so also man is born of woman. But everything comes from God (11:12). Paul states an important principle that both men and women ultimately come from God.

Does not the very nature of things teach you that if a man has long hair, it is a disgrace to him (11:14). Nature (*physis*) was thought to be the determining factor in the way society expressed itself. Long hair for men was unusual in ancient society. It was common in the representation of the deities Apollo and Dionysos (Bacchus), but not for other gods. Men were expected to wear their hair short.

If a woman has long hair, it is her glory? For long hair is given to her as a covering (11:15). Portraits of women, and in particular female members of the imperial family, show that their hair was carefully braided and arranged.[113]

Divisions at the Lord's Supper (11:17–34)

Paul moves from issues of dress and status in the gatherings of the people of God at Corinth to issues of much more pressing importance.

In the following directives I have no praise for you, for your meetings do more harm than good (11:17). Paul contrasts the praise for the Corinthian Christians

---

▶ Women in Corinth

A number of women from the Roman colony are known by name, either in their own right or because they wished to honor their husbands by erecting some monument. For example, a possible Augustan marble statue base from the southeastern part of the forum recorded the erection of a (now lost) portrait statue of Sextus Olius Secundus by his son Sextus and by his wife Cornelia.[A-31] A first century A.D. inscription also from the southeastern part of the forum honored Cornelius Pulcher, who had helped to organize the Isthmian games, by his wife.[A-32]

Archaeology has also revealed inscriptions relating to women who were prominent in their own right. A statue base from Corinth was inscribed with this text:

> To Polyaena, daughter of Marcus, priestess of Victory. The high priest [Publius] Licinius Priscus Juventianus, [while still living, (set up this monument)] with the official sanction of the city council to (this) excellent woman.[A-33]

Polyaena held a specific religious role within the life of the colony. Perhaps one of the most extensive documents for women in the Greek east during the first century was found on a stele that had been used in a late antique tomb near Corinth.[A-34] The text consists of a transcript of a number of decrees from the Lycian confederation, the cities of Myra, Patara, and Telmessos, and a letter to the Corinthians from the Lycian confederation. They relate to Iunia Theodora,

> living in Corinth, a fine and worthy woman, and devoted to the nation, [who] continuously shows her zeal and her munificence towards the nation and being full of goodwill both to individual Lycians and to all in general has gained for the nation the friendship of many of the authorities, employing her assistance in all areas which most directly interest all the Lycians.[A-35]

Iunia Theodora was specifically praised "since . . . very many of our people in exile were welcomed by her with magnificence."[A-36] These Lycian exiles were probably linked either to the civil strife in Lycia when it became a Roman province in A.D. 43,[A-37] or perhaps in A.D. 57, when the Lycian federation unsuccessfully prosecuted the governor, Titus Clodius Eprius Marcellus.[A-38] Iunia Theodora's residence at Corinth, though her family came from Lycia, may have a commercial reason, and this may explain why individual cities of Lycia were grateful to her for looking after their interests in one of the major ports of the Mediterranean.

over holding onto the teaching he has communicated to them (11:2) with a refusal to praise them for their actions at the Lord's Supper.

When you come together as a church, there are divisions among you (11:18). Paul has already noted the divisions within the church (1:10), but here they are manifest when the church comes together. The word Paul uses to describe the church (*ekklēsia*) is the same one that was commonly used in Greek cities for describing the political body.[114] The political assembly was where oratorical skills could be displayed, sometimes with the goal of creating factions and divisions to further civic or political ends. Perhaps the Corinthian Christians thought that the politicking of the citizen body in Corinth was a role model for their own assembly. The church met as a body in a house of one of its members, such as the house of Gaius (Rom. 16:23).

To some extent I believe it (11:18). Earlier in the letter Paul made it clear that he knows about the divisions because of the reports he received from "Chloe's household" (1:11). Now it appears that Paul is only partially informed. The clause can in fact also be translated as "and I believe a certain report."[115] This "report" (translating the Greek word *meros*) would be the one from Chloe's household.

There have to be differences among you to show which of you have God's approval (11:19). Those who wave "God's approval" are in fact those who have passed the "examination" or "test." Such a "test" reappears in 2 Corinthians 2:9: "The reason I wrote you was to see if you would stand the test and be obedient in everything." The "test," and thereby "God's approval," is adherence to Paul's teaching as an apostle. The implication is that within the Corinthian church there are some who do not accept Paul's apostolic authority. It has been argued that the group separating themselves from the rest may in fact be the social elite.[116]

When you come together, it is not the Lord's Supper you eat, for as you eat, each of you goes ahead without waiting for anybody else (11:20–21). The Greek phrase implies that either some at the Lord's Supper start eating before anybody has had a chance, or that some have brought their own meals along and do not share them. The implication for the Lord's Supper is that while some members of the Christian community dine rather well—some even get drunk—others have nothing to eat. Clearly there are some who have brought food and others who have none to bring.

The "Lord's Supper" refers to the meal that commemorates the supper Jesus ate with his disciples in the Upper Room in Jerusalem before his arrest. Luke refers to the Christians at Troas (Troy) in northwestern Turkey coming together "to break bread" on the first day of the week (i.e., Sunday) (Acts 20:7). The fact that Jesus asked his disciples to have such a meal "in remembrance of me" (Luke 22:19) seems to have led to the creation of a regular gathering of Christian disciples that included a meal known as "the Lord's Supper," where the events and significance of Christ's death on the cross could be recalled.[117]

Don't you have homes to eat and drink in? Or do you despise the church of God and humiliate those who have nothing? What shall I say to you? Shall

I praise you for this? Certainly not! (11:22). Paul now asks some searching questions of the Corinthian Christians. Those bringing their own food (and wine) to the Lord's Supper and treating it like one of the banquets common in the city[118] have their own homes. The Greek word *oikia* ("house, home") can be translated "household"; it may reflect the fact that those abusing the Lord's Supper are part of the social elite of the colony who are accustomed to hosting lavish banquets in their villas. Paul is critical of those who have been despising those who "have nothing" (lit., the "have nots"). These "have nots" may represent the urban poor of the Roman colony who had not fallen under the patronage of the leading families of the city. Such patronage was a common feature of Roman society. If Paul was writing at a time of food shortage in the colony— "the present crisis" (7:26)—some in the church may have been facing starvation. In contrast, some of the wealthy may have had estates across Greece—some of the wealthy Corinthians came from Sparta, and another is recorded as having grazing rights on the Methana peninsula in the Saronic gulf—and would have been cushioned from crop failures or drought in a specific area.

For I received from the Lord what I also passed on to you (11:23). Paul now recounts the story of the Last Supper on the night of Jesus' arrest in Jerusalem. It affirms that at this early stage the Christian church had formulated an account of the events of that night as it gave meaning to the act of holding a Lord's Supper as a commemoration of that event. Paul's version of the events is similar to that which appears in Luke's account:

The Lord Jesus, on the night he was betrayed, took bread, and when he had given thanks, he broke it and said, "This is my body, which is for you; do this in remembrance of me." In the same way, after supper he took the cup, saying, "This cup is the new covenant in my blood; do this, whenever you drink it, in remembrance of me." (1 Cor. 11:23–25)

And he took bread, gave thanks and broke it, and gave it to them, saying, "This is my body given for you; do this in remembrance of me." In the same way, after the supper he took the cup, saying, "This cup is the new covenant in my blood, which is poured out for you." (Luke 22:19–20)

The covenant recalls the Exodus of the people of Israel from Egypt, marked by the Passover and the sprinkling of the blood of the lambs (Ex. 12), but it also looks back to the original covenant made with Abraham, who would be a blessing for all people (Gen. 12:2–3). The "new covenant" picks up on the prophecy of Jeremiah (Jer. 31:31), when the Lord says that he "will put my law in their minds and write it on their hearts" (31:33). This "new covenant" was important to the early church as seen by the discussion in the letter to the Hebrews (Heb. 8:8).

For I received from the Lord what I also passed on to you (11:23). Paul is alluding either to receiving this teaching as part of the revelation of Jesus Christ as he made his way to Damascus, or through subsequent teaching (by the apostles) at Jerusalem.

The Lord Jesus ... took bread, when he had given thanks (11:23–24). The common Jewish form of blessing was, "Blessed are you, O Lord our God, king of the universe, who brings forth bread from the earth."[119]

This is my body, which is for you; do this in remembrance of me (11:24). During the Passover meal, the person presiding at the meal would take up the unleavened bread—the "bread of affliction" (Deut. 16:3)—and make a statement about it, recalling the Exodus from Egypt. Although the words used at the Passover in the first century A.D. are not known, a later common formula was, "This is the bread of affliction which our fathers ate in the land of Egypt; let all who are hungry come and eat."[120] Jesus as president of this Passover meal thus transformed the words and applied them to himself. The act of remembrance at the Passover of the Exodus was now applied to the *exodus* of Jesus, "which he was about to bring to fulfillment at Jerusalem" (Luke 9:31).

This cup is the new covenant in my blood; do this, whenever you drink it, in remembrance of me (11:25). The cup referred to here is likely the "cup of blessing" that came in the Passover meal. The

words used evoked the words of Moses: "This is the blood of the covenant that the Lord has made with you" (Ex. 24:8).

For whenever you eat this bread and drink this cup, you proclaim the Lord's death until he comes (11:26). Christ's death on the cross was a selfless act. Those members of the Corinthian church who abuse the Lord's Supper by bringing their own food and allow fellow Christians to starve in their very presence can be considered as selfish.

Whoever eats the bread or drinks the cup of the Lord in an unworthy manner will be guilty of sinning against the body and blood of the Lord (11:27). Paul places the focus of the actions of the Lord's Supper on our attitudes toward those who share the meal together. The wealthy elite, who place such an emphasis on worth and status, are being accused of having the unenviable attribute of being "unworthy."

A man ought to examine himself before he eats of the bread and drinks of the cup (11:28). The examination looks back to attitudes toward divisions within the church and toward those less well off in the Christian community.

Anyone who eats and drinks without recognizing the body of the Lord eats and drinks judgment on himself (11:29). The "judgment" is in fact the (guilty) verdict passed down by a judge at a trial. This emphasizes the seriousness with which believers should treat the celebration of the Lord's Supper.

That is why many among you are weak and sick, and a number of you have fallen asleep (11:30). Illness in the Chris-

tian community is seen here as perhaps a consequence of wrongdoing, in the way that the Jews were judged during their exodus from Egypt. This may indicate the presence of a number of people familiar with the Old Testament in the Christian community at Corinth. "Fallen asleep" refers to the death of believing Christians (cf. 1 Thess. 4:14–15).

But if we judged ourselves, we would not come under judgment. When we are judged by the Lord, we are being disciplined so that we will not be condemned with the world (11:31–32). The gods of the pagan world had to be appeased in order to avert evil; the Roman writer Pausanias noted a temple in the agora at Athens dedicated to Apollo Alexikakos ("Averter of Evil"), the god perceived as bringing the late fifth-century B.C. plague in the city under control (Pausanias, *Descr.* 1.3.4). Piety toward the gods was a possible route to an untroubled life; Paul presents the Lord's judgement in contrast to that generally accepted in the ancient world.

When you come together to eat, wait for each other (11:33). The phrase "wait for each other" can also mean that the Corinthian Christians should share their food together, thus avoiding the situation of some who eat well and some who have no food at all.

If anyone is hungry, he should eat at home, so that when you meet together it may not result in judgment (11:34). Food shortages, not famines, were a major feature of the ancient world.[121] This was especially true of large urban populations, and a number of riots are known at Rome. Emperor Claudius is even said to have been pelted with hunks

of bread in the Forum at Rome.[122] Such a food shortage may lie behind the "present crisis" mentioned in 7:26.

When I come I will give further directions (11:34). Paul anticipates his own visit, which is briefly described in Acts 20:2–3. His stay in "Greece" (i.e., the province of Achaia as opposed to Macedonia) lasted three months, and Corinth is likely to have been one of the main centers.

Now About Spiritual Gifts (12:1–13)

Paul now turns from the Lord's Supper to the way that meetings of the Christian fellowship are conducted. One of the key issues is the use of the gift of "tongues," which is referred to throughout the next three chapters (12:10, 28, 30; 13:1, 8; 14:5, 6, 18, 22, 23, 39).

Now about spiritual gifts, brothers (12:1). "Spiritual gifts" can in fact also be translated "spiritual people." Such a view would develop Paul's arguments from earlier in the letter (2:15; 3:1), to which he will again turn (14:37). The emphasis he places on these issues is the same as he placed on the lessons from Israel's past (10:1).

You know that when you were pagans, somehow or other you were influenced and led astray to mute idols (12:2). "Pagans" identifies the members of the church at Corinth as coming from the Gentile, that is to say, the non-Jewish, world (though see comments on 1:8; "Jews at Corinth" at 1:23). The city of Corinth was dominated by a range of cults, from the temple of Aphrodite on the top of Akrocorinth overlooking the city to the archaic temple above the forum and various temples dedicated to the imperial cult. Within each sanctuary was a representation of its deity, often created by famous craftsmen. Yet these idols, with all their costly art, were unable to speak, just as is stated in the Old Testament times about idols (e.g., Hab. 2:18–19).

Paul presents a similar idea in Romans 1:23, where he notes that some have "exchanged the glory of the immortal God for images made to look like mortal man and birds and animals and reptiles." Such "mute idols" or deities were viewed as making utterances through oracles, the most famous of which was the oracle of Pythian Apollo at Delphi, which continued to be active in the Roman period (see comments on 14:28).

No one who is speaking by the Spirit of God says, "Jesus be cursed," and no one can say, "Jesus is Lord," except by the Holy Spirit (12:3). Curses were part of Roman cult practice, and adherents of a particular god might leave a short note in a temple or sanctuary, asking him or her to act on their behalf. Some of these have survived, most commonly on lead tablets. One from the sanctuary of Demeter at Corinth reads, "Hermes of the underworld [grant] heavy curses."[123] The curse that some in Corinth seem to have been using is "Jesus [is] a curse [*anathema*]." Members of the church may have been adopting the normal Corinthian practice of using the gods to forward their cause by casting a curse on those opposing them. Paul encourages the Corinthians to make the statement that "Jesus [is] Lord." Paul later calls down an *anathema* on those who do "not love the Lord" (16:22).

There are different kinds of gifts, but the same Spirit . . . the same Lord . . . the same God works all of them in all men (12:4–6). From the same "Spirit," "Lord," and "God" come the means for the church to carry out its function through gifts, service, and working. Pagans might consider what they could do for the deity concerned through offering sacrifices and making dedications in a sanctuary, but in Christian terms it is God, through the Holy Spirit and through Jesus Christ, who equips his church.

ACROCORINTH

(left) The Acrocorinth with some of the ruins of ancient Corinth in the foreground.

(right) Roman, Byzantine, and Turkish walls on the top of the Acrocorinth.

▼

To each one the manifestation of the Spirit is given for the common good (12:7). The Corinthian community was used to rich individuals in the colony providing benefactions of food, festivals, or buildings for the "common good" or "welfare of the community." Thus by the theater in Corinth the magistrate Erastus laid a piazza from his own money as a benefaction to the city (see "Paul Quotes an Athenian Playwright" at 15:33).[124] Such benefactions gave status to the individual, especially if the new building or facility carried a Latin inscription, sometimes with the letters fitted with bronze. Paul is reminding the Corinthian Christians that the Holy Spirit is given for the benefit or welfare of the community, not for personal glorification.

To one there is given through the Spirit the message of wisdom, to another . . . to another speaking in different kinds of tongues (12:8–10). Paul draws attention to the diversity of gifts. Notice how the gifts are not given to the same person but are spread throughout the Christian community ("another"). "Tongues" can also be translated as "languages."

All these are the work of one and the same Spirit, and he gives them to each one, just as he determines (12:11). The diversity of gifts is derived from one Spirit. Some may have thought that different gifts reflected a diversity of belief.

The body is a unit . . . and though all its parts are many, they form one body. So it is with Christ (12:12). The use of the body as an image of diversity but unity was well used in the ancient world. The Roman philosopher Seneca, the brother of the Corinthian governor Gallio, noted: "All that you behold, that which comprises both god and man, is one—we are the parts of one great body."[125]

For we were all baptized by one Spirit into one body—whether Jews or Greeks, slave or free—and we were all given the one Spirit to drink (12:13). Paul has moved from the Old Testament parallel drawn from Exodus where the people of God "drank the same spiritual drink" (10:4) to the New Testament experience of the Holy Spirit.

The Body of the Church (12:14–31)

This discussion of body parts recalls the way that in the ancient world small models of parts of the body were dedicated in sanctuaries of the healing god Asklepios.[126] One of the most famous sanctuaries of the god was at Epidauros in the Argolid, some forty kilometers (twenty-five miles) southeast of Corinth. Corinth itself had a sanctuary of Asklepios, called the Asklepieion.[127] It is perhaps not coincidental that Paul links the body parts to gifts of healing.

If the foot should say . . . if the ear should say (12:15–16). Paul uses a series of rhetorical questions to make his point.

God has arranged the parts in the body . . . just as he wanted them to be (12:18). As God created the body, so God has initiated the church with all its diversity.

The eye cannot say to the hand, "I don't need you!" And the head cannot say to the feet, "I don't need you!" (12:21). The idea of speaking eyes and listening hands and feet might amuse, but one suspects that some of the elite members may have been formulating these phrases when confronted with poorer members of the Christian community as they met together to celebrate the Lord's Supper.

On the contrary, those parts of the body that seem to be weaker are indispensable (12:22). No part of the body is redundant, in the sense that the diversity of the Christian community reinforces the fact that Christ died for all people.

The parts that we think are less honorable we treat with special honor. And the parts that are unpresentable are treated with special modesty (12:23–24). In the Roman colony of Corinth, the norm was to show individuals draped.[128] This was in marked contrast to the Greek honorific statues, especially of victorious athletes, erected in sanctuaries such as Olympia or Isthmia or in public spaces of their home towns, where an individual might be shown naked. An exception at Corinth was the pair of statues to Gaius and Lucius, the intended heirs of the emperor Augustus, who were shown naked. However, nakedness was also linked to divinity and hinted at the cult of the imperial family. One of the scandals in the Jewish world was the introduction of Greek

games to Jerusalem, where male individuals were expected to compete naked.

There should be no division in the body, but . . . its parts should have equal concern for each other (12:25). Once again Paul refers to the division within the Christian community at Corinth (see 1:10; 3:3; 11:18).

If one part suffers, every part suffers with it; if one part is honored, every part rejoices with it (12:26). A similar lesson is found in the Jewish historian Josephus: "If one part suffers, all parts suffer together."[129]

You are the body of Christ, and each one of you is a part of it (12:27). Whereas it was only possible to take an active part in the life of a colony like Corinth if you were a male Roman citizen and had sufficient wealth to stand for public office, all could play a role in the life of the church. No one can say he or she does not have a part; passivity is not an option!

In the church God has appointed first of all apostles, second prophets, third teachers, then workers of miracles, also those having gifts of healing, those able to help others, those with gifts of administration, and those speaking in different kinds of tongues (12:28). Church order is ordained by God. The first three form a group consisting of specific individuals in the church, beginning with apostles (like Paul), who hold first place because of their special role as communicators of teaching. The appearance of "teachers" suggests that "teaching" (and with it learning and maturity) were integral to the life of the early church. The second group consists of those holding specific gifts, also men-

PARTS OF THE BODY

People who claimed healing by Asclepius offered representations of their healed body part to the god. These are on display in the Corinth Museum.

▼

DO WE FEEL THAT WE HAVE SOME-thing to offer the life of our local church? Is there just scope for the confident, the musicians, the public speakers? We need to remember that God has equipped *each one of us* for a role in the life of our church community. Perhaps it is to give that welcoming smile at the church door, which helps to reassure the newcomer. Or it may be to ensure that the building is clean and fresh for a Sunday service. All gifts enhance the body and life of the church. What can I offer?

tioned in 12:8–10. Paul mentions teachers and leadership in Romans 12:6–8, written from Corinth: "If your gift . . . is teaching, then teach; . . . if it is leadership, then govern diligently."

Eagerly desire the greater gifts. And now I will show you the most excellent way (12:31). Paul does not want the Corinthians to rank their spiritual gifts but to look at those that will build up their body and bring a widespread understanding of the good news that has been proclaimed among them.

The Priority of Relationships over Achievements (13:1–13)

But have not love (13:1). The word Paul uses for love here is *agapē*, a word used in the LXX to translate God's love. The Christian concept of love contrasts with the two other Greek words: *erōs*, which can be translated as a love of passion or "desire," and *philia*, defined as "friendly love" or "affection."[130] It is perhaps ironic that Paul writes an essay on love to a city whose patron deity was in fact Aphrodite, the goddess of love, whose temple was situated on the Akrocorinth. Aphrodite (the Roman god Venus) was thought to be the ancestor of Julius Caesar, and a temple to her was a central feature of the Julian Forum at Rome. Augustus, as the adopted son of Julius, also promoted his links with Aphrodite.

I am only a resounding gong or a clanging cymbal (13:1). The "resounding gong" is in fact literally "echoing bronze." Corinth was famous in the ancient world for a special bronze alloy (made of copper and tin) that was even used on the doors of the temple at Jerusalem.[131] The "cymbal" was an instrument that could be used in pagan worship; reliefs of the cult of the Anatolian deity Cybele show worshipers using cymbals.[132] The bronze gong was the musical accompaniment to the gods who are no gods (cf. 8:5), and the tongues or languages of men and of angels are equally meaningless in the worship of the living God if love is absent.

Can fathom all mysteries and all knowledge (13:2). "Mysteries" (*mystēria*) and "knowledge" (*gnōsis*), echo Daniel 2:19–23, 28, especially in the LXX.

If I have a faith that can move mountains (13:2). This may be a reference to Jesus' own teaching: "I tell you the truth, if anyone says to this mountain, 'Go, throw yourself into the sea,' and does not doubt in his heart but believes that what he says will happen, it will be done for him" (Mark 11:23; see also Matt. 17:20).

If I give all I possess to the poor (13:3). This phrase may pick up on the teaching of Jesus: "If you want to be perfect, go, sell your possessions and give to the poor, and you will have treasure in heaven. Then come, follow me" (Matt. 19:21; cf. Luke 12:33). The Greek word for "property" is the same in Jesus' teaching and Paul's writing.

Surrender my body to the flames (13:3). This may refer to the persecution of Jews by fire, such as Daniel's three friends in the fiery furnace (Dan. 3), or it may allude to Christian martyrdom. In the 60s, Nero persecuted Christians in Rome by igniting them as burning torches.[133]

Love . . . does not boast (13:4). This is the first instance of the verb *perpereuomai* in Greek literature, though the adjective is found in Polybius relating to "windbags."[134]

[Love] is not proud (13:4). The pride addressed here was characteristic of parts of the Corinthian church (4:6, 18–19 ["arrogance"]; 5:2). Literally the Greek means "puffed up"; earlier Paul contrasted knowledge and love by using the two verbs "to puff up" and "to build up": "Knowledge puffs up, but love builds up" (8:1).

REFLECTIONS

IN THE ANDREW LLOYD-WEBBER musical *Aspects of Love* this line occurs: "Love, love changes everything." Paul sees love as providing the most excellent way for the life of the church. Yet so often our emphasis is on biblical teaching (important though that is!) or on social concern (vital though that is!); we forget to concentrate on encouraging each other to allow love to permeate our Christian ministry and service. Where can I start?

[Love] is not rude (13:5). Paul uses a verb that carries with it the concept of shame; the same verb in his section on virgins ("acting improperly" in 7:36). Such shaming was unacceptable in Roman elite society and should not be allowed to become acceptable in the Christian community.

[Love] is not self-seeking (13:5). Earlier Paul used this phrase when discussing the freedom of the Christian in the context of attending pagan festivals (10:24)—in particular of his own ministry: "For I am not seeking my own good but the good of many" (10:33).

[Love] keeps no record of wrongs (13:5). The record-keeping of wrongs uses a Greek phrase that resonates with the LXX of Zechariah 8:17, which is translated (from the Hebrew) as "do not plot evil against your neighbor."

Love never fails (13:8). The Greek sense implies "to fall" or "to fall short."

Prophecies . . . will cease . . . tongues . . . will be stilled . . . knowledge . . . will pass away (13:8). Paul returns to the group of issues he addressed earlier (12:8, 10; 13:2).

For we know in part and we prophesy in part, but when perfection comes, the imperfect disappears (13:9–10). The gifts familiar to the church will no longer be important when the end time comes. Gifts for edification will no longer be required.

When I was a child, I talked like a child, I thought like a child, I reasoned like a child. When I became a man, I put childish ways behind me (13:11). Paul is perhaps alluding to the classical form of education that placed an emphasis on clear thinking processes and public oratory. Children were expected to learn how to develop arguments and to present sophisticated cases.

Now we see but a poor reflection as in a mirror; then we shall see face to face (13:12). Mirrors in the Roman world were formed by a disc of polished metal, perhaps silver or bronze, placed on a handle. The viewing side might be convex and the reverse patterned.[135] The cult statue of Aphrodite on the Akrocorinth showed the deity, who in the Greek period had had a military role in protecting the city, admiring herself in the reflection of a shield.

Now these three remain: faith, hope and love. But the greatest of these is love (13:13). The combination of faith, hope, and love may have been a feature of the Christian gospel; see, for example, Paul's use of these three characteristics in Romans 5:1–5, written from Corinth. Love needs to be worked out in the life of believers, as Paul has tried to explain through this chapter.

Functioning in the Secular and Christian *Ekklēsia* (14:1–25)

Paul now develops how the concept of love will apply to the use of individual gifts in the life of the church community.

Eagerly desire spiritual gifts (14:1). This picks up on the argument from 12:31: "But eagerly desire the greater gifts."

Everyone who prophesies speaks to men for their strengthening, encouragement and comfort (14:3). Paul clearly sees

◀
ROMAN MIRROR

prophecy as a ministry focusing on the people of God, with the result that they are strengthened, encouraged, and comforted. Such a role was unusual in the religious framework of the ancient world. The word for "strengthening" (*oikodomē*) is drawn from architecture, where it means a "building." Thus the New Testament prophet is envisaged as the architect who lays the foundation and builds his structure in a systematic way. The buildings given to the Roman colony by rich benefactors were a credit to the city; in the same way the "strengthening" of the church at Corinth was to the glory of God.

What good will I be to you, unless I bring you some revelation or knowledge or prophecy or word of instruction? (14:6). Knowledge here translates the Greek *gnōsis*, a word often used in Greek philosophy.

In the case of lifeless things that make sounds, such as the flute or harp, how will anyone know what tune is being played unless there is a distinction in the notes? (14:7). Musical events were one aspect of some of the cultural events that came to be attached to athletic events in the Greek cities of the east. Thus proficiency in these musical forms was expected. The word translated "harp" (*kithara*) denotes a stringed instrument, often depicted in classical art as played by the god Apollo.

If the trumpet does not sound a clear call, who will get ready for battle? (14:8). This military allusion is derived from the way troops were controlled in battle. A trumpet would need to be heard over the din of fighting. Trumpets were also part of athletic festivals, often forming the first event so that the winner could have the privilege of "announcing" or trumpeting subsequent actions.

Unless you speak intelligible words with your tongue (14:9). The emphasis in the Greek is on clearly distinct words uttered by individuals.

▶

KITHARA

A marble representation of a *kithara* on a statue of Apollo.

There are all sorts of languages in the world, yet none of them is without meaning (14:10). Corinth itself was at the very least a bilingual city, with Latin as the official language, but Greek was in common usage (even the graffiti cut on pottery from the first century A.D. uses Greek). Paul's letter was itself written in Greek. With the ports of Lechaeum and Cenchrea, languages from all over the Mediterranean were likely heard in the city. Paul may have in mind the Jewish view that languages were created at the time of the tower of Babel (Gen. 11:9).

I am a foreigner to the speaker, and he is a foreigner to me (14:11). The Greek word for "foreigner" (*barbaros*) is suggestive. To the Corinthians foreigners speak languages that sound like "bar-bar."

Since you are eager to have spiritual gifts, try to excel in gifts that build up the church (14:12). The Corinthian Christians are seen as (lit.) "zealots" in their eagerness to acquire spiritual gifts. Paul instructs them to direct the energy of their seeking to the building up of the church, just as those in the wider Corinthian society sought to promote themselves through the building projects in the colony.

Anyone who speaks in a tongue should pray that he may interpret what he says (14:13). Paul's emphasis is not on seeking for a different type of gift to build up the church, but rather clarity on the use of gifts in the worshiping life of the Christian community.

If I pray in a tongue, my spirit prays, but my mind is unfruitful (14:14). For some the working of the Spirit in their lives may lead to praying "in a tongue."

So what shall I do? I will pray with my spirit, but I will also pray with my mind; I will sing with my spirit, but I will also sing with my mind (14:15). We could paraphrase this question as, "What are the implications for me?" Although an individual may "pray in a tongue," the use of the "mind" suggests that Paul encourages those with the gift of tongues to use an intelligible language like Greek or Latin in the meetings so that all can understand.

How can one who finds himself among those who do not understand say "Amen" to your thanksgiving? (14:16). The Hebrew word "Amen"—meaning "that which is sure and valid"[136]—was one used by those gathered in a Jewish synagogue to give endorsement to what was said; it is used here in the context of Christian worship.

You may be giving thanks well enough, but the other man is not edified (14:17). Thanksgiving is an appropriate part to Christian worship, but the encouragement of fellow believers is more significant.

I speak in tongues more than all of you (14:18). Presumably this side of Paul was largely unknown to the Christian community in Corinth. While he was with them, he had emphasized building up the Corinthian church rather than using this special gift of tongues. If the apostle Paul can show restraint, so can members of the congregation.

In the church I would rather speak five intelligible words to instruct others than ten thousand words in a tongue (14:19). "Ten thousand" (*myrias*) was the largest number that could be expressed in Greek, so its use here implies innumerable—in today's language, "a trillion, trillion."

Stop thinking like children. In regard to evil be infants, but in your thinking be adults (14:20). Children (*paidia*) suggests young people in training. Paul is

◄

HARBOR AT LECHAEUM

The western port of Corinth.

suggesting that the believers in Corinth be more mature and developed in their thinking.

"Through men of strange tongues and through the lips of foreigners I will speak to this people, but even then they will not listen to me" (14:21). The quotation is an abridged form of Isaiah 28:11–12: "Very well then, with foreign lips and strange tongues God will speak to this people, to whom he said, 'This is the resting place, let the weary rest'; and, 'This is the place of repose'—but they would not listen." Paul may also have had in his mind a verse from Deuteronomy 28:49: "The LORD will bring a nation against you from far away, from the ends of the earth, like an eagle swooping down, a nation whose language you will not understand."

Tongues, then, are a sign, not for believers but for unbelievers; prophecy, however, is for believers, not for unbelievers (14:22). Paul's mature reading of the Jewish law and the Old Testament in general leads him to conclusions about the gifts of tongues and prophecy.

So if the whole church comes together and everyone speaks in tongues, and ... some unbelievers come in, will they not say that you are out of your mind? **(14:23).** The verb translated "are out of your mind" (*mainomai*) is one that was used to describe the frenzy of mystery religions (see comments on 4:1), such as that of the Greek god of wine, Dionysos. Paul wants the church to be different from these mystery cults.

If an unbeliever ... comes in while everybody is prophesying, he will be convinced by all that he is a sinner. ... So he will fall down and worship God (14:24–25). The purpose of Christian worship is to include and to draw people to God. This is in marked contrast to mystery cults, such as that surrounding the worship of Demeter and Persephone at Eleusis in Attica, where the uninitiated were excluded from the events and those who participated were forbidden from speaking of what went on. This is well illustrated by the usually informative Pausanias, who was clearly an initiate: "My dream forbade the description of the things within the wall of the sanctuary [of Demeter at Eleusis], and the uninitiated are of course not permitted to learn that which they are prevented from seeing."[137]

Ordering Corporate Worship (14:26–40)

The Corinthian Christians needed to think about the implications of meeting together in worship on a regular basis. How can they strengthen the body of the church?

When you come together, everyone has a hymn, or a word of instruction, a revelation, a tongue or an interpretation. All of these must be done for the strengthening of the church (14:26). Paul returns to the architectural image of building the

▶

DIONYSUS

A mosaic of the god at the Corinth museum.

church. The buildings of the Roman colony could be placed on terraces or on podia, supported by columns, and roofed in marble. These elements created the building but would look odd standing without the others (as indeed a reconstructed column can look lost in the midst of an archaeological site). So each element of the worship needs to complement the other.

If anyone speaks in a tongue, two—or at the most three—should speak, one at a time, and someone must interpret (14:27). Some of the cults of antiquity allowed ecstatic utterances, which were incomprehensible to those attending the rites. If these utterances in the Christian worship are from God, they must be treated in an orderly way so that they can be understood.

If there is no interpreter, the speaker should keep quiet in the church and speak to himself and God (14:28). The oracles of antiquity were well-known for giving ambiguous messages, which could be misinterpreted by those who had sought advice from the gods (in particular, from Apollo at Delphi). Christians must

ensure that any message from God is interpreted by somebody in the community so that the community can benefit.

You can all prophesy in turn so that everyone may be instructed and encouraged (14:31). Two key elements of Christian worship, instruction and encouragement, were largely absent from the worship of the pagan deities in the colony. This type of worship was new.

The spirits of prophets are subject to the control of prophets (14:32). Christian worship is subject to control and order by designated leaders.

For God is not a God of disorder but of peace (14:33). Disorder was one of the negative characteristics of the church at Corinth, which Paul addresses in 2 Corinthians 12:20.

Women should remain silent in the churches. They are not allowed to speak (14:34). This verse needs to be balanced with what Paul has said earlier, where he expects women to be praying and prophesying in the fellowship (11:6).

Women . . . must be in submission . . . as the Law says (14:34). Paul is clearly alluding to the Garden of Eden, where God tells Eve, "Your desire will be for your husband, and he will rule over you" (Gen. 3:16b). The Greek word *gynē* can be translated as "woman" or "wife." Thus, Paul is most likely addressing the proper function of wives in the Christian assembly, where proper respect for their husbands needed to be shown. It should be noted that the specific context for these comments comes from Paul's addressing the issue of public prophecy for the edification of the church.

If they want to inquire about something, they should ask their own husbands at home; for it is disgraceful for a woman to speak in the church (14:35). If a husband were to make a prophecy, it would perhaps be inappropriate for the wife to question the prophecy in a public gathering; according to social expectations, the wife should ask questions at home. This makes sense if Paul does not want wives to prophesy when their husbands are present.

Did the word of God originate with you? Or are you the only people it has reached? (14:36). The balance for the Corinthian Christians is that they are one of a number of churches that now stretch across the cities of the eastern Roman empire. They may live in one of the most important cities of the province, but they need to learn humility.

What I am writing to you is the Lord's command (14:37). Paul the apostle (1:1) is writing these words to the Corinthians at God's command. He brings his apostolic authority to bear on this issue of order in the service of worship.

Be eager to prophesy, and do not forbid speaking in tongues (14:39). Public teaching needed to be encouraged ("be eager" is lit. "be zealous").

Everything should be done in a fitting and orderly way (14:40). The word "fitting" is a word with elite overtones and can be translated as seemly or honorable. Meetings of the *ekklēsia* needed to be conducted in a dignified fashion.

Evidence and Belief (15:1–11)

When Paul addressed the Areopagus at Athens, the pagan hearers sneered at the ridiculous suggestion of a bodily resurrection (Acts 17:32). But those Greeks and Romans trained in Greek, and especially Platonic philosophy, would understand about the immortality of the soul.

I want to remind you of the gospel I preached to you, which you received and on which you have taken your stand (15:1). Paul's starting point is to find the common belief that all Christians shared, especially in the light of the pagan world around them. Note also his similar message to Christians in Galatia: "I want you to know, brothers, that the gospel I preached is not something that man made up" (Gal. 1:11). The gospel of Jesus is not like the fantastic stories connected with the pagan gods. The Roman travel writer Pausanias, for example, later recounted the story of the miraculous preservation of the baby Kypselos—the future tyrant of Corinth—when his mother placed him in a chest at birth; a chest that supposedly could still be seen at Olympia in Pausanias's day.[138] The gospel of Jesus is based on fact, not fiction.

By this gospel you are saved, if you hold firmly to the word I preached to you. Otherwise, you have believed in vain (15:2). The Corinthian Christians had understood the vanity, the emptiness, of the pagan deities that filled their city and required acts of piety. Paul brings them back to the essentials of the Christian gospel through which they received salvation.

For what I received I passed on to you as of first importance (15:3). Paul's argument is parallel to an earlier one in the letter concerning the Lord's Supper: "For I received from the Lord what I also passed on to you" (11:23). This type of language probably reflects the Jewish form of instruction. What follows appears to be an early Christian creed that contains the "basic" Christian doctrines (15:3–5).

Christ died for our sins according to the Scriptures (15:3). The Scriptures Paul is alluding to are the books of the Old Testament; in other words, these books point to the need for the Messiah to die for our sins. Paul perhaps had in mind the picture of the Suffering Servant of Isaiah, who "was pierced for our transgressions, he was crushed for our iniquities" (Isa. 53:5). This language resonates with the words of Jesus at the Last Supper: "This is my body, which is for you" (1 Cor. 11:24). Paul emphasizes the fact that Jesus died for our sins as the Christ, the anointed Messiah.

He was buried . . . he was raised on the third day according to the Scriptures (15:4). The doctrine of the resurrection of Jesus Christ was central to the early Christians. Peter's speech in Jerusalem at Pentecost emphasized how the resurrection had been predicted by David in Psalm 16:10b (quoted in Acts 2:27). Similar to the present passage is 1 Thessalonians 4:14, probably written on Paul's first visit to Corinth: "We believe that Jesus died and rose again." "The third day" may be derived from Jesus' own teaching to his disciples about his resurrection in connection with the temple at Jerusalem: "Destroy this temple, and I will raise it again in three days" (John 2:19; see also Matt. 26:61; Mark 15:58). The "third day" may also pick up on Hosea 6:2: "After two days he will revive us; on the third day he will restore us, that we may live in his presence." Burial presupposes death and excludes misunderstanding about Jesus' physical death on the cross. Matthew recalled the misleading story derived from the guards that Jesus' disciples "came during the night and stole him away while we were asleep," an account that "has been widely circulated among the Jews to this day" (Matt. 28:13, 15).

He appeared to Peter, and then to the Twelve (15:5). As burial presupposed death, so resurrection was confirmed by appearances to trustworthy witnesses. These were no vague appearances that formed part of a folklore or mythology about Jesus; at the time of writing, Peter and the other disciples could be pressed about what they had seen and witnessed. The appearance to Peter was a cry of the early disciples: "It is true! The Lord has risen and has appeared to Simon" (Luke 24:34). Paul's language here resembles Jesus' words when he appeared to the disciples: "This is what is written: 'The Christ will suffer and rise from the dead on the third day'" (24:46).

He appeared to more than five hundred of the brothers at the same time (15:6). This appearance is not recorded in any of the Gospel accounts of the post-resurrection appearances of the risen Jesus. There

---

REFLECTIONS

IF WE THINK BACK TO OUR FIRST SCHOOL, WE CAN probably recall (hopefully with affection!) our first teachers. They were the ones who set us off on the path of learning, on the way to adulthood. Paul takes the Corinthians back to the point when they first believed. It is so easy for people to forget why they first trusted Jesus Christ as their Lord and their Savior. Perhaps they want to look "mature" in the eyes of their friends. Yet our Christian life started when we realized what it meant for Jesus Christ to die on the cross for our sins: "By this gospel you are saved" (15:2).

were others available in the first century besides those recorded in the Gospels.

Then he appeared to James, then to all the apostles (15:7). Paul had met James, "the Lord's brother," at Jerusalem at the start of his ministry (Gal. 1:19). The "apostles" may be another way of referring to the "Twelve" (15:5), though it might include others who had seen their risen Lord.

Last of all he appeared to me also, as to one abnormally born (15:8). Paul has already referred to meeting Jesus on the road to Damascus (9:1; see Acts 9). "Abnormally born" translates a word that can denote either a miscarriage or an abortion. Perhaps some of the Christians at Corinth dismissed Paul's position as an apostle because he had not been one of the Twelve or questioned his becoming an apostle in an abnormal route after having been a chief persecutor of Christians.

For I am the least of the apostles and do not even deserve to be called an apostle (15:9). Paul had come to the Corinthians in "weakness and fear, and much trembling" (2:3), hardly what was considered to have been the stature for an apostle.

But by the grace of God I am what I am, and his grace to me was not without effect. No, I worked harder than all of them—yet not I, but the grace of God that was with me (15:10). Paul's earlier hard work had gone into pursuing the early followers of Jesus: "as for zeal, persecuting the church" (Phil. 3:6). Yet Paul was transformed by the grace of God.

Whether . . . I or they, this is what we preach, and this is what you believed (15:11). Paul's preaching on the resurrection was in keeping with other teachers of the church, presumably including Apollos and Cephas (cf. 1:12); the Corinthians are the ones who have moved away from that teaching.

Immortality (15:12–34)

Paul now develops a series of six "ifs" relating to the beliefs of some of the Corinthian Christians. This rebuffs the view held by some that there was no resurrection of the dead.

How can some of you say that there is no resurrection of the dead? (15:12). The resurrection was central to the preaching and teaching of the church from the earliest days. For example, Peter on Pentecost proclaimed that "God raised [Jesus of Nazareth] from the dead, freeing him from the agony of death, because it was impossible for death to keep its hold on him" (Acts 2:24). Both Jewish and Roman authorities had had ample opportunity to reject this teaching by presenting an alternative to the Christian message of the resurrection, but none had presented a convincing case to the contrary.

If there is no resurrection of the dead, then not even Christ has been raised (15:13). A commonly held view in the ancient world at the time, and in the province of Achaia in particular (see Acts 17:32a), was a disbelief in the possibility of dead people rising back to life. Paul uses this mistaken view to show that it was incompatible with Christian belief.

If Christ has not been raised, our preaching is useless and so is your faith (15:14). However eloquent the teaching, however vibrant the outworking of faith, the core of Christian belief and life is the resurrection of Jesus Christ.

More than that, we are then found to be false witnesses about God (15:15). The integrity of Paul and the apostles is now at stake. Paul sees the presentation of the resurrection in legal terms with witnesses bearing testimony.

If the dead are not raised, then Christ has not been raised either (15:16). The logical extension of the argument presented by some of the Christians at Corinth is that Christ in whom they had placed their trust had not been raised. The resurrected Christ and the general resurrection of the dead are linked.

If Christ has not been raised, your faith is futile; you are still in your sins (15:17). Without the resurrection, there is no forgiveness of sins.

Then those also who have fallen asleep in Christ are lost (15:18). Those who have abandoned the worship of pagan deities are now addressed. The (flawed) logic is that the gods that the Corinthian Christians have rejected in response to the good news of Jesus Christ would save them. Paul is reducing the argument to the absurd so that the Corinthians can see afresh the power of the Christian gospel.

If only for this life we have hope in Christ, we are to be pitied more than all men (15:19). The logical conclusion of the argument held by some of the Corinthian Christians means that the Christian faith has no place or relevance against the multiplicity of religious expression found in the colony; Paul wants the Christian community to see the error in their argument.

But Christ has indeed been raised from the dead, the firstfruits of those who have fallen asleep (15:20). The Christian view of death is in marked contrast to that held in the ancient world. The Christians perceived death as no more than sleep, whereas pagan society saw it was important to protect the dead in the next life by sometimes placing apotropaic images (i.e., images to ward off evil) above the grave. The "firstfruits" was a concept familiar to both Jews and Gentiles; they were often offered to the gods in the sanctuaries of the Greek world.

Since death came through a man, the resurrection of the dead comes also through a man (15:21). The allusion is to the fruit of "the tree of the knowledge of good and evil" in the Garden of Eden; "for when you eat of it you will surely die" (Gen. 2:17).

As in Adam all die, so in Christ all will be made alive (15:22). This alludes to the curse on Adam: "For dust you are and to dust you will return" (Gen. 3:19).

Then the end will come, when he hands over the kingdom to God the Father after he has destroyed all dominion, authority and power (15:24). Such words must have been disturbing when Paul wrote them to the Christians at Corinth. The familiar authority structures they are accustomed to—the emperor, the Roman senate, the provincial governor, the Roman army, the civic magistrates—will all disappear. These structures, which brought peace to the Mediterranean world in their lifetime, will be no more.

He must reign until he has put all his enemies under his feet (15:25). This view picks up on Psalm 110:1: "Sit at my right hand until I make your enemies a footstool for your feet." Residents of Corinth know how enemies of Rome are brought before the emperor in chains.

The last enemy to be destroyed is death (15:26). Roman emperors might look for new territory to acquire on the fringes of the existing empire. For the Christian the ultimate battle and victory is over death. The resurrection serves the same function as the triumphal arches at the city of Rome, which marked the final defeat of a foe.

For he "has put everything under his feet" (15:27). The quotation is from the Psalms (8:6) which affirms, "O LORD, our Lord, how majestic is your name in all the earth!" It is also a psalm that speaks of "the son of man," a title of the Messiah or Christ (see Heb. 5–9).

Then the Son himself will be made subject to him who put everything under him, so that God may be all in all (15:28). The Corinthian Christians are brought back to the Psalms: "You have made him ruler over the works of your hands; you put everything under his feet" (Ps. 8:6). God's authority will be in force.

Now if there is no resurrection, what will those do who are baptized for the dead? (15:29). It seems as if members of the church at Corinth were conducting baptism services for those—probably members of their families—who had already died. The precise details are unclear and there is no obvious precedent from the pagan world.

As for us, why do we endanger ourselves every hour? (15:30). Travel in the ancient world was a dangerous thing, and Paul himself experienced shipwreck in his travels (cf. 2 Cor. 11:23–28; Acts 27). Yet it was dangerous to speak out against the beliefs and views of the ancient world, and Paul had faced arrest and a beating at Philippi and a trial at Athens before the Areopagus. Ultimately, he was to lose his life in speaking of his risen Lord.

I die every day—I mean that, brothers— just as surely as I glory over you in Christ Jesus our Lord (15:31). Paul imposes a firm discipline on himself rather than

▶Paul Quotes an Athenian Playwright

Paul's pithy observation, "Bad company corrupts good character" (15:33) is actually a quotation from a work of Menander, where the immediate context is prostitution.[A-39] Menander was an Athenian comic playwright, whose first play was produced in 321 B.C. He is known to have written at least a hundred plays. Thus, Paul is using a quotation that would be familiar to a Greek-speaking audience. Plays were an important part in the cultural life of the Roman colony at Corinth. The theater lay to the northwest of the forum. It had been an integral part of the original Greek city and had been restored in the early part of the Roman settlement.[A-40] It has been estimated to hold some 15,000 people. One of the benefactions to enhance the theater was the donation by an *aedile* of the city, Erastus, who paved a piazza at the east entrance; his benefaction was recorded by an inscription cut into the slabs and filled with bronze letters.[A-41]

adopting an attitude, common in the ancient world, that self-indulgence was important.[139]

If I fought wild beasts in Ephesus for merely human reasons (15:32). Hunts were often a feature of games established in the Greek east on a Roman model. They were an unusual feature in the first century A.D., but an inscription from the Roman colony of Pisidian Antioch records the gift of such an event by Caius Albucius Firmus in his will.[140] Animal games are likely to have formed part of the civic life at Ephesus. Paul is writing this letter to the Corinthian church from Ephesus, and this imagery reflects the opposition that he is facing.

Let us eat and drink, for tomorrow we die (15:32). Paul quotes here from Isaiah 22:13. The belief in eating and drinking (i.e., self-indulgence) was part of Epicurean belief.

Come back to your senses as you ought, and stop sinning; for there are some who are ignorant of God (15:34). Paul may be suggesting here that those who deny the bodily resurrection feel they can adopt the ethical standards of the pagans in the Roman colony.[141] But Christians will stand before the judgment throne of God, where they will be accountable for their actions. If they look ahead to this day, they will change their lifestyle.

Resurrection (15:35–58)

The emphasis in the chapter moves from the "dead" to the word "body." The Corinthian Christians are presented with questions and answers about death.

With what kind of body will they come? (15:35). The roads leading to the gates of cities in the ancient world were lined with cemeteries, often with images of the deceased. It was not uncommon for families to visit graves and leave offerings, and it must have troubled Corinthians who knew from firsthand experience that bodies decomposed. How could these bones be turned into bodies?

How foolish! (15:36). This translates the Greek word *aphrōn* ("foolish man"; lit., "without sense"). It was often used to

bottom left

CORINTH AND EPHESUS

Ephesus was just across the Aegean Sea from Corinth.

bottom right

THE MEDITERRANEAN WORLD

Paul would travel from Ephesus to Macedonia and on to Corinth as he gathered the collection to take to Jerusalem.

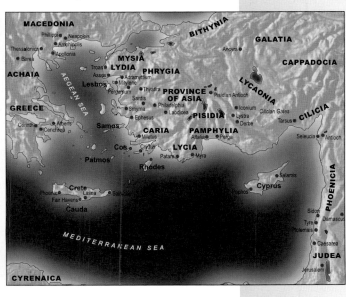

describe inanimate statues. But the word would also resonate with Greek-speaking Jews, who would recognize it as the one used in the LXX for "fool," especially in Proverbs.

When you sow, you do not plant the body that will be, but just a seed (15:37). Paul uses the agricultural imagery to explain the transformation. The Corinthia was an area suitable for growing large amounts of grain to support the large population of the colony.

But God gives it a body as he has determined, and to each kind of seed he gives its own body (15:38). God the Creator lies behind this resurrection, just as he lies behind the natural world.

All flesh is not the same: Men . . . animals . . . birds . . . fish (15:39). These four different types also appear in the created order in Genesis but in the reverse of how they appear in here: "Let the water teem with living creatures, and let birds fly above the earth" (Gen. 1:20); "let the land produce living creatures . . . livestock . . . and wild animals" (1:24); and "let us make man in our image" (1:26). Such a view is derived from Paul's view of the Old Testament.

Heavenly bodies and . . . earthly bodies (15:40). Science was well developed in the ancient world. "Heavenly bodies" may relate the sun and other bodies.

The sun has one kind of splendor, the moon another and the stars another; and star differs from star in splendor (15:41). The Greek scientist Empedokles from Akragas in southern Sicily had written about the cosmos in the fifth century B.C. He attempted to explain night and day. Such views formed part of Roman education.[142]

The body that is sown is perishable, it is raised imperishable (15:42). The analogy of the transformed seed is used for the transformation of the body that decays in the grave but is transformed through the resurrection.

"The first man Adam became a living being"; the last Adam, a life-giving spirit (15:45). The allusion is to the creation of Adam and specifically to when God "breathed into his nostrils the breath of life" (Gen. 2:7).

The spiritual did not come first, but the natural, and after that the spiritual (15:46). The emphasis is on the sequence of the natural then the spiritual, rather than some philosophical idea that there is a spiritual state in conjunction with the physical.

The first man was of the dust of the earth (15:47). The earlier city of Corinth made use of the surrounding clay beds to produce fine figure-decorated pottery, which

GREEK COUNTRYSIDE NEAR THE ACROCORINTH
▼

is found in some quantity around the shores of the Mediterranean. Such an allusion to Adam made of clay may have had special significance to the Corinthian Christians.

As was the earthly man, so are those who are of the earth; and as is the man from heaven, so also are those who are of heaven (15:48). Ancestry was important in a city like Corinth, where status was valued; important ancestors meant high status. The ancestry that matters for the Corinthian Christians is that they are now descendants of Jesus Christ by faith.

Just as we have borne the likeness of the earthly man, so shall we bear the likeness of the man from heaven (15:49). If the Corinthians looked at the portraits of the Roman emperors, in particular those of Augustus and his heirs (Gaius and Lucius), they would see a family likeness in the treatment of the hair. No doubt Roman sculptors intended this so that people could be convinced by the legitimacy of rule. For Christians, they need to show the characteristics of Jesus Christ in their community to emphasize the validity of their professed faith.

I tell you a mystery (15:51). Unlike the mystery cults, such as Demeter and Kore at Eleusis in Attica at the other end of the isthmus of Corinth, where mysteries were kept quiet, the Christian gospel, the good news of the resurrection, must be told.

For the trumpet will sound, the dead will be raised imperishable, and we will be changed (15:52). Paul may have in mind Zechariah 9:14, a prophecy about the Lord's appearing: "The Sovereign LORD will sound the trumpet."

For the perishable must clothe itself with the imperishable, and the mortal with immortality (15:53). In the Greek east there was a philosophical belief about the immorality of the soul. For the Christian the resurrection of Christ allows the individual to be "clothed" with eternal life.

Then the saying . . . will come true: "Death has been swallowed up in victory" (15:54). This appears to be an adapted form of Isaiah 25:8: "He will swallow up death forever," though the word "victory" does not appear.

"Where, O death, is your victory? Where, O death, is your sting?" (15:55). The context for this quotation is a modified version of Hosea 13:14: "I will ransom them from the power of the grave; I will redeem them from death."

The sting of death is sin (15:56). The result of Adam and Eve's disobeying God and eating the fruit from the tree of the knowledge of good and evil was death (Gen. 2:17).

God . . . gives us the victory through our Lord Jesus Christ (15:57). Corinthian Christians would be familiar with the way the Roman emperor celebrated famous victories, especially when new provinces were acquired. Such secular celebrations—though with religious overtones, such as sacrifices—pale into insignificance with Christian rejoicing. The emperor Augustus passed through Corinth after the fall of Alexandria in 30 B.C. on his way to celebrate a triple triumph at Rome in August, 29 B.C.

Always give yourselves fully to the work of the Lord, because you know that your labor in the Lord is not in vain (15:58).

Paul develops this theme more completely in 2 Corinthians 5:8: "For we must all appear before the judgement seat of Christ, that each one may receive what is due to him for the things done while in the body, whether good or bad."

The Issue About the Collection for God's People (16:1–4)

In this closing section Paul focuses on Jerusalem, but he places his message within the Roman provincial structure; notice the stress on Galatia, Macedonia, and Asia.

Now about the collection for God's people: Do what I told the Galatian churches to do (16:1). Paul is picking up on the fifth of the issues put in the letter to him by the Corinthian church (see comments on 7:1). Under the Roman empire Jewish communities sent money to Jerusalem. Philo in his *Embassy to Gaius* records a letter of the proconsul Gaius Norbanus Flaccus to the magistrates at Ephesus: "Caesar has written to me saying that it is a special ancestral custom of the Jews, wherever they live, to meet and contribute money which they send to Jerusalem. He does not wish them to be prevented from doing this."[143] The difference with Corinth is that this is a Christian community with strong, though not exclusively, Gentile features. Paul is encouraging the Corinthian believers to identify with their Jewish-Christian fellow believers in Judea; the destination of Jerusalem for the collection is made clear (16:3).

The collection was a feature of Paul's third missionary journey. Starting from Antioch in Syria, Paul presumably took the Roman road up from Cilicia, which took him to such places as the key Roman colony of Pisidian Antioch in the Roman province of Galatia (Acts 18:23). If Paul wrote 1 Corinthians from Ephesus during the events described in Acts 19, he would have just passed through Galatia before entering Asia.

On the first day of every week, each one of you should set aside a sum of money in keeping with his income, saving it up (16:2). The calendar implies that the early Christians are following a Jewish pattern; the Roman calendar was dominated by feast days. The first day of the week was the day that Christ was found to have risen from the tomb—in other words, the day after the Jewish Sabbath. Note, for example, how the Christians in Troas met together "on the first day of the week . . . to break bread" (Acts 20:7). Presumably the Corinthian church follows a similar pattern of meeting on the day after the Jewish Sabbath, on what we now term Sunday. Paul is here advocating a planned and regular scheme of putting aside a sum of money (or perhaps even items in kind) for the benefit of the Christian community in Jerusalem. It is important to remember that the Corinthian church includes slaves and women, who probably do not have access to cash in their own right.

I will give letters of introduction to the men you approve (16:3). Few letters have survived from the ancient world because of their fragile nature. Some of the best examples written on papyri have been obtained from Egypt, though excavations at Vindolanda just south of Hadrian's Wall in northern England have revealed first century A.D. correspondence from the archive of the fort.[144] The gift Paul is collecting is to be accompanied to Jerusalem by members chosen by the Corinthian church; they will be responsible for the safety of the gift, but

PAUL ASKS THE CORINTHIAN CHURCH to respond to the needs in Jerusalem on a weekly basis. What Christian causes can we support in a regular and planned way? How can we develop our links with the bodies we support? How can we use our resources to help those of our Christian brothers and sisters in need?

they will also be able to carry personal messages between the two churches. It was common, even during the empire, for cities to send embassies to the emperor; this may be the model Paul has in mind for the delegation. The use of such messengers ensures Paul's integrity so that there will be no question whether he is acquiring the money for his own benefit.[145]

Your gift to Jerusalem (16:3). Paul describes this gift for Jerusalem and its purpose in Romans 15:25–28, where he notes that the provinces of Macedonia and Achaia (which includes Corinth) "were pleased to make a contribution for the poor among the saints in Jerusalem."

If it seems advisable for me to go also, they will accompany me (16:4). In 2 Corinthians 1:16 Paul records his intention for the Corinthian church to "send me on my way to Judea" with the collection.

Paul's Plans (16:5–9)

After I go through Macedonia, I will come to you—for I will be going through Macedonia (16:5). The journey that Paul is planning to make here is described in Acts 20:1–3. He deliberately chose the land route rather than sailing from Asia to Achaia. Macedonia was a Roman province in what is now northern Greece. It was a key province as its western frontier was defined by the Adriatic, and through the port of Dyrrachium gave access to Brundisium (modern Brindisi) and Italy. Macedonia also gave access to the Aegean on its south side. The whole province was traversed by the strategic Egnatian way, the Roman road that gave access to the eastern provinces. There is a possibility that Paul may have reached Corinth by sailing down the west coast of mainland Greece from Dyrrachium. In Romans 15:19, written from Corinth, perhaps during this intended stay, Paul notes that "from Jerusalem all the way around to Illyricum, I have fully proclaimed the gospel of Christ." Illyricum is the area to the north of Dyrrachium, and such a visit would make sense of the journey across Macedonia. Such a route would allow him to visit other important cities in the Peloponnese, such as the colony at Patras.

Perhaps I will stay with you awhile, or even spend the winter, so that you can help me on my journey (16:6). In Acts 20:3 Paul is recorded as staying three months in Greece (which presumably means the Roman province of Achaia). Most likely most of this time was spent in Corinth. Paul would avoid the dangerous winter season for sailing in the Mediterranean. The verb translated "help me on my journey" implies that the Corinthian Christians will provide Paul with the means to complete his journey, which may include traveling companions.[146]

I do not want to see you now and make only a passing visit; I hope to spend some time with you, if the Lord permits (16:7).

If Paul sails directly from Ephesus to Corinth, he will have to press on for Macedonia and will only be able to stay a short time in Corinth. If he goes by the land route, he will have opportunity for a longer stay at Corinth by wintering there.

I will stay on at Ephesus until Pentecost (16:8). This gives us the information that Paul is writing from the province of Asia in early spring, perhaps of A.D. 56. Pentecost was the Jewish festival, fifty days after Passover. (In the Christian calendar, Pentecost is calculated as fifty days from Easter and thus always falls on a Sunday.) Pentecost is also the time that the apostles were filled with the Holy Spirit (Acts 2:1), the day usually recognized as the birthday of the church. By Pentecost of the following year Paul planned on being in Jerusalem (Acts 20:16).

A great door for effective work has opened to me, and there are many who oppose me (16:9). The door is an image Paul uses elsewhere (2 Cor. 2:12; Col. 4:3). The effective work in Ephesus and the magnitude of the opposition is described in the account in Acts 19:23–41, where Demetrius the silversmith initiates a riot. Interestingly the account is placed between the dispatch of Timothy and Erastus for Macedonia and Paul's own departure (19:22; 20:1).

Timothy's Planned Visit (16:10–11)

If Timothy comes (16:10). Timothy's mission has been noted earlier in 4:17.

Send him on his way in peace so that he may return to me. I am expecting him along with the brothers (16:11). Peace may be an allusion to the Jewish *shalom*.

The "brothers" may include Erastus, who was sent with Timothy from Ephesus (Acts 19:22).

Apollos and the Appointment of Leaders in the Church (16:12–18)

Now about our brother Apollos: I strongly urged him to go to you with the brothers . . . he will go when he has the opportunity (16:12). This is the sixth issue raised by the Corinthian church. Apollos is clearly with Paul in Ephesus, and the Corinthian church has presumably requested his return. Paul is urging him to return to Corinth with the delegation from the church (presumably those mentioned in 16:17). Given the earlier tensions and perceived rivalries at Corinth (1:12), Paul's urging of Apollos demonstrates his confidence in his "brother" and coworker in the gospel of Jesus Christ.

The household of Stephanas were the first converts in Achaia, and they have devoted themselves to the service of the saints (16:15). "The household of Stephanas" (mentioned also in 1:16) were the "first converts" of Paul's ministry in the province of Achaia. Achaia was the name of the Roman province covering southern Greece and the Peloponnese; it was created in Augustus's reorganization of the provinces in 27 B.C. In A.D. 15 it was reunited with Macedonia (northern Greece), but in 44 it became a province again in its own right. The word translated "first converts" (*aparchē*) is in fact the word used in the Greco-Roman world for the "firstfruits" that were sacrificed to one of the gods or offered as a dedication in a sanctuary. For example, the famed king Kroisos made special offerings in the sanctuary of Apollo at Delphi, which were the *aparchē* of the wealth he inherited.[147] It may be that the household's ministry was a model for other Christians in the province. The "service [*diakonia*] for the saints" may allude to the use of the household for acts of worship, including hosting the Lord's Supper.

To submit to such as these and to everyone who joins in the work (16:16). This refers not to submission as recognized in the Roman colony, that is to say, by class or status, but rather to the Christian role in the ministry of the church.

I was glad when Stephanas, Fortunatus and Achaicus arrived, because they have supplied what was lacking from you (16:17). The three men are presumably the delegation with whom Apollos should return to Corinth (16:12). Fortunatus is a Latin name meaning "lucky." As a personal name it was often used of slaves, though it would be retained if freedom had been obtained. The name Achaicus is derived from the name of the province of Achaia, and it too may suggest a servile origin for this person. Both men may be connected to the household of Stephanas.

Greetings and Salutations (16:19–21)

The churches in the province of Asia send you greetings (16:19). The province of Asia consists of what today is western Turkey and included the city of Ephesus. It had become a province on the death of king Attalos III of Pergamon in 133 B.C. The churches of Asia may have included the communities at Miletus, Colosse, Smyrna, Sardis, Pergamum, and Troas.

Aquila and Priscilla greet you warmly in the Lord (16:19). Aquila was a native of Pontus; the province of Bithynia and Pontus was in northern Turkey on the shores of the Black Sea. He and his wife, Priscilla, had fled from Rome during the time of Claudius (Acts 18:2), perhaps c. A.D. 49, and had settled in Corinth. Shortly after Paul wrote this letter to Corinth, Aquila and Priscilla seem to have returned to Rome (Rom. 16:3). It should be noted that Paul uses the shorter form, Prisca, though some translations give the full form (Rom. 16:3; 1 Cor. 16:19; 2 Tim. 4:19), whereas in Acts 18:2, 18, 26 she is referred to as Priscilla. In most New Testament references, Priscilla's name occurs first.

The church that meets at their house (16:19). At this time the church usually met in a private house; it was not until Constantine that specific buildings tended to be built for holding services of worship. Plans of houses of this period suggest that the numbers who could come together at one time were quite limited.

Greet one another with a holy kiss (16:20). The kiss may have had its origins in Jewish culture, perhaps an allusion to the fact that members of the church needed to be reconciled with each other, just as Jacob was reconciled to Esau with a kiss (Gen. 33:4). Paul uses the same request in 2 Corinthians 13:12 as well as in Romans 16:16 and 1 Thessalonians 5:26.

I, Paul, write this greeting in my own hand (16:21). Although the beginning of the letter suggests that Paul and Sosthenes have jointly written the letter, this final valediction is in Paul's own hand. In

Romans 16:22 Paul's scribe Tertius adds his greetings at the end of the letter. Paul makes a similar point in Galatians 6:11 and Colossians 4:18. Some scholars have posited attempts to pass off other letters under Paul's name; thus, by adding his own postscript in his own handwriting, Paul gives this letter authenticity.

Cursings and Blessings (16:22–24)

Paul draws the letter to a close with the unusual feature of a curse followed by a blessing.

If anyone does not love the Lord (16:22). Paul uses the verb *phileō* ("to love") instead of *agapaō* (also "to love"), which he has used elsewhere in the letter (see comments on 13:1). One of the few other places where *phileō* occurs in Paul's letters is Titus 3:15: "Greet those who love us in the faith." The contrast between the two Greek words also recalls the conversation between the resurrected Jesus and Simon Peter by the Sea of Galilee (John 21:15–17).

A curse be on him (16:22). For the use of set curses see comments on 12:3.

Come, O Lord! (16:22). The phrase "Come, O Lord" translates the Greek form of the Aramaic phrase *Maran atha*.

The grace of the Lord Jesus be with you (16:23). These words are similar to those used at the end of other Pauline letters (e.g., Rom. 16:20; 2 Cor. 13:14; Phil. 4:23; Philem. 25). A more standard letter, concluding with a simple "Farewell," was sent by the Council of Jerusalem to the Christian believers in Antioch, Syria, and Cilicia (Acts 15:23–29).

My love to all of you in Christ Jesus (16:24). In a letter that includes Paul's essay on love (13:1–13), it is fitting that love (*agapē*) is the closing word.

ANNOTATED BIBLIOGRAPHY

Commentaries

Bruce, F. F. *1 and 2 Corinthians*. NCBC. London: Oliphants, 1971.

A commentary from a scholar sensitive to the classical texts of the Greek and Roman world.

Fee, Gordon D. *The First Epistle to the Corinthians*. NICNT. Grand Rapids: Eerdmans, 1987.

A comprehensive commentary on the letter complete with footnotes and discussion of the Greek text. His magisterial commentary remains one of the most useful works on this letter.

Green, Michael. *To Corinth With Love: The Vital Relevance Today of Paul's Advice to the Corinthian Church*. London: Hodder and Stoughton, 1982.

A popular discussion of the Corinthian correspondence, which draws on relevant background material.

Prior, David. *The Message of 1 Corinthians*. BST. Leicester: Inter-Varsity, 1985.

An exegetical commentary on the letter rooted in parish ministry in South Africa and Oxford, England.

Thiselton, Anthony C. *The First Epistle to the Corinthians*. NIGTC. Grand Rapids: Eerdmans, 2000.

The most comprehensive commentary available on 1 Corinthians.

Winter, Bruce W. "1 Corinthians." *New Bible Commentary: 21st Century Edition*. Eds. D. A. Carson, R. T. France, J. A. Motyer, and G. J. Wenham. Downers Grove, Ill.: InterVarsity, 1994.

Although this commentary lacks critical apparatus, there are some important windows on the relevant cultural background.

Special Studies

Clarke, Andrew D. *Secular and Christian Leadership in Corinth: A Socio-Historical and Exegetical Study of 1 Corinthians 1–6*. Leiden: E. J. Brill, 1993.

A sensitive and methodological discussion of Paul's letter against the background of the Roman colony.

Engels, Donald. *Roman Corinth: An Alternative Model for the Classical City*. Chicago: University of Chicago Press, 1990.

The only short discussion of the Roman colony, the study draws on the results of the excavations by the American School of Classical Studies at Athens.

Gill, David W. J., and Conrad Gempf, eds. BAFCS 2. *The Book of Acts in its Graeco-Roman Setting*. Grand Rapids: Eerdmans, 1994.

A series of essays that provides key discussions of the Roman provincial structure and religious background during the first century A.D.

Winter, Bruce W. *Philo and Paul Among the Sophists*. SNTSMS. Cambridge: Cambridge University Press, 1997.

This study includes important comments on the Corinthian material against the background of public oratory in the eastern Mediterranean during the first century A.D.

CHAPTER NOTES

Main Text Notes

1. For the most recent study of the colony, see D. Engels, *Roman Corinth: An Alternative Model for the Classical City* (Chicago: Univ. of Chicago Press, 1990). However, this work should be read alongside the searching reviews: A. J. S. Spawforth, *Classical Review* 42.1 (1992): 119–20; R. Saller, *Classical Philology* 86.4 (1991): 351–57. For a survey of the archaeology, see M. E. H. Walbank, "The Foundation and Planning of Early Roman Corinth," *Journal of Roman Archaeology* 10 (1997): 95–130. Results of the excavations appear in the *Excavations at Corinth* monograph series (see note 21).

2. Strabo, *Geography* 8.6.23 (trans. Loeb).

3. Cicero, *Fam.* 4.5.4.

4. Cicero, *Tusc.* 3.22.53.

5. L. Foxhall, D. Gill, and H. Forbes, "The Inscriptions of Methana," in C. B. Mee & H. Forbes (eds.), *A Rough and Rocky Place: The Landscape and Settlement History of the Methana Peninsula, Greece* (Liverpool: Liverpool Univ. Press, 1997), 273–74, no. 15; *IG* 4.853; *SEG* 37 (1987): 321. The dating of the inscription to the Actian era (commemorating Augustus's victory at Actium) is discussed by A. J. Gossage, "The Date of *IG* V (2) 516 (*SIG*³ 800)," *Annual of the British School at Athens* 49 (1954): 53, 56.

6. Favorinus's speech has been preserved by Dio Chrysostom (*Orations* 37.34).

7. Strabo, *Geography* 8.6.20.

8. Ibid., 8.6.20.

9. J. H. Kent, *The Inscriptions, 1926–1950* (Corinth: Results of Excavations Conducted by the American School of Classical Studies at Athens 8.3; Princeton, N.J.: American School of Classical Studies at Athens, 1966), pl. 8, no. 56.

10. Pausanias, *Descr.* 2.2.8.

11. M. E. H. Walbank, "Evidence for the Imperial Cult in Julio-Claudian Corinth," in Alastair Small (ed.), *Subject and Ruler: The Cult of the Ruling Power in Classical Antiquity. Papers Presented at a Conference Held in the University of Alberta on April 13–15, 1994, To Celebrate the 65ᵗʰ Anniversary of Duncan Fishwick* (Journal of Roman Archaeology Supplement 17; Ann Arbor, Mich.: Journal of Roman Archaeology, 1996), 201–12.

12. Suetonius, *Nero* 19.

13. Engels, *Roman Corinth*, 102–6. The sanctuary of Isis at Cenchreae has been excavated.

14. I. F. Saunders, *Roman Crete* (Warminster, U.K.: Aris & Phillips, 1992). Other cults of Isis are known around the Saronic Gulf.

15. In addition to the works cited in the bibliography, I am also indebted to Rev. David Holloway, who first opened the letter to me in a series of sermons at Jesmond Parish Church, Newcastle upon Tyne, UK.

16. The inscription is published by Kent, *Inscriptions*, no. 165.

17. Favorinus is generally considered to have been the author of *Oration* 37 attributed to Dio Chrysostom. This sophist is discussed in B. W. Winter, "Favorinus," in B. W. Winter and A. D. Clarke (eds.), *The Book of Acts in its Ancient Literary Setting* (BAFCS 1; Grand Rapids: Eerdmans, 1993), 296–305.

18. For the initial publication, see D. I. Pallas, S. Charitonidis, and J. Venencie, "Inscriptions lyciennes trouvées à Solômos près de Corinthe," *Bulletin de correspondance hellénique* 83 (1959): 496–508. For discussion, see L. Robert, "VII. Décret de la confédération lycienne à Corinthe," *Revue des études anciennes* 62 (1960): 324–42.

19. The inscription is conveniently illustrated in M. Lang, *Cure and Cult in Ancient Corinth: A Guide to the Asklepieion* (American Excavations in Old Corinth, Corinth Notes 1; Princeton, N.J.: American School of Classical Studies at Athens, 1977), 3, fig. 2.

20. This position is argued Winter, *Philo and Paul*, 186–94.

21. V. Ehrenberg and A. H. M. Jones, *Documents Illustrating the Reigns of Augustus and Tiberius* (2d ed., Oxford: Clarendon, 1955), no. 98a (Greek text); translated in N. Lewis and M. Reinhold, *Roman Civilization; I: The Republic and the Augustan Age* (New York: Columbia Univ. Press, 1990), 627.

22. Herodotus, *Histories* 4.77.1.

23. See, e.g., Pliny, *Letters* 10.96.

24. On the rhetorical construction, see Winter, *Philo and Paul*, 193.

25. For a full discussion, see Winter, *Philo and Paul*, 149–51.

26. Favorinus, *Orations* 37.1.

27. Dio Chrysostom, *Orations* 47.22. See Winter, *Philo and Paul*, 151.

28. These words feature in Aristotle's discussion of rhetoric (*Rhetoric* 2.2.7).

29. Ibid., 519. See Winter, *Philo and Paul*, 157–58.

30. Winter, *Philo and Paul*, 155, observes that "rhetoric is the art of persuasion."

31. Cicero, *Academica* 2.8.

32. Quintilian, 5.10.7. For a discussion of the oratorical setting of this word, see Winter, *Philo and Paul*, 154.

33. Dio Chrysostom, *Orations* 33.3. For further discussion on this, see Winter, *Philo and Paul*, 154–55.

34. Epictetus, 2.16.39.

35. Philo, *Agriculture* 9.

36. For an overview (with bibliography), see D. W.J. Gill, "Mines and Quarries," in G. Speake (ed.), *Encyclopedia of Greece and the Hellenic Tradition* (Chicago: Fitzroy Dearborn) 2.1059–61.

37. A convenient range of such building accounts in translation can be found in J. J. Pollitt, *The Art of Ancient Greece: Sources and Documents* (Cambridge: Cambridge Univ. Press, 1990), 190–93.

38. Dio Cassius, 57.10.1–3 (trans. Pollitt).

39. Pagan gods might appear to have several expressions in one city. They were differentiated by different epithets. Thus at Corinth there were several cult centers of the Greek god Apollo, one being Clarian Apollo (Pausanias, *Descr.* 2.1.8), named after the god's oracle center, not at Delphi, but at Claros in Anatolia.

40. For the description of this event, see the account by the Roman historian Livy, 29.14.10–14.

41. Philo, *Worse* 33. See further: Winter, *Philo and Paul*, 107.

42. The title was used from the late second century A.D., though the concept of the emperor having dominion across the empire and beyond is found in the *Res Gestae* ("Achievements") of the emperor Augustus, inscribed on columns outside his mausoleum at Rome. This inscription even notes contact with India.

43. For a summary of the archaeological issues, see M. B. Walbank, "The Foundation and Planning of Early Roman Corinth," *Journal of Roman Archaeology* 10 (1997): 115, fig. 9 (aerial photograph), 124–25, fig. 10.

44. Dio Chrysostom, *Orations* 31.121. Ancient cemeteries do in fact adjoin the amphitheater.

45. A. J. S. Spawforth, "Corinth, Argos, and the Imperial Cult: Pseudo-Julian, *Letters* 198," *Hesperia* 63 (1994): 211–32; with corrigendum, *Hesperia* 63 (1994): 522.

46. For a detailed consideration of this section of the letter see A. D. Clarke, *Secular and Christian Leadership in Corinth: A Socio-Historical and Exegetical Study of 1 Corinthians 1–6* (Leiden: Brill, 1993), ch. 6.

47. Philo, *Sacrifices* 32.

48. B. W. Winter, *Seek the Welfare of the City: Christians as Benefactors and Citizens* (Grand Rapids: Eerdmans, 1994), 105–21, provides a full discussion of this section of 1 Corinthians.

49. E.g., Dio Cassius, 52.7.5.

50. *SEG* 9.8, decree I (see also note 73, below).

51. Winter, *Seek the Welfare of the City*, 110. For the Augustus decree, see *SEG* 9.8, decree I; K. Chisholm and J. Ferguson (eds.), *Rome: The Augustan Age. A Source Book* (Oxford: Oxford Univ. Press/The Open Univ. Press, 1981), 128 no. C20: "There exist certain conspiracies to oppress the Greeks in trials on capital charges. . . . I myself have ascertained that some innocent people have in this way been oppressed and carried off to the supreme penalty."

52. E.g., Dio Chrysostom, *Orations* 8.9; Favorinus, *Orations* 37.16–17; Apuleius, *Metam.* 9.33.

53. Winter, *Seek the Welfare of the City*, 107 n. 7 provides a useful list of what was covered by criminal law.

54. Ibid., 107.

55. Winter, *Seek the Welfare of the City*, 116.

56. B. W. Winter, "Homosexual Terminology in 1 Corinthians 6:9: The Roman Context and the Greek Loan-word," in A. N. S. Lane (ed.), *Interpreting the Bible: Historical and Theological Studies in Honor of David F. Wright* (Leicester, U.K.: Apollos, 1997), 275–90 (ch. 14).

57. This law was passed by the tribune Scantinius c. 146 B.C. See S. Lilja, *Homosexuality in Republican and Augustan Rome* (Helsinki: Societas Scientiarum Fennica, 1982), 112–21.

58. For a selection of recipes from Apicius's cookbook, see J. Shelton, *As the Romans Did: A Sourcebook in Roman Social History* (New York: Oxford Univ. Press, 1988), 86–88, nos. 93, 94, 95, 96, and 97.

59. Winter, "Homosexual Terminology," 287; idem, "Gluttony and Immorality at Elitist Banquets: The Background to 1 Corinthians 6:12–20," *Jian Dao* 7 (1997): 55–67.

60. *CIL* 1.2.1221. A translation may be found in Shelton, *As the Romans Did*, 37, no. 47, 48, no. 57.

61. Winter, "1 Corinthians," 1171.

62. Soranus, *Gynecology* 1.60.4 (trans. Shelton). On contraception in the ancient world, see Shelton, *As the Romans Did*, 26, nos. 27–28.

63. Fee, *Corinthians*, 287–88.

64. Pliny the Younger, *Letters* 8.5.1–2.

65. *BGU* 1103 (A. S. Hunt and C. C. Edgar, *Select Papyri* [Loeb Classical Library; Cambridge,

Mass.: Harvard Univ. Press, 1956], 6). A translation may be found in Shelton, *As the Romans Did*, 50, no. 61; Lewis and Reinhold, *Roman Civilization*, 2:344.

66. *BGU* 1103 (*Select Papyri* 6). A translation may be found in Shelton, *As the Romans Did*, 50, no. 61.

67. For this section see Winter, *Seek the Welfare of the City*, 145–64.

68. See ibid., 160–61.

69. Celsus, *De Medicina* 7.25. Epispasm is discussed by Winter, *Seek the Welfare of the City*, 147–52.

70. See Winter, *Seek the Welfare of the City*, 155–57.

71. Part of the oath taken by the new slave was to the *genius* of the master (see Winter, *Seek the Welfare of the City*, 159).

72. S. Treggiari, *Roman Marriage: Iusti Coniuges from the Time of Cicero to the Time of Ulpian* (Oxford: Clarendon, 1991), 153–55.

73. B. Winter, "'The Seasons' of This Life and Eschatology in 1 Corinthians 7:29–31," in K. E. Brower and M. W. Elliott (eds.), *"The Reader Must Understand": Eschatology in Bible and Theology* (Leicester, U.K.: Apollos, 1997), 331.

74. B. Winter, "Secular and Christian Responses to Corinthian Famines," *TynBul* 40.1 (1989): 86–106.

75. Peter Garnsey, *Famine and Food Supply in the Graeco-Roman World: Responses to Risk and Crisis* (Cambridge: Cambridge Univ. Press, 1988).

76. Tacitus, *Annals* 3.25.

77. *IG* IV. 853. See now L. Foxhall, D. Gill, and H. Forbes, "The Inscriptions of Methana," in C. Mee and H. Forbes, *A Rough and Rocky Place*, 273–74, no. 15.

78. See Winter, "Seasons of This Life," 323–34.

79. This follows the meaning in LSJ, ἀσχημονέω.

80. B. Winter, "Puberty or Passion? The Referent of ὑπέρακμος in 1 Corinthians 7:36," *TynBul* 49.1 (1998): 78–79.

81. Treggiari, *Roman Marriage*, 159.

82. See LSJ, ὑπέρακμος. For a discussion of this term, see Winter, "The Seasons of This Life," 333; idem, *After Paul Left Corinth: The Impact of Secular Ethics and Social Change* (Grand Rapids: Eerdmans, 2000), ch. 8. Winter suggests that the term "refers . . . to the growing sense of physical closeness and expectation of sexual intimacy naturally felt as the actual marriage grew closer."

83. Soranus, *Gynecology* 1.22. For the English translation see O. Temkin, *Soranus' Gynaecology* (Baltimore: Johns Hopkins Univ. Press, 1956). The passage is discussed by Winter, "Puberty or Passion?" 75.

84. Hesychius. For a discussion: Winter, "Puberty or Passion?" 76.

85. *Acta Divi Augusti* (Rome, 1945), 187. A convenient translation is found in Shelton, *As the Romans Did*, 29, no. 33.

86. Kent, *Inscriptions*, no. 153. For a convenient summary of his career, see Clarke, *Secular and Christian Leadership*, 143, no. 59.

87. Plutarch, *Quaest. Conviv.* 723A: "During the Isthmian games, the second time Sospis was president, I avoided the other banquets, at which he entertained a great many foreign visitors at one, and several times entertained all the citizens" (trans. Winter).

88. See Winter, *Seek the Welfare of the City*, 132, for the grammatical structure of this section.

89. Spawforth, "Corinth, Argos, and the Imperial Cult," 522. For its application to the Christian church at Corinth, see Winter, *Seek the Welfare of the City*, 126.

90. See Winter, *Seek the Welfare of the City*, 174.

91. Strabo, *Geography* 8.3.30.

92. See on this section Winter, *Seek the Welfare of the City*, 165–77.

93. Some of the best known dining rooms come from the sanctuary of Demeter and Kore on the lower slopes of Akrocorinth. However, archaeological evidence suggests that the rooms were not in use at this time. Equally impressive dining rooms come from the extramural sanctuary at Perachora at the northwestern end of the Isthmus. See R. A. Tomlinson, "Perachora: The Remains Outside the Two Sanctuaries," *Annual of the British School at Athens* 64 (1969): 155–258.

94. M. S. Kos, "A Latin Epitaph of a Roman Legionary from Corinth," *Journal of Roman Studies* 68 (1978): 22–25.

95. Another soldier known at Corinth is the *optio* Aurelius Nestor of the 4th Flavian legion; see A. B. West, *Latin Inscriptions, 1896–1926* (Corinth: Results of Excavations Conducted by the American School of Classical Studies at Athens 8.2; Princeton, N.J.: American School of Classical Studies at Athens, 1966), no. 10. See also R. K. Sherk, "Roman Imperial Troops in Macedonia and Achaia," *American Journal of Philology* 78 (1957): 52–62.

96. See the discussion in H. Bowden and D. Gill, "Roman Methana," in Mee and Forbes, *A Rough and Rocky Place*, 80–81, and Foxhall, Gill, and Forbes, "Inscriptions of Methana," ibid., 273–74, no. 15. The inscription is *IG* 4:853; *SEG* 37 (1987): 321. For an earlier discussion, see Gossage, "The Date of *IG* V (2) 516 (*SIG*³ 800)," 53, 56.

97. Translation from Fee, *Corinthians*, 417.

98. E. R. Gebhard, "The Isthmian Games and the Sanctuary of Poseidon in the Early Empire,"

in T. E. Gregory (ed.), *The Corinthia in the Roman Period* (Journal of Roman Archaeology Supplement 8; Ann Arbor, Mich.: Journal of Roman Archaeology, 1994), 78–94. See also D. J. Geagen, "Notes on the Agonistic Institutions of Roman Corinth," *Greek, Roman and Byzantine Studies* 9 (1968): 69–80; W. R. Biers and D. J. Geagen, "A New List of Victors in the Caesarea at Isthmia," *Hesperia* 39.2 (1970): 79–93.

99. Philostratus the Elder, *Apollonius of Tyana* 5.43. Translation from J. Swaddling, *The Ancient Olympic Games* (London: British Museum Press, 1980), 35.

100. The pine wreath is shown on dedications from the sanctuary of Poseidon.

101. Dio Chrysostom, *Orations* 77/78.4.

102. Philo *Spec. Laws* 1.221.

103. See Winter, *Seek the Welfare of the City*, 168.

104. The term can be translated as "welfare"; see Winter, *Seek the Welfare of the City*, 174–75.

105. D. W. J. Gill, "The Meat-Market at Corinth (1 Corinthians 10:25)," *TynBul* 43.2 (1992): 389–93.

106. F. F. Bruce, *1 and 2 Corinthians* (NCB; Grand Rapids: Eerdmans, 1971), 99, cites *t. Ber.* 4.1 as endorsement of the use of Ps. 24 in the context of eating.

107. As suggested by Fee, *Corinthians*, 485.

108. See the two articles by W. Grudem: "Does κεφαλή ("Head") Mean 'Source' or 'Authority Over' in Greek Literature? A Survey of 2,336 Examples," *TrinJ* NS 6 (1985): 38–59; "Catherine Kroeger, IVP, Liddell-Scott, and Others on the Meaning of κεφαλή ('Head'): An Evaluation of New Evidence, Real and Alleged," *JETS* (forthcoming, 2001). However, see Fee, *Corinthians*, 502–3.

109. In a discussion of an aureus (gold coin) of Claudius (A.D. 51) showing the portrait of Agrippina the Younger: D. E. E. Kleiner and S. B. Matheson, *I Claudia: Women in Ancient Rome* (New Haven, Conn.: Yale Univ. Press, 1996), 65 no. 18.

110. For a funerary relief of the Augustan period showing Vesinia Iucunda flanked by two male freedmen, see Kleiner and Matheson, *I Claudia*, 199–200, no. 150; for a free-standing portrait statue possibly from the late republic or early Augustan period, see ibid., 197, no. 145.

111. Tacitus, *Germania* 19 (though the context regards Germanic tribes).

112. See R. MacMullen, "Women in Public in the Roman Empire," *Historia* 29 (1980): 208–18.

113. See Kleiner and Matheson, *I Claudia*.

114. A. H. M. Jones, *The Greek City from Alexander to Justinian* (Oxford: Clarendon, 1940), 176–78.

115. Winter, "1 Corinthians," 1179.

116. R. A. Campbell, "Does Paul Acquiesce in Divisions at the Lord's Supper?" *NovT* 33 (1991): 61–70. He suggests the translation: "For there actually has to be discrimination in your meetings, so that (if you please!) the elite may stand out from the rest."

117. For a helpful discussion, see I. H. Marshall, "Lord's Supper," *DPL*, 569–75.

118. The discovery of animal bones near the theater has suggested that food was being served for communal banquets, and that these may have been eaten in the theater itself.

119. Adapted from Bruce, *1 and 2 Corinthians*, 111.

120. Quoted by ibid., 113.

121. Garnsey, *Famine and Food Supply*.

122. Suetonius, *Claudius* 18–19.

123. Cited by Winter, "1 Corinthians," 1180.

124. See D. W. J. Gill, "Erastus the Aedile," *TynBul* 40 (1989): 293–301. The piazza was laid at the private expense of Erastus.

125. Seneca, *Epistles* 95.52.

126. See, e.g., A. E. Hill, "The Temple of Asclepius: An Alternative Source for Paul's Body Theology," *JBL* 99 (1980): 437–39; G. G. Garnier, "The Temple of Asklepius at Corinth and Paul's Theology," *Buried History* 18 (1982): 52–58. Fee, *Corinthians*, 602 n. 11, dismisses the Asklepieion as a possible source for this illustration.

127. C. Roebuck, *The Asklepieion and Lerna* (Corinth 14; Princeton, N.J.: American School of Classical Studies at Athens, 1951).

128. Winter, "Puberty or Passion?" 81.

129. Josephus, *J.W.* 4.7.2 §406.

130. The translation suggested by LSJ, φιλία.

131. D. M. Jacobson and M. P. Weitzman, "What Was Corinthian Bronze?" *American Journal of Archaeology* 96.2 (1992): 237–47.

132. See the marble container in the Fitzwilliam Museum, University of Cambridge, England, which is decorated with scenes of Cybele: L. Budde and R. Nicholls, *Catalogue of Greek and Roman Sculpture in the Fitzwilliam Museum, Cambridge* (Cambridge: Cambridge Univ. Press, 1964), 77–78, pl. 41, no. 125.

133. Fee, *Corinthians*, 634, suggests that there may have been a manuscript change that substituted the Greek word for "burning" instead of "boasting." The suggestion is in part based on similarities with the text of Clement of Rome in his letter to Corinth. For Nero's persecution of the Christians at Rome, see Tacitus, *Annals* 15.44.

134. See LSJ, περπερεύομαι.

135. For a silver mirror from the first century A.D., said to be from Egypt, see D. von Bothmer, *A*

Greek and Roman Treasury (New York: Metropolitan Museum of Art, 1984), 69, no. 129. The mirror was inscribed with the owner's name, "Iris."

136. See Fee, *Corinthians*, 672, esp. n. 37.
137. Pausanias, *Descr.* 1.38.7 (trans. Loeb).
138. For a description of the chest of Kypselos, which included many of the Greek myths, see ibid., 5.17.5–5.19.10.
139. A suggestion I owe to Bruce Winter ("1 Corinthians," 1184).
140. Further games were held at the extra-mural sanctuary of Mên Askaenos (a local deity often associated with the Roman deity Luna, the personification of the Moon) outside Pisidian Antioch at Kara Kuyu. For details of the games (though placing them much later than is necessary) see J. G. C. Anderson, "Festivals of Mên Askaênos in the Roman Colony at Antioch of Pisidia," *Journal of Roman Studies* 3 (1913): 267–300.
141. Winter, "1 Corinthians," 1184–85.
142. See, e.g., Quintilian's comments on the importance of Empedokles (*Inst. Or.* 1.4.1–5).
143. Philo, *Embassy* 40.314 (trans. Lewis and Reinhold, *Roman Civilization*, 2:314).
144. For a convenient overview, see P. G. Bahn, "Vindolanda: Letters from Rome," in P. G. Bahn (ed.), *Wonderful Things: Uncovering the World's Great Archaeological Treasures* (London: Weidenfeld & Nicolson, 1999), 182–85.
145. On this question of integrity, see Winter, *Philo and Paul*, 219.
146. See also, e.g., Rom. 15:24; 2 Cor. 1:16.
147. Herodotus, *Histories* 1.92.2.

Sidebar and Chart Notes

A-1. Strabo, *Geography* 8.5.21.
A-2. Ibid., 8.6.19.
A-3. A helpful discussion on Pausanias as a source is to be found in C. Habicht, *Pausanias' Guide to Ancient Greece* (Sather Classical Lectures 50; Berkeley: Univ. of California Press, 1985, 1998).
A-4. E.g., Pausanias, *Descr.* 5.13.7.
A-5. Ibid., 5.1.2.
A-6. Ibid., 2.2.6.
A-7. The excavations are published in the monograph series *Corinth: Results of Excavations Conducted by the American School of Classical Studies at Athens* (Cambridge, Mass., and Princeton, N.J.: American School of Classical Studies at Athens). Preliminary reports also appear in *Hesperia*, the journal of the American School. S. Dyson, *Ancient Marbles to American Shores: Classical Archaeology in the United States* (Philadelphia: Univ. of Pennsylania Press, 1998), 85, has observed that "Corinth's

association with St. Paul's mission and the development of early Christianity provided another major incentive for raising financial support for what the School hoped would be long-term excavations."

A-8. The results have been published in the monograph series *Kenchreai: Eastern Port of Corinth* (Leiden: Brill, 1976–1981). For a color photograph of the harbor, see R. V. Schoder, *Ancient Greece from the Air* (London: Thames & Hudson, 1974), 111–13. For a history of the excavations, see L. S. Meritt, *History of the American School of Classical Studies at Athens 1939–1980* (Princeton, N.J.: American School of Classical Studies at Athens, 1984), 171.
A-9. E.g., D. I. Pallas, "Anaskaphai ereunai en Lechaio," *Praktika* (1965): 137–66; idem, "Anaskaphai Lechaiou," *Archaiologikon Deltion* 17.2 (1961–62): 69–78 (both in Greek).
A-10. The excavations appear in the monograph series *Isthmia Excavations* (Princeton, N.J.: American School of Classical Studies at Athens). Preliminary reports appeared in *Hesperia*. For a history of the excavation, see Meritt, *History of the American School*, 169–71.
A-11. Philo, *Embassy* 281.
A-12. The text of Favorinus's speech can be found in the Loeb edition of Dio Chrysostom (*Discourses* 4.37). For a discussion of Favorinus, see Winter, *Philo and Paul*, 132–37.
A-13. Favorinus, *Orations* 37.8 (trans. Loeb).
A-14. Philostratos, *Lives of the Sophists* 490–91.
A-15. Kent, *Inscriptions*, no. 322.
A-16. A. B. West, *Latin Inscriptions, 1896–1926*, nos. 2, 3, 98–101, 132; Kent, *Inscriptions*, no. 155.
A-17. A helpful table showing building activity at Corinth may be found in Engels, *Roman Corinth*, 169, table 11.
A-18. *SEG* 9.8, decree IV. The translation comes from Chisholm and Ferguson, *Rome: The Augustan Age*, 129 no. C20. For such juries operating within the context of a province see A. H. M. Jones, *The Greek City from Alexander to Justinian* (Oxford: Clarendon, 1940), 122.
A-19. Martial, 7.82.
A-20. See Winter, *Seek the Welfare of the City*, 149.
A-21. Agonistic festivals were established at Jerusalem in the Hellenistic period when Judea fell under the control of the Seleucids. This required the establishment of institutions such as a gymnasium, where the young men were trained as well as met for educational purposes. As yet we have no

archaeological evidence for a gymnasium or for that matter a stadium at Jerusalem. For a convenient summary of the later evidence, see D. Sperber, *The City in Roman Palestine* (New York/Oxford: Oxford Univ. Press, 1998), 85–89.

A-22. West, *Corinth*, 8.2, nos. 86–90; Kent, *Inscriptions*, nos. 158–63.

A-23. E.g., Tacitus, *Annals* 12.43.1 (A.D. 51). See also Garnsey, *Famine and Food Supply*, 261.

A-24. Biers and Geagan, "A New List of Victors," 79–93 (dating to the early second century A.D.). For other lists, see Meritt, *History of the American School*, 8.1, nos. 14 (A.D. 3), 19 (Claudian), and 18 (early empire).

A-25. Plutarch, *Moralia* 675d–677b.

A-26. F. P. Johnson, *Sculpture 1896–1923* (Corinth 9; Cambridge, Mass.: American School of Classical Studies at Athens, 1931). See also C. L. Thompson, "Hairstyles, Head-Coverings, and St Paul: Portraits from Roman Corinth," *BA* 51.2 (June 1988): 99–110.

A-27. Johnson, *Sculpture*, 72. For a helpful discussion of Roman portraiture, see S. Walker, *Greek and Roman Portraits* (London: British Museum Press, 1995).

A-28. Plutarch, *Quaest. Rom.* 266 D. For more on this, see D. J. Gill, "The Importance of Roman Portraiture for Head-Coverings in 1 Corinthians 11:2–16," *TynBul* 41.2 (1990): 246–51.

A-29. Johnson, *Sculpture*, 76–77. For a convenient overview of the portraiture of Nero, see D. E. E. Kleiner, *Roman Sculpture* (New Haven, Conn.: Yale Univ. Press, 1992), 135–39.

A-30. Johnson, *Sculpture*, 86, no. 160.

A-31. Kent, *Inscriptions*, no. 156.

A-32. Ibid., no. 173.

A-33. Ibid., no. 199.

A-34. Pallas, Charitonidis, and Venencie, "Inscriptions lyciennes trouvées à Solômos près de Corinthe," 496–508; L. Robert, "VII. Décret de la confédération lycienne à Corinthe," *Revue des Études Anciennes* 62 (1960): 324–42. For a convenient translation and discussion, see R. A. Kearsley, "Women in Public Life in the Roman East: Iunia Theodora, Claudia Metrodora and Phoibe, Benefactress of Paul," *Ancient Society* [Macquarie Ancient History Association] 15, 3 (1985): 124–37; idem, "Women in Public Life in the Roman East," *TynBul* 50.2 (1999): 189–211.

A-35. Decree 1, ll. 1–7 (trans. Kearsley).

A-36. Decree 4, ll. 57–58.

A-37. Suetonius, *Claudius* 25.9.

A-38. Tactius, *Annals* 13.33.4.

A-39. Menander, *Thais*. For the context of this citation see Winter, "Homosexual Terminology," 288.

A-40. R. Stillwell, *The Theater* (Corinth 2; Princeton, N.J.: American School of Classical Studies at Athens, 1965).

A-41. Gill, "Erastus the Aedile," 293–301.

2 CORINTHIANS

by Moyer Hubbard

Corinth and the Corinthians

See Introduction to 1 Corinthians.

Developments Between 1 and 2 Corinthians

When Paul wrote 1 Corinthians (probably from Ephesus), he promised to send Timothy to Corinth (1 Cor. 4:17; 16:11) to guide the struggling community through some difficult issues that had arisen since his departure. These included factionalism (1 Cor. 3), immorality (1 Cor. 5), continued participation in pagan religious feasts (1 Cor. 8; 10:14–22), and questions related to theology and church practice (1 Cor. 11–15). Although what happened next is not entirely clear, it seems likely that Timothy returned with news that the situation had worsened, which forced Paul to abandon the travel plans he announced in 1 Cor. 16 and make an abrupt visit to Corinth (cf. 2 Cor. 13:1–2). This was a painful experience for Paul (2:1), who found himself personally attacked by a member of the congregation (2:5–11; 7:12). Upon returning to Ephesus, Paul wrote an

THE SUMMIT OF THE ACROCORINTH

In the location of the notorious temple of Aphrodite.

◀

▶ **2 Corinthians**
IMPORTANT FACTS:

- **AUTHOR:** Paul the apostle.
- **DATE:** A.D. 55.
- **OCCASION:** Written to reaffirm his affection for the Corinthians, to re-ignite enthusiasm for the collection, and to rebuff intruding opponents.
- **THEMES:**
  1. The new covenant ministry of the Spirit.
  2. Strength in weakness.
  3. The inner dynamic of the Christian life.

emotional letter, now lost, which he conveyed through Titus (2:4, 12–13; 7:6–7).

Titus eventually brought Paul news that the Corinthians had responded favorably to that letter written "with many tears" (2:4) and had taken disciplinary action against the offender (2:5–11; 7:5–12). However, Titus also reported a new threat: flamboyant missionaries from churches in Judea had arrived in Corinth and challenged Paul's legitimacy as an apostle (see "Paul's Opponents" at 11:6). Paul responded by dispatching Titus from Macedonia with the letter we now call 2 Corinthians (around A.D. 55), while he made preparations for his third visit to the troubled community (13:1–2).

Unity of 2 Corinthians

The historical reconstruction sketched above assumes that the canonical form of 2 Corinthians represents a single correspondence written by Paul, addressing a complex set of circumstances in Corinth. This is hardly universally accepted, however. In particular, the dramatic change of tone in chapters 10–13 seems to many impossible to reconcile with the confident and hopeful tenor of chapters 1–9. This has led some to propose that these later chapters are a portion of the earlier

tearful letter (2:4), or perhaps comprise a letter written subsequent to chapters 1–9, after Paul had been more fully appraised of the situation in Corinth. Many other partition theories have been offered, though it is beyond the scope and focus of this commentary to examine these in any detail. Recent discussions of this issue tend to favor the unity of 2 Corinthians.[1] The following arguments are especially pertinent:

1. **Lack of textual support**. There is no evidence that 2 Corinthians ever existed in any form other than its present canonical form.

2. **Unifying motifs**. Certain key themes occur throughout our canonical 2 Corinthians and suggest a rhetorically unified composition: *strength in weakness* (2:14–16; 4:7–18; 11:30–33; 12:10; 13:3); *Paul's style and philosophy of preaching* (2:17; 4:2–5; 5:11–13; 10:10–12; 11:5–6; 13:2–3); *testing one's faith* (2:9; 8:8; 13:5–6);

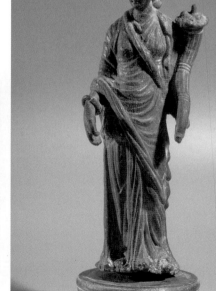

proper and improper boasting (1:12, 14; 5:12; 7:4, 14; 8:24; 9:2; 10:8–17; 11:10–30; 12:1–10); *commendation* (3:1–3; 4:2; 5:12; 7:11; 10:18; 12:11), and so on.

3. **Chapters 1–9 preparatory to 10–13.** In significant ways, chapters 10–13 presuppose the argumentation of 1–9.[2] In both sections Paul is defending himself before the Corinthians, and his direct confrontation of his opponents in 10–13 is almost expected, given his allusions to their activity in 1:12–13; 2:17; 4:2–4; 5:12. It is simply not true that chapters 1–9 contain no hint of simmering problems between Paul and the Corinthians.[3]

4. **Various contexts, various strategies.** From the Corinthian correspondence we know there were those in Corinth who questioned Paul's leadership (1 Cor. 3–4), some who were Paul's supporters (1:11; 16:15–17), at least one person who had openly attacked Paul (2 Cor. 2:5; 7:12), others who had a change of heart over their opposition to Paul (7:9–12), not to mention intruders who wished to undermine Paul's authority (2 Cor. 10–13). In other words, there was a variety of situations and groups to address. Thus, to evaluate the integrity of this letter on problematic notions of "restricted coherence, focused consistency, and unitary intentionality"[4] is to fail to grasp the complexity of the situation on the ground in Corinth.

Problems in Corinth

According to 1 Corinthians, the fundamental problem in Corinth was the Corinthians themselves. In Paul's view they were worldly, immature, and still not ready for the "solid food" of advanced discipleship (1 Cor. 3:1–4). Although some improvements are evident by the time of 2 Corinthians, it is clear that many of the same problems persist. Paul again has to confront those who continue to frequent pagan temples (2 Cor. 6:14–7:2; cf. 1 Cor. 8; 10:14–22), and again has to address Corinthian dissatisfaction with his oratory (2 Cor. 10:10; 11:6; cf. 1 Cor. 2:1–5). The Corinthians are also somewhat embarrassed by Paul's insistence on plying his trade as a tentmaker rather than accepting their patronage, thus elevating his social status. When Paul speaks of "lowering himself" through pursuing his craft (2 Cor. 11:7), he certainly echoes the Corinthian perspective on his trade, and the picture that begins to emerge is one of a superficial, status-conscious community that has failed to grasp the cruciform character of the Christian life.

The Purpose of 2 Corinthians

Given the problems outlined above, it is not surprising that most of Paul's theological argumentation in 2 Corinthians is aimed at correcting an inverted value system. In chapters 3–6 Paul emphasizes the transforming work of the Spirit (3:3–6, 7, 17–18; 5:4, 17), the priority of inner reality over outward display (3:1–3, 6; 4:6–7, 16, 18; 5:7, 12), and the radical newness of life in Christ: "You are a new creation" (5:17). In chapters 10–13 Paul takes this argument one step further by demonstrating that what the Corinthians regard as weakness is actually the very strength of

God (12:9–10). In short, what Paul attempts in this letter is nothing less than a theological program of re-enculturation.

There are, of course, other reasons for this lengthy letter. Paul's ever-changing travel plans have brought charges of indecision and suspicions of waning affection, and Paul is eager to set the record straight (1:15–2:4). He also needs to reignite enthusiasm for the collection, a beneficent gift on behalf of the Gentile churches to their brothers and sisters in Judea (chs. 8–9). The Corinthians had already pledged their support (1 Cor. 16:1–4), and Paul needs to act quickly in order to capitalize on the momentum of Titus's recent efforts on this front (2 Cor. 8:6). And then there are Paul's opponents—recently arrived emissaries from Judea who seem determined to undermine Paul's authority and presumptuously foist themselves on the vulnerable community (chs. 10–13). Their version of the gospel places themselves at the center, rather than Christ, and Paul exposes this anemic, truncated pseudo-gospel for the sham that it is.

THE
MEDITERRANEAN
WORLD OF THE
ROMAN ERA
▼

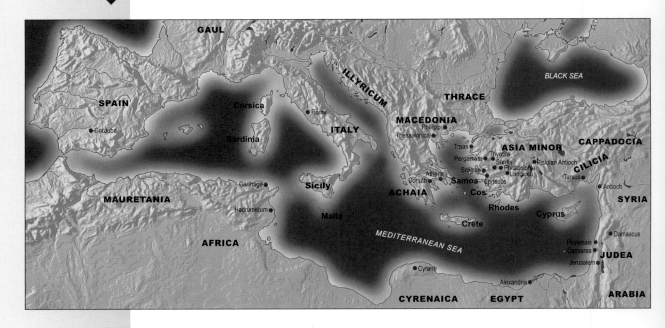

If we were to summarize these disparate interests under one rubric, we might identify *reconciliation* as the dominant concern of Paul in 2 Corinthians. In what may be his most personal letter (cf. 6:11–13), Paul aims to regain the support of key groups in Corinth in order that the community as a whole can grow to maturity in Christ. Although Paul's language is at times harsh and scolding, it issues from genuine parental affection: "I speak as to my children—open wide your hearts also" (6:13).

Greeting and Opening Blessing (1:1–7)

The opening paragraphs of Paul's letters usually set the tone for what follows and contain important clues to the main themes of the letter. In this introductory segment Paul emphasizes his *authority as an apostle* (1:1–2) and expresses his deep *relief and joy* (1:3–7) over the successful mission of reconciliation carried out by Titus (see 7:5–6).

To the church of God in Corinth (1:1). The earliest Christian groups met in private homes, and in this respect "the church" in Corinth was actually a collection of household assemblies. Acts 18:7 mentions Titius Justus as the first host of the fledgling community in Corinth, and later we learn that Gaius was able to accommodate "the whole church," apparently meaning all of the household assemblies (Rom. 16:23). We know from 1 Corinthians 14:23 that such gatherings did occur, though we can only speculate how often. Meeting in individual homes afforded privacy (though they were not closed gatherings; see 1 Cor. 14:23), and contributed to a sense of community,

though there were some obvious drawbacks.

Recent excavations in Corinth have uncovered a number of elegant villas from the Roman era, but the maximum number of guests that an atrium (a formal reception room) and triclinium (the dining room) together could have held was not more than fifty.[5] According to common Roman practice, guests of higher social standing were given preferential treatment at mealtime, so that the Roman satirist Martial complains to his host, "Why is not the same dinner served to me as to you? You take oysters fattened in the Lucrine lake, I suck a mussel through a hole in the shell. . . . Why do I dine without you although, Ponticus, I am dining with you?"[6] One wonders if the divisions that arose in Corinth in connection with the Lord's Supper ("one remains hungry, another gets drunk," 1 Cor. 11:17–22) were not partially the result of the chosen mechanism of fellowship, the private home.

▶ **Corinth**
IMPORTANT FACTS:

- Population: About 100,000.
- Religion: Aphrodite, Poseidon, and the Imperial Family worshiped, along with many other deities.
- Society: Cosmopolitan, ethnically diverse, relatively prosperous.
- Politics: Roman form of government, capital city of the province of Achaia.
- Culture: Competitive, status conscious.
- Economy: Port city; host of the Isthmian Games, important center of trade and tourism.

Together with all the saints throughout Achaia (1:1). At the time of the writing of 2 Corinthians, the Roman province of Achaia extended well beyond Athens, but Paul's usage elsewhere suggests he has in mind here a smaller geographical region. His earlier ministry in Athens resulted in at least a few conversions (Acts 17:32–34), yet he refers to the household of Stephanas of Corinth as the "firstfruits of Achaia" (1 Cor. 16:15). Even so, the clear implication of this verse is that the gospel had not only taken root in Corinth, but had spread to some of the surrounding communities. Romans 16:1 names Phoebe as a deaconess of the church in nearby Cenchrea, and presumably this letter is to be copied and dispatched to other household assemblies in the area.

Grace and peace to you from God our Father and the Lord Jesus Christ (1:2). The standard opening salutation in Greek letters of this era was *chairein!* (Greetings!). In a clever play on words, Paul christianizes this formulaic greeting and changes it to *charis!* (Grace!). This is expanded by a wish of "peace" (Gk. *eirēnē*; Heb. *shalom*), which was the typical Hebrew/Aramaic greeting.[7] The Hellenistic form is filled with Christian/Jewish content, and this perfectly expresses the complexity of Paul's biography and thought.

The Father of compassion and God of all comfort (1:3). Paul's Jewish faith is especially evident in his designation of God as "Father." From his study of the Torah, the young Saul of Tarsus learned that God was "the Father and Creator" of Israel (Deut. 32:6; cf. 8:5, 14:1). With the prophets he called on God as "Lord, Father, Redeemer of old."[8] Reflecting the same intimacy that characterized the prayer of Jesus, Paul addressed his heavenly Father as "Abba."[9] Although such affectionate language was not widely used by Jewish writers in this era, the hymns from Qumran offer this heartwarming parallel:

> *Because you are Father to all the*
>   *sons of your truth.*
> *In them you rejoice,*
>   *like one full of gentleness for*
>   *her child,*
>   *and like a wet-nurse,*
> *you clutch to your chest all your*
>   *creatures.*[10]

It is important to remember, however, that the Roman conception of fatherhood was considerably more harsh and authoritarian than our modern Western ideal. As the head of his family, the Roman father held absolute legal authority (*patria potestas*) over his children as his property. Unwanted infants could be discarded, and older children could be sold as slaves. The Roman historian Tacitus regards as eccentric the Jewish conviction that it was criminal "to kill any newly-born infant."[11] Although the exposure of infants was held in check by pub-

MACEDONIA
Pella
Thessalonica
Amphipolis
Apollonia
Berea
Mt. Olympus ▲
AEGEAN SEA
Larisa
EPIRUS
Nicopolis
Delphi
CORINTHIAN GULF
Isthmia
Eleusis
Athens
ACHAIA
Lechaeum
Corinth
Cenchrea
SARONIC GULF
Mycenae
Olympia
Epidaurus
Sparta
MEDITERRANEAN SEA

lic opinion and eventually outlawed under Christian emperors, both pagan and Christian writers from this period protest against this act of cruelty, which confirms its widespread practice.[12] In describing God as a "compassionate Father," Paul is assuring the Corinthians that, whatever their earthly fathers may have been like, the head of the Christian family is a responsive and loving Father, who exercises his authority in the best interests of his children.

Who comforts us in all our troubles (1:4–7). Comfort in affliction is the dominant theme of Paul's introductory blessing and one that resonates throughout chapters 1–9 (see esp. 2:14–16; 4:8–12; 5:4–5; 6:2–12). The depth of emotion so obvious in 2 Corinthians renders it perhaps Paul's most personal letter. At one point in the letter Paul himself comments on his candid self-disclosure, "O Corinthians, we have poured out our hearts to you" (6:11).

Paul's Change of Plans (1:8–2:13)

Paul's change in his travel itinerary raised the accusation in Corinth of fickleness and worldliness (1:12–22). In order to correct this misperception, Paul explains that it was out of concern for them that he decided to postpone his third visit to Corinth (1:23–2:4), allowing them time to discipline the person who had offended Paul (2:5–13).

The province of Asia (1:8) The province of Asia, bordered on the west by the Aegean, and on the east by Galatia, included such towns as Colosse, Smyrna, Pergamum, Troas, and Ephesus. Paul visited these cities on his second and third missionary journeys. Ephesus, an important sea port in the province, became one of the strategic centers of his missionary endeavor.

The hardships we suffered in the province of Asia . . . in our heart we felt the sentence of death (1:8). As the hardship catalogs of 6:3–6 and 11:23–29 illustrate, there is much about Paul's biography that we do not know, and the precise nature of the hardship (the Greek is singular, indicating one specific hardship) mentioned here remains obscure. Paul may be referring to the Ephesian riot related in Acts 19, though there is no indication in Acts of a sentence of death. Because this official verdict (*apokrima*; NIV, "sentence") was experienced "within," some feel Paul is speaking figuratively of a personal distress or perhaps a physical illness (see 12:7). If this were the case, however, his use of first-person plural ("we," "our") is unusual.

In holiness and sincerity . . . not according to worldly wisdom (1:12). In contrasting

REFLECTIONS

IN PONDERING THE HARDSHIP HE EXPERIENCED IN Asia, Paul senses a divine purpose involved, which he relates in verse 9: "But this happened that we might not rely on ourselves, but on God." Paul recognizes that the painful experiences of life are not random, pointless happenings, but divinely intended opportunities for growth. The lesson Paul needed to learn is not to rely on his own strength, intelligence, or natural abilities, but to trust wholly on God (Zech. 4:6). Not only is this a lesson that we need to learn (and relearn) today, but Paul's candid admission of his own need for growth serves as an important reminder that spiritual leaders do not come preassembled from the factory. They are grown from saplings through seasons of heat, frost, and rain, and require years of cultivation and pruning to reach maturity.

his own "simplicity" (*haplotēs*; NIV, "holiness") and "sincerity" with the "fleshly" (*sarkikos*; NIV, "worldly") conduct of others, Paul alludes to the practice of many self-styled philosophers who were in fact charlatans out for their own interests. Many writers of the period heap contempt on this ever burgeoning throng of pretenders who, "in the guise of philosophers [operate] with a view to their own profit and reputation, and not to improve [their followers]"(see comments on 1:24; 2:17; 4:2, 5; 5:11; 10:5; 11:20).[13]

The day of the Lord Jesus (1:14). The "day of the LORD" was a prominent motif in Israel's prophetic traditions, where it usually connoted a dark and foreboding day of judgment (Isa. 2:12–21; Amos 5:18–20; Zech. 14:1–2). This day of judgment would lead to the vindication and restoration of Israel (Amos 9:11–15; Zech. 14:6–21). Both positive (Matt. 16:27) and negative (Rom. 2:5) aspects of "the day of the Lord" are present in the New Testament; in this verse the emphasis lies on the hopeful prospect

of receiving the approval of the Lord on the day of his visitation (see Phil. 2:16).

I planned to visit you. . . . do I make my plans in worldly manner? (1:16–17). Paul's change of plans provoked strong criticism in Corinth (see the introduction), which forces the apostle to give a detailed defense of his apparently fickle disposition (1:12–2:4). The strength of the reaction in Corinth may be due, in part, to fashionable Stoicism, which considered decisiveness a defining virtue of the wise man:

> Nor do [the Stoics] assume that a man with good sense changes his mind, for changing one's mind belongs to false assent, on the grounds of erring through haste. Nor does he change his mind in any way, nor alter his opinion, nor is he confused. For all these things are marks of those who waver in their beliefs, which is alien to the person with good sense.[14]

He anointed us (1:21). Although the Greek word for "anoint" could be used of lotion massaged into an athlete or of oils used after bathing, Paul's vocabulary here is drawn from the Greek Old Testament, where the word refers to consecration to sacred office. Kings, priests, prophets, and other leaders were commissioned to service through a ceremony involving anointing with oil.[15] This anointing set them apart from their peers and authorized them to carry out their divinely ordained task.

In the present context, Paul's claim that the anointing of the Spirit extends to *all* believers ("he anointed *us*") has both sociological and theological implications. Given the prominence of this imagery in the Old Testament, Jewish converts in Corinth like Crispus (Acts

PAUL'S INTENDED ITINERARY

▼

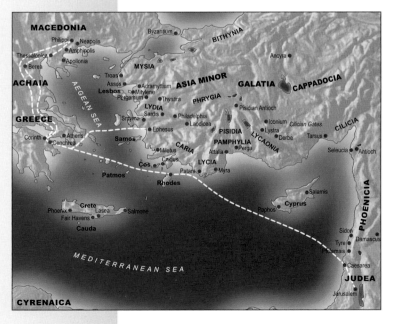

18:8) and God-fearers like Titius Justus (Acts 18:17) would have marveled at this bold democratization of a sacred rite once reserved for select individuals within the community of faith. This anointing, however, is not to a position of privilege, but to a position of service, as Paul himself modeled in Corinth (2 Cor. 4:4; 6:2–10; 11:23–29).

Set his seal of ownership on us (1:22). Unlike today, where seals are more decorative than functional, seals in antiquity were widely used and extremely important in commerce and everyday life. On a document, the seal serves as a signature, guaranteeing its authenticity. Parcels could be sealed to ensure that their contents were not disturbed in transit. The seal itself was made of stone, metal, or ivory, which was then pressed into soft wax or lead to make a distinctive impression. The imprint might bear the name of the owner, a unique symbol, or perhaps the image of a mythological figure or deity. Seals became objects of detailed craftsmanship in the Roman era and commonly imprinted the image of the one to whom they belonged.

In light of this, Paul's reference here to the divine seal of ownership impressed on every believer may include a subtle allusion to the believer's transformation into the image of God. The Corinthians were already familiar with this idea from Paul's previous correspondence (1 Cor. 15:42–49), and Paul will soon take up the issue explicitly (2 Cor. 3:18; 4:4–6). Philo, Paul's contemporary in Alexandria, was particularly fond of this analogy. Commenting on the creation of Adam in the divine image he writes, "He that was made according to the divine image was like . . . a seal."[16]

And put his Spirit in our hearts as a deposit, guaranteeing what is to come (1:22). Like the English word "deposit," the Greek term Paul employs here (*arrabōn*) is taken from the world of finance and denotes an initial down payment in promise of full payment at a later date. This precise phrase occurs again in 5:5, where we learn that the full payment involves being clothed with our "heavenly dwelling," when at last "what is mortal may be swallowed up by life" (5:4). In a parallel passage in Romans, Paul refers to the Spirit as "the firstfruits," guaranteeing our ultimate adoption and the redemption of our bodies (Rom. 8:23). For Paul, the Spirit was the power of the

ANCIENT SEALS

(left) Agate seal found in Mizpah (seventh century B.C.).

(right) Jasper seal bearing the inscription "Amos the Scribe" (seventh century B.C.).

future working in the present to renew, transform, and recreate God's people from the inside out (2 Cor. 3:3, 18; 4:6, 16, 5:5, 17).

I call God as my witness (1:23). Paul's Greek is more forceful than the NIV and can be accurately rendered, "I summon God as a witness *against me*."[17] This phraseology resembles the Old Testament oath formula, "May the LORD deal with me ever so severely if I do not do such and such. . ." (cf. Ruth 1:17; 2 Sam. 3:9). Oaths were more important in the ancient world than in modern Western societies and often carried the weight of a legally binding contract. In the Greco-Roman context, invoking the name of a deity added special gravity to the vow, and Zeus became known as "the god of oaths" among the ancients. The city of Assos (see Acts 20:13–14) in the province Asia publicly displayed this solemn oath of allegiance to the emperor Caligula on a bronze tablet: "We swear by Zeus the Savior and the God of Caesar Augustus . . . that we are loyally disposed to Gaius Caesar Augustus. . . . If we observe this oath, may all go well with us; if not, may the opposite befall."[18] Closer to Corinth, Pausanias tells of the oaths sworn before Palaemon, the mythological hero honored by the Isthmian Games: "Whosoever swears falsely here, whether Corinthian or stranger, can by no means escape from his oath."[19]

Paul's unusually strong language, subpoenaing God himself as a potential witness *against him*, indicates the seriousness of the issue in his mind. Far from being indecisive or unconcerned about the Corinthians (see 1:17), Paul's change of plans issued solely from his parental desire to spare his children another unpleasant confrontation.

Not that we lord it over your faith, but we work with you (1:24). Paul's determination to distance himself from those who would "lord it over" the Corinthians is rooted in his knowledge of the concrete reality of daily life in Corinth. Charlatans parading as philosophers and preying on the vanities of the populace blighted the cities of the Roman world during this period, so much so that the Emperor Vespasian felt justified in expelling all so-called philosophers from Rome in A.D. 71.[20] The sharp-tongued Roman satirist Lucian offers us this description:

> There is a class of men which made its appearance in the world not long ago, lazy, disputatious, vainglorious, quick-tempered, gluttonous, doltish, addle-pated, full of effrontery. . . . These people, dividing themselves into schools and inventing various word-mazes, have called themselves Stoics, Academics, Epicureans, Peripatetics, and other things much more laughable than these. . . . They amass biting phrases and school themselves in novel terms of abuse, and then they censure and reproach their fellow-men.[21]

Although Paul is not afraid to make use of his authority as an apostle when circumstances demand it, his preferred stance is that of a "coworker" (Gk. *synergos*; NIV, "we work with you"), working alongside his converts as a father with his son (cf. Phil. 2:22).

Another painful visit . . . through many tears I wrote to you (2:1–4). See "Developments Between the Letters" in the introduction.

The punishment inflicted on him by the majority is sufficient (2:6). A possible implication of Paul's wording is that there remains a minority who are not in agreement with the decision of "the majority" regarding the sentence passed on the offender, even though this person has admitted guilt and is grieved by his sin (2:7). Equally likely, however, is that the term *pleiones* (NIV, "majority") means simply "the rest of the community" as opposed to the one offender.[22] This seems to be the meaning of *pleiones* in 9:2 and Philippians 1:14; a similar idiom was also employed by the Qumran community, where "the Many" is equivalent to the entire congregation: "And to any in Israel who freely volunteers to enroll in the council of the Community, the Instructor who is at the head of the Many shall test him with regard to his insight and his deeds."[23]

In order that Satan might not outwit us. For we are not unaware of his schemes (2:11). In keeping with his Jewish contemporaries and unlike most moderns, Paul is acutely aware of Satan's intrigues and of the influence of the demonic realm on human affairs. Jewish literature of the pre-Christian era reveals an increased sensitivity to the activities of Satan and his cohorts, and in some quarters this heightened awareness led to a kind of demonic paranoia.

The author of the book of *Jubilees* (ca. 150 B.C.) went so far as to rewrite the book of Genesis in an attempt to iron out its theological wrinkles while implicating the demonic realm. According to this Jewish writer it was Satan, not Yahweh or his angel, who was responsible for the near sacrifice of Isaac, who planned to slay Moses on his way to confront Pharaoh, who killed the firstborn of Egypt, and who hardened Pharaoh's heart.[24] While Paul avoids this extreme, his Jewish heritage has endowed him with a deeper understanding of the spiritual nature of the conflict between good and evil, and it is this broader perspective that surfaces here (see comments on 2 Cor. 4:4).

Now when I went to Troas . . . I still had no peace of mind. . . . So I said good-by to them (2:12–13). Acts records that Paul's departure from Ephesus and journey to Greece occurred after a serious riot in that city, instigated by the guild of silversmiths, whose financial livelihood was threatened by the advance of the gospel (Acts 19:1–20:3). Paul probably journeyed to Troas by ship, and after the tumult in Ephesus he must have been pleased to find that "the Lord had opened a door" for the gospel in Troas. Yet Paul's concern for the Corinthians and how they had responded to his strongly worded letter carried by Titus compelled him to move on when Titus did not arrive in Troas on schedule. Paul was unwilling to foster a new family in Troas at the expense of his children in Corinth, and his decision to leave behind a potentially fruitful ministry in Troas is a poignant testimony to the genuineness of his words in 1 Corinthians 4:15: "For

REFLECTIONS

ACCORDING TO THE BOOK OF JOB, SATAN ROAMS ALL over the earth looking for those he can ruin (Job 1:6–12), and according to 1 Peter 5:8 he is like a lion continually on the prowl. Paul shares this conviction, and so he enjoins the Corinthians to reaffirm their love for the unnamed brother who sinned. In Paul's view, failure on the part of the Corinthians to make every effort to restore this penitent sinner would render them unwitting participants in the schemes of the enemy. The estrangement of a fallen saint is the victory of Satan, and the first line of defense for the believing community is to become aware of the enemy's designs.

in Christ Jesus *I became your father* through the Gospel" (italics added).

Ministers of the New Covenant (2:14–3:6)

The anxiety of verse 13 breaks into thanksgiving in verse 14 ("Thanks be to God"), as Paul is reminded of the good news that Titus brought of the Corinthians' reconciliation (7:5–16). This line of thought will be resumed in 7:5. The intervening material (2:14–7:4) constitutes a profound theological excursus on the nature of Paul's life, ministry, and message, as one of strength displayed through weakness, life revealed through death, and hope in the midst of despair.

▶ The Triumphal Procession

In 2:14–16 Paul alludes to one of the most spectacular and important celebrations in antiquity, the Roman triumph. Awarded by the senate to honor a victorious general, the triumph was essentially an enormous parade through the heart of Rome. It was designed to display the glory of the Roman general and offer thanks to Jupiter, the chief deity of the Roman pantheon, for granting the victory.[A-1] The festivities could last several days, and not only did the entire populace of Rome turn out to view the spectacle, but Rome itself was copiously adorned to embrace her conquering hero.

Josephus, an eye-witness to one such Triumph, remarks, "It is impossible to describe the multitude of the shows as they deserve, and the magnificence of them all."[A-2] The pageant would include all manner of plunder taken from the enemy, the victorious soldiers, and also captured soldiers and leading officers of the enemy. The captives would be led before the chariot of the conquering general, to the mockery and taunts of the onlookers. In recounting the events of his reign, Augustus boasted, "I waged wars on land and on sea.... In my Triumphs nine kings or children of kings were led before my chariot."[A-3] The climax of the procession involved a sacrifice to the Roman deities and the execution of any eminent captives in the Forum, as Josephus recounts:

Now the last part of this pompous show was at the temple of Jupiter Capitolinus, whither when they were come, they stood still; for it was the Romans' ancient custom to stay, till somebody brought the news that the general of the enemy was slain. This general was Simon, the son of Gioras, who had then been led in this triumph among the captives; a rope had also been put upon his head, and he had been drawn into a proper place in the forum, and had withal been tormented by those that drew him along, and the law of the Romans required that malefactors condemned to die should be slain there.[A-4]

Although the triumphal procession itself was confined to Rome, the imagery of the conquest and the triumph was disseminated throughout the empire on coinage, which depicted vanquished foes, victorious generals, triumphal arches, and so on. Triumphal arches, which served as veritable billboards advertising the conquest, were also scattered throughout the provinces. The first-century visitor to Corinth would have entered its main market through a magnificent triumphal-style arch.[A-5] By the second century A.D. (and perhaps earlier), the adjoining basilica was supported by columns carved in the shape of captured barbarian soldiers.[A-6]

◀

COIN DEPICTING CAPTIVES OF JULIUS CAESAR

Who always leads us in triumphal procession (2:14–16). While some translations of verse 14 give the impression that Paul is portraying himself as one of the victors marching in a triumphal procession, this rendering is linguistically impossible. If we were to fill out the NIV translation above in light of the triumphal imagery (see "The Triumphal Procession") and in accordance with the only attested meaning of this Greek construction, we would render this clause, "Thanks be to God who always leads us *as conquered foes* in his triumphal procession."[25] Paul makes a similar statement in 1 Corinthians 4:9: "For it seems to me that God has put us apostles on display at the end of the procession, like men condemned to die in the arena." Although formerly an "enemy of the cross" (Phil. 3:18; see Gal. 1:13; 1 Tim. 1:13), Paul now sees himself as Christ's slave (Rom. 1:1; 2 Cor. 4:5), whose suffering and ministry are offered as a continuous testimony to the glory of Christ and as a fragrant sacrifice (see below) of thanks to God.

And through us spreads everywhere the fragrance of the knowledge of him (2:14). One of the standard features of religious or civic rituals in antiquity was the use of incense and other fragrant materials. Religious processions, the arrival of an important dignitary, the triumphal return of a Roman general, and so on, were all occasions on which such aromatics might be used. In describing the triumphal procession of Aemelius Paulus, Plutarch tells us that "every temple was open and filled with garlands and incense."[26] Continuing the image of the Roman triumph, Paul portrays his crushed and vanquished apostolic existence as the means through which the

aroma of the crucified Christ is mediated to those around him. Paradoxically, God's strength is most potently displayed through Paul's weakness. Already the apostle is preparing the ground for his startling declaration in 12:10, "For when I am weak, then I am strong."

For we are to God the aroma of Christ among those who are being saved and those who are perishing (2:15). Embedded within the imagery of the triumphal procession is an allusion to the Levitical sacrifices of the Old Testament, where the terms *euōdia* (NIV "fragrance") and *osmē* (NIV "aroma") combine to refer to a sacrificial "aroma pleasing to the LORD" (Lev. 2:2, 12; 6:14, etc.). As elsewhere (e.g., Col. 1:24), Paul portrays his apostolic suffering as an extension of the suffering of Christ, and he will make this point more explicitly in 4:10: "We always carry around in our body the death of Jesus."

To the one we are the smell of death; to the other, the fragrance of life (2:16).

TRIUMPHAL ARCH

The Arch of Titus commemorating his Roman triumphal procession after defeating Judea and Jerusalem in the Jewish War.

▼

Although the transitions between metaphors is abrupt, Paul returns to the spectacle of the triumph and notes the differing effects the aroma-filled parade route would have on those involved. For the cheering crowds, the victorious soldiers, and the gloating general, this was the sweet fragrance of victory. But to the unfortunate captives destined for the auctioneer's block or execution in the forum, this was the scent of death itself.

Unlike so many, we do not peddle the word of God for profit (2:17). Preaching the gospel for mere financial gain has been a problem from the earliest days of the Christian movement. Already by the time of the *Didache* (ca. A.D. 80–150) Christian communities were exhorted to judge itinerant Christian teachers with reference to their desire for monetary gain: "And when the apostle leaves, he is to take nothing except bread until he finds his next night's lodging. But if he asks for money he is a false prophet."[27] Paul may have in mind the intruders addressed in chapters 10–13, or he may be referring more generally to that familiar brand of itinerant philosopher who would peddle his teaching for a hefty profit.

The Greek verb Paul uses for "peddle for profit" (*kapēleuō*) was regularly used as an indictment against the Sophists, the popular rhetoricians of Paul's day. As early as Socrates we find the Sophists described as those who "take their doctrines the round of our cities, hawking them about (*kapēleuō*) to any odd purchaser."[28] Philo, Paul's contemporary in Alexandria, makes a similar disparaging assessment of the Sophists: "And the wisdom must not be that of the systems hatched by the word-catchers and Sophists who sell their tenets and argu-

ments like any bit of merchandise in the market."[29] Dio Chrysostom describes this lot as those who come "in the guise of philosophers," yet whose pretentious oratory was displayed solely "with a view to their own profit and reputation."[30]

But the charge of avarice was leveled against a variety of schools of philosophy whose practitioners earned their livelihood from attracting a crowd and then gaining a following. Indeed, the Cynics sometimes fared little better than the Sophists:

> These Cynics, posting themselves at street-corners, in alleyways, and at temple-gates, pass around the hat and play upon the credulity of lads and sailors and crowds of that sort, stringing together rough jokes and much tittle-tattle and that low bandage that smacks of the market-place.[31]

Paul's point is that unlike so many who proclaim their "religion" for a price, he and his companions preach Christ for altruistic reasons.

Are we beginning to commend ourselves again? . . . You yourselves are our letter . . . written not with ink . . . not on tablets of stone (3:1–3). No doubt Paul's initial ministry in Corinth involved a sincere effort to win the trust of these new believers, to "commend" himself to them. Paul's denial of any need for continual self-commendation is grounded in the obvious reality of their transformed lives: "You show that you are a letter from Christ" (3:3).

To the Corinthians, surrounded on all sides by monuments of self-commendation, Paul's words may have been heard as a friendly barb. Many of Corinth's civic structures were donated by wealthy patrons, and inscriptions of self-commendation, engraved in stone and proudly heralding the name of the benefactor, have been found on monuments, temples, market stalls, and pavements (see "The Erastus Inscription"). Although slightly later than Paul, an inscription on a statue that the orator Herodes Atticus allowed to be erected in his honor bears witness to the indulgent nature of some of these self-commendations: "Given by great Herodes Atticus, pre-eminent above others, who had attained the peak of every kind of excellence . . . famous among Hellenes and furthermore a son [of Greece] greater than them all, the flower of Achaia."[32]

Do we need, like some people, letters of recommendation to you or from you (3:1)? Although letters of reference are common enough today, they played a far more important role in ancient Roman society. Travelers, wishing to avoid the grubby and often sordid environment of roadside inns, relied on local hospitality. To help them obtain it, they carried letters of recommendation from people familiar with the region being traversed. Letters of reference were also written to introduce one party to another, frequently with a view to social advancement or to other practical assistance.[33] Such letters presume a relationship of friendship or authority, or perhaps both

(cf. the letter to Philemon, written by Paul on behalf of the runaway slave Onesimus). Most commentators see here a veiled reference to certain Christian missionaries who arrived in Corinth with letters of recommendation, perhaps from prominent members of the church in Jerusalem, and who subsequently caused trouble for Paul (see "Paul's Opponents in Corinth" at 11:6). This is plausible, but the additional phrase "to you or from you" may indicate simply an innocent reference to the familiar practice of sending and receiving letters of recommendation.

Ministers of a new covenant (3:6). The clear allusions to Jeremiah and Ezekiel in

REFLECTIONS

A MISSIONARY IN A PREDOMINATELY HINDU COUNTRY once related the story of a devout Hindu who admired Christ and studied the Gospels, and who frankly admitted to her, "I would become a Christian if it were not for Christians." This person's experience of Christians had left a bitter taste in his mouth and had led him to reject the faith he sensed, deep within, to be true. In telling the Corinthians that they are "a letter from Christ" read by all (3:2–3), Paul reminds us that our personal conduct and daily witness should authenticate the faith we proclaim. Any disjunction between our faith and our practice will cause our message to fall on deaf ears. Seeing is believing.

▶ The Erastus Inscription

One of the most remarkable discoveries from the excavations in Corinth is the Erastus inscription. Engraved on the pavement between the theatre and the market, the inscription reads, "Erastus in return for his aedileship laid [this pavement] at his own expense." This same Erastus is mentioned by Paul in Rom. 16:23 and is called the "city treasurer."

Both the Greek term used by Paul (*oikonomos*), and the Latin term found in the inscription (*aedile*) refer to one of the chief administrators of Roman Corinth. Elected magistrates were expected to make public benefactions in gratitude for their election, and Erastus's pavement was an appropriate token of appreciation to the local citizenry.

3:3 (see Jer. 17:1; 31:33; Ezek. 36:26–27) lead to a direct citation of Jeremiah's memorable "new covenant" (Jer. 31:31), as Paul explains that his ministry is the fulfillment of the prophetic expectation of the inner renewal of God's people. The newness of Jeremiah's "new covenant" and Ezekiel's "everlasting covenant" (Ezek. 37:26) was its inwardness: "I will write my law on their hearts" (Jer. 31:33); "I will give you a new heart and put a new spirit in you" (Ezek. 36:26). The scrolls from Qumran similarly describe entrance into that community as entering into the "new covenant," though membership in this sect entailed full and complete obedience to the Mosaic law and the rules of the community:[34]

> All who enter the council of holiness of those walking in perfect behavior as he commanded, anyone of them who breaks a word of the law of Moses impertinently or through carelessness will be banished.[35]

The new covenant Paul announces, however, is not of "the letter," which is unable to produce obedience, but of the life-giving Spirit, who energizes from within.

Not of the letter but of the Spirit; for the letter kills, but the Spirit gives life (3:6). In Jewish thought, the connection between "spirit" and "life" was as ancient as Genesis itself (Gen. 1:2; 2:7; 6:17), and Jewish writers regularly linked "spirit" with "life" as the substance that animates humanity: "'Spirit' is the most life-giving, and God is the author of life."[36] But the life Paul describes here is not biological, but ethical, spiritual life, and the roots of the idea go back to the prophet Ezekiel: "I will put my Spirit in you *and you will live*" (Ezek. 37:14). Moral renewal through the infusion of God's Spirit was the hope of the prophets and is the reality of the new covenant community.

The Transforming Glory of the New Covenant (3:7–18)

The letter/Spirit antithesis of 3:6 (see also Rom. 2:29; 7:6) requires elaboration. Thus, in 3:7–18 Paul reflects on the inadequacies of the old covenant in contrast to the transforming power of the new covenant.

The ministry that brought death . . . the ministry that condemns (3:7–9). Paul begins with a description of the Mosaic era that surely must have startled and angered his Jewish contemporaries. Far from a "ministry of death," Jews of the period thought of the Torah as an "eternal law," "made for the sake of righteousness to aid the quest for virtue and the perfecting of character."[37] A common prayer in the ancient synagogue, which Paul himself may have recited, blesses "the Torah of life."[38] It is no wonder that Paul's message encountered fierce opposition from his Jewish kinsmen, including those in Corinth (Acts 18:12–17).

For what was glorious has no glory now in comparison with the surpassing glory . . . how much greater is the glory of that which lasts (3:10–11). Paul is careful to affirm that the Mosaic law did possess a kind of glory. When viewed from the perspective of its origin and purpose, Paul can describe the law as "holy, righteous and good" (Rom. 7:12). Yet when viewed from the standpoint of its efficacy, Paul calls it "the law of sin and death" (8:2). From his post-Damascus vantage point Paul now sees that the glory of the new covenant surpasses the glory of the old in the same way as the sun outshines a candle.

Once again, this is entirely at odds with the views of his fellow-Jews, who described the law as "an eternal light," "a lamp that will abide forever."[39] Paul is consciously rejecting the cherished Jewish notion of the abiding and perpetual glory of the law: "For we who have received the law and sinned will perish . . . the Law, however, does not perish but remains in its glory."[40]

We are very bold . . . not like Moses, who would put a veil over his face (3:12–13). Moses' practice of veiling himself (Ex. 34:29–35) is contrasted with Paul's candid, open proclamation, which Paul is seeking to defend in 2 Corinthians. The Greek word *parrēsia* (NIV, "very bold") is usually associated with speech and denotes frank and candid expression, especially in contrast to duplicitous flattery. The swelling ranks of disingenuous Sophists prompted a renewed concern for sincerity in word and deed, and *parrēsia* became a popular topic for discourses during this period of Roman history:

> But to find a man who in plain terms and without guile speaks his mind with *frankness* (*parrēsia*), and neither for the sake of reputation nor for gain makes false pretensions, but out of good will and concern for his fellow-man stands ready, if need be, to submit to ridicule and to the disorder of the mob—to find such a man is not easy, but rather the good fortune of every great city, so great is the dearth of noble, independent souls and such is the abundance of toadies, mountebanks and sophists.[41]

Paul's spoken proclamation was heavily criticized in Corinth (1 Cor. 2:1–5; 10:10; 11:6; 13:3), and this verse echoes his introductory statement in 2:17: "We speak before God with sincerity."

For to this day the same veil remains when the old covenant is read (3:14–15). Paul coins the phrase "old covenant" in deliberate antithesis to the new covenant prophesied by Jeremiah (Jer. 31:33), inaugurated by Christ (Luke 22:20; 1 Cor. 11:25), and heralded by

◄

VEIL

A veiled Bedouin woman.

Paul (2 Cor. 3:6). The context indicates that the apostle is thinking of the Mosaic law in particular, as verse 15 confirms, "Even to this day when Moses is read, a veil covers their hearts." The primary setting for the reading of the Jewish Scriptures was the local synagogue, and Philo provides an illuminating description of a first-century synagogue gathering:

> [When the Jewish community gathers in the synagogue] they sit according to their age in classes, the younger sitting under the elder, and listening with eager attention in becoming order. Then one, indeed, takes up the holy volume and reads it, and another of the men of greatest experience comes forward and explains what is not very intelligible, for a great many precepts are delivered in enigmatical modes of expression.[42]

Especially prominent in the synagogue was the reading of the law, as this inscription, dated to the first century and found in Jerusalem, illustrates: "Theodotus Vattanus, priest and synagogue leader . . . built this synagogue for the purpose of the reading of the Law and for instruction of the commandments of the Law."[43]

And we, who with unveiled faces all reflect the Lord's glory (3:18). The Greek term behind the NIV's "reflect" (*katoptrizō*) means literally "to gaze upon as in a mirror"; in this passage it denotes studied contemplation of a something—in this case God's glory. Mirrors in antiquity were made of polished metal and did not produce the kind of clear and vivid reflection of modern mirrors. More than a casual glance was needed for personal grooming, and Paul's words here seem carefully chosen to emphasize the believer's steady, transforming contemplation of the glory of the Lord.

▶

SEAT OF MOSES

Stone-carved seat from the Chorazim synagogue in lower Galilee.

right ▶

SYNAGOGUE OF THE HEBREWS INSCRIPTION

▶ Synagogue of the Hebrews

The presence of a Jewish community in Corinth is noted by Philo, and a synagogue is explicitly mentioned in Acts 18.[A-7] A broken inscription found in Corinth and dated to the third century A.D. reads, "Synagogue of the Hebrews." Another fragmentary inscription has been reconstructed to refer possibly to "The teacher and ruler of the synagogue of Corinth."[A-8] According to Acts 18:8, Crispus, the ruler of the synagogue in Corinth, was converted under Paul's ministry.

We are being transformed into his likeness with ever-increasing glory, which comes from the Lord, who is the Spirit (3:18). Paul describes two transformative events in his letters: a present, progressive, moral transformation (Rom. 12:1–2; 2 Cor. 3:18; 4:16–17), and an instantaneous, eschatological, physical transformation (Rom. 8:21–25; 1 Cor. 15:51–54; 2 Cor. 5:1–5; Phil. 3:20–22). Jewish writers of the period looked forward to a glorious transformation in the future, but true parallels to what Paul describes here are hard to find.[44] Paul's new covenant conviction that the life-giving Spirit was presently operative in the believing community led him to use language that would have sounded odd to many of his contemporaries. According to Paul, the renewing Spirit was, even now, restoring

the divine image (NIV, "likeness"), marred by Adam's transgression (see comments on 4:4–6).

Glorious Treasure in Jars of Clay (4:1–18)

Continuing his discussion of the transforming power of the new covenant ministry of the Spirit, Paul reflects on the paradox of the Christian life: inner renewal in the midst of outer decay and life concealed in death.

We have renounced secret and shameful ways; we do not use deception (4:2). The accusation of trickery and deceit was commonly leveled against Sophists and certain philosophers; thus, Paul's words here may not reflect an accusation leveled against him by his detractors in Corinth. Paul is probably trying to distinguish himself and his colleagues from these other itinerant preachers, because on the surface they looked similar: traveling from city to city, speaking on moral themes, gathering a following, soliciting funds, and so on. Using the same terminology as Paul, Lucian (c. A.D. 120–180) describes this brand of philosophers as those who "sell their lessons as wine merchants . . . most of them adulterating and cheating and giving false measure."[45] Both Paul and Lucian use the word *doloō* (to "distort, adulterate, water down"), and the image evoked is of a crafty wine merchant selling a pathetic and diluted concoction.

The god of this age (4:4). Canonical and extracanonical literature reveals a wide variety of designations for Satan (devil, Mastema, Azael, Samael, prince of error, angel of light, etc.), though only here is the evil one referred to with the word "god" (Gk. *theos*). The contrast between this present evil age and the age to come was rooted in the eschatology of the prophets, where phrases such as "in that [coming] day" are commonplace.[46] This antithesis became part of the eschatological idiom of Paul's day and was particularly popular in apocalyptic writings, where the present evil age of foreign domination was contrasted with the day when Israel would throw off the yoke of Gentile oppression and finally "be the head, and not the tail."[47]

Has blinded the minds of unbelievers (4:4). Paul's deep-seated conviction of the power of Satan and his cohorts is echoed throughout Jewish literature of the period, where prayers for protection are common:

- And Abram prayed, "Save me from the hands of evil spirits which rule over the thought of the heart of man."[48]

- Strengthen your servant against fiendish spirits so that he can walk in all that you love, and loathe all that you hate.[49]
- Let not Satan rule over me, nor an evil spirit.[50]

Yet while Paul was keenly aware of the spiritual battle, he was also confident of the believer's victory in Christ (Rom. 8:38–39; Col. 1:13), and it is this sober optimism that separates him from many of his contemporaries.

The light of the gospel of the glory of Christ, who is the image of God (4:4). In 3:18 Paul spoke of transformation into the "likeness" of the Lord; here he identifies Christ as the "image of God." This motif is rooted in Genesis, where Adam is said to have been created in God's image (Gen. 1:26–27). As 1 Corinthians 15:14–49 demonstrates, Paul thought of Christ as a kind of second Adam, rectifying the failure of the first.

Many of Paul's Jewish contemporaries longed for the eschatological restoration of Adam's prefall glory, and the scrolls from Qumran document this sect's intense expectation of inheriting "all the glory of Adam."[51] Paul, however, leaves no room for the veneration of Adam: "In Adam all die ... in Christ all will be made alive" (1 Cor. 15:22; cf. Rom. 5:12–21). Christ has supplanted Adam in the apostle's eschatology. Paul does not look back to the garden, but ahead to Christ's return and the complete conformation of the believer to the image of Christ (Phil. 3:21).

For we do not preach ourselves, but Jesus Christ as Lord (4:5). Once again Paul is carefully distinguishing himself from many of the popular teachers of his day, whose pretentious oratory served mainly as an exercise in vanity. Dio Chrysostom

---

R E F L E C T I O N S

PAUL'S ANALYSIS OF THE HUMAN DILEMMA IS BOTH similar to and different from other Jewish thinkers of his day. Jewish literature of the period accounts for the presence of evil in three primary ways: Satan, the Gentiles, and the evil inclination (i.e., the flesh). Especially important was the influence of the demonic realm, and in the early apocalypses of *1 Enoch* and *Jubilees*, it is the evil angelic host that is held responsible for the entrance of sin, not Adam.

In contrast to these, Paul reserves his most poignant, gripping analysis of the human predicament for his discussion of *the flesh* (Rom. 6–8; Gal 5–6). In his view, it is the life-giving presence of the Spirit (Rom. 8; 2 Cor. 3) that enables believers to successfully resist both the temptations of the flesh and the enticement of the evil one. To be sure, Satan represents an ever-present threat to the believer (2 Cor. 1:11; 1 Thess. 1:18). Those outside of Christ, however, remain helpless pawns in the clutches of these dark powers, blinded by "the god of this age."

(c. A.D. 40–120), who also struggled to distance himself from the Sophists, voices the same complaint to the Athenians: "Now the great majority of those styled philosophers proclaim themselves."[52] According to Epictetus (c. A.D. 50–120), the Sophist implores his listeners, "But praise me! . . . Cry out to me 'Bravo!' or 'Marvelous!'"[53] Seneca (4 B.C.-A.D. 65) is equally scornful of those orators whose "ostentatious gate" and "desire to show off" rendered their trivial discourses useless for the common good: "But speech that deals with the truth should be unadorned and plain. This popular style has nothing to do with the truth; its aim is to impress the common herd."[54]

Your servants for Jesus' sake (4:5). Paul refers to himself in a variety of ways in 2 Corinthians (apostle, minister/servant, ambassador, coworker with God); the term he uses here, *doulos*, is better trans-

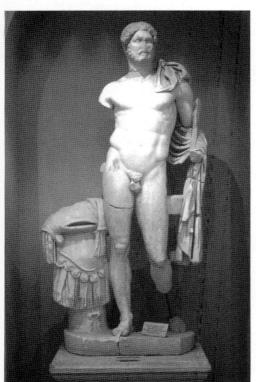

lated "slave" than "servant." While the duties of Roman slaves ranged from farm laborer to physician, the slave was regarded as the lowest order of the social class, "a tool that speaks" (*instrumentum vocale*), with none of the rights of citizens or freedmen. Paul's willingness to wear this label, even metaphorically, is illustrative of his indifference to such distinctions of social rank (1 Cor. 7:20–24; Gal. 3:28) and his readiness to spend and expend himself (2 Cor. 12:15) on behalf of his churches. The qualifying phrase "for Jesus' sake" delimits the sphere of Paul's servitude.

For God . . . made his light shine in our hearts to give us the light of the knowledge of the glory of God in the face of Christ (4:6). Most New Testament scholars rightly believe that Paul's description of a shining light that revealed the glory of God on the face of Christ betrays the apostle's vivid memory of his encounter with the risen Christ on the road to Damascus. In reflecting on his own conversion and applying it to believers generally, Paul strips his story of its nonparadigmatic elements (external light, a voice from heaven, blindness; see Acts 9:3–6; 22:6–18) in order to highlight its most crucial feature: "God . . . made his light shine *in our hearts*." Although the external phenomena associated with Paul's conversion were indeed striking, he presents the significance of this momentous revelation not in terms of what happened *around* him, but in terms of what happened *within* him, which constitutes the true miracle of authentic conversion.

Treasure in jars of clay (4:7). Jars and other kinds of containers were manufactured from a wide variety of materials,

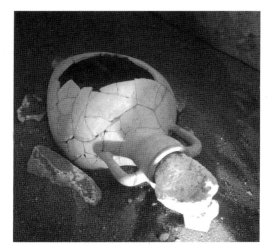

▶

"WE HAVE THIS TREASURE IN JARS OF CLAY..."

though clay was by far the most common. Archaeological digs at ancient sites, including Corinth, unearth vast amounts of pottery fragments, providing a contemporary illustration of Paul's point: the fragile, ephemeral character of earthenware contrasts sharply with the eternal nature of the treasure within. Also implicit in this word picture is the irony of an inestimable fortune concealed in a common clay jar. Corinth had a widespread reputation for the production of exquisite bronze vessels,[55] and this metaphor may have had a

▶ Jesus Christ as Lord: Paul's Counter-Imperial Gospel

"Why, what harm is there in saying 'Caesar is Lord,' and offering incense, and thereby saving yourself?"[A-9] This question, addressed to the aged bishop Polycarp by the local magistrates in Smyrna (c. A.D. 155), is a question that many believers faced during the first three hundred years of the Christian movement. The followers of Jesus proclaimed him as Lord, Savior, and Son of God, yet each of these titles was also claimed by another sovereign, the Roman emperor.

Emperor worship began in earnest sometime after the posthumous deification of Julius Caesar (42 B.C.), and by the middle of the first century the imperial cult was firmly established in Rome and the provinces. By the late A.D. 80s the emperor Domitian was demanding to be addressed as *dominus et deus*, "Lord and God."[A-10]

The veneration of the emperor and the imperial family was not undertaken solely for religious purposes. Significant economic and political benefits accrued to a city with a strong imperial cult, which left municipalities and the upwardly mobile citizenry competing to display their devotion to Caesar.[A-11] Corinth itself had a vibrant imperial cult, with an impressive temple above the forum and an active priesthood.[A-12] Statues of the emperors were scattered throughout the city, as were portraits and honorific inscriptions. All manner of deific titles are

found on these dedications, and the following may be regarded as typical:

The Achaeans erected this monument in honor of the Emperor Caesar Trajan Hadrian Augustus, son of the deified Trajan Parthicus, grandson of the deified Nerva Pontifex Maximus, holder of the tribune power for the eighth time, Consul for the third time, Restorer and Savior and Benefactor of Greece.[A-13]

The epigraphic evidence indicates that the imperial cult was particularly popular with the upper class in Corinth,[A-14] which is not surprising considering the enormous debt the aristocracy owed Julius Caesar for establishing, populating, and supporting the colony. Although Paul instructed his churches to respect Roman authority (Rom. 13:1–7), his message of the impending epiphany from heaven of the Lord Jesus was ultimately deemed politically subversive.

By the first decade of the second century, Christians were routinely executed for failing to pay homage to the Roman gods and the Roman emperor.[A-15] As for Polycarp, after repeatedly being urged to "revile Christ," he finally replied to his inquisitors: "For eighty-six years I have been his servant and he has done me no wrong. How can I blaspheme my King who saved me?" He was subsequently burned at the stake.[A-16]

special poignancy for the proud makers of famed Corinthian bronze.

We are hard pressed on every side, but not crushed; perplexed, but not in despair; persecuted, but not abandoned; struck down, but not destroyed (4:8–9). In Paul's day this style of argumentation was in vogue among the Stoics and Cynics, and the Corinthians would have certainly recognized this antithetical formulation. Plutarch's essays on Stoicism contain the following caricature of the Stoic, who, "being mutilated, is not injured, and taking a fall in wrestling, is unconquerable, and under siege, is impregnable, and being sold into slavery by his enemies, is not taken captive."[56] In each instance, the anticipated negative outcome is unexpectedly truncated, and the intent is to create empathy and respect for the one undergoing such trials. Although similar in form, the presuppositions behind Paul's hardship catalogs are very different from those of the Stoics and Cynics, as 6:3–10 and 11:23–33 will reveal.

We always carry around in our body the death of Jesus. . . . For we who are alive are always being given over to death for Jesus' sake, so that his life may be revealed in our mortal body (4:10–11). In other contexts, Paul forcefully emphasizes the past, completed nature of the believer's death with Christ (Rom. 6:1–11), though here he depicts this event as one that continues to characterize his daily experience. A passage with verbal similarities to 4:10–11 comes from Seneca's "On Despising Death":

> I remember one day you [Lucilius] were handling the well known commonplace—that we do not suddenly fall on death, but advance towards it by slight degrees; *we die every day*. For every day a little of our life is taken from us; even when we are growing, our life is on the wane. We lose our childhood, then our boyhood, and then our youth . . . the final hour when we cease to exist does not of itself bring death; it merely of itself completes the death-process. We reach death at that moment, but we have been a long time on the way.[57]

Seneca refers to the "commonplace" notion that death is a daily experience of life. Paul, however, far from viewing his temporal pilgrimage and sacrificial ministry as the gradual ebbing of life, believed his apostolic suffering to be the means of experiencing and mediating true life—the life of the risen Jesus—in fullest form. For Paul, dying not only *initiates* the believer's new life (Rom. 6:1–11), it also *sustains* the believer's new life and has a redemptive effect on the believing community: "So then, death is at work in us, but life is at work in you" (4:12).

It is written: "I believed; therefore I have spoken." . . . We also believe and therefore speak (4:13). In this verse Paul offers a profound theological rationale for his spoken proclamation, which was under attack in Corinth (cf. 10:10; 12:19; 13:3). While placing himself in continuity with his Old Testament predecessors, Paul explains that his speech issues from the same Spirit that inspired the psalmist and is rooted in faith. Introduced in 2:17 ("we speak in Christ"), this theme will be taken up in 5:11 ("We persuade people").

Though outwardly we are wasting away, yet inwardly we are being renewed day by day (4:16). The distinction between the "outer person" and the "inner person" (NIV, "outwardly," "inwardly") was commonly made in Greco-Roman literature, especially as a means of disparaging humanity's physical component (see comments on 5:1–5). Marcus Aurelius (A.D. 121–180), for example, describes the body as "this dead thing" and exhorts his readers, "Remember that this which pulls the strings is the thing which is hidden within . . . this is life, this, if one may so say, is man."[58] While affirming the priority of the inner over the outer (4:16–17) and the eternal over the transitory (4:17), Paul offers no denigration of the decaying physical body. By means of this familiar language, Paul begins the process of reshaping his readers' anthropology, which will be continued in the verses that follow.

Our Eternal Dwelling (5:1–10)

Paul's confidence in an unseen eternal reality (4:18) leads him to elaborate on the transitory nature of our present earthly condition and the certainty of a transformed physical existence that will come (5:1–5). The apostle's assurances of a future, bodily, immortal existence inspire perseverance and good works (5:6–10), but are at odds with much of the popular eschatology of the period.

Earthly tent . . . eternal house (5:1–4). Paul depicts the temporary status of our present bodily condition through the imagery of a tent. Tents were commonly used by soldiers, herdsmen, and other nomadic tradesmen camping in the open field, but also by attendees at religious feasts and athletic games. As the host of the pan-Hellenic Isthmian games, the environs of Corinth swelled with these temporary dwellings every two years, and

the image in verse 1 of a tent suddenly collapsing (Gk. *katalyō*) would have been familiar to the Corinthians. Equally appropriate is the contrast with a permanent edifice, "a building from God . . . an eternal house" (vv. 1–2). The impressive stone structures of Roman Corinth, some of which are still visible, served as an imposing and daily reminder to the Corinthians of the incorruptible nature of the eternal state, when "mortality is swallowed up by life" (v. 4). Paul's confident present tense in verse 1, "*we have* a building from God," is not intended to indicate the *immediacy* of the new physical state upon death, but its *certainty* (see vv. 6–8).

Longing to be clothed with our heavenly dwelling (5:2). A more precise rendering of this verse might be, "longing to put on our heavenly dwelling as an overgarment." The Greek word Paul uses (*ependysasthai*) indicates a type of clothing that is put on *in addition to* something already being worn. Clothing styles varied only slightly in the Mediterranean basin in the period, consisting of outer garments and inner garments.[59] The outer garments were draped over or wrapped around the inner garment, and it is this layered manner of attire that Paul envisions. The apostle indicates his desire to survive until the second coming of Christ and so to put on his heavenly garment *over* his earthly garment, his physical body.

When we are clothed, we will not be found naked (5:3). Nakedness was more distasteful to Jews than to Gentiles, for both theological and historical reasons. Theologically, it was associated with Adam's transgression and the shame that followed (Gen. 3:7). Historically, Jews of the period viewed nakedness as one of the defining features of Hellenistic culture, and the construction of a gymnasium in Jerusalem—where Jewish men exercised naked like their Greek counterparts—prompted a violent reaction from Jews of the Maccabean era (1 Macc. 1:10–14; 2 Macc. 4:7–20). The (Jewish) author of the book of *Jubilees*, writing around 140 B.C., concludes from the judgment imposed on Adam and Eve in the Garden of Eden: "Therefore it is commanded in the heavenly tablets to all who know the Law that they should cover their shame and not go about naked as do the Gentiles" (*Jub.* 1:31).

Paul, in contrast to the popular dualism of Greek thinking (see "The After-Life"), feels a strong aversion to the separation of the material and immaterial components of personhood, and thus he chooses a word with a negative connotation to describe this condition, "naked." Yet the full force of his point would not have been felt by many of his readers in Corinth, who probably did not share his Jewish scruples on this subject. Nude figures graced the pottery, sculptures, artwork, and coinage of Roman Corinth, and nakedness per se was not considered objectionable. The public baths, the gymnasiums (from the Gk. word *gymnos*, "naked"), and the athletic events were important features of everyday life in Corinth, and in all these venues nudity was taken for granted.

In this tent, we groan and are burdened (5:4). Greek writers often described the body as a prison or tomb of the soul, which would be finally discarded upon death. Popular Greek philosophy viewed the physical component of human existence with contempt, believing it to be a lower nature, capable of only base desires and instincts. Although writing later than Paul, Plotinus perfectly summarizes this significant strand of Greek thought: "The body is brute beast touched to life. The true man is the other . . . the Soul which even in its dwelling here may be kept apart."[60]

In contrast to his pagan contemporaries, Paul's view of humanity is rooted in Genesis and affirms the goodness of the material creation, including humanity's

◀

THE TABERNACLE

This is a model of the "tent" where the people of Israel worshiped God in their desert wanderings.

physical component. Paul's "groaning" is not for release from the shackles of bodily existence, but for the transformed physical state that will occur at Christ's second coming (Phil. 3:20–21) or the resurrection (1 Cor. 15:35–49). As Paul's encounter with the council of the Areopagus illustrates (Acts 17:16–34), this was not an easy proposition for the philosophically trained Greek mind to accept.

The Spirit as a deposit (5:5). See comments on 1:22.

Away from the body and at home with the Lord (5:8–9). Although Paul prefers to bypass the intermediate "naked" state, when the soul and/or spirit is temporarily separated from the body, he comforts himself with the knowledge that during this period he will be "at home" with the Lord. Paul chooses two picturesque words to describe this dilemma, both drawn from the vocabulary of the traveler. The Greek word *ekdēmeō* (NIV "away from") was used of a person who journeyed abroad, be it voluntarily or even in exile. In view of civic duties, the conscientious citizen might notify the proper authorities of an impending journey: "If we change our residence, or go abroad [*ekdēmeō*], we shall give notice."[61]

Its antonym, *endēmeō* (NIV, "at home"), describes someone living in his or her homeland, among friends and family. At this point in his missionary career, Paul has traversed innumerable miles of Roman roads, endured harrowing shipwrecks, spent countless months in foreign lands, and even experienced rejection from his own people (Gal. 5:11; 1 Thess. 2:14–16). It is no surprise that he should come to see the Christian life as a journey toward a home as yet unseen: "for we walk by faith, not by sight" (2 Cor. 5:7).

The judgment seat of Christ (5:10). Of Corinth's many impressive structures, its

GRECO-ROMAN ATTIRE

Terracotta fiture of a woman wearing a *chitōn* (tunic) and *himation* (cloak).

right ▶

GREEK ATHLETE

Statue of an athlete stooping to throw the discus.

bēma (NIV, "judgment seat") was certainly one of the finest. Located in the center of the large marketplace, Corinth's bēma was modeled after the bēma built by Caesar Augustus in Rome and was originally covered in marble with elaborately carved molding.[62] The bēma had two primary functions in the civic life of Corinth: It served as the seat for judicial pronouncements and, more commonly, as the platform for public oration.

During his initial ministry in Corinth, Paul was forced to stand before the Roman Governor Gallio seated on the bēma and face accusations from his fellow Jews (Acts 18:12–17). No doubt both Paul and the Corinthians had vivid memories of this event, and it may be that Paul is purposefully drawing on this shared recollection. Paul's concern, however, is with the bēma of Christ, not that of Gallio. In employing this image, the apostle invests this important municipal structure with a new significance, making it an object lesson for the judgment to come. The thoughtful Corinthian believer would probably be reminded of these words on his or her next visit to the marketplace.

Paul's Ministry of Reconciliation (5:11–6:2)

In 5:11–21 Paul offers a summary of his message and ministry, and the pivotal word in this ten-verse synopsis is "reconciliation" (vv. 18–20). Paul relates *his motives*, which include both fear (v. 11) and love (v. 14), and also explains *the results* of his ministry: inwardly transformed people ("a new creation," v. 17)

▶ The After-Life

The average citizen of first-century Corinth was familiar with a wide variety of views concerning the after-life. The popular Homeric legends spoke of the dreary underworld of Hades, to which all mortals are destined (*Odyssey* 11). Plato reasoned that the soul of the noble philosopher would survive death and attain perfect knowledge (*Phaedo*). Epicureans and Stoics were skeptical about *any* post-mortem existence (Epicurus, *Principal Doctrines*; Marcus Aurelius, *Meditations*), while the mystery religions (like the Isis cult in nearby Isthmia) promised their initiates a blissful celestial immortality.

One of the more common inscriptions on grave markers in this period is the epitaph: "I was not, I was, I am not, I care not." Funerary reliefs and artifacts also reveal the primitive but enduring notion that the spirit of the deceased lived on in the tomb. In defense of his plans for an elaborate funerary monument, one wealthy Roman reasons, "It is quite wrong for a man to decorate his house while he is alive, and not to trouble about the house where he must make a longer stay."[A-17]

With no clear conception of the after-life, it is no wonder that Paul could refer to unbelievers in Thessalonica as "those who have no hope" (1 Thess. 4:13). While vastly different, these pagan belief systems were united in their rejection of a bodily resurrection. But neither was first-century Judaism in complete agreement on this issue (Matt. 22; Acts 23). Some Jewish thinkers of the period, influenced by Hellenistic ideas, affirmed the immortality of the soul apart from any physical resurrection.[A-18] Others, including Jesus, Paul, and the Pharisees, vigorously defended the notion of a bodily resurrection.[A-19] Amidst this cacophony of voices, Paul's clear instructions to the Corinthians on the resurrection (1 Cor. 15) and the intermediate state (2 Cor. 5:1–10) provided hope for the discouraged ("Take courage!," 2 Cor. 5:6) and motivation for all toward godly living: "for we must all appear before the judgment seat of Christ" (v. 10).

▶

GALLIO INSCRIPTION

The text mentions Gallio, the Roman governor of Achaia, before whom Paul stood at the Corinthian *bēma*.

with a new orientation ("no longer living for ourselves," vv. 15–16). *The basis* of Paul's new covenant ministry of reconciliation is expressed in terms of the centripetal event of human history: the death and resurrection of Christ (vv. 15, 21).

We try to persuade [people] (5:11). The art of "persuasion" was deeply rooted in Greek society, and the Greek term *peithō* (NIV, "persuade") enjoyed a cultural and literary heritage in the Greco-Roman world that few other words can rival.[63] So important was *persuasion* to the Greeks that she was deified as a goddess and worshiped. Writing around A.D. 175, Pausanius describes the "Sanctuary of Persuasion" located in the center of the marketplace in Corinth.[64] The Roman orator Cicero (106–43 BC) articulates the ideal to which so many aspired:

> I mean the kind of eloquence which rushes along with the roar of a mighty stream, which all look up to and admire, and which they despair of attaining. This eloquence has power to sway men's minds and move them in every possible way. Now it storms the feelings, now it creeps in; it implants new ideas and uproots the old.[65]

Especially prominent in the first and second centuries were the Sophists, whose persuasive oratory dazzled the crowds while lining their own pockets. Not only was Corinth familiar with this class of high-powered rhetoricians, they also erected statues to their favorite Sophists and became the beneficiaries of public buildings from the wealthier practitioners of the art. Although some scholars have wondered about the connection between verses 10 and 11, from the perspective of the Corinthians the link between the *bēma* and Paul's "persuasion" would have seemed natural. In a speech in Tarsus, the philosopher-Sophist Dio Chrysostom (A.D. 40–120) asked his audience why they wanted so much to hear "sweet-voiced songbirds" like himself, and concluded:

> Do you believe that we possess a different power in word and thought alike, a power of *persuasion* [*peithō*] that is keener and truly formidable, which you call rhetoric, a power that holds sway both in the market place and on the *bēma?*[66]

Compared to the crowd-pleasers the Corinthians are so accustomed to, Paul receives poor marks: "For some [of you] say, 'His letters are forceful . . . but his speaking amounts to nothing'" (10:10; cf. 11:6; 12:19; 13:3). Paul has already defended his unadorned style in a previous letter to the Corinthians, where he explains that he did not come with "eloquence" or "persuasive words" lest their faith rest on mere human ingenuity (1 Cor. 2:1–5). As we will see, however, he does not succeed in silencing his critics.

An opportunity to take pride in us (5:12). Seen in the context of Paul's continuing dialogue with the Corinthians over his unimpressive public speaking,[67] his concern to give them a reason to be proud of him is easily understood. In the typical Greco-Roman city, the local Sophist was an object of civic pride, as were buildings, coinage, canals, and other municipal achievements. Not unlike professional sports today, vicious rivalries sometimes developed between cities over whose representative was superior, as illustrated by the famous dispute between Polemo, hero of Smyrna, and Favorinius, spokesman for Ephesus.[68] Philostratus, the historian of the sophistic movement, goes to great lengths to recount the various exploits and entrepreneurial acts of the Sophists, all in service of one essential point: "For not only does a city give a man renown, but the city itself gains it from the man."[69]

Those who take pride in what is seen rather than in what is in the heart (5:12). A more exact translation of this phrase is "those who boast in externals." Again, it is the arrogant, self-commending Sophists Paul has in mind. Boasting, in fact, was a prime characteristic of the Sophists, and in a rare moment of unpartisan candor, Philostratus labels the entire Sophistic vocation "a profession prone to egotism and arrogance."[70] Particularly relevant is the speech of self-commendation that the Sophist Favorinus (A.D. 80–150) delivered in Corinth after he discovered that a statue the Corinthians had erected in honor of his eloquence had been removed. Given his superior lineage, athletic prowess, wisdom, and eloquence, Favorinus concludes, "Ought [I] not have a bronze statue here in Corinth? Yes! And in every city!"[71]

If we are out of our mind (5:13). The way Paul has constructed this sentence (in Greek) indicates he is responding to an accusation, and scholars have long puzzled over what activity could possibly warrant the charge that Paul has been "out of his mind." Is it his untiring zeal (2 Cor. 6:3–10)? His ecstatic experiences (1 Cor. 14:18; 2 Cor. 12:1–10)? His alleged fondness for self-commendation (2 Cor. 3:1; 5:12)? In all likelihood Paul's terminology reflects the language of his detractors in Corinth, those whose rhetorical sensitivities are easily offended.[72]

Indeed, Paul's unusual word for being out of his mind (*existēmi*) is found in popular rhetorical handbooks to describe an orator who fails to persuade because of his unpolished delivery.[73] Paul knows, as the Corinthians do not, that when form dominates over content, the result is misplaced faith. Thus, he is determined not to pattern his ministry after the self-serving style of the Sophists. Yet his straightforward, no-frills oratory does not sit well with some in Corinth and has become a running joke among this group (2 Cor. 10:10).

New creation (5:17). Although Paul introduces the phrase "new creation" into Christian vocabulary in his letter to the Galatians (Gal. 6:15), it was already current in the Judaism of his day. The apocalyptic visionaries spoke of a "new creation" in which Gentile oppression would end and Israel herself would finally be vindicated over the nations.[74] Somewhat later, the rabbis became fond of referring to a convert to Judaism as "a new creature," and this language probably had first-century antecedents.[75] Particularly illuminating, and contemporary with Paul, is the imagery found in *Joseph and Aseneth*, a Hellenistic romance of Diaspora Judaism. In this fictitious work, the patriarch Joseph prays for the conversion of Aseneth, a pagan priestess who had fallen hopelessly in love with him, and whom he later marries (cf. Gen. 41:45):

> *You, O Lord, bless this virgin,*
> *make her new through your Spirit*
> *re-create her by your hidden hand*
> *give her new life through your life . . .*
> *and number her with your people.*[76]

Given the emphasis in 2 Corinthians 3–5 on *the Spirit, newness,* and *life,* this text offers an illuminating parallel to 2 Corinthians 5:17. Depicting conversion as a dramatic *new creation* underscores a complete and irrevocable break with the past, and so is an ideal expression to apply to converts from a pagan environment like Corinth. Paul's point is to remind the Corinthians who they are in Christ: a renewed humanity, already being transformed into the image of Christ through the Spirit (3:17–18).

The ministry of reconciliation (5:18–19). What Paul earlier refers to as the "ministry of the Spirit" (3:8) and the "ministry of righteousness" (3:9), he calls here "the ministry of reconciliation." The word group *katallagē* (NIV, "reconciliation") is drawn from the Greco-Roman political arena, where it referred to removal of enmity between two aggrieved parties.[77] Diplomatic envoys ("ambassadors," see below) between warring nations or communities in conflict hoped to achieve reconciliation and so gain a reputation for successful arbitration.

After a crushing defeat by the Romans, the first-century B.C. historian Dionysius of Halicarnassus records how the Sabines "sent ambassadors to the consul to sue for peace . . . and with difficulty obtained a reconciliation."[78] The reconciliation Paul describes, however, is initiated and accomplished by only one party, God, who has appointed his apostles (and ultimately all believers) as his emissaries in the task of reconciliation.

Christ's ambassadors (5:20). Continuing the imagery of Greco-Roman diplomacy, Paul explains that he and his coworkers are Christ's "ambassadors, as though God were making his appeal through us." The task of ambassador in Roman society fell, naturally, to the educated and eloquent, the *literati* who could best represent the interests of the polis. By the first and second century A.D. these prestigious assignments had become so monopolized by Sophists that historians today regularly identify this movement of Paul's day with ambassadorial service.

According to Philostratus, the crowning achievement of a Sophist's career was

REFLECTIONS

IN THE LAST TWO CHAPTERS WE HAVE SEEN PAUL using common imagery in the Greco-Roman world ("inner man/outer man," "reconciliation," "ambassadorial service"), in order to more effectively communicate the gospel in this context. Each of these themes could have been articulated using Jewish categories and symbols, yet Paul purposefully chooses concepts familiar to the Corinthians so that the good news of Christ may take root more easily in the Greek soil of the Peloponnese. While the substance of the gospel remains unchanged, Paul's shrewd use of culturally appropriate symbolism gives his message an indigenous quality crucial for it to truly flourish.

Theologians and missiologists call this "contextualization," and it is just as important today as it was in the first century. The message of God's love and saving work in Christ is for all humanity, and it is our task as "ambassadors for Christ" to translate this message into culturally sensitive forms, without allowing the content of the message to be shaped by the culture. This translation is important not only for our neighbors across the globe, but also for our neighbors across the street.

to be chosen as an ambassador, especially in making a petition to the emperor. The ancient historian recounts famous embassies by Sophists to Domitian (81–96 A.D.), Trajan (98–117), and Hadrian (117–138),[79] revealing the influence and power of these individuals in Greco-Roman society. According to Favorinus, Corinth's strategic position as "the promenade of Hellas" meant that "every year crowds of travelers, pilgrims, merchants, and *ambassadors*" passed through its gates.[80]

Heard within this context—as it would have been in Corinth—the polemical edge to Paul's argument is considerably sharpened. Unlike so many who aspired to represent the Corinthian community as its spokesman before the emperor, Paul turns this venerated tradition upside down and claims to represent the Great Emperor to the Corinthians—"as if God himself were making his appeal through us" (5:20). Indeed, in appropriating the terminology of Greek diplomacy and employing it as a vehicle for the Gospel, we see Paul the missionary at his finest.

Paul's Hardships (6:3–13)

Having summarized the *nature* of his message and ministry (5:10–6:2), Paul now focuses on the *character* of the minister. By means of the familiar hardship catalog, he demonstrates his altruistic motives and self-sacrificing labor.

As servants of God we commend ourselves in every way: in great endurance; in troubles, hardships and distresses (6:4). In 4:8–9, 6:3–10, and 11:23–33 Paul presents the Corinthians with his apostolic credentials, a partial list of hardships he has endured on their behalf. These "hardship catalogs," as they are called, were part of the standard repertoire of Stoic and Cynic instruction and served to demonstrate the moral character of the teacher. Through these inventories of adversity the teacher sought to

◀

CORINTH

The Lechaeon Road leading into the Roman city with the Acrocorinth in the background.

exemplify three primary virtues: fortitude, self-sufficiency, and indifference to external circumstances.

In using this form of argument Paul also offers himself as a model to emulate, but he qualifies these virtues in significant ways. Fortitude and strength, perhaps; but more important, weakness (11:30; 12:10). Dependence on self? Absolutely not! Rather, dependence on God (6:6–7; 12:9). Unaffected by circumstances? Not really. While patiently enduring pain, Paul is not ashamed to admit profound emotion (1:8–9; 6:9; 11:28). Most of the following hardships are repeated in 11:23–33, and the details of each ordeal will be discussed there. At the present we will focus on comparing the perspective of Paul's hardship catalogs with some of his Greco-Roman contemporaries.

In beatings, imprisonments and riots; in hard work, sleepless nights and hunger (6:5). "Hardships . . . put virtue to the test" and successfully enduring hazardous trials demonstrated the philosopher's strength and superiority.[81] According to the *Epitome of Stoic Ethics* compiled by Arius Didymus (first century B.C.), the noble Stoic is "great, powerful, eminent and strong . . . because he has possession of the strength which befalls such a man, being invincible and unconquerable" (11g). In language similar to Paul, Epictetus refers to "exile and imprisonment, and bonds and death and disrepute" as matters of no concern.[82]

Like the Stoics, Paul believes physical hardships are of some value (1 Cor. 9:27; 1 Tim. 4:8), though his concern is not to parade Stoic bravado and claim "invincibility." Rather, he needs to make the Corinthians aware—especially those who question his leadership—of his tireless labor on their behalf. Contrary to the Stoic

emphasis on invulnerable strength, Paul focuses his attention on his weakness (see comments on 12:10).

In purity, understanding, patience and kindness; in the Holy Spirit and in sincere love; in truthful speech and in the power of God (6:6–7a). The ideal sage, according to popular Stoic (and Cynic) representation, is one who relies solely on his own inner resources to face the deprivations and calamities that fortune supplies. According to Stoic doctrine, "he makes the whole matter [of happiness] depend upon himself" and is enjoined by God, "If you wish any good thing, get it from yourself."[83] Paul, by contrast, is adamant that his strength rests in "the Holy Spirit . . . and in the power of God" (cf. 3:1–6; 12:9–10); this is the most fundamental difference between the valiant Stoic and the follower of Christ.

With weapons of righteousness in the right hand and in the left (6:7b). Military imagery occurs frequently in Paul's letters, and the description here is of a well-equipped Roman legionary.[84] The offensive weapon in the right hand is either a medium-length javelin (infantrymen carried two) or a short thrusting

sword, while the left hand holds the defensive weapon, a sturdy shield. Roman field tactics called for both javelins to be discharged from a short distance, whereupon the soldier rushed upon the wounded enemy to finish him off with a quick thrust of his sword.

Through glory and dishonor, bad report and good report; genuine, yet regarded as impostors; known, yet regarded as unknown; dying, and yet we live on; beaten, and yet not killed (6:8–9). In the ancient Mediterranean world, honor and shame were core values, and within the highly stratified social structure of Roman society a great deal of daily energy was expended avoiding shame and accumulating honor. As a group value, honor was gained through public recognition (formally or informally) of personal worth. In expressing his indifference to public opinion, Paul dons the mantle of the suffering sage willing to endure contempt for the good of the community. Such a role was actually honored in Mediterranean society, and contemporary philosophers often adopted this posture:

- Hunger, exile, loss of reputation, and the like have no terrors for [the noble sage]; nay he holds them as mere trifles.[85]
- These are examples of indifferent things: life, death, reputation, lack of reputation, toil, pleasure, riches, poverty, sickness, health.[86]

Sorrowful, yet always rejoicing; poor, yet making many rich; having nothing, and yet possessing everything (6:10). Once again, Paul's argument reflects both continuity and discontinuity with his Greco-Roman contemporaries. Unlike the Stoic, who strove to "view with unconcern pains

and losses, sores and wounds . . . wholly unchanged amid the diversities of fortune," Paul freely admits his sorrow (cf. 1:8–9; 7:5; 11:28–29).[87] The display of emotion during hardship was considered an indication of moral weakness, hence Epictetus extols the man "who though sick is happy, though in danger is happy, though dying is happy, though condemned to exile is happy, though in disrepute, is happy."[88] Yet Paul does advocate contentment in all circumstances (Phil. 4:11–13), and the final words of 2 Corinthians 2:10, "having nothing, and yet possessing all things" echo an important Stoic principle:

> Alone and old, and seeing the enemy in possession of everything around me, I, nevertheless, declare that all my holdings are intact and unharmed. I still possess them; whatever I have had as my own, I have. . . . So far as my [true] possessions are concerned, they are with me, and ever will be with me.[89]

The Temple of God and the Temple of Idols (6:14–7:1)

The plea of 6:1 not to receive God's grace in vain is now given concrete expression in a prohibition against nurturing harmful relationships with unbelievers. Paul treated this topic in 1 Corinthians 8; 10:14–22, but apparently his advice was treated too lightly.

Do not be yoked together with unbelievers (6:14). The scene evoked by Paul's words is less obvious to those living in industrialized Western societies, where a team of oxen plowing a field is an unimaginable sight. The term *heterozygeō*, to yoke differently, refers to placing two animals of different species under the same yoke (e.g., an ox and a donkey). The obvious difference in strength, height, and disposition could lead to disastrous consequences. Although one *application* of this verse relates to believers marrying unbelievers, Paul's purview is much broader and includes all manner of spiritually detrimental social intercourse, especially pertaining to the practice of frequenting pagan temples (see below).

What harmony is there between Christ and Belial? . . . between the temple of God and idols? . . . Dear friends, let us purify ourselves from everything that contaminates body and spirit (6:15–7:1). In 1 Corinthians 8:1–13 and 10:14–30, Paul dealt extensively with problems relating to dining in pagan temples and eating meat sacrificed to idols. These activities were not simply a function of pagan religiosity from which the new believer could easily abstain. Rather, they were an integral part of the social fabric of Roman society and were often associated with the fulfillment of civic responsibilities. Since only the well-to-do had homes large enough for a formal dining room, the abundant temples of Corinth

► **THE TEMPLE OF GOD AND THE TEMPLE OF AN IDOL**

(right) The Apollo temple in Corinth.

(bottom right) A model of the Jerusalem temple.

REFLECTIONS

FOR JEWS OF PAUL'S DAY, THE TEMPLE IN JERUSALEM was a symbol of God's favor, of his choice of Israel, and a visual reminder of God's presence with his people. In line with the perspective of the prophets (Jer. 7, Mic. 3:9–12), Jesus (John 4:20–24), and other New Testament writers (Heb. 8:1–6; 1 Peter 2:4–10), Paul undermines the significance of this physical structure by claiming that the Christian community now constitutes the true dwelling place of God: "We are the temple of the living God" (2 Cor. 6:16). As with the temple of old, the sacredness of the Christian assembly issues from the presence of the Holy One—a continual testimony of God's amazing grace.

provided facilities for entertaining dinner parties. The related fees were naturally used for the support of the temple and cult. Numerous invitations to these ancient cocktail parties survive:

> Herais asks you to dine in the (dining-)room of the Serapeion at a banquet of the Lord Serapis tomorrow, the 11th from the 9th hour.[90]

Drunkenness, gluttony, and sexual promiscuity were part and parcel of such affairs, and against this backdrop Paul's harsh warning against the "contamination of body and spirit" (7:1) becomes more

comprehensible.[91] Also understandable is Paul's insistence that Christ and Belial (Satan) cannot consort. Not only were offerings and toasts made to the god, but the deity was believed to be present at the meal and sometimes even sent the invitation: "The god calls you to a banquet being held in the Thoereion tomorrow from the 9th hour."[92] Given Paul's conviction that the worship of pagan deities is actually the worship of demons (1 Cor. 10:20–22), no participation in such rituals could be tolerated. But in a culture where religion and the social order walked hand in hand, such separation was a delicate and dangerous task. It is not surprising that Christians were later charged with misanthropy, antisocial behavior.[93]

Paul's Joyful Reunion with Titus (7:2–16)

Paul now returns to the thought he left dangling in 2:13 and expresses his great joy at the good news Titus brought him in Macedonia of the Corinthians' reaffirmation of their affection for Paul and their commitment to his leadership. The momentum of this positive memory carries Paul into chapters 8 and 9 and helps prepare the ground for his appeal concerning the collection.

◀ *left*

SERAPIS

▶ The Asclepion of Corinth

Dedicated to Asclepius, the god of healing, the Asclepion of Corinth was the ancient equivalent of the modern hospital. Here the ailing person offered a sacrifice and waited for a vision from the deity prescribing a cure. The remains of the temple of Aclepius in Corinth reveal spacious courtyards, baths, fountains, kitchens, and dining rooms. The dining facilities were used for both religious and social functions. Within the main sanctuary stood the cult statues of Asclepius and Hygieia (goddess of health), along with a table for offerings. Located at the entrance of the temple was a stone collection box, in which archaeologists have discovered thirteen copper coins. Also unearthed from the Asclepion was a vast collection of terra-cotta ex-votos, representing bodily parts in need of healing: hands, ears, feet, breasts, and so on.[A-20]

Make room for us in your hearts . . . you have such a place in our hearts that we would live or die with you (7:2–3). Paul does not want his appeal for reciprocated affection to be interpreted as a veiled criticism, and so he reiterates the depth of his commitment to their well-being by means of one of his favorite images, life and death. As a pastor, Paul's unrestrained self-investment in the lives of the Corinthians serves as a cord that binds their fates together. When they suffer, so does Paul; when they rejoice, so does Paul (see 11:28–29). Popular Stoicism, a philosophy vying for the attention of the Corinthians, would have despised such vulnerability as moral weakness:

> This is what you ought to practice from morning till evening: Begin with the most trifling things . . . like a pot, or a cup, and then advance to a tunic, a paltry dog, a mere horse, a bit of land; thence to yourself, your body, and its members, your children, wife, brothers. Look about on every side and cast these things away from you. Purify your judgments, for fear lest [you] be attached to them or grown together with them, and may give you pain when it is torn loose.[94]

I have great confidence in you (7:4). Many commentaries and translations recognize a technical expression in the opening phrase of verse 4 and so render

it, "I can speak quite candidly with you" (cf. 6:11). In the Greco-Roman world of Paul's day, *parrēsia*, candid speech (NIV "confidence"), was the right of every citizen and one of the defining virtues of true friendship. The glories of sincere *parrēsia* were commonly extolled by philosophers; according to Musonius Rufus, the chief disadvantage of being enslaved or in exile was the loss of *parrēsia* (Fragment 9). Perhaps the most detailed treatment of the subject comes from the pen of Philodemus (c. 110–35 B.C.) in his essay "On Frank Criticism" (*Peri parrēsia*), who remarks:

> In short, a wise man will employ frankness (*parrēsia*) toward his friends. . . . Although many fine things result from friendship, there is nothing so grand as having one to whom one will say what is in one's heart and who will listen when one speaks.[95]

As 11:11–12 will reveal, the Corinthians have begun to doubt Paul's affection for them. His choice of words in this verse would be heard by the Corinthians as a profound compliment and a reaffirmation of his committed friendship.

For when we came into Macedonia . . . we were harassed at every turn—conflicts on the outside, fears within (7:5). We have no information on the precise nature of these stressful events, though the "fears within" undoubtedly include his concern over Titus's reception (see comments on 2:12–13).

But God, who comforts the downcast, comforted us by the coming of Titus. . . . He told us about your longing for me, your deep sorrow (7:6–7). Comfort in affliction is a central theme in 2 Corinthians (1:3–11; 2:2–3, 14–17; 4:7–12,

MACEDONIA

16–17; 6:3–10) and arises from the relief Paul felt at the gracious treatment Titus received in Corinth. As Paul's emissary, Titus was charged with a difficult task: to confront the Corinthians with Paul's forceful letter, to heal the broken relationship without ignoring the grievous offense, and to rekindle enthusiasm for the stalled collection.

Paul's choice of Titus was shrewd. He was Greek (Gal. 2:3) and so shared many cultural affinities with the Corinthians. He was also experienced in politically sensitive missions, having accompanied Paul on his embassy to Jerusalem in resolution of the Gentile question (Gal. 2:1–10). His splendid success in Corinth is perhaps one reason why we later see him commissioned to go to Crete and "straighten out what was left unfinished" (Titus 1:5).

Even if I caused you sorrow by my letter, I do not regret it . . . because your sorrow led you to repentance (7:8–9). The rebuke that aims at edification was commended in Hebrew wisdom literature (Prov. 3:11–12; Sir. 30:1–13) and was considered crucial for moral formation by Greco-Roman philosophers. It was closely associated with *parrēsia*, "frank criticism," and was called "a caring admonition" by Philodemus.[96] According to Plutarch, the painful wound of frank criticism "is healed by the very words which inflicted the hurt. For this reason he who is taken to task must feel and suffer some smart, yet not be crushed or dispirited."[97] Paul's fatherly affection required fatherly discipline, and on this point the Hebrew sage and the pagan moralist were in hearty agreement.

Godly sorrow brings repentance that leads to salvation and leaves no regret, but worldly sorrow brings death (7:10–11). "Salvation" (Gk. *sōtērion*) commonly refers to deliverance from calamity. In this context it may denote fullness of life rather than final eternal life. The sincere repentance described here is delightfully illustrated by one of Paul's Jewish contemporaries, who pictures repentance as a beautiful angel who "renews all who repent and waits on them herself forever and ever."[98]

You were all obedient, receiving him with fear and trembling (7:15). Cultural protocol—Jewish and Roman—dictated that an envoy be afforded the same respect as the person he or she represented.[99] Thus, the Corinthians' warm reception of Titus is particularly comforting for Paul. Philo expresses the matter like this: "Whatever insults ambassadors are subjected to are at all times referred to those who sent them."[100] The principle was stated positively by Jesus: "Whoever receives me, receives the one who sent me" (John 13:20).

REFLECTIONS

CHRISTIANS TYPICALLY THINK OF REPENTANCE AS something necessary for beginning the Christian life, but it should also be an activity that characterizes the Christian life. Like the pilot who continually makes slight course adjustments to keep his aircraft on track, repentance and renewal should characterize our daily walk with Christ. In this passage Paul commends the Christians in Corinth for repenting when confronted with their sin, and in the process makes an important distinction between healthy and unhealthy remorse. In contrast to genuine contrition ("godly sorrow," 7:10), which restores life, stands disingenuous, worldly sorrow, which is closer to resentment than repentance. This kind of sorrow regrets the discovery of the sin more than the sin itself and leads to bitterness and ultimately death (7:11).

Remembering the Poor (8:1–9:15)

The collection for the poor in Jerusalem is a critical venture for Paul, one that the Corinthians have already committed themselves to (see "The Collection"). However, the unstable situation in Corinth, especially the church's strained relationship with Paul, has caused their enthusiasm for the project to wane. The earlier visit of Titus with the "tearful letter" helped get the Corinthians back on board, and in these two chapters Paul gives further advice on the subject prior to his arrival.

The grace that God has given the Macedonian churches (8:1). Paul's ministry in Macedonia began as a result of a vision the apostle received while in Troas, in which he saw a Macedonian pleading for help (Acts 16:6–10). Paul and his companions established churches in Philippi, Thessalonica, and Berea (Acts 16:6–17:15), and by the time of this writing the Macedonians were now offering help to others, in the form of a monetary donation to the Jerusalem fund.

Out of the most severe trial, their overflowing joy and their extreme poverty welled up in rich generosity (8:2).

▶ The Collection

Although Paul is remembered primarily as an evangelist and theologian, he also devoted a great deal of time and energy to organizing a collection to help relieve the economic hardship of the churches in Judea. Following the request of Peter and the leadership of the Jerusalem church that he "continue to remember the poor" (Gal. 2:10; cf. Acts 11:27–30), Paul began actively promoting this charitable contribution in his ministry throughout the Aegean basin.

The scope of this endeavor was truly significant. In the letters that have survived, Paul first explicitly mentions it in 1 Corinthians 16:1–4, though it is clear from this reference that the Corinthians have already been participating in the project, as were the churches in Galatia. In Romans 15:26 Paul confirms that the churches of Achaia are contributing, as well as those of Macedonia (cf. 2 Cor. 8:1–5). From 2 Corinthians 8:19–20 (cf. 1 Cor. 16:3–4) we learn that the apostle himself is going to accompany delegates from the churches to deliver the relief aid to Jerusalem.

As Paul sets out for Jerusalem, Acts records that he is accompanied by representatives from Derbe, Lystra, Berea, Thessalonica, and Ephesus (Acts 20:4). It is commonly assumed that these men are the local delegates chosen to travel with Paul and the collection. According to Romans 15:28–29, Paul's plan is to escort the gift to Jerusalem and then journey to Rome "in the full measure of the blessing of Christ."

While the primary purpose of this charitable gift is to relieve the poverty of the Jerusalem church, in 2 Corinthians 9:12–14 Paul indicates that more is involved than mere financial assistance: "In their prayers [of thanksgiving] for you their hearts will go out to you because of the surpassing grace God has given you."[A-21] Paul reasons that such a generous gift will cause the Jewish believers in Jerusalem to grow in their affection for the expanding Gentile church, thus promoting the unity of Jew and Gentile in Christ and, by implication, strengthening his Gentile mission.

Although the goals of this philanthropic endeavor are noble, the outcome of the collection is not what Paul has anticipated (but see Rom. 15:30–31). After a warm reception by the leaders of the Jerusalem church (Acts 21:17–25), Paul's visit to the temple causes a riot that led to his arrest and subsequent transferal to Rome to stand trial. Paul does indeed make it to Rome, but he arrives there in shackles.

Although Paul does not mention the details of the severe trials in Macedonia or the cause of their poverty, his letters to the Christian communities in this province confirm these hardships. Intense persecution accompanied Paul's proclamation of the gospel in the Macedonian city of Thessalonica, and it seems likely that this contributed significantly to their economic deprivation.[101]

It is important to remember that the distribution of wealth in ancient Mediterranean society was enormously lopsided compared with modern Western societies, and Paul's report of the Macedonians' "extreme poverty" needs to be understood in this light. Considering that there was virtually no middle class in the first-century Roman world of Achaia and Macedonia and that the vast majority of the population lived at or below the subsistence level, the colloquialism "dirt poor" would not be an inappropriate description of the Macedonian communities responsible for this generous gift.

They gave as much as they were able, and even beyond their ability (8:3). Perhaps it was their own low estate that allowed the Macedonians to feel more keenly the deprivation of their brothers and sisters in Judea. Dio Chrysostom, who was once clothed, fed, and given shelter by a local peasant and his family after being shipwrecked on Euboea (an island south of Macedonia, off the coast of Greece) reflects on the openhanded generosity of the poor:

> They light a fire more promptly than the rich and guide one on the way without reluctance . . . and often they share what they have more readily. When will you find a rich man

who will give the victim of a shipwreck his wife's or his daughter's purple gown or any article of clothing far cheaper than that: a mantle, a tunic, though he has thousand of them, or even a cloak from one of his slaves?[102]

This service to the saints (8:4). The word rendered "saints" represents the Greek term *hagioi* (lit., "holy ones"), which is one of Paul's favorite designations for those who have placed their faith in Christ.[103] This language is common in the Old Testament, where it denotes persons or objects separated and consecrated to the Lord's service.[104] It later came to refer to God's elect people as a whole, particularly in distinction from the pagan nations.[105] Paul's frequent use of such rich and powerful language serves to reinforce the new personal identity of the believer ("a new creation," 2 Cor. 5:17), while also helping to reorient the social identity of the believing community as God's elect and holy people.

So we urged Titus, since he had earlier made a beginning, to bring also to completion this act of grace on your part (8:6). Apparently during his previous visit, after successfully representing Paul's grievance, Titus was also able to revive the stalled collection. Paul's decision to

ERASTUS INSCRIPTION IN CORINTH

Erastus was a well-known patron in Corinth, a city administrator, and a Christian.

send Titus ahead of him with the present letter may have been a result of his progress on this front.

But just as you excel in everything—in faith, in speech, in knowledge . . . see that you also excel in this grace of giving (8:7). Paul probably refers here to those remarkable manifestations of the Spirit discussed in his earlier correspondence: glossalalia (1 Cor. 12:10; 14:1–19), miracle-working faith (12:9–10; 13:2), and supernatural discernment (12:8; 13:2). Paul uses the same word here (*perisseuō*) to describe the Corinthians' excelling in charismata as he did earlier (2 Cor. 8:3) to describe Macedonians' excelling in generosity. He wants the Corinthians to abound not only in the spectacular gifts that inspire awe and are focused on the local assembly, but also in the less dramatic gifts that benefit the larger body of Christ.

For if the willingness is there, the gift is acceptable according to what one has (8:12). The sentiment expressed here was widely held in the Jewish and Greco-Roman world and is illustrated in the story of "the widow's mite" in Mark 12:41–44. On the Jewish side, Tobit 4:8 is relevant: "Measure your alms by what you have; if you have much, give more; if you have little, do not be afraid to give less in alms." The enlightened pagan moralist Dio Chrysostom thought along similar lines: "No gift is inadequate which is prompted by affection."[106]

Our desire is . . . that there might be equality (8:13). "Equality" was deeply

▶ Social Stratification in Ancient Mediterranean Society

Most people in the first-century were relatively poor by modern standards.[A-22] At the top of the social hierarchy were the Roman imperial aristocracy, senators, equestrians, the provincial aristocracy, and the (relatively few) men and women who had made their fortune through successful trade, or other skills. Those dependent on the elite upper strata for their livelihood included slaves, freedmen, and some freeborn who assumed important offices for their master or patron—administrative, cultic, or military. Beneath these were those artisans, teachers, small landowners, shopkeepers, and certain members of the military establishment, who worked hard and enjoyed seasons of modest success, but were still relatively poor by today's standards.

Roughly 70 percent of the populace survived at or below the subsistence level. They lived hand to mouth and spent their day hoping to earn enough to feed themselves and their dependents. In this group we would find less successful craftsmen, clients of patrons, day laborers, slaves, and tenant farmers. Lucian vividly depicts the unhappy lot of this large majority of the populace: "Toiling and moiling from morning till night, doubled over their tasks, they merely eke out a bare existence."[A-23] At the very bottom were the outcasts: orphans, widows, and those unable to work because of illness or physical impairment.

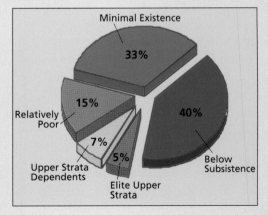

imbedded in the ideals of Greek democracy and was copiously extolled by the great thinkers of Greece: Plato, Aristotle, Demosthenes, Isocrates, and so on. The playwright Euripides advised: "It is better, my son, to honor Equality, who always joins friend to friend, city to city, allies to allies . . . but the lesser is always in opposition to the greater, and so begins the dawn of hatred."[107] Philo, Paul's older contemporary in Alexandria, devoted a lengthy essay to this theme, defining equality as "the parent of peace."[108] In a similar vein, Paul also understands that extreme economic disparity will engender discord and disunity, and this recognition seems to have played a role in his strenuous campaign for this relief fund.

Your plenty will supply what they need, so that in turn their plenty will supply what you need. Then there will be equality (8:14). Paul's concern for equality should not be construed in terms of strict economic parity. Paul does not command wealthy converts to liquidate their assets. Rather, he exhorts them not to put their trust in ephemeral wealth but instead to be eager to share (1 Tim. 6:17–19). Both Paul and the local assemblies benefited from the hospitality of wealthy church members (Rom. 16:23), and Paul himself experienced seasons of plenty (Phil. 4:12). As the citation of Ex. 16:18 in verse 15 indicates, Paul's concern is that everyone's basic needs are met.

More important are the implications of these verses for Paul's theology of work. According to Paul, the goal of work is not the *accumulation* of wealth, but its

R E F L E C T I O N S

IN ROMANS 12:8 PAUL MENTIONS THE SPIRITUAL gift of philanthropy, though in 2 Corinthians 8 and 9 he speaks more generally of a Christian grace in which all believers are called to abound: generosity. Paul couches his discussion in language designed to communicate that generosity as an act of spirituality and a necessary consequence of faith in Christ. He calls it a *grace* (8:1, 6) and a *spiritual endowment* (8:7) *given from God* (8:1). It is a *ministry* (9:12) and *service to the saints* (8:4–7; 9:1), modeled on *the sacrificial offering of Christ* (8:8) which brings *glory to God* (8:19; 9:14). In Paul's view, willingness to contribute financially to the needs of others is a concrete measure of the sincerity of the believer's love (8:9). This judgment is a natural application of the principle enunciated by Jesus: "For where your treasure is, there your heart will be also" (Matt. 6:21).

▶ *Aequitas* ("Equality")

Roman imperial society, with its elitist oligarchy and rigid hierarchical structure, showed little enthusiasm for the democratic principles of Greek culture. The Roman emperors, however, made shrewd use of the virtue of Equality (Lat., *Aequitas*) on their coinage, which served as imperial propaganda. *Aequitas* is personified as a beautiful woman holding scales (symbolic of justice and equity) and a cornucopia (symbolic of prosperity). The inscription on many coins depicting *Aequitas* typically reads "Augustan Equality." It is entirely possible that at least some coins of this type were contributed to the Jerusalem relief fund, whose goal, Paul tells us, was "equality."

◀
THE GODDESS AEQUITAS

dissemination: "He who has been stealing . . . must work, doing something useful with his hands, *that he might have something to share with those in need.*"[109] Paul ardently commends personal industry, not for personal gain, but in order to be a blessing to others: "You will be made rich . . . so that you can be generous on every occasion."[110]

The brother who is praised by all the churches . . . [and] our brother who has often proved to us in many ways that he is zealous (8:18, 22). It is curious that Paul does not mention the names of the brothers he is recommending. Some commentators suppose that their names were recorded in the original, but were subsequently expunged after some moral failure on their part. This is an unnecessary conjecture. Since these individuals will be present with Titus when this letter is delivered and read, there is no need for their names to be mentioned here. To us, their identity will remain a mystery, though Luke, Timothy, and Apollos are frequently suggested as possibilities. The brother of verse 22 may have been one of the representatives from Macedonia who accompanied Paul to Jerusalem with the collection: Sopater, Aristarchus, or Secundus (Acts 20:4).

He was chosen by the churches to accompany us as we carry the offering (8:19). The method of selection used by the Macedonian churches was probably some kind of an electoral procedure, as suggested by the verb *cheirotoneō*, which originally meant to elect by a show of hands. This would have been a natural course of action for the democratically oriented Macedonian assemblies; it was also practiced in the primitive church: *Didache* 15:1; Ignatius, *To the Philadelphians* 10:1; *To the Smyrneans* 11:2. Other methods of selection attested in New Testament include direct appointment (Titus 1:9), casting lots (Acts 1:26), and direct revelation from the Spirit (13:2–3). The selection of this traveling companion ensures that all propriety is observed in handling the donations (8:20–22), as well as for safety along the journey.

For if any Macedonians come with me and find you unprepared . . . we would be ashamed of having been so confident (9:4). The possible embarrassment felt by Paul and the Corinthians will be all the greater, given the poverty of the Macedonians and the relative prosperity of at least some of the members of the Achaean-Corinthian assemblies. Erastus was able to donate an expensive pavement near the theater in return for his election to public office (see "Erastus Inscription" at 3:1). Titius Justus owned a home near the synagogue and hosted Paul (Acts 18:7). The home of Gaius was large enough to accommodate all the Corinthian house churches at once (Rom. 16:23).

The ability to travel is a good indicator of financial means, and we see many Corinthians on the move. Phoebe, a deaconess and patroness of the assembly in Cenchrea,[111] had the resources to travel to Rome (on business?) and deliver Paul's letter to the Romans (Rom. 16:1–2). Chloe was able to dispatch servants or family members to Ephesus (perhaps on other business) and keep Paul abreast of developments in Corinth (1 Cor. 1:11). Stephanas is also able to visit Paul in Ephesus, along with Fortunatus and Achaicus (his slaves?), and offer encouragement (16:15–18). Certainly the Corinthians had the wherewithal to contribute to those destitute believers in Jerusalem.

The generous gift you had promised (9:5). Not only were some of the Corinthians evidently persons of substance, but the region itself was almost legendary for its prosperity. Corinth's location, commerce, festivals, and fertile agricultural regions provide the background for the assessment of Favorinus (A.D. 85–155) that the city was "both prow and stern of Hellas, having been called prosperous and wealthy and the like by poets and gods from olden days."[112] This is not to say that the Corinthian church as a whole was affluent (see 1 Cor. 1:26–29; 11:22). Yet the evidence from Paul's letters suggests that they were better off than the Macedonian assemblies and more than capable of a generous donation.

Whoever sows sparingly will also reap sparingly, and whoever sows generously will also reap generously (9:6). Although the local economy of Roman Corinth was not agriculturally based, nor was Paul, as far as we know, ever deeply involved in rural life, ancient societies were more vitally connected to the field and farm than modern Western societies and so also with the agrarian wisdom that thrived in such a setting. The image of a farmer sowing seed in the field, harvesting, and bearing his produce to the market would have been a daily reality for both Paul and the Corinthians.

He who supplies seed to the sower and bread for food . . . will increase your store of seed (9:10). Paul takes for granted that the Creator has supplied his creation with everything necessary for life and abundance. Yet this Jewish conviction clashes dramatically with the religious ideas of Greece and Rome, and this collision provides an opportunity for Paul to reeducate his pagan converts. In Corinth and throughout the Greco-Roman world, Demeter was worshiped as the goddess of grain, agriculture, and bountiful harvests,

FARMING IMPLEMENTS

A sickle, scraper, hoe, and other tools found in Samaria.

along with her daughter Kore. An ancient temple dedicated to these two goddesses was located on the north slope of the Acrocorinth and was remodeled during the first century B.C. This cult was especially popular among the poor of Corinth, judging from the large number of inexpensive votives found in the excavation.[113] Demeter is commonly pictured with grain, fruit, cornucopia, and other symbols of agricultural fertility.

Paul Defends His Ministry (10:1–18)

In chapters 10–13 Paul focuses his attention on the claims of his opponents, certain Jewish-Christian missionaries who have recently arrived in Corinth and are challenging Paul's apostolic credentials. While formally addressing the Corinthians, Paul takes up the objections of his rivals, and the tone of the polemic often bristles with sarcasm. Such an approach was deemed appropriate for the moralist when the souls of his listeners hung in the balance: "partly by persuading and exhorting, partly by abusing and reproaching, in the hope that he may thereby rescue somebody from folly . . . with gentle words and at other times harsh."[114]

By the meekness and gentleness of Christ, I appeal to you (10:1). The character of the Messiah (Gk. *Christos*) as gentle, meek, and lowly was anticipated in many Old Testament prophecies and was exemplified in the life and teaching of the earthly Jesus.[115] In Peter's recollection of Jesus he was a "lamb" (1 Peter 1:19), and this image dominates the apocalypse of John.[116] Not surprisingly, this picture was carried on in the writings of the early church fathers:

For Christ is with those who are humble, not with those who exalt themselves over his flock. The majestic scepter of God, our Lord Jesus Christ did not come with the pomp of arrogance or pride, but in humility . . . like a sheep he was led to the slaughter.[117]

I, Paul, who am "timid" when face to face with you, but "bold" when away! (10:1). The words placed in quotation marks in the NIV indicate that Paul is probably alluding to accusations of his opponents that he is courageous only from a distance (see comments on 10:10–12). Paul's opponents have confused his Christ-like demeanor with weakness, and it is this inverted value system he seeks to correct.

Some people who think that we live by the standards of this world (10:2). We encounter here another charge, which can be translated literally as "walking according to the flesh." This language represents Paul's assessment of his opponents' accusation(s), which he leaves unspecified.[118] It may relate to his seemingly fickle change of travel plans (2 Cor. 1:15–2:4), to an alleged mishandling of the collection (12:16–18), or to something else altogether. It is certain, however, that Paul's character is under indictment.

We do not wage war as the world does. The weapons we fight with are not the weapons of the world (10:3b–4a). The warfare imagery Paul adopts was particularly popular among philosophers of the Stoic-Cynic variety, who depicted their way of life and philosophy in terms of a battle for moral advancement. According to Dio Chrysostom, the wise man continually fights "a stubborn battle against lusts and opinions and all mankind."[119] The development of character could be likened to capturing "the citadel within" and expelling the inner tyrants: "How then is a citadel destroyed? Not by iron, nor by fire, but by sound judgments."[120] The ultimate goal of the contest against the inner and outer foe is eloquently described by Seneca: "Though earthworks rise to match the loftiest citadel, yet no war-engines can be devised that will shake the firm-fixed soul."[121]

They have divine power to demolish strongholds (10:4b). By the first century A.D., Roman siege warfare had developed sophisticated machinery and treacherous tactics. Siege equipment included a complex variety of artillery, catapults, battering rams, mobile towers, mechanical ladders, movable protective sheds, and vehicles and tools specifically designed for maintaining a siege. The remains of an impressive siege ramp are still visible at Masada, and if the Romans could not go over or through a wall, they also developed methods for tunneling under the wall. Sometimes tunnels were constructed simply to undermine the foundation of the defensive fortification. Corinth itself was besieged and ravaged by the Roman General Lucius Mummius in 146 B.C., though by Paul's day the city walls had been restored. However, the walls of the Acrocorinth, the fortress situated above Corinth, still lay in rubble and served as a poignant illustration of a "demolished stronghold".

We demolish arguments and every pretension that sets itself up against the knowledge of God (10:5). In speaking of pretentious reasoning that exalts itself over the truth, Paul echoes a common caricature of the Sophists, who were known for their crafty argumentation and affected style. In an earlier letter Paul refers to them as "the debaters of this age" whose (pseudo-)wisdom God has shown as foolishness (1 Cor. 1:20).

Philo is especially scornful of these "lovers of disputations," who "raise themselves up to heaven in pride and arrogance" and who are constantly "stirring up a quarrelsome confusion, which tends to the adulteration of the truth."[122] These pseudo-philosophers "annoy the ears of those whom they meet by discussing with minute accuracy . . . all expressions of a double and ambiguous character."[123] Through convoluted argumentation they erect "impregnable fortifications" and labor "to devise what is persuasive for the establishment of a false opinion."[124] Indeed, Philo labels the entire Sophistic

endeavor as "studying the art of words in opposition to truth."[125] Like many Greco-Roman cities, Corinth was deeply influenced by the Sophistic movement,[126] which compelled Paul to adopt an anti-Sophistic posture in Corinth in order to distinguish himself clearly from these other traveling preachers.[127]

We take captive every thought to make it obedient to Christ (10:5). Continuing the combat imagery, Paul pictures himself as a commander who has vanquished his foe and presented the survivors to his Lord as captives. The military success of Rome from 200 B.C.-A.D. 100 produced vast numbers of captives who were then sold as slaves in the slave markets. Like Rome itself, Corinth was undoubtedly teeming with these kinds of slaves or descendants of such captured slaves. One of the more common images on imperial coinage and other imperially commissioned statuary was the captive, bound and stooped under the boot of imperial Rome.

The authority the Lord gave us for building you up rather than pulling you down (10:8). In Galatians 1:15 Paul describes his conversion in terms reminiscent of the prophet Jeremiah's call from the womb (Jer. 1:5); here he depicts his ministry in language that also echoes Jeremiah's commission (1:10). As the herald of Jeremiah's new covenant (2 Cor. 3:6; cf. Jer. 31:31), Paul takes this heroic prophet as a role model exemplifying perseverance in opposition. It is not surprising, then, to see Paul look to Jeremiah for an indictment of his boasting adversaries: "Let him who boasts boast in the Lord."[128]

For some say, "His letters are weighty and forceful" (10:10). This verse is significant if for no other reason than that it is the only time Paul actually cites his opponents. It is difficult to determine, however, which group is voicing this objection. We know that the Corinthians themselves were already grumbling about Paul's unimpressive oratory, which

DEFENSIVE WALLS ON THE ACROCORINTH

he defends in 1 Corinthians 1–4. Yet we also know that subsequently other missionaries arrived in Corinth and challenged Paul's leadership (2 Cor. 11–13).

Paul's opposition concedes that his letters are impressive examples of persuasive discourse, and this perspective is borne out by modern research on the structure and strategy of Paul's letters.[129] While far from the rhetorical showpieces of Cicero and Seneca, Paul's letters creatively adapt conventional features of Hellenistic letter-writing to address the needs of his churches and provide a powerful witness to the genius and passion of Paul the apostle.

"But in person he is unimpressive" (10:10). A more literal translation reads, "but his bodily presence is weak," indicating that some in Corinth are criticizing Paul's personal appearance—be it the opposing missionaries or the disgruntled among the Corinthians. The only physical description of Paul from antiquity comes to us from the second-century document, *The Acts of Paul and Thecla:* "small of stature, with a bald head and crooked legs, in a good state of body, with eyebrows meeting and nose somewhat hooked." While certainly fictitious, this depiction corresponds to what we might expect of a hard-working artisan, a tentmaker who labored at his workbench "night and day" (1 Thess. 2:9) in the cities he evangelized, including Corinth.[130]

But it is precisely this kind of public image that would repel those from the privileged classes in Corinth. Some of these may have agreed with the elitist perspective of Cicero, who looked down on all manual laborers, small shopkeepers, and artisans engaged in "vulgar trades, for no workshop can have anything liberal about it."[131] Often it was the dress and physical appearance of such workers that was deemed so distasteful. Lucian, in choosing his profession, purposely opts for the "dignified appearance" of the orator over the "servile appearance" of a sculptor, with his tunic covered in marble dust, hunched over his work, toting sledges and chisels in his calloused hands.[132]

To be sure, the working class judged matters differently, as did some philosophers, who believed certain kinds of manual labor could be good for the body and soul.[133] Yet even an enlightened spirit like Epictetus argued that in order for the philosopher-moralist to be compelling, "such a man needs also a certain kind of body, since if a consumptive man comes forward, thin and pale, his testimony no longer carries the same weight" (*Discourses* 3.22.86). Epictetus goes on to explain that in order to gain a hearing for his message, the philosopher should be able to say, "Look, both I and my body are witnesses to the truth of my contention" (3.22.88). Such a maxim would have carried much weight in Corinth,

REFLECTIONS

IN 10:7 PAUL ACCUSES THE CORINTHIANS OF "LOOKing only on the surface"; this may be regarded as the fundamental problem in Corinth. Like many today, the Corinthians were more concerned with externals, such as social status, physical appearance, and flashy demonstrations of the Spirit, and neglected the deeper issues of character, humility, and the inner beauty of a Spirit-filled life. Even mature believers struggle with this from time to time. It is somewhat comforting to recall that even the prophet Samuel had to be reminded of this fundamental spiritual principle: "But the LORD said to Samuel, 'Do not consider his appearance or his height. . . . The LORD does not look at the things man looks at. Man looks at the outward appearance, but the LORD looks at the heart'" (1 Sam. 16:7).

where physical appearance was valued at a premium.[134]

In his discourse *On Personal Adornment*, Epictetus describes a young student of rhetoric from Corinth who was "elaborately dressed . . . and whose attire in general was highly embellished" (3.1.1). Bedecked in jewelry and sporting a lavish hairstyle (3.1.14), this Corinthian even plucked out all his bodily hair to enhance his physical appeal (3.1.27–35). Martial's description of another Corinthian, Charmenion, is similar: "You stroll about with sleek and curled hair. . . . You are smoothed with depilatory [hair removal lotion] daily."[135] It is no wonder that Paul began this section with the reproof, "[O Corinthians,] you are looking only on the surface of things" (10:7).

And his speaking amounts to nothing (10:10). The accusation of poor rhetorical ability permeates Paul's extant correspondence with this church and appears to be the main complaint leveled against Paul in Corinth.[136] The Corinthians, like typical citizens of any Greco-Roman city in this era, had been fed a rich diet of oratory from birth and were true connoisseurs of the art (see comments on 5:11–13). What Dio Chrysostom says of the Phrygians was even more true of the Corinthians: "You are devoted to oratory . . . and you tolerate as speakers only those who are very clever."[137]

The Corinthians prided themselves on their expertise in evaluating public speakers, who were expected to be exemplary in word and appearance. Lucian advises anyone aspiring to be a Sophist, "First of all, you must pay special attention to outward appearance," which reveals why Paul's physical appearance and his rhetorical ability are both under attack here: The Corinthians are comparing Paul to the orators who entertain them at their banquets and in their lecture halls, and are giving him poor marks on their scorecards.[138]

When they measure themselves by themselves and compare themselves with themselves, they are not wise (10:12). The art of comparison was taught as a rudimentary exercise of rhetorical technique and is defined by Paul's contemporary Quintilian as the determination of "which of two characters are the better or worse."[139] The practice was particularly common among the Sophists as a means of self-advertisement. Indeed, Plutarch virtually defines Sophists by the excessive use of comparison in attracting

---

▶ Reflections of a Jewish Scribe on Leisure and Manual Labor (c. 180 B.C.)

The wisdom of the scribe depends on the opportunity of leisure; only the one who has little business can become wise. How can one become wise who handles the plow, and who glories in the shaft of a goad, who drives oxen and is occupied with their work, and whose talk is about bulls? . . . So it is with every artisan and master artisan who labors by night as well as by day; those who cut the signets of seals . . . the smith . . . the potter. . . . All these rely on their hands, and all are skillful in their own work. Without them no city can be inhabited, and wherever they live, they will not go hungry. Yet they are not sought out for the council of the people, nor do they attain eminence in the public assembly. They do not sit in the judge's seat, nor do they understand the decisions of the courts; they cannot expound discipline or judgment, and they are not found among the rulers. (Sir. 38:24–33)

attention: "For it is not like friendship, but sophistry to seek for glory in other men's faults."[140] A good example of what Paul is opposing comes from Lucian, who sarcastically relates the words of a Sophist recruiting a student: "Do not expect to see something that you can compare with So-and-so, or So-and-so. . . . Indeed you will find that I drown them out as effectively as trumpets drown flutes."[141]

The field God has assigned to us, a field that reaches even to you (10:13). From the time of his calling on the Damascus road, God made clear to Paul that his commission was primarily to the Gentiles.[142] This was confirmed by Peter, James, and John, the leadership in Jerusalem (Gal. 2:7–9). In introducing the gospel to a Gentile city, Paul often began by preaching in the local synagogue, as he did in Corinth (Acts 18:4; cf. Acts 17:1–2). This approach allowed him to proclaim the Messiah first to his fellow Jews, while also gaining a hearing for his message among the God-fearing Gentiles who frequented the synagogue.

God-fearers were not full converts to Judaism, yet they were attracted to the faith, tradition, and ethic of the Jewish religion. In this verse and in one that follows, Paul is reminding the Corinthians that God himself has assigned him apostolic jurisdiction among the Gentiles. No matter what his opponents may claim, in bringing the gospel to Corinth he is not reaching beyond his divinely granted commission.

As your faith continues to grow . . . we can preach the gospel in the regions beyond you. For we do not want to boast about work already done in another man's territory (10:15–16). Two principles of Paul's missionary strategy are enunciated here: to use established churches as a base for further advancing the gospel, and to preach Christ in regions hitherto unevangelized, "where Christ is not known" (Rom. 15:20). Paul also implies that a healthy church will be a *sending church*, one whose growing faith inevitably involves a desire to see Christ's kingdom expand.

Paul's passion for evangelism was particularly focused on unreached peoples, so that he could claim in Romans 15:19–23: "From Jerusalem all the way around to Illyricum, I have fully proclaimed the gospel of Christ . . . there is no more place for me to work in these regions"—referring to a vast swath of the Roman world in which there was certainly more work to be done. As a pioneer evangelist, Paul's goal was to proclaim the gospel *extensively*, in as many regions as possible, rather than *intensively*, to everyone within a particular region. Of course, Paul made a great effort to ensure that churches were established and believers nourished. But as his letters indicate, with their frequent travel itineraries, visions of Spain, and so on, Paul's eye was ever on the road, always planning his next missionary enterprise.

Let him who boasts boast in the Lord (10:17). See comments on 10:8.

Paul's "Foolish" Boasting (11:1–12:13)

Continuing his defense of his ministry, Paul is forced into the awkward position of adopting a practice he has just censured in his opponents: boasting. Paul calls this maneuver "foolishness" (11:1) and being "out of [his] mind" (11:23), but the effectiveness of his opponents' libel campaign compels him to fight fire with fire. Paul refuses, however, to engage in petty Sophistic one-upmanship. Rather, he peppers his boasting with tongue-in-cheek irony in order to expose the absurdity of his opponents' position: They arrogantly proclaim a Messiah who, in fact, exemplified meekness and humility in his earthly life!

The climax of this parody is Paul's preposterous (to his rivals) insistence on boasting in his weakness (11:30) and his nonsensical contention that weakness is strength (12:10). But concealed in the apostle's hand is a trump card his opponents are not expecting: the example of Jesus, crucified in weakness (13:4). Paul concentrates his boasting in three areas: his proclamation of the gospel free of charge (11:7–15), his suffering as an apostle (11:16–33), and his mystical experiences (12:1–10).

I am jealous for you with a godly jealousy. I promised you to one husband, to Christ (11:2). In order to communicate his outrage at the infatuation that some in Corinth feel toward the intruding missionaries, Paul portrays himself as a father who has pledged his daughter (the Corinthians) in marriage, only to hear rumors that she has transferred her affections. The imagery is that of a betrothal (*harmozō*; NIV, "I promised"). While both Roman and Jewish marriage customs included a betrothal period, Paul is probably assuming a Jewish framework, which involved a ceremony with witnesses and an exchange of gifts and could precede the actual marriage by as much as twelve months.

Not all these details are relevant here, but the Jewish betrothal differs from our modern Western engagement period in that it was legally binding. As we see with Joseph and Mary, terminating the relationship constituted a divorce (Matt. 1:18–20). According to the Mishnah, the death of the betrothed male prior to the wedding rendered the virgin a widow and prohibited her from marrying a high priest.[143]

So that I might present you as a pure virgin to him (11:2). Following the betrothal, the bride was presented to the groom by her family and friends, which sometimes involved a joyous procession to the groom's house (1 Macc. 9:39; Matt. 25:6–10). It was the obligation of the father of the bride to safeguard his daughter's chastity, which was a serious matter. The sages of the Mishnah provided detailed legislation regarding the bride's obligation to furnish proof of her purity after cohabitation and the husband's right to sue her family if such evidence was not forthcoming.[144] Purity during the betrothal period was especially revered in Jewish circles, and the mishnaic rabbis stipulated that any man violating a betrothed virgin still under the protection of her father should be stoned or strangled.[145]

These Jewish sources help us understand the gravity of the situation in Corinth as Paul sees it and the appropriateness of his analogy to illustrate the matter. Paul feels the outrage of a father whose daughter has been seduced by another man on the eve of her wedding. The analogy also alludes to the consummation of redemptive history, when the presentation of the bride (the church) to the groom (Christ) is made (Eph. 5:27; Rev. 19:6–9; 21:2).

As Eve was deceived by the serpent's cunning (11:3). Jewish writers of the period describe the serpent of Genesis 3 as Satan, as his mouthpiece, or as one of the fallen angels.[146] The context (esp. 2 Cor. 11:13–15) suggests that Paul may be making a similar assumption. The abundant evidence—archaeological and literary—of a pervasive Jewish presence throughout the Mediterranean leaves little doubt that the average Roman was familiar with the major stories and characters of the Jewish Scriptures, including the serpent in Eden.

A Jesus other than the Jesus we preached . . . a different spirit . . . a different gospel . . . "super-apostles" (11:4–5). See " Paul's Opponents in Corinth" at 11:6 and comments on 12:11.

I may not be a trained speaker, but I do have knowledge (11:6). Once again Paul singles out his oratory as one of the central points of contention between him and his detractors. The NIV captures well the sense of the Greek expression *idiōtēs tō logō* ("not a trained speaker"), which indicates only that Paul has not received formal training as a rhetorician; he is an amateur. Yet we need not suppose that he is a complete bungler, rhetorically. Acts presents the apostle as a competent speaker, if not always compelling (Acts 17:18; 20:9), and we can assume that after many years of preaching in synagogues and in other public venues he developed some proficiency in his delivery. As 2 Corinthians 10:10–12 indicates, the problem is that the Corinthians, perhaps encouraged by Paul's opponents, are comparing Paul with polished professional orators and judging him inadequate.

But Paul is not merely battling snooty Corinthians with overly sensitive rhetorical tastes. Rather, he is confronting a cultural value that judges a person's knowledge and character on the basis of his or her oratorical prowess. From the time of Isocrates (436–338 B.C.), who reasoned that "the power to speak well is the surest index of sound understanding," to the time of Aristides (A.D. 117–181), who contended that "the title of 'wise' and the ability to speak well are attributes of the same man," wisdom and eloquence were intimately connected; this helps explain Paul's insistence that he does in fact possess knowledge, even though his oratory may be less than brilliant.[147] Stoic philosophy in particular connected oratory and knowledge, and in such way as to make eloquence a gauge of character:

- What is he [the listener] to think of their souls, when their speech is sent into the charge in utter disorder, and cannot be kept in hand?[148]
- They [the Stoics] say that only the wise man is a good prophet, poet, and orator.[149]

Aristides, quoting a widely circulated proverb, makes the connection explicit and illustrates well the difficulty Paul finds himself in: "As character is, such is the speech. The reverse is also true."[150]

Was it a sin for me to lower myself in order to elevate you by preaching the gospel of God to you free of charge? (11:7–10). Paul is responding to a complaint issuing from his refusal to accept financial remuneration from the Corinthians. As the context indicates, what the Corinthians are objecting to is Paul "lowering himself" through manual labor in order not to be "a burden" on any of them (11:8).[151] Paul's insistence on plying his trade as a leather worker in order to support himself is a source of embarrassment to some in Corinth (see comments on 2 Cor. 10:10). While manual labor was more esteemed in Jewish circles, even here it had its cultured despisers (see "Reflections of a Jewish Scribe" at 10:10).

Among Greeks and Romans in Paul's day there was a fair amount of debate concerning the appropriate means of livelihood for philosophers and ethical moralists.[152] Cynics begged, Sophists charged fees, philosophers attached themselves to wealthy patrons, and Stoics might do any of the above but were also known to support themselves through

---

▶ Paul's Opponents in Corinth

The identity of Paul's opponents in Corinth has been a major point of dispute among New Testament scholars for much of the twentieth century. The various profiles that have been offered include Jewish-Christians from Palestine who want Gentile Christians to keep the law, Gnostics, and Christian evangelists with roots in Hellenistic Judaism. Deciding among the alternatives requires reckoning with a whole host of methodological and historical issues, as well as a circumspect analysis of the text. Any reconstruction must recognize that, while 2 Corinthians 10–13 provide firm evidence of intruders, we know from 1 Corinthians that complaints about Paul had already been voiced among the Corinthians themselves, so we cannot assume that every objection Paul answers in 2 Corinthians is directed toward a single front.

What we do know about Paul's opponents can be summarized briefly. (1) They are Jewish (11:22), but there is no evidence that they are advocating obedience to the Mosaic law. (2) They profess Christ (11:23) and claim the title "apostle" (11:5, 13; 12:11). (3) They relish oratorical display (11:5–6) and rhetorical technique (11:12). (4) They boast excessively (10:12–17; 11:16–12:11) and are abusive in their leadership style (11:20). (5) They take money from the Corinthians (11:7–15, 20; 12:14–15).

Paul never attacks their teaching but focuses rather on their arrogant, bombastic style. This suggests that the primary heresy of these intruders, in Paul's eyes, is not one of doctrine, but one of demeanor. Based on what we know with certainty about these interlopers, it appears that they are Jewish-Christian evangelists who have adopted the methods and style of the popular Hellenistic Sophist-philosophers for their own financial gain and have severely compromised the gospel in the process.

Paul, by contrast, understands that the medium and the message are inextricably connected, so that proclaiming a humble, self-sacrificing Messiah in an inflated, self-promoting way represents a distortion of the message itself. It is, in fact, preaching another Jesus and proclaiming another gospel (11:4). Paul resolved to preach Christ "not with eloquent words of wisdom" lest the gospel be robbed of its power and attention be focused on the preacher rather than on the one preached (1 Cor. 2:1–5). As James Denny put it, "No man can give the impression that he himself is clever, and that Christ is mighty to save."[A-24] Anyone who pretends otherwise, in Paul's view, is a mere charlatan with a counterfeit faith and truncated gospel (11:13–15).[A-25]

manual labor.[153] The exorbitant fees charged by Sophists frequently led to accusations of greed and avarice.[154] Sophists were widely known as lovers of luxury who were "strangers to labor," and Paul was certainly not willing to be confused with this lot.[155]

Yet cultivating a relationship with a wealthy patron as a means of financial support would involve Paul in a whole host of reciprocal obligations that would severely limit his freedom (see below). This kind of relationship was regarded by Paul's contemporaries as virtual slavery, turning the philosopher into his patron's yes-man.[156] On this issue Paul is in agreement with his Stoic contemporary Musonius Rufus: "One should endure hardships and suffer the pains of labor with his own body, rather than depend upon another for sustenance" (Fragment 11).

Paul is willing to accept limited support from the Macedonians to make up for his lack (11:9), but the support the Corinthians offer either had patron-client strings attached or was offered merely as a way of avoiding the shameful spectacle of their founding apostle setting up shop in the market. Paul, however, is less concerned about offending patrician sensibilities than he is about modeling the servanthood of Christ (Phil. 2:6–11), who made himself poor so that others might become rich (2 Cor. 8:9).[157]

Why? Because I do not love you? God knows I do! (11:11–12). In justifying his refusal to accept the Corinthians' offer of financial support, Paul inadvertently divulges their interpretation of his action: It is tantamount to rejecting their friendship.

Greco-Roman society was governed by a complex system of patronage and benefaction, in which the offer of a gift constituted an offer of friendship and obligated the recipient to respond in some tangible and proportionate fashion.[158] Often gifts were proffered to a weaker party in order to create a power relationship, thus enhancing the status and honor of the benefactor. There was something of a moral obligation to accept such gifts when offered, and refusal could result in animosity on the part of the one declined. A person might refuse benefaction if the giver were deemed unworthy, if the recipient was unwilling to return the favor, or if accepting might put the recipient in a difficult situation with respect to some other party. In refusing their support, Paul has violated certain cultural conventions relating to giving and receiving gifts, and some Corinthians have taken grave offense.

False apostles, deceitful workmen, masquerading as apostles of Christ ... [Satan's] servants (11:13–15). Although many questions would be answered had Paul specifically identified the targets of his attack, his use of polemical epithets to describe his opponents is widely

MASK

Flask in the form of the head of an actor wearing a female mask.

attested in the literature of Second Temple Judaism. In *Jubilees*, the oppressing Gentiles are labeled as "sons of Beliar," "children of perdition," "idol worshipers," and "the hated ones," among other things. In the Dead Sea Scrolls the chief opponent of the sect at Qumran (presumably the high priest in Jerusalem) is never actually named, but instead is referred to contemptuously as "the Scoffer," "the Liar," "the Spouter of Lies," and "the Wicked Priest." While Paul's invective may sound harsh to our ears, the situation in Corinth demands a sharp response from him, which he renders in accordance with the polemical conventions of his day.

Satan himself masquerades as an angel of light (11:14). In some Jewish traditions, Satan transformed himself into an angel of light and deceived Eve a second time:

> Then Satan was angry and transformed himself into the brightness of angels and went away to the Tigris River to Eve and found her weeping. And the devil himself, as if to grieve with her began to weep and said to her, "Step out of the river and cry no more . . . come out to the water and I will lead you to the place where your food has been prepared."[159]

Since many are boasting in the way the world does, I too will boast (11:18). Although Paul does not explicitly reveal who the "many" are who are boasting "according to the flesh" (NIV, "as the world does"), we can safely assume he has one eye on the Sophists and other fashionable rhetoricians, who made boasting a regular feature of their oratorical repertoire, and another eye on his opponents, who have adopted this trendy style of declamation (see "Paul's Opponents in Corinth" at 11:6).

Like Paul, Plutarch regarded Sophistic self-praise as "odious and offensive," yet accepted that boasting could be legitimately employed when done in the service of a noble cause or in defense of one's character.[160] Self-praise could be rendered inoffensive if one's own shortcomings are also mentioned, if the speaker recounts his or her hardships, or if credit is given to others or to God.[161] The correspondences between Plutarch's advice and Paul's self-acknowledged foolish boasting ("I am out of my mind to talk like this," 11:23) are remarkable, though the basis of their abhorrence of boasting is very different. For Plutarch, boasting was tasteless self-display. For Paul, informed by the Jewish Scriptures (Ps. 94:4–7; 103:3–4; Jer. 9:23), it represents the quintessential expression of humanity in opposition to God (Rom. 3:27; 1 Cor. 1:28–31).

You even put up with anyone who enslaves you or exploits you or takes advantage of you or pushes himself forward or slaps you in the face (11:20). Paul provides important information on the deportment of the intruding missionaries, which essentially amounts to an abusive manner, with overtones of financial exploitation. Although it may sound incredible that some in Corinth would tolerate such a demeanor, this kind of hard-hitting public persona was very much in vogue in Paul's day. Cynic philosophers had a reputation for verbally accosting passersby, and Sophists likewise were known to be ruthless in advancing their point of view.

Dio Chrysostom describes a scene in Isthmia, some six miles from Corinth, in which "crowds of wretched sophists [stand] around Poseidon's temple shouting and reviling one another, and their disciples too ... fighting with one another."[162] Philo paints a similar picture of Sophists as "lovers of self" who, like gladiators, descend into the arena to battle men of virtue and "never cease struggling against them with every kind of weapon, till they compel them to succumb, or else utterly destroy them."[163] What Paul describes is a heavy-handed leadership style, which is the antithesis of what he has modeled for the Corinthians in his own ministry (10:1; 11:22).

Are they Hebrews ... Israelites ... Abraham's descendants? So am I (11:22). "They" refers to the intruders, and it seems that one of their boasts concerned their pristine Jewish lineage (see "Paul's Opponents in Corinth" at 11:6). The terms Paul uses here are roughly synonymous in this context and are piled up for rhetorical effect. If Paul's opponents are *Palestinian* Jewish-Christians, which seems likely, it is conceivable that they drew attention to Paul's Diaspora roots (Tarsus, Acts 21:39; 22:3) in contrast to their own origins in the Jewish heartland, so as to discredit him. This kind of comparison was a routine practice of Sophists and rhetoricians (see comments on 10:12) and is explained by Theon (late first century A.D.) in the following way:

In the comparison of people, one firstly juxtaposes their status, education, offspring, positions held, prestige and physique; if there is any other physical matter, or external merit, it should be stated beforehand in the material for the encomia.[164]

In the face of such carnal self-promotion, Paul counters that he is every bit as "Jewish" as they are.

I have worked much harder (11:23). Hardship catalogs, like the one that follows, were commonly employed by Stoics in order to demonstrate their superior character and fortitude. For a discussion of Paul's hardship catalogs in relation to his Stoic contemporaries, see comments on 6:3–13.

In prison more frequently (11:23). Acts mentions only one imprisonment prior to the time of this letter (in Philippi, Acts 16:16–40), which illustrates the selective nature of Luke's account. Imprisonment could occur for reasons other than being judged guilty (with or without a trial) of some criminal offence.[165] Confinement sometimes took place to protect an individual or to hold an accused offender on remand while authorities determined if charges were appropriate. At other times imprisonment was used by magistrates to coerce a stubborn provincial to divulge information or to comply with a command.

The conditions in which prisoners were typically held would be considered inhumane by modern standards.[166] Locked away in over-crowded, lice-infested, unsanitary, and lightless hovels, prisoners routinely contracted disease through incarceration and sometimes died as a result of a prolonged stay in a Roman jail. Heavy iron manacles were

bound around wrists, feet, and often the neck, which grated through the flesh and caused all manner of pain and infection. Paul's frequent mention of his "chains," should conjure up images too distressful to contemplate.[167]

Five times I received from the Jews the forty lashes minus one. Three times I was beaten with rods, once I was stoned, three times I was shipwrecked (11:24–25). Paul's words read like a parody of the famous inscription of Augustus in which he catalogs the glories of his reign, the achievements he wanted all to remember:

> Twice have I had the lesser triumph . . . three times the [full] curule triumph; twenty-one times have I been saluted as "Imperator." . . . Fifty-five times has the Senate decreed a thanksgiving unto the Immortal Gods . . . Nine kings, or children of kings, have been led before my chariot in my triumphs . . . thirteen times had I been consul.[168]

The original inscription was erected on bronze pillars at the emperor's mausoleum in Rome, and copies were distributed throughout the provinces. Portions have been found in Ancyra (capital of Galatia), Apollonia (in Illyricum), and Antioch (in Pisidia). Such chronicles of glory would have been familiar to Paul and the Corinthians, rendering Paul's "boast" all the more ironic.

Forty lashes minus one (11:24). Deuteronomy 25:2–3 prescribes flogging as a means of punishment, up to a maximum of forty strokes. Receiving one less than forty may have been to ensure that the Mosaic stipulations were not exceeded through miscount. The later

mishnaic rabbis offered detailed instruction on what crimes were punishable by flogging, which included moral, cultic, and civil infractions.[169] As the passage from the Mishnah indicates, this was a painful and humiliating ordeal:

> How do they flog him? One ties his two hands on either side of a pillar, and the minister of the community grabs his clothing—if it is torn, it is torn, and if it is ripped to pieces, it is ripped to pieces—until he bares his chest. A stone is set down behind him, on which the minister of the community stands. And a strap of cowhide is in his hand, doubled and redoubled, with two straps that rise and fall [fastened] to it. . . . And he who hits him hits with one hand, with all his might.[170]

That Paul received this "from the Jews" indicates his continued missionary activities in the synagogues (Acts 17:1–3).

Beaten with rods (11:25). This punishment was a distinctively Roman way of dealing with a malefactor. The rods were made of wood, and the sentence would be executed by the *lictor*, who assisted the magistrate with the enforcement of corporal punishment. Acts records that Paul and Silas were severely beaten with rods in Philippi (Acts 16:22–23), even though it was illegal to flog a Roman citizen. Numerous examples can be found where the law was ignored by a magistrate.[171] As Romans, the Corinthians would have been keenly aware of the social stigma attached to this punishment, which underscores again Paul's determination to undermine the inverted value system of the Corinthians by boasting in the very things they would have regarded as shameful (11:30; 12:9–10).

Once I was stoned (11:25). Stoning was a common brand of punishment among Jews and was occasionally practiced by Romans.[172] While it could be an officially administered form of capital punishment, it was more often the result of mob violence.[173] The specific incident Paul refers to occurred in Lystra at the instigation of Jews from Antioch and Iconium (14:19).

Three times I was shipwrecked, I spent a night and a day in the open sea (11:25). Although Acts records only one shipwreck involving Paul (during his later journey to Rome), it mentions a number of other voyages on which such calamities may have occurred. Even these, however, do not comprise all of Paul seafaring journeys. Traveling by ship was especially dangerous in the first century, and countless instances of nautical misfortune are chronicled in the surviving literature and inscriptions.[174]

Since passenger ships were not in existence, Paul would have booked passage on a merchant ship heading to his desired destination and slept on the deck with other passengers and crew. Only the captain had a separate sleeping quarters. The causes of maritime disasters were numerous. Ancient merchant ships were considerably less sturdy than later sailing vessels and were propelled by only one mainsail, with possibly a smaller sail on the bowsprit. The ability to sail into the wind (tacking) was a later achievement, which meant that ancient mariners were largely at the mercy of prevailing winds.

In addition, these vessels were controlled by a steering oar, not a rudder, which further inhibited maneuverability. If one combines all this with the absence of (modern) detailed navigational charts, which display currents, depths, and hazards, the abundance of dedicatory epigrams like the following is not surprising:

> To Glaucus, Nereus, and Melicertes, Ino's son [mythological figures associated with the sea], to the Lord of the Depths, the son of Cronos, and to the Samothracian gods, do I, Lucillius, saved from the deep, offer these locks clipped from my head, for I have nothing else.[175]

> Dionysius, the only one saved out of forty sailors, dedicates here the image of a cele [possibly part of the ship's rigging], tying which close to his thighs he swam to shore. So even a cele brings luck on some occasions.[176]

251

2 Corinthians

bottom left

MERCHANT SHIPS

A column in Rome in honor of the emperor Marcus Aurelius (A.D. 161–180) depicting Roman merchant ships.

bottom right

ST. PAUL'S BAY, MALTA

The place where Paul survived a dramatic shipwreck.

I have been constantly on the move. I have been in danger from rivers . . . from bandits . . . from my own countrymen . . . from Gentiles . . . in danger in the city, in danger in the country (11:26). Paul recounts in short staccato salvos the occupational hazards of an itinerant evangelist. These center around travel, which has always (until recent history) been a risky undertaking. Like most, Paul would have traveled on foot and been subject to cold, heat, dust, mud, and all the vicissitudes of capricious weather.[177]

For accommodation, Paul and his traveling companions (he would not have traveled alone, if at all possible) would have relied on the hospitality of local residents, inns, or sleeping in the open, if need be. Horace (65–8 B.C.) describes a journey that involved all three at various points.[178] Though decent lodging could occasionally be found, inns were notorious for bed bugs, rough characters, and promiscuity.[179] Bandits, too, were a perennial threat (Luke 10:30–35), and every precaution was taken to ensure safe passage:

> This is the way also with the more cautious among travelers. A man has heard that the road which he is taking is infested with robbers; he does not venture to set forth alone, but he waits for company, either that of a quaestor or proconsul, and when he has attached himself to them he travels along the road in safety.[180]

The first-century traveler, well aware of the all the dangers involved, would have made vows to his/her patron deity for protection while traveling and looked for roadside shrines en route, as this inscription attests:

> Artemis, goddess of the road, Antiphilus dedicates to thee this hat from his head, a token of his wayfaring; for thou hast hearkened to his vows, thou has blessed his paths. The gift is not great, but given in piety, and let no covetous traveler lay his hand on my offering; it is not safe to despoil a shrine or even little gifts.[181]

I have labored and toiled and have often gone without sleep; I have known hunger and thirst and have often gone without food; I have been cold and naked (11:27). Choosing to support himself through his trade, Paul was forced to work longer hours than other artisans and to face even worse deprivation. The observation of Jesus ben Sirach that all craftsmen could be found "toiling day and night" (Sir. 38:27) would have been even more true of a bivocational evangelist. Paul labored "night and day" (1 Thess. 2:9; 2 Thess. 3:7–10) in the cities he evangelized in order to be a model for the Christian communities he established. His policy was to "gladly spend . . . and expend [himself]" on behalf of his spiritual children (12:15). On Paul's life as a tentmaker, see comments on 10:10 and 11:7–10.

I face daily the pressure of my concern for all the churches. Who is weak, and I

do not feel weak? Who is led into sin, and I do not inwardly burn? (11:28–29). As a pastor, Paul identifies with his flock to the point of suffering with them through their weaknesses and temptations. As we emphasized in our comments on 6:3–13, although both Paul and his Stoic contemporaries make use of hardship catalogs to commend themselves to their followers, the underlying presuppositions of each are very different.

For the Stoics, the whole point of adversity was to render the philosopher impervious to sorrow, fear, anxiety, or distress. According to Epictetus, philosophy beckons her pupils with the words, "Men, if you heed me, wherever you may be, whatever you may be doing, you will feel no pain, no anger, no compulsion, no hindrance, but you will pass your lives in tranquility and in freedom from every disturbance."[182]

Paul's open admission of anxiety is diametrically opposed to the doctrine and ideals of popular Stoic teaching and reflects a level of transparency that many of his day would despise as weakness. According to Dio Chrysostom, Diogenes represented the model to which all should aspire:

> . . . disclosing no weakness even though he must endure the lash or give his body to be burned . . . he holds [hardships] as mere trifles, and while in their very grip the perfect man is often as sportive as boys with their dice and their colored balls.[183]

With irony as his chief weapon, Paul is redefining for the Corinthians what true strength is. As the following verses illustrate, weakness and vulnerability play a major role in his definition.

In Damascus the governor under King Aretas had the city of the Damascenes guarded in order to arrest me. But I was lowered in a basket from a window in the wall and slipped through his hands (11:32–33). This incident is also related in Acts 9:23–25, which implicates the Jews of Damascus in the plot as well. Aretas was the ruler of the Arabic kingdom of the Nabateans to the south of the ancient city of Damascus, and it is unclear what kind of authority he exercised in Damascus at this time. The Greek word *ethnarch*, however, has a much broader range of meanings than the NIV's "governor" and may indicate simply that Aretas's consul in Roman controlled Damascus.[184] If Paul's time in Arabia (Gal. 1:17) included an unwelcomed mission among the Nabateans, this could explain the hostility on the part of Aretas.

The biting irony of Paul's boast becomes clear when we understand that the highest military honor in the Roman army was the *corona muralis*, the "wall crown," given to the first soldier to scale the wall and enter a besieged city. The pitiful picture of Paul being lowered in a basket contrasts dramatically with the glorious image of soldier battling his way over the wall and is offered as a scolding parody of the Corinthians' inverted value system.

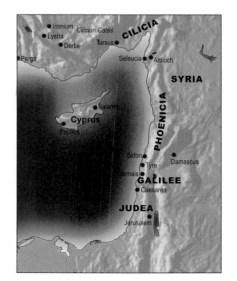

I know a man in Christ (12:2). Paul adopts the third person to relate an experience we later discover is his own (12:6–10). This is indicative of his reticence to "boast" of such remarkable occurrences in his own life and his commitment to proclaim Christ, not himself (2 Cor. 4:5). Interestingly, the experience of Paul's heavenly ascent has many parallels in Jewish literature, and there too the revelation is always ascribed to another, usually a hero of Israel's past.[185]

Fourteen years ago (12:2). That Paul must go back a full fourteen years to this occurrence indicates it is not a regular feature of his religious experience. If 2 Corinthians was written in the mid–50s, then the event Paul narrates occurred around 40 A.D., some seven years after his conversion and at least several years before he founded the church in Corinth.

Caught up to the third heaven . . . to paradise (12:2–4). Jewish literature of the period refers to one, three, five, seven, and even 955 heavens.[186] In each instance—and this seems to be the case here as well—the point is that the one ascending has reached the *highest* heavens, the very abode of God. In this passage, "third heaven" and "paradise" refer to the same locale.

He heard inexpressible things, things that man is not permitted to tell (12:4). Quite contrary to other heavenly ascent texts of Second Temple Judaism, whose whole point was to reveal the cosmological secrets of the universe or describe the ineffable mysteries of God, Paul comes back with nothing to say. Once again, the irony of Paul's "boast" is barely concealed by the exceptional nature of the event he recounts.

A thorn in my flesh, a messenger of Satan, to torment me (12:7). In order to keep Paul humble, God allows him to be plagued by a "thorn in [his] flesh." Many have suggested that this was some type of physical or mental ailment (poor eyesight, a speech impediment, epilepsy, depression), while others have seen in the mention of Satan an allusion to Paul's opponents and his persecution for the gospel (cf. 11:13–15). The reference to the "flesh" makes one think of a physical impairment of some kind, though anything beyond this is conjecture. Paul must have been of reasonably sound physical constitution in order to endure the hardships he has just described (11:23–28) and to maintain his arduous travel itinerary. Whatever this ailment was, it is probably more of a chronic burden than a completely debilitating affliction.

For Christ's sake, I delight in weaknesses . . . for when I am weak, then I am strong (12:10). This single, most important verse in 2 Corinthians crystallizes the argument of chapters 10–13 in a paradox of profound magnitude. In the crucible of affliction Paul has learned that the presence of the crucified Christ is mediated more perfectly through suffering and weakness than through glory and strength. This principle he has made emblematic of his ministry. Living his life in the shadow of the cross, Paul's ministry assumes a cruciform character, which rejects the path of status, position, power, and prestige and embraces the folly and humiliation of the cross as God's deepest wisdom (cf. 1 Cor. 1:18–2:5).

I am not in the least inferior to the "super-apostles" (12:11). "Super-apostles" represents Paul's own cynical designation of the intruders—with their imposing manner, pretentious oratory, and eccentric claims to apostolic status. See "Paul's Opponents in Corinth" at 11:6.

Signs, wonders and miracles (12:12). Part of Paul's proof of his apostleship is the miraculous deeds he performs in the service of the gospel. Acts attributes to Paul various healings (14:8–10; 28:7–9), exorcisms (16:16–18), and even raising the dead (20:7–12), though none of those described in Acts occurred in Corinth.

Paul's Impending Visit and a Final Warning (12:14–13:13)

In concluding his letter, Paul warns the Corinthians of his upcoming visit and exhorts them to perform a thorough spiritual inventory, lest he have to deal with them more harshly than he would like.

Now I am ready to visit you for the third time (12:14). Paul's first visit was his founding visit (Acts 18), and his second visit was the painful visit described in 2:1–5 and 7:12.

Not your possessions, but you (12:14). In reiterating his determination to support himself, Paul again alludes to the

REFLECTIONS

PERHAPS NOTHING IS MORE PAINFUL THAN TO HEAR God say "No." We can be sure that Paul's earnest prayers that this unnamed physical burden be removed were offered for all the right reasons. How could he endure the rigors of his ministry—the preaching, the travel, the public debates—if his own body often recoiled at the mundane tasks of daily life? We can also be certain that the outcome of this affliction—experiencing the power of the risen Christ—was the deepest desire of Paul's heart (Phil. 3:10), even though the means God chose to accomplish this end sent him staggering to his knees for relief. As Jesus was made perfect through suffering (Heb. 2:10), so too must his followers. The lesson Paul learned came at a heavy price, and it is one we all must face in our journey toward Christ-likeness. God cannot use a person greatly until he wounds him deeply.

mercenary tactics of his opponents, who proclaim the gospel with a view to monetary gain (see 2:17; 11:7–15).

Children should not have to save up for their parents, but parents for their children (12:14). As today, Greek, Roman, and Jewish societies emphasized the parents' responsibility in providing for their children. A variety of formal and informal laws of inheritance guarded this custom. The proverbial nature of Paul's statement reflects the universality of the principle, which the apostle applies to himself (the parent) and the Corinthians (the children). Whereas the Corinthians would have liked to have been Paul's patron/benefactor, providing for his needs and thus placing him under certain obligations, Paul explains their relationship with the metaphor of a family. Within this model, the emphasis lies on self-sacrifice and love, not on debits, credits, and reciprocal obligations.

Did I exploit you through any of the men I sent you? (12:17). Likely concealed beneath this rhetorical question is the suspicion on the part of some in Corinth that Paul has been siphoning funds from the collection (see "The Collection" at 8:1). While giving the appearance of financial propriety (they allege), the third parties involved are really working in concert with Paul to defraud them. Paul's confident, even incredulous tone in 12:16–18 indicates his certainty that few in Corinth will take this charge seriously.

Quarreling, jealousy, outbursts of anger, factions, slander, gossip, arrogance and disorder (12:20). Vice catalogs, like the one here, were a traditional component of first-century ethical discourse and have many parallels in the New Testament and in pagan philosophical literature.[187] This should caution us against assuming that the scenario Paul is contemplating in Corinth upon his arrival is truly as bleak as it may appear from this verse. Yet there is evidence in 1 Corinthians that many of these vices were wreaking havoc in the community, and we can understand why Paul is bracing himself for the worst.

"The testimony of two or three witnesses" (13:1). Paul intends to arbitrate disputes and put to rest any allegations against him when he arrives. He invokes the juridical principle of Deuteronomy 19:5, which he also applies in relation to church discipline in 1 Timothy 5:19 (cf. Matt 18:16).

Since you are demanding proof that Christ is speaking through me (13:3). One more time before he signs off Paul brings up the Corinthian complaint regarding his oratory and their skepticism concerning his claim to be a divine spokesman. Yet Paul's continued insistence that Christ (2:17; 12:19; 13:3) or God (5:21) is speaking through him can only have provided his skeptics with fuel for their fire.

Sophists and professors of rhetoric regularly ascribed their eloquence to divine giftedness, portraying the orator as "a god among men."[188] In an address to the Corinthians, the Sophist Favorinus (A.D. 80–150) explains that his wisdom and eloquence are evidence that he has been "equipped by the gods for this express purpose."[189] Given the popular understanding of oratory as "a divine thing,"[190] anyone claiming to be a divine spokesman would have fairly large sandals to fill. When seen in this light, the Corinthian expectation that Paul should excel in the rhetorical arts is not as eccentric as it may at first appear.

He was crucified in weakness (13:4). The Roman practice of crucifixion was a gruesome and agonizing form of capital punishment, typically reserved for slaves and noncitizens. The ordeal began with the flogging of the condemned, who was then forced to carry the cross-beam to the place of execution. The victim's wrists would be nailed or bound with cords to the horizontal cross-beam, and the feet were similarly bound to the vertical beam.

Often there was a small ledge affixed to the vertical beam to partially support the body and prolong the torture. The

victim would not die from the wounds inflicted during the crucifixion, but from exhaustion or suffocation. Recent archaeological excavations near Jerusalem uncovered the tomb of a certain Jehohanan, crucified sometime between A.D. 7 and 66.[191] During his crucifixion Jehohanan's legs were shattered with a heavy object, probably to prevent him from being able to raise himself up for breath,

thus hastening death. The large nail used to secure Jehohanan's legs to the cross was still lodged in the heel bone. As a portrait of "weakness," no more potent image could be offered than the humiliating spectacle of a victim of crucifixion.

Examine yourselves . . . test yourselves . . . do what is right (13:5–7). The exhortation to self-scrutiny was popular among Hellenistic philosophers from at least the time of Socrates, as witnessed by Epictetus (A.D. 55–135): "Socrates used to tell us not to live a life unsubjected to examination."[192] The goal of this moral introspection was knowledge of "the good" (*to kalon*; NIV, "what is right"), which should lead to right conduct:

> For the gods did not withhold from non-Greeks the ability to know the good. It is possible, through reasoned examination, to test whether

◀ *left*

HEELBONE OF A CRUCIFIED MAN

The iron nail that pierced the bone is still fixed in the heel. The bone was found in an ossuary in a Jerusalem tomb.

▶ Weakness and Strength: A Corinthian Perspective

In a city whose heritage, culture, and worldview were shaped by athletic competition and the triumph of strength over weakness, Paul's proclamation of a Savior crucified in weakness and his insistence that weakness is strength must have left many Corinthians staring in confused bewilderment. As the proud host of the Isthmian games, the victorious athlete stood at the center of Corinth's civic pride. A visitor to first-century Corinth would stroll past exquisite marble statues of wrestlers grappling, sprinters poised for flight, plaques enumerating victors, and a colossal sculpture of the goddess herself, Nike/Victoria, with triumphant wings outstretched.

The coins exchanged in the market bore similar images of contestants and victors' wreaths, and upon leaving the forum along the Lechaeum road, an imposing bronze of Herakles/Hercules would bid

the traveler farewell. In fact, Hercules, the "savior of the earth and humanity," performed six of his famous twelve labors in the region and served as the patron saint of the Peloponnese.[A-26] Embodying the ideal of bravery and brute strength, his brawny physique graced Corinthian coins and statuary, and his temple was located near the center of the city. Half mortal, half divine, this mythic hero conquered death itself by descending into the underworld and bringing back the infernal watchdog, Cerberus. In death he was equally glorious, for he mounted his own funeral pyre, set it alight, and offered himself sacrificially to Zeus, his father.

When compared to mighty Hercules or the victors at the games, Jesus the crucified criminal cut a rather poor figure, and Paul's strenuous campaign in 2 Corinthians 10–13 to redefine strength and weakness is actually a daring exercise in resocialization.

we think good thoughts, and to investigate whether our words correspond to our actions, and whether we are like those who live morally.[193]

Paul has phrased this bold challenge in the parlance of popular Greco-Roman philosophy in order to render his appeal all the more intelligible and convicting to his Greco-Roman audience.

Do you not realize that Christ Jesus is in you—unless, of course, you fail the test? (13:5). While the form of Paul's exhortation conforms to the general pattern of Hellenistic philosophers (see above), the criterion for evaluation is not inner fortitude or moral progress, but the presence of the indwelling Christ: "If anyone does not have the Spirit of Christ, he does not belong to Christ" (Rom. 8:9).

This is why I write these things when I am absent, that when I come I may not have to be harsh in my use of authority (13:10). It is probably right to read this verse in reference to the entire letter (see 2:3–4). Paul's fatherly affection leads him to take every measure possible to avoid an unnecessary display of his parental authority, including penning this lengthy letter. From this verse we can conclude that 2 Corinthians has been written primarily to preempt another "painful visit" and to effect reconciliation with the minority, who have come under the influence of the intruding missionaries.

For building you up, not tearing you down (13:10). See comments on 10:8.

Finally, brothers, good-by. Aim for perfection, listen to my appeal, be of one mind, live in peace. And the God of love and peace will be with you (13:11).

Using brief maxim-like exhortations, Paul summarizes his prayer for the Corinthians: *maturity* ("aim at perfection"), *obedience* ("listen to my appeal"), *unity* ("be of one mind"), and *harmony* ("live in peace"). Sadly, many of the same problems Paul addressed in 1 and 2 Corinthians were still present a generation later. According to *1 Clement*, written around A.D. 95 by the leadership of the church in Rome to the congregation in Corinth, once again the Corinthian church was torn by "jealousy and envy, strife and sedition, persecution and anarchy."[194]

Greet one another with a holy kiss (13:12). In Paul's day, kisses were given to express affection (between relatives, close friends, or lovers), homage (to the emperor or a patron), congratulation (to the victor in athletic competition), and sometimes upon entrance to a guild or religious sect. There is some evidence that rural communities differed from urban populations with respect to kissing, as evidenced by the embarrassing situation recounted by Dio Chrysostom, in which a farmer greets an old acquaintance he meets in the city with a kiss, only to be laughed at by bystanders: "Then I understood that in the cities, they do not kiss."[195]

REFLECTIONS

PAUL'S PROMISE THAT THE GOD OF love and peace would make his presence felt in the lives of the Corinthians (13:11) is contingent on their active pursuit of holiness. The blessings of God's love and peace can be hindered by obstinacy and spiritual laziness, which is why Paul enjoins his readers, "Examine yourselves!" (13:5).

Paul elsewhere recommends a kiss of greeting between believers, which later became a regular part of community worship.[196] This expression of intimacy cut across social barriers and served to both promote and symbolize the genuine sense of community experienced among believers, regardless of rank or status.

All the saints send their greetings (13:13). Although the precise identity of "the saints" is uncertain, more than likely Paul refers to the Macedonian believers in his company as the letter was penned. Paul typically includes greetings from others in his farewell.[197] This serves to reinforce the unity of the dispersed body of Christ, while also placing the local community in the context of something much larger, the church universal.

The grace of our Lord Jesus Christ, and the love of God, and the fellowship of the Holy Spirit (13:13). This final blessing is expressed in a Trinitarian formula that suggestively unites Father, Son, and Spirit as coworkers in the process of sanctification. Such triadic expressions are not uncommon in Paul's letters and imply a Trinitarian conception of the Godhead, at least in embryonic form.[198]

ANNOTATED BIBLIOGRAPHY

Commentaries

Barrett, C. K. *A Commentary to the Second Epistle to the Corinthians*. BNTC. London: Black, 1973.

A concise and circumspect exegesis of 2 Corinthians from one of the leading New Testament scholars of this century.

Furnish, Victor Paul. *II Corinthians*. AB 32A. New York: Doubleday, 1984.

A detailed, technical commentary rich in primary source research. Includes a fresh translation of the text.

Garland, David E. *2 Corinthians*. NAC 29. Nashville: Broadman & Holman, 1999.

A full-scale exegetical commentary mindful of the contemporary application of the text. Pastoral and theological in tone.

Witherington, Ben III. *Conflict and Community in Corinth: A Socio-Rhetorical Commentary on 1 and 2 Corinthians*. Grand Rapids: Eerdmans, 1995.

Focuses on the rhetorical dimensions of 1 and 2 Corinthians and the social context of Paul's ministry. Contains numerous helpful excurses on important issues.

Important Studies

Hafemann, Scott J. *Suffering and Ministry in the Spirit: Paul's Defense of His Ministry in II Corinthians 2:14–3:3*. Grand Rapids: Eerdmans, 1990.

A detailed exegesis of 2 Corinthians 2–3 with profound insights into Paul's perception of his apostolic ministry.

Hubbard, Moyer. *New Creation*. SNTSMS. Cambridge: Cambridge University Press, forthcoming.

An examination of the motif of new creation in 2 Corinthians and Galatians, with special reference to the Jewish background of this theme.

Savage, Timothy B. *Power Through Weakness: Paul's Understanding of the Christian Ministry in 2 Corinthians*. SNTSMS 86, 1996.

An exploration of the motif of strength in weakness in 2 Corinthians, with an illuminating depiction of Corinth and the Corinthians.

Sumney, Jerry L. *Identifying Paul's Opponents: The Question of Method in 2 Corinthians*. JSNTSup 40. Sheffield: JSOT Press.

A level-headed, textually based study of one on the most difficult issues in 2 Corinthians: the identity of Paul's opponents.

Winter, Bruce W. *Paul and Philo Among the Sophists*. SNTSMS 96. Cambridge: Cambridge University Press, 1997.

An examination of Paul and the Corinthian correspondence in light of the rise of the second Sophistic movement.

CHAPTER NOTES

Main Text Notes

1. For example, Francis Young and David Ford, *Meaning and Truth in 2 Corinthians* (London: SCM, 1987); Ben Witherington, *Conflict and Community in Corinth* (Grand Rapids: Eerdmans, 1995); Paul Barnett, *The Second Epistle to the Corinthians* (NICNT. Grand Rapids: Eerdmans, 1997); Jerry McCant, *2 Corinthians* (Sheffield: Sheffield Academic, 1999); J. D. H. Amador, "Revisiting 2 Corinthians: Rhetoric and the Case for Unity," *NTS* 46 (2000): 92–111.
2. On this see Amador, "Revisiting 2 Corinthians."
3. See 1:17–23; 6:1–3, 11–13; 6:14–7:2.
4. Amador, "Revisiting 2 Corinthians," 94.
5. Jerome Murphy-O'Connor, *St. Paul's Corinth* (Collegeville, Minn.: Liturgical), 161–69.
6. Martial, *Epigrams* 3.60.
7. See Dennis Pardee, "Hebrew Letters," *ABD*, 4:282–85; Paul E. Dion, "Aramaic Letters" *ABD*, 4:285–90.
8. Isa. 63:16; cf. 64:8; Jer. 31:9; Mal. 2:10.
9. Rom. 8:15; Gal. 4:6; cf. Mark 14:36.
10. 1QH 17:35–36; see also Sir. 23:1; *T. Job* 33:3, 9; *Jos. Asen.* 12:7–11.
11. Tacitus, *Hist.* 5.3.
12. For the Christian objection, see *Didache* 2:2; 5:2. More forceful is the moving essay by the first-century Stoic philosopher Musonius Rufus entitled, "Should Every Child That Is Born Be Raised?"
13. Dio Chrysostom, *Oration* 32.10.
14. Arius Didymus, *Epitome of Stoic Ethics* 11m.
15. 1 Sam. 16:13; 1 Kings 19:16; Ps. 105:15; Zech. 4:14.
16. *Planting* 18; cf. *Creation* 134; *Alleg. Interp.* 1.133–33; *Flight* 11–13.
17. Cf. Rom. 1:9; Phil. 1:8. On this construction see BAGD, 288.
18. Cited in Walter A. Elwell and Robert W. Yarborough, *Readings from the First-Century World* (Grand Rapids: Baker, 1998), 136.
19. *Description of Greece* 2.2.1.
20. See the account by Dio Cassius, *Roman History* 65.13, who notes that Musonius Rufus was exempted.
21. Lucian, *Icarmenippus* 29–30. See also his *A Professor of Public Speaking* and *The Runaways*.
22. See BAGD, 689, which cites 2 Cor. 9:2 and Phil. 1:14 as further instances of this usage. Note also Paul's use of "all" as a synonym for "the many" in Rom. 5:15–21.
23. See James C. VanderKam, *The Dead Sea Scrolls Today* (Grand Rapids: Eerdmans, 1994), 164–65; 1QS 6:13–14.
24. *Jub.* 17:16; 18:12; 2 Cor. 48:1–4; cf. Ex 4.24–25; 49:2–4; 48:9.
25. Scott J. Hafemann, *Suffering and Ministry in the Spirit: Paul's Defense of his Ministry in II Corinthians 2:14–3:3* (Grand Rapids: Eerdmans, 1990), 16–34.
26. *Aemelius Paulus* 32.
27. *Did.* 11:6.
28. Plato, *Protagoras* 313D.
29. *The Life of Moses* 2.212.
30. *Oration* 32.10.
31. Ibid., 32.9.
32. John Harvey Kent, *Corinth, Volume 8, Part 3: The Inscriptions, 1926–1950* (Princeton: American School of Classical Studies at Athens, 1966).
33. Numerous examples of such letters survive. See the examples in Chan-Hie Kim, *The Familiar Greek Letter of Recommendation* (SBLDS 4; Missoula, Mont.: Society of Biblical Literature, 1972). For relevant New Testament references, see Acts 9:2; 15:23–29; 18:27; 22:5; Rom. 16:1–2; 1 Cor. 16:10–11; 2 Cor. 8:22–24; Col. 4:10.
34. CD 6:19; 8:21; 20:12; 1QpHab 2:3–4.
35. 1QS 8:20–22.
36. See also 2 Macc. 7:23; Wisd. Sol. 15:11; *T. Abr.* 18:11; Philo, *Creation* 32.
37. *1 En.* 99:2; *Let. Aris.* 144–45.
38. *Eighteen Benedictions*; cf. Wisd. Sol. 17:11; 45:5; *4 Ezra* 14:30; *2 Bar.* 38:2.
39. *2 Bar.* 78:16; Ps. Philo 9:8.
40. *4 Ezra* 9:37.
41. Dio Chrysostom, *Oration* 32.11. See also Plutarch's amusing "How to Tell a Friend from a Flatterer" and the lengthy treatise by Philodemus, *On Frank Criticism.*
42. Philo, *Good Person* 81–82.
43. Cited in Elwell and Yarbrough, *Readings*, 87.
44. *1 En.* 90:37–39; *2 Bar.* 51:1–3; 1QS 4:6–8; Wisd. Sol. 3:7; *Jos Asen.* 8–21; 1QH; 4Q434–37.
45. Lucian, *Hermotimus* 59.
46. Gal. 1:4; cf. Rom. 12:2; 1 Cor. 1:20; Eph. 1:21; also Isa. 19–20; Hos. 2:18; Amos 9:11.
47. *1 En.* 16; CD 6:10–14; *4 Ezra* 4:9; *2 Bar.* 15:8; *Jub.* 1:16.
48. *Jub.* 12:20.
49. 1QH 4:24.
50. 11Q5 19.
51. 1QS 4:22–23; CD 3:18–20; 1QH 4:15.
52. Dio Chrysostom, *Discourse* 13:11.
53. *Discourses* 2:28.

54. Seneca, *Ep.* 40.4, 8, 14.
55. Cicero, *Tusc. Disp.* 4.14; Propertius 3.5.6; Petronius, *Satyr.* 50; Josephus, *J.W.* 5.5.3 §201; Suetonius, *Aug.* 70.
56. Cited in Margaret Thrall, *The Second Epistle to the Corinthians* (Edinburgh: T. & T. Clark, 1994), 1:326.
57. Seneca, *Epistle* 24.19–20 (italics added).
58. Marcus Aurelius, *Meditations* 10.
59. See Albert A. Bell Jr., *A Guide to the New Testament World* (Scottsdale, Pa.: Herald, 1994), 214–17.
60. Plotinus, *The Animate and the Man* 10.
61. From a letter dated A.D. 99. See MM, 192.
62. Oscar Broneer (ed.), *Ancient Corinth: A Guide to the Excavations* (Athens: Hestia, 1947), 55.
63. On the background and influence of *peithō* in Greek literature see R. G. A. Buxton, *Persuasion in Greek Tragedy: A Study of Peitho* (Cambridge: Cambridge Univ. Press, 1982); George Kennedy, *The Art of Persuasion in Greece* (London: Routledge and Keegan Paul, 1963).
64. *Descriptions of Greece* 2.7.7–9.
65. Cicero, *Orator* 97.
66. Dio Chrysostom, *Discourses* 33.1.
67. For an excellent discussion of this subject, see Duane Litfin's *St. Paul's Theology of Proclamation* (SNTSMS 79; Cambridge: Cambridge Univ. Press, 1994).
68. See the account by Philostratus, *Lives of the Sophists* 491.
69. Philo, *Lives of the Sophists* 532.
70. Ibid., 616.
71. This speech has been passed down under the name of Dio Chrysostom (see his *Discourses* 37.26).
72. See Moyer Hubbard, "Was Paul Out of His Mind? Re-reading 2 Cor 5:13," *JSNT* 70 (1998) 39–64.
73. See Aristotle's influential *The Art of Rhetoric* 1408b; 1418a.
74. *Jubilees* 1:15–29; cf. *1 En.* 72:1.
75. *Gen. Rab.* 39:4.
76. *Jos. Asen.* 8:9.
77. See Cilliers Breytenbach, *Versöhnung: Eine Studie zur paulinischen Soteriologie* (WMANT 60; Neukirchener: Neukirchen-Vluyn, 1989).
78. *Rom. Ant.* 5.49.6.
79. *Lives of the Sophists* 489, 520–33.
80. Dio Chrysostom, *Oration* 37.7–9.
81. See Seneca's "On Despising Death" (*Epistle* 24), or Musonius Rufus's "That One Should Disdain Hardships" (*Fragment* 7); Dio Chrysostom, *Oration* 3.3.
82. Epictetus, *Discourses* 30.2–3.
83. Musonius Rufus, *Fragment* 9; Epictetus, *Discourses* 1.29.4.
84. Rom. 13:12; Eph. 6:10–18; 1 Thess. 5:8; 1 Tim. 3:3–4.
85. Dio Chrysostom, *Oration* 8:16.
86. Arius Didymus, *Stoic Ethics* 5a.
87. Seneca, *On Firmness* 6.3.
88. Epictetus, *Discourses* 2.19.24.
89. Seneca, *On Firmness* 6.5–6.
90. See *New Documents Illustrating Early Christianity*, ed. Richard Horsley (New Ryde: Macquarie University), 1.5.
91. For details and primary sources see Ramsay MacMullen, *Paganism in the Roman Empire* (New Haven: Yale Univ. Press, 1981), 18–48.
92. From *New Documents Illustrating Early Christianity*, 1.5. The Thoereion was probably a banquet room connected to the temple of Isis or Serapis.
93. Tacitus, *Ann.* 15.44; Tertullian, *Apology* 35–37.
94. Epictetus, *Discourses* 4.1.111–12.
95. Philodemus, *On Frank Criticism* 15, 28.
96. Ibid., 26.
97. Plutarch, *On Listening to Lectures* 47A.
98. *Jos. Asen.* 15:7.
99. See Margaret M. Mitchell, "New Testament Envoys in the Context of Greco-Roman Diplomatic and Epistolary Conventions: The Example of Timothy and Titus," *JBL* 111 (1992): 641–62.
100. Philo, *Embassy* 369.
101. 1 Thess. 1:6; 2:14; 3:2–4; 2 Thess. 1:4–10; cf. Phil. 1:29–30.
102. *Oration* 7.82.
103. Rom. 12:15; 1 Cor. 1:2; Eph. 1:18.
104. Ex. 19:6; Lev. 21:7; Ex. 28:2; Lev. 16:32–33.
105. Ps. 34:9; Dan. 7:18–27; cf. Tobit 8:15.
106. Dio Chrysostom, *Oration* 7.93.
107. Although a fifth-century B.C. playwright, Euripides's perennial popularity is illustrated by Dio Chrysostom (A.D. 40–120), who cites this passage from memory in *Oration* 17; Euripides, *Phoenician Women* 535.
108. Philo, *Heir* 162.
109. Eph. 4:28, italics added; cf. Rom. 12:13; 1 Tim. 6:18.
110. 1 Thess. 4:11–12; 2 Thess. 3:6–13; 1 Tim. 6:6–10; 2 Cor. 8:11; cf. Phil. 4:10–19.
111. On the patroness status of Phoebe, see Wayne Meeks, *The First Urban Christians* (New Haven: Yale Univ. Press, 1983), 60.
112. This oration has been passed down under Dio Chrysostom's name (see his *Discourses* 37.36).
113. Donald Engels, *Roman Corinth: An Alternative Model for the Classical City* (Chicago: Univ. of Chicago Press, 1994), 101.

114. Dio Chrysostom, *Oration* 77.38.
115. E.g., Ps. 45:4; Isa. 40:11; 42:3; 53:7; Zech. 9:9 (cited in Matt. 21:5); Matt. 5:5; 11:29; John 1:29.
116. Rev. 5:6–13; 6:1–7; 21:9–22.
117. *1 Clem.* 16:1, 7; cf. *Barn.* 5:2.
118. Cf. Rom. 8:4–5, 12–13; 2 Cor. 1:17; 5:16; 11:18.
119. Dio Chrysostom, *Oration* 77/78.40.
120. Epictetus, *Discourses* 4.1.86.
121. Seneca, *On the Firmness of the Wise Man* 6.4.
122. Philo, *QG* 3.27; *Migration* 172; *Planting* 159.
123. Philo, *Planting* 136.
124. Philo, *Rewards* 25; *Cherubim* 9.
125. Philo, *Posterity* 101.
126. See Litfin, *Proclamation*.
127. See Bruce Winter, *Paul and Philo Among the Sophists* (SNTSMS 96; Cambridge: Cambridge Univ. Press, 1997).
128. 2 Cor. 10:17; cf. Jer. 9:24; 1 Cor. 1:31.
129. An insightful treatment of this topic can be found in Calvin Roetzel, *Paul: The Man and the Myth* (Philadelphia: Fortress, 1999), ch. 3, "The Letter Writer."
130. Acts 18:1–3; 1 Cor. 4:12; 9:3–18; 2 Cor. 11:7–9.
131. Cicero, *Off.* 150.
132. Lucian, *Dream* 6–13.
133. The life of the farmer was particularly admired; see Musonius Rufus, *Fragment* 11; Dio Chrysostom, *Oration* 7.103–52.
134. On the importance of beauty in Corinth see Timothy B. Savage, *Power Through Weakness: Paul's Understanding of the Christian Ministry in 2 Corinthians* (SNTSMS 86; Cambridge: Cambridge Univ. Press, 1996), 46–47.
135. Martial, *Ep.* 10.65.
136. 1 Cor. 1–4; 2 Cor. 2:17; 5:11–13; 10:10; 11:6; 12:19; 13:3.
137. Dio Chrysostom, *Oration* 35.1.
138. Lucian, *Professor of Public Speaking* 16.
139. Cited in Peter Marshall, *Enmity in Corinth: Social Conventions in Paul's Relations with the Corinthians* (WUNT 2.23; Tübingen: J.C.B. Mohr [Paul Siebeck] 1987), 54; Quintilian, *Inst. Or.* 2.4.21.
140. Plutarch, *How to Tell a Friend from a Flatterer* 71.
141. Lucian, *Professor of Public Speaking* 13.
142. Acts 22:21; 26:17–18; Gal. 1:16.
143. *m. Yebam.* 6:4.
144. *m. Ketub.*
145. Deut. 22:22–27; Philo, *Spec. Laws* 1.107; 3.72; *m. Sanh.* 7:9.
146. Wisd. Sol. 2:24; *Apoc. Mos.* 16; *1 En.* 69:6, which names the angel Gader'el.
147. Isocrates, *Nicoles* 7; Aristides, *To Plato* 391.
148. Seneca, *Ep.* 40.6.
149. Arius Dydimus, *Epitome* 5b12.
150. Aristides, *To Plato* 392. This proverb surfaces in one form or another in Plato, Cicero, Seneca, Quintilian, and Juvenal. Seneca, in fact, devoted an entire essay to its exposition: "On Style as a Mirror of Character" (*Epistle* 114).
151. Cf. Acts 18:1–3; 1 Cor. 4:12; 9:3–18; 2 Cor. 12:15.
152. See, e.g., Musonius Rufus, Fragment 11, "What Means of Livelihood Is Appropriate for a Philosopher?"; Dio Chrysostom, *Oration* 7; Arius Didymus 11m; Diogenes Laertius 7.188.
153. For a more nuanced appraisal, see Ronald F. Hock, *The Social Context of Paul's Ministry: Tentmaking and Apostleship* (Philadelphia: Fortress, 1980), 50–65.
154. Dio Chrysostom, *Oration* 4.132; Philo, *Posterity* 150; Lucian, *Professor of Public Speaking* 6–8.
155. Philo, *Worse* 34.
156. See, e.g., Lucian, *On Salaried Posts*; Dio Chrysostom, *Oration* 77/78.37.
157. For the view that Paul refused support primarily to model a life of self-imposed poverty before the materialistic Corinthians, see Savage, *Power Through Weakness*, 80–99.
158. On Greco-Roman gift-giving conventions, see Peter Marshall's *Enmity in Corinth*. My comments rely on his detailed analysis.
159. *Life of Adam and Eve* 9:1–5.
160. Plutarch, *On Inoffensive Self-Praise* 547 D; 539 E-F; 540 C.
161. Ibid., 543 F–544 C; cf. 12:9–10; 544 C; cf. 11:23–29; 542 E–543 A; cf. 11:32–33; 12:9–10.
162. Dio Chrysostom, *Oration* 8:9.
163. Philo, *Worse* 33.
164. Cited in C. Forbes, "Comparison, Self-Praise, and Irony: Paul's Boasting and the Conventions of Hellenistic Rhetoric," *NTS* 32 (1986): 7.
165. For a full discussion, see Brian Rapske's study, *The Book of Acts and Paul in Roman Custody* (BAFCS 3; Grand Rapids: Eerdmans, 1994), 10–20.
166. Ibid., 195–225.
167. Eph. 6:20; Phil. 1:7, 13–17; Col. 4:3, 18; 2 Tim. 2:9; Philem. 10, 13.
168. *Acts of Augustus* 1.4.
169. *m. Makkot* 3:1–16; *m. Šebuᶜot* 3:7–11.
170. *m. Makkot* 3:12–13.
171. See Rapske, *Paul in Roman Custody*, 48–56.
172. Josh. 7:25; *Jub.* 30:7–9; *Lives of the Prophets* 2:1; Philo, *Flaccus* 66, 174; Petronius, *Satyr.* 90.
173. Deut. 13:7–12; *m. Sanh.* 6:1–4; John 10:31–33; Acts 7:58; 14:19.

174. E.g., Dio Chrysostom, *Oration* 7; Petronius, *Satyr.* 113–16; Seneca, *Ep.* 53; For inscriptional evidence see Horsley, *New Documents Illustrating Early Christianity*, 4. #26.

175. Lucillius, *Greek Anthology* 6.164.

176. Dionysius, *Greek Anthology* 6.166.

177. Cf. Seneca, *On the Trials of Travel.*

178. Horace, *Satires* 1.5.

179. Ibid.; Petronius, *Satyr.* 16–26.

180. Epictetus, *Discourses* 4.1.91.

181. Antiphilus, *Greek Anthology* 6.199.

182. Epictetus, *Discourses* 3.13.11.

183. Dio Chrysostom, *Oration* 8.15–16.

184. A comprehensive survey of this issue can be found in Rainer Riesner's, *Paul's Early Period: Chronology, Mission Strategy, Theology* (Grand Rapids: Eerdmans, 1998), 75–89.

185. E.g., *1 En.* 1–36; *2 En.; 3 Bar.; The Apocalypse of Zephaniah.*

186. One heaven: *1 En.;* three heavens: *T. Levi* 3:1; *Apoc. Mos.* 37; five heavens: *3 Bar.* 11:1–2; seven heavens: *2 En.* 20:1; *Apoc. Ab.* 19:5–6; *Ascen. Isa.* 9:6; *3 En.* 17:1; 955 heavens: *3 En.* 48:1.

187. E.g., Rom. 1:29–30; 1 Tim. 6:4–5; Arius Didymus, *Epitome* 11k; Ps.-Anacharsis, *Ep.* 1.

188. Cicero, *De Oratore* 3.53.

189. This speech is found in the orations of Dio Chrysostom, 37.27.

190. Aelius Aristides, *In Defense of Oratory* 113.

191. James H. Charlesworth, "Jesus and Jehohanan: An Archaeological Note on Crucifixion," *ExpTim* 84/6 (February, 1973), 147–50.

192. Epictetus, *Discourses* 3.12.15.

193. Ps-Anacharsis, *Epistle* 2.

194. *1 Clem.* 3:2.

195. Dio Chrysostom, *Oration* 7.59.

196. Rom. 16:16; 1 Cor 16:20; 1 Thess. 5:26; cf. 1 Pet. 5:14.

197. Rom. 16:21–23; 1 Cor. 16:19–20; Phil. 4:22; Philem. 23–24.

198. Rom. 15:30; 1 Cor. 12:4–6; Gal. 4:4–6.

Sidebar and Chart Notes

A-1. See the extensive treatment by Hafemann in *Suffering and Ministry in the Spirit.*

A-2. Josephus, *J.W.* 7.5.5 §132.

A-3. *Acts of Augustus* 1.4.

A-4. Josephus, *J.W.* 7.5.6 §§153–54.

A-5. See the description of Pausanius, *Descriptions of Greece* 2.3.1–2.

A-6. Oscar Broneer (ed.), *Ancient Corinth: A Guide to the Excavations*, 39–40.

A-7. Philo, *Embassy* 281.

A-8. See *New Documents Illustrating Early Christianity*, 4:213–20.

A-9. Polycarp, *Martyrdom of Polycarp* 8:2.

A-10. Suetonius, *Dom.* 13.

A-11. Paul Zanker, "The Power of Images," in *Paul and Empire: Religion and Power in Roman Imperial Society*, ed. Richard A. Horsley (Harrisburg, Pa.: Trinity, 1997), 72–86.

A-12. Donald Engels, *Roman Corinth*, 101–2.

A-13. Kent, *Corinth: The Inscriptions*, #102.

A-14. Engels, *Roman Corinth*, 102.

A-15. Pliny, *Letters* 10.96–97.

A-16. Polycarp, *Mart. Pol.* 9–15.

A-17. Trimalchio, a fictitious character from Petronius' *Satyricon* (71).

A-18. Philo, *Creation* 135; Wisd. Sol. 3; *4 Macc.* 18:23.

A-19. Matt. 17:22–23; 1 Cor. 15; cf. 2 Macc. 7:14; *2 Bar.* 49–51.

A-20. On the Asclepion in Corinth, see Broneer, *Ancient Corinth*, 100–105; James Wisemann, "Corinth and Rome I: 228 BC–AD 267" in *ANRW* 2.7.1 (Berlin: Walter de Gruyter, 1979): 438–548.

A-21. Acts 24:17; Rom. 15:26; Gal. 2:10; 2 Cor. 8:13–15.

A-22. This data has been adapted from Ekkehard W. Stegemann and Wolfgang Stegemann, *The Jesus Movement: A Social History of its First Century* (Minneapolis: Fortress, 1999), 5–95. See also James S. Jeffers, *The Greco-Roman World of the New Testament Era: Exploring the Background of the New Testament* (Downers Grove: InterVarsity, 1999), 181–96.

A-23. Lucian, *Runaways* 17.

A-24. Cited in John Piper, *The Supremacy of God in Preaching* (Grand Rapids: Baker, 1990), 55.

A-25. The classic treatments of Paul's opponents in Corinth are those of C. K. Barrett ("Paul's Opponents in II Corinthians," *NTS* 17 [1971]: 233–54) and Ernst Käsemann ("Die Legitimität des Apostels: Eine Untersuchung zu II Korinther 10–13," *ZNW* 41 [1942]: 33–71]. My own appraisal is closest to Jerry Sumney's in *Identifying Paul's Opponents: The Question of Method in 2 Corinthians* (JSNTSup 40; Sheffield: JSOT Press, 1990).

A-26. Dio Chrysostom, *Oration* 1.84.

GALATIANS

by Ralph P. Martin and Julie L. Wu

Introduction

The letter to the Galatians is one of the key documents of the New Testament and the Christian faith. It is written in polemical style and tone, yet with a clear rhetorical structure[1] and deep pastoral concern for the readers, to enforce the twin themes of *faith* and *freedom*. Pivotal verses are, therefore, 2:16: "we, too, have put our faith in Christ Jesus that we may be justified by faith in Christ and not by observing the law," and 5:1: "It is for freedom that Christ has set us free. Stand firm, then, and do not let yourselves be burdened again by a yoke of slavery" (cf. 5:13).

In Christian history this letter has played a significant role as we recall its influence on such leaders as Luther and John Wesley. We may appreciate the richness of its teaching if we set the letter in its context. To do so, we need to ask three questions—two of which may be treated summarily, while the third requires more extended treatment.

PISIDIAN ANTIOCH

Remains of a Byzantine church built on the site of the first-century Jewish synagogue.

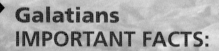

Galatians
IMPORTANT FACTS:

- **AUTHOR:** Paul.
- **DATE:** 48–49 (if from Antioch).
- **OCCASION:**
  - To counter the threat to the Galatian churches.
  - To defend Paul's apostleship.
  - To set forth the basis of the law-free gospel of grace.
  - To remind the readers of the obligations of Christian living.
- **KEY THEMES:**
  1. Faith and freedom centered in Christ.
  2. The centrality of the cross for salvation and the life of believers.
  3. The role of the Holy Spirit.
  4. The Old Testament example of Abraham points forward to Christ and his people.

Who Were the Galatian Readers?

This is not easy to answer, since the region called Galatia covered a wide area of Asia Minor, embracing a large portion of the modern country of Turkey. The term Galatia, as used in Acts 16:6; 18:23, refers to the southern part of this territory and included such cities as Antioch in Pisidia and Iconium, where Paul preached during his first missionary journey and formed churches (see Acts 13–14).

But other ancient sources tell us that the Galatians inhabited the region to the north and east of this territory, and from the second century A.D. the area of Lycaonia Galatia became detached from Galatia proper. Thus, patristic writers read 1:2 in a sense familiar to them and considered "Galatia" as the northern parts of the Asian province. This identification was championed, in classic fashion, by J. B. Lightfoot in 1865[2] and has been supported by many modern scholars, of whom J. Murphy-O'Connor gives the latest set of arguments to link the readers' home with the area of the river San-garius (see map)[3], around Pessinus (modern Balahissar).

The work of William M. Ramsay,[4] however, also in the late nineteenth century, broke new ground in defense of the southern Galatia identification on the basis of a study of epigraphy, classical literature, and a personal survey he made of the terrain of Asia Minor and its archaeological significance. In particular he appealed to the data of historical geography and to Paul's missionary strategy of concentrating on main trade routes and centers like Pisidian Antioch.

The tide of scholarly opinion has begun to flow in the direction of this identification proposed by Ramsay, thanks to the support given by commentators like F. F. Bruce[5] and R. N. Longenecker.[6] The former comments, "The burden of proof lies on those who understand Galativa and Galavtai [Galatia/Galatians]. . . in other than the provincial sense" (i.e., as referring to the districts covered in Paul's journeys of Acts 13–14). The letter is taken, then, to refer to these places and congregations because "we have important historical, geographical, literary and epigraphic data which

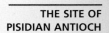

provide material for [the letter's] better understanding." Recent epigraphists like S. Mitchell concur that only the South Galatia setting will hold up.[7]

When Was the Letter Written?

How we answer the question of Galatians' identity in part affects our fixing a date for the letter. If we assume the Southern Galatia destination, covering the area of Paul's first mission tour, it becomes possible to suggest a date as soon as possible after that journey and so before the apostolic conference of Acts 15 (c. A.D. 49). The alternate proposal, on the view that the events of Galatians 2 are the same as those recorded in Acts 15, is that the letter must be dated later in Paul's ministry. The usually accepted view, on the ground of common ideas and terminology, is to put Galatians in the period of 2 Corinthians and link it with the composition of Romans, that is, during Paul's Ephesian ministry, Macedonian visit, and sojourn in Corinth (Acts 19:1–20:2).

Later in the commentary we suggest that the first visit to Jerusalem (spoken of in Gal. 1:18) is that of Acts 9:26 and the consultation of Galatians 2:1–10 is to be equated with Paul's visit in Acts 11:30; this proposal makes the mention of his coming to Jerusalem in response to a "revelation" (Gal. 2:2) to agree with Agabus's prophecy in Acts 11:28. If so, then the churches referred to in 1:2 were founded on Paul's mission of Acts 13:14–14:21. His second visit to the area is that of Acts 14:21b–23, and the mention of a preaching of the gospel at "first" or on a former occasion (Gal. 4:13) looks back to the initial evangelism of Acts 13–14:21.

The letter is thus early in terms of Paul's letters, likely the first one he wrote that has survived, and is to be dated prior to the Jerusalem council of A.D. 49, perhaps sent from Antioch in Syria.

Who Were the Agitators in 5:12?

Obviously all was not well within the Galatian congregations. Paul writes to address problems caused by someone "who is throwing you into confusion" (5:10) by trying to pervert the gospel of Christ as brought to the Galatians by Paul; thus, they are branded as "agitators" (5:12; cf. 1:7). But who are these teachers and what are they seeking to do?

H.-D. Betz has correctly seen this as the main issue. "How [was it] possible for the anti-Pauline forces to get a foothold among the Galatian Christians?"[8] Again, no easy answers are possible, and only a mirror-reading of the text will give us the data we need to construct a profile of them. Yet even that characterization is how Paul views them. We have no independent evidence of what they stand for nor a statement of their arguments in their own words. Clearly Paul perceives

ASIA MINOR

The map shows the cities of southern Galatia where Paul planted the churches: Antioch, Iconium, Lystra, and Derbe.

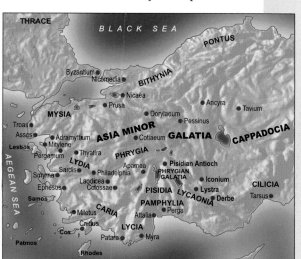

these teachers to be a serious threat to his gospel (1:6–10) since what they have introduced poses a rival message—one the Galatians are in danger of embracing to their eternal peril (5:2–6). Their presence in Galatia may be inferred, even if their number is small (5:9–10); nonetheless it is destructive and requires from Paul serious attention and sustained refutation.

Among the variety of possibilities as to their identity, one designation stands out as eminently reasonable. These agitators are Jewish-Christian emissaries (possibly from Jerusalem, 2:12) who insist that Paul's gospel for the Gentiles by faith alone and without the identity badge of circumcision is insufficient for salvation and living the Christian life. They seem to imply that after his initial evangelization, Paul left behind only "half Christians," who lacked full status within God's covenant people derived from Abraham, a proselyte whom God called to be the founder of a new, elect race with circumcision as their marker (Gen. 17:1–14).

Alongside this doctrinal controversy vitally related to becoming members of the elect people and staying in as his own people in the world—and indeed as part of it—they are conducting a smear campaign against Paul, alleging that he is no true apostle, and is dependent on (and so inferior to) the Twelve, especially the outstanding trio (called "pillar" apostles, 2:9), Peter, James the Lord's brother, and John. Moreover, Paul speaks (they insinuate) with a double voice over circumcision, not requiring it in Galatia but permitting it on occasion because he wants to make it easy for non-Jewish males to enter the church; they will thus owe allegiance to him as a leader sent out from Antioch, not to the mother church in Jerusalem (see 1:10; 5:11; 6:12–16).

A historical sidelight[9] should be noted at this point in the reconstruction of the Judaizers' pitch. Evidence from Jewish-Roman political tensions in Judea in the 40s suggests this was a time of nationalist unrest and a mounting desire to throw off Roman rule in the province. Thus, Jewish Christians may well have been

LYSTRA

The tel of the ancient city (center right).

reacting to the pressure to show themselves as true Jews, faithful to Abraham and such covenant heroes as Moses, Phinehas, and Judith, all of whom were "jealous" for the ancestral faith. Paul seemed, in this light, to be renegade, verging on apostate. There is a rumbling of this accusation of his disloyalty over non-circumcision in Acts 21:20–21.

In any case, Paul's response to these insinuations is to champion the cause of *faith* as the sole gateway of becoming a Christian and *freedom* as the hallmark of staying in the covenant community. Both slogans, however, need to be set in the context of some control, articulated in 5:6, "faith expressing itself through love," which is not a ticket to license (5:13), since the Holy Spirit who leads believers to faith (4:6–7) also works to yield a moral harvest of good social and personal behavior (5:16, 22–26).

With some indignation at the ready welcome given to the false teachers' appeal (1:6; 4:15–16; 5:7), Paul rebuts all charges of dependence on human authority (1:1, 11–12) and presses home the need of justification—that is, acceptance into God's favor and family as the covenant community of the new Israel (6:16). One receives this gift by trusting God's promise ratified in Christ, who came (4:4), died (3:13), and sent the Spirit to make salvation available to all who follow Abraham's faith (3:14). The cross of Jesus is the sign of that promise (1:4; 3:13), and any bid to add to its saving value destroys it (2:21; 5:2–6; 6:14).

Thus, "the law" with its external code and practice of circumcision only leads to a false hope. It yields either frustration (since no one can fully comply, 3:10) or self-confidence as a reliance on the "flesh," a badge of identity in which religious claims become a source of pride (3:21). The "law" leads us to Christ; when it does so, its function is completed (3:23–25). What the law sought to achieve—love of God and one's neighbor—is made possible in the new age of Messiah's salvation by the Holy Spirit, who provides moral energy to empower human conduct (3:14; 5:16–26). In this way, "the law of Christ" (6:2) is fulfilled.

The sufficiency of Christ and his saving grace in addition to the dynamic of the Spirit—these are the leading themes of the letter, and they give it a timeless (and timely) relevance needed in every age.

Greeting and Address (1:1–5)

Paul, an apostle (1:1). At the outset Paul states his credentials and his case to address the Galatian problems. His commission is directly from both Jesus Christ and God the Father. "Apostle" means one sent by the risen Lord to be his representative and messenger (as the Galatians acknowledged when Paul first came to evangelize, 4:14).

Grace and peace (1:3). This is a greeting that unites the two cultural and linguistic worlds of early churches. "Grace" is a Greek word denoting charm, beauty, goodwill, benefit, and gratitude. Attractive speech and the beauty of the human form are typical examples. Such ideas are virtually absent from the New Testament (but cf. Luke 4:22; Col. 4:6). The Graces are the virgin daughters of Zeus, who hand out feminine charm; occasionally "charm" is linked with magical amulets.[10] Here, however, the term is christianized to describe God's favor and condescension to rescue sinners (Gal. 1:4). "Peace" reflects the outcome in God's plan to restore men and women to wholeness

(Heb. *shalom*) of living. Thus, both Greco-Roman culture and Old Testament-Judaic motifs merge in this common Pauline greeting.

Present evil age (1:4). The evil age from which believers are delivered is one where astrological powers hold sway in Hellenistic society. Life was uncertain and held in a tyrannical grip of cosmic forces, called the "elemental spirits" (cf. 4:3, 9).

Paul Defends His Gospel (1:6–10)

I am astonished that you are so quickly deserting the one who called you (1:6). Paul expresses here in moving terms the issues at stake as he views the situation in the Galatian churches. The central problem is the inroad of a teaching of which he strongly disapproves, branding it a "different gospel."

A different gospel—which is really no gospel at all (1:6–7). Paul uses two

words to denote the gospel: One is the gospel he preached, the other what the Judaizers offered. In Hellenistic Greek *allos* and *heteros* are not always distinguished, but here they must be: "a different (*heteros*) gospel—which is really no gospel (*allos*) at all"—is how the NIV makes the point. The opponents' message is not an alternative to Paul's gospel, but a rival to it and a substitute for it.

Some people are throwing you into confusion (1:7). These troublemakers are more than mischievous, and they do more than preach the gospel in a way that irritates Paul (cf. Phil. 1:15–19). Rather, they are opponents who profess to be gospel preachers, but their message is so at variance with the apostolic preaching the Galatians have received and by which they were both saved and given the Holy Spirit (Gal. 3:1–5) that they are self-condemned (see 2 Cor. 11:4, 13–15) as *anathema* (see comments on 1:8).

But even if we . . .should preach a gospel other than the one we preached (1:8). If Paul were to forsake the apostolic message and resort to an insistence on circumcision as necessary for Gentile converts to enjoy a place in God's covenant, then he too would be under divine judgment (see 5:11). The sole sufficiency of the cross as God's power for new life is the issue at stake.[11] See 6:14 for Paul's settled determination, though the price he is willing to pay is a heavy one (6:17).

Let him be eternally condemned (1:8). The Greek *anathema* (NIV "eternally condemned" in 1:8, 9) is the usual translation in the LXX for the Hebrew *ḥerem*, "ban, outside the covenant," a sentence

IMAGES OF ANGELS

Artistic representation of cherubim on the tabernacle coverings.

meted out to Achan (Josh. 7:1–26). Perhaps Paul implies a disciplinary action here, excommunicating the teachers from the church and consigning them to Satan's realm.

Divine Revelation (1:11–12)

The gospel I preached (1:11). The reason for Paul's claim to be a herald of the only gospel (i.e., the good news of God) stems, in part, from the following facts: He did not invent his gospel, he is not indebted to any human source for its substance, nor did he get it by instruction from others (namely, the apostles before him, 1:17).

I received it by revelation from Jesus Christ (1:12). The gospel came from God as an act of special revelation from or about Jesus Christ. "Revelation" (Gk. *apokalypsis*) stresses the divine initiative in God's unfolding plan, which is otherwise shrouded in mystery.

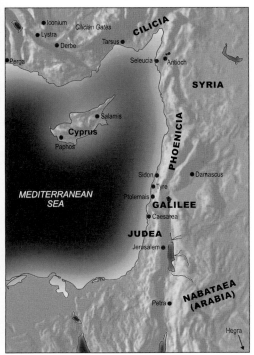

Paul calls this "revelation" God's choice "to reveal his Son in [or to] me" (1:16). Yet this phrase equally implies a commission to proclaim this good news, since the expression can also mean "through me." This defines the nature of the uniqueness Paul claims for his gospel. What came to him in his conversion/call experience on the Damascus road was God's plan *for the Gentiles*. At the same time, he received the shared traditions about Jesus from his Jewish-Christian predecessors (1 Cor. 15:3–8), while the new understanding of God's inclusion of the non-Jews was God's special gift in making him "the apostle to the Gentiles" (see Rom. 15:17).

Paul's Early Life (1:13–14)

My previous way of life in Judaism (1:13). "Judaism" here connotes the practice of living as a Jew, adopting Jewish customs as national badges and identity markers. This definition plays a significant role in Paul's later argument in refusing to grant salvific or covenantal status to such practices as circumcision, regarded by him when imposed on Gentile believers as "works of the law" (2:16; NIV, "observing the law").

To repel the charge that his credentials as a Jew are defective, Paul rehearses the attested claims of his preconversion life. Those claims (amplified in Phil. 3:4–6) are marked by his thorough knowledge of Jewish traditions, learned at the school of rabbi Gamaliel (Acts 22:3; 26:5), and his zeal in rooting out all who compromised the distinctiveness of the ancestral faith and practice.

Extremely zealous for the traditions of my fathers (1:14). "Zealous" (1:14) is another key term, summing up the earnestness, courage, and devotion of Jewish women like Judith and men like Phinehas, Elijah, and the Maccabean freedom fighters, in opposing the inroads of pagan, immoral influences that would have destroyed the distinctive faith of Judaism ("the traditions of my fathers").[12] In particular, Paul dedicated his zeal, like these Jewish exemplars, to opposing the church of the Hellenists (Hellenistic Jewish Christians, who had begun to catch the vision of Stephen as his followers, see Acts 11:19–21).

His Apostolic Call and Sequel (1:15–17)

The turning point for Paul came in what is usually called his conversion, narrated in graphic detail three times in Acts (9:1–19; 22:3–21; 26:1–23). The autobiography gives the reader the *theological* dimension, spelled out in terms of God's prenatal choice and summons to be his prophet to the nations. Yet it was more than a prophetic calling to which he responded on the road to Damascus. He entered into a personal union with the living Lord, of which he writes movingly in Galatians 2:20 (cf. also Phil. 3:12).[13]

Nor did I go up to Jerusalem . . . but I went immediately into Arabia (1:17). Once transformed and turned in a new (opposite) direction, Paul did not seek approval of human authorities, not even from the leaders in Jerusalem, but went off to preach in "Arabia" (i.e., Nabatea, ruled by King Aretas IV, alluded to in 2 Cor. 11:32–33). After that, Paul returned to Damascus.

Aretas reigned at Petra from 9 B.C. to A.D. 39/40. He was father-in-law of Herod Antipas, who divorced Aretas's daughter to marry Herodias (Mark 6:17–18), a move that enraged Aretas. Thus it is not surprising that in A.D. 36 Aretas defeated Herod's army and thereafter, with Emperor Tiberius's connivance, took control of Damascus until the early years of Caligula's reign, the next Roman emperor. Most modern historians date Aretas's control of Damascus from A.D. 37 until his death in 39/40; thus, Paul's experiences in that city fall within this two- to three-year time span.[14]

Paul's escape is prior to Aretas's death (see 2 Cor. 11:32–33), but his chronology is silent as to exactly when it occurred; hence the "after three years" of Galatians 1:18 is presumably to be reckoned from this flight, variously dated from between 31 to 37 (though the "three years" may be dated from his conversion[15]; see comments on 1:18).

Encounter with Jerusalem Leaders (1:18–20)

Then . . .I went up to Jerusalem (1:18). After three years following his conversion (around A.D. 34) Paul visited Jerusalem to make the acquaintance of Peter, with whom he lodged for only a two-week period. Notice that he had already begun his preaching and apos-

R E F L E C T I O N S

LUKE RECORDS PAUL'S DRAMATIC ENCOUNTER WITH the risen Lord three times in the book of Acts. As Paul tells his own story here in Galatians, he is concerned to pinpoint the *theological* significance of his new life in Christ. His reflection centers on God's sovereign act of choice in claiming him as his servant, and the redirecting of his zeal in the cause of Christ, his new inspiration and goal in living (see also Phil. 1:21; 3:7–14). What we call his conversion, happening in a moment, led to a change of direction; and this, we may say, is the test of genuine experience of Christ today.

tolic ministry, and his time with Peter was brief. No implication that he received his gospel from this apostolic source is possible.

Paul admits to no other contact with the apostles, with the exception of James, the brother of the Lord, to whom the risen Jesus appeared (1 Cor. 15:7).[16] This mention is important since it appears that the emissaries to Galatia may have claimed the authority of James when they came to Antioch to challenge Peter (Gal. 2:12). Paul wishes to head off any idea that he is indebted to or in disagreement with James, the head of the Jerusalem church (Acts 12:17; 15:13).

James (1:19). James, the Lord's brother, played a significant role in early Christianity, much more than the fleeting allusions to him in Acts suggest.[17] Paul only occasionally mentions him, but at crucial points in his letters (e.g., 1 Cor. 15:7; Gal. 1:18; 2:12).[18]

Mission in Syria, Cilicia (1:20–24)

Later I went to Syria and Cilicia (1:21). This is obviously a compressed account of Paul's early ministry, to be filled out by what is contained in Acts 9:19–25 as well as his own autobiographical story in 2 Corinthians 11:32–33.

Titus Was Not Circumcised When He Went to Jerusalem (2:1–5)

Paul is continuing his story of relations with the church at Jerusalem. He now recalls his second visit to Jerusalem "fourteen years later." His actions and interactions with the Jewish Christian leaders there provided additional powerful messages reinforcing the kind of gospel (i.e.,

justification by faith alone) he had been preaching in the Gentile communities.

Fourteen years later I went up again to Jerusalem (2:1). Two questions are involved here: (1) Which visit to Jerusalem in the book of Acts matches the description given here? (2) When Paul counts "fourteen years," what is his starting point? "Fourteen years later" than when?

The view taken here is that Paul is referring to the visit of Acts 11:29–30, and that he reckons from the time of his conversion-call, which probably occurred in A.D. 33–34. This would bring the date to A.D. 47–48 for the second Jerusalem visit. While these are fascinating and complicated matters, they are incidental to the chief point Paul is wishing to establish, namely, that his two short visits to the Jerusalem apostles could hardly have meant that he was going "hat in hand" to gain their approval for his ministry. The geographical note in 1:21–22 suggests that Paul had already gained considerable experience as an evangelist in Syria and Cilicia, especially at Antioch (a city that will play a significant role in his discussion at 2:11). This tallies with

the descriptions in Acts (9:30; 11:25) of Paul's ministry in his own city of Tarsus in Cilicia.

With Barnabas (2:1). Barnabas was Paul's mentor when Paul first returned to Jerusalem after his conversion (Acts 9:27). But he was also Paul's colleague (11:24–26, 30; 12:25) at the time of the mission to Galatia (chs. 13–14).

I took Titus along (2:1). Who was Titus?[19] In the New Testament, his name is only mentioned by Paul.[20] Apparently, Titus was a Gentile who resided in Antioch and became a Christian through Paul's evangelistic activities there. When Paul and Barnabas brought the famine relief fund to Jerusalem (Acts 11:30), they took Titus along as a test case.

A revelation (2:2). The biblical word "revelation" (*apokalypsis*)[21] connotes an unveiling of supernatural origin. A revelation may come to a person directly (cf. Gal. 1:12), through a group of church leaders (cf. Acts 13:2), or through a prophet such as Agabus (cf. 11:28; 21:10–11). Paul clearly states that his second visit to Jerusalem was not due to the Jerusalem leaders' invitation or his own ambition to have a direct confrontation with them concerning his Gentile mission.

Set before them the gospel (2:2). "Set before" literally connotes the idea of "laying something before for one's own interest or purpose." After fourteen years of evangelistic activities among the Gentiles in the Syria and Cilicia regions, Paul realizes that the advancement of this mission invites the recognition or endorsement (not approval) of the Jewish Christian leaders in Jerusalem (see 2:9 for the outcome).

To those who seemed to be leaders (2:2). This phrase refers to James, Peter, and John (2:9), who were the influential persons in the Christian community in Jerusalem. The first was a member of the family of Jesus; the latter two were part of the original apostolic band.

That I was running or had run my race in vain (2:2). Paul often uses athletic imagery (see Phil. 3:12–14 for his picture of the Christian life as a race; cf. 2 Tim. 4:7). Here "running" describes his apostolic service (cf. Phil. 2:16), though he will return to the race image in Galatians 5:7 in his gentle rebuke of his readers as in danger of being deflected from their loyalty to Christ.[22]

Yet not even Titus . . . was compelled to be circumcised (2:3). Titus's presence clearly sharpened the issues that lay at the heart of the debate: Ought Gentile Christians to be received into the church's fellowship on equal terms with Jewish Christians without insisting on the rite of circumcision? Paul preaches a message that answers that question with a strong yes (2:2), but he is aware that

TARSUS

The recently excavated Roman road (*cardo*) in Tarsus.

▼

this practice is open to criticism from "false brothers" (2:4; see 2 Cor. 11:13–15 for a strong condemnation of these intruders) who dog Paul's footsteps and challenge his apostolic work. Although under pressure, Paul stood firm and refused to concede the need for Titus's circumcision.

Because some Greek manuscripts from the Western tradition (e.g., codex D) omit the word "not" before "Titus," we face an obvious ambiguity: Was Titus circumcised under pressure or not? If he was, the wording is at least clear that the surgical operation, practiced to admit Gentile converts to Judaism as a "rite of passage," was not carried out as a result of "giving in" (2:5) or capitulating to Paul's opponents. Rather, it was done out of deference to the tender feelings and convictions of Jewish Christian leaders in the capital city (1 Cor. 9:19–23 is often appealed to for Paul's willingness to be accommodating). The conclusion, however, that Titus was not circumcised is to be preferred.

False brothers had infiltrated our ranks (2:4). The expression "false brothers" here refers to some Jewish Christians who are treated as insincere people. They have gate-crashed into what was a private meeting between Paul and the Jewish Christian leaders (2:2). Their motives were to challenge Paul's gospel of freedom in Christ and to introduce "bondage" in its place (see 5:1 for the exact wording) so that they might undermine Paul's adherence to the "truth of the gospel" he had brought to Galatia (2:5).

To spy on our freedom . . . and to make us slaves (2:4). Slavery was a common practice in the Greco-Roman world during Paul's lifetime.[23] By law slaves were considered "human tools" (Aristotle). In the first century some slaves wished to be manumitted and became freed persons (cf. 1 Cor. 7:20–24). Paul uses this slavery concept to illustrate the harm these false teachers were doing in trying to impose their ideas on him and Barnabas and especially the Galatians. If Gentile believers must also be circumcised in order to be saved, then Paul and Barnabas themselves have become slaves to Jewish ways, a setback to the gospel message they presented in the Gentile communities.

We did not give in . . . for a moment (2:5). Paul was under extreme pressure to give in to the false brothers' persuasion (see also the use of "compelled" in 2:3), but he held firm to his conviction.

The truth of the gospel (2:5). In this letter, the truth of the gospel refers to the conviction that justification is founded on God's grace (2:21) through faith in Christ Jesus (2:16) apart from circumcision (5:2–3) or the observance of the Mosaic law (2:16; 5:4).

Paul's Ministry Was Acknowledged by the Key Leaders in Jerusalem (2:6–10)

Though facing tremendous pressure before the Jewish Christian leaders in Jerusalem fourteen years after his conversion (possibly because of pro-Zealot pressure in Judea that made conforming to Jewish customs a clear signal of the loyalty of Jewish messianic believers to the ancestral faith), Paul boldly declared that his Gentile mission was of equal footing with Peter's Jewish mission (both men had been commissioned by God and were apostles, 2:7–8). Most significant, the chief leaders of the Jewish-Christian communities unanimously acknowledged his work.

Makes no difference to me (2:6). In the Greco-Roman world, networking and partnership were commonly done through letters of recommendation (cf. Rom. 16:1; 1 Cor. 16:10–11).[24] Itinerant teachers usually acquired these letters of recommendation from conspicuous figures to establish their credentials in order to pave their ways to foreign communities. Paul did not rely on this device (cf. 2 Cor. 3:1; see Acts 18:27 for illustration).

Peter . . . to the Jews (2:7). According to Luke's account in Acts, when Paul and Barnabas were in Jerusalem for the famine relief (11:30), Peter had already evangelized Cornelius (a Gentile) and his household (ch. 10). But that was a unique occasion,[25] which the Jewish Christians willingly accepted after Peter's explanation (see Acts 11:18). Overall, Peter's evangelistic activities were aimed at the Jews.

Pillars (2:9). "Pillars" (*styloi*) was a metaphor commonly used by the Jews in speaking of the great teachers of the law.[26] The church is here regarded as the house or temple of God held up and supported by pillars, that is, these key apostolic leaders (James, Peter, and John).

Right hand of fellowship (2:9). It may be equivalent to the modern greeting. But the use of "fellowship" (*koinōnia*) connotes more than just a friendly handshake. Paul was eager to inform his readers that there was an expression of partnership[27] in this Gentile mission when James, Peter, and John shook hands with him and Barnabas in Jerusalem.

To remember (2:10). This is also an expression of actual actions involved (cf. Phil. 1:3).[28]

The poor (2:10). Why were the Jerusalem saints (1 Cor. 16:1) stricken by poverty? Famine was only one of the factors, though a key one.[29] Other factors also contributed: (1) Many new believers had liquidated their assets by selling their properties to form a common fund for communal life after their conversion (Acts 2–4); (2) there was an increasing number of widows (Acts 6) living in Jerusalem; (3) believers were persecuted following Stephen's martyrdom (Acts 8:1–2).[30]

The very thing I was eager to do (2:10). Paul had already started this famine relief with Barnabas in Antioch. The reasons are clear: (1) Paul, a man of compassion, was always willing to help needy people. (2) He understood that this project could strategically help to cement the relationship between the Jerusalem Christians and the Gentile churches and to promote their unity. (3) He saw that this was an eschatological fulfillment of Isaiah's

"PILLARS"

Columns from the temple of Apollo at Corinth.

▼

ANTIOCH

▼

▶ Antioch

The place of Antioch in early Christianity is important. It was a bastion of Hellenism in the Syrian lands, the inevitable meeting point of the two worlds. In the time of the Maccabees many of the Jews of Jerusalem showed their adoption of Greek ways by becoming honorary citizens of Antioch. It is easy to imagine, then, how a liberal, tolerant spirit prevailed there. Peter (called here by his Aramaic name Cephas) at first fell in with the practice of sharing a common table with Christian Gentiles.[A-1]

prophecy that Gentiles would bring gifts to the holy mountain in the last days (Isa. 66:20).

Peter's Action Was Rebuked (2:11–13)

In order to demonstrate further the independent authenticity of the message he proclaimed, Paul recalls an unpleasant encounter he had with Peter occurring not long ago before the writing of this letter. He gives an account of Peter's action, the reason behind it, and its impact on other Jewish Christians. His purpose, evidently, is not to expose Peter's weakness. Rather, he wants to show his readers how he went beyond his safety zone to defend the authenticity of this gospel of grace. No one, including Peter, can cause him to yield or compromise (cf. 1:10) when truth is being undermined. This is true in spite of Paul's acknowledgment that Peter is one of the pillars of the Jerusalem church, whom he once made an effort to get acquainted with (1:18) and who had extended the right hand of fellowship not long ago (2:9).

When Peter came to Antioch (2:11). The time of Peter's visit possibly took place after Paul and Barnabas completed their first missionary journey in A.D. 48.[31] Peter came to Antioch to learn about as well as to show support to this unprecedented Gentile outreach program launched by the Gentile-Christian church. "Came to Antioch" may suggest that Paul was at

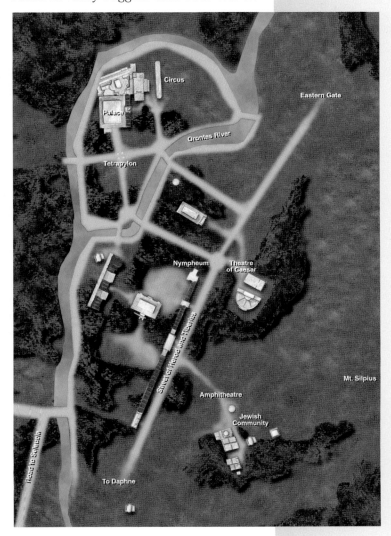

Circus

Eastern Gate

Palace

Orontes River

Tetrapylon

Nympheum

Theatre of Caesar

Street of Herod and Tiberius

Mt. Silpius

Amphitheatre

Jewish Community

Road to Seleucia

To Daphne

Antioch at the time of his writing of Galatians.

I opposed him to his face (2:11). There was a face-to-face confrontation between Paul and Peter. "I opposed" suggests that Paul is reacting to Peter, who initiates this conflict by his improper behavior toward the Gentile Christians.

Certain men came from James (2:12). These people are evidently not the "false brothers" of 2:4. They were commissioned by James or at least claimed his authorization. They were of the circumcision group (2:13) and possibly came with a special assignment to learn about Paul and Barnabas's Gentile mission (as Peter did). James, we will remember, is the Lord's brother, who became the leader of the Jerusalem church[32] after Peter took on a wider ministry base (Acts 9:32).

He began to ... separate himself (2:12). Literally, "he cut himself off"—a possible pun, meaning "he played the Pharisee" ("Pharisee" is built on a Semitic root meaning "to separate"). These Jewish leaders were self-styled "separated ones," anxious to preserve their ritual purity and ethnic distinctiveness as elites within God's covenant people.

He was afraid (2:12). Why? Having been commissioned by God to evangelize Cornelius (a Gentile, Acts 10:20) and having witnessed God's saving mercy among the Gentiles (11:4–17), Peter takes an action that is perplexing and betrays his vacillating character. Presumably Peter is trying to avoid another direct conflict with these Jewish brothers. In 11:2–3 he was once criticized[33] by the circumcision group in Jerusalem for eating with uncircumcised people.

The other Jews joined him in his hypocrisy (2:13). Peter's giving in may be due to an unpleasant experience in the past. But the others' behavior, standing up in the midst of a meal and walking away, is intolerable to Paul. Labeling Peter with the word "hypocrisy" (*hypokrisis*) associates him with the Pharisees. According to Paul, Peter not only "played the Pharisee" (see 2:12); he actually behaved "like the Pharisee" in this matter. *Hypokrisis*, however, may have more serious overtones here since the LXX uses it to refer to Israel's enemies as "ungodly people."

Even Barnabas (2:13). Barnabas is mentioned by name because the Galatians know him personally (Acts 13–14). But instead of protecting Barnabas's reputation, Paul chooses to reveal the details so that the readers can appreciate his own integrity. When Paul says he does not please people (Gal. 1:10) for the sake of the gospel, he means it. Barnabas's giving in to the situation reflects the reality of peer pressure in daily life.

ANTIOCH

The ruins of the temple of Augustus at Pisidian Antioch.

▼

Peter's Reasoning Challenged (2:14–17)

Paul carefully rehearses his conversation with Peter to explain to his readers the reason for his harsh attitude toward Peter. At the same time, he endeavors to persuade them about the uselessness of seeking justification by means of observing the law.

I said to Peter (2:14). Paul follows Peter the moment he sees him and other Jewish Christians leave their seats (cf. 2:5, "did not give in to them for a moment"). Instead of lecturing to the crowd, he directly talks to Peter, the leader as well as the initiator of this misconduct. Paul is using a rhetorical device here since his real "audience" is the Judaizers and/or the Galatians influenced by them.

You are a Jew . . . live like a Gentile and not like a Jew (2:14). Peter, being a Jew by nationality, has been able to liberate himself from the restrictive Jewish dietary regulations (cf. Lev. 11). He has learned his freedom as a Christian based on the teaching of Jesus in Mark 7:1–21 and lived like a Gentile, enjoying table fellowship with the Gentile Christians.

[To] force Gentiles to follow Jewish customs (2:14). The verb used here, *ioudaizō* (lit., "to judaize"; NIV, "to follow Jewish customs"), occurs only here in the New Testament. According to Josephus, it means "to live like a Jew" or "to adopt Jewish customs."[34] In this context, Jewish customs specifically refer to the areas of circumcision and strict observance of the Mosaic law. When Peter was eating with them, his action communicated a strong sense of acceptance and fellowship. Paul considers Peter's inconsistent behavior as an indirect way of forcing Gentiles to follow Jewish customs. The harm this might bring to these new Gentile Christians is immeasurable. This explains Paul's fierce reaction in challenging Peter.

Gentile sinners (2:15). This is a general attitude of the Jews toward the Gentiles.[35]

To be justified in Christ . . . we ourselves are sinners (2:17). This may be a charge raised by the false brothers according to their way of reasoning. They claim Paul is teaching that to be justified in Christ, it is necessary to abandon the law (cf. 2:16), and to abandon the law is to become a sinner. That means, in effect, that Christ promotes sin (lit., Christ is the minister or agent of sin). Paul refutes this argument.

In Conclusion: A Personal Note (2:18–21)

Notice a change of pronoun from "we" (2:15–17) to "I" (2:18–21). Before closing this section, Paul adds a personal note, sharing his own spiritual experience in this new relationship to Christ after breaking off from the Jewish way of salvation, which he used to treasure as a Pharisee.

A lawbreaker (2:18). Literally, "a transgressor," that is, one who goes beyond or violates the rules established. In this incident, perhaps Peter should be the speaker who fell short by turning completely under pressure from the presence of James' representatives. Paul, however, may also intend to justify his own actions in not circumcising Titus even under extreme pressure and in rebuking Peter. If he had given in at these crucial points, he would have proved himself to be "a lawbreaker."

Through the law I died to the law (2:19). "To die to the law" means "to break off from a relationship."[36] Through his own legalistic efforts Paul has realized that no one can be justified by observing the law (cf. Rom. 7:7–11). Therefore, he must break off from it for salvation. It is only through faith in Christ that a person can be justified and liberated to a true relationship with God. This is exactly what Paul experienced on the road to Damascus, where he gave up all hope of self-justification and came to a new understanding of the way God saves people.

I have been crucified with Christ (2:20). The verb here is perfect tense, denoting a past action with a continuing effect. The old life of self-effort has been condemned and put on the cross. By using the cross imagery, Paul gives testimony to his new relationship with Christ and his new purpose in living. Now by faith he lives (present tense, denoting a moment-by-moment fellowship) in union with a living Lord, who henceforth controls him and lives out his resurrection life in him.

By faith in the Son of God (2:20). This critical and controversial expression may mean (1) by my trust in Christ, or (2) by Christ's faithfulness to me.

The grace of God (2:21). Above all, it is God's grace that makes it possible for sinners to be justified. It is unthinkable for anyone to set aside what God has already provided and to return to the old ways. Doing so would devalue the cross as the center of our hope (6:14). No wonder in the following statement (3:1), Paul began with an outburst, "you foolish Galatians!"

Paul Confronts His Readers (3:1–5)

Paul's discussion now turns from the past episode at Antioch to the present situation in Galatia. The closing part of his rehearsal of the earlier incident is clear in stating that (1) there is no hope or value in seeking acceptance with God by observing the law (2:21), and (2) in any case, God has himself made full provision for human, specifically Gentile, need in the cross of Jesus, who did not die "for nothing." These twin affirmations are the grounds for Paul's impassioned appeal (3:1).

You foolish Galatians! Who has bewitched you? (3:1). This direct address is unusual for Paul and marks his emotional appeal. He charges that his Galatian friends are under the spell of an "evil eye," a Greek expression to denote the placing of a curse on someone, as

R E F L E C T I O N S

IN WRITING GALATIANS 2:19–20, PAUL OPENS UP HIS inner soul in a way he does only rarely. Sometimes this is called "the mysticism" of Paul (as in Albert Schweitzer's well-known title), but it is doubtful if this description is accurate. Rather, it is a revelation of Paul's Christ-centered life, based on a death-to-self reality but issuing in newness that he attributes to "Christ living in me." Commentators note how the pronoun "I" (typical of the old life of striving to please God in one's own strength) has been inflected to "me" to whom God's blessing came as a grateful recipient of grace (2:21). The person Paul knows as his life-changing power is none other than "the Son of God, who loved me and gave himself up for me." Have you opened up your life to the same person who poured his love and grace into the apostle Paul's life?

illustrated in contemporary execration texts and amulets.[37] One such text illustrates the ostensible magical power of the curse known as the "evil eye": "Above all, I pray that you may be in health unharmed by the evil eye and faring prosperously."

Jesus Christ was clearly portrayed as crucified (3:1). Paul harks back to his earlier amazement (1:6) that his readers have succumbed to this spell. He is especially puzzled when he recalls how clearly the picture of the crucified Lord has been presented to them, presumably by his vivid preaching of the cross. "Portrayed" literally means to post a notice in public, like a modern bulletin board—the ancient method of giving out notices of a political or social event.[38]

Paul continues to press home his appeal by a series of questions, each of which concerns the Christian experience of the Galatians. How did they become believers at the beginning? How do they hope to make progress and come to their final salvation (3:3)? How do they explain God's manifest presence and power among them (3:5)?

Give you his Spirit (3:5). The Greek word for "give" here is *epichorēgeō*, from which *chorēgia* ("supply") played an important role in Attic Greek drama. The verb means "to provide for the chorus," whose narration carried the story line for the audience in Greek plays. It thus came to refer to patriotic and generous citizens in Athens who gave contributions to aid the state. One classicist notes: "The importance of the choral element is shown by the fact that the main responsibility of each of the financial sponsors (*chorēgoi*) was the recruiting and maintenance, costuming and training of the chorus."[39]

Because you observe the law, or because you believe what you heard? (3:5). This is the stark alternative, leading to only one conclusion (as Paul's logic insists).

Abraham as Model Believer (3:6–9)

The Jewish teachers who had unsettled the Galatians (1:7; 5:12) are the real persons addressed. They evidently made much of Abraham in their approach, offering a seemingly plausible argument: You Gentiles wish to inherit the blessing of righteousness that our ancestor Abraham received (a common belief found in Philo and the rabbinic sources;[40] for Abraham as an example for future generations, see Sir. 44:19–21); why then do you hesitate to follow his example and get circumcised, as he was told to do (Gen. 17:9–14)?

Abraham, Paul retorts, did indeed receive divine approval, and God put him "in the right" (called justification) with himself. But on what basis? The patriarch was, above all, a person of "faith" (3:6, appealing to Gen. 15:6 and a promise that *precedes* the command to circumcise all Abraham's family). Romans 4:9–12 makes this even clearer.

All nations will be blessed through you (3:8). A second Scripture citation is needed to oppose the Judaizers' argument and their appeal to Abraham. Earlier still in the Genesis story of Israel's ancestors God had given a first promise to Abraham (Gen. 12:3, repeated in 18:18) that he was to be ancestor, not of Jewish people only but of "all nations," a wide inclusion quoted by Paul in Galatians 3:8. The word for "nations" in the Greek Bible can also mean "Gentiles"; here it refers to the Galatians. How then can the Judaizing teachers claim that the Galatians must become Jews in order to be complete Christians? Paul's logic is clear and leads to 3:9—those who believe are blessed in the same way as Abraham the believer.

The Law Cannot Bring Salvation (3:10–14)

One further argument will lead to the same conclusion—stated in 3:14 with even sharper focus on the readers as former pagans (4:8–10).

The law is not based on faith (3:12). The gist of Paul's argument is that religion based on law, so far from being required to gain salvation/justification, lies under judgment. The only exception to this verdict would be if a person could be found who perfectly kept the law. But that possibility is excluded by the sinful human nature, called "flesh" (in 6:13) and is endorsed by the verdict of Deuteronomy 27:26 (quoted in Gal. 3:10). Later on, Paul will develop the way nomistic religion (i.e., "law-oriented" religion), based on an observance for Gentiles of circumcision in order to gain a place in God's covenant, is really a no-win situation, since nomism leads either to frustration and condemnation when we fail (as here), or to pride when we succeed (Phil.

3:6). Either way, it leads to a false hope and a bitter result, as is clear (cf. "clearly" in Gal. 3:11).

Christ redeemed us from the curse of the law (3:13). Yet there is hope once we renounce all attempts to be our own savior, and it centers in the cross of Christ, where he bore our judgment by dying the sinner's death.

Law Versus Promise (3:15–22)

Paul here faces an objection. To be sure, so his opponents argued, God gave Abraham a promise that included his family (3:16)—but we know this refers to the Jewish people by the fact that some centuries later God made a covenant (agreement) with Israel. So, they reasoned, the

REFLECTIONS

ONE OF THE CLEAREST STATEMENTS Paul gives for the basis of our salvation is in Galatians 3:13. Christ has set us free from all vain attempts to win our redemption; he has paid the cost by his death on the cross (2:20–21)—where he assumed our curse as sinners and died as our vicarious Redeemer. We now live with him in freedom, dead to sin's curse.

▶ Redemption

"Redeemed" is the terminology used for the way slaves gained their freedom in Greco-Roman society as well as for Israel's deliverance from bondage in Egypt (Ex. 15:13; Ps. 77:15) and servitude in Babylon (Isa. 42:1). The former worldview was exceedingly common in the ancient world. For example, at Delphi the names of former slaves set free by payment of their savings and deposited in the temple of Apollo as by a fiction (since the owners received the money in payment) are recorded on several temple walls. In Roman society slaves' redemption and gaining of freedom was common. The freed slave was also promised Roman citizenship.[A-2]

law of Moses supersedes the Abrahamic covenant.

Paul gives a firm "No" to this conclusion in a series of counterarguments: (1) The allusion to Abraham's "seed' (i.e., offspring) turns on the fact that the word is singular in number (in Gen. 12:7; 13:15–16; 17:8; 24:7) and so must be understood in a collective sense (Gal. 3:16), meaning the Messiah and his people, including both Gentiles and Jews (cf. 1 Cor. 12:12). (See comments below on Gal. 3:16.)

(2) The giving of the law at a *later* period does not invalidate the earlier promise made to Abraham (3:17), any more than a codicil added to a human will destroys the terms of the original document once it has been ratified (3:15). Paul is familiar with the making of wills in Greco-Roman society and uses a technical term (in 3:17: "does not set aside"), evidenced in the papyri for "void by illegality."[41] Yet his understanding of family inheritance based on the principle of primogeniture (the right of the eldest son to inherit) is not the same as Athenian law provided, where the inheritance of property (a person's *klēros* or lot) was divided equally by lot between surviving sons.[42] God's "promise" (a word found eight times in 3:14–19) to Abraham is what the Gentile believers have inherited, thereby bypassing the law's requirement (here circumcision).

(3) The Mosaic law, though coming later in time than the promise to Abraham, has all the marks of inferiority: It was given to define human sin without giving the power to overcome it (3:21), and it came by various intermediaries since it was handed down from God via Moses via the angels to the people.[43] By contrast, the promise to Abraham was given directly from God himself (Gal. 3:20).

The Scripture does not say "and to seeds," meaning many people, but "and to your seed," meaning one person, who is Christ (3:16). Paul's line of reasoning, beginning with the fact that "seed" is singular, has precedent in rabbinic interpretation.[44] It is his extension of this interpretation as messianic and individual that is unusual, since "seed" does not normally refer to one person. Morris observes that it points to the one person as outstanding (not like Isaac over against Ishmael, a discussion to come later in 4:21–31). "It is not one descendant among many but *the* descendant." So, Paul concludes, what is vital is not that "Abraham's descendants became a nation . . . but that . . . God's chosen one, the Christ, appeared in due course and that the covenant God made centres on him."[45]

Added because of transgressions (3:19). This unexplained addendum may be Paul's way of saying that the law gave definition and focus to sin (as in Rom. 3:20; 4:15), as the REB takes it, "to make wrongdoing a legal offence" or simply to point to human need of pardon and atonement that the law was powerless to meet (as 2 Cor. 3:6 may imply, and is seen in Paul's conclusion at Gal. 3:21). Above all, the law is propaedeutic and prophetic, both preparing people for the gospel message (Gal. 3:8) and pointing them to Christ as the promised Redeemer (3:22).

By a mediator (3:19). Literally, "in the hand of a mediator." This phrase evidently refers to Moses since it was by Moses that the Torah was given.[46] Some think the allusion to Moses' hand relates to the tables of the law placed into his hands at Sinai (Ex. 32:19). The function of Moses the lawgiver as a human intermediary is a sign of the law's inferiority in contrast to the direct giving of the promise to Abraham.

Is the law, therefore, opposed to the promises of God? (3:21). It seems the answer must be yes; but Paul replies, "Absolutely not!" The law did have a role to play, such as providing a definition of sin as transgression, i.e., stepping across the line of God's will.

Why the Law? (3:23–29)

The law was put in charge (3:24). The law was temporary, like a custodian, keeping people in check as a disciplinarian (3:23–24). The Greek word is *paidagōgos*, describing a slave in Hellenistic society who acted as tutor and guardian to children as well as imposing discipline. The slave also led the children to the school, "helped to bring up the child and at school must have been a helpful overseer."[47] Hence, the *paidagōgos* was a trusted member of the family

and even sometimes had charge of "home-schooling" before group schooling became accepted.[48]

In any case that job lasted only until the children reached the age of maturity. Then his responsibility was at an end. Now, Paul insists, "faith came" and brought our time with the law to an end, since it pointed to Christ, who alone can set us right with God (3:24) and place us in God's family as his adult children (3:26).

You are all sons of God (3:26). Mention of family life leads Paul to rehearse the benefits of belonging to God's new order by various steps. (1) The first step was believing in Christ Jesus (3:26). (2) Then came baptism into him as an act of identification when candidates stripped off old clothes and were given new garments. This was a picture of putting on Christ's character (3:27); (3) In this new family life of believers all the age-old barriers of race, social position, and gender are overcome in Christ, who unites believers as "one" in him. This does away with the pride that thanks God (as in Jewish prayers[49]) that male Jews are not created as Gentiles, slaves, or women (3:28). (4) As a triumphant conclusion, Paul addresses his Gentile audience as Christ's people and so as the family of Abraham and inheritors of God's promise to him (3:29).

God's Children—Not Slaves (4:1–7)

This section shows what inheritance means. The contrast is a direct one between "slaves" and "sons" (4:7), and so what believers are as inheritors. Roman society—with its institution of slavery and its family life, where children had no

▶

"BAPTISMAL" POOL

A traditional Jewish purification bath (*miqveh*) discovered in the southern wall excavations at Jerusalem just south of the Temple Mount.

rights or little significance until they grew up to adulthood—is reflected here. Paul uses this framework to argue for spiritual applications, which we may tabulate: (1) Childhood is a time under control (4:2); (2) it is akin to slavery (4:3); (3) yet it holds the promise of reaching adulthood, just as some slaves hoped to be set free by manumission (see earlier on 3:13).

"Abba, Father" (4:6). *Abba* is Jesus' familiar name for God as "dear father"(Mark 14:32–39; Luke 11:2–4).

No longer a slave, but a son (4:7). (1) Slavery induces fear and can represent the human condition under the power of bad religion, called "the basic principles of the world" (4:3). Here, however, it is more likely a reference to star worship. The cosmic "elements" were thought to control human beings and to lead to uncertainty about human fate, as 4:8–9 makes clear. (2) Slavery pictures men and women in bondage to sin and needing to be "redeemed." This has happened in Christ's coming and death (1:4; 3:13). (3) The outcome is a new life of "sonship," enjoying our full inheritance (4:1, 5) and freedom as God's children who know intimately the smile of their Parent.

Paul's Expression of Concern (4:8–20)

Slaves to those who by nature are not gods (4:8). This is a clear indication that the Galatians were pagan before entering God's family in Christ. Paul marvels (as he does at 1:6) that they should wish to revert to the slavery brought on by fear of cosmic powers—such as the star deities that once ruled their lives—by imposing a regime of observing "special days" when good luck may be expected for an enterprise (a typical sentiment of Greco-Roman religion with its recourse to magic, omens, and horoscope predictions). Their interest was in what "days" were good for business or travel or marriage and which "seasons" were favored by the gods to produce fertile ground or harvest yield.

Because of an illness that I first [or, on a former occasion] preached the gospel to you (4:13). Paul's first visit to Galatia (in Acts 13–14) is the background here. He was evidently a sick person at that time and suffered a disfiguring or debilitating illness that could have made the Galatians reject him as the opposite of a divine messenger. Instead, they welcomed him as a

---

▶ **Elements**

The use of the Greek word *stoicheia* in this context is much discussed. Its basic meaning is what stands in a line, like a row of peas or the characters of the alphabet. Hence it comes to mean rudimentary "elements" or the ABCs in educational theory among Greco-Roman teachers. This is sometimes thought to link it with the reference to *paidagōgos* in Galatians 3:23–24.

Yet the way Paul proceeds in **4:8** to associate these *stoicheia* with pagan religion from which the Galatians have been delivered suggests that he has in mind the cosmic powers, thought to be expressed in the stars, which in turn control human destiny. Diogenes Laertius speaks of "twelve immortal stoicheia," meaning the signs of the zodiac; he refers to human fear of uncertainty in the astrological-magical realm when human life is held in the grip of these planetary powers (see comments on Gal. 4:8).[A-3]

► HERMES

person sent from God (like Hermes/Mercury in Acts 14:12) and obeyed the gospel call as if Christ himself were speaking.

You welcomed me as if I were an angel of God (4:14). The surnaming of Paul as a "messenger [*angelos*] of God" combines the two cultural ideas of (1) Jewish representatives (Heb. *seluḥim*) of the synagogues of the Dispersion, charged to carry funds to Jerusalem, and (2) the Hellenistic depiction of a messenger of the gods, notably Hermes in the Homeric pantheon.[50] A son of Zeus and the nymph Maia, Hermes played many roles, notably as a guide for divine children, leading them to safety, and as a *psychopōpos*, i.e., one who escorts souls to the underworld of Hades. But he is best known as a messenger god who is obedient to the king of the gods, Zeus, and executes his orders.

Torn out your eyes (4:15). Some take this to mean that Paul's sickness was ophthalmic—possibly a migraine headache that affected his vision; this is why, perhaps, he had to write in large letters (6:11).

My dear children, for whom I am again in the pains of childbirth until Christ is formed in you (4:19). This sentence is a remarkable window into Paul's pastoral care for his converts. He likens his role as a birth-mother undergoing labor to deliver her child. His goal as an apostle is to see people reflect the likeness of Christ (2 Cor. 3:18). Children were regarded in low esteem in Greco-Roman society.[51] Paul's more positive attitude is given in Colossians 3:18–4:1.

Two Women—Two Covenants (4:21–31)

Paul reverts to an argument from scriptural exegesis, employing an allegorical method familiar in Philo. In Abraham's household two women lived uneasily together: Hagar (Gen. 16:5) and Sarah (21:2). Paul's chief interest is with them as mothers of two children, Ishmael and

R E F L E C T I O N S

SOMETIMES PAUL IS VIEWED AS RATHER AUSTERE and aloof from his readers, too authoritarian and browbeating the opposition in severe tones and with a temper. True, he can be harsh in this letter (e.g., 1:6–10; 5:12), but his stern face is usually directed to the teachers who were undermining the Christian faith and experience of his congregation. Toward his converts, he is tender and solicitous; and never more so than at 4:12–20 (esp. 4:19). His role as a mother, caring for her young children and desiring only their best interests, is vividly portrayed. It is one of several places where Paul appears in this light comparing himself to a mother's love for her child.[A-4] This word to pastors and church leaders is especially relevant in any age.[A-5]

Slavery	Freedom
• Hagar was a slave woman	• Sarah was a "free" wife
• Ishmael, born of the flesh, a trademark of the Judaizers (6:13-14)	• Isaac, born through promise (4:23) and the Spirit (4:29)
• Mount Sinai, Jerusalem of the Judaizers (4:25), is a symbol of slavery	• Mount Zion (4:26; Heb. 12:22) stands for joyous freedom (based on Isa. 54:1)
• "Ishmael" is in slavery and opposes his brother	• "Isaac" (Paul and his converts) suffers persecution (Gal. 6:12-13)
• But the Judaizers are to be refused since Ishmael did not gain an inheritance (4:30)	• Rather, Paul's gospel connects believers with the "free woman" and the promise of liberty (4:31)

Isaac. He develops two lines of descent and connects them to a spiritual/figurative meaning. This interpretation is based on his desire to show that only one son was "born as the result of a promise" (4:23) and that this line leads to freedom, not slavery (4:31). That is the key to Paul's thought. We may note that he uses the term "covenant" to include both lines of development from Ishmael as well as Isaac, whereas in 3:15–16 he kept "covenant" to relate to promise, not law.

The table above may help set out the issues as Paul sees them:[52]

Recent study of these verses has helped our understanding of Paul's argument in introducing this extended allegory or illustration of Hagar and Sarah.[53] The Jewish scribes used this story from Genesis to praise the line from Abraham/Sarah to Israel,[54] but Paul's purpose is different. The climax comes at 4:30, where he cites Genesis 21:10. The citation in this verse shapes his conclusion in answer to the question, "Are you not aware of what the law says?" (4:21).

The examples given of Hagar and Ishmael (who represent slavery and the life of servitude "under the law") and Sarah and Isaac (who stand for the covenant of grace and freedom) are targeted at the Judaizers, who sought to impose legalism on Paul's Gentile converts. Yet the conclusion in 4:30—"get rid of the slave woman and her son"—is not directed at Judaizers or Jews, but at

MOUNT SINAI
▼

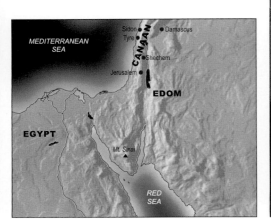

the covenant of Sinai. The old covenant leads to bondage since it is based on "flesh" and not the Spirit. It belongs to the old order, not the new age of messianic salvation brought by Christ and endorsed by the Spirit.

Paul will develop this line of reasoning at length later when he writes 2 Corinthians 3:1–18. There the same conclusion is reached as in Galatians 4:31: "We are . . . children . . . of the free [one]," Christ Jesus, and we have a spiritual parentage, "the Jerusalem that is above [which] is free" (4:26), the mother of both believing Jews and Gentiles. Paul's use of the figure of the holy city of Jerusalem to relate to a spiritual home, the church of God's new creation, not any geographical or ethnic location, is to be noted, and is parallel with Hebrews 12:22 and Revelation 21:1–5.

Conclusion (5:1)

It is for freedom that Christ has set us free. Stand firm . . . and do not let yourselves be burdened again by a yoke of slavery (5:1). Here Paul concludes his theological argument by driving home the issue of freedom that many of his readers understand well from their own experiences as slaves (cf. 1 Cor. 1:26; 7:21). They are well aware of the essential differences between them and their free masters, who have the freedom to own property, to schedule their own daily activities, to earn as well as to spend their own living in ways they like, and to live wherever they wish. No one would tolerate the reversion to become a slave again, once redeemed and set free. A person's spiritual condition is similar (cf. Gal. 4:8–9), Paul argues. Christ has paid a high price in redeeming sinners and setting them free (1:4; 3:13). No one should therefore return to the state of slavery, whether to be under the yoke of the law (as the Jews) or under the bondage of the *stoicheia* of this world (as the pagans, 4:8–10).

Freedom in Christ: What It Implies (5:2–12)

Apparently, the matter of circumcision (mentioned five times in 5:2, 3, 6, 11) is at stake here. It is the first time in this letter Paul directly addresses this topic to his readers. Paul emphatically declares (5:2) that freedom in Christ *excludes* the requirement of circumcision (5:6).[55]

If you let yourselves be circumcised, Christ will be of no value to you at all (5:2). Paul makes it clear that circumcision and Christ are incompatible with one another. If there is any saving value in religious ordinances (e.g., circumcision) apart from the cross of Christ, then Christ's death has been in vain (cf. 2:21).

Every man who lets himself be circumcised . . . is obligated to obey the whole law (5:3). Circumcision and keeping the law are two integral components of Judaism. No one can observe one requirement and dismiss the other. Many have argued that Paul's statement about obeying the whole law reflects only his own Christian understanding of Torah. There are, however, many evidences both from rabbinic literature and other literature showing that the conviction of keeping the whole law was adopted prior to and after Paul's time.[56]

For example, a Gentile proselyte was required to offer a gift, to be baptized, to vow to observe the Mosaic law, and to be circumcised (for male proselytes). At the same time, no amount of law-keeping or conformity to Jewish ways mattered in the eyes of stricter Jews unless circumcision had been accepted.[57] Thus, to be circumcised implies an obligation to obey the whole law.

You who are trying to be justified by law have been alienated from Christ (5:4). This is the logical conclusion to which Paul intends to lead the Galatians. If they seek justification by obeying the whole law, they are actually alienated (*katergēthēte*, lit., "you are made impotent," see 3:17; 5:11; 1 Cor. 1:28; 2 Tim. 1:10) from Christ. In other words, their relation with him as the Redeemer is severed.

You have fallen away from grace (5:4). "Fallen away" (*ekpiptō*) originally refers to the falling out of a flower. Later, it also means to be loosened from something. This phrase further illustrates the serious consequence of those who seek justification by keeping the law and allow themselves to be circumcised. Paul emphatically warns his readers not to let go of something too good to be loosed from (i.e., Christ and his grace) for something (i.e., circumcision and law-keeping) that is unable to help them gain acceptance before God (2:15–16; 3:11).

But by faith we eagerly await . . . righteousness (5:5). This refers to the hope of a favorable verdict in the last judgment (cf. Rom. 2:5–16). It marks the key difference between Paul and the Judaizers. Paul has already moved from the entrance of salvation onto the future hope while the Judaizers were still trying to teach people how to get into the door of salvation.

For in Christ Jesus neither circumcision nor uncircumcision has any value (5:6). This is a bold statement guaranteed to evoke an offense in the Judaizers. Paul, who once was a serious Jew (circumcised and striving to observe the whole law, 1:14; Phil. 3:5–6; cf. Acts 26:4–5) is most qualified to testify from his own experiences the fruitlessness of these religious practices (Rom. 7:18–24; cf. Phil 3:7–8).

The only thing that counts is faith expressing itself through love (5:6). Faith is the *only* criterion for justification—a theme emphasized repeatedly in this first canonical letter of Paul (2:16; 3:3, 8, 14, 24; 5:5). His strong conviction on this subject matter first came from a revelation (Gal. 1:11–12).[58] Yet Paul makes it clear that the faith that leads to justification is not merely a cognitive recognition or a matter of mental exercise. It entails actions that stem out of love. Saving faith is, in essence, a practical faith—a message shared by the three pillars (James, Peter, and John, 2:9) of the Jerusalem church (James 2:14–26; 1 Peter 1:22; 1 John 3:18–19).

You were running a good race (5:7). The use of an athletic metaphor in describing the Christian life is frequently found in Paul's writing.[59] It reflects (1) the popularity of athletic sports in the Greco-Roman world that most people would have had no difficulty in understanding; and (2) the strenuous quality of Christian service and life as likened to a race. The Galatians are commended for their beginning steps in the Christian race (see Gal. 4:13–15; cf. 3:2–3).

Who cut in on you and kept you from obeying the truth? (5:7). "To cut in" (*enkoptō*) suggests a breaking into or obstruction of the Galatian Christians in their course of following the truth. The picture is that of a runner who has allowed his or her progress to be blocked or who is still running but on the wrong course.[60] In the track race of the Greek festivals there were rules against tripping or cutting in on an opponent.[61] In the case of the Galatians, they have allowed the Judaizers to come in and distract them.

That kind of persuasion does not come from the one who calls you (5:8). The word persuasion (*peismonē*, found only here in the New Testament) opens a window to the method of the Judaizers in approaching the Galatians, that is, by a form of "contrived persuasiveness."[62] In the Greco-Roman world, politicians, religious leaders, or philosophers were known for their rhetorical speech, which was used to impress as well as to attract the hearers.[63] Paul, however, intends to distinguish himself from the common practice of his time in his apostolic ministry.[64]

Perhaps these Judaizers have tried to allure the Galatians (just as the false

teachers did the Corinthians, 2 Cor. 11:3, 13–15) to receive circumcision because it is not only necessary for a complete salvation, it is also commendable in that Christ himself was circumcised (see Luke 2:21). Paul's identifying himself with Christ's crucifixion (Gal. 2:20; cf. 6:14) may suggest a correction to the Galatians' desire to identify with Christ's circumcision as something they can boast of (cf. 6:13b).

A little yeast works through the whole batch of dough (5:9). Jewish people saw yeast as a symbol of evil and sin after the Passover event when their ancestors were commanded to eat only unleavened bread (Ex. 12:15, 17–20; Deut. 16:3–8). Paul applies this analogy to the Judaizers, whose influence on the Galatians is considered both evil and corrupting.[65]

The one who is throwing you into confusion (5:10). There was perhaps one person leading this group of agitators (1:7; 5:12) in persuading Gentile believers to be circumcised.[66] He will most surely be punished by God.

The offense of the cross has been abolished (5:11). "Offense" (*skandalon*) literally refers to the arm or stick on which bait was fixed in a trap,[67] that which trips one up, a cause of stumbling.[68] During Paul's apostolic ministry, he repeatedly confronted the same difficulty in winning the Jews to Christ. For in the mind of Jewish people, Christ's death on the cross symbolized his being under a curse.[69] The cross was thus an offense to them. Paul insists, however, that to preach circumcision as a means for salvation is to validate the keeping of the law for justification (5:4). It will in effect nullify the preaching of Christ crucified.

CYBELE

The "Great Mother" goddess of Asia Minor.

As for those agitators, I wish they would go the whole way and emasculate themselves (5:12). Did Paul borrow from the residents of the southern Galatia region a crude expression to express a challenge to the agitators to cut themselves off from the church, the body of Christ on the basis of the fact that emasculation is prohibited by the Mosaic law[70] (Deut. 23:1)? Yet in fact, sacral castration or emasculation was commonly known in the ancient world. It was frequently practiced by pagan priests in the cult of Cybele, which was prominent in Asia. Here Paul is possibly making a sarcastic challenge[71] to his opponents, who are so eager in persuading the Galatians to be circumcised. They should actually mutilate themselves like priests of Cybele.

Freedom in Christ: What It Means (5:13–26)

Having stated the implication of freedom in Christ, Paul moves on to define the meaning of this freedom. There are two aspects. On the negative side, it is not the freedom to indulge one's sinful nature; positively, it is the freedom to serve one another in love (5:13). But how can Christians do that? In the following statements (5:16–23), Paul provides his readers a way to reach this goal, that is, to live by the Spirit (5:16a). He is confident that when people live by the Spirit, they will not gratify the desires of the "sinful nature" (i.e., "flesh," *sarx*; 5:16b). They will, on the contrary, be able to "serve [*douleuō*, performing the duties of a slave] one another in love" (5:13), because love is part of the fruit or harvest of the Holy Spirit (5:22). The use of a singular noun "fruit" (*karpos*) in 5:22 to include nine virtuous elements of conduct is better considered "a harvest" that

includes various kinds of produce. A list of personality traits or activities are spelled out to further help readers identify the characteristics of the sinful nature (5:19–21) and the harvest of the Spirit (5:22–23). A logical exhortation leads to the conclusion: "Since we live by the Spirit [cf. 3:3], let us keep in step with the Spirit" (5:25).

You … were called to be free … do not use your freedom to indulge the sinful nature (5:13). This statement reconnects to the earlier statement in 5:1 on Christian freedom. Paul began with an encouragement to stand firm (5:1); now he voices a warning against indulgence. "Sinful nature" translates the Greek word *sarx*, which may simply refer to a person's physical body, just like the Hebrew word *basar*.[72] Paul, however, also uses it in an ethical sense, referring to a person's "desires and passions" (Gal. 5:16–17, 24; cf. 1 Cor. 3:3) that is essentially self-centered.[73]

The entire law is summed up in … "Love your neighbor as yourself" (5:14). Being well aware of the Judaizers' emphasis on the law, Paul also makes a reference to the Mosaic law in Leviticus 19:18b (a command to love one's neighbor) as the background of his call to serve one another in love (Gal. 5:13). The emphasis on love as the *summary* of all law was first introduced by Jesus himself.[74] It was later reinforced by Paul[75] as well as the three pillars of the Jerusalem church[76] as a primary Christian virtue and a hallmark of Christian identity.

If you keep on biting and devouring each other (5:15). The two verbs "to bite" (*daknō*) and "to eat up" (*katesthiō*) usually refer to fighting among wild animals.[77] Coupled with the warning given in 5:26, "let us not become conceited, provoking and envying each other," we have a glimpse of the internal situation within the Galatian churches. Ramsay has observed that there was a close connection between the lifestyle of the South Galatian cities and the new converts. He points out, owing to (1) the national religion, (2) their position in a municipality, and (3) the customs of society in Hellenistic cities, these new converts are liable to be led astray by habits and ways of thought known to them.[78] Therefore, this unpleasant picture of "biting" and "eating up" may indeed explain Paul's choice of conduct listed as the acts of the sinful nature in 5:19–21.

The sinful nature (5:17). The literal translation of the Greek word is "flesh" (*sarx*). The rabbinic background and terminology of the two "impulses" (denoted in Paul by "flesh" and "Spirit") are well-attested (W. D. Davies has the seminal discussion of the rabbinic texts[79]). Yet more recently there is a move to locate Paul's dichotomy in the world of apocalyptic dualism.[80] On this reading Paul is contrasting not simply the good and evil parts of human nature ("higher"/"lower," as in NEB), but more profoundly the contrasted setting of sinful humankind in the domain of moral and cosmic evil (and expressed as opposition to God) and the Christian released to new life in Christ by the Spirit.

Contrary to the Spirit. . . . They are in conflict with each other (5:17). These statements may be derived from rabbinic teaching. The rabbis contended that every human being has two desires, the *yetser tob* (good impulse) and the *yetser ra`* (bad impulse). These desires are in conflict with each other.[81] As a Pharisee, Paul could testify from his own experience about the constant struggle between the good and the bad impulses within himself (cf. Rom. 7:7–24).

The acts of the sinful nature (5:19–21). In order to clarify what he means, Paul provides a list of behaviors classified as stemming from the sinful nature. These behaviors may be divided into four categories: (1) irregular sexual practices (5:19, "sexual immorality, impurity and debauchery"); (2) perverted religion (5:20, "idolatry and witchcraft"); (3) antisocial behavior (5:20, "hatred, discord, jealousy, fits of rage, selfish ambition, dissensions, factions"); and (4) personal lapses (v. 21, "envy; drunkenness, orgies, and the like").

The fruit [harvest] of the Spirit (5:22–23). The Holy Spirit's transforming power in a person's life, on the other hand, produces a harvest of ethical characteristics that cover a threefold relationship: (1) with God (love, joy, peace); (2) with fellow believers (patience, kindness, goodness); and (3) with oneself (faithfulness, gentleness, self-control).

The acts of the sinful nature are essentially self-centered, gratifying a person's

MAENAD WITH TWO SATYRS

The Bacchic (Dionysiac) rituals embodied many features of Paul's list of the acts of the sinful nature. ▼

R E F L E C T I O N S

THE ITEMS PAUL MENTIONS IN Galatians 5:19–23 may also be employed as a "spiritual thermometer" for measuring one's own spiritual health: "How am I doing as a Christian? Am I living according to my sinful nature (*sarx*) or walking according to the Spirit? How can I tell?" A chart of comparison may help to identify the contrasts between the two ways of life:

physical and emotional desires. They are destructive of community life. The fruit of the Spirit, on the other hand, is a list of actions that promote community life.[82] As mentioned above, some of the Galatians were beset by severe conflict and competition (cf. 5:15, 26). Thus Paul's teaching here can be understood as directly addressing the problems and needs of these new Christian communities.[83]

Freedom in Christ: How It Works (6:1–10)

After mentioning the meaning of freedom in Christ (5:13) and spelling out the qualities of the harvest of the Spirit (5:22–23), Paul adds several practical instructions as ways of applying these principles to the Galatians' daily life as well as church life.[84]

Restore him gently (6:1). The word "restore" (*katartizō*) is a medical term for setting a fractured bone. Those who are spiritual (i.e., who live by the Spirit, 5:16, 25) are those who care enough to help other members when they fall and who are able to deal with it with *gentleness* (5:23). By this kind of mutual helping (carrying each other's burdens) for spiritual restoration, believers are fulfilling (in action) the law of Christ, which is the law of *love* (5:22; cf. 5:14).[85]

Each one should carry his own load (6:5). Spiritual people are able to be responsible for their own needs. The word "burden" here (*phortion*) is different from the burden in 6:2 (*barē*). *Phortion* is a common term for a soldier's pack.[86] Bearing one's own burden is a traditional maxim. Paul adopted this idea to exhort the Galatians to see themselves as soldiers of Christ, setting out on their march and discharging their own obligations (i.e., *faithfulness*, 5:22) rather than taking pride in their current achievements through comparison or competition (6:4, which is an act of sinful desire such as *selfish ambition*, 5:20). Ultimately at the final judgment, each believer is responsible for his or her "pack" (life and service) before God.[87]

Share all good things with his instructor (6:6). By using *koinōneō*, Paul perceives the relationship between the catechumen (the

Acts of the Sinful Nature	Harvest of the Spirit
• Sexual immorality, impurity & debauchery	• Love, joy, peace
• Idolatry and witchcraft	• Patience, kindness, goodness
• Hatred, discord, jealousy, fits of rage	• Faithfulness, gentleness, self-control
• Selfish ambition, dissensions, factions	
• Envy, drunkenness, orgies, and the like	

learner) and the teacher in a form of partnership,[88] especially in the area of material possessions. Although pagan priests often received fees for their sacrificial services, Paul prefers to train his converts in voluntary liberality as distinguished from payments received from performing sacrificial rites.[89] This is also a concrete manifestation of the fruit of the Spirit in *kindness* and *goodness* (5:22).

Let us do good to all people (6:10). "Doing good" in Paul's mind may be a direct fund-raising drive to the Galatians to participate in the Jerusalem famine relief fund project, which is now under his care (2:9; cf. 2 Cor. 9:6–9).[90] This exhortation is compared to sowing and reaping for the purpose of assuring the Galatians that good results will be guaranteed from kind actions.[91]

Closing Remarks and Final Greeting (6:11–18)

This section not only sums up Paul's letter, but is also important for the interpretation of the letter. "It contains the interpretive clues to the understanding of Paul's major concerns in the letter as a whole and should be employed as the hermeneutical key to the intentions of the Apostle."[92]

Large letters I use as I write to you with my own hand (6:11). Large letters appearing in ancient correspondence are often seen as an indicator calling for special attention.[93] It is like using bold type in modern printing or double underlining in a manuscript. Paul wants his swayed readers to pay special attention to his concluding remarks (6:12–18), which he now pens personally.

To avoid being persecuted for the cross of Christ (6:12). In the first century of the Christian era, Jewish Christians in Jerusalem evidently faced social pressure from the Zealots, the nationalists. They made efforts, therefore, to persuade the Gentile Christians to accept circumcision with the hope of preserving the Jerusalem church and other Christian churches in Judea from falling into the hands of Zealot-minded militants by having connection with uncircumcised Gentiles.[94]

May I never boast except in the cross (6:14). The Greeks and the Romans considered the cross a symbol of shame and unspeakable horror. Death in this way was not mentionable in polite Roman society.[95] Paul, as a Roman citizen, knew well the meaning and implication of the cross. Yet he was able to embrace it as the most worthwhile goal in life with the knowledge of the crucified Christ and boasted in his cross (cf. 2:20; Phil. 3:8–10). For it was at the "cross" where salvation was wrought and it is the "cross" that sets the pattern of self-denial.[96]

Peace ... to all who follow this rule, even to the Israel of God (6:16). The word "rule" (*kanōn*, lit., a measuring rod) refers to the principle of justification by faith in this letter. Paul pronounces his greeting of peace to all God's people, whether

Jews or Gentiles. As long as they follow the *kanōn* of salvation (i.e., justification by faith on the basis of God's grace), they are the true Israel of God (cf. Heb. 11:17).[97]

For I bear on my body the marks of Jesus (6:17). In the Greco-Roman world, slaves were usually marked with the mark (*stigma*) or name of their master as a sign of ownership.[98] Marks or scars can also be seen as symbols of loyalty. For example, Josephus refers to an incident in which Antipater (Herod's father) strips off his clothes and exhibits his many scars as witnesses to his loyalty to Caesar.[99] Likewise, in contrast to the mark of circumcision, which the Judaizers have insisted on for Gentile converts, Paul asserts that he has marks/scars on his body that were acquired in his service for Christ. He possibly received these when he was in Iconium and Lystra during his first missionary journey (Acts 14:5, 19). They are the true marks of Christian identity, not circumcision.

The grace of our Lord Jesus Christ be with your spirit. . . . Amen (6:18). Paul now follows the epistolary custom of his time by ending his letter with a wish. The mention of "your spirit" instead of "you" may be intended to remind the Galatians, who have been influenced by the Judaizers to put too much attention on the *sarx* (flesh or body), the importance of their spirit, which is to be led by the Holy Spirit.[100]

The insertion of a liturgical "Amen" (from Heb. *ʾmn*, meaning "firmness and certainty" or "so let it be") at the end unquestionably places this letter in a public worship setting, where all believers are given an opportunity to affirm what they have just heard (the truth of the gospel) in unison.

ANNOTATED BIBLIOGRAPHY

Betz, H-D. *Galatians*. Hermeneia. Philadelphia: Fortress, 1979.

  A learned and detailed commentary on Greco-Roman and Jewish backgrounds.

Bruce, F. F. *The Epistle to the Galatians*. NIGTC. Grand Rapids: Eerdmans, 1982.

  An excellent commentary, covering all the exegetical problems and options, but requiring some knowledge of Greek.

Burton, E. *A Critical and Exegetical Commentary on the Epistle to the Galatians*. ICC. Edinburgh: T. & T. Clark, 1921.

  A solid commentary, strong on word studies and historical background.

Dunn, J. D. G. *The Epistle to the Galatians*. Peabody, Mass.: Hendrickson, 1993.

  A highly readable commentary with good insight into the text.

———. *The Theology of Paul's Letter to the Galatians*. NTT. Cambridge: Cambridge Univ. Press, 1993.

  An excellent survey of the key theological themes in Galatians.

Elliot, Susan M. "Choose Your Mother, Choose Your Master: Galatians 4:21–5:1 in the Shadow of the Anatolian Mother of the Gods." *JBL* 118 (1999): 661–83.

  An article that provides important background information for interpreting the letter.

Hansen, G. W. "Galatians, Letter to" in *Dictionary of Paul and His Letters*. Downers Grove: InterVarsity Press, 1993, 323–34.

  A mine of information on Galatians.

Longenecker, R. N. *Galatians*. WBC. Dallas: Word, 1990.

  A detailed discussion of all the issues and full of scholars' opinions as well as the author's preferences.

Morris, L. *Galatians*. Downers Grove: InterVarsity, 1996.

  This is probably the most serviceable commentary for the general reader with many insights and much helpful comment.

CHAPTER NOTES

Main Text Notes

1. For an accessible discussion of the rhetorical setting of the letter as deliberative and an example of "the art of persuasion," see B. Witherington III, *The Paul Quest* (Downers Grove, Ill.: InterVarsity, 1998), 119–22.

2. J. B. Lightfoot, *Saint Paul's Epistle to the Galatians* (1865; reprint, Grand Rapids: Zondervan, 1957).

3. J. Murphy-O'Connor, *Paul: A Critical Life* (Oxford: Clarendon, 1996), 160, 187.

4. W. M. Ramsay, *A Historical Commentary on St. Paul's Epistle to the Galatians* (London: Hodder & Stoughton, 1899; reprint, Grand Rapids: Baker, 1979).

5. F. F. Bruce, *The Epistle to the Galatians* (NIGTC; Grand Rapids: Eerdmans, 1982), 15.

6. R. N. Longenecker, *Galatians* (WBC 41; Dallas: Word, 1990).

7. S. Mitchell, "Population and Land in South Galatia," *ANRW* II.7.2 (1980): 1053–81.

8. H.-D. Betz, *Galatians: A Commentary on Paul's Letter to the Churches in Galatia* (Hermeneia; Philadelphia: Fortress, 1979), 8.

9. See R. Jewett, "The Agitators and the Galatian Congregation," *NTS* 17 (1970–1971): 198–212.

10. C. Spicq, *TLNT*, 3.500–506; Pindar, *Ol.* 14.5; cf. Philo, *Migration* 31.

11. J. D. G. Dunn, *The Theology of Paul's Letter to the Galatians* (NTT; Cambridge: Cambridge Univ. Press, 1993) 65.

12. Judith 9:3–4; Num. 25:6–13; Sir. 45:23–24; 1 Macc. 2:54; Sir. 48:2; 1 Macc. 2:58; 1 Macc. 2:15–28.

13. Paul's new life and career have been intensively studied in recent times. See M. Hengel and Anna Maria Schwemer, *Paul Between Damascus and Antioch* (Louisville: John Knox/Westminster, 1997); *The Road from Damascus*, ed. R. N. Longenecker (Grand Rapids: Eerdmans, 1997).

14. See D. F. Graf, "Aretas," *ABD*, 1.373–76.

15. The options are listed in R. P. Martin, *2 Corinthians* (WBC 40: Waco, Tex.: Word, 1986), ad loc.

16. See also the apocryphal *Gospel of the Hebrews* and the gnostic *Gospel of Thomas* 12.

17. See Acts 12:17; 15:13ff.; 21:18ff.

18. These verses and the picture of James in both Jerusalem Christianity and at Antioch are surveyed, along with the developing trajectory that traces the part he played in Jewish-Christian relations and later in gnostic circles, in R. P. Martin, *James* (WBC 48; Waco, Tex.: Word, 1988), Introduction.

19. For a more detailed introduction of Titus, see C. K. Barrett, "Titus" in *Neotestamentica et Semitica*, eds. E. Ellis and M. Wilcox (Edinburgh: T. & T. Clark, 1969), 1–14.

20. In 2 Cor. 2:13; 7:6, 13–15; 8:6, 23; also his letter to Titus.

21. Colin G. Kruse, *Paul, the Law, and Justification* (Peabody, Mass.: Hendrickson, 1996), 59.

22. V. C. Pfitzner, *Paul and the Agon Motif* (Leiden: Brill, 1967).

23. See A. A. Rupprecht, "Slave, Slavery," *DPL*, 881–82; S. S. Bartchy, "Slave, Slavery," *DLNT*, 1098–1102.

24. See C. W. Keyes, "The Greek Letter of Introduction," *AJP* 56 (1935): 28–44.

25. See A. W. F. Blunt, *The Epistle of Paul to the Galatians* (Oxford: Clarendon, 1960), 75 for a different explanation.

26. Cf. *Clem Hom*.18:14, where the patriarchs are called *styloi*. For more detailed explanation of this word, see Ulrich Wilckens, "στύλος," *TDNT*, 7.732–36.

27. See E. de Witt Burton, *Galatians* (ICC; Edinburgh: T. & T. Clark, 1980), 95–96.

28. D. Georgi, *Remembering the Poor* (ET, Nashville: Abingdon, 1992), 40.

29. Acts 11:27–28; see also Josephus, *Ant.* 20.2.5 §§51–53; 20.5.2 §101.

30. Ibid., 43–48.

31. F. F. Bruce, *Paul, Apostle of the Heart Set Free* (Grand Rapids: Eerdmans, 1977), 176.

32. See Acts 12:17; 15:13. In later church tradition, James is known as the bishop of the Jerusalem church (Eusebius, *Eccl. Hist.* 2.1). See also comments on 1:18.

33. Louw and Nida, eds., *Greek-English Lexicon of the New Testament* (New York: United Bible Societies, 1989), 1:435.

34. Josephus, *J.W.* 2.17.10 §454.

35. Burton, *Galatians*, 119.

36. Cf. Rom. 7:1–4, where Paul uses the death of one's spouse to illustrate the breaking off from the law when one is in Christ. See also Burton, *Galatians*, 132.

37. G. Milligan, *Selections from the Greek Papyri*, #14.

38. See *New Documents Illustrating Early Christianity*, vol. 8, *A Review of the Greek Inscription and Papyri*, ed. S. R. Llewelyn (Grand Rapids: Eerdmans, 1998), 23, 62, 64.

39. See "The Greek Tragedy," in *The Oxford Companion to Classical Civilization*, ed. S. Horn-

blower and A. Spawforth (Oxford: Oxford Univ. Press, 1998), 733–39, esp. 736.

40. *Jub. 23:10* describes Abraham as a model Jew, "perfect in all his actions with the Lord." As Dunn (*The Theology of Paul's Letter to the Galatians*, 81) remarks, he is important in Paul's response because he was in effect "the first proselyte and type of true conversion"; Dunn shows this by appealing to Philo, *Abraham* 60–88; Josephus, *Ant.* 1.7.1 §155; *Apoc. Abr.* 1–8. See too Nancy L. Calvert, "Abraham," *DPL*, 1–9.

41. MM, s.v.

42. O. Murray, "Life and Society in Classical Greece," in *Greece and the Hellenistic World*, ed. J. Boardman et al. (Oxford: OUP, 1991 ed.), 249 therefore comments: "This is one important reason for the instability of the Athenian family."

43. Gal. 3:19–20; see Acts 7:38, 53; Heb. 2:2, based on Deut. 33:2.

44. Str-B, 3.553.

45. Morris, *Galatians*, 110.

46. Philo, *Moses* 2.166; *Dreams* 143.

47. OCCC, 245.

48. Xenophon, *Mem.* 2.2.6.

49. See *b. Ber.* 13b for the Jewish prayer, where the male worshiper thanks God he was not made a woman, a slave, or a Gentile.

50. Hermes (in Greek vase motifs) is often portrayed as winged and shod (as befits a messenger).

51. See the evidence, mainly Stoic, in A. J. Malherbe, *Moral Exhortation: A Greco-Roman Sourcebook* (Philadelphia: Westminster, 1986); see also W. A. Strange, *Children in the Early Church* (Carlisle, Eng.: Paternoster, 1996), which covers a wider field.

52. C. K. Barrett's essay, "The Allegory of Abraham, Sarah and Hagar in the Argument of Galatians," in *Essays on Paul* (London: SPCK, 1982), 118–32, has a good discussion. See also A. C. Perriman, "The Rhetorical Strategy of Galatians 4:21–5:1," *EvQ* 65 (1993): 27–42; P. Borgen, "Some Hebrew and Pagan Features in Philo's and Paul's Interpretation of Hagar and Ishmael," in *The New Testament and Hellenistic Judaism*, eds. P. Borgen and S. Giversen (Peabody, Mass.: Hendrickson, 1997), 151–64.

53. Most notably by Perriman, "Rhetorical Strategy," 27–42.

54. See Longenecker, *Galatians*, 200–206.

55. Frank J. Matera points out that chs. 5–6 are the climax of Paul's deliberative argument aimed at persuading the Galatians not to be circumcised. Paul employs the paraenesis of these chapters to support his argument and bring it to its culmination. See "The Culmination of Paul's Argument to the Galatians: Gal. 5:1–6:17," *JSNT* 32 (1988): 79–91.

56. See Bruce, *Galatians*, 230–31; Longenecker, *Galatians*, 227; Kruse, *Paul*, 102, n. 121; e.g., *b. Sanh.* 81a; *Midr. Tehillim* 15.7; Sir. 7:8; *4 Macc.* 5:20–21.

57. Cf. Josephus, *Ant.* 20.2.4 §§44–48.

58. Possibly during his conversion experience on his way to Damascus; see Seyoon Kim, *The Origin of Paul's Gospel* (Grand Rapids: Eerdmans, 1982), for a full discussion about the connection between Paul's gospel and his conversion experience.

59. Acts 20:24; 1 Cor. 9:24–27; Gal. 2:2; Phil. 3:14; cf. 2 Tim. 4:7.

60. See Carl E. De Vries, "Paul's 'Cutting' Remarks About a Race: Galatians 5:1–12," in *Current Issues in Biblical and Patristic Interpretation: Studies in Honor of M. C. Tenney*, ed. G. F. Hawthorne (Grand Rapids: Eerdmans, 1975), 115–20; Rogers & Rogers, *New Linguistic and Exegetical Key to the Greek New Testament* (Grand Rapids: Zondervan, 1998), 430.

61. See E. N. Gardiner, *Greek Athletic Sports and Festivals* (Oxford: Clarendon, 1955), 146.

62. Longenecker, *Galatians*, 230.

63. See *The Oxford History of Greece and the Hellenistic World* and *The Oxford History of the Roman World*, 2 vols., eds. J. Boardman, J. Griffin, and O. Murray (Oxford: Oxford Univ. Press, 1986).

64. 1 Cor. 2:1–5; cf. 2 Cor. 10:10; 1 Thess. 1:5.

65. Cf. 1 Cor. 5:6–8; later *1 Clem.* 5:6; Ignatius, *Mag.* 10.2; and Justin, *Dial.* 14.2.3.

66. See D. C. Arichea Jr. and Eugene A. Nida, *A Translator's Handbook on Paul's Letter to the Galatians* (London: UBC, 1976), 127.

67. Cf. Josh. 23:13 LXX; Ps. 69:22; 141:9; 1 Macc. 5:4.

68. Cf. Judith 5:20; Sir. 7:6; 27:23. See also Michael B. Thompson, "Stumbling Block," *DPL*, 918–19.

69. Deut. 21:22–23; 1 Cor. 1:23; Gal. 3:13.

70. Ramsay, *Galatians*, 437–39; Arichea and Nida, *Galatians*, 129–30.

71. Lightfoot, *Galatians*, 207; Burton, *Galatians*, 289–90; Bruce, *Galatians*, 238; Longenecker, *Galatians*, 234; R. A. Cole, *Galatians* (TNTC; Grand Rapids: Eerdmans, 1989 rev. ed.), 201–2; Dunn, *Galatians*, 1.

72. Gal. 2:20; Phil. 3:4; Gen. 2:21; 40:19; Ex. 21:28; 33:31.

73. F. T. Gench, "Galatians 5:1, 13–25," *Interp* 46 (1992): 294. For a more detailed discussion of *sarx* in the New Testament, see R. Jewett,

Paul's Anthropological Terms (Leiden: Brill, 1971).

74. See Matt. 22:35–40 (cf. 7:12); Mark 12:28–31; Luke 6:27–38; John 13:34–35. See also J. Nissen, "The Distinctive Character of the New Testament Love Command in Relation to Hellenistic Judaism," in *The New Testament and Hellenistic Judaism*, eds. Borgen and Giversen, 123–50.

75. See Rom. 13:8; 1 Cor. 8:1b; 13:13; Gal. 5:14; Col. 3:14; 1 Tim. 1:5.

76. See James 2:8; 1 Peter 4:8; 1 John 3:11, 23; 2 John 5.

77. Arichea and Nida, *Galatians*, 132.

78. Ramsay, *Galatians*, 447. See also John Matthews, "Roman Life and Society," *OHRW*, 380–87.

79. W. D. Davies, *Paul and Rabbinic Judaism* (Philadelphia: Fortress, 1980). A more recent discussion is in R. J. Erickson, "Flesh" in *DPL*, 303–6.

80. E.g., at Qumran and *T. Jud.* 19:4; *T. Zeb.* 9:7.

81. See S. McKnight, "Galatians," *NIVAC* (Grand Rapids: Zondervan, 1995), 264; cf. *T. Ash.* 1:6.

82. Cf. Gench, "Galatians," 294–95.

83. See P. F. Esler, "Group Boundaries and Intergroup Conflict in Galatians: A New Reading of Galatians 5:13–6:10," in *Ethnicity and the Bible*, ed. M. Brett (Leiden: Brill, 1996), 215–40; cf. C. D. Stanley, "'Neither Jew Nor Greek,': Ethnic Conflict in Graeco-Roman Society," *JSNT* 64 (1996):101–24.

84. Longenecker, *Galatians*, 271.

85. Bruce, *Galatians*, 261; Dunn, *Galatians*, 114; Kruse, *Paul*, 106.

86. Xenophon, *Mem.* 3.13.6.

87. David W. Kuck, "'Each Will Bear His Own Burden': Paul's Creative Use of an Apocalyptic Motif," *NTS* 40 (1994): 295–97; see also Betz, *Galatians*, 303–4.

88. Arichea and Nida, *Galatians*, 150.

89. Ramsay, *Galatians*, 459.

90. L. W. Hurtado, "The Jerusalem Collection and the Book of Galatians," *JSNT* 5 (1979): 53; Ramsay, 460–61.

91. The metaphor of sowing and reaping for conduct and its results is a frequent one, e.g., Job 4:8; Prov. 22:8; Hos. 8:7; 10:12; Luke 19:21; 2 Cor. 9:6; Plato, *Phaedr.* 260c; Sir. 7:3; Philo, *Confusion* 21.7. See also J. L. North, "Sowing and Reaping (Gal. 6:7b): More Examples of a Classical Maxim," *JTS* 43 (1992): 523–27, esp. 526; Frank Stagg, "Galatians 6:7–10," *RevExp* 88 (1991): 247–51.

92. Betz, *Galatians*, 313. See also J. A. D. Weima, "Gal. 6:11–18: A Hermeneutical Key to the Galatian Letter," *CTJ* 28 (1993): 90–107.

93. Ramsay, *Galatians*, 466.

94. Josephus, *J.W.* 4.5–7 §§ 305–437 provides some information about the military actions of the Zealots before the Fall of Jerusalem; also R. Jewett, "Agitators," 205.

95. Cicero, *Pro Rabirio* 16.

96. See M. Hengel, *Crucifixion in the Ancient World and the Folly of the Message of the Cross* (Philadelphia: Fortress, 1977); see also Bruce, *Galatians*, 271.

97. Lightfoot, *Galatians*, 225; Longenecker, *Galatians*, 299; Arichea and Nida, *Galatians*, 159.

98. Bruce, *Galatians*, 361; Luther, *Galatians* (Wheaton, Ill.: Crossway, 1998 ed.), 303.

99. Josephus, *J.W.* 1.10.2 §197; W. Klassen, "Galatians 6:17," *ExpTim* 81 (1970): 378.

100. Lightfoot, *Galatians*, 226; Arichea and Nida, *Galatians*, 160.

Sidebar and Chart Notes

A-1. For more information about Antioch, see J. McRay, "Antioch on the Orontes," *DPL*, 23–25.

A-2. See J. Griffin, "Introduction," in *The Roman World*, eds. J. Boardman, J. Griffin and O. Murray (*OHCW*; Oxford: Oxford Univ. Press, 1997), 4.

A-3. Diogenes Laertius 6.102.

A-4. 1 Cor. 4:14–16; 2 Cor. 6:13; 12:15; Phil. 2:22; 1 Thess. 2:7–8.

A-5. See P. Beasley-Murray, "Pastor, Paul as," *DPL*, 654–58; M. J. Wilkins, "Pastoral Theology," *DLNT*, 876–82.

EPHESIANS

by Clinton E. Arnold

Ephesus and Western Asia Minor

The city of Ephesus was the leading city of the richest region of the Roman empire. With a population of about 250,000 people, only Rome and Alexandria were larger. Ephesus served as the Roman provincial capital of Asia Minor and was a prosperous commercial center. As the principal port for Asia Minor, merchant and cargo vessels from all over the Mediterranean docked there to unload passengers and goods as well as to transport products from Asia Minor to Rome and throughout the empire. The first-century writer Strabo called Ephesus "the greatest commercial center in Asia this side of the Taurus river."[1]

The city was cosmopolitan and multiethnic. In addition to the indigenous Anatolian peoples of Ionia, Lydia, Phrygia, Caria, and Mysia, Ephesus was home to Egyptian, Greek, and Roman settlers. There was also a strong Jewish community in the city since Seleucid times (3d century B.C.). It appears that the Jews of the city had a fairly cordial relationship with the civic

EPHESUS
The countryside around the city.

▶ **Ephesians**
IMPORTANT FACTS:

- **AUTHOR:** The apostle Paul and Timothy.
- **DATE:** A.D. 58–59 (Paul imprisoned in Rome).
- **OCCASION:**
  - To give new believers converted from a background in Judaism, local religions, magic, and astrology a positive grounding in the gospel of Christ.
  - To help and admonish believers to cultivate a distinctively Christian lifestyle.
- **KEY THEMES:**
  1. Christ is supreme over all of creation, especially the powers of darkness.
  2. Believers participate with Christ in his death, resurrection, and fullness.
  3. The church is the one body of Christ and is composed of Jews and Gentiles.

officials and the local populace since there is no evidence of the kind of ethnic strife that rocked Alexandria and Rome. According to Josephus, they had been granted freedom to practice their religion according to their own traditions.[2]

The Introduction of Christianity to the City

Paul started the church at Ephesus after his eighteen-month sojourn in Corinth and following a visit to Jerusalem. He was aided significantly by the help of a Jewish-Christian couple from Rome, Priscilla and Aquila.

Luke provides us with a few of the highlights of Paul's ministry there in Acts 19. Following the typical pattern of his missionary outreach, Paul began proclaiming the gospel in the synagogue until opposition to his preaching grew too strong. He then moved to a lecture hall in the city where he taught regularly. The Western text of the book of Acts preserves the tradition that he taught there daily between 11:00 A.M. and 4:00 P.M. Most significantly, Luke claims that not only did people in Ephesus and its environs hear the gospel during these two years, but "all the Jews and Greeks who lived in the province of Asia heard the word of the Lord" (Acts 19:10). It was during this time that churches began in various other cities of western Asia Minor including Colosse, Laodicea, Pergamum, Smyrna, Sardis, Magnesia, Tralles, and elsewhere.

The original church of Ephesus thus consisted of many converted Jews and Gentile God-fearers and sympathizers to the Jewish faith, as well as many Gentiles coming directly from the pagan cults of the city, particularly the cult of Artemis. If the silversmith guild had experienced such a sharp decline of revenues for their images of Artemis, there was probably a sizeable group of Gentiles who embraced the one true God and the Lord Jesus Christ.

It is highly unlikely that the church met as a large group in one central location. Groups of believers probably met in homes every Lord's day in various parts of the city and in the local villages (e.g., Hypaipa, Diashieron, Neikaia, and Koloe).

The Spiritual Climate of the Area

There are some distinctive features of the religious environment of the area that help us better understand the discipleship issues these new believers faced and why Paul addressed certain topics and stressed others in his letter.

A religiously pluralistic environment. Although best known as the sacred home

to the Artemis cult, up to fifty other gods and goddesses were worshiped in Ephesus. Among those worshiped in Ephesus were Zeus, Athena, Aphrodite, Asclepius, Apollo, Dionysus, Demeter, Hekate, Tyche, Theos Hypsistos, Meter Oreia, and Hephaistos.[3] The two Egyptian deities Isis and Sarapis were also popular in the city.[4] There was a spirit of religious tolerance among the people. In fact, people typically worshiped more than one deity.

The pervasive influence of the Artemis cult. Artemis of Ephesus was undeniably the most important deity to the people living in the city. Her relationship to the city was forged in terms of a divinely directed covenant relationship. One month of the year was named after her, Olympic-style games were held in her honor (the Artemisia), and the cult was the major savings and loan institution for the entire region. The temple of Artemis was lauded by ancient writers as one of the seven wonders of the ancient world.[5]

Magic and spirit powers. Ephesus also bore a reputation in antiquity for magic, shamanism, and the occult arts. The practice of magic was predicated on an animistic worldview in which good and evil spirits were involved in practically every area of life. Magic represented a means of harnessing spiritual power through rituals, incantations, and invocations.[6] Luke informs us that many believers gathered their magical books together and burned them after a fear fell on them following Sceva's failed exorcism of a demonized man (Acts 19:17–20). His account demonstrates the difficulty new Christians had in turning completely away from their former practices in the process of discipleship. It would have been tempting for them to continue using magical incantations and invoking other deities and helper spirits for issues in daily life.

A Portrait of the Situation

Paul engaged in his Ephesian ministry in the mid–50s (perhaps A.D. 52–55). During this time the church was established and numerous other churches in a radius from Ephesus were planted. After his abrupt departure from the city precipitated by the silversmiths and adherents

CURETES STREET

(left) At the beginnng of the street, the columns depict Hercules draped in a lion skin.

(right) The well-preserved street passes by the principal civic buildings of Ephesus.

to the Artemis cult, Paul traveled to Macedonia and Greece. From there he went to Jerusalem, where he was arrested (see Acts 20–21). From that point on, Paul was incarcerated by the Romans—in Caesarea and then, after his harrowing sea voyage, in Rome (A.D. 60–62). It is from his imprisonment in the capital city that Paul writes this letter, probably shortly after he writes to the Colossian believers.

In the five years or so since his departure, a lot has happened in the churches of Ephesus and its environs. The believers have continued to proclaim the gospel in the area and many more Gentiles have put their faith in Christ and joined the Christian community. These new believers have never met Paul, but they have certainly heard of him and respected his authority as an apostle of Christ.

Coming to Christ from a background of animism, goddess worship, magical practices, and a variety of other religions, these people need a more extensive grounding in the gospel and its implications for life. Paul writes the letter to support the Ephesian leadership in addressing a variety of concerns. Three issues in particular surface as the most prominent:

1. When these people turned to Christ and joined the community, their fear of evil spirits and demonic powers did not vanish. They would have been greatly tempted to hold onto some of their household idols and their magical texts in spite of the precedent set by the original believers of Ephesus in the historic book-burning episode. These dear believers need reassurance as to the preeminence of Christ in relationship to other spiritual forces and their own access to the power of God for resisting the hostile powers.
2. Because of their immoral pre-Christian lifestyle, they need help and admonishment in cultivating a lifestyle consistent with their salvation in Christ—a lifestyle free from drunkenness, sexual immorality, lying, stealing, bitterness, and many other vices.
3. With a large influx of Gentiles into the Ephesian house churches,

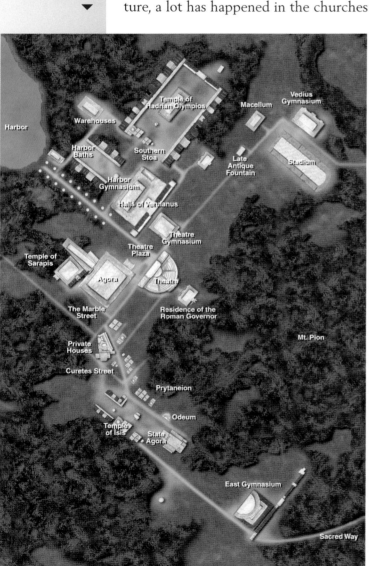

a situation was created for a heightening of tensions between Gentiles and Jews. Not only was there already a natural tension between Jews and Gentiles, but Gentile converts often lacked an appreciation for the Jewish heritage of their new faith.

Paul therefore sets out to write a general letter to the network of house churches in Ephesus and the churches of the region to address these and other issues. There does not appear to be a specific crisis (such as he addressed at Galatia or Corinth), but he nevertheless speaks in a pastoral and apostolic manner to a variety of real needs of which he has become aware through Tychicus and others.

Introduction to the Letter (1:1–2)

Paul, an apostle of Christ Jesus (1:1). Whereas Timothy is named as cowriter of Colossians and Philemon (written just before Ephesians), Paul names himself as the sole author of this letter. It is uncertain if Timothy is still in Rome or has departed to serve in another area. We do know that he becomes a key leader among the churches in Ephesus shortly after this letter is written (see 1 Timothy).

To the saints in Ephesus (1:2). The text of the NIV places a footnote here that reads, "Some early manuscripts do not have *in Ephesus*." There are only six manuscripts that omit Ephesus, but three of these are generally regarded as very reliable (Sinaiticus [Å], Vaticanus [B], and a second-century papyrus [p^{46}]. This has led some scholars to think that Ephesians was not originally written to believers in the city of Ephesus, but rather was a circular letter intended for a number of churches. This is unnecessary, however, because the vast majority of manuscripts and early translations into other languages support the inclusion of "in Ephesus" and also because there is a reasonable explanation for its omission from 1:2 very early. The contents of Ephesians are especially well-suited to a broad readership. It is likely that a scribe deliberately omitted "in Ephesus" for the purpose of the public reading of Scripture in another location (e.g., in Egypt). A similar omission, likely for the same reason, occurs in Romans, where several manuscripts omit "in Rome" in 1:7. Thus, it is probable that the letter was originally addressed by the apostle Paul to believers residing in the third largest city of the Roman empire, Ephesus.

Praise to God For His Remarkable Plan of Redemption (1:3–14)

Paul begins his letter with a poetically crafted exclamation of praise to the Father. The style of this section is quite different from the rest of the letter and has affinities to the Psalms and Jewish hymns that we know from the Dead Sea Scrolls. The language is designed to evoke an attitude of praise and thanksgiving to our great God and Lord. The apostle Paul could not teach theology in a dry and detached way. To reflect on the plan and work of God provoked an emotional response that led him into praise and worship.

This passage speaks of the overall plan of God, conceived before he created the world and now brought into effect by the Lord Jesus Christ. The passage highlights the overall sovereignty of God. His plan is unfolding just as he purposed.

▶ Fate and Astral Powers

People living in Ephesus and western Asia Minor lived in constant dread of astral powers that controlled fate. The Stoic writer Manilius (first century A.D.) writes:

> They [the Egyptian priests] were the first to see, through their art, how fate depends on the wandering stars. Over the course of many centuries they assigned with persistent care to each period of time the events connected with it: the day on which someone is born, the kind of life he shall lead, the influence of every hour on the laws of destiny, and the enormous differences made by small motions .... From long

observation it was discovered that the stars control the whole world by mysterious laws, that the world itself moves by an eternal principle, and that we can, by reliable signs, recognize the ups and downs of fate.[A-1]

The beautiful cult statue of the Ephesian Artemis depicts the goddess as wearing the signs of the zodiac as a necklace, expressing that as Queen of Heaven she had the power to break the bonds of fate. Even some Jewish writings from the Roman period display a concern about fate and the spirits associated with the sun, moon, planets, and stars.

Praise be to the God and Father of our Lord Jesus Christ (1:3). The term "praise" (*eulogētos*) has often been translated "blessed." Throughout the Old Testament, the people of God responded to him in praise for delivering them from their enemies and for providing salvation. For instance, in response to God's marvelous redemption of Israel from bondage in Egypt, Moses' father-in-law exclaimed, "Praise be to the LORD, who rescued you from the hand of the Egyptians and of Pharaoh, and who rescued the people from the hand of the Egyptians. Now I know that the LORD is greater than all other gods" (Ex. 18:10–11). Because of his salvation, the psalmist bursts forth in praise: "The LORD lives, and blessed be my rock; And exalted be the God of my salvation" (Ps. 18:46 NASB). Paul cannot contain himself as he ponders the ultimate act of redemption in Christ.

Jesus is named in this verse alongside the Father as both Lord and Messiah. He is the agent of redemption and the focus of God's eternal plan.

[He] has blessed us in the heavenly realms (1:3). Paul conceives of heaven not only as a place where believers will live after they die, but also as a spiritual realm. It is the place where God and the resurrected Christ currently live (1:3, 20; 2:6) as well as where the powers of darkness continue to operate (3:10; 6:12). Because of Christ's work of redemption on the cross and their present relation-

ARTEMIS ADORNED WITH THE ZODIAC

▼

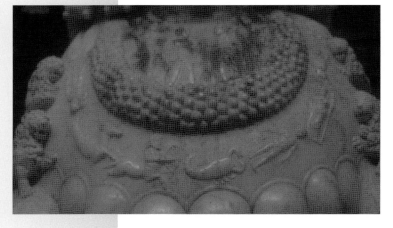

ship with him, believers now have access to spiritual power to aid in their struggle against the evil one.

He chose us in him before the creation of the world (1:4). Paul's teaching here communicates relevant and extraordinary truth about ultimate reality for these believers in Asia. Contrary to popular belief, their fate was not wrapped up in the stars and the planets, but in the one true almighty God, who made the sun and the stars. God had in fact chosen them to be in Christ before he made the heavens and the earth. What a tremendous comfort this teaching must be to new believers still worried about their foul horoscopes or the threat of astral powers to their daily lives.

To be holy and blameless in his sight (1:4). God's purpose for his people has always been for them to become like him in holiness. When he gave the Israelites the law after delivering them from Egypt, he declared, "I am the LORD who brought you up out of Egypt to be your God; therefore be holy, because I am holy" (Lev. 11:45).

Adopted as his sons (1:5). The adoption of a child was a practice that everyone in the Greco-Roman world would have been familiar with. Under Roman law, an adopted child acquired all of the legal rights of a natural born child and lost all rights held in his former family. The child also received the adopting parents' family name and shared in the status of the new family.[7] The most decisive influence on Paul's thought, however, is in the promise of adoption God made to David by Nathan the prophet: "I will be his father, and he will be my son" (2 Sam. 7:14). Jesus himself has fulfilled this promise as the descendant of David who sits on the throne. By virtue of union with Jesus, believers share in this adoption and truly become children of God.

To the praise of his glorious grace (1:6). Variations of this refrain of praise punctuate this passage at three intervals (1:6, 12, 14). Reflecting on the awesome and gracious plan of God involving Jesus, Paul exults in the same way as the psalmist who exclaimed, "My tongue will speak of your righteousness and of your praises all day long" (Ps. 35:28). (On grace, see comments on 2:7.)

In him we have redemption through his blood (1:7). The people of Israel were once delivered from oppressive slavery to corrupt rulers and taskmasters in Egypt. The Old Testament repeatedly refers to this as Israel's redemption (see Deut. 7:8; 9:26; 13:5). Now God has delivered his people from the much more deadly and enslaving power of sin. He has done this by Christ's sacrificial death on the cross—a costly ransom price. Believers can therefore experience the forgiveness of sins.

He made known to us the mystery of his will (1:9). "Mystery" was a term widely known in the ancient world. Many of the Gentile converts in the Ephesian churches have probably experienced ritual initiation into one or more of the mystery cults, such as the cult of Artemis, Isis, Cybele, or Dionysus. They are called "mysteries" because the adherents were sworn to secrecy about what they experienced. The mystery Paul is talking about here is substantially different from this. He is speaking about God's plan that can only be known through revelation. This same use of the word occurs in the book of Daniel to describe Nebuchadnezzar's divinely inspired dream about God's plan for the ages.[8] The word Paul uses for "made known" (*gnōrizō*) also occurs in Daniel for God's revelatory activity.[9]

When the times will have reached their fulfillment (1:10). The Greek and Roman world generally thought of time as unending. The world will continue on and on. The Old Testament, by contrast, is clear that time is measured and fixed (see Dan. 9:24–27). At some point in time history as we know it will be drawn to a conclusion. This period of fulfillment will represent the climax of God's redemptive plan.

To bring all things in heaven and on earth together under one head, even Christ (1:10). There has been a significant rupture in God's creation. Angels in heaven have rebelled against the Lord. Sin has emerged as a power that not only enslaves God's creation, but also causes people to revolt against him and his purposes. Paul declares here that this condition will not continue forever. All of creation—both heavenly principalities and every person—will someday be forced to submit to the righteous and all-powerful reign of the Messiah. All will be brought under the universal "headship" of Jesus. The initial realization of this plan has already taken place in Jesus' incarnation, proclamation of the kingdom, death, and exaltation to the right hand of God. Believers now await the complete fulfillment.

The word of truth, the gospel of your salvation (1:13). First-century Ephesus had nearly fifty gods and goddesses claiming to be true. There were also a wide variety of philosophies that laid claim to providing knowledge of the truth. In this environment, Paul does not shrink back from insisting that the good news of Jesus as the revelation of ultimate reality is *the* truth (the Greek text has the article). This was not just a matter for the satisfaction of intellectual curiosity. Jesus revealed insight into the plight of humanity and their need for deliverance.

You were marked in him with a seal, the promised Holy Spirit (1:13). Seals were used widely in the ancient world as the primary way of indicating ownership. They were typically made of hard stones or precious metals and had a distinctive image engraved on them (usually the representation of a favorite deity, a hero, or a portrait). All of a person's significant possessions were marked with the impression of the seal. Even slaves and livestock were marked by the owner.[10] In some cases, people declared themselves the possession of a deity by the imprint of a seal.[11] The one true God has also marked his possessions by means of a seal, yet his seal does not leave a physical impression. He has given his people the gift of the Holy Spirit as a sign of their belonging to him.

ANCIENT SEALS

Hebrew signet rings from the seventh or eighth century B.C.

▼

A deposit guaranteeing our inheritance (1:14). The Spirit is also represented as a down payment on the full future inheritance believers will receive. The word *arrabōn*, here translated "a deposit guaranteeing," is familiar to Paul's readers from the context of business and trade. In much the same way that we put a down payment on a car or a home, in the ancient world someone could put a down payment on an item to secure a legal claim on it. Although believers have nothing to offer but themselves, God so values his people that he has put down a deposit and will complete the transaction in the future. The Spirit, then, is a guarantee of the full experience of salvation—the inheritance—that believers have yet to receive.

A Prayer for an Increased Awareness of God's Power (1:15–23)

Following immediately after his sentence of praise, Paul expresses thanksgiving to God for his Asia Minor converts and reports how he and his companions have been interceding for them.

Ever since I heard about your faith (1:15). About five to seven years have passed since Paul was last with the Ephesians. He engaged in further mission work, was arrested in Jerusalem, spent nearly two years in prison in Caesarea, experienced a harrowing voyage and shipwreck on his way to Rome, and is now imprisoned in the capital city. A lot has happened in Asia Minor since he was with them. Nevertheless, he has received word from his coworkers that their faith is growing and their love is abounding. Probably many others have become Christians in this period of time and their

faith is flourishing. For this, Paul gives thanks to God.

The Spirit of wisdom and revelation (1:17). The heart of Paul's request for these dear people is for their knowledge of God to increase. Paul knows that this is not just a matter of intellectual apprehension. The Holy Spirit needs to be operative in their lives to impress the truths about God and his plan of salvation onto their minds and into their hearts.

This is also necessary because "the ruler of the kingdom of the air" is still at work, endeavoring to disrupt what God is doing in the lives of these people. Paul speaks of the work of the Spirit in terms similar to how Isaiah prophesied that the Spirit would work in the Messiah: "The Spirit of the LORD will rest on him—the Spirit of wisdom and understanding, the Spirit of counsel and of power, the Spirit of knowledge and of the fear of the LORD" (Isa. 11:2).

The eyes of your heart (1:18). This is a fascinating (and somewhat humorous) metaphor because hearts do not have eyes, yet the intent is clear. It appears that Paul himself has created this image since it does not appear in any literature prior to him. The closest statement comes from the Dead Sea Scrolls: "May he illuminate your heart with the discernment of life."[12] In the Old Testament and Judaism, "heart" was used metaphorically as the place of a person's intellectual and spiritual life. Paul is here using colorful language to pray for the people to receive a deep-seated awareness of God.

The hope (1:18). This is the first of three specific requests Paul reports praying for the Ephesians. Given their previous background in non-Christian religions largely devoid of future hope as well as their previous deep-seated beliefs about astral fate, this was very important.

His glorious inheritance in the saints (1:18). This is Paul's second request. He has already mentioned the future inheritance of the Ephesians in 1:14, which consists of their hope, but here he speaks of them as *God's* valuable inheritance. The love of God is a significant theme in this letter. How wonderful it must feel to these people, accustomed as they have been to worshiping capricious and self-serving gods and goddesses, now to be in a relationship with a God who dearly loves them and values them as his choice inheritance.

REFLECTIONS

WHEN GOD LOOKS AT YOU, HE DOES not shrink back in horror and disgust. He sees a person of inestimable value and beauty. He loves you so much that he gave the costliest gift imaginable to obtain you as his own "glorious" inheritance. You will be his cherished son or daughter forever.

His incomparably great power (1:19). This letter has more to say about power than any of Paul's other letters. His final request is for the Ephesians to be able to grasp the vastness of the one true God's mighty power at work in their lives. Why does he pray for this? Because spiritual power is a huge issue for these people. They are accustomed to seeking spiritual power through their magical practices. Based on Luke's account we know it has been difficult for many of these people to let loose of their magical incantations and

formulas. With language that is emphatic, Paul assures them that God's power is beyond that of any competing spirit power, god, or goddess. Not only do they serve the most powerful God, but he manifests his power in their lives for protection, growth, and service.

Seated him at his right hand (1:20). Jesus not only died for our sins and rose from the dead, but he has been installed at God's right hand on the heavenly throne. This was an important conviction of the early Christians, evidenced in part by the fact that Psalm 110:1—cited here as fulfilled in Christ—is quoted more than any other Old Testament passage by New Testament writers.

The setting of Psalm 110 was the enthronement of a king. The right hand of God occurs frequently in the Old Testament as a way of describing a position of power (see Ex. 15:6) and favor (Ps. 80:17). The enthronement of Christ establishes his identity as the messianic king and highlights his sovereignty over all of creation. The enemies that this victorious king has subjugated are not the Romans or any other physical army, but the spiritual forces of evil.

Far above all rule and authority, power and dominion (1:21). Paul now elaborates on these spiritual enemies by listing a few of them. These labels are just a few of many possible terms Paul could have used to describe demonic spirits. Although these terms do not occur in the Old Testament, they were well known in the Judaism of the time.[13] They had become part of the common vocabulary for spirit powers not only in Judaism, but to some degree also in the Greco-Roman world. The terms may indicate some kind of hierarchy within the demonic realm, but there is no way of determining this. The texts outside of the New Testament that use these terms make no attempt at classifying these angelic powers. Paul uses these words here to convey the fact that these are powerful supernatural forces. They serve to highlight the superiority of Christ because his is "far above" these forces in power and sovereignty.

Every title that can be given (1:21). This phrase (lit., "every name that is named") is loaded with significance for people who have been converted out of a background of participation in magical practices. Discerning and using the names of spirit powers was central to the use of magic. Note the calling of names in lines from three magical papyri:

- "I conjure you by the great names."
- "You, these holy names and these powers, confirm and carry out this perfect enchantment."
- "A phylactery, a bodyguard against demons, against phantasms, against every sickness and suffering, to be written on a leaf of gold or silver or tin or hieratic papyrus. When worn it works mightily, for it is the name of power of the great god and his seal, and it is as follows: . . . [fourteen magical names are given]. . . . These are the names."[14]

Paul wants to assure these new believers they that need not concern themselves with discerning the names of spirit entities or with worrying about some being that may rival Christ in power and authority. There is no conceivable spiritual force outside of the dominion of Christ. The name of Jesus alone, not his name in addition to others, is sufficient for them.

Not only in the present age but also in the one to come (1:21). Paul sees history as divided into two ages—this present evil age and the age to come (see Gal. 1:4). This perspective is one of the standard features of Jewish theology and appears in the book of Daniel. The age to come corresponds to the time when God will restore David's kingdom on the earth.[15]

◀ *left*

NAMING POWERFUL NAMES

Someone wrote the names of five deities on this potsherd (*ostracon*): Sambathis, Artemis, Koura, Dionysus, and Demo.

▶ **The Ephesian Names**

There is a long tradition of six magical names that was associated with Ephesus: *Askion, Kataskion, Lix, Tetrax, Damnameneus,* and *Aisia.* Known as the "Ephesian Letters" (*Ephesia grammata*), these were the names of six powerful beings who could be called upon for assistance and protection. Plutarch says that the "magi" instructed people who were possessed by evil spirits to repeat to themselves the magic words in order to drive the demons out.[A-2] Even athletes wore the "Ephesian letters" to ensure success.

Head over everything (1:22). The metaphor of headship clearly indicates the sovereignty of Jesus. As the exalted Lord, he possesses ruling authority over everything. Particularly meaningful for the Ephesian readers is the fact that Jesus reigns as supreme over all the supernatural powers that they so deeply feared.

The church, which is his body (1:22–23). Jesus also is "head" in relationship to his "body," which Paul here identifies as the church. Head-body imagery abounded in the ancient world, especially in the medical writers and in some of the philosophers. In these texts, this image stresses a person's function of giving leadership and providing for his people. This image flows naturally out of the observation of human anatomy, where the head coordinates the movements of the members of the body and provides nourishment as well.

The fullness of him who fills everything in every way (1:23). Under the old covenant, God manifested his presence in the temple. The *Shekinah*—the essence, glory, power, and presence of God—filled the temple. Biblical writers could therefore exclaim, "Behold, the house of the Lord is full of his glory."[16] Under the new covenant, God now fills believers directly with his presence through the promised Holy Spirit (Eph. 1:13–14).

This verse also indicates that believers have a mission. God is setting out to fill all of creation with the good news of redemption available in the Messiah Jesus. "In every way" is perhaps better translated "totally" or "in all parts." God manifests his presence in believers so they can move out to reach every corner of the world with the gospel of Christ and then to help each of these new believers grow and mature in every way before God.

The Desperate Human Plight (2:1–3)

From his exultant praise of God and his prayer for the readers, Paul moves to a description of the horrible condition humanity faces: death, slavery, and condemnation. This plight results from the pervasive and powerful influence of evil, which impinges on people in three different but related forms.

The ways of this world (2:2). The literal wording of this phrase is "the age of this world." Paul thereby sets sinful behavior into the context of "this present evil age" (see comments on 1:21). He also speaks of "the world" in a similar way (see 1 Cor. 3:19; 5:10). Paul understands the physical creation and humanity as belonging to the present evil age. The social structures and the value systems of corporate humanity have been corrupted by sin and exert a powerful influence on people.

The ruler of the kingdom of the air (2:2). The second evil influence is the devil, whom Paul describes here as a "ruler"

EPHESUS

The façade to the library of Celsus.

▼

(*archōn*). This is a common term for human rulers throughout the Greek Old Testament (LXX) as well as documents and inscriptions from the first century. This *archōn* is clearly not a human ruler, but a supernatural power because his domain is "the air" and he is subsequently characterized as a spirit. The Greek text of Daniel also uses this word to refer to angelic powers: the "prince" of Persia and the "prince" of Greece.[17] The Synoptic Gospels describe the devil as "the prince of demons," and John's Gospel terms him "the prince of this world."[18]

The "air" was widely spoken of as the dwelling place of evil spirits in antiquity. One magical papyrus reads: "Protect me from every demon in the air."[19] A Jewish text from the first century also illustrates this belief: "For the person who fears God and loves his neighbor cannot be plagued by the aerial spirit of Beliar since he is sheltered by the fear of God."[20] Satan is here understood, then, to be the ruler of an army of evil spiritual powers who work at promoting disobedience to the purposes of God among humanity.

The cravings of our sinful nature (2:3). This third form of evil influence is literally translated, "the lusts of our flesh." Central to Jewish thinking among the rabbis at the time of Paul was the notion that every person struggled with an inner propensity toward evil. They called this the *yetzer hārāʿ*, "the evil impulse."[21] Paul spoke of this impulse as "the flesh" (*sarx*) and conceived of it as a power welling up from within the person, prompting him or her to act in ways displeasing to God.

The combination of these three evil influences—the world, the devil, and the flesh—exerts a compelling pull on people to sin and transgress God's commandments. People need deliverance and freedom from the overwhelming power of these forces.

We were by nature objects of wrath (2:3). All humanity, having succumbed

◀

to the influence of evil, faces the wrath of God for violating his righteous directives. The Old Testament prophets point to a future day, called a "day of wrath," when God will exercise judgment (Zeph. 1:15, 18; 2:2–3). "By nature" reveals that human culpability before God can be attributed to the fact that every person stands in solidarity with Adam, the progenitor of the human race and the first to sin (see Rom. 5:12–14). This resulted in a sinful tendency that spreads like a disease to every single human being.

The Merciful Saving Action of God (2:4–10)

God has responded in his love to the dreadful situation of humanity. He has delivered people from captivity to evil based on the work of Christ. Those who are redeemed are brought into close relationship with Christ and a solidarity with the events of the cross.

His great love for us (2:4). In spite of how undeserving and how unlovely sin-tainted people are, God has a tremendous love for them. This has been true from the beginning. God told Israel: "The LORD did not set his affection on you and choose you because you were more numerous than other peoples, for you were the fewest of all peoples. But it was because the LORD loved you" (Deut. 7:7–8). John's Gospel tells us that it was because God loved the world so much that he sent his Son (John 3:16).

Made us alive with Christ . . . raised us up with Christ . . . and seated us with him (2:5–6). God has brought believers into a relationship with himself through Christ. He has mercifully created a plan whereby people can participate in the events of the cross—Jesus' death (not explicitly stated here but assumed)—his resurrection, and his ascension/exaltation (see also Rom. 6:4–8). The work of Christ that Paul expresses praise for in chapter 1, he now makes relevant to the plight of believers. This benefit is predicated on entering a relationship of solidarity with Jesus Christ. Not only do people experience forgiveness of sins and life after death, but they presently share in Christ's authority. This is a particularly relevant and important message for these Asia Minor readers who are deeply concerned about how to respond to the unseen world of evil forces.

You have been saved (2:5, 8). No longer are God's people destined for wrath, for they have been saved from this dreadful fate. The experience of salvation goes beyond this future deliverance; it is a present experience based on participation in this past event.

Incomparable riches of his grace (2:7). "Grace" (*charis*) was not a widely used term in Greek philosophical or religious writings, but it was a significant way of describing God's overwhelming love in Jewish circles. It corresponds to the Hebrew word *hesed*, which was used commonly in the Old Testament to express the kindness and favor God demonstrated to his people through the covenant.[22] The incredible love of God manifested in the sacrifice of his Son is indeed incomparably great.

Through faith—and this not from yourselves (2:8). A decisive feature of the new covenant that runs counter to many popular misconceptions about divine salvation in Paul's day is that there is nothing a person can do to earn favor with

God. Some Jews, for instance, believed that ultimately the sum total of their works would be weighed on the Judgment Day and God would determine if they had sufficient merit to be saved. This belief is illustrated in one Jewish document that depicts two angels as holding the scales of judgment and recording sins as well as righteous deeds. At the end of time, the aggregate of each person's deeds is tested by fire. The person whose remaining good works outweigh his evil deeds "is justified and the angel of righteousness takes him and carries him up to be saved in the lot of the righteous."[23] Paul here strongly emphasizes that salvation is based entirely on the merits of Christ's work—not ours. We are urged merely to put our faith in Christ.

Created in Christ Jesus to do good works (2:10). The idea that God created people to live righteously and perform good works was well-rooted in Judaism. Rabbi Johanan ben Zakkai (first century A.D.) is reported in the Mishnah to have customarily said, "If thou has wrought much in the Law claim not merit for thyself, for to this end was thou created."[24] Believers in Christ perform these good works based on their relationship with Christ and the power and direction he provides. They do so out of a heart of gratitude for all that Christ has accomplished for them.

The Unity of Jews and Greeks in One Body (2:11–17)

Paul now specifically addresses the Gentiles among his readers. He calls them to remember their former alienation from God and from the Jews. All of that has been changed by the sacrificial death of Christ, who now unites them all into one unified body.

Behind this passage may be a situation of tension between Jewish and Gentile Christians among the house churches of Ephesus and Asia Minor. Perhaps a flood of Gentile new believers entering the churches has led over time to a lack of appreciation for the Jewish heritage of their faith. Note too that throughout the Roman empire a growing anti-Jewish sentiment led to intense flare-ups of racial tension in the cities.

Remember (2:11). God has always called his people to remember their past condition. The intent is not to provoke sorrow, grief, or self-hatred, but to help them appreciate all the more the greatness of God's grace, mercy, and love. The Israelites, for instance, were instructed by God to remember their deliverance from Egypt by an annual feast called "Unleavened Bread": "Then Moses said to the people, 'Commemorate [lit., "remember"] this day, the day you came out of Egypt, out of the land of slavery, because the LORD brought you out of it with a mighty hand. Eat nothing containing yeast'" (Ex.13:3). The sins and difficulties

EPHESUS

Hadrian's temple.

the Israelites got themselves into could in part be attributed to the fact that "they did not remember" the wondrous works of God and his past acts of deliverance (see Ps. 78:42; 106:7).

You who are Gentiles by birth (2:11). Paul singles out and addresses the non-Jews among the believers in Ephesus. It is important to recognize that Ephesus was a multiethnic city. The reference to Gentiles would include people of many different ethnicities, including Anatolians, Egyptians, Romans, Persians, Syrians, and others.

"Uncircumcised" . . . "the circumcision" (2:11). Jews commonly distinguished themselves from Gentiles by the fact that their males were circumcised—the mark of their covenant with God (Gen. 17:9–14). This became a matter of inappropriate ethnic pride for many Jews, who referred to Gentiles as "the uncircumcision" (lit., "those with foreskins").

Foreigners to the covenants of the promise (2:12). Paul is speaking here of the series of covenants God made with his people: Abraham, Isaac, Jacob/Israel, and David.[25] The singular "promise" is

the Messiah, in whom all of the covenants find their fulfillment. Gentiles have not shared in these covenants nor have they been included in God's special relationship to Israel.

Without God (2:12). There is incredible irony in Paul's referring to a formerly *polytheistic* group of people as "godless" (*atheoi*). What Paul has in mind is the fact that they did not have a relationship with the one true God.

You who once were far away have been brought near (2:13). The language of this verse echoes Isaiah 57:19 ("'Peace, peace, to those far and near,' says the LORD"), which Paul here and more explicitly in Ephesians 2:17 declares as fulfilled by the work of Jesus on the cross. Those "far" are understood to be the Gentiles and those "near" are the Jews. Yet both now have access to the Father only through the blood of Christ.

He himself is our peace (2:14). Peace is found in a person—the Lord Jesus Christ. He is truly the "Prince of Peace" (Isa. 9:6) and has established a kingdom that is characterized by "peace" (Isa. 9:7). Yet it was his sacrifice of himself that serves as the source of this peace. Isaiah prophesied of the Servant of the Lord: "The punishment that brought us peace was upon him, and by his wounds we are healed" (Isa. 53:5). The peace Jesus makes possible is first and foremost with the Father. But this peace extends to human relationship within the body of Christ.

The barrier, the dividing wall of hostility (2:14). Gentiles were allowed to enter the temple enclosure in Jerusalem. This large paved area surrounding the

---

WARNING INSCRIPTION

A first-century inscription from the balustrade around the Jerusalem temple warning Gentiles not to enter on the pain of death.

▼

temple and its inner courts was itself enclosed by a double colonnade of pillars standing thirty-seven feet high. The perimeter of this area measured nearly three-quarters of a mile. This outer court was also called the Court of the Gentiles. Gentiles were not allowed access to the inner courts or the temple. A four and a half foot high barrier surrounding the inner courts served as a dividing wall.

The Jewish historian Josephus informs us that thirteen stone slabs written in Greek and Latin stood at intervals on the barrier, warning Gentiles not to enter.[26] Archaeologists have discovered two of these tablets.[27] The inscription reads: "No foreigner is to enter within the forecourt and the balustrade around the sanctuary. Whoever is caught will have himself to blame for his subsequent death."[28] The fact of this barrier recently impressed itself upon Paul's mind because he was falsely accused in Jerusalem for taking a Gentile, Trophimus, into the temple (Acts 21:28–29). This was the reason for his initial imprisonment in Jerusalem and then Caesarea.

Paul's language in this verse appears to make allusion to this barrier—a symbol of the alienation of Gentiles from the Jewish people, from citizenship in Israel, from the promises of the covenants, and, more important, from access to the one true God. Paul declares that the barriers separating Gentiles from God and from Jews have now been destroyed. The physical balustrade at the temple still stood (until the temple was destroyed in A.D. 70), but there is no longer any fence prohibiting direct access to God.

The law with its commandments and regulations (2:15). By his death on the cross, Jesus has fulfilled the law and thus brought to an end the ceremonies and rituals associated with the temple. No longer are the bloody sacrifices, ritual purity, and circumcision essential for the worship of God.

In this one body to reconcile both of them to God (2:16). The word "reconciliation" was widely used in the Greek-speaking world to describe the restoration of a relationship after some kind of rupture through hostility or displeasure. God has not only brought about the possibility of a close relationship with himself, but between two groups formerly at enmity with one another. This does not take place in society at large, but within the church.

We both have access to the Father (2:18). Access to the Father is no longer through the temple priesthood or based on being a Jew. Gentiles and Jews alike now gain direct access to God through the work of Christ and by the indwelling Spirit, the very presence of God with his people.

REFLECTIONS

CHRIST HAS NOT ONLY OVERCOME the divisions separating Jews from Gentiles, but also every barrier that separates people from one another today. This includes race, social status, denominations, and every other dividing wall that we may choose to erect. Our churches should showcase to the world the unifying power of the gospel. How is your church doing? Do you harbor any pride, bitterness, or animosity toward other believers in your heart? The gospel demands that we work toward unity.

God's Citizens, Family, and Temple Indwelt by the Spirit (2:19–22)

Paul now uses three images well known to the people of that time to describe the nature of the church: fellow citizens of a kingdom, members of a family, and a temple.

Fellow citizens (2:19). The background of the word (*politeia*) Paul uses here (as also in 2:12) is in Greek texts that refer to a government, state, or a commonwealth. It never appears in the LXX, although it is used in Judaism leading up to the time of Christ. It is reminiscent of the "kingdom" language used by Jesus. The principal idea is that believers have gained a new citizenship (see Phil. 3:20) in a divinely constituted commonwealth. This is not a private matter, but a corporate experience, in that they join a group of other believers.

Members of God's household (2:19). Paul moves from the image of citizenship to the image of family (see also Gal. 6:10 and 1 Tim. 5:8, where the same Greek word is used). The picture of the "household" conveys a deeper level of intimacy and belonging. Central to the idea of the

church is the creation of strong and supportive relationships.

Built on the foundation of the apostles and prophets (2:20). Now Paul begins to develop a picture of the church as a building under construction. The foundation for this building was laid in the first century with the initial leadership of the church. The "apostles" are those directly commissioned by the Lord Jesus and sent by him to plant churches and root them deeply in his word. These include primarily the Twelve and Paul. The "prophets" are not the Old Testament prophets such as Isaiah and Jeremiah, but the New Testament prophets, who were inspired by the Spirit, gave direction and encouragement to the church, and provided leadership (see the leadership role of the prophets in Antioch in Acts 13:1–3).

The chief cornerstone (2:20). The most significant part of the foundation of any large building was the cornerstone. This stone bore much of the weight of the building. Archaeologists have recently discovered five enormous building stones that helped form the foundation of the Jerusalem temple. The largest stone measures fifty-five feet long, eleven feet high, and fourteen feet wide and is estimated to weigh 570 tons.[29] The prophet Isaiah spoke of the importance of the cornerstone in a passage understood in both Judaism and early Christianity as referring to the Messiah: "See, I lay a stone in Zion, a tested stone, a precious cornerstone for a sure foundation; the one who trusts will never be dismayed" (Isa. 28:16). In his development of the image of the church as a temple, Paul presents Jesus as this significant cornerstone. The whole building is established on him,

LARGE FOUNDATION STONES OF THE JERUSALEM TEMPLE

▼

◄

THE JERUSALEM TEMPLE

A model of the temple and its courts. The court of women is in the foreground.

including the foundation laid by the apostles and the prophets.

A holy temple (2:21). The Jerusalem temple provided a fitting analogy to the church. It was the place where God manifested his presence to the people of Israel. The Jerusalem temple of Paul's day was also a long time in the making. Josephus informs us that construction on Herod's temple began around 20 B.C. and work on the temple precincts was not completed until the early 60s.[30] In other words, work is still continuing as Paul writes this letter. God is finished, however, with the physical temple in Jerusalem. He is replacing it with a "temple" comprised of people filled with his Spirit. This temple is also still under construction. People are being added to it, and they are being crafted and refashioned by God to reflect his holiness and purity.

▲

Paul's Apostolic Ministry (3:1–13)

Paul begins to relate to these Asia Minor believers how he has been praying for them, but he abruptly digresses and explains the nature of his ministry as an apostle.

The prisoner of Christ Jesus (3:1). For the first time in this letter, Paul makes explicit reference to the fact that he is incarcerated. He was arrested and is awaiting trial because of his ministry for the cause of Christ.

The administration of God's grace that was given to me (3:2). "Administration" (*oikonomia*) is a colorful word taken from the management of everyday affairs of life in a household (*oikos*). The administrator (*oikonomos*) was a person who managed an estate in accordance with the wishes of the owner (see Luke 16:2–4). Paul compares himself to this domestic official who has been entrusted with a significant responsibility and will ultimately be called to account by the owner. Paul sees himself as a steward of the grace of God manifested in his marvelous plan of salvation.

As I have already written briefly (3:3). Paul is not speaking of a different letter, but what he has already written up to this point.

The mystery of Christ (3:4). "Mystery," as we have already noted in 1:9, is God's plan for the ages that cannot be known apart from revelation. God has revealed his plan of salvation to Paul, the heart and essence of which is Christ, the Messiah. Because Christ is *the* mystery, the definitive revelation of the one true God, the readers can forsake all of their pseudo-mysteries—the rituals of the gods and goddesses they have worshiped all of their lives.

This mystery is that through the gospel the Gentiles are heirs together ... members together ... and sharers together (3:6). The center point of God's plan of salvation is Christ, but he has unfolded the plan of salvation in a way that the people of Israel could not previously discern. God has brought Jews and Gentiles together into one corporate entity, dynamically united to Christ. The threefold stress on "together" brings out that this obliteration of any distinctions is the radical change in God's way of bringing salvation to people. God's people will now be identified based on a dynamic relationship with the risen Christ and their togetherness in a multiethnic and loving group, not by circumcision, ritual purity, and bloody sacrifices.

I became a servant of this gospel (3:7). Consistent with the image of himself as a manager of a household (3:2), Paul now characterizes his ministry as that of a "servant" (*diakovos*), who is under orders from his master (cf. 6:5–9). Paul thereby once again deflects any praise he might receive and points people to Christ.

The manifold wisdom of God should be made known to the rulers and authorities in the heavenly realms (3:10). The evil principalities and powers had tried to thwart God's plan of redemption by inspiring human rulers to put the Messiah to death.[31] They profoundly underestimated the incredible wisdom of God because it was by Jesus' sacrificial death on the cross that God can now forgive the sins of humanity and thereby take away the power of Satan to justly accuse. Jews and Gentiles, formerly held in slavery by the "elemental spirits of the world," have now been redeemed (Gal. 4:3–5 NRSV). The very existence of the church provides a constant witness to the evil angelic realm of God's extraordinary wisdom.

In him we may approach God with freedom and confidence (3:12). The sentence can more literally be translated, "in him we have the freedom [or boldness] and access in confidence." The "freedom/boldness" (*parrēsia*) that Paul speaks of here was common in Greek literature for describing the kind of communication that would occur among close friends. One may address a friend openly, frankly, and confidently. "Access" (*prosagōgē*) is now repeated from 2:18. Believers not only have the right to approach God, but they can approach him with candidness and freedom, much as one would address a close friend.

Prayer for a Deeper Experience of God's Power (3:14–21)

Paul now resumes his prayer request for the Ephesians. He tells these dear believers that he has been praying for a profound realization of the power of God in their lives. This request builds on what he prayed in chapter 1, where the focus was more on gaining an awareness of God's great power available to them. He concludes his prayer with a beautiful doxology—an ascription of praise to God.

I kneel before the Father (3:14). This is one of the few times that Paul describes his posture in prayer. Kneeling was a symbol of deep respect for the person addressed. The man with leprosy paid Jesus this respect when he knelt before

him and asked for healing.[32] Paul knelt on the beach and prayed with the leaders of the Ephesian church the last time he saw them. When Jesus prayed he often stood and looked into the sky (see Mark 7:34; John 17:1).

From whom his whole family in heaven and on earth derives its name (3:15). This unusual description of God characterizes him as the source of all life. The bestowing of a name means the granting of power and authority. God has made the whole of humanity in all of its diversity. He is also the creator of the heavenly angelic realm—in all its diversity in authorities and roles. In spite of the fact that part of the angelic realm has rebelled against him, God remains sovereign; he is the One who has granted them life and power. This should bring reassurance to people who fear that hostile powers might disrupt what has been asked for them in prayer.

He may strengthen you with power through his Spirit (3:16). The emphasis on the Holy Spirit as the agent for dispensing God's power stands in rather

EPHESUS

The marketplace (*agora*).

stark contrast to the religious climate of the area. In the Greco-Roman world, power was often seen as an impersonal force (like electricity) that could be manipulated, harnessed, or controlled. The power of God comes to his people by means of a *relationship*—a relationship with God by virtue of union with the exalted Christ and with the Holy Spirit residing in each believer.

In your inner being (3:16). The "inner being" is another way of referring to the heart. Paul understands the inner being to be that part of the self in conflict with the power of sin (see Rom. 7:22–23). When personified as a power, sin stands for the three evil influences Paul has already described in Ephesians 2:1–3: the world, the flesh, and the devil. Paul knows very well that believers cannot resist these overwhelmingly powerful evil influences in their own strength.

That Christ may dwell in your hearts through faith (3:17). These people have already received Christ into their lives. Paul is therefore not praying that they will become Christians, but that they will grow in their Christian lives. He prays that Christ will increasingly manifest his reign over every area of their lives and push back the footholds that evil has maintained.

Being rooted and established in love (3:17). Paul mixes metaphors here by combining an agricultural image (a plant taking root) with a construction image (a foundation laid for a building). The net result is an emphasis on love as the primary feature of the Christian life and experience. He subsequently prays, with irony, that believers will come to know something that cannot be fully known— the incredible love of Christ. Love was not a virtue that characterized the workings of the gods and goddesses in the various cults of Asia Minor.

How wide and long and high and deep is the love of Christ (3:18). "The love of Christ" is not in the Greek text. It is a matter of interpretation to decide what the object of the four dimensional terms are. Most commentators have suggested that it is "love" because of the emphasis on love in the surrounding context. A case could be made, however, that this is a reference to the vastness of the power of God. Surprisingly, the only other time that these four words appear together in the Greek language is in a magical text where they speak of the great power of another deity.[33] The readers may well have been familiar with this expression as a way of extolling the power of a god.

Such an interpretation does not diminish the emphasis on love in the passage, but it couples the love of God with his vast power. Love alone is insufficient for God to fulfill his eternal intent for the salvation of humanity. He needs the power and ability to carry it out. Such an emphasis on the cosmic scope of God's power fits with the emphasis of the prayer in Ephesians 1 on the surpassing greatness of his power and the concerns of Paul's readers, who continue to entertain questions about the power of the gods, goddesses, and spirits they formerly worshiped.

To him who is able to do immeasurably more than all we ask or imagine (3:20). In an emotive outburst of praise at the conclusion of the prayer, Paul once again highlights the superabundance of God's power. The overt emphasis on the enabling power of God here and throughout the letter likely comes to expression because Paul is addressing a group of believers on the nature of the Christian life in light of the continuing presence and hostility of the evil principalities and powers. This is a deep concern for Christians in Ephesus and Asia Minor because of the widespread influence of magic, the mysteries of underworld deities, and astrology.

Call to Unity (4:1–6)

The Lord wants his people to live together in harmony. Yet this is not a tolerance of anything. Paul has warned the Ephesian elders a few years earlier that "men will arise and distort the truth in order to draw away disciples after them" (Acts 20:30). Paul calls these people to live and work together in a unity that flows out of Christlike attitudes and a common core of beliefs.

As a prisoner of the Lord (4:1). Paul begins his appeal to unity with a reminder that he is held by chains in Rome. There is irony in the fact that the political structure known for peace (*pax romana*, "the peace of Rome") imprisoned a man for proclaiming the gospel of peace. Paul saw his true Lord as Jesus and not the Roman emperor.

I urge you (4:1). This expression actually stands first in the Greek text and marks the beginning of the second half of his letter. Paul appeals to these new believers to bring their behavior into conformity with the pure and righteous God whom they now serve.

To live a life worthy (4:1). The literal wording behind "to live" is "to walk." Throughout the Old Testament and in Jewish literature, "walking" was used to describe how a person conducted one's life. When he appealed to God to prolong his life, Hezekiah prayed, "Remember, O LORD, how I have walked before you faithfully and with wholehearted devotion and have done what is good in your eyes" (2 Kings 20:3). In Jewish tradition, *Halakah* (from the Hebrew word *hlk*, "to walk") was the set of laws and traditions governing daily life.

Humble . . . gentle . . . patient (4:2). These virtues give practical help toward the goal of maintaining unity among believers. Although Gentile philosophers and moral teachers sometimes spoke of the importance of "gentleness," they rarely, if ever, extolled "humility" and "patience." Throughout the Old Testament, God tells his people how he wants for them to have a spirit of brokenness before him (see Ps. 34:18; Isa. 66:2). The Lord Jesus himself begins his Sermon on the Mount with a call to humility (see Matt. 5:3–5): "Blessed are the poor in spirit, for theirs is the kingdom of heaven."

Make every effort to keep (4:3). Paul does not urge believers to keep working toward an ideal of unity. He assumes that it is already there by virtue of believers sharing a common experience of being united by one Spirit. The task for believers is to preserve the unity that God has given his people.

The bond of peace (4:3). Paul represents the peace that Christ supplies as a chain that ties people together. This idea may have come to Paul as he considered the way his chains bound him to his guard.

One . . . one . . . (4:4–6). The word "one" appears seven times in these three verses. The basis for unity is found in the common core of beliefs of the one church Jesus has created.

REFLECTIONS

UNITY IS IMPORTANT, BUT NOT AT any cost. This is why Paul follows his exhortation with a confession of faith. Church unity needs to be rooted in a shared commitment to the essentials of the faith. The problem we often face is in allowing personality conflicts and disputes over nonessentials to shatter the bond of peace.

One Spirit (4:4). Non-Christians living in this environment believed in many different spirits and were accustomed to making distinctions between helpful and harmful spirits. Paul is not denying the reality of the spirit realm by saying that there is only one Spirit. Rather, he is placing emphasis on the one true Spirit from God, who joins believers to the one body of Christ and indwells their lives. This is the only Spirit that they should concern themselves with now.

Who is over all and through all and in all (4:6). God, who is "over all," is sovereign over heaven, earth, and all the so-called gods and goddesses. Although on the surface, "through all and in all" may appear to be a pantheistic notion of God (he is in everything), this expression stops short of affirming the pantheistic notion of "the one God *is* the all." The wording is rooted in the Old Testament statements about the omnipotence of God over all creation (e.g., Isa. 6:3, "the whole earth is full of his glory"; see also Ps. 8:6–9).

Each Member Contributes to the Growth of the Body (4:7–16)

Jesus himself is powerfully at work in the new community uniting it, strengthening it, and enabling it to appropriate Christian virtues and resist evil influences from the world. By virtue of his exaltation to the right hand of God, Christ has bestowed spiritual giftings on his people.

To each one of us grace has been given (4:7). Whereas Paul speaks of spiritual gifts (*charismata*) in 1 Corinthians and Romans, here he refers to a special grace (*charis*) each believer receives. He created the word *charismata* on the basis of *charis* as a way of referring to the varied and specific manifestations of God's grace to each individual for serving others in the body of Christ.

This is why it says, "When he ascended on high" (4:8). As a lead-in to his discussion about spiritually gifted people, Paul cites Psalm 68:18. This is appropriate because the original setting of this psalm celebrates God's triumphant ascent of Mount Zion after delivering his people (through his earthly king). In appropriating this psalm, Paul sees Jesus as the victorious king who has vanquished his enemies through his death on the cross and his resurrection. As the victor, he now provides gifts to his people.

He led captives in his train (4:8). The captives Jesus led were the evil principalities and powers. Colossians 2:15 uses the imagery of a Roman triumphal procession to describe Jesus' victory over them by means of the cross.

[He] gave gifts to men (4:8). This passage differs from the Hebrew and Greek versions of Psalm 68:18, which read, "You received gifts from men." Paul here appears to be citing an early Aramaic version of the psalm (preserved in a Targum—a written Aramaic translation of the Old Testament) that contains "he gave." The Targum interprets the giving as a reference to Moses' giving of the law.[34]

What makes Psalm 68 all the more significant to this context is that Jews were accustomed to hearing this passage read aloud each year in their synagogues at Pentecost as a designated reading for the day. The law of Moses is no longer to be seen as the focal point and fulfillment of this psalm, but rather the incarnation (descent) and resurrection/exaltation (ascent) of Christ.

Because of Christ's ascent to the right hand of God, he could send the Holy Spirit at Pentecost to incorporate believers into the body of Christ and endow them with special abilities for the building up of the body.

He also descended to the lower, earthly regions (4:9). Although some think this refers to Christ's incarnation or his coming in the presence of the Spirit at Pentecost, it is best to understand this as a reference to the underworld (or, Hades). Christ went there following his death on the cross to proclaim his victory to the imprisoned powers of darkness (1 Peter 3:19). When Christ returns to earth, every knee will bow before him of those

EPHESUS

The 24,000-seat theater.

"in heaven and on earth *and under the earth*" (Phil. 2:10, italics added).

Pastors and teachers (4:11). In addition to the apostles, prophets, and evangelists, God gives the church pastors and teachers. The two terms stand under the same article in the Greek text and should therefore be seen as two functions of the same gifted person: a pastor/teacher. Surprisingly, this is the only time that Paul uses the word "pastor" in the New Testament. In the common language of the day, a "pastor" was a sheepherder. Jesus applied this image to himself in John 10, when he spoke of himself as "the good shepherd" (John 10:11). Paul now takes the image and applies it to those who lead and teach in the body of Christ.

To prepare God's people for works of service (4:12). The gifted leaders of the church are called primarily to help prepare the various members of Christ's body to serve one another with the overall goal of assisting each person to know Christ better and reflect his character in their lives.

Tossed back and forth by the waves (4:14). A boat in the middle of a tempest in the Mediterranean Sea was unstable and out of control—as Paul knew so well in his recent dramatic voyage to Rome. Believers not sufficiently grounded in the teachings of the Scripture and in a solid relationship with Christ are easy prey for deceitful teachers.

Every wind of teaching (4:14). Various kinds of false teachings constantly threatened the churches that Paul planted (see also Acts 20:29–30). Paul does not appear to have a specific false teaching in mind here; rather, he is seeking to immunize the Ephesians from those who will assuredly come.

The whole body, joined and held together by every supporting ligament (4:16). The proper functioning of the church is comparable to the human body. The head provides leadership, direction, and guidance to the body, but it is essential for every supporting ligament to do its part. The terminology Paul uses here for this elaborate metaphor has its roots in the medical language of the day (as can be seen in Galen, a doctor who lived in Pergamum). The image highlights the unity of the church, but also the fact that God empowers each member to contribute to the overall edification of the entire body.[35]

▶ Some False Teachings That Threatened the Churches

- **Judaizing Influences**—a group of Jewish Christians that told the Galatians they needed to be circumcised and obey certain features of the Jewish law to be saved.
- **Syncretistic Teachings**—a faction in the Colossian church that mixed Christianity with local folk beliefs.

- **Docetism**—in subsequent years at Ephesus, a faction that surfaced within the church proclaiming that Jesus did not really come in the flesh.
- **Gnosticism**—late in the first century and throughout the second, a heresy that became a serious threat to the churches in Asia Minor.

Developing a Distinctively Christian Lifestyle (4:17–24)

Christ leads his people into a different lifestyle from the environment that surrounds them.

You must no longer live as the Gentiles do (4:17). Paul makes it clear that these believers must make a clean break with the patterns of thinking and behavior that characterized their lives before they became followers of Christ. He focuses particularly on the Gentile believers because they have come from a background of worshiping false deities and leading immoral lives.

In the futility of their thinking (4:17). Jewish wisdom tradition of Paul's time viewed Gentiles as utterly foolish in the way they ignored the signs of the one true God in creation. Much of Paul's language here and in Romans 1:21–24 reflects Wisdom of Solomon 13:1: "For all people who were ignorant of God were foolish by nature; and they were unable from the good things that are seen to know the one who exists." Their empty and darkened thinking has resulted in estrangement from their Creator and the Source of all life.

The hardening of their hearts (4:18). In the Old Testament, a heart was said to be "hardened" when the will and thinking of a person had become insensitive to God and actually withstood him. "Hardness" is used repeatedly in Exodus to describe the condition of Pharaoh's heart—he hardens his own heart (e.g., Ex. 7:13, 22; 8:19; 9:35) and ultimately God hardens it (e.g., 4:21; 7:3; 14:4).

They have given themselves over to sensuality (4:19). Paul places the miserable condition of these Gentile sinners squarely on their own shoulders. They have immersed themselves in an undisciplined lifestyle of gratifying every self-oriented and unholy pleasure.

Indulge in every kind of impurity (4:19). Jews in the first century were deeply concerned about ceremonial purity—avoiding "common" or unclean foods, not touching a corpse, and keeping a variety of other purity regulations based on the Mosaic law and Jewish tradition. Paul, however, stresses only the importance of moral purity for followers of Christ. He insists that all his churches renounce the various kinds of moral impurities that were so rampant in the culture in which they lived.

You were taught ... to put off your old self ... and put on the new self (4:22–24). Paul calls these believers to a transformed life. He roots this in the fact that God has bestowed on them a new life in the Spirit—they possess a new self, a new identity. As a way of expressing the struggle between the new and the old, Paul uses the imagery of taking off and putting on clothing, a picture anyone in the ancient world—or now—can understand.

In Romans, Paul spoke of clothing oneself with the Lord Jesus Christ and not gratifying the desires of the evil inclination (i.e., the flesh) (Rom. 13:14). The same idea is present here. When someone becomes a Christian, that person is supernaturally transformed by entering a close relationship with Jesus Christ. Nevertheless, sinful tendencies remain present and believers must become in their daily lives what they truly already are in Christ. Paul urges them to get rid of sinful practices and practice virtuous behavior instead.

Being corrupted . . . made new (4:22–23). There is no middle ground of neutrality in the Christian life. Either one is succumbing to the powerful influences that cause moral corruption or one is being empowered by the Lord to appropriate righteous and pure attitudes and behavior.

Specific Moral Exhortations (4:25–5:2)

In the next portion of his letter, Paul gives concrete examples of where this renewing activity needs to take place in the lives of these Asia Minor believers. Most of these exhortations have to do with the area of social relationships. People today sometimes overglamorize the life of the early church. This passage helps bring us back to reality. The believers in these house churches struggle with lying, anger, stealing, dirty talk, hard feelings, and even bitterness. There is nothing here that is unique to the churches of Asia Minor. These are tendencies that Christians everywhere have had to deal with.

Do not let the sun go down while you are still angry (4:26). The Old Testament designates sunset as the time limit for a number of items, such as paying the wages of a day laborer (Deut. 24:15). Throughout the Old and New Testaments, anger is viewed as something to be avoided, if at all possible. James, for example, urges believers to "be slow to become angry."[36] The quotation from Psalm 4:4 used here in Ephesians 4:28 does not give permission to vent anger, but cautions that when it comes, one should get a handle on it quickly.

Jewish tradition, as expressed in the Dead Sea Scrolls, encouraged community members not to let anger spill over into the next day in any case of discipline: "They shall rebuke each man his brother according to the commandment and shall bear no rancor from one day to the next" (CD 7:2–3).[37] Even non-Christian Greeks living in the first century understood the danger of allowing anger to continue unabated—even overnight. Plutarch writes, "We should next pattern ourselves after the Pythagoreans, who,

though related not at all by birth, yet sharing a common discipline, if ever they were led by anger into recrimination, never let the sun go down before they joined right hands, embraced each other, and were reconciled."[38]

Do not give the devil a foothold (4:27). The term "foothold" (*topos*) could refer to a "chance" or "opportunity," but in line with the use of spatial language throughout Ephesians it is probably better to understand it in the sense of "space" for the operation of an evil spirit. The same word appears in the teaching of Jesus to refer to a spirit looking for a place to go: "When an evil spirit comes out of a man, it goes through arid places seeking rest [*topos*, i.e., a resting place] and does not find it. Then it says, 'I will return to the house I left'" (Luke 11:24). First-century Judaism saw anger as a magnet that attracts the working of an evil spirit: "Anger and falsehood together are a double-edged evil, and work together to perturb the reason. And when the soul is continually perturbed, the Lord withdraws from it and Beliar rules it."[39]

Do not grieve the Holy Spirit of God (4:30). The Holy Spirit does not leave a believer, but the Spirit may be grieved by sinful behavior and what influence the Spirit had is quenched (cf. 1 Thess. 5:19).

Live a life of love, just as Christ loved us and gave himself up for us (5:2). The high point and foundation of all Christian ethics is love, patterned on the example of Christ's sacrificial death. While it is true that the Greek word *agapaō* is used in this passage (versus *eroō* or *phileō*) there is no example of this magnitude of love in all of Greek literature.

It is not the word that is important, it is the example.

Darkness and Light (5:3–14)

But among you there must not be even a hint of sexual immorality (5:3). Sexual immorality (Paul here uses the word *porneia*) was an enormous problem in the early church among the Gentiles. Adulterous relationships, men sleeping with their slave girls, incest, prostitution, "sacred" sexual encounters in the local temples, and homosexuality were all a part of everyday life in that culture. There was no pervasive social standard with regard to sexual relations. Jews had long been appalled at the behavior of the Gentiles in this regard and considered them "impure." The Mishnah even prohibits a Jewish woman from ever being left alone with a Gentile because he cannot be trusted sexually.[40] The word *porneia* is a broad term covering all kinds of illicit sexual behavior, not just fornication or premarital sex. The term is used abundantly in Jewish literature written in Greek with reference to sexual sin of all kinds.[41]

Obscenity, foolish talk, or coarse joking (5:4). Not only are Christians called to a high standard of sexual purity, they are urged not to cheapen and demean sexuality by making it the topic of crude

REFLECTIONS

TELEVISION TALK SHOWS, SIT-COMS, and call-in radio have majored in the kind of coarse humor that Paul cautions us to avoid. Our "old selves" are drawn to this form of entertainment, but it is destructive to our souls.

jokes, as so often happened in Gentile society. Paul uses three colorful words here—not found in the Old Testament, but from the context of Gentile moral exhortation. The only proper way to respond to God for sexuality is to practice it in the right context and give thanks to him for this wonderful gift.

Such a man is an idolater (5:5). Ephesus and its environs abounded with idolatry—the worship of the images of gods and goddesses in place of the one true God. Here Paul takes idolatry a step further by associating it with sexual immorality and the greedy pursuit of wealth. This is not an innovation with Paul, for other Jewish writers had made this connection: "My children, love of money leads to idolatry, because once they are led astray by money, they designate as gods those who are not gods";[42] "The sin of promiscuity is the pitfall of life, separating man from God and leading on toward idolatry, because it is the deceiver of the mind and the perceptions."[43] Philo sharply criticized the "money lovers" who would "procure gold and silver coins from every side and treasure their hoard like a divine image in a sanctuary, believing it to be a source of blessing and happiness of every kind."[44]

Let no one deceive you with empty words (5:6). Paul is not thinking here of a group of heretics, but simply of unbelievers who attempt to justify their immoral behavior and pull these new Christians back into an improper lifestyle.

You were once darkness but now you are light (5:8). Darkness and light were images commonly used in all ancient religions. The image is especially prominent in an entire document of the Dead Sea Scrolls that speaks of an impending end-time battle between "the sons of light" (the faithful covenant people of God) and "the sons of darkness" (the devil, his angels, and all of God's human enemies).

Paul shows frequent indebtedness to the book of Isaiah, however, and light-darkness imagery is also prominent there. The Lord says through the prophet: "Arise, shine, for your light has come. . . . See, darkness covers the earth and thick darkness is over the peoples, but the LORD rises upon you and his glory appears over you. . . . The LORD will be your everlasting light" (Isa. 60:1–2, 19). Paul describes one's coming to Christ as a radical change of identity—from darkness to light, from the kingdom of darkness to the kingdom of light. There are echoes here of the teaching of Jesus as represented in John's Gospel: "I am the light of the world. Whoever follows me will never walk in darkness, but will have the light of life" (John 8:12).

"Wake up, O sleeper, rise from the dead, and Christ will shine on you" (5:14).

Paul introduces this quotation in the same way he introduces a citation from the Old Testament (see 4:8), yet this is not a verse from the Old Testament. What is he then quoting? Most likely he is citing oral tradition that was passed on in the early church—here from the context of Christian worship and exhortation.[45] Unfortunately, we have no means of verifying this conclusion since no written texts of first-century Christian liturgy have survived (if they were ever even written down). The essence of this passage is to admonish believers to be morally vigilant and deal with the problem of sin, receiving the grace of Christ to help them in their struggle.

Wise and Spirit-Filled Living (5:15–20)

As wise (5:15). Paul commends to these believers the vast Old Testament teaching about wisdom, especially as represented by the books of Proverbs and Ecclesiastes. There they can find ethical insight into God's will.

Do not get drunk on wine (5:18). Wine and drunkenness were central features of the worship of Dionysus (also known as Bacchus).[46] In the frenzied and ecstatic Dionysiac rituals, intoxication with wine was tantamount to being filled with the spirit of Dionysus. It is therefore conceivable that some of the new believers in Asia Minor were carrying this form of worship with them into the church by associating wine with the filling of the Holy Spirit. Paul repudiates such a notion by denouncing drunkenness and associating the filling of the Spirit with other activities. The problem of drunkenness, however, went far beyond the practices of one cult. It was a societal problem.

Paul's comments on drunkenness denounce intoxication for any reason.

Be filled with the Spirit (5:18). The coming and presence of the Holy Spirit fulfill the Old Testament promise concerning the new covenant and the future messianic age of blessing.[47] The followers of Jesus were "filled with the Holy Spirit" on the day of Pentecost (Acts 2:4), and Peter proclaimed this as the fulfillment of expectation. The Spirit is constantly present with believers, but Paul here urges a regular appropriation of the Spirit's power. The following context suggests some of the means by which believers receive a fuller manifestation of the Spirit's presence in their lives.

◄

DIONYSUS

The god is leaning on a satyr while holding a column adorned with grapes and the god Pan. Cupids are at his feet.

Psalms, hymns, and spiritual songs (5:19). The three terms that Paul chooses here—*psalmos*, *hymnos*, and *ōdē*—stress the variety of forms of music in the early church. All three words occur in the LXX of Psalms, but *psalmos* is particularly at home in a Jewish context. *Hymnos* was a term used extensively by Gentiles in their pagan worship; they were accustomed to singing *hymnoi* in praise of their gods and goddesses. There are many papyrus examples of hymns sung in honor of Isis, Asclepius, "The Great Mother," Apollo, and many other deities. Verses of hymns were sung every morning at the entrance of the temple of Asclepius. Choruses of hymn singers customarily sang words of praise to Apollo at his temple at Claros, just north of Ephesus.[48] For Christians, it is not the musical form that is important, it is the object of worship. Christians worship the one true God and the Lord Jesus Christ.

Husbands and Wives (5:21–33)

This passage marks the beginning of a set of instructions to various members of the Christian household (see "Household Duties" at 1 Peter 2:11). Paul addresses husbands and wives, parents and children, and slaves and masters. His most extensive remarks have to do with marriage. Male and female relationships fell far short of the mark of God's ideal in antiquity.

Submit to one another. . . . Wives, submit to your husbands (5:21–22). In a first-century context, to "submit" (*hypatassō*) is a word for order that was used to designate role relationships in various kinds of social structures. In contrast to the word "obey" (*hypakouō*), "submit" implies a voluntary yielding to one who has authority in a leadership structure. Submission is thus used in contexts where soldiers follow their commanders, members of the church yield to their leaders (see 1 Peter 3:5), and all people to the governing authorities of the state (see Rom. 13:1).

LYRE

This Jewish coin dates to A.D. 134–135, the year of the Bar Kochba revolt in Judea. The lyre may be reminiscent of those used in the Jerusalem temple ceremonies.

▶Josephus and Philo on Marriage

First-century Jewish writers Josephus and Philo provide insight into some common Jewish attitudes about the wife's responsibility in marriage. Both stress blind obedience (versus submission) and say nothing of a husband's responsibility to love and serve his wife:

> For saith the Scripture, "A woman is inferior to her husband in all things" [in reality, there is no such verse anywhere in the Old Testament]. Let her, therefore, be obedient to him; not so that he should abuse her, but that she may acknowledge her duty to her husband; for God hath given the authority to the husband.[A-3]

> Wives must be in servitude to their husbands, a servitude not imposed by violent treatment but promoting obedience in all things.[A-4]

> ▶ **Aemilius Paulus and Papiria**
>
> The absence of the kind of love Paul describes as essential in marriage is well illustrated by the attitude of Aemelius Paulus toward his wife, as told by Florence Dupont:
>
> > Aemilius Paullus had married Papiria, daughter of a former consul. Papiria was the perfect wife and gave her husband two sons, both of whom proved exceptional men.... Socially, Papiria was everything that was expected of her: she was beautiful, virtuous and fertile. Aemelius Paullus, however, decided to divorce her. "Why?" he was asked. "Is she not discreet? Is she not beautiful? Is she not fruitful?" Aemelius Paullus then held out his shoe, saying: "Is this not handsome? Is it not new? But not one of you can see where it pinches my foot." So he married another woman.[A-5]

In the first occurrence, Paul takes the dramatic step of enjoining a mutual submission. This flows out of the teaching of Jesus, who calls his disciples to serve one another and resist the temptation to "lord it over" each other (Mark 10:42–45). Elsewhere, Paul encourages believers to defer to the needs and interests of others by considering fellow believers even more highly than they consider themselves (Phil. 2:2–3). This involves subduing pride and self-oriented pursuits.

Nevertheless, Paul does not eliminate the social structuring of submission. He clearly maintains a role distinction between men and women in the marriage relationship and expects the man to assume a role of leadership. Yet Paul carefully qualifies the kind of leadership the husband is to provide.

The husband is the head of the wife as Christ is the head of the church (5:23). Paul has already used head-body imagery twice in this letter to describe the role of Christ in relationship to the church (see comments on 1:22–23 and 4:16). Here he applies the imagery to the role of the husband in the marriage relationship. Just as Christ provides leadership to the church and is its principal source of provision, the husband is called to the same function on behalf of his wife.

Husbands, love your wives, just as Christ loved the church and gave himself up for her (5:25). The kind of leadership the husband should exert is not defined by the prevailing cultural trends, but by the example of Christ himself. Above all the husband's leadership is governed by a self-sacrificial love. This admonition to the men flew in the face of many heavy-handed and demeaning attitudes of men toward their wives in antiquity—both in Judaism and in Greco-Roman culture (see "Josephus and Philo On Marriage" and "Aemelius Paulus and Papiria").

The washing with water (5:26). Paul is alluding here to the image of a marital covenant that Yahweh entered with Jerusalem. The Lord told his people, "'I gave you my solemn oath and entered into a covenant with you', declares the Sovereign LORD, 'and you became mine. I bathed you with water and washed the blood from you ... you became very beautiful and rose to be a queen'" (Ezek. 16:8–13). The church is not cleansed by literal water (although there may be an allusion to baptism here); rather, the effective factor for salvation is the Word of God, the gospel, rooted in the blood of Christ that cleanses believers from all sin.

He feeds and cares for it (5:29). Both of these words appear in a papyrus marriage contract that delineates the husband's responsibilities for his wife: "to cherish and nourish and clothe her."[49]

This is a profound mystery (5:32). Paul is not referring to marriage as a deep mystery (and thus to marriage as a sacrament) or even mystery as it was used in the mystery religions of the area. The *mystery* he speaks of here is the intimate relationship of Christ to the church. This is consistent with his usage of this term throughout the letter (1:9; 3:3, 4, 9; 6:19), where it always speaks of something concealed that God has now revealed in Christ.

Children and Parents (6:1–4)

Children, obey your parents in the Lord (6:1). This command upholds the household authority structure common in the ancient world. In Jewish homes as well as Roman or Greek families, it was taken for granted that children should respond to their parents with total obedience. The distinctive contribution of this passage is that children are given an added incentive. The Lord himself expects children to have an attitude of obedience to parents. This is proper and essential for a Christian household.

Honor your father and mother (6:2). Paul now cites the fifth of the ten commandments to provide further support and perspective on children's obedience to their parents (Ex. 20:12; Deut. 5:16). Honoring and respecting parents was a social expectation that cut across all cultures in first-century society. In Gentile circles, honoring one's parents is regarded as important as honoring the gods. In Judaism, the fifth commandment is upheld by many writers, especially the wisdom literature. Note, for example, Sirach 3:8–11:

> Honor your father by word and deed,
>   that a blessing from him may come
>   upon you. . . .
> Do not glorify yourself by dishonoring
>   your father,
>   for your father's dishonor is no
>   glory to you.
> The glory of one's father is one's own
>   glory,
>   and it is a disgrace for children not
>   to respect their mother.

The first commandment with a promise (6:2). "Honor your father and mother" is the first of the Ten Commandments that treats human relationships (following the first four, which deal with one's relationship to God). It is also the only one of the ten that specifically has a promise attached to it.

Fathers, don't exasperate your children (6:4). In the exercise of authority and discipline, fathers are called to exercise sensitivity and moderation. This is consistent with the advice of some other ancient writers. The Greek writer Menander, for instance, says, "A father who is always threatening does not receive much reverence," and "One should correct a child by not hurting him but persuading him." Another writer cautions, "Do not be harsh with your children but be gentle."[50]

The training and instruction of the Lord (6:4). The ultimate responsibility for nurturing the children in the Christian faith lies with the father. He needs to pass on to them the apostolic tradition about Christ and his kingdom and help mold his children's lives into conformity with the will of God.

Slaves and Masters (6:5–9)

Slavery in the Roman world differed significantly from slavery in the New World. Yet slaves in antiquity were still considered possessions over which the owner had powerful rights. Centuries earlier, Aristotle could say, "A slave is a man's chattel" and "a living tool."[51] Given the fact that one-third or more of the population consisted of slaves, fifteen to twenty people in a house church of forty-five may have been slaves. In this passage, Paul assumes that slaves are full members of the church and share equally with their masters in all of the blessings of new life in Christ.

Obey your earthly masters (6:5). At this time and in this letter, Paul does not challenge the social order with respect to the institution of slavery, but gives perspective on how Christian slaves can live out their faith within this Roman social structure.

Like slaves of Christ (6:6). Paul clarifies that their allegiance and ownership does not lie ultimately with their human masters, but with Christ himself. They belong to him and are obligated to serve him.

Serve wholeheartedly (6:7). Some ancient writers spoke of "wholehearted service" or "enthusiasm" (*eunoia*) as a virtue for slaves.[52] One second-century A.D. papyrus even refers to a number of slaves who were set free because of their enthusiasm and affection in serving their master.[53]

Do not threaten them (6:9). Close to the same time that Paul was writing this letter, a Roman lawyer named Gaius Cassius Longinus addressed the Roman senate seeking retribution on the slaves of a former consul who was murdered by one of his slaves in his own home. Longinus cannot believe that the man's other slaves knew nothing of the plot or did anything to stop the murder. He pleads, "the only way to keep down this scum is

---

▶ Why There Wasn't a Massive Slave Revolt in the First Century

There is no evidence in ancient literature of a slave rebellion with the abolition of slavery as its goal. Why? Not only was Roman-era slavery a nonracial institution (there were slaves of all races), but most slaves could reasonably expect emancipation by the time they reached thirty years of age. Nor was the work of a slave limited to hard labor; slaves worked in a variety of different occupations—including household management, teaching, business, and industry—and many even owned property. Because of the poverty of many free laborers, the economic and living conditions of slaves were often far better. This led many free laborers to sell themselves into slavery as a means of economic advancement.[A-6] This is not to say that slavery was essentially an ungodly structure that deprived a person of freedom and dignity. It is simply to affirm that Roman era slavery did not share all of the same features of New World slavery that would ignite a rebellion.

▶ # The Story of the Ephesian Wrestler

An ancient writer named Pausanias relates an interesting and relevant parable about an Ephesian wrestler who traveled to Olympia, Greece, to compete in the games. The athlete was unbeateable in the wrestling event, winning match after match. During one of the competitions, however, the referee discovered he was wearing an anklet inscribed with the six Ephesian Grammata—the magical words invoking spiritual powers. This was immediately removed, whereupon his opponent from Miletus proceeded to three consecutive victories over him because of his loss of magical power.[A-7]

by intimidation."[54] Certainly not all Roman slave owners had this attitude or threatened their slaves. Jewish slave owners were in fact warned against undue severity.[55]

There is no favoritism with him (6:9). Paul reminds the wealthy slave owners that they will curry no special favor with God based on their social status. God is impartial and defers to no one according to social position. The Torah reveals that "the LORD your God is God of gods and Lord of lords, the great God, mighty and awesome, who shows no partiality" (Deut. 10:17).

Spiritual Warfare (6:10–20)

Paul says more about the struggle believers have with the evil supernatural realm here than anywhere else in his other letters. This may be due in large measure to the fact that most of these believers came to the Lord from a background in magic, astrology, witchcraft, goddess worship, and various mystery cults. Paul now prepares these believers for resisting the ongoing hostile work of the powers of darkness.

Be strong in the Lord (6:10). The emphasis of this command lies not with the verbal form of *dynamis* ("be strong"), but on "in the Lord." The people of this area are well aware of spiritual power, but they have been accustomed to receiving it from the wrong means— through helper spirits, incantations, rituals, formulas, and calling on their gods and goddesses. God desires to strengthen his people through a dynamic relationship to the Lord Jesus Christ.

Put on the full armor of God (6:11). Paul elaborates on his admonition to "be strong in the Lord" by using the imagery of the armor of God. The word that he uses for "full armor" (*panoplia*) never appears in the Old Testament, but it is used in Jewish wisdom literature.[56] Interpreters have often looked to the Roman soldier and his gear as the background for Paul's delineation of the six elements in the armor listed in 6:14–17. Yet each of the elements Paul lists is found in the Old Testament, especially in the book of Isaiah (see the chart).[57] It is also conspicuous that Paul does not mention weapons typically used by Roman soldiers, such as the heavy javelin (*pilum*) and greaves (leg armor).[58] It is important not to overinterpret the metaphors, but rather focus on the spiritual gifts and virtues associated with them.

So that you can take your stand (6:11). Forms of the verb "stand" appear four times in the next four verses. Paul stresses

the fact that there is a supernatural being who is bent on promoting the demise of God's people.

Our struggle (6:12). Paul shifts the image from warfare to wrestling. Wrestling (*palē*) was a popular event in the games held in Ephesus, Smyrna, Pergamum, and all over Asia Minor. This image communicates more of the directness of the struggle.

Against the powers of this dark world (6:12). For his third expression in this list of powers (see comments on 1:21), Paul uses a word that appears nowhere else in the New Testament or the LXX—the term *kosmokratores* (lit. trans., "world powers"). The word does appear, however, in the Greek magical papyri (used

◄

ARMOR

Model reconstructions of a Roman breastplate and sword.

Spiritual Warfare Imagery		
Image	Background	Spiritual Weapon
1. Belt . . . buckled around your waist	Isa. 11:5	Truth
2. Breastplate	Isa. 59:17	Righteousness
3. Feet fitted	Isa. 52:7	Gospel of peace
4. Shield	(Isa. 21:5; Ps. 35:2) —23 times in the Old Testament	Faith
5. Helmet	Isa. 59:17	Salvation
6. Sword	(Isa. 49:2) —178 times in the Old Testament	Spirit/Word of God Prayer

of the gods Helios, Ra, Hermes, and Sarapis), some astrological texts (used of the planets), and a Roman inscription, where it refers to the gods Sarapis and Mithras.[59] The term is also used in a Jewish magical text, where it refers to the astral-demonic powers of the zodiac, who afflict people in a variety of ways.[60] The word is therefore known both to Gentile and Jewish readers. It is possible that Paul intends this word to be understood as his interpretation of the Ephesian Artemis and the other gods and goddesses worshiped in that city. Far from being beneficial or helpful deities, they should be regarded as evil spirits of "this dark world" (see also 1 Cor. 10:20).

When the day of evil comes (6:13). The Old Testament prophets anticipated a period of evil that they spoke of as "the day of disaster."[61] Apocalyptic Judaism spoke frequently of the evil character of the last days. Paul also speaks in these terms, but understands this time to be now. He speaks of "the present evil age" (Gal. 1:4) and encourages the Ephesians to redeem the time "because the days are evil" (Eph. 5:16). Although he still anticipates a time when Christ will return in judgment and wrath—"the day of the Lord," the present days are filled with evil and are a time of struggle and conflict

right ▶

ARMOR

An Ephesian monument of a soldier with a helmet, shield, boots, and a sword.

with the demonic.[62] The singular "day of evil" probably refers to particular periods within this time when demonic attack, manifestations of evil, and temptation are unusually strong.

With which you can extinguish all of the flaming arrows of the evil one (6:16). Flammable arrows were common and effective weapons in antiquity. They were used by Israelites and other Middle Easterners (see Ps. 7:13), Greeks, and Romans. The arrows typically had a clump of fiber attached near the point that had been dipped in pitch and set on fire. According to the Greek historian Thucydides (2.75.5), wooden shields were sometimes coated in leather and soaked in water before a battle so that they could not be ignited and could effectively subdue flaming arrows. The image of the devil hurling fiery arrows at God's servants is reminiscent of his angry opposition to the Seventy as they were

REFLECTIONS

HOW DOES ONE PUT ON THE ARMOR OF GOD? THE corporate dimension of the passage and the way Paul reflects on the role of prayer—not only here, but also in Ephesians 1 and 3—suggest that a key part of spiritual warfare is in joining other Christians in praying for each other. Just as a soldier would need help in putting on his armor, we are called to arm each other through prayer. This passage sets an agenda for small group prayer times!

sent by Jesus on a mission. Jesus said, "I saw Satan fall like lightning from heaven" (Luke 10:18).

I am an ambassador in chains (6:20). Paul reminds the readers that he is bound as a prisoner in Rome.

Pray that I may declare it fearlessly (6:20). Twice at the end of this spiritual warfare passage Paul asks these dear believers to pray for God to make him bold in declaring the gospel. Although we are not accustomed to thinking of the apostle Paul as capable of intimidation, it appears that he may have some fear and a loss of nerve that he attributes to the work of the evil one through his circumstances in Rome. Paul does not hesitate to ask his fellow believers to intercede in prayer for him.

Personal Remarks and Closing (6:21–24)

Paul concludes his letter in the most personal of touches. He indicates that he will send his trusted colleague Tychicus to fill the Ephesians in on his circumstances. He draws his letter to an end by prayerfully wishing for them a manifestation of God's peace, love, and grace.

Tychicus (6:21). Tychicus is one of Paul's missionary colleagues with him in Rome as he writes this letter. According to Acts, Tychicus was from the province of Asia, which may very well mean that he was actually from Ephesus.[63] He is not mentioned in the account of Paul's ministry in Ephesus (Acts 19) nor did he accompany Paul on his harrowing sea voyage to Rome. This means he probably journeyed from Ephesus to Rome specifically to help Paul. Paul's warm description of him as "a dear brother and faithful servant in the Lord" indicates that the Lord has used him to encourage Paul in his difficult circumstances. Now out of his concern for the Asia Minor Christians, Paul sends Tychicus back home to Asia Minor, where he will deliver the letter to the Colossians (see Col. 4:7) and this letter to the Ephesians.

ANNOTATED BIBLIOGRAPHY

Arnold, Clinton E. *Power and Magic: The Concept of Power in Ephesians*. Grand Rapids: Baker, 1997 (formerly titled *Ephesians: Power and Magic*; originally published as SNTSMS 63; Cambridge: Cambridge Univ. Press, 1989).

This is a detailed background study of Ephesians focusing on the theme of power and spirit powers. The book highlights and explains the relevance of the local occultism, magical practices, astrology, and the cult of the Ephesian Artemis (Diana) for explaining the emphasis on the power of God and spiritual warfare in Ephesians.

Bruce, F. F. *The Epistles to the Colossians, to Philemon, and to the Ephesians*. NICNT. Grand Rapids: Eerdmans, 1984.

As always, Bruce provides helpful commentary on each passage with useful historical background information.

Lincoln, Andrew T. *Ephesians*. WBC 42. Dallas: Word, 1990.

This five-hundred-page volume is one of the best detailed commentaries available on Ephesians. There are abundant historical and cultural insights scattered throughout this commentary.

Moritz, Thorsten. *A Profound Mystery: The Use of the Old Testament in Ephesians*. NovTSup 85. Leiden: Brill, 1996.

An outstanding study of the use of the Old Testament throughout Ephesians.

O'Brien, Peter T. *Ephesians*. PNTC. Grand Rapids: Eerdmans, 1999.

This is the best all-around commentary on Ephesians.

Snodgrass, Klyne. *Ephesians*. NIVAC. Grand Rapids: Zondervan, 1996.

Snodgrass does an excellent job of interpreting Ephesians and discerning the implications of the text for contemporary life.

Stott, John R. W. *The Message of Ephesians*. The Bible Speaks Today. Downers Grove: InterVarsity, 1979.

In finding a commentary on Ephesians that combines exegetical insight with good application, it is hard to beat the work of John Stott.

CHAPTER NOTES

Main Text Notes

1. Strabo 14.1.24.
2. Josephus, *Ant.* 14.10.11–12 §§223–27; 14.10.25 §§262–64.
3. See Richard E. Oster, "Ephesus As a Religious Center Under the Principate, I. Paganism Before Constantine," *ANRW* 2.18.3 (1990): 1661–726.
4. See James Walters, "Egyptian Religions in Ephesus," in *Ephesos: Metropolis of Asia* (HTS 41; Valley Forge, Pa.: Trinity Press International, 1995): 281–309.
5. Antipater, *Anthologia Graeca* 9.58.
6. See C. E. Arnold, "Magic," *DPL*, 580–83; idem, "Magic and Astrology," *DLNT*, 701–5.
7. See "Adoption," *OCD*[3], s.v.
8. See Dan. 2:18, 19, 27–30, 47.
9. See Dan. 2:28, 29, 45.
10. See R. Schippers, "Seal," *NIDNTT*, 3:497.
11. Herodotus 2.113; *3 Macc.* 2:29–30.
12. 1QS 2:3.
13. See *1 En.* 6:7–8; 61:10; *2 En.* 20:1; *T. Levi* 3:8; *T. Sol.* 3:6; 20:15; *3 Bar.* 12:3; *T. Ab.* 13:10 (shorter recension).
14. *PGM* 61.2; CI.52; 7:580–90.
15. See Dan. 2:44; 7:14, 18, 27.
16. Cf. Ezek. 44:4; also Isa. 6:1; Hag. 2:7.
17. Dan. 10:13, 20–21; 12:1.
18. Matt. 9:34; 12:24; Mark 3:22; Luke 11:15; John 12:31; 14:30; 16:11.
19. *PGM* CI.39.
20. *T. Benj.* 3:4.
21. The best explanation of this can be found in W. D. Davies, *Paul and Rabbinic Judaism. Some Rabbinic Elements in Pauline Theology* (3d ed.; London: SPCK, 1970 [originally published in 1948]), ch. 2: "The Old Enemy: The Flesh and Sin," 17–35.
22. See Deut. 5:10; 7:9, 12; Ps. 89:28.
23. *T. Ab.* 13:1–14. See also *4 Ezra* 9:7 and 13:23.
24. *m.* ʾ*Abot* 2:8 (Danby, 448).

25. Gen. 15:7–21; 17:1–21; 26:2–5; 28:13–15; Ex. 24:1–8; 2 Sam. 7.
26. Josephus, *J.W.* 5.5.2 §§193–94; 6.2.4 §§124–26; *Ant.* 15.11.5 §417.
27. One complete tablet written in Greek is on display in the Archaeological Museum in Istanbul, Turkey. Half of another is housed in the Rockefeller Museum in Jerusalem.
28. An English translation is given and discussed in Barrett, *Background*, 53 (no. 50). See also the discussions in Douglas R. Edwards, "-Gentiles, Court of the," *ABD* 2.963; Schürer, *History*, 2.222.
29. See "Temple Foundation Stone Discovered," *Christianity Today* 36 (May 18, 1992): 52.
30. Josephus, *Ant.* 15.11.1 §380; 20.9.7 §§219–23.
31. 1 Cor. 2:6–8; cf. Luke 22:3; John 13:27.
32. Mark 2:40; see also Matt. 9:18; 15:25.
33. See *PGM* 4.964–74, 979–85.
34. For the Aramaic text and translation as well as an in-depth discussion, see W. Hall Harris III, *The Descent of Christ. Ephesians 4:7–11 and Traditional Hebrew Imagery* (AGJU 32; Leiden: Brill, 1996), 65, 97.
35. For further details, see Clinton E. Arnold, "Jesus Christ: 'Head' of the Church," in *Jesus of Nazareth: Lord and Christ. Essays on the Historical Jesus and New Testament Christology*, eds. M. M. B. Turner and J. B. Green (Grand Rapids: Eerdmans, 1994), 346–66.
36. James 1:19–20; see also Prov. 15:1, 18; 22:24; 29:11; Eccl. 7:9.
37. Translation from G. Vermes, *The Complete Dead Sea Scrolls in English* (New York: Penguin Press, 1997), 132.
38. Plutarch, *Moralia* 488c (as cited in Lincoln, *Ephesians*, 302).
39. *T. Dan* 4:7.
40. *m. ʿAbod. Zar.* 2.1.
41. See, e.g., *T. Reu.* 1.6; 2.1; 3.3; 4.6; 5.1, 3; 6.1; *T. Sim.* 5.3; *T. Iss.* 7.2.
42. *T. Jud.* 19:1.
43. *T. Reu.* 4:6.
44. Philo, *Spec. Laws* 1.23.
45. See R. P. Martin, "Hymns, Hymn Fragments, Songs, Spiritual Songs," *DPL*, 419–23.
46. See Albert Heinrichs, "Dionysus," *OCD*, 479–82; Walter Burkert, *Ancient Mystery Cults* (Cambridge, Mass.: Harvard Univ. Press, 1987), 109–11.
47. Isa. 32:15; 44:3; Ezek. 36:25–27; 39:28–29; Joel 2:28–29.
48. See Ramsay MacMullen, *Paganism in the Roman Empire* (New Haven, Conn.: Yale Univ. Press, 1981), 15–18.
49. The text is quoted in Best, *Ephesians*, 550.
50. Cited in Lincoln, *Ephesians*, 406 (Menander as quoted in Stobaeus, *Anthologia* 4.26.7, 13; Ps.-Phocylides 207).
51. Aristotle, *Eth. Nic.* 5.1134b, 8.1161b.
52. See the texts cited in Lincoln, *Ephesians*, 422.
53. P.Oxy. 494.6.
54. Tacitus, *Ann.* 14.44
55. Sir. 4:30; 7:20; 33:31.
56. See Wisd. Sol. 5:17–20.
57. See Thorsten Moritz, *A Profound Mystery. The Use of the Old Testament in Ephesians* (NovTSup 85; Leiden: Brill, 1996), 178–212.
58. See Jonathan C. N. Coulston, "Arms and Armour (Roman)," in *OCD*[3], 174.
59. See Arnold, *Power and Magic*, 65–68.
60. *T. Sol.* 8:2; 18:2.
61. Jer. 17:17–18; Obad. 13.
62. 1 Cor. 1:8; 5:5; 1 Thess. 5:2.
63. The Western text of Acts (codex D) specifically adds that he was an Ephesian.

Sidebar and Chart Notes

A-1. From Manilius 1.25–112, as cited in Georg Luck, *Arcana Mundi* (Baltimore: John's Hopkins Univ. Press, 1985), 325.
A-2. Plutarch, *Quaest. conv.* 7.5.
A-3. Josephus, *Ag. Ap.* 2.25 §201.
A-4. Philo, *Hypothetica* 7.3.
A-5. Florence Dupont, *Daily Life in Ancient Rome* (Oxford: Blackwell, 1989), 114. The original source is Plutarch, *Aemilius Paullus* 5.
A-6. On slavery in the Roman world, see S. Scott Bartchy, "Slavery," in *ABD*, 6:65–73 and his book, *MALLON CHRESAI: First Century Slavery and the Interpretation of 1 Cor 7:21* (SBLDS 11; Missoula, Mont., 1973 [repr. 1985]).
A-7. Pausanias as cited in Eustathius, *Comm. ad Hom.* 19.247. The account is also cited in The Suda.

PHILIPPIANS

by Frank Thielman

First Century Philippi

In Paul's time Philippi was an important city in the Roman province of Macedonia. It was located on a fertile plain in the highlands about ten miles northwest of the port city Neapolis (modern Kavalla in northern Greece), and the Via Egnatia—the primary road linking Italy with Asia—ran through the city. After the Romans conquered Macedonia at the Battle of Pydna in 167 B.C. they divided it into four districts.[1] Philippi was located in the first of these districts and probably contended with Amphipolis (the district's capital) and Thessalonica for the coveted title of "leading city" of its region.[2]

Mark Anthony and Octavian designated Philippi a Roman colony and enlarged its territory after their defeat of Brutus and Cassius in a famous battle fought on the plains and hills surrounding the city in 42 B.C.[3] From that time the city and its surrounding regions became a favorite location for settling Roman soldiers whose term of service in the

PHILIPPI

▶ **Philippians**
IMPORTANT FACTS:

■ **AUTHOR:** Paul (with Timothy).

■ **DATE:** A.D. 53 (if from Ephesus), or A.D. 62 (if from Rome).

■ **OCCASION:**
- To thank the Philippians for a gift.
- To commend Epaphroditus for completing his assigned task.
- To warn the Philippians against theological error.
- To encourage the Philippians to strive for unity.

■ **KEY THEMES:**

1. The progress of the gospel as the basis for joy despite suffering.
2. Attaining Christian unity by following the selfless example of Christ.
3. A right standing with God available by faith in Christ alone.
4. Mature faith as working faith.

army had ended.[4] As a result, by Paul's time, Philippi had a decidedly Roman character. In first-century inscriptions found at the site of Philippi, Latin is the dominant tongue. Some of these inscriptions mention duumviri, aediles, and quaestors, all Roman terms for city officials—and clear evidence that in Paul's time the city was administered according to Roman custom. Moreover, the architectural remains of buildings and monuments from the first century are reminiscent of Rome: a Roman forum, Roman baths, and an arch marking the limit of the city's sacred, uncultivated area (*pomerium*).[5]

Important commercial centers, with their wide variety of influences, teemed with religious activity, and Philippi was no exception. Inscriptions from around Paul's time show the presence of a sanctuary dedicated to Dionysius (Bacchus) and other deities associated with him: Liber, Libera, and Hercules.[6] Themes of fertility often accompanied worship of Dionysius, and the Dionysian mystery cult seems to have given him a role in assuring a happy life for the dead. Women played an especially prominent role in the worship of Dionysius and his associates in Philippi.[7] Nearly eighty depictions of the goddess Diana appear in reliefs carved into the hill above Philippi, and although they come from a period after Paul, they probably reflect religious convictions current during his time. Diana was associated with fertility, childbirth, and children, typical concerns of ancient women. Most of her followers, both priestesses and devotees, seem to have been women.[8] The Thracian Horseman also appears in seven hillside reliefs. He was especially connected with the safe conduct of the soul into the afterlife.[9] In addition, archaeologists have turned up an altar dedicated to the emperor Augustus and a sanctuary dedicated to the worship of some 140 Egyptian deities.[10]

The Gospel Comes to Philippi

Into this cacophony of religious activity, Paul and his friends Silas, Timothy, and Luke brought the gospel. Taking the gospel to Philippi had not been Paul's idea. After traveling through central Asia Minor, Paul, Silas, and Timothy had wanted to continue north to Bithynia, but "the Spirit of Jesus would not allow them to" (Acts 16:7), and they had been

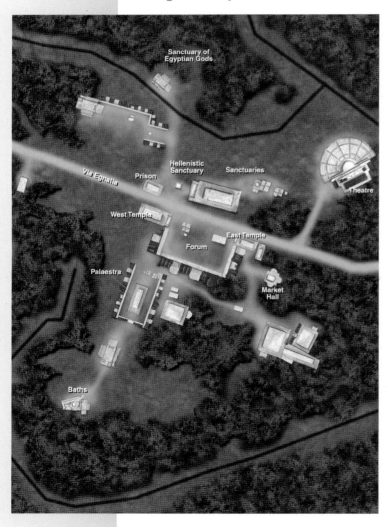

Sanctuary of Egyptian Gods

Via Egnatia

Prison

Hellenistic Sanctuary

Sanctuaries

Theatre

West Temple

East Temple

Forum

Palaestra

Market Hall

Baths

forced to turn east toward Troas. There Paul had a vision of a man from Macedonia, who begged him to "come . . . and help us" (16:9), and Paul and his friends, now accompanied by Luke, obediently went (16:10–12). Their ship from Troas landed at Neapolis, and from there they followed the Via Egnatia to Philippi.

Paul discovered no synagogue in the city, but only a place of prayer where a few women gathered to call on the name of the God of Abraham, Isaac, and Jacob. Luke tells us that this place was "outside the city gate" (Acts 16:13). Could this mean that their gathering place lay outside the sacred precincts of the Roman *pomerium*, marked by a marble arch?[11] Paul explained the gospel to the group of women gathered there, and a woman named Lydia, together with her household, believed. She must have been wealthy, for not only was she a businesswoman, but she owned a house large enough to accommodate Paul and his companions during their visit to Philippi (16:14–15).

Before long, however, storm clouds gathered over Paul's ministry in the city: The apostle angered the owners of a slave girl by exorcising her of a demon that enabled her to earn "a great deal of money for her owners" by telling fortunes (Acts 16:16–19). The enraged slaveholders dragged Paul and Silas before the city magistrates and charged them with being Jews and creating a stir by advocating "customs unlawful for us Romans to accept or practice" (16:20–21). At the

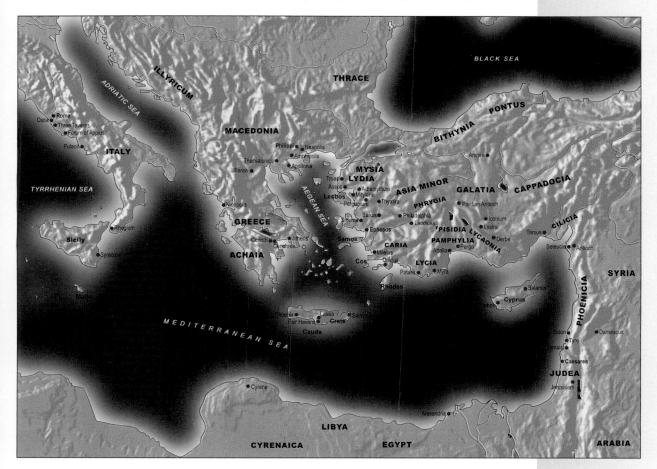

magistrates' orders, Paul and Silas were stripped, beaten, and thrown into prison (16:22). Despite the conversion of the jailer (16:31–34) and an apology to Paul from the magistrates for failing to give Roman citizens a proper trial (16:35–37), the persecution of the fledgling Philippian church continued (Phil. 1:27–30).

The Reasons for Paul's Letter

We do not know exactly where Paul was when he wrote Philippians. He was in a city large enough to have a *praetorium* or official government headquarters (Phil. 1:13, NIV, "palace guard"), but whether this was Rome, Ephesus, or Caesarea has been a matter for scholarly debate over the years. Whatever the city, however, Paul was in prison when he wrote (1:7,

13–14, 17), and he wrote in part to thank the Philippians for gifts that they had sent to him through their messenger Epaphroditus: "I am amply supplied," he says, "now that I have received from Epaphroditus the gifts you sent" (4:18; cf. 1:5; 2:25; 4:10, 14).

The Philippians' gifts and Paul's need to thank them provided a context in which to address four other concerns.

1. Paul intended to send Epaphroditus back to the Philippians earlier than they expected because he had become ill and the Philippians had become worried about him. In doing so, Paul wanted the Philippians to know that Epaphroditus had not failed in his duty, but instead deserved rich commendation, "because he almost died for the work of Christ" (2:30).

2. Paul had left a persecuted community behind after his initial visit. That persecution had continued unabated, and Paul, since he was in prison himself, wanted to provide an example to the Philippians of how a believer should respond to physical suffering and social ostracisim for the faith. He tells them, "You are going through the same struggle you saw I had, and now hear that I still have" (1:30; cf. 2:17–18; 3:17). Paul's example shows that the believer's joy should be tied to the progress of the gospel, not to physical comfort or social acceptance (1:18).

3. Paul wanted to warn the Philippians against two errors that he has seen tear apart other churches under his care: thinking that the boundaries of Christianity are defined by the Mosaic law (cf. Galatians) and that Christians who have "arrived" spiritually can do anything they like with their bodies (cf. 1 Corinthians). If the letter was written from Ephesus, the wounds created by these problems

were fresh, and Paul warned the Philippians against them in 3:1–4:1. Christianity is a matter of faith in Christ, Paul says (3:1–11), and mature Christians know that they must never rest on their laurels (3:12–4:1).

4. Paul had apparently learned from Epaphroditus that the Philippians were quarreling with one another. Paul is concerned that this may lead to a tarnished witness to the outside world where the Philippian Christians "shine like stars in the universe" (2:15; cf. 1:27; 2:1–11, 14; 4:2). In light of this, he urged the Philippians to have the mind of Christ, who in obedience to God and in service to others, humbled himself and suffered death on the cross (2:1–11).

Introduction (1:1–2)

Ancient letters typically began with the name of the sender, followed by the name of the recipient and the common salutation *charein* ("Greetings!"). Paul changes *charein* to *charis*, the Greek word for "grace," and adds the typical Jewish greeting, "peace." Such changes in the opening lines of letters were as rare in ancient times as they are today, but they were not wholly unknown. The ancient moral philosopher Epicurus (341–270 B.C.) apparently modified the openings of his letters so that they reflected his belief that pleasure was the highest of life's ideals. "Live well," he sometimes wrote in the salutation.[12] Nothing was more important to Paul, however, than the "grace of our Lord Jesus Christ" (2 Cor. 8:9) and the "peace with God" effected by that grace (Rom. 3:24–25; 5:1). Accordingly, the salutations in all thirteen of Paul's letters refer to "grace" and "peace."

Paul and Timothy (1:1). Paul couples his name with Timothy's name in this letter as he does at the beginning of five other letters (2 Corinthians, Colossians, 1 Thessalonians, 2 Thessalonians, and Philemon). Despite this, Paul alone composed the letter, as his frequent use of "I" and his

commendation of Timothy in 2:20–22 show. Why then mention Timothy at all? Perhaps Timothy served as Paul's secretary, recording the letter as Paul dictated it. *Amanuenses*, as they were called in Greek, were commonly used to compose letters at the dictation of others. In addition, Paul probably wanted the Philippians to know that his most trusted coworker ("I have no one else like him," 2:20) and their friend ("you know that Timothy has proved himself," 2:22) joined him in the expression of friendship represented by the letter and in the admonitions that Paul wanted the Philippians to hear (see "Timothy Among Paul's Coworkers," below).

Servants of Christ Jesus (1:1). The term "servants" might give the impression that Paul's metaphor refers to hired household help. Paul calls himself and Timothy not "servants" in this sense, however, but "slaves" of Christ Jesus. Like every major urban center in the Roman empire, Philippi would have had a large slave population, and the Philippians would have inevitably heard in the term "slaves" overtones of humility and submission. Is Paul modeling here the attitude of humble service that he encourages the Philippians to adopt toward one another in 2:3–4?

Overseers (1:1). Two hundred miles to the southeast of Philippi, at the southern end of the Aegean Sea, was the island of Rhodes. Here the term "overseers" was used on an inscription from the second or first century B.C. of the five community officials that formed a kind of town council. Another inscription from the island also refers to an official in the temple of Apollo as an "overseer."[13] As religious communities, it is natural that the churches Paul founded in Ephesus (Acts 20:28; 1 Tim. 3:2) and on Crete (Titus 1:7) had an analogous office of "overseer." These officials were to tend carefully the churches over whom God had placed them as stewards (1 Tim. 3:2; Titus 1:7). As part of this task, they were to take special care to keep false teachers at bay (Acts 20:28; cf. Phil. 3:1–11).

Deacons (1:1). In the city of Magnesia, an ancient Greek inscription includes a "cook" and a "deacon" among local temple officials.[14] In early Christianity too churches served meals and chose certain people from within the church to wait tables (*diakoneō*; Acts 6:1–2). The duties of these helpers must have quickly broadened to include a variety of charitable and administrative tasks—responsibilities that required deacons to be people of unblemished character (1 Tim. 3:8–13). Unlike the deacons in pagan religions, Christian deacons would have patterned their service after that of Jesus who "did not come to be served [aor. pass. inf. of *diakoneō*], but to

DIONYSUS AND ATHENA

Both deities were worshiped in Philippi.

(left) Dionysus
(right) Athena

▼

serve [aor. act. inf. of *diakoneō*], and to give his life as a ransom for many" (Mark 10:45).[15]

Thanksgiving Prayer (1:3–8)

Paul typically follows the introductions to his letters with a section in which he tells the congregation to whom he is writing why he thanks God for them. These thanksgivings briefly mention themes that Paul will develop in the course of the letter. If the Philippians had received other letters from Paul (3:1), they may have understood this characteristic of his letters and may have known to listen carefully for the letter's leading themes as Epaphroditus read the thanksgiving to them.

Your partnership from the first day until now (1:5). When Paul speaks of partnership, he is speaking of the practical hospitality and material help that the Philippians had given to him ever since he first met them. The first Philippian convert, Lydia, had invited Paul and his companions to stay at her house during their visit to the city (Acts 16:15). When Paul left Philippi and pressed westward along the Egnatian Way to Thessalonica, the Philippians more than once sent him gifts to help him in his work (Phil. 4:16). Even after he left the province of Macedonia, they and they alone continued to help him in practical ways (4:15). Although poor, they contributed generously to the collection for the saints in Jerusalem (2 Cor. 8:1–5), and they had most recently sent Paul both money and the companionship of Epaphroditus (2:25; 4:18). It is no wonder that as some Christians where Paul was imprisoned sought his harm (1:17), he longed for this beloved congregation (1:8; 4:1).

The day of Christ Jesus (1:6, 10). Some of the Philippian Christians, such as Lydia, were familiar with Judaism (Acts 16:13–14) and would have probably readily understood the Old Testament background of this phrase. For others, Paul would have explained the ideas necessary for understanding it when he first preached among the Philippians. "Christ" in Greek means "anointed one" and refers to the anointed descendant of David—the Messiah—who would sit on David's throne forever, purge God's people of wickedness, and rule justly (Isa. 9:7; Jer. 23:5–6; see "God's Righteousness in Paul's Bible," below).[16] The gospel that Paul preached in Philippi proclaimed that the Messiah was Jesus of Nazareth and that although he had been crucified, God had raised him from the dead. He was still present with his people by his Spirit (1:19) and was at work among them to make them pure and blameless for the day when he would come again (1:10).

Defending and confirming the gospel (1:7). "Defending" is a technical term for mounting a defense in court against legal accusations. "Confirming" is also a technical legal term; it refers to a legal guarantee that, for example, a piece of property to be sold has no liens against it.[17] Paul's own legal situation, as he waited in prison for trial, may have suggested this imagery to him.

Intercessory Prayer (1:9–11)

Ancient letters between friends, family members, and business associates frequently included a brief statement that the person sending the letter prayed for the prosperity and health of the recipient. In a letter from the second century A.D. a young soldier named Theonas writes home to his mother Tetheus and after the letter's introduction says, "Before all else I pray that you are well; I myself am well and make obeisance on your behalf to the gods here."[18] Another letter from a military veteran named Papirius Apollinarius to an apparent business associate greets the recipient and then assures him that Papirius bows daily on his behalf "before the lord Serapis."[19] Paul prays to the God of Abraham, Isaac, Jacob, and Christ Jesus, and, unlike prayer after prayer in ancient pagan correspondence, he prays not for the material prosperity of the Philippians or even for their physical health, but that they might know God and live in ways that please him.

Pure and blameless (1:10). Paul prays that the Philippians might have knowledge and insight, enabling them to choose what is best from the various moral options that confront them. If they do this consistently, they will be "pure" and "blameless" on the day when the Messiah returns. The term "pure" means "unmixed" and could be used in the Attic period to refer to ethnic purity. Plato, for example, speaks of being "purely Greek and without barbarian mixture."[20] Paul uses the word in a figurative way typical of the Koine period to mean "unmixed with evil."[21] The word "blameless" means similarly doing no injustice or evil, and is a quality that pious Jews of the period could use of God. It was a divine quality, said one third-century B.C. Jew, that Gentiles should seek to imitate.[22]

Paul's Circumstances (1:12–18a)

Now I want you to know (1:12). In ancient letters to friends and family a phrase similar to this sometimes marked the beginning of a section of the letter that would give the recipients the latest news of their loved one. Young soldiers separated from their families by many miles frequently wrote such letters. Theonas, for example, wrote to his mother from his military camp to let her know that he was not seriously ill, as she had mistakenly heard, but was doing well. After the standard greetings, he says, "I want you to know that the reason I have not sent you a letter for such a long time is because I am in camp and not on account of illness; so do not worry yourself about me."[23] Paul begins the section of Philippians that gives news about his own circumstances (1:12–26) in the same way. Significantly, however, this section of the letter tells more about the progress of the gospel in the midst of Paul's circumstances than about the details of his health, the conditions of his imprisonment, or his strategy for defending himself at trial. Paul's life was so wrapped up with Christ and the gospel that to give news about himself was always to say how God was at work in Paul's circumstances to advance the gospel.

What has happened to me has really served to advance the gospel (1:12). The

moral philosopher Epicurus believed that when tragedy struck, he could still be happy if he turned his mind away from his unpleasant circumstances and concentrated on pleasurable thoughts. He put this principle into action during his final illness when, in the midst of excruciating pain, he wrote letters to his disciples Idomeneus and Hermarchus. Here he tells these two followers that he is turning his thoughts away from the pain of his circumstances to the pleasure of the philosophical discussions that they all had enjoyed in more pleasant times.[24] Later in Philippians, Paul will advocate that the Philippian Christians turn from the worries of their own persecutions to the contemplation not of pleasure but of the virtues: whatever is true, noble, right, pure, lovely, admirable, excellent, and praiseworthy (4:4–8).[25] He will also tell them that they should look to him as an example to follow in doing this (4:9). In 1:12–18a he provides that example. Here Paul mentally turns aside from his imprisonment and from his enemies to concentrate on God's advancement of the gospel through these difficult circumstances.[26] Like Epicurus, Paul is mentally turning away from pain to pleasure, but Paul found pleasure in the advancement of the gospel and the glory of God (1:11–12).

The whole palace guard (1:13). The phrase "palace guard" translates the Latin loanword *praetorium*, which literally means "military headquarters." Paul gives the word a figurative meaning: "the people who work in the *praetorium*." If he wrote from Rome, he probably meant "the praetorian [or palace] guard." If he wrote from Ephesus, he meant the staff who worked in the governor's headquarters, where he was imprisoned. News of

the advancement of the gospel among the praetorians in Rome would have been especially welcome to the Philippians. Since during Paul's time the praetorians were required to come either from Italy itself or from Rome's most sympathetic colonies, some of them may have come from Philippi. The Philippian Christians knew about them and, in the midst of their own experience of persecution, must have been cheered by the news that the gospel had even advanced to this elite enclave of the Roman world.

In chains for Christ (1:13). Roman custody was of four basic types: imprisonment (with or without chains), military custody (which might include being chained to a soldier), release into the custody of a trustworthy person, and release on one's own recognizance. Paul may have been under military guard, possibly chained to a soldier. This must have been an extraordinarily uncomfortable situation, since Paul would have to ask permission from the soldier guarding him to make any significant physical movement. The Christian bishop Ignatius shows just how unfriendly such guards could be. In a letter written in the early second century while on his way from Syrian Antioch to Rome for execution, Ignatius says that he is chained night and day to "wild beasts. . .[who] become worse when treated well."[27]

Put here for the defense of the gospel (1:16). Exactly why some who preached Christ in the city of Paul's imprisonment opposed the apostle and tried to make his affliction worse remains a mystery. When Paul says that his supporters know that he is in prison "for the defense of the gospel" (1:16), he may provide a clue to the reasoning of his opponents. Ancient Roman society placed immense value on public honor, and therefore imprison-

ment was profoundly shameful. Thus, when people of honor were led to prison, they sometimes tried to cover or hide their faces and were forced to lift or expose them in order to intensify their shame.[28] It is possible that Paul's rivals considered his imprisonment shameful and an embarrassment to the gospel (cf. 2 Tim. 1:16–17). His supporters knew, however, that Paul had no reason to be ashamed—he had been imprisoned because of his faithfulness in defending the gospel.

Selfish ambition (1:17). Prior to the New Testament, the only known use of this term is in Aristotle's *Politics* (5.3), where the philosopher used it to describe a greedy grasp for public office through unjust means.[29] Paul seems to use the expression in a similar way here to say that his opponents are not preaching Christ in order to promote the cause of the gospel, but are unfairly using Paul's imprisonment as a means of promoting their own agenda.

Paul Reflects on His Future (1:18b–26)

Will turn out for my deliverance . . . and . . . that I will in no way be ashamed (1:19–20). Although Paul nowhere indicates that he is quoting Scripture when

---

REFLECTIONS

CHRISTIANS IN EVERY GENERATION HAVE HAD TO take courageous stands for the gospel against the prevailing winds of the societies in which they have lived. In the last generation the Confessing Church in Germany stood against the so-called "German Christians" who had sold out to the evil policies of the Third Reich. Where will the church of the twenty-first century be tempted to swim with the tide of society when the church ought to stand against it?

▶ The Praetorians

The "palace guard" or "praetorians" were the bodyguards of the Roman emperor. Whether Paul wrote Philippians from Ephesus during the reign of Claudius or from Rome during the reign of Nero, the praetorians would have consisted of twelve cohorts, possibly of 1,000 soldiers each.[A-1] The praetorians were extremely powerful. Only a few years prior to Paul's imprisonment among them they had succeeded in having Claudius proclaimed emperor after the assassination of Caligula in A.D. 41. Their purpose was to retain their position of power rather than relinquish it to the Roman senate and a republican form of government.[A-2]

he uses this phrase, it is a word-for-word citation of the Greek version of Job 13:16. Job says that he knows, contrary to his accusers, that his own iniquity is not the cause of his suffering. He uses the metaphor of standing trial before God and says that he is confident that after God has cross-examined him he will be saved. Similarly, Paul knows that whatever the outcome of his trial, when he stands before God he will have no cause for shame but will experience "salvation" (NIV, "deliverance").

Whether by life or by death . . . what shall I choose . . . I am torn between the two (1:20–23). The Philippian Christians lived within a culture that was deeply concerned with death and the meticulous care of the deceased. Paul's approach to death and life in 1:20–23 must have seemed extraordinarily casual to those in the Philippian church who were accustomed to such practices. Physical death was of little importance to him—living meant Christ, and because to die involved going to be with Christ eternally, this too was a gain.

Your progress (1:26). In 1:12 Paul spoke of the "advancement" (*prokopē*) of the gospel through his own circumstances. Now he uses the same word, translated "progress" in the NIV, to anticipate the discussion in the rest of the letters of the gospel's "advancement" among the Philippians. This is a rare word, used in the New Testament only in these two places and in 1 Timothy 4:15. By using it in this way, Paul is marking off the major divisions of his letter for those who will hear it read aloud. The ancients called this rhetorical device *inclusio*.

The Philippians' Circumstances (1:27–2:18)

Conduct yourselves (1:27). This phrase translates a single Greek verb (*politeueomai*) that appears only here and in Acts 23:1 in the New Testament. In both places it refers to one's conduct as a citizen. The Philippians were conscious of their privileged status as a Roman colony, one of only five cities in Macedonia granted the *ius Italicum*—the right to be governed by Roman law and to be

exempt from direct taxation.[30] The Philippian Christians must have stuck out like a sore thumb in this society. They were not willing to participate in the popular cult of the Roman emperor, nor were they willing to conduct the traditional funerary rites at the graves of their ancestors (see "Rock Reliefs and the Afterlife in Ancient Philippi," above). Neither step would have endeared them to government officials or to unbelieving family members. Both groups would have viewed them as bad citizens, a cause for shame to both city and family. With this admonition to live as citizens who are worthy of the Christian gospel, Paul is telling the Philippians that they are citizens of another, heavenly country (cf. 3:20) and should take their sense of shame and honor from it rather than from Philippi.

Contending (1:27). Here and in verse 30, where Paul speaks of his past and present "struggle," he uses athletic imagery to describe the conduct of Christians in the face of opposition. Around the time of Paul, the author of *4 Maccabees* used this imagery in a similar way to describe the "contest" that Jewish martyrs faced under the wicked Seleucid King Antiochus IV.[31] Like the labor of athletes, the struggle of persecuted Jews and Christians was often both physical and public. The persecuted people of God, however, engaged in this struggle for different reasons from their counterparts in the athletic arena. "They do it," Paul says in another place, "to get a crown that will not last; but we do it to get a crown that will last forever" (1 Cor. 9:25).

Encouragement . . . comfort . . . fellowship . . . tenderness . . . compassion (2:1). Like many people today, people in the Greco-Roman world often lived in anxiety about the future. Would they be victims of disease, famine, war, and an untimely death, or would Fate deal them a better hand? The ancients used magic to try to control the powers that they believed decided their future. But (they must have worried) would their incantations, sacrifices, and amulets work? Into all this the gospel brought the "encouragement" and "comfort" that a loving God created and controlled the world. It brought the good news that this God had shown his love through Jesus Christ, who in "tenderness" and "compassion" healed the sick and raised the dead in anticipation of a day when disease and death would disappear. The preaching of the gospel also established a "fellowship" of

▶ Rock Reliefs and the Afterlife in Ancient Philippi

On the hill that towers above Philippi ancient Philippians often carved into the living rock reliefs of goddesses and gods who would help them in the afterlife. Nine reliefs of the Greek goddess Diana show her in close proximity to a lunar crescent, a symbol of death and the afterlife. The hill also features carvings of the Thracian Horseman, who was thought to lead the deceased to heaven after death. Gravestones from the vicinity of Philippi also depict the Thracian Horseman and tell survivors of the deceased to visit the grave each year to conduct special ceremonies for the dead. Some devotees of the Horseman gathered in funerary associations whose task was to keep watch over the graves of deceased members. Although these reliefs and inscriptions come from about a century after Paul, the cults that produced them would have been thriving during the period of Paul's ministry.[A-3]

▶ Is 2:6–11 an Early Christian Hymn?

The early Christians sang not only the Psalter but "hymns and spiritual songs" also (Eph. 5:19; Col. 3:16). Paul may quote such songs in Colossians 1:15–20 and 1 Timothy 3:16. In the late nineteenth century, a few scholars began suggesting that Philippians 2:6–11 was also a hymn about the humiliation and exaltation of Christ, and during the twentieth century a number of detailed studies seemed to confirm this notion.[A-4] Like the other two passages, these verses begin with the pronoun "who," possibly a clue that they are an excerpt from a larger composition. They also use several words that appear nowhere else in Paul's letters, and they seem to fall naturally into two balanced parts, verses 6–8 describing Christ's humiliation and verses 9–11 his exaltation.

Other scholars, however, continue to maintain that these verses reflect a moment of impressive rhetoric created by Paul himself precisely to drive home the point that the Philippians should strive for unity by imitating the unselfishness of Christ. These scholars point out that the passage does not have the characteristics of either Greek or Hebrew poetry, that the sentences are structured in a way common to Paul, and that Paul breaks into this kind of "exalted prose" elsewhere in passages that cannot be hymnic quotations (e.g., 1 Cor. 1:22–25).[A-5]

Whether originally composed by Paul or not, 2:6–11 shows that from an early time Christians affirmed the preexistence of Christ, his equality with God, and his full humanity. The later explanation of these matters in the great ecumenical creeds of the fourth and fifth centuries were only developments of what the orthodox church believed from the first.

believers who, if they followed Jesus' example, would help one another in the troubles of life until that final day.

Selfish ambition . . . humility (2:3). Paul contrasts the greedy grasp for what one should not rightfully have (see comments on 1:17) with the humble willingness to put the needs of others first. The term "humility" often had bad overtones in ancient literature outside the New Testament. The Stoic philosopher Epictetus (A.D. 55–ca.135), for example, used it to refer to weakness of character.[32] Wherever the term appears in the New Testament, however, it carries a positive sense. Here Paul uses it to refer to a sacrificial willingness to give up one's rights and work for the good of others. The supreme example of this was Jesus, who "humbled himself" in obedience to God and suffered death by crucifixion (2:8).

Taking the very nature of a servant (2:7). The word translated "servant" in the NIV is the common word for "slave" (see comments on 1:1). But in what sense did Jesus take the form of a slave? From the standpoint of the Romans, Jesus was a common Jew, a member of a people whom the Roman general Pompey had conquered in 63 B.C. and over whom the Romans had ruled ever since, sometimes directly through governors and sometimes indirectly through puppet kings such as Herod the Great, his son Archelaeus, and his grandson Herod Agrippa I. From the Jewish perspective, however, rule by a foreign power was slavery—well-deserved punishment for breaking God's law (Deut. 28:68; Ezra 9:9). Jesus became just such a slave, sharing the curse of the law that had fallen on God's people (Gal. 3:10; 4:4), although he alone among God's people had broken none of God's laws.

Even death on a cross! (2:8). Opponents of Christianity regularly pointed out the scandal of the Christian worship of a crucified man. "God does not suffer, and God cannot be humiliated," smirked the second century anti-Christian philosopher Celsus.[33] Paul's gospel paints a different picture of God as he is revealed in Jesus Christ, however. Christ suffered not because he deserved it but because he selflessly refused to exploit his divinity and instead substituted his own death for the death of those who justly deserved God's wrath.

In heaven and on earth and under the earth (2:10). Ancient people often lived in fear of various invisible powers residing in the heavens and under the earth. Sometimes they attempted to defend themselves against these forces through the use of magic or sacrifices. The ancient geographer Strabo says that one morning off the coast of Sicily people saw the sea rise to a great height, smelled a noxious odor, and then saw flames, smoke, and mud emerge from the sea's surface to form an island. The governor of Sicily responded to this unnerving spectacle by sending a deputation to the newly created island so that sacrifices might be offered to turn aside the wrath of the gods who lived "under the earth" and in the sea.[34] The Philippians must have taken comfort in the knowledge that Jesus had triumphed over all inimical powers, and that every knee in heaven, on earth, and under the earth would one day, whether willingly or in subjection, bow before him and acknowledge him as Lord. As Peter puts it, Jesus "has gone into heaven and is at God's right hand—with angels, authorities, and powers in submission to him" (1 Peter 3:22; cf. Col. 1:22).

Do everything without complaining (2:14). The Greek word for "complaining" appears in only three other places in the New Testament, and this is its only appearance in Philippians. The Greek translators of the Old Testament often

▶ Crucifixion: The Slave's Punishment

Crucifixion was widely regarded in the ancient Roman world as "the slave's punishment" (*supplicium servile*). The victim of crucifixion served as a living public placard, warning all who passed by of what would happen to those who rebelled against their station in life, whether as a literal slave or as a member of a conquered, and therefore symbolically enslaved, nation. After the defeat of the rebellion under Spartacus (73 B.C.), in which many renegade slaves fought, six thousand prisoners were crucified.[A-6] Under Nero (emperor A.D. 54–68)

a law was revived that allowed the crucifixion of all slaves within a household if their master had been murdered.[A-7] During the unrest in Judea following the death of Herod the Great, the Roman legate of Syria crucified two thousand Jews.[A-8] As the punishment reserved for slaves and the lower classes of conquered peoples, crucifixion was widely despised. The word was not even mentioned in polite company and was used by the lower classes, at least from the third century B.C. on, as a vulgar insult.[A-9] used it, however, to refer to the "complaining" of the Israelites against Moses in the desert.[35] Paul may be making a subtle comparison between the disobedience of God's people under the old covenant and the dissension that apparently infected the Philippian church.[36]

Shine like stars in the universe (2:15). Israel was supposed to be "a light for the Gentiles" (Isa. 49:6; cf. 42:6–7), calling them to the worship of the one God. It failed in this vocation, however, and became itself a "warped and crooked generation" (Deut. 32:4–5). Here Paul calls on the Philippian church to drop their differences and to fulfill their calling as God's people.

Did not run . . . for nothing (2:16). Paul's metaphor of running is borrowed from the world of ancient athletics. He frequently used this kind of imagery to describe the strenuous nature of his apostolic labors and to stress that their reward lay in the future.[37] The Isthmian games were held every two years in Corinth, and Paul's many months of ministry in that city may have overlapped with the celebration of these games. Victorious athletes in the games received a crown of dry celery.[38] Like a runner in these games Paul focused all his energy on the goal that lay ahead (Phil. 3:13). The goal was the heavenly finish of his race (3:14), and the prize that awaited him he could variously describe as the imperishable crown of eternal life (1 Cor. 9:25), the crown of righteousness (2 Tim. 4:8), or the crown of his churches whom he hoped to present to God, blameless and pure, on that final day (Phil. 4:1; 1 Thess. 2:19).

Poured out like a drink offering (2:17). Many ancient cultures practiced sacrifi-

REFLECTIONS

WE OFTEN THINK OF THE PURITY of the church as more important than the peace of the church. Paul considered the church's purity important—chapter 3 shows that!—but he also recognized that needless disunity in Christ's body tarnishes the church's witness. A clear-headed understanding of the essentials of the gospel, derived from a deep level of familiarity with Scripture, will help us to tell the difference between sane and silly disagreements within the church.

cial rituals in which libations were poured over a slaughtered animal. In the Old Testament (e.g., Num. 15:1–10) libations are sometimes made in addition to other offerings rather than poured over them. Paul probably has the Old Testament model in mind here and speaks of how his own suffering and possible death joins with the sacrificial suffering (1:28) and giving (1:7; 2:26; 4:15–18) of the Philippians to make a sacrifice pleasing to God.

PHILIPPI

An inscription of a Byzantine-era cross from the remains of a basilica in the city.
▼

The Travel Plans of Paul and His Coworkers (2:19–30)

Paul often refers in his letters to the movements of his coworkers and sometimes mentions his own travel plans also. This information can appear at the beginning of the letter, within its body, or at its conclusion. In Philippians, Paul has special reasons for locating his comments on Timothy and Epaphroditus right on the heels of his admonitions to unity in 2:1–18. These two coworkers provide examples of what it means to put the interests of others ahead of one's own interests. Paul wants the Philippians to turn from their "grumbling and complaining" against each other and to follow the path of unselfishness that these two valued friends have chosen.

You know that Timothy has proved himself (2:22). A more literal translation of this sentence might read, "His proven character you know." The noun rendered here as "proven character" (*dokimē*) refers to the quality of having remained faithful through difficult circumstances. The Jewish historian Josephus uses a verbal form of this word to describe how God put Abraham's faithfulness to the test when he commanded him to sacrifice his son Isaac.[39]

Epaphroditus . . . your messenger . . . to take care of my needs (2:25). Epaphroditus's mission was apparently twofold: to bring a financial gift from the Philippians to Paul (4:18) and to stay with Paul to care for him in prison. Roman prison officials made little, if any, provision for prisoners' food, clothing, bath, or bedding, and the meager amount of these basic necessities that the prisoner might receive had to be purchased at the prisoner's expense. Thus, prisoners were sometimes allowed to keep a small amount of money on them in prison and to receive gifts of food and clothing from friends and family.[40] The Philippians' concern that Paul would need these physical necessities seems to have been the primary reason that they sent Epaphroditus to him.

He was ill, and almost died (2:27). We can only speculate how and where Epaphroditus became ill. Did he contract

▶

PHILIPPI

Temple ruins.

malaria as he traveled overland to the place of Paul's imprisonment? If he traveled by sea, did he become infected with disease by a fellow traveler in the close quarters of a Roman grain ship?[41] It is certainly possible that he became sick while tending to Paul's needs in prison. Ancient literature that refers to Roman imprisonment regularly mentions the "squalor of long captivity" (Lucan, 87 B.C.), "the squalor of the dungeon" (Cyprian, A.D. 250), and the appearance of prisoners as "foul and disfigured with filth and dirt" (Cyprian, A.D. 257).[42]

A Warning Against Theological Error (3:1–4:1)

If Paul was in prison in Ephesus when he wrote to the Philippians, then just before writing the letter he may have also written to the Galatians and to the Corinthians. In Galatians Paul appeals to several of his churches not to be convinced by a group of itinerant teachers that they must add observance of the Jewish law to faith in Christ in order to be acquitted before God's tribunal on the final day. In 1 Corinthians Paul battles against the notion, prominent in the Middle Platonism of the time, that the physical element of reality is to be shunned or demeaned but spiritual and intellectual elements are to be elevated to positions of primacy. In 3:1–4:1 Paul warns the Philippians against both errors, probably not because they had already infected the Philippian community, but because he hopes to prevent the problems he had encountered in Galatia and Corinth from cropping up in Philippi also.

Watch out for . . . dogs . . . men who do evil . . . mutilators of the flesh (3:2). The force of Paul's rhetoric in this statement

> ## ▶ Timothy Among Paul's Coworkers

Paul depended heavily for the success of his missionary labors on the help of a close circle of coworkers. Friends such as Priscilla, Aquila, and Apollos aided Paul in the proclamation of the gospel, in the establishment of his churches, and in earning enough income to provide practical support for his missionary work.[A-10] Occasionally coworkers such as Epaphroditus were his hands and feet while the apostle himself was in prison (Phil. 2:25; cf. Philem. 13). When relations between Paul and the Corinthians became strained, Titus carried Paul's "tearful letter" to Corinth (2 Cor. 2:1–14; 7:5–16). Later, while Paul labored in Macedonia, Titus traveled to Corinth again to encourage the Christians there to contribute to Paul's collection for the famine-plagued believers in Jerusalem (2 Cor. 8:16–24). In addition, he helped to organize Paul's newly established churches on Crete, freeing the apostle to work in other regions (Titus 1:5; 3:12).

Paul's most valued coworker, however, was Timothy. Paul had such confidence in him that he considered Timothy's presence in one of his churches as good as his own presence there. Thus, when Paul could not bear to think how the newly-established Thessalonian church might be faring in his absence, he sent Timothy to encourage them (1 Thess. 3:1–2). When the Corinthians began a downward spiral into dissension and immorality, Paul sent Timothy to remind them of Paul's "way of life in Christ Jesus" (1 Cor. 4:17; 16:10). Paul and Timothy were also close friends, as Paul's terms of endearment for his colleague reveal. Timothy is Paul's "beloved and faithful child in the Lord" (1 Cor. 4:17, RSV), his "true son in the faith" (1 Tim. 1:2), and his "dear son" (2 Tim. 1:2). Paul has no words of commendation for any of his coworkers more endearing, however, than his description of Timothy in Philippians 2:20–22.

is nearly impossible to communicate in English translation. In Greek, the statement consists of three clauses all beginning with the same verb ("watch out"!) and each verb's direct object begins with a "k" sound. We can almost catch the rhetorical effectiveness of the phrase with the translation, "Beware the curs! Beware the criminals! Beware the cutters!" Paul is referring to Jewish Christians who teach that circumcision, dietary observance, and Sabbath-keeping are all necessary requirements, in addition to faith in Christ, for salvation. By calling them "dogs" Paul is turning their own advocacy of ritual purity back upon them. Because ancient streets were often home to dogs (Ps. 59:6, 14), who ate whatever they found, they may have been considered a symbol of nonobservance in matters of diet. The term "mutilators" (*katatomē*) is a play on the term "circumcision" (*peritomē*), which Paul uses in the next verse. Since circumcision was not necessary for salvation, those who promoted it were only mutilating the flesh, something that Leviticus 21:5 forbids as a pagan ritual.

No confidence in the flesh (3:3). Paul uses the term "flesh" here to mean any human credential that one might use to try to gain God's acceptance on the final day. The emphasis of his opponents on the fleshly rite of circumcision made it an especially appropriate metaphor.

Circumcised on the eighth day (3:5). The Mosaic law mandated the eighth day of life as the time for the circumcision of a male child (Gen. 17:12; Lev. 12:3), and although it involved work, this commandment was to take precedence over keeping the Sabbath (John 7:22–23). "Great is circumcision," said Rabbi Jose, "which overrides

even the rigor of the Sabbath."[43] Paul's circumcision on this day shows that he was not a proselyte but the son of observant Jews (cf. Luke 1:59; 2:21).[44]

Of the tribe of Benjamin (3:5). We know only from Acts that Paul also bore the Jewish name Saul. His namesake was the first king of Israel and the most famous member of the tribe of Benjamin.[45]

A Hebrew of Hebrews (3:5). The fourth-century bishop of Antioch John Chrysostom took this phrase to mean that Paul was raised to speak Aramaic, the native language of first-century Judaism, and most modern scholars believe that this is correct.[46]

In regard to the law, a Pharisee (3:5). The Jewish historian Josephus tells us that the Pharisees had the reputation of excelling all other Jews in the painstaking accuracy with which they interpreted the traditional laws of Judaism.[47] He also tells us that they wished to be righteous in everything.[48] We must not tar all Pharisees with the same brush, but these characteristics led some Pharisees to place confidence in themselves rather than in God (Luke 18:9). As a pre-Christian Pharisee, Paul had placed his confidence in what he calls "a righteousness of my own" (3:9). He seems to have thought that his own status and efforts were good enough to play some part in his acquittal on the final day.

As for zeal, persecuting the church (3:6). Paul identifies himself here and in Galatians 1:13–14 with a tradition of zealotry in Judaism that stretches back to Simeon and Levi (Gen. 34), Phinehas (Num. 25), and Elijah (1 Kings 18–19). Its chief characteristic was a concern for the Jewish law so intense that it could sometimes be expressed as violence against anyone who opposed it. Zeal for the law, for example, drove Mattathias Maccabeus to take up arms against the vast Seleucid army in the second century B.C. (1 Macc. 2:27).[49] The pre-Christian Paul probably persecuted the church because of its willingness to admit Gentiles to the people of God apart from conformity to the Mosaic law. He correctly saw that the gospel implied the end of the law as a boundary marker for the people of God, but incorrectly believed that this development was not from God.[50]

Profit . . . loss (3:7). The terms "profit" and "loss" are financial terms. They could be used in a legal setting to speak of the injured party's "loss" that had become the criminal's "gain."[51]

The righteousness that comes from God (3:9). Paul believed that in Jesus Christ God had effected the final display of his righteous, saving activity on behalf of his people. He had done this through Christ's death on the cross (Rom. 3:21–26), where he exchanged Christ's righteousness for our sinfulness (2 Cor. 5:21). On the cross, to use Jeremiah's phrase, the Lord had become "Our Righteousness" (Jer. 23:6).

Already been made perfect (3:12). Striving for perfection through intellectual and spiritual enlightenment was a common religious ideal in Greco-Roman antiquity. Those who responded positively to the preaching of this message "became perfect men, since they had received a complete mind."[52] Paul had seen such ideas infect the church at Corinth, where some believers claimed that they had already been perfected by their spiritual knowledge and

denied the goodness of the physical world. He would encounter this "knowledge which is falsely so called" (1 Tim. 6:20 ASV) again at Ephesus. Here in Philippians he is perhaps taking precautions against the misinterpretation of Philippians 3:7–11 as support for such false teaching.

I press on toward the goal to win the prize (3:14). The imagery of this verse comes from the athletic arena (see comments on 2:16), where runners would fix their eyes on the post that marked the end point of the race and winners received a prize. The term "goal" was often used figuratively of an object on which one could fix his or her eyes and so be guided safely to a final destination. In the third-century B.C. *Letter of Aristeas*, for example, the author says that "life is rightly guided when the pilot knows the *goal* toward which he must make his way" (251).[53]

Enemies of the cross of Christ (3:18). Opponents of Christianity in antiquity regularly mocked Christians for their worship of a man who had died by crucifixion. The early Christian apologist Minucius Felix puts these words on the lips of an imaginary, but typical, opponent: "To say that their ceremonies centre

REFLECTIONS

IT IS WORTH ASKING FROM TIME TO TIME WHERE OUR confidence lies. Do we think that God loves us because of all that we do for him—teaching Sunday school, ministering to the poor, serving in the offices of the church? Or do we know that God loves us—regardless of what we do—because of what he has done for us on the cross of Jesus Christ? If our confidence before God lies in anything but his love for us, we have made the mistake of the pre-Christian Paul, and like him, we need to trust solely in the righteousness that comes from God for our salvation.

on a man put to death for his crime and on the fatal wood of the cross is to assign to these abandoned wretches sanctuaries which are appropriate to them and the kind of worship they deserve."[54] Under such circumstances some Christians succumbed to the temptation to play down the significance of Christ's crucifixion (see, for example, 1 John 5:6). Paul's emphasis on the folly of the cross in 1 Corinthians 1:18–2:5 may mean that the Corinthians were moving in this direction, and here in Philippians 3:18 he seems to be taking precautions against such influences among the Philippians.

Our citizenship is in heaven (3:20). The word translated "citizenship" (*politeuma*) was sometimes used generally to speak of the political rights of a particular group. The third-century Macedonian King Philip V, for example, commented that the Romans, when they freed their slaves, welcomed them "into *citizenship*." The same word could also refer to a distinct ethnic group that lived away from its homeland and was governed by its own constitution—"a city within a city."[55] An inscription from the town of Bernike in Cyrenaica, for example, speaks of "the *community* of Jews in Bernike" (13 B.C.), and the third-century

B.C. *Letter of Aristeas* can speak of a group of Jews in Egypt as "some from the Jewish *community*."[56] Here Paul reminds the Philippians that although they have been marginalized by the society in which they live, they are not people without a country. They form a distinct group with its own loyalties, its own homeland (see also comments on 1:27), and, as we see below, its own "Savior."

We eagerly await a Savior from there (3:20). In Hellenistic and Roman society, the ruler was frequently called "savior." This term was especially common for Roman emperors. Plutarch says that the Greeks use "the designation 'savior'" for the ruler because of his accomplishments (*De Coriolano* 11).[57] Thus, an inscription from Ephesus dated to A.D. 48, only a few years before Paul wrote Philippians, speaks of Julius Caesar as "a visible god and political savior of human life." Another inscription from Egypt, this time perhaps from a few years after Philippians, calls Emperor Nero "savior and benefactor of the world." Paul wants the Philippians to know that the "Savior" of their "community" (*politeuma*, see above) is none other than Jesus, who will bring "everything under his control" (3:21; cf. 2:10).[58]

▶ God's Righteousness in Paul's Bible

Paul's Bible was filled with references to God's willingness to rescue his covenant people from peril. It sometimes referred to this saving work as God's "righteousness." For example, the psalmist says, "The LORD has made his salvation known and revealed his righteousness to the nations. He has remembered his love and his faithfulness to the house of Israel" (Ps. 98:2–3a). Occasionally, the Scriptures refer to a righteous king through whom God will act decisively and finally for the good of his people. Jeremiah, for example, prophesies, "'The days are coming,' declares the LORD, 'when I will raise up to David a righteous Branch, a King who will reign wisely and do what is just and right in the land.... This is the name by which he will be called: The LORD Our Righteousness'" (Jer. 23:5–6).[A-11]

My . . . crown (4:1). This is probably a metaphorical reference to the wreath of dry celery worn by athletes after they had reached their goal and won the race (see comments on 2:16 and 3:14).

Concluding Admonitions (4:2–9)

Near the end of several letters Paul includes a section of short, pithy exhortations similar to what we find here. For example, Paul draws his first letter to the Thessalonians to a close with a series of brief admonitions to respect the church's leaders, to live in peace with each other, to be joyful, to pray, to be thankful, to be sensitive to the Spirit, to listen to prophecies, to test everything, to hold on to what is good, and to avoid evil (1 Thess. 5:12–22). Here in Philippians, he calls the names of some of his readers for the first time (Phil. 4:2–3) and applies the admonitions to unity in 1:27–2:30 specifically to a dispute between Euodia and Syntyche. In addition, he employs but modifies an Epicurean philosophical convention to summarize for his readers the attitude that they should have toward the persecution they are facing (cf. 1:27–30).

Contended at my side (4:3). This phrase translates a word (*synathleō*) that in Greek is a compound of the preposition "with" (*syn*) and a verb that can mean "to contend in battle" or "to compete in athletic games" (*athleō*).[59] Paul is probably continuing to use the athletic imagery that has appeared so often in his previous argument (2:16; 3:13–14; 4:1).

Loyal yokefellow (4:3). At least since the early third-century church father Clement of Alexandria, some people have thought that Paul was addressing his wife with this phrase (*Miscellanies* 3.6). The word "yokefellow" (*syzygos* in Greek) can mean "wife," but that cannot be its meaning here since Paul qualifies the word with the masculine form of the adjective "loyal" (*gnesie*). If Paul were referring to his wife, he would have used the feminine form of the adjective (*gnesia*).[60]

Fellow workers (4:3). This is the term Paul uses for Timothy, Epaphroditus, Titus, Prisca (Priscilla in Acts), Aquila, Apollos, and others who formed the inner circle of his helpers (see "Timothy Among Paul's Coworkers," above). Paul's language implies that Euodia and Syntyche were members of this group. How did they have the leisure to contend at Paul's side in the cause of the gospel? We cannot know definitely, but Euodia and Syntyche may have been wealthy women, like Lydia (Acts 16:14), who naturally assumed positions of prominence in the Philippian church because they had held some position of responsibility commensurate with their social rank in the political or religious institutions of Philippi prior to their conversion. Euodia and Syntyche are both Greek names, and at least in Asia, Greek women sometimes held important political positions.[61] In Philippi, women probably occupied leading roles in the worship of the goddess Diana.[62]

The book of life (4:3). The Old Testament sometimes refers to a record, kept by God, of those who belong to God's people. Moses pleads with God to blot his own name from it rather than the names of the rebellious desert generation of Israelites (Ex. 32:32–33). David calls it "the book of life" (Ps. 69:28), and Isaiah carries the idea into the future when he speaks of the blessings that will come to those "who are recorded among the living in Jerusalem" at the time of the restoration of God's people (Isa. 4:3). John frequently refers to a "book of life," kept by Jesus himself, that contains the names of those who belong to God's people and will be citizens of the heavenly Jerusalem.[63] Probably lying in the background of all these references is the civic practice of record-keeping; the names of citizens were commonly recorded on lists in antiquity.[64] Thus, in the command of the Macedonian King Philip V referred to above (see comments on Phil. 3:20), Philip tells the city officials of Larisa to restore to the "community" the names that they have erased, apparently from some list of citizens.[65] By using the phrase "book of life" here, Paul may be reminding his Philippian coworkers that although their status as good citizens of Philippi is in jeopardy, they are nevertheless enrolled on the citizen list of God's heavenly society.[66]

Let your gentleness be evident to all (4:5). The term "gentleness" was often used to describe an attitude of kindness where a normal response would be retaliation. Thus in the apocryphal book Wisdom of Solomon, a group of evil people decide to persecute a righteous man whose virtuous life is a rebuke to them. "Let us test him with insult and torture," they say, "so that we may find out his *gen-*

tleness, and make trial of his forbearance."[67] This is probably also the nuance of the term in 2 Corinthians 10:1, where Paul implies that the origin of his own gentle conduct with the recalcitrant Corinthians is "the meekness and *gentleness* of Christ." Similarly, Paul wants the persecuted Philippians (Phil. 1:28–29) to return evil with good (cf. Rom. 12:21).

Think about such things (4:8). Ancient moral philosophers often consoled those who were grieving or otherwise plagued with difficult circumstances to turn their minds away from their difficulties (*avocatio*) and to turn them to pleasurable or virtuous thoughts (*revocatio*). Epicureans (see comments on 1:12) advocated turning one's thoughts from the painful to the pleasurable. Stoics, such as Cicero and Seneca, advocated replacing painful thoughts with the contemplation of virtue. Cicero's list of virtues for contemplation is similar to Paul's list here: "all that is lovely, honourable, of good report."[68] Paul may have taken over this convention and, varying the approach represented by Cicero and Seneca, advocated that the Philippians commit the worries that accompany their persecution in prayer to God (4:6) and turn their minds to the contemplation of the virtues.[69]

A Word of Thanks (4:10–20)

Paul draws his letter to a close with an expression of appreciation for the Philippians' gift to him through Epaphroditus. Paul's use of financial metaphors in this part of the letter (4:15–18) implies that the gift consisted primarily of money, although it may have included clothes and other basic necessities that would ease the harsh conditions of his imprisonment (see comments on 2:25). Whereas Paul is clearly appreciative of these gifts (4:10, 14–16, 18–20), he qualifies his thanks in vv. 11–13 by saying that he really did not need them and in v. 17 that he did not seek them. He did not want the Philippians to think either that he preached the gospel for money or that they were the benefactors of his ministry.

Content (4:11). This word translates a widely discussed virtue in ancient Greek moral philosophy (*autarkēs*). Aristotle defined contentment as "possessing all things and needing nothing."[70] The word became especially important to the Stoics, among whom it represented the highest of Stoic ideals—complete self-sufficiency. Marcus Aurelius, who describes his adoptive father as the ideal Stoic man, claims that he was "self-sufficient in all things."[71] Paul's understanding

of contentment could hardly have been more different from this. He was content not because he needed nothing or because he was self-sufficient, but because he was utterly dependent on a God who gave him everything he truly needed. Through Paul's suffering God had taught the apostle, "My grace is sufficient for you, for my power is made perfect in weakness" (2 Cor. 12:9).[72]

The matter of giving and receiving (4:15). These are common financial terms for credit (*dosis*) and debit (*lēmpsis*). Sirach 42:7, for example, advises, "Whatever you deal out, let it be by number and weight, and make a record of all that you give out [*dosis*] or take in [*lēmpsis*]." The language was sometimes used metaphorically among friends to refer to the mutual "give" and "take" of friendship. These connotations probably lie beneath

---

▶ # Sophistry, Philosophy, and Chicanery in the Greco-Roman World

Giving material wealth, especially to teachers and lecturers, was fraught with significance in ancient Greco-Roman society. For example, the group of itinerant teachers known as "Sophists" charged a fee for teaching their pupils how to succeed in life. Their lectures ran the gamut of self-help topics from memory improvement to effective oratory. All Sophists were skilled speakers and many had an impressive physical presence, often enhanced by a stunning wardrobe. Their trade was frequently lucrative, and although there were exceptions, their profession was somewhat cynically oriented toward a life of material success irrespective of any search for truth.[A-12]

Although less impressive in outward appearance and more oriented toward the pursuit of truth, Cynic philosophers also depended on the generosity of benefactors to support their life of itinerant philosophical teaching. Not infrequently the ability

of con artists to ape the costume and manner of Cynic teachers enabled them to defraud the gullible of considerable sums and then to leave town without a trace. The second-century satirist Lucian parodied these swindlers in his play The Runaways. "They collect tribute," he says, "going from house to house, or, as they themselves express it, they 'shear the sheep': and they expect many to give, either out of respect for their cloth or for fear of their abusive language" (14).[A-13]

Paul's reserved expression of thanks in Philippians may be an effort to distance himself both from any hint that his teaching is motivated by a desire for financial gain and from the possibility that the Philippians were his benefactors. Paul preached the gospel not for money but because God had called him to preach (1 Cor. 9:15–18), and his authority as an apostle came from no human being but from God himself (Gal. 1:1).[A-14]

Paul's use of the language here since Paul's point is that he had entered into a unique relationship with the Philippians: He had allowed no other church but theirs to give financial support to his Gentile mission (2 Cor. 11:8–9). Elsewhere Paul had worked with his hands for his own support (1 Cor. 4:12; 2 Thess. 3:7–10).[73]

I have received full payment (4:18). Paul is again using technical commercial language for writing a receipt of payment. One example of the literal financial use of this language—and it could be multiplied many times—comes from an ostracon dated A.D. 32–33 and stating that Pamaris the son of Hermodorus has "received full payment" from a man named Abos of a tax levied on aliens in the city of Thebes.[74]

Conclusion (4:21–23)

Letters to friends and family in ancient times typically contained a simple conclusion, often using nothing more than the word "farewell" (*errōso*). Occasion-ally, however, especially in letters from the first century, the conclusion was expanded to include a brief wish for the health of the recipient.[75] Sometimes conclusions included greetings to third parties and greeted the recipient on behalf of someone in the sender's company. The soldier Apollinarios writes to his mother, for example, and closes the letter this way: "I greet (salute) my brothers much, and Apollinarios and his children, and Karalas and his children. I greet Ptolemy, and Ptolemais and her children. I greet all your friends, each by name. I pray that you are well."[76] And in a letter written within a few years of the time Paul wrote Philippians, Herennia concludes a letter to her father Pompeius with best wishes "to Charitous and her children" and greetings from Herennia's younger brother, "Pompeius junior."[77] Paul follows the same custom in Philippians, sending greetings to all the Philippian Christians and greeting them on behalf of everyone with him (4:21).

Especially those who belong to Caesar's household (4:22). The phrase "Caesar's household" refers to slaves and freed slaves who served the emperor either as part of his entourage of personal attendants in Rome or as part of the more widely dispersed group of servants who supervised his financial affairs. Both groups were proud of the status that their work in the emperor's service accorded them, and they often added to their names an abbreviation showing that they were slaves or freedmen of the emperor.[78] Paul may intend these greetings as an encouragement to the persecuted Philippians that he knows of people even within the structures of imperial power who have been touched by the gospel.

REFLECTIONS

PAUL COULD BE CONTENT EVEN IN PRISON BECAUSE he was content when the gospel was making progress, and the gospel was making progress because of his imprisonment (1:12). Paul could also be content when other preachers of the gospel increased his suffering. "What does it matter?" he says, "the important thing is that Christ is preached" (1:18). When we are discontent, perhaps we should ask ourselves where the origin of contentment lies for us. Does it lie in the progress of the gospel (if so, we need never fear that God will fail to see it progress) or does it lie in physical comfort or emotional security?

Bockhuehl, Markus. *The Epistle to the Philippians.* BNTC. Peabody, Mass.: Hendrickson, 1998.

A well-written, concise exposition marked by insights from both Jewish and Greco-Roman sources and informed by a mastery of the best social and cultural studies of ancient Philippi.

Bruce, F. F. *Philippians.* GNC. New York: Harper & Row, 1983.

A short, lucid explanation of the letter with frequent insights from the history and culture of Paul's time.

Caird, G. B. *Paul's Letters from Prison (Ephesians, Philippians, Colossians, Philemon) in the Revised Standard Version.* Oxford: Oxford University Press, 1976.

A brilliant exposition of Philippians within only a few pages, from the author of the classic *The Language and Imagery of the Bible.*

Fee, Gordon D. *Paul's Letter to the Philippians.* NICNT. Grand Rapids: Eerdmans, 1995.

A sound exposition of the letter with constant reference to its character as an ancient letter of friendship, to its effectiveness as an effort at oral communication, and to its theological significance for the present-day church.

Hawthorne, Gerald F. *Philippians.* WBC. Waco, Tex.: Word, 1983.

An insightful exposition of the Greek text by a revered and erudite professor of the Greek language.

Martin, Ralph P. *Philippians.* NCBC. Grand Rapids/London: Eerdmans/ Marshall, Morgan & Scott, 1976.

A short, clear, and exegetically sane exposition, based on the RSV.

Murphy-O'Connor, Jerome. *Paul: A Critical Life.* Oxford: Clarendon, 1996.

Although sullied by its skeptical attitude toward the historicity of Acts, its truncated Pauline canon, and its frequent speculativeness, this book is filled with rich insights on the historical and cultural background of Paul's ministry.

O'Brien, Peter T. *The Epistle to the Philippians: A Commentary on the Greek Text.* NIGTC. Grand Rapids: Eerdmans, 1991.

The most detailed exposition of the Greek text in over a century and a reliable guide to virtually every exegetical problem in the letter.

Rapske, Brian. *Paul in Roman Custody.* Grand Rapids: Eerdmans, 1994.

A gripping account of every facet of ancient imprisonment with special attention to the record of Paul's imprisonments in Acts.

Silva, Moisés. *Philippians.* BECNT. Grand Rapids: Baker, 1992.

A theologically sensitive explanation of the letter with sound insights into the meaning of the text from the field of linguistics.

Thielman, Frank. *Philippians.* NIVAC. Grand Rapids: Zondervan, 1995.

A commentary that focuses both on the original meaning and on the application of this letter of Paul.

White, John L. *Light from Ancient Letters.* Foundations & Facets: New Testament. Philadelphia: Fortress, 1986.

A collection of 117 ancient papyrus letters from Egypt and an illuminating account of how and why they were written.

Witherington, Ben III. *Friendship and Finances in Philippi: The Letter of Paul to the Philippians.* The New Testament in Context. Valley Forge, Pa.: Trinity Press International, 1994.

A clearly written exposition of the Philippians in light of ancient rhetorical and cultural conventions.

CHAPTER NOTES

Main Text Notes

1. David W. J. Gill and Conrad Gempf, *The Book of Acts in Its Graeco–Roman Setting* (Grand Rapids: Eerdmans, 1994), 401.
2. See Richard S. Ascough, "Civic Pride at Philippi: The Text–Critical Problem of Acts 16.12," *NTS* 44 (1998): 93–103.
3. Appian, *Civil Wars* 4.13.105–32.
4. Strabo, *Geogr.* 7.41; Dio Cassius, *Roman History* 51.4.6.
5. Holland L. Hendrix, "Philippi," *ABD*, 5:315.
6. Ibid., 315.
7. Nils Martin Persson Nilsson, Herbert Jennings Rose, and Charles Martin Robertson, "Dionysius," *OCD²*, 352–53; Hendrix, "Philippi," 5:315.
8. Valerie Abrahamsen, "Christianity and the Rock Reliefs at Philippi," *BA* 51 (1988): 48–50.
9. Ibid., 51.
10. Gill and Gempf, *Greco–Roman Setting*, 412; cf. Markus Bockmuehl, *The Epistle to the Philippians* (BNTC; Peabody, Mass.: Hendrickson, 1998), 6–8.
11. As suggested by Paul Collart, *Philippes: Ville de Macédoine* (Paris: École française d'Athènes, 1937), 323, 458–60. But see Peter Pilheifer, *Philippi* (WUNT 87; Tübingen: Mohr, 1995), 167–74.
12. Stanley K. Stowers, *Letter Writing in Greco-Roman Antiquity* (LEC 5; Louisville, Ky.: Westminster/John Knox, 1986), 66.
13. MM, 244.
14. Ibid., 149.
15. A. Weiser, "διακονέω," *EDNT*, 1:302.
16. Arland J. Hultgren, *Paul's Gospel and Mission: The Outlook from His Letter to the Romans* (Philadelphia: Fortress, 1985), 21–26.
17. On "confirming" (*bebaiōsis*) see BAGD, 138, and MM, 108.
18. John L. White, *Light from Ancient Letters* (Philadelphia: Fortress, 1986), 104.
19. Ibid., 173.
20. Plato, *Menexenus* 245d.
21. Ceslas Spicq, *TLNT*, 1:420–23.
22. *Letter of Aristeas* 210.
23. White, *Light from Ancient Letters*, 158.
24. Quoted in Cicero, *On the Ends of Goods and Evils* 2.30.96.
25. cf. Cicero, *Tusculan Disputations* 3.16.35–3.17.38; cf. 5.23.6.
26. I am indebted for these insights to Paul A. Holloway, "*Bona Cogitare*: An Epicurean Consolation in Phil 4:8–9," *HTR* 91 (1998): 89–96.
27. Brian Rapske, *The Book of Acts and Paul in Roman Custody* (Grand Rapids: Eerdmans, 1994), 20–35; Ignatius, *Romans* 5.1.
28. Ibid., 290.
29. Spicq, *TLNT*, 2:70–71.
30. J. A. O. Larsen, "Roman Greece," in *An Economic Survey of Ancient Rome*, ed. Tenney Frank (Baltimore: Johns Hopkins Univ. Press, 1933–40), 4:459.
31. Elthelbert Stauffer, "ἀγών," *TDNT*, 1:136; *4 Macc.* 11:20; 16:16; 17:10–16.
32. Walter Grundmann, "ταπεινός," *TDNT*, 8:5; Epictetus, *Discourses* 3.24.56.
33. Celsus, *On the True Doctrine: A Discourse Against the Christians* (New York: Oxford Univ. Press, 1987), 107.
34. Strabo, *Geogr.* 6.2.11.
35. Ex. 16:2–9; 17:3; Num. 11:1; cf. 14:2.
36. Phil. 4:2; cf. 1 Cor. 10:1–13.
37. 1 Cor. 9:24–27; 2 Tim. 4:6–8; cf. Gal. 2:2.
38. Jerome Murphy-O'Connor, *Paul: A Critical Life* (Oxford: Clarendon, 1996), 259.
39. *Ant.* 1.13.4 §233; cf. Gen. 22:1–19; Spicq, *TLNT*, 1:355.
40. Rapske, *Paul in Roman Custody*, 196–97, 209–19.
41. On the many dangers that ancient travelers faced, see Murphy-O'Connor, *Paul*, 96–101.
42. Rapske, *Paul in Roman Custody*, 217.
43. The translation is from Herbert Danby, *The Mishnah* (Oxford: Oxford Univ. Press, 1933), 268; *m. Nedarim* 3.11.
44. Peter T. O'Brien, *Commentary on Philippians* (NIGTC; Grand Rapids: Eerdmans, 1991), 369.
45. 1 Sam. 9:21; 10:20–21; 2 Sam. 21:14.
46. Chrysostom, *Homilies on Philippians* 10.
47. Josephus, *Life* 38 §191; *J.W.* 2.8.14 §162.
48. Josephus, *Ant.* 18.1.3 §15.
49. Terence L. Donaldson, *Paul and the Gentiles: Remapping the Apostle's Convictional World* (Minneapolis: Fortress, 1997), 285–86.
50. Ibid., 273–92.
51. Aristotle, *Nicomachean Ethics* 5.4, 1132a.
52. C. K. Barrett, *The New Testament Background: Selected Documents* (rev. and exp. ed.; San Francisco: HarperCollins, 1987), 101; *Corpus Hermeticum* 4; *The Bowl* 3–7.
53. See MM, 579.
54. Martin Hengel, *Crucifixion* (Philadelphia: Fortress, 1977), 1–10: Minucius Felix, *Octavius* 9.

55. E. Mary Smallwood, *The Jews under Roman Rule from Pompey to Diocletian: A Study in Political Relations* (Leiden: Brill, 1981), 225.

56. MM, 525–26. See also Smallwood, *Jews under Roman Rule*, 225–30.

57. Werner Foerster, "σωτήρ," *TDNT*, 7:1007.

58. MM, 621–22.

59. LSJ, 32.

60. Murphy-O'Connor, *Paul*, 64.

61. Ben Witherington III, *Friendship and Finances in Philippi: The Letter of Paul to the Philippians* (The New Testament in Context; Valley Forge, Pa.: Trinity Press International, 1994), 108.

62. Abrahamsen, "Christianity and the Rock Reliefs at Philippi," 46–56.

63. E.g., Rev. 20:12, 15; 21:27.

64. H. Balz, "βιβλίον," *EDNT*, 1:218.

65. MM, 525.

66. Gerald Hawthorne, *Philippians* (WBC 43; Waco, Tex.: Word, 1983), 181.

67. Wisd. Sol. 2:19 RSV modified.

68. Cicero, *Tusc. Disp.* 5.23.67; The translation is from the Loeb Classical Library edition of Cicero's works.

69. I am indebted for these insights to Holloway, "*Bona Cogitare*," 89–96.

70. Aristotle, *Politics* 7.5, 1326b; Gerhard Kittel, "αὐτάρκεια," *TDNT*, 1:466–67.

71. Marcus Aurelius, *Meditations* 1.16.11; J. N. Sevenster, *Paul and Seneca* (Leiden: E. J. Brill, 1961), 114.

72. B. Siede, "Suffice, Satisfy," *NIDNTT*, 3:728.

73. Gordon D. Fee, *Paul's Letter to the Philippians* (NICNT; Grand Rapids: Eerdmans, 1995), 439–47.

74. Adolf Deissmann, *Light from the Ancient East* (Grand Rapids: Baker, 1978 [reprt.]), 111.

75. White, *Light from Ancient Letters*, 199–200.

76. Ibid., 196.

77. Ibid., 141.

78. P. R. C. Weaver, *Familia Caesaris: A Social Study of the Emperor's Freedmen and Slaves* (Cambridge: Cambridge Univ. Press, 1972), 1–8.

Sidebar and Chart Notes

A-1. Henry Michael Denne Parker and George Ronald Watson, "Praetorians," *OCD*², 873–74.

A-2. Anthony A. Barrett, *Caligula: The Corruption of Power* (New Haven, Conn.: Yale Univ. Press, 1989), 172–74.

A-3. See Abrahamsen, "Christianity and the Rock Reliefs at Philippi," 51.

A-4. Ralph P. Martin, *A Hymn of Christ: Philippians 2:5–11 in Recent Interpretation and in the Setting of Early Christian Worship* (Downers Grove, Ill.: InterVarsity, 1997), 24–41.

A-5. Gordon Fee, "Philippians 2:5–11: Hymn or Exalted Pauline Prose?" *BBR* 2 (1992): 29–46.

A-6. Caesar, *Civil Wars* 1.120.

A-7. Tacitus, *Ann.* 13.32.1; Martin Hengel, *Crucifixion*, 51–63.

A-8. Josephus, *Ant.* 17.10.10 §295.

A-9. Ibid., 9–10.

A-10. Acts 18:2–4, 18, 24–28; Rom. 16:3–9; 1 Cor. 3:9.

A-11. See Hultgren, *Paul's Gospel and Mission*, 12–46.

A-12. See Guy Cromwell Field, "Sophists," *OCD*², 1000, and Bruce W. Winter, "Is Paul Among the Sophists?" *RTR* 53 (1994): 28–29.

A-13. The translation is from the Loeb Classical Library edition of Lucian's works.

A-14. See the helpful discussion in Witherington, *Friendship and Finances*, 123–24.

COLOSSIANS

by Clinton E. Arnold

The City of Colosse

Colosse was a small agrarian town in western Asia Minor (modern Turkey).[1] It was located about 120 miles east of Ephesus in the Lycus River Valley of the territory of Phrygia. The city lay near the base of Mount Cadmus (elevation 8,435 feet) and was only eleven miles southeast of Laodicea.

Because of the sparse historical records, we have no way of determining the approximate size of the city. We do know that Colosse was rather insignificant in Roman history; it is mentioned only by a handful of writers. The city was largely overshadowed by the larger and more prosperous Laodicea. Even nearby Hierapolis (fifteen miles northwest) figures more prominently in the historical record.

The distinctive color of the wool produced at Colosse, commonly called *colossinus,* aided the success of the textile industry there. The economic position of the city was

COLOSSE

Alongside the tel of the ancient city.

◀

▶ **Colossians**
IMPORTANT FACTS:

- **AUTHOR:** The apostle Paul and Timothy.
- **DATE:** A.D. 60–62 (Paul imprisoned in Rome).
- **OCCASION:**
  - To warn believers about the dangers of a spiritualistic teaching being pushed by some influential people in the church.
  - To provide positive Christian teaching to facilitate the spiritual growth of the Colossian believers.
- **KEY THEMES:**
  1. The supremacy of Christ over all of creation, especially the powers.
  2. Believers participate with Christ in his death, resurrection, and fullness.

also enhanced by its location on the major trade route leading from the Aegean coast (to the west) to the heartland of Asia Minor and on to Syria and the east.

There is evidence of a sizeable Jewish population in the area around Colosse, and thus probably in the city of Colosse. This is based on a reference in Cicero to the amount of tax collected for the Jerusalem temple from this district in the first century B.C.[2] No synagogue has yet been discovered.

Two different ancient writers attest to a severe earthquake that rocked this region in the early 60s of the first century A.D.[3] Laodicea suffered extensive damage, and we can only surmise that Colosse suffered the same. It appears that the quake may have struck shortly after Paul wrote his letter to the church. Paul's eloquent words about Christ as Lord of creation must have been especially meaningful to the believers after this tragic event.

Archaeological Prospects at Colosse

Colosse has never been excavated, although groups have applied to the Turkish government for permission. The site was discovered in 1835 by explorer W. J. Hamilton. Members of the Near East Archaeological Society and others have conducted site surveys, which have yielded evidence of an acropolis, a theater on the south bank of the Lycus River, a necropolis (a graveyard), and the remains of other ancient buildings on the northern bank of the river.[4] The excavation of Colosse could yield important finds with implications for the interpretation of the letter. This is particularly important because of the influence of local religious traditions on the teaching of the faction that Paul opposes in the letter. The excavation of temples and discovery of religious inscriptions would provide helpful insight about the nature of these cults and the folk religious beliefs of the area. Of course, any discoveries of Jewish inscriptions or symbols would greatly assist in clarifying the picture of what Judaism was like in this area.

The Spiritual Climate of the Area

Because of the nature of the problem facing the Colossian church, it is important to have an awareness of some of the spiritual beliefs of the people living in this area who became Christians. There were no secular humanists at this time. In fact, most of the people living in this country area could aptly be described as animists. They believed in the reality of the gods and goddesses as well as in the pervasive influence of good and evil spirits. Here are a few specific features of their beliefs that will help to better understand the nature of the issue the church is struggling with:

A religiously pluralistic environment. Like any other city in the Roman empire

COLOSSE AND EPHESUS

Colosse was about 100 miles due east of Ephesus.

▼

at this time, Colosse was religiously pluralistic. We know this because of the variety of gods and goddesses depicted on a few coins that have been discovered originally minted in the city.[5] They suggest that among the deities the Colossians worshiped were the Ephesian Artemis, the Laodicean Zeus, Artemis (the huntress), the local moon-god Men, the lunar goddess Selene, the Egyptian deities Isis and Sarapis, as well as a number of well-known Greek divinities, including Athena, Demeter, Hygieia, Helios, and Tyche. It is likely that other distinctively Asia Minor deities would have been worshiped there as well, such as the mother goddess, Cybele, and the goddess of witchcraft, Hekate.

Blending of religious beliefs. It was common for a person at this time not only to worship more than one god or goddess (polytheism), but also for the religions themselves to reflect a borrowing of ideas and forms of worship from one another. Such a blending of religious ideas is called *syncretism.*

A strong belief in dangerous spirits and powers. In their belief, not all gods, goddesses, and spirits were benevolent. Most were to be feared. Even the good deities, if offended, could manifest their anger toward the people in some kind of disaster. People also had to worry about the potential of being cursed (and not in the sense of someone uttering a four-letter word at them). In this context, curses involved the summoning of supernatural beings to harm the life of another person. Archaeologists have discovered curse tablets in Asia Minor that illustrate these dark arts.[6]

The people also feared the many spirits associated with the wildlife, agriculture, and the intersection of roads. Spirits were associated with some objects that could pose a significant threat to one's safety. They believed that astral spirits, the zodiac, planetary deities, and the constellations (such as Pleiades and the constellation of the bear—Arktos) held sway over fate and influenced the affairs of day-to-day life. They were also fearful of the underworld and the gods and goddesses such as Hades and Hekate. Not least, they had to be wary of the spirits of deceased ancestors and of the untimely dead who haunted and could wreak terror.

An appeal to "angels" and other divine beings for protection. There is abundant evidence that people in Asia Minor tended to invoke various spirit beings for protection and deliverance.[7] Numerous inscriptions have been discovered in the area illustrating the fact that people called on angels for help. This was true in the pagan cults and in Judaism.

Ecstatic forms of worship. One final aspect of the religious practice of the area is the manifestation of extreme forms of behavior in the context of worship. This often led to the abuse of the body. This is best illustrated by the nature of the worship directed to the Great Mother goddess of Asia Minor, Cybele, and her consort, Attis. Worshipers often engaged in rites of self-mutilation and flagellation.[8] We may also add to this the fact that fasting and other forms of self-denial were a part of the preparation for initiation into some of the mystery cults in the region.

The Introduction of Christianity to the City

In the mid–50s, the apostle Paul spent considerable time in the city of Ephesus. Luke informs us that during this time all "Asia heard the word of the Lord" (Acts 19:10). This was the most likely time that a man named Epaphras journeyed from Colosse to Ephesus, heard Paul's preaching about the Messiah Jesus, became a Christian, and was instructed in the way of the Lord by Paul. This new believer then returned to his home city and zealously spread the news about Christ. If he was a Jew, which seems probable, he would have gone immediately into the synagogue(s) and proclaimed Christ. Here a number of Jews and many Gentile "God-fearers" and proselytes (Gen-

▶ Plutarch's *Dread of the Gods*

Plutarch, a well-known first-century writer, wrote an entire essay on the common fear of the gods among the common people of the Roman empire. In *Deisidaimonia* (*Dread of the Gods*), Plutarch describes how the people are terrified by the gods and worried about potential attacks by evil spirits.[A-1] They experience awful dreams and see frightening and horrible apparitions. They also live in the fear of life beyond the grave, imagining that they will descend to the abysmal underworld and face countless numbers of woes. This dread prompts people to wear protective amulets and to use magical charms and spells, to seek the assistance of magicians and conjurers, to severely abuse their bodies as they confess their errors, to offer sacrifices and perform purifications, and to pray with quivering voices. For all these people, hope is fleeting.

tiles who had undergone the rite of circumcision) would have turned to the Lord. The proclamation of the gospel would then have extended to the Gentile population of the city, with perhaps many turning to the Lord right out of the various cults. Also at this time the gospel probably spread to the nearby city of Laodicea.

It is uncertain whether Paul ever visited the city himself. If he did, such a visit would have occurred during his lengthy stay at Ephesus. The apostle takes no credit for the establishment of the church in Colosse. Note 1:7, where he writes that they learned the gospel from Epaphras.

Among those who came to know Christ in the city is a man named Philemon. To him Paul writes a brief letter to intercede on behalf of his runaway slave Onesimus, who has encountered Paul in Rome and has come to know Christ (see 4:9; see commentary on Philemon).

These Christians gathered in homes for worship, teaching, and fellowship. There are at least two house churches that we know of—one in the home of a lady named Nympha (4:15), who lives in Laodicea, and the other in the home of Philemon (Philem. 2). There are probably a number of house fellowships in both of these cities. Nearly all believers throughout the Mediterranean world met in homes during the first century of the church's existence.

The Problem in the Church at Colosse

Paul writes this letter to counteract the inroads of a new and dangerous teaching in the church at Colosse. He denounces the teaching as empty, deceitful, and in accordance with elemental spirits (2:8).

What exactly are the contours of this teaching that the apostle finds objectionable? This question has been one of the most controversial issues surrounding the interpretation of this letter. The previous generation of scholarship thought the letter reflected the incursion of Gnosticism into the church.[9] This is unlikely because it is doubtful that Gnosticism as a religion of redemption yet existed at this early stage and the letter does not take on some of the key features of Gnosticism, such as the two-god theology.

In recent years, many scholars have suggested that the problem reflects a Jewish mysticism involving a visionary ascent to heaven and glimpses of angels surrounding the heavenly throne.[10] This view is more on the right track because there appears to be clear Jewish aspects to the teaching, such as the observance of Sabbaths and New Moon festivals (see 2:16). Yet this perspective does not explain all of the evidence, especially that which suggests the influence of local religions and religious practices. The Colossian problem is best described as a *syncretism*—a blending of religious ideas from a variety of local traditions.

A Portrait of the Situation

Word has reached the apostle Paul, perhaps through Epaphras, that trouble is brewing in the Colossian church. An influential leader—perhaps a shaman-like figure—is attracting a following among the believers. This spiritual guide claims superior insight into the spirit realm and is insisting on certain rites, taboos, and practices as a means of protection from evil spirits and for deliverance from afflictions and calamities. Paul characterizes his teaching as a "philosophy" (2:8).

One of the distinctive features of this teaching is "the worship of angels" for assistance and protection (2:18). This resonates well with the people who were accustomed to invoking spirit mediator beings in their pre-Christian lives. Although these people have received Christ as their Redeemer and Lord, they have not drawn out the full implications of this for their daily lives. Rather than relying directly on their powerful Lord, they invoke spirit assistants, or angels, to protect them from curses, to drive away spirits causing fevers, headaches, or horrible nighttime apparitions. Part of this probably involves the wearing of magical amulets, which normally bear the names of angels and spirits who they believe will provide protection.

The outspoken leader of the faction appears to be basing his unique spiritual insight, in part, on his prior experience of initiation into one or more of the local mystery cults. Paul alludes to this in 2:18 when he describes the deviant teaching using a rare word (*embateuō*) that is part of the technical vocabulary of a local cult. On the basis of his prior initiation, the shaman claims a certain immunity to the hostile powers and a superior understanding of the realm of gods and spirits.

In the teaching of this spiritualistic "philosophy," one must also observe a variety of taboos, such as fasting, avoidance of certain foods, and possibly also sexual regulations. In essence, there is such a rigor of discipline that Paul speaks of it as an unsparing or "harsh treatment of the body" (2:23).

Some other features of the teaching ultimately come from Judaism. Sabbath observance, festivals and New Moon celebrations, "humility" (probably referring to fasting), and "wisdom" all suggest Jewish roots. One must remember, however, that we should not always think of Judaism through the lenses of the Pharisees. There is clearly a dimension of what we may call "folk Judaism" in this countryside setting of western Asia Minor. In folk Judaism, there is a form of "wisdom" informing Jews about how to command and manipulate demons, especially by calling on angels.

After hearing about the spreading influence of this esoteric philosophy, Paul feels compelled to write to the Colossians and respond to this deviant teaching by pointing them to a proper perspective on the exalted Christ. In essence, he disqualifies the ringleaders of this teaching from leadership and urges the Colossians to desist from these practices, to cling to Christ, and to ignore their damning criticisms.

Introduction to the Letter (1:1–2)

Paul . . . and Timothy (1:1). The first line of the letter explicitly says that it is written not just by Paul, but also by Timothy, Paul's close companion. Paul's contribution far overshadows that of Timothy, especially when he switches to the first person ("I, Paul . . .") in 1:23 and writes autobiographically. Timothy is most likely functioning as Paul's secretary (a position the Greeks called an *amanuensis*).[11] In this role, Timothy may very well have had an active part in crafting the letter.

Grace and peace to you from God our Father (1:2). The standard convention in Greek letter-writing was to begin by pronouncing greetings (using the word *chairein*). Paul varies from this convention by using the word *charis* ("grace"). By this, he deepens the greeting by calling on the one true God to manifest his dynamic generosity upon these dear believers. He also adds to this the typical Jewish greeting of "peace" (Heb. *shalōm;* Gk. *eirēnē*). The peace of God is a key part of the eschatological blessings of the new covenant.

Thanksgiving and Prayer (1:3–14)

As almost all commentators concur, Paul shapes his thanksgiving and prayer to address the real situation of the readers. Paul feels a pastoral responsibility for this church because it was planted during his ministry in Ephesus by one of his converts. He genuinely prays for this group and gives thanks to God for them.

We always thank God when we pray (1:3). Paul often describes his prayer as unceasing. We can assume that at the minimum this means that he prays three times a day, as was common in Jewish practice. Beyond this, he probably finds many hours to pray for the many churches and people he cared for during his long days as an incarcerated prisoner. Apparently Timothy joins him for many extended times of prayer.

Love you have for all the saints (1:4). The emphasis on tangible manifestations of love is the distinctive trait that set Christianity apart from all of the other religions of the time. The self-sacrificial love of Christ is the benchmark for Paul's definition of love (see Eph. 5:1–2).

Hope that is stored up for you in heaven (1:5). To a people worried about life after death and the fate-determining stars in heaven, the notion that God is sovereign and is ultimately in control of their fate, granting them an eternal hope, is especially comforting. The threefold repetition of hope in the first chapter (1:5, 23, 27) may suggest that some of the Colossians still struggle with feelings of hopelessness.

Truth (1:5–6). In affirming that the Colossians have received a *true* gospel and that they now know the grace of God in *truth,* Paul anticipates his later comments about the *deceit* of the new teaching in the church (2:8) as well as the deceitfulness of the various idolatrous religions in the area.

All over the world this gospel is bearing fruit and growing (1:6). The gospel has literally spread into almost every reach of the Roman empire by the time Paul writes. The apostle is probably familiar with many incredible stories of the penetration of the gospel into places like Egypt, North Africa, and Persia.

You learned it from Epaphras (1:7). Here Paul credits this important Colossian leader as the first to bring these people the gospel. He not only evangelized the Lycus Valley cities, but the term "learned" implies that he continued to instruct them in the faith. Epaphras has just reported to Paul the good news about the spiritual vitality of the Colossian believers, but has also related the threat posed to the stability and well-being of the church by the faction that has developed.

That you may live a life worthy of the Lord (1:10). Literally, Paul writes, "that you *walk* worthily of the Lord." Walking is a metaphor for one's conduct, which he uses three other times in Colossians (2:6; 3:7; 4:5). Paul encourages conduct that honors the Lord and is appropriate for Christians. The metaphor is Jewish (see Ex. 18:20; Deut. 13:4–5) and was not commonly used by Greeks. The Hebrew term *halak* is the root of the rabbinic term *Halakah*, rules or statutes designed to guide the daily life of an individual (see comments on Eph. 4:1). Many of the Pharisaic regulations were written down in the second century A.D. in the Mishnah.

Being strengthened with all power according to his glorious might (1:11). Paul links four terms conveying the idea of divine power. God's awesome power is available to his people. Folks in the Greco-Roman world sought power for a variety of reasons—for protection from evils or to acquire wealth or influence. Here God's power is manifested to believers to enable them to have patience and endurance as they experience suffering, temptation, deceitful teachers, and various difficulties in this present evil age.

Who has qualified you to share in the inheritance of the saints in the . . . light (1:12). The image that stands behind the language of this verse is the anticipation of God's people as they wandered in the desert and waited to receive their inheritance in the Promised Land (see Num. 18:20; Deut. 10:19). The book of Daniel speaks of a future allotted inheritance (Dan. 12:13). The way Paul expresses himself here is similar to the way the Qumran community spoke of an eschatological inheritance: "God has caused them to inherit the lot of the Holy Ones. He has joined their assembly to the Sons of Heaven."[12] The difference, of course, is that Paul sees this fulfilled in the work of the Messiah, Jesus.

He has rescued us (1:13). The Exodus is once again the image that stands behind the words here. Paul compares God's deliverance of his people from their bondage in Egypt (Ex. 6:6; 14:30) to his mighty work now of rescuing believers from their bondage to the power of the evil one. Paul views his proclamation of the gospel as the means God uses for unbelievers "to open their eyes and turn them from darkness to light, and from the power of Satan" (Acts 26:18).

The dominion of darkness (1:13). The phrase refers to the sphere over which Satan and his demonic powers rule.

Brought us into the kingdom (1:13). The translation of the NIV does not bring out the color of the Greek verb Paul chooses here. *Methistēmi* was frequently used with the sense of transferal and often describes the massive dislocation of a group of one people from one region to another. The terminology may have reminded the Jewish readers of the time when the Syrian king Antiochus transferred several thousand Jews to Asia Minor in the second century B.C.[13] The believing community has not only been rescued from this evil domain, but they have been transplanted into a new dominion—the kingdom of God.

Redemption (1:14). Anyone in the Roman empire was readily familiar with this term because it commonly referred to the purchase of a slave. Readers who knew the Old Testament would rightly see an allusion here to God's freeing his people from their slavery in Egypt.[14] So much of the language of this passage points to a comparison between the first exodus from Egypt and now the second exodus of God's people from the more ultimate power of evil.

Poetic Praise to Christ (1:15–20)

This is one of the most beautiful and eloquent poems of praise to Christ in all of the New Testament. The piece magnificently celebrates Christ's sovereignty over all of creation and his supremacy over all powers, most notably the hostile angelic powers. Christ is truly Lord of heaven and earth.

The language and style of this passage have led many interpreters to regard the passage as a quotation of an actual hymn from the worship of the early church.[15] Colossians 3:16 intimates that this church regularly sang hymns of praise to Christ that were rich with statements about his identity and work. There is no doubt that this passage has many poetic features, but it is impossible for us to know with certainty that it is an actual hymn. If it were, it teaches us two important lessons: (1) The lyrics of the early Christian hymns were heavy with theological content, especially about Christ, and (2) Paul not only appeals to the intellect of his readers, but also to their hearts through the language of worship.

People in the Lycus Valley fear the influence of astral powers, terrestrial spirits, and underworld powers that raise problems for them in day-to-day life. This fear did not instantly go away for the Colossian believers after they turned to Christ. They know the reality of these powers and must still deal with them. The question for them is: What difference does Christ make? For the ringleader of the new teaching at Colosse, Christ is functionally no more powerful than the angels they invoke for protection. For Paul, Christ is the exalted Lord, Creator of the universe, preeminent in everything, and infinitely superior to any kind of angelic power.

He is the image of the invisible God (1:15). In the book of Proverbs, wisdom is personified and said to be with God at the creation of the world: "I was there when he set the heavens in place. . . . I was the craftsman at his side" (Prov. 8:27, 30). In the Jewish wisdom literature just before the New Testament era, this personified divine wisdom is described as the image of God: "For she is a reflection of eternal light, a spotless mirror of the working of God, and an image of his

goodness" (Wisd. Sol. 7:26). It was difficult for Jewish Christians to reconcile the deity of Jesus Christ with their one-God theology (monotheism). Paul uses the language of wisdom to help clarify the nature and work of Christ in his existence before his incarnation.

The firstborn over all creation (1:15). This expression does not mean that Christ is the first being God created. The Old Testament background is decisive here. This is a title that belongs to Christ as a descendant of David who reigns as king. The psalmist reports what God said of David: "I will also appoint him my *firstborn*, the most exalted of the kings of the earth" (Ps. 89:27, italics added). The emphasis falls on Christ's ruling sovereignty and the closeness of his relationship to the Father.

Whether thrones or powers or rulers or authorities (1:16). These terms were commonly used in Jewish literature to speak of angelic powers, good or evil. Out of these sources, a passage in one first-century document uses three of the four terms: "I tell you, in all the creation which God created, there is not to be found one like you [Abraham]. For he searched among the angels and archangels, and principalities and powers, as well as thrones."[16] Although a hierarchy of angels may be assumed in Colossians 1:16, we have no way of discerning what that is. Although some have thought these are good angels, Paul consistently speaks of the "rulers" and "authorities" in a negative way in this letter (see 2:10, 15). By expanding on the invisible realm, Paul emphasizes to the Colossians that Christ is by no means an angel nor is he on the same level as an angel; he is Creator of this realm, and he is incomparably greater.

In him all things hold together (1:17). Christ not only brought all things into being, but he maintains the creation. J. B. Lightfoot once said that Christ is the One who makes creation "a cosmos instead of a chaos."[17] Not only does Christ keep the world from falling apart as a result of earthquakes, floods, plagues, and cosmic disturbances, he maintains a check on the awful workings of the demonic powers.

He is the head of the body, the church (1:18). Paul elaborates on his metaphor of the church as the body of Christ by now asserting that Christ functions as the head of this body. The image of a head in relationship to a body was common during Paul's time, especially in medical writers, some philosophers, and the Jewish writer Philo. Christ not only provides leadership and direction for his people, but he is the source of the church's life energy for its growth.[18]

God was pleased to have all his fullness dwell in him (1:19). The term "fullness" (*plērōma*) echoes the many places in the Old Testament where the essence, power, and glory of God inhabit the place he has chosen to dwell. The prophet Ezekiel exclaimed, "I looked and saw the glory of the LORD filling the temple" (Ezek. 44:4). This word may very well be another way of referring to the Holy Spirit, who dwelt in Jesus and empowered his ministry.

To reconcile to himself all things, whether things on earth or things in heaven (1:20). This passage holds out the promise of universal peace. The Messiah, as "Prince of Peace" (Isa. 9:6), will finally and ultimately bring worldwide peace and quell every upheaval and rebellion in all of creation. For the evil principalities and powers this means pacification as enemies of Christ, not a reconciliation to him as friends (see Col. 2:15).

Reconciliation (1:21–23)

Once . . . now (1:21–22). Paul elaborates on the nature of reconciliation by applying it particularly to the Gentile members of the Colossian church. In doing so he contrasts their former life ("once") with their present life in Christ ("now"). The "once–now" language appears frequently in early Christian literature to describe conversion.[19]

You were alienated from God and were enemies (1:21). Because they had given their devotion to idols such as Cybele, Apollo, and Aphrodite and lived in bondage to sinful practices, the Colossian Gentiles were estranged from the one true God.

To present you holy in his sight, without blemish and free from accusation (1:22). The aim of reconciliation goes beyond the enjoyment of a relationship with the living God. He wants to purify his people. The language of this verse comes from the context of sacrifice in Judaism. As an unblemished sacrificial animal was presented at the Jerusalem temple, so the Lord seeks to present his people to himself as pure. "Without blemish" was used to describe the animal offerings that the Lord required from his people and to characterize Christ in his self-sacrifice.[20] Paul shifts from the sacrificial language to a judicial image when he says "free from accusation." This was used in the common language of the day, as the papyri show, to refer to a person against whom no blame or fault could be brought.[21]

Not moved (1:23). Paul is deeply concerned that some of the Colossian believers are moving away from the core of the gospel. This is one of his principal reasons for writing the letter and the essential burden of Colossians 2.

Paul's Labor for the Gospel (1:24–29)

I fill up in my flesh what is still lacking in regard to Christ's afflictions (1:24). In Judaism and early Christianity, there was a conviction that a set amount of suffering must be endured by God's people before the final events of history are set in motion. This is clearly evident in Revelation 6:9–11, where the souls of the martyrs under the altar ask the Lord how much longer he will tarry before executing his work of judgment. They are told "to wait a little longer, until the number of their fellow servants and brothers who were to be killed . . . was completed." In a similar way, Jewish apocalyptic writers conceived of an appointed measure of suffering that must be fulfilled before the end of the age. One first-century Jewish writer puts it this way: "For [God] has weighed the age in the balance, and measured the times by measure, and

COLOSSE

Looking west from the top of the tel.

▼

numbered the times by number; and he will not move or arouse them until that measure is fulfilled" (*4 Ezra* 4:36–37).

What Paul clearly does not mean in this passage is that Christ's sufferings were in any way deficient for securing salvation for his people. Christ's sufferings are "still lacking" only in that they do not fill the appointed measure to usher in the end of the age. It appears that Paul saw his sufferings as contributing to the sum total that would hasten the coming of the Lord in judgment and final salvation.

By the commission God gave me (1:25). Paul here describes himself as an appointed steward in the unfolding of God's plan of salvation. The term *oikonomos* was widely used in Greco-Roman society for the work carried out by the administrator of a large household or an estate. In many contexts, the *oikonomos* was actually a slave.

The mystery (1:26–27). Paul is not referring here to the local religions that have mystery initiation rituals. He contrasts these with *the* mystery—the person of Christ. Jesus is the One who comes in fulfillment of the mystery spoken of in the book of Daniel (Dan. 2:18, 19, 27–30, 47), which is revealed to Nebuchadnezzar in a dream yet requires interpretation by divine insight. Jesus is the rock that was cut out "not by human hands," who has set up a kingdom that fills the whole earth and will never be destroyed (2:34–35, 44).

Christ in you, the hope of glory (1:27). As the core and essence of God's mystery, Christ indwells his people. He is directly and personally present in the lives of his people, who now constitute his body. This contrasts with Stoic notions of an impersonal and pantheistic immanence. Paul will build on this teaching in chapter 2 to raise the question of why they feel a need to call on angelic mediators when they are in a present and dynamic relationship with the risen Christ. The fact of Christ's presence also ensures them of a future life with him when he returns.

Admonishing and teaching everyone (1:28). Paul has invested enormous time and energy in teaching those who have come to Christ. This involved explaining the Old Testament in light of Jesus as the Messiah, passing on the teaching of and about Jesus, and explaining the kingdom of God. He has spent far more time teaching than simply an hour on Sunday morning and an hour on Wednesday evening. He has invested many hours of intensive sessions with small and large groups. Included with his teaching is direct and pointed criticism, admonition, and correction of the people. This would have been directed at engaging false beliefs as well as challenging these new believers to change their lifestyles.

Struggling with all his energy (1:29). In order to convey the significant effort involved in his ministry, Paul makes use of the athletic image of struggle (*agōn*). Paul's ministry on behalf of the church is comparable to the self-discipline and exertion of an athlete in training for competition. Yet Paul makes it clear that he does not depend only on his own strength, but on the supernatural enabling power that God bestows on him.

Paul's Labor for the Colossians (2:1–5)

In spite of his personal absence from the Colossians, Paul is deeply concerned about them and labors for them in prayer. For the first time, he mentions that he does not want them to be victimized to a teaching that is contrary to the gospel of Christ.

For those at Laodicea (2:1). Laodicea was only eleven miles down the Lycus River from Colosse. The church there was probably established at the same time as the church in Colosse by Epaphras (see 4:12–13; cf. 1:7). It is also addressed as one of the seven churches in the book of Revelation (Rev. 3:14–22), where it is called into account for its lukewarmness in the context of their material affluence and self-sufficiency.

Laodicea was in fact wealthy. Some of its leading citizens gained notoriety for their generous benefactions to the city. It was much larger than Colosse and served the area as a center for banking and finance. Much of the revenues for the city came from the production of textiles. The medical school of Laodicea, associated with the local deity Memn Karou, was also well known.[22]

For all who have not met me personally (2:1). Since Paul has never been to Colosse, only those who heard him preach the gospel in Ephesus would have had the opportunity to meet him personally. In spite of the fact that Paul did not plant this church, he has a deep and loving concern for their spiritual well-being. He labors in prayer for them, writes to them, and sends one of his trusted associates to minister to them.

Full riches of complete understanding (2:2). Paul wants to encourage the community and promote their unity in love, but this needs to be built on a foundation of proper knowledge. The word "com-

plete" can more precisely be translated "full assurance" or "certainty." The writer of Hebrews uses this expression when he urges believers to "draw near to God with a sincere heart in *full assurance* of faith" (Heb. 10:22, italics added). This assurance is based on the forgiveness of sin and a knowledge of the Christian faith, to which he urges his readers to hold unswervingly (10:23).

In whom are hidden all the treasures of wisdom and knowledge (2:3). Christ, as the mystery of God, is the source of knowledge. Paul here draws on the personification of "wisdom" in the Old Testament (as well as in later Jewish literature) and transfers its functions to Christ:

> *If you call out for insight*
> *   and cry aloud for understanding,*
> *and if you look for it as silver*
> *   and search for it as for hidden*
> *   treasure,*
> *then you will understand the fear of*
> *   the LORD*
> *   and find the knowledge of God.*
> *For the LORD gives wisdom,*
> *   and from his mouth come*
> *   knowledge and understanding.*
> *   (Prov. 2:3–6)*

RUINS AT LAODICEA

That no one may deceive you by fine-sounding arguments (2:4). Paul does not state this hypothetically. He is genuinely concerned that the Colossians are being deceived. In Greek writers such as Aristotle, Plato, and Epictetus, *pithanalogia* ("fine-sounding arguments") was not used with negative connotations, but with the sense of plausible and persuasive speech. The idea is similar to Paul's comments to the Corinthians that his preaching was "not with wise and persuasive words, but with a demonstration of the Spirit's power" (1 Cor. 2:4).

How orderly you are and how firm your faith in Christ is (2:5). Paul appeals to military imagery here, as he so often does in his letters (see Eph. 6:14–17), to convey the reality of the threat posed by the variant teaching. "Order" (*taxis*) is used in Greek literature and in the Old Testament for troops drawn up in battle formation. "Firm" (*stereōma*) was often used to designate the strength of troop units in resisting the enemy. In the LXX, it is used to describe God as a place of refuge against the enemy: "The LORD is my rock, my fortress and my deliverer" (Ps. 18:2; cf. 71:3). Once again, the strength and ability for Christians to stand strong is through Christ.

Live in Christ! Don't Fall Prey to Seductive Teaching (2:6–8)

Rooted and built up in him (2:7). Paul combines the images of a tree and a building here to describe the stability of the foundation believers have already received in Christ (see also 1 Cor. 3:9).

See to it that no one takes you captive (2:8). The apostle uses a rare and colorful word to speak of the danger facing the Colossian believers. Greek dictionaries, in fact, report only two other occurrences of the word *sylagogeō* in the language: In one instance it is used for stealing property and in the other for taking a captive.[23] One of the root words (*syla*) was commonly used to refer to booty or plunder that was seized from a cargo ship.

Hollow and deceptive philosophy (2:8). Paul is not condemning here the traditional Greek philosophies, such as Platonism, Epicureanism, or Stoicism. The language of this passage points to a faction within the church who spoke of their own set of teachings as "philosophy." This usage accords with the broad way the word *philosophia* was used in antiquity to refer to anything from occult traditions to the Jewish sects and to the traditional Greek philosophies. The fact that Paul characterizes the teaching of the factional group as "hollow and deceptive" underlines the danger and threat that he sees it posing to the church.

The basic principles of this world (2:8). "Basic principles" is a translation of the Greek word *stoicheia*. The term may indeed have the idea of the rudiments of science or an institution (such as the fundamental principles of religion), but it can also be a designation for spirit beings (as it is translated by the NRSV: "elemental spirits of the universe"). It is this latter sense that best fits the context here and in 2:20.[24]

Stoicheia is used for spirit beings in Persian religious texts, magical papyri, astrological texts, and some Jewish documents. The word thus represents still another term in Paul's reservoir of terminology to refer to the powers of darkness in Colossians, along with principalities, powers, authorities, and thrones. The basic point of

▶ *Stoicheia* in Jewish Occultism

This word features prominently in a Jewish occult document known as the *Testament of Solomon*. The original form of this document was probably composed in the first-century A.D. and may have originated in Asia Minor. An astrological portion of this work probably circulated independently as early as the first century B.C. It provides significant insight into the usage of the term:

Then I [Solomon] commanded another demon to appear before me. There came to me thirty-six heavenly bodies [*stoicheia*], their heads like formless dogs.... When I, Solomon, saw these things, I asked them, saying, "Well who are you?" All at once, with one voice, they said, "We are thirty-six heavenly bodies [*stoicheia*], the world rulers of the darkness of this age."

Paul's teaching here is that the dangerous teaching at Colosse has a demonic root. Although it is passed along as human tradition, it can ultimately be traced to the inspiration of demonic spirits.

Your Resources in Christ (2:9–15)

You have been given fullness in Christ (2:10). Not only does the power and authority of God belong to the resurrected Christ, but believers share in it by virtue of their incorporation into him. The Colossian believers do not need to fear the evil supernatural realm or rely on the teaching of "the philosophy." They have direct and immediate access to the power of God through Christ.

The head over every power and authority (2:10). Many of the Colossian believers continue to live in the daily fear of the workings of underworld spirits, terrestrial spirits, and astral spirits, as they have been accustomed to throughout their lives. Because of their union to Christ, however, they now share in his authority over the powers of darkness. The word "head" clearly indicates here the

sense of "authority over." This is in line with its usage in the Old Testament and other Jewish documents.[25]

In him you were also circumcised (2:11). In an unusual twist, Paul introduces his remarks on baptism by first speaking of it metaphorically as circumcision. He here draws on and adapts the Old Testament teaching about the "circumcision of the heart."[26] Even the Qumran community referred to circumcision metaphorically, illustrated by a passage in the Dead Sea Scrolls that speaks of circumcision of the foreskin of evil inclination and stiffness of neck.

In the putting off of the sinful nature (2:11). "Sinful nature" is the NIV's translation of *sarx* (flesh). For Paul, literal

R E F L E C T I O N S

PART OF THE REASON THAT WE STUMBLE AND LOSE heart in the midst of our struggles is because we do not recognize and fully appreciate our position in Christ. Our knowledge about Christ and his work impacts how we live and see ourselves. Recognizing the meaning and implications of our relationship to Christ should have a profound impact on how we live day-to-day.

circumcision is no longer a necessary or valid practice for the new covenant people of God, but a spiritual circumcision is vitally essential. This is the removal of believers' solidarity with Adam, which Paul refers to as "the body of sin" in Romans 6:6. Christ removes the determining power of sin and death and, in its place, asserts his own lordship.

Buried with him in baptism and raised with him (2:12). Paul calls on the Colossian believers to remember the meaning of their baptism as an identification with the death and burial with Jesus. They are no longer identified with Adam, but with Christ and his victory over sin and its power. The idea of dying and rising with Christ is central to Paul's theology and receives its fullest expression in Romans 6:3–11.

The concept of co-resurrection receives a much stronger emphasis here and in Ephesians (see Eph. 2:4–6) than in Romans. By emphasizing the Colossians' participation in the resurrection of Christ, Paul demonstrates their share in his authority over the realm of demons and evil spirits. Christ alone is sufficient to protect them from the "powers." They no longer need to rely on their former means of control offered by occultism, nor do they need to rely on the solution presented by "the philosophy."

God made you alive with Christ (2:13). Some of the mystery cults claimed to offer an experience of rebirth and new life through ritual initiation. A papyrus document called the "Mithras Liturgy" (although probably not actually linked to Mithraism) purports to prescribe the proper rites and invocations for an initiate to become immortal, be reborn, be unified with the deity, and enter a new

life.[27] By contrast, Paul declares that new life is only found through union with the resurrected Christ.

Having cancelled the written code (2:14). Paul illustrates God's complete forgiveness of all the sins of believers by a colorful image derived from the world of business in the first century. The "written code" (*cheirographon*) was a note of indebtedness. The term is used many times in the papyri and is even well attested in Jewish literature. One Jewish document well illustrates how it was used: "'Let us find how we might be able to repay you.' Without delay, I would bring before them the note (*cheirographon*) and read it granting cancellation."[28]

Jesus has cancelled the note of indebtedness believers have with God. Consequently, all of the penalties God has threatened because humanity has defaulted in its obligations to him are declared null and void because of Christ's work on the cross. Paul creatively takes the image one step further by saying that Christ has taken the note away from us and nailed it to the cross.

Having disarmed the powers and authorities (2:15). The death and resurrection of Christ marked a decisive victory over the evil supernatural realm. They have

---

REFLECTIONS

WE DO NOT NEED TO BROOD OVER the past. We realistically experience a new life in Christ. The imagery of "the written code" nailed to the cross reminds us that every single transgression against our God has been completely forgiven on the basis of the work of Christ.

been deprived of any effective power against Christ himself or against those incorporated into him and appropriating his power. The Greek word translated "disarmed" is found in other literature simply in the sense of "strip off," as one removes clothing (see the use of this verb in 3:9 and the related noun in 2:11). The evil powers are not totally divested of their power. They continue to be hostile and active, but they are powerless against the Colossian Christians insofar as these believers recognize and appropriate their authority in Christ.

He made a public spectacle of them (2:15). The idea here is of a public exposure leading to disgrace. The verb used here (*deigmatizō*) is used of Joseph's plan to expose Mary's pregnancy and thus bring public shame on her (Matt. 1:19). An ancient historian cites a Cyprian law that mandates an adulteress to cut her hair and thus be subject to contempt by the community (Dio Chrysostom 47[64]3). The powers of darkness are exposed as weak and ineffective against God. Their efforts to put Christ to death and thereby ruin the redemptive plan of God (1 Cor. 2:6–8) were exposed as futile in light of God's power in raising Jesus from the dead. Their plotting was unmasked as ineffective in light of God's wisdom, who used Jesus' death as the means of reconciling people to himself.

Triumphing over them by the cross (2:15). Paul takes the idea of public exposure one step further by adopting the vivid image of a Roman triumph. When a general led his army to victory in battle, the returning army would celebrate their conquest with a "triumphal procession" (*thriambeuō*). The successful general led a tumultuous procession marching through the streets of Rome, followed by his army singing hymns of victory and jubilantly reveling in their conquest. The defeated king with all of his surviving warriors together with the spoils of war were also paraded along as a spectacle for all to see.[29]

By analogy, God has put the principalities and powers on public display as defeated enemies through Christ's death and resurrection. The demonic rulers and evil spirits are led in the celebration as vanquished enemies. The Lord Jesus Christ is due all praise, honor, and glory as the victorious general. E. F. Scott aptly

▶The Triumphal Procession of Aemilius Paulus

The first-century writer Plutarch tells the story of the parade led by the victorious general Aemelius Paulus. Depicted in this passage was the disheartened king Perseus along with all of his arms, riches, children, and attendants:

He [Perseus] was followed by a company of friends and intimates whose faces were heavy with grief. ... The whole army also carried sprays of laurel, following the chariot of their general [Aemilius] by companies and divisions, and singing, some of them divers songs intermingled with jesting, as the ancient custom was, and others paeans of victory and hymns in praise of the achievements of Aemilius, who was gazed upon and admired by all, and envied by no one that was good.[A-2]

comments that the safety of the Colossian believer

was to be found in the conciliation of the friendly powers by means of offerings, sacred rites, spells, and talismans, so that they would protect him against the opposing demons . . . but Paul insists always that this protection is offered by Christ and that all else is useless. . . . We have a power on our side which can overcome everything that is against us.[30]

▶ **MAGICAL AMULET**

This is a Christian amulet depicting a rider slaying a demon. The reverse side has the inscription: "Guard from every evil him who carries this amulet."

Don't Be Victimized by the Variant Teaching (2:16–23)

Paul now takes up a direct and incisive criticism of many features of the variant teaching at Colosse. His basic complaint is that these heretics have lost their connection to Christ by replacing him with their syncretistic practices and calling on angels.

Do not let anyone judge you (2:16). A group of believers within the church at Colosse are, in fact, judging and demeaning others who do not subscribe to their teachings (see 2:18, 20). The language of this passage (esp. the Gk. pronoun *tis*, "a certain person"), may point to an influential teacher—perhaps a shaman-like figure—who is ringleader of this emerging faction.

A religious festival, a New Moon celebration or a Sabbath day (2:16). These are distinctively Jewish observances found together repeatedly in the Old Testament

---

▶ The Combination of Jewish Observances with Pagan Cult Practices

The church father Hippolytus describes the teaching of a Christian leader named Elchasai, who lived at the end of the first century. Elchasai was not from Colosse, but his teaching is an example of how a Christian could mix Jewish, Christian, and pagan cult practices. Hippolytus quotes an important aspect of this teaching of Elchasai:

> There exist wicked stars of impiety . . . beware of the power of the days of the sovereignty of these stars, and engage not in the commencement of any undertaking during the ruling days of these. And baptize not man or woman during the days of the power of these stars, when the moon, (emerging) from among them, courses the sky, and travels along with them.

> Beware of the very day up to that on which the moon passes out from these stars, and enter on every beginning of your works. But, moreover, honour the day of the Sabbath, since that day is one of those during which prevails (the power) of these stars. Take care, however, not to commence your works the third day from a Sabbath, since when three years of the reign of the emperor Trajan are again completed from the time that he subjected the Parthians to his own sway,—when, I say, three years have been completed, war rages between the impious angels of the northern constellations; and on this account all kingdoms of impiety are in a state of confusion.[A-3]

and ardently advocated by the proponents of the Colossian "philosophy."[31] There is evidence in Josephus and from inscriptions that Sabbath observance was important to the Jews of Asia Minor.[32] There is also testimony from the inscriptions that Jews in Asia Minor customarily observed the important Jewish festivals (such as Passover and Pentecost).[33]

The adherents of "the philosophy" are apparently not law-abiding Jews from the local synagogue. They are Christians (some of whom are ethnically Jewish) who are holding on to certain aspects of the Jewish law and yet combining it with local folk beliefs. It is even possible that they are giving these festivals and observances a new interpretation.

Religious festivals of various kinds were important in the local religions of Colosse. Also, the observance of the New Moon was integral to the performance of certain mystery initiation rituals. A popular deity in the region (also attested in the coins of Colosse) was the moon god Memn. The various phases of the moon were important to the worship of this god. Interestingly, another deity worshiped at Colosse was the goddess Selene. Her name, in fact, is the Greek word for the moon; she was closely associated with Artemis and Hekate. In popular belief these three goddesses were believed to protect their worshipers from hostile spirits.

A shadow of the things that were to come (2:17). The Jewish festivals and observances, as they were taught in the Old Testament, were essentially a foretaste of a future reality, realized now in the Lord Jesus Christ (see Heb. 10:1).

False humility (2:18). The word "false" is not in the Greek text, but it is inferred from the context. In Jewish texts, the word for "humility" could be used for fasting and may refer to that discipline here. In both Jewish and pagan circles, fasting is seen as important for driving off evil spirits. One Jewish text illustrates this well: "But a pure fast is what I created, with a pure heart and pure hands. It releases sin. It heals diseases. It casts out demons."[34] Fasting was also a precondition in many religious contexts for successful visionary experience (something we know was part of the Colossian "philosophy").

The worship of angels (2:18). This expression provides us with a significant insight into an important feature of the deviant teaching at Colosse. Although some have suggested that we need to interpret it in terms of the angels performing the worship, it makes better sense to view the angels as the object of the veneration. The group in Colosse is apparently calling on angels for assistance and protection from evil spirits. This was the way people commonly sought angels in the first century—in folk Judaism, in local folk belief, and later, even in segments of early Christianity.[35] It is doubtful that the group had splintered off from the church and were worshiping angels as they would worship God and Christ. Rather, the unique word for "worship" (*thrēskeia*) should be understood in the sense of "invoking" or "calling on."

[Don't] let anyone ... disqualify you for the prize (2:18). The Greek word translated here (*katabrabeuō*) was used in the context of the games and reflected the decision of the judge (*brabeus*) against someone. An athlete who did not receive a favorable decision by the judge could be disqualified or deprived of the prize.

Paul hereby says that the people involved in this church faction have no right to set themselves up as judges over the Colossian believers. Rather, they should resist the insistence of these teachers to invoke angels and engage in ascetic practices, in spite of their visionary claims.

Such a person goes into great detail (2:18). This is a highly disputed translation of a Greek word that is rare in the language, but is vital to understanding the nature of the teaching of the Colossian "philosophy." The basic meaning of *embateuō* is "entering," which has led to the extended meanings of "entering into an investigation of something" or "entering into the possession of something." The great difficulty is that no explicit object for entering is given in the Greek text.

Our understanding of the religious usage of this word was enhanced significantly by the discovery of the Apollo temple at Claros, about thirty miles north of Ephesus. The interior walls of the temple preserve many Greek inscriptions of official delegations coming to consult the oracle. In the process of consultation, the delegations often went through the mystery initiation ritual associated with the cult. There were two stages to the ritual: (1) the reception of the mysteries (or the initiation), and (2) an entering (*embateuō*) of the innermost sanctuary of the temple for the consultation. *Embateuō* thus functions as a technical term to refer to the second and highest stage of the ritual initiation.[36]

This suggests that the leader and perhaps others in this "philosophy" have experienced some form of mystery initiation ritual into one of the local cults. This may have bolstered their claim to spiritual authority based on the knowledge and visionary experiences they presumably received.

About what he has seen (2:18). Visionary experience was a core feature of mys-

▶ Calling on Angels for Protection

There are many inscriptions from Asia Minor mentioning angels. Most of these are invocations to angels for protection, deliverance, or assistance. An inscribed amulet found near the city of Cyzicus illustrates this tendency:

> Michael, Gabriel, Ouriel, Raphael, protect the one who wears this. Holy, holy, holy. PIPI RPSS. Angel, Araaph, flee O hated one. Solomon pursues you.[A-4]

Another inscription found on a tablet in Patras (Achaia) illustrates the same tendency in a way that highlights the connection to daily life:

> O angels, protect the household and lives of John and Georgia . . . Sabaōth, Eloeein, Ariēl,

Gabriēl, Michaēl, Raphaēl, Thelchiēl, Sisiēl, Ouriēl, Raphaēl, Daniēl, Ouriēl, Boreēl, Iaō, Sabaōth, Chariēl . . . O power of these angels and characters, give victory and favor to John and Georgia and this household while they live.[A-5]

AMULET INVOKING ANGELS

This amulet calls upon Michael, Raphael, Gabriel, and Ouriel.

▶ Finding the Right Angel to Thwart a Demon

The *Testament of Solomon* (see *"Sto-icheia* in Jewish Occultism" at 2:8) contains Jewish folk tradition on dealing with demons. One portion of the text ostensibly helps a person discern what demon is causing a particular ailment. The remedy typically involves calling on the appropriate angel who can thwart the evil workings of that demon. Here are a few examples:

- Then I, Solomon, summoned the first spirit and said to him, "Who are you?" He replied, "I am the first decan of the zodiac and I am called Ruax. I cause heads of men to suffer pain and I cause their temples to throb. Should I hear only, 'Michael, imprison Ruax,' I retreate immediately."

- The third said, "I am called Artosael. I do much damage to the eyes. Should I hear, 'Ouriel, imprison Artosael,' I retreat immediately."
- The fourth said, "I am called Oropel. I attack throats, result in sore throats and mucus. Should I hear, 'Raphael, imprison Oropel,' I retreat immediately."
- The eleventh said, "I am called Katanikotael. I unleash fights and feuds in homes. If anyone wishes to make peace, let him write on seven laurel leaves the names of those who thwart me: 'Angel, Eae, Ieo, Sabaoth, imprison Katanikotael,' and when he has soaked the laurel leaves in water, let him sprinkle his house with the water and I retreat immediately."[A-6]

tery initiation ritual. The first-century writer Pausanias reports that the underworld deities near the Meander River in western Asia Minor would send visions to all whom they wished to enter their inner sanctuaries in ritual initiation (Pausanias 32.13). The so-called "Mithras Liturgy" illustrates what the initiate might see (using the same verb for seeing that appears in this verse):

> You will *see* yourself being lifted up and ascending to the height, so that you seem to be in midair . . . you will *see* all immortal things. For in that day and hour you will *see* the divine order of the skies: the presiding gods rising into heaven, and others setting. Now the course of the *visible* gods will appear through the disk of god. . . . And you will *see* the gods staring intently at you and rushing at you

. . . but rather going about in their own order of affairs.[37]

He has lost connection with the Head (2:19). The great problem with all of these highly spiritualistic practices is that

◀

A CAPTIVE OF WAR

A colossal statue of a Phrygian captive used as a pier in Corinth.

these people have got their eyes off of Christ. They are not holding on tight to the Lord Jesus. In his place, they have inserted many kinds of observances and practices from Judaism and local folk belief that are not only unnecessary, but are animated by demonic spirits. Paul's use of the word "Head" in this passage stresses Jesus' role as leader of his church; he is the One they should be looking to for direction, guidance, strength, and protection.

You died with Christ to the basic principles of this world (2:20). The best understanding of the word *stoicheia* (trans. here as "basic principles" of the world) is as a reference to hostile spirit powers or demons (see comments on 2:8). The idea of dying to the influence of the powers is a natural extension of Paul's thought on the implications of being united with Christ (Rom. 6:3–11; see comments on Col. 2:12).

Paul thus presents a message of freedom. Identification with Christ's death necessarily implies immunity from demonic tyranny. It does not come automatically for believers; it must be appropriated by struggling with the unseen realm (see his exhortation in the following verses). If the Colossian Christians are immunized against the demonic realm, there is now no reason for them to be tempted to follow the regulations of "the philosophy," which, ironically, Paul claims were inspired by the spirit powers themselves.

Do not handle! Do not taste! Do not touch! (2:21). Paul here apparently quotes from his opponents. These commands represent the taboos that characterized the lifestyle teaching of this movement within the church. Paul does not specify exactly what they prohibit, but it probably has to do with abstinence from various foods and drinks and may be understood in connection with fasting and "humility" (see comments on 2:18).

An appearance of wisdom (2:23). The kind of "wisdom" exhibited by the leaders of the faction is not traditional Jewish wisdom (of the type recorded in Proverbs, Ecclesiastes, Wisdom of Solomon, or Wisdom of Jesus ben Sirach), nor is it a traditional Greek form of wisdom as represented by the philosophers. This was esoteric wisdom for dealing with spiritual powers. There was a strong tradition within folk Judaism of a wisdom for handling evil spirits that purportedly went back to Solomon. This tradition of Solomon's great wisdom for dealing with evil spirits is best illustrated by Josephus:

> Now so great was the prudence and *wisdom* which God granted Solomon that he surpassed the ancients, and even the Egyptians, who are said to excel all men in understanding, were not only, when compared with him, a little inferior but proved to fall far short of the king in sagacity. . . . There was no form of nature with which he was not acquainted or which he passed over without examining, but he studied them all philosophically and revealed the most complete knowledge of their several properties. And God granted him knowledge of the art used against demons for the benefit and healing of men. He also composed incantations by which illnesses are relieved, and left behind forms of exorcisms with which those possessed by demons drive them out, never to return. And this kind of cure is of very great power among us

▶ Prohibitions in a Jewish Magical Text

In Jewish folk belief, someone seeking a visionary experience typically needed to adhere to certain taboos and purity regulations. The *Sepher Ha-Razim* (*Book of Mysteries*), a collection of incantation texts from popular Judaism that invoked angels, cautions a careful observance of all the necessary taboos to elicit an appearance of the god Helios: "Guard yourself, take care, and keep pure for seven days from all impure food, from all impure drink, and from every unclean thing. Then on the seventh day . . . invoke seven times the names of the angels that lead him during the day."[A-7]

to this day, for I have seen a certain Eleazar, a countryman of mine, in the presence of Vespasian, his sons, tribunes and a number of other soldiers, free men possessed by demons, and this was the manner of the cure. . . . And when this was done, the understanding and *wisdom* of Solomon were clearly revealed.[38]

Harsh treatment of the body (2:23). This refers to the ascetic practices associated with the teaching of "the philosophy"— including fasting, various taboos, and other regulations. It is doubtful, though not impossible, that this included the self-flagellation and self-mutilation that characterized the local cult of Attis.

Seek the Things Above (3:1–4)

Based on their participation in the death and resurrection of Christ, believers partake of a new life. Here there is security, freedom of fear, and power for dealing with the influences of hostile powers.

Set your hearts on things above (3:1). The language and thought here are reminiscent of Jesus' exhortation to "seek first his kingdom" (Matt. 6:33). When Paul speaks of the "above," he is not so much thinking literally as spiritually. He has in mind all that characterizes "the age to come," life in the new covenant, and citizenship in heaven (see Phil. 3:20).

The right hand of God (3:2). There is an echo here of the language of Psalm 110:1: "The LORD says to my Lord: 'Sit at my right hand until I make your enemies a footstool for your feet.'" This passage was understood by Paul and the early Christians to be a messianic promise that God's Anointed One would be exalted to a position of prominence and authority after he defeated his enemies. Paul calls on Christians to meditate on the fact that they live in a vital connection to a sovereign Lord who has defeated his supernatural enemies—the same enemies they now face—and now sits enthroned in a position of preeminent authority.

Your life is now hidden with Christ in God (3:3). Paul stresses that the position of believers in Christ is a place of security. He employs the language of Isaiah and the Psalms to express the security of God's people as they trust in him when they face their enemies. In Psalm 27:5–6, the psalmist says, "For in the day of trouble he will keep me safe in his dwelling; he will hide me in the shelter of his tabernacle and set me high upon a rock." Isaiah 49:2 says, "In the shadow of his hand he hid me; he made me into a polished arrow and concealed me in his quiver" (see also Ps. 31:19–20).

Put Away the Sins of the Past (3:5–11)

Put to death, therefore, whatever belongs to your earthly nature (3:5). Using common physiological terminology, Paul creates a metaphor to describe the process of developing moral purity. Every believer needs to kill off the body parts that lead to sin. The language is reminiscent of Jesus' own teaching when he said, "If your right eye causes you to sin, gouge it out and throw it away" (Matt. 5:29).

Sexual immorality (3:5). Lists of vices were common in the moral exhortation of ancient writers, especially among the Stoics. Paul lists five items for the Colossians to work on, all of which have to do with sexual purity. This is not surprising given the sexual promiscuity of the time. *Porneia* is a broad term referring to every kind of sexual encounter outside of the bond of marriage.

REFLECTIONS

SINS OF DESIRE ARE PART OF THE past life that God wants us to bring under control. Greed involves constantly acquiring new "toys," spending large amounts of our money on entertainment and nonessentials, and planning our lives around the acquisition of wealth. A greedy spirit is ignored by mislabeling desires as needs.

Greed, which is idolatry (3:5). Greed applies to sex because it involves an insatiable appetite. Paul may not be limiting this word strictly to matters of sexuality here. In a cultural context rampant with idolatry, it is somewhat surprising to find Paul referring to greed as idolatry. In Paul's mind, however, anything (including unbridled sexual pleasures) that usurps the proper place of God in one's devotion is idolatry (see comments on Eph. 5:5).

The wrath of God is coming (3:6). Everyone will be called to accountability in the future about their misappropriation of God's gift of sexuality, as well as every other form of idolatry. This period of God's judgment is customarily called "the day of the LORD" in the Old Testament prophets. The prophet Zephaniah warns, "The great day of the LORD is near. . . . That day will be a day of wrath, a day of distress" (Zeph. 1:14–15; see also 1 Thess. 5:1–3).

Anger (3:8). Paul now addresses another group of five vices that focus on the nature of personal interaction among fellow believers. "Anger, rage, malice, slander, and filthy language" are destructive to the unity that should characterize the church and inconsistent with the kind of love that Christ models.

Since you have taken off your old self . . . and put on the new (3:9–10). The image of taking off and putting on clothing was widespread in the ancient world. The Old Testament speaks frequently of being clothed with strength, righteousness, and salvation, but there is never any mention of the removal of a sinful and corrupt nature.[39] Paul now gives the Colossians a better understanding of how a virtuous life is possible by speaking of conversion as a decisive supernatural event that reaches to the core of one's being.

The "old self" (one's identity in solidarity with the sin of Adam) has been removed and a "new self" (one's identity in union with Christ) has replaced it. This change of identity serves as the basis of dealing with vice and appropriating virtue. There is thus also a sense in which believers now need to actualize what has already taken place spiritually—they need to take off the old self and put on the new self (see also comments on Eph. 4:22–24).

Barbarian (3:11). Among the Greeks and Romans, "barbarians" were people who lacked the civility of Greek or Roman culture. A barbarian could be any foreigner who spoke a language other than Greek or Latin and was different in appearance, manners, and behavior.[40]

Scythian (3:11). Historically, the Scythians were northern people located along the northern coast of the Black Sea in the area of what is today southern Ukraine. To the Greeks, the Scythians were a violent, uneducated, and uncivilized people. Josephus reflects a common view of the Scythians when he says, "Now, as to the Scythians, they take a pleasure in killing men, and differ little from brute beasts."[41] For those who have been incorporated into the body of Christ, there is no longer a distinction between people based on ethnicity, culture, gender, or social status.

Put On the Virtues of Christ (3:12–17)

Paul calls on the Colossian believers to cultivate a variety of Christian virtues that are essential for life in their new community. He carefully weaves into his admonitions the reasons why they are now able to change their attitudes, lifestyle, and behavior. Not only have they participated in Christ's death and resurrection and received a new self, but they are also chosen by God and have received purity, love, forgiveness, peace, and the word of Christ.

Bear with each other (3:13). This needs to be tempered by what Paul has said in Colossians 2. The false teaching should not be patiently endured. Yet if the leaders of the faction turn away from their teaching in accordance with Paul's instructions, the Colossians should be quick to forgive and embrace them in love.

Let the peace of Christ rule in your hearts (3:15). "Rule" does not capture the full significance of the word *brabeuō* (see comments on 2:18). This is a metaphor that comes from the context of athletic games where an official would serve as an umpire in judging a conflict. The Colossians are not only living in fear of the realm of the demonic, but they are now in turmoil because of the teaching of "the philosophy," not to mention all of the other concerns of day-to-day life. These internal fears and storms should be adjudicated by the wonderful gift of peace from the Messiah (see also John 14:27; Phil. 4:6).

The word of Christ (3:16). At this early time, it is doubtful that the Colossians possess any of the four Gospels, yet they have plenty of teaching about Jesus. They have received this from the oral tradition stemming from Palestine that was passed on to them from Paul via Epaphras. As we have already mentioned, part of this may have been hymns that were rich in teaching about Jesus (as 1:15–20 may have been). Paul here encourages them to continue meditating on the teaching about Christ, especially as it is imparted to them in their hymns of praise to Christ.

Psalms, hymns and spiritual songs (3:16). This expression describes the full range of forms in use in the Colossian church. It is possible that "psalms" represents more of a Jewish style and "hymns" a Greek form. Both terms, however, are used in the book of Psalms. The word "spiritual" goes with all three and characterizes the work of the Holy Spirit in moving Christians to write lyrics and songs in praise of Jesus in the early church (see comments on Eph. 5:19).

Proper Behavior in the Christian Household (3:18–4:1)

This is the earliest example of a set of instructions to the various members of a Christian household (see "Household Duties" at 1 Peter 2:11). There are many examples of these kinds of instructions in antiquity, both in Hellenistic Judaism and in Hellenistic popular philosophy (such as Stoicism). One of the key distinguishing features of this household code from non-Christian codes is the new basis and motivation. Seven times in these eight verses Paul roots his instructions "in the Lord." It is crucial to recognize that Paul is not admonishing these believers to conform to the prevailing cultural patterns, but rather to evaluate everything they do in light of the teaching about Jesus and the pattern he left for his people to emulate.

Wives, submit to your husbands, as is fitting in the Lord (3:18). Paul urges wives to recognize that there is an order of authority in the Christian household. There was a strong cultural patriarchy in the homes of antiquity. The first-century writer Plutarch comments, "If they [the

---

▶ Obeying and Honoring Parents in a Jewish Home

Philo, a first-century Jew living in Alexandria, Egypt, writes about the obligation of children in the home to honor their parents.

> Parents have not only been given the right of exercising authority over their children, but the power of a master.... For parents pay out a sum many times the value of a slave on their children. They also invest in nurses, tutors and teachers, in addition to the cost of their clothes, food and care in sickness and health from their earliest years until they are full grown.
>
> Given all these considerations, children who honor their parents do nothing deserving of praise since even one of the items mentioned is in itself quite a sufficient call to show deep respect. And on the contrary, they deserve blame, a sharp reprimand, and extreme punishment who do not respect them as seniors nor listen to them as instructors nor feel the duty of repaying them as benefactors nor obey them as rulers nor fear them as masters.
>
> Therefore, honor your father and mother next to God, he [Moses] says [Ex. 20:12].... For parents have little thought for their own personal interests and find their fulfillment and happiness in the high excellence of their children, and to gain this the children will be willing to listen to their instructions and to obey them in everything that is just and profitable; for the true father will give no instruction to his son that is foreign to virtue.[A-8]

wives] subordinate themselves to their husbands, they are commended, but if they want to have control, they cut a sorrier figure than the subjects of their control."[42] Another writer states the role of wives quite simply: "For it is proper for a wife to be subject to her husband."[43]

In a Roman household, the eldest male was in authority as the *paterfamilias*. What is vitally significant here is that Paul qualifies the submission by "as is fitting in the Lord." Once again, culture is not the guide, but God's revelation on issues of role relationships and order. In Ephesians 5, Paul bases this order in the marriage relationship on the pattern of Christ's relationship to the church.

Husbands, love your wives and do not be harsh with them (3:19). Christian husbands are to avoid being insensitive and overbearing with their wives. This contrasts significantly to many Roman households. Plutarch speaks of Roman men who "rage bitterly against their wives."[44] Paul goes one step further by enjoining men to love their wives—with the kind of love modeled to us by the Lord Jesus (see 3:12, 14; Eph. 5:25).

Children, obey your parents in everything (3:20). The fifth commandment instructs children to "honor" their parents (Ex. 20:12). In a Jewish context where children were still minors, honor was demonstrated by obedience.

Fathers, do not embitter your children (3:21). Because of their position in the household, fathers may be tempted to be severe with their children. Paul advises restraint for the practical reason of not overly discouraging the children. Even Roman writers at times admonished fathers to exercise restraint and sensitiv-

ity. Plutarch advises, "I do not think they [fathers] should be utterly harsh and austere in their nature, but they should in many cases concede some shortcomings to the younger person, and remind themselves that they once were young."[45]

Slaves, obey your earthly masters (3:22). The very presence of this admonition reminds the modern reader that the small church at Colosse consisted of both slave owners and slaves. Philemon is probably one of these slave owners (see Philemon). Although Paul may have objected to the institution of slavery, he advises Christians on how to live within the parameters of this thoroughly entrenched economic and social structure. He urges slaves to obey their masters. He pens these remarks at a time when he has recently come in contact with the disobedient slave, Onesimus, who fled Colosse and his master, Philemon. One must always remember to sharply distinguish the features of slavery in the Roman era from slavery in the ante-bellum South (see comments on slavery in the commentary on Philemon and at Eph. 6:5–9).

Working for the Lord (3:23). Slaves could potentially lack motivation for their work and engage in their responsibilities with an attitude of drudgery. Paul prescribes a new motivation. Ultimately they serve a different master, and it is him that they should seek to please.

Anyone who does wrong will be repaid for his wrong (3:25). This would encourage slaves who had been unfairly treated by their masters. There is a time of judgment for the recompense of every injustice. This was also a warning for the slaves to conduct their service with integrity.[46]

Masters, provide your slaves with what is right and fair (4:1). Paul now appeals to the slave owners not only to respond to their slaves with a sense of justice, but also to treat them with "equality" (*isotēs*). Paul clearly sows the seeds for the eventual dismantling of this unjust social structure.

The Roman writer Seneca also advocated treating slaves with justice: "Be moderate in what you tell slaves to do. Even with slaves, one ought to consider not how much you can make them suffer without fearing revenge, but how much justice and goodness allow" (Seneca, *On Mercy* 1.18).[47] Notably absent from Seneca, however, is any reference to treating slaves with "equality." In the Christian community, slaves are "no longer a possession subject to their master's caprice, but brothers in Christ."[48] A Jewish group called the Essenes denounced slavery as an outrage to the principle of "equality" (*isotēs*).[49]

Final Instructions (4:2–6)

Devote yourselves to prayer (4:2). Paul urges the Colossian believers to maintain a constant attitude of prayer. This continuance in prayer probably includes but goes well beyond maintaining a schedule of set times to pray during the day. In Judaism, it was typical to pray three times a day—at morning, noon, and night. The word for "devote" (*proskartereō*) is used in Mark 3:9 to describe a boat that was being kept ready for Jesus. Prayer is especially vital at this juncture for the Colossians as the means of staying in close contact with the Head of the church, who can give them counsel, guidance, and strength regarding their threatening situation.

Being watchful (4:2). This expression echoes the teaching of Jesus. The Lord admonished his disciples to "watch and pray" so that they would not fall into temptation (Mark 14:38). This is wise counsel to the Colossian believers who are tempted to follow the teachings of "the philosophy."

That God may open a door for our message (4:3). The image of an "open door" to represent an opportunity for some activity was widely used in the ancient world. The Stoic writer Epictetus uses the image in the sense of, "I am free to go anywhere."[50] Paul uses the image elsewhere to speak of an opportunity for the presentation of the gospel (1 Cor. 16:9; 2 Cor. 2:12). He can only rely on God to provide opportunities, since his freedom is being severely restricted by imprisonment.

I am in chains (4:3). The reference to "chains" reminds the Colossians that Paul is in Roman custody, awaiting trial. He has been imprisoned for up to three years now (two years in Caesarea and for up to a year in Rome). Most likely Paul is literally in shackles of some sort. A Roman jurist once advised, "If the officer in charge of a prison is bribed to keep someone in custody without chains . . . he must be punished by the court."[51]

Be wise in the way you act toward outsiders (4:5). "Outsiders" is a Jewish manner of expression for those who are outside of the community of the covenant people of God. Here it refers to unbelievers in the city of Colosse and the surrounding countryside. Paul urges the Colossian believers to exercise God-given wisdom in their interactions with people they encounter at the marketplace, at work, and at civic functions. These new believers would be under scrutiny by people wondering why they have left the synagogue or have forsaken their allegiance to the local cults.

Seasoned with salt (4:6). Job asks rhetorically, "Is tasteless food eaten without salt?" (Job 6:6). Everyone in the ancient world used salt to season their food. A discussion "seasoned with salt" became a way of referring to an interesting, stimulating, and enjoyable conversation or discourse. One ancient writer bemoaned the presentations of certain philosophers as "unsalted."[52]

Whenever the Colossian Christians have opportunity to interact with unbelievers, Paul wants them to engage in lively and interesting conversation. The image that he provides us of the Colossian church is not of a group who have disengaged from the world and are huddling together in isolation. His comments presuppose a group of people involved in the community and bearing a vibrant testimony.

Personal Greetings and Instructions (4:7–18). Paul extends greetings to the Colossians from eight coworkers currently serving with him in Rome.

Tychicus (4:7). A trusted colleague of Paul's originally hailing from Asia Minor (see Acts 20:4) and possibly known by the Colossians, Tychicus will carry the letter and share further details with them personally (see comments on Eph. 6:21).

Onesimus (4:9). This is Philemon's fugitive slave (see Philem. 10). Somehow this runaway slave has encountered Paul, become a Christian, and ministered to the apostle faithfully in his imprisonment. It is striking that Paul can commend him to the Colossian congregation

REFLECTIONS

ARE YOU A "LONE RANGER" OR A team player? The apostle Paul seldom worked alone. He always had a strong team of people surrounding him who shared in the ministry. Differently gifted people enhance our ministries and similarly gifted people need to be raised up, encouraged, and provided with opportunities to cultivate their gifts for the sake of the kingdom.

as a "dear brother." Colosse was the hometown of Onesimus.

My fellow prisoner Aristarchus (4:10). Paul is not the only believer imprisoned in Rome. His companion Aristarchus shares the same plight. Although we do not know the circumstances of this man's imprisonment, presumably it stems from his bold proclamation of the gospel (Acts 20:4). Aristarchus, a Jewish Christian, was part of the fruit of Paul's ministry at Thessalonica. He subsequently joined Paul for at least a part of his work at Ephesus, where he was a victim in the mob

HIERAPOLIS

Hillside pools in terraces formed by lime deposits from calcareous spring water.

CHAPTER NOTES

Main Text Notes

1. For more information about the city of Colosse, see C. E. Arnold, "Colosse," *ABD*, 1:1089–90.
2. Cicero, *Flac.* 28.68.
3. Tacitus, *Ann.* 14.27; Eusebius, *Chronica* 1.210.
4. See W. H. Mare, "Archaeological Prospects at Colosse," *NEASB* 7 (1976): 39–59. Professor Daria de Barnardi Ferrero, director of the Italian group currently excavating Hierapolis, clarified for me by letter that she is not aware of any group that has recently gained permission to excavate the site.
5. The coins have been published (with photographs) by Hans von Aulock, *Münzen und Städte Phrygiens* (Part 2; Istanbuler Mitteilungen, Beiheft 27; Tübingen: Ernst Wasmuth, 1987), 24–27, 83–93 (nos. 443–595).
6. Many of these have now been published with an English translation and discussion by J. G. Gager, *Curse Tablets and Binding Spells from the Ancient World* (New York/Oxford: Oxford Univ. Press, 1992).
7. See ch. 3 ("The Local Veneration of Angels") in C. E. Arnold, *The Colossian Sycretism* (Grand Rapids: Baker, 1996), 61–89.
8. On the cult of Cybele, see M. J. Vermaseren, *Cybele and Attis* (London: Thames and Hudson, 1977).
9. This view is advocated, e.g., by William Barclay, *The Letters to the Philippians, Colossians, and Thessalonians* (Daily Study Bible; rev. ed.; Louisville: Westminster, 1975).
10. See, e.g., the commentaries by F. F. Bruce (*The Epistles to the Colossians, to Philemon, and to the Ephesians* [NICNT; Grand Rapids: Eerdmans, 1984], 17–26) and P. T. O'Brien (*Colossians, Philemon* [WBC 44; Waco, Tex.: Word, 1982], xxx–xxxviii).
11. See H. Y. Gamble, "Amanuensis," *ABD*, 1:172. An entire book has now been devoted to this theme; see E. R. Richards, *The Secretary in the Letters of Paul* (WUNT 2/42; Tübingen: J. C. B. Mohr, 1991).
12. 1QS 11:7–8.
13. Josephus, *Ant.* 12.3.4 §149.
14. See Ex. 6:6; 13:15; 15:13; Isa. 51:10.
15. There is more written about this passage in Colossians than any other. For a recent and detailed discussion about the passage as a hymn, see M. Barth and H. Blanke, *Colossians* (AB 34B; New York: Doubleday, 1994), 227–46.
16. *T. Ab.* 13:10.
17. J. B. Lightfoot, *Saint Paul's Epistles to the Colossians and to Philemon* (Grand Rapids: Zondervan, 1977; originally printed in 1879), 156.
18. See C. E. Arnold, "Jesus Christ: 'Head' of the Church," in *Jesus of Nazareth: Lord and Christ*, eds. M. M. B. Turner and J. B. Green (Grand Rapids: Eerdmans, 1994), 346–66.
19. See Rom. 11:30–31; Gal. 4:8–9; Eph. 2:2–3, 11–13; 1 Peter 2:10.
20. See Lev. 22:21; Num. 19:2; Heb. 9:14; 1 Peter 1:19.
21. Walter Grundmann, "ἀνέγκλητος," *TDNT*, 1:356–57.
22. For more information on Laodicea, see F. F. Bruce, "Laodicea," *ABD*, 4:229–31.
23. See MM, 596.
24. For a detailed discussion and a listing of the primary-source evidence, see my *Colossian Syncretism*, 158–94.
25. See Deut. 28:13; Judg. 10:18; 11:8, 9; Philo: *Creation* 119; *Flight* 110, 182; *Dreams* 2.207; *Life of Moses* 2.30, 82; *Special Laws* 3.184; *Questions on Genesis* 1.3, 10; 2.5; *Questions on Exodus* 2.124.
26. See Lev. 26:41; Deut. 10:16; Jer. 4:4; Ezek. 44:7, 9.
27. The text is found in the Great Paris Magical Papyrus, *PGM* 4.475–829.
28. *T. Job* 11:11.
29. For additional detailed discussion on this and the previous two images, see my *Colossian Syncretism*, 277–87. See also L. Williamson, "Led in Triumph: Paul's Use of Thriambeuo," *Int* 22 (1968): 317–32.
30. E. F. Scott, *Epistles to the Colossians, to Philemon, and to the Ephesians* (London: Hodder & Stoughton, 1936), 50.
31. See 1 Chron. 23:31; 2 Chron. 2:4; 31:3; Ezek. 45:17; Hos. 2:11.
32. For references, see Paul Trebilco, *Jewish Communities in Asia Minor* (SNTSMS 69; Cambridge: Cambridge Univ. Press, 1991), 17–18, 198–99.
33. Ibid., 199, note 70.
34. *Apoc. Elijah* 1:20–21.
35. See Part I: "The Worship of Angels," in my *Colossian Syncretism*, 8–102.
36. For the texts, translation, and a detailed discussion of these inscriptions, see ch. 5 in my *Colossian Syncretism*, 104–57.
37. *PGM* 4.539–85.
38. Josephus, *Ant.* 8.2.5 §§ 41–49.
39. See 2 Chron. 6:41; Ps. 132:9; Isa. 51:9; 52:1.

40. See Thomas E. J. Wiedemann, "Barbarian," in *OCD*[3], 233.
41. Josephus, *Ag. Ap.* 2.38 §269; see Karen S. Rubinson, "Scythians," in *ABD*, 5:1056–57.
42. Plutarch, *Conjugalia praecepta* 33.
43. Both texts are cited from E. F. Lohse, *Colossians and Philemon* (Hermenia; Philadelphia, Fortress, 1971), 157, note 18; Pseudo-Callisthenes 1.22.4.
44. Ibid., 158, note 30; Plutarch, *De Cohibenda Ira* 8.
45. Plutach, *Moralia* 1.13d; as cited in Barth and Blanke, *Colossians*, 444, note 37.
46. See Dunn, *Colossians*, 258.
47. As cited in Scott Bartchy, "Slavery (Greco-Roman)," *ABD*, 6:69.
48. E. Beyreuther, "Like, Equal," *NIDNTT*, 2:499.
49. See Philo, *Good Person* 79.
50. See J. Jeremias, "θύρα," in *TDNT*, 3:174.
51. *Digesta* 48.3.8 (as cited in Brian Rapske, *The Book of Acts and Paul in Roman Custody* [BA1CS 3; Grand Rapids: Eerdmans, 1994], 27).
52. Timon as presented in Diogenes Laertius 4.67 (as cited in BAGD, 35).
53. See Eusebius, *History of the Church* 3.39.
54. W. Schneemelcher, ed., *New Testament Apocrypha* (Louisville, Ky.: Westminster/John Knox, 1992), 2.42–46.

Sidebar and Chart Notes

A-1. Plutarch, *Moralia* 164E–171F.
A-2. Plutarch, *Aemilius Paulus* 32–34.
A-3. Hippolytus, *Haer.* 9.11. Translation by J. H. MacMahon in *The Ante-Nicene Fathers*, vol. 5 (Grand Rapids: Eerdmans, n.d. [repr. 1990]).
A-4. For the Greek text and translation, see ibid., 64–66.
A-5. *Corpus Inscriptionum Judaicarum* 717.
A-6. *T. Sol.* 18:4, 7, 8, 15.
A-7. *Sepher Ha-Razim*, 4.25–30; cf. also 4.43–45. (The text is in: Michael Morgan, *Sepher Ha-Razim: The Book of Mysteries* [SBL Texts and Translations 25, Pseudepigrapha Series 11; Chico, Calif.: Scholars, 1983].)
A-8. Philo, *Spec. Laws* 2.233–36; trans. by F. H. Colson, *Philo* (LCL; Cambridge, Mass.: Harvard Univ. Press, 1984), with some modifications based on the Greek text.

1 THESSALONIANS

by Jeffrey A. D. Weima

The City of Thessalonica

A noble history. Cassander, a former general of Alexander the Great and later king of Macedonia, founded the city of Thessalonica in 315 B.C. He named the new community after his wife, the half sister of Alexander. The city was captured in 167 B.C. by the Romans and made the capital of one of their four newly created districts in this region. When the Romans reorganized these four districts into a single province in 146 B.C., Thessalonica was designated as the capital city. Just over a century later in 42 B.C., the city was rewarded for helping the victorious Mark Antony and Octavian in the Roman civil wars by being made a "free city." This favored status resulted in such privileges as a measure of autonomy over local affairs, the right to mint its own coins, freedom from military occupation, and certain tax concessions.

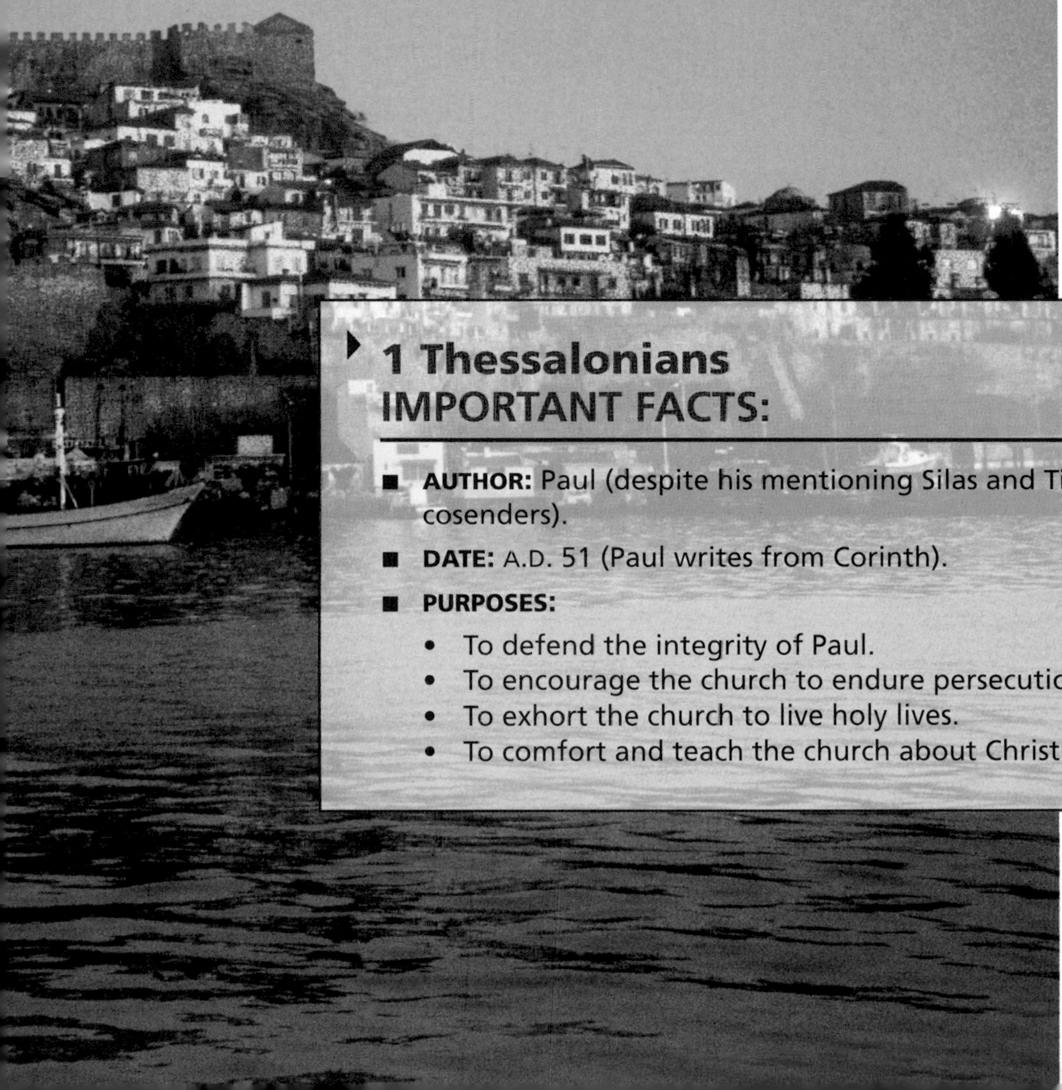

NEAPOLIS, MACEDONIA

The modern harbor of the city where Paul arrived in Macedonia.

◄

▶ 1 Thessalonians
IMPORTANT FACTS:

- **AUTHOR:** Paul (despite his mentioning Silas and Timothy as cosenders).
- **DATE:** A.D. 51 (Paul writes from Corinth).
- **PURPOSES:**
  - To defend the integrity of Paul.
  - To encourage the church to endure persecution.
  - To exhort the church to live holy lives.
  - To comfort and teach the church about Christ's return.

A strategic location. Two geographical factors resulted in Thessalonica's quickly becoming the most populous (100,000 people), wealthy, and thus important city in Macedonia.[1] First, the city possessed a natural harbor that was the best in the entire Aegean Sea. Second, the city was located on the juncture of the Via Egnatia (the major east-west highway that extended from Asia Minor all the way to Rome) and the road north to Danube. Thessalonica was thus ideally situated for both commercial and military enterprises. As Meletius observed so many years ago: "So long as nature does not change, Thessalonica will remain wealthy and fortunate."[2]

▶

POLITARCHAI INSCRIPTION

An inscription discovered at Thessalonica referring to this distinctive office.

A unique political structure. Thessalonica, as a free city, was allowed to keep its traditional structure of a democratic civil administration, unlike its neighboring communities. The lowest level involved a citizen assembly that handled public business. The Jews initially attempted to bring Paul and Silas before this assembly (Acts 17:5). The higher level of administration involved the city council, which consisted of five or six local authorities called "politarchs" (the NIV simply refers to them as "city officials"), the city treasurer, and the gymnasiarch. The Jews, after enlisting the aid of certain disreputable men, seized Jason and some other converts and brought them not to the citizen assembly but to the politarchs (17:6–8).

A religiously pluralistic environment. Like other major urban centers in the ancient world, Thessalonica had plenty of religious competitors to the Christ proclaimed by Paul.[3] A religiously pluralistic environment is indicated by the apostle's words that the majority of the Thessalonian believers had "turned to God from idols" (1 Thess. 1:9). Archaeological and inscriptural evidence also reveals the popularity of various mystery religions dedicated to such Greco-Roman and Egyptian deities as Dionysius, Serapis, Isis, Aphrodite, Demeter, Zeus, and Asclepius. The most important deity in Thessalonica, however, was Cabirus—the

▶ **Politarchs**

The office of politarch, mentioned twice by Luke in his description of Paul's ministry in Thessalonica (Acts 17:6, 8), is unique to the province of Macedonia and found only rarely in other cities. Archaeologists have so far discovered twenty-eight references to this distinctive office in Thessalonica.[A-1] These findings prove that Luke was familiar with the political structure of the different cities in Paul's journeys and thus suggest that his recording of these travels in Acts is historically reliable.

patron god of the city. This Cabirus figure was a martyred hero, murdered by his two brothers, buried with symbols of royal power, and expected to return to help the oppressed poor in general and the citizens of Thessalonica in particular. It has been suggested that similarities between Cabirus and the story of Jesus account for the success of Paul's ministry in this city.[4]

The diverse religious context of Thessalonica included a Jewish synagogue. The size and influence of this synagogue are suggested by the presence of "a large number of God-fearing Greeks" (Gentiles who converted to Judaism but who did not allow themselves to be circumcised) as well as "not a few prominent women" (Acts 17:4).

The imperial cult with its worship of Rome and the emperor also played a key role in the religious life of Thessalonica. On the one hand, the imperial cult served to ensure the ongoing favor of the current Roman emperor by visibly demonstrating the city's allegiance to his leadership. On the other hand, the imperial cult also helped to sustain Roman rule over the local populace by stressing the divine nature of the emperors as well as the benefits the city enjoyed under their rule. In this political and religious context, it is not surprising that Paul's preaching about "another king . . . Jesus" would alarm civic sensibilities and lead to the accusation that he was violating "Caesar's decrees " (Acts 17:7). Similarly, the failure of the Thessalonian believers to continue to participate in the imperial cult and in the worship of other pagan deities aroused the anger of their fellow citizens and quickly led to the persecution of this newly planted church.

Paul and the Thessalonian Church

Philippi to Thessalonica. Paul's relationship with the Thessalonian church began during the middle of his second missionary

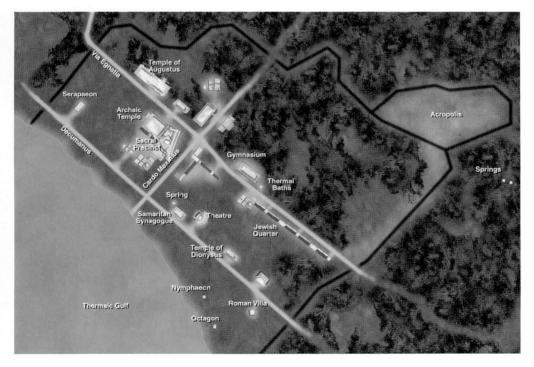

journey. The apostle, along with Silas and Timothy, departed from Philippi, leaving Luke behind to pastor the newly founded church there. This small group of missionaries traveled some ninety miles along the Via Egnatia, passing through two cities of lesser importance, Amphipolis and Apollonia, and arriving on the third day in Thessalonica (Acts 17:1; 1 Thess. 2:1–2).

Thessalonica. Paul began his evangelistic activity in the local synagogue, where he preached for three Sabbaths. This resulted in the conversion of some Jews and even more Gentiles, including a number of wealthy women from leading families in the community (Acts 17:2–4). These Gentiles had earlier been attracted to Judaism but now underwent a second conversion to Christianity. During the rest of the week, Paul and his co-missionaries supported themselves by working as tentmakers (cf. 18:3). In this way, they not only provided the church with a good example of proper conduct in the area of work but also avoided any potential charges that they preached the gospel only to win followers and to obtain financial gain (1 Thess. 2:9; 2 Thess. 3:7).

It is commonly assumed that Paul won converts by preaching in the marketplaces ("street corner" evangelism). Nevertheless, there is good evidence that his missionary work took place in the workshop and the private home.[5] We can picture the apostle in Thessalonica laboring in a local workshop, perhaps one owned by Jason (Acts 17:5). During the long hours at his workbench, cutting and sewing leather to make tents, Paul would have had opportunities to share the gospel with fellow workers, customers, and other citizens who were interested in this tentmaker-philosopher newly arrived in the city. Those who wanted to know more about Paul and his message would have returned for individual instruction (1 Thess. 2:11, lit., "we exhorted *each one of you*"), either in the workshop or a believer's private home. Many accepted Paul's message as the word of God (2:13) and so turned from idols to serve the living God (1:9). These Gentile converts from paganism soon made up the major-

ity of the believers in the Thessalonian church.

Paul's success, however, quickly aroused opposition. The synagogue leaders were upset by the loss of its members and the city officials were similarly alarmed by the conversion of its wealthy women to a cult that worshiped an alternate emperor. The unbelieving Jews acted first and, with the help of some troublemakers, managed to start a city riot against the infant church. The crowd originally intended to bring Paul, Silas, and Timothy to the lowest level of administration: the popular assembly (Acts 17:5). But when they could not find the missionaries, they instead seized Jason, their host, and a few other congregational members and brought them to the higher officials: the politarchs (17:6). Two charges—one general, the other specific—were laid against the missionaries in absentia: first, they were disturbing the peace; second, they had violated the decrees of Caesar (17:7).

Thessalonica to Berea. In order to protect Jason and the other converts, Paul and his two traveling companions had no option but to leave quietly in the middle of the night. They traveled for two or three days southwest to Berea (Acts 17:10). Here, in sharp contrast to the hostility of the Jews in Thessalonica, Paul received a warm reception from his countrymen (17:11).

Berea to Athens. The peaceful ministry setting of Berea was soon disturbed by Thessalonian Jews who once again forced Paul to leave town in a hurry. The apostle was escorted by some believers all the way to Athens, likely traveling by road to the port city of Dion and by sea the remainder of the journey. Silas and Timothy stayed behind briefly in Berea, rejoining Paul in Athens shortly thereafter (Acts 17:13–15; 1 Thess. 3:1–2).

Athens. During his stay in Athens, Paul continued to worry about his young converts in Thessalonica and the persecution they were enduring. Therefore, he sent Timothy back to Thessalonica (1 Thess. 3:1–5) and Silas possibly to Philippi. Paul dearly wanted to revisit the Thessalonians himself but was prevented from doing so (2:18).

Athens to Corinth. After a frustrating ministry in Athens, Paul arrived in Corinth for an eighteen-month stay. Timothy and Silas rejoined Paul after their trip to Macedonia (Acts 18:5), apparently with donated funds from the Thessalonian and Philippian churches, which allowed the apostle to quit his tent-making work and preach full time. Timothy gave Paul an initially good report about the Thessalonian church but also informed him of a few problems (1 Thess. 3:6–10). This news caused Paul to write his first letter to the church in A.D. 51. A short time later the apostle received an alarming report about the spread of a false teaching to the effect that "the day of the Lord has already come" (2 Thess. 2:2), as well as a reoccurrence of the problem of believers who refused to work. Paul, therefore, felt the need to write to the Thessalonian church for a second time.

Later visits to Thessalonica. Paul had ongoing contact with the believers in Thessalonica in his later years of ministry. He visited them twice on his third missionary journey, both on his way to Corinth via Macedonia (Acts 19:21) and on his way back from that city (20:1–6).

He may have also visited them during his fourth missionary journey, following his prison journey to Rome and subsequent release. That Paul enjoyed good relations with the Thessalonian church in the years after his two letters to them is clear from the fact that they contributed to the collection he was gathering for the needy churches in Palestine (Rom. 15:26; 2 Cor. 8:1–5; 9:4) and also apparently supported him in his own evangelistic work (2 Cor. 11:9).

Why Did Paul Write 1 Thessalonians?

After Timothy returned from his second visit to Thessalonica, he gave Paul an essentially good report about the spiritual health of the young church (1 Thess. 3:6–9). Yet, Timothy also informed the apostle about some concerns that caused Paul to write 1 Thessalonians:

Concern about Paul's integrity: Non-Christians in Thessalonica (1 Thess. 2:14, "your own countrymen") accused Paul of having impure, selfish motives. Paul, therefore, spends much of the first half of the letter defending himself, first for his past conduct in their midst (2:1–16), and second for his present inability to revisit them (2:17–3:10).

Concern about persecution: The Thessalonian Christians not only accepted the gospel "in spite of severe suffering" (1 Thess. 1:6), they also continued to endure opposition for their faith after their conversion.[6] Paul, therefore, seeks to encourage his persecuted readers.

Concern about proper conduct: When the Thessalonian Christians "turned . . . from idols to serve the living and true God" (1 Thess. 1:9), their conversion involved a radically different lifestyle. Paul, therefore, emphasizes throughout the letter, but especially in the second half (4:1–5:22), the Thessalonians' need to live a holy or sanctified life.

Concern about Christ's Return: The Thessalonian Christians had questions concerning the fate of believers who die before Jesus' second coming (1 Thess. 4:13–18) as well as the "times and dates" of Christ's return (5:1–11). Paul, therefore, writes 1 Thessalonians in order to clarify these and other matters connected with Christ's return.

Letter Opening (1:1)

The opening section of letters in the ancient world follows a fixed pattern consisting of three elements: the sender, the recipient, and the greeting. It is clear that Paul has been influenced by this pattern as he begins his first letter to the Thessalonians with the same three elements in their expected order. But

VIA EGNATIA
▼

instead of slavishly following the epistolary custom of his day, Paul has "Christianized" somewhat his letter opening. He takes the typical Greek greeting *chairein* ("Greetings!") and replaces it with the similar sounding word *charis* ("grace"). The apostle also adds to this salutation the typical Jewish welcome of "peace," thereby creating a distinctively Christian greeting ("Grace and peace to you") that honors both Gentile and Jewish believer alike.

Paul, Silas and Timothy (1:1). Paul differs from the typical letter opening of his day by including as cosenders the names of others who were with him. This, along with the frequent use of the plural "we" throughout the letter, has led some to conclude that 1 Thessalonians was written by all three of the individuals named in the letter opening. The use of the first person "I" (2:18; 3:5; 5:27), however, reveals that Paul is the real author of this letter. The names of Silas and Timothy are included because of their substantial role in the establishment and later support of the Thessalonian church.

Thanksgiving (1:2–10)

Paul's letters typically include a thanksgiving that is located after the letter opening and before the letter body. This part of the letter is called a "thanksgiving" because of the main verb that introduces this section ("I/We give thanks. . .") as well as its general content: thanksgiving to God for the believers to whom Paul is writing.

Some ancient letters similarly open with a brief thanksgiving to the gods. For example, this third century B.C. letter begins: "Toubias to Apollonios, greeting. If you are well and if all your affairs and everything else is proceeding according to your will, many thanks to the gods."[7] Paul's thanksgivings, however, differ from such ancient letters in that his deal with the spiritual rather than the physical well-being of his recipients and are much longer and formally complex.

The Pauline thanksgiving possesses at least three important functions. First, it has a *pastoral* function: The thanksgiving reestablishes the apostle's relationship with his readers by means of a positive expression of gratitude to God for their faith and work. This is important if Paul wants his letters to be accepted and his exhortations to be obeyed by his readers. Second, it has a *paraenetic* function: There is an implicit (or even, at times, explicit) challenge for the readers to live up to the praise that the apostle is giving them in his words of thanksgiving. Third, the thanksgiving has a *foreshadowing* function: It anticipates the main themes to be developed in the body of the letter.[8]

Your work produced by faith, your labor prompted by love, and your endurance inspired by hope (1:3). The first or immediate reason why Paul gives thanks to God focuses on three things that the Thessalonian Christians are doing. The first is "your work produced by faith." Although Paul was vehemently opposed to "legalism"—the belief that salvation

◄

MACEDONIAN COIN

This Greek coin highlights the prominence of Macedonia with the inscription: "Macedonia is first!"

comes through the works of the law—he was by no means antinomistic (i.e., against the law). This allows him to pair the words "work" and "faith" together to refer to that Christian activity that results from faith—what Paul elsewhere refers to as "faith expressing itself through love" (Gal. 5:6). The second phrase, "your labor prompted by love," somewhat similarly refers to those Christian deeds that stem from love. The third phrase, "your endurance inspired by hope," refers to the hope that the Thessalonians continue to have in the imminent return of Christ.

He has chosen you (1:4). The second or ultimate reason why Paul gives thanks shifts the focus from what the Thessalonian Christians are doing to what God has done: "He has chosen you." The Greek phrase literally means "your election" and ought to be interpreted in light of the language elsewhere in the letter of God's "calling" and "appointing" the Thessalonians (2:12; 4:7; 5:9, 24). By identifying his readers as God's elect, Paul applies language reserved exclusively for Israel to the predominantly Gentile church in Thessalonica. The fact that the apostle uses the term *election* without any accompanying explanation suggests that this subject must have been an integral part of his original preaching in the Thessalonian church.

Because our gospel came to you (1:5). The apologetic reference to Paul's original preaching ministry in Thessalonica in 1:5a ("because our gospel came to you not simply with words, but also with power, with the Holy Spirit and with deep conviction") as well as the defense of his integrity in 1:5b ("You know how we lived among you for your sake") foreshadows the lengthy defense of his

integrity in 2:1–16. The honest and sincere character of the apostle should be evident to the Thessalonians, first in his powerful and passionate preaching, which was likely accompanied by miracles and second, in the personal knowledge they have of how he acted in their midst.[9]

You became imitators of us and of the Lord (1:6). The individualism that characterizes our modern society might easily lead to the notion that imitating another person involves the denial of one's true and unique identity such that he or she is really a "phony." In the ancient world, however, the idea of imitating others was common.[10] Thus, not only is Paul following a widespread practice of his day but his failure to make use of the imitation theme may have opened himself up to charges that he considered himself an unworthy teacher for his followers to emulate.

In spite of severe suffering (1:6). The reference here and elsewhere to the suffering experienced by the Thessalonian church does not likely refer to physical persecution but to social harassment.[11] There is virtually no evidence that Christians anywhere in the Roman empire during the 50s suffered from any organized opposition or physical oppression. Many sources do indicate, however, the offense, even disgust, felt by non-Christian neighbors and fellow citizens when converts to Christianity declined to take part in normal social and cultic activities (see "Social Harassment of Christians in the Greco-Roman World").[12]

The Lord's message rang out (1:8). Paul uses the rare verb *exēcheō* here, from which the English word "echo" is ultimately derived. The image that the apostle presents is that of a sound—the gospel message—that emanates from the Thessalonian Christians and echoes throughout the hills and valleys of Macedonia, Achaia, and beyond.

How you turned to God from idols (1:9). A variety of pagan deities were worshiped in Thessalonica. Archaeologists have discovered a temple dedicated to the Egyptian god Serapis, where a board of some fourteen priests ensured that the rites of the Nile were performed diligently. Inscriptions unearthed from this temple indicate that the Egyptian goddess Isis, who is associated with culture and mysteries, was also worshiped here. Epigraphic evidence reveals that Dionysus, the god of wine and joy, was among the more influential religious cults in Thessalonica. The patron god of the city, however, was Cabirus, about whom unfortunately little is known (see the Introduction). Other gods worshiped in Thessalonica included Aphrodite, Demeter, Zeus, and Asclepius. The ceremonies associated with these diverse cults offered regeneration, immortality, a measure of equality and self-respect for an initiate, relief from ills and misfortune, and the promise of sexual fulfillment—concerns addressed to some degree in Paul's two letters to the Thessalonians.[13]

To wait for his Son from heaven (1:10). The eschatological subjects of Christ's return in 1:10a ("to wait for his Son from heaven") and the final judgment in 1:10b ("who rescues us from the coming wrath") anticipate well the discussion of these matters in 4:13–18 and 5:1–11.

Defense of Paul's Past Visit to Thessalonica (2:1–16)

The central theme of 2:1–16 is a defense of Paul's integrity during his past visit to Thessalonica. That this defense of his integrity was a major concern to the apostle is clear from the fact that it is the first topic he chooses to take up in the body of the letter. The importance of this subject is also evident from the way in which he foreshadowed his defensive concern in the thanksgiving (see comments on 1:5).

From whom is Paul defending himself? Paul's opponents come from *outside* the church. The good report of Timothy about the congregation (3:6), the exemplary character of the Thessalonian believers' life (1:6–7), Paul's description of them as "our glory and joy" at Christ's return (2:19–20), and his frequent reference to them as "brothers" (1:4; 2:1, 9, 14, 17; 3:7; 4:1, 13; 5:1, 4, 12, 14, 25) make it impossible to conclude that Paul was facing attack from believers inside the church. The best candidate for opponents

REFLECTIONS

THE THESSALONIAN CHRISTIANS exemplify a healthy balance between ethics and eschatology. Some contemporary believers emphasize only serving God in the present and so fail to anticipate the glorious return of Christ in the future. Others today stress the Second Coming so much that they devote little thought or energy to serving God in this world. In contrast, the Thessalonians' passion for serving God and so living a holy life in the present (1:9) is matched by their fervent hope in the future and glorious return of Christ (1:10).

outside the church are "your own countrymen"(2:14): unbelieving citizens of Thessalonica who not only persecuted the church but also attacked the church's leader, Paul, who was, in their minds, the source of the problem.

What were the charges brought against Paul? A careful reading of 2:1–16 reveals that Paul is defending himself against attacks on his integrity and the genuineness of his motives. Non-Christians in Thessalonica accused Paul of being no different than other wandering philosopher-teachers of his day: those who taught and spoke only to receive money and praise. There are enough clues available to see how unbelievers in Thessalonica opposed to this new religious movement founded by Paul might "spin" certain facts in a way in which the apostle's integrity would be questioned. The fact that Paul received money at least twice from the Philippian church during his original ministry in Thessalonica (Phil. 4:16), the fact that Paul converted among others in Thessalonica "not a few prominent [i.e., wealthy] women" (Acts 17:4) as well as Jason, who was rich enough to host the missionaries and post bond for them (17:5–9), the fact that Paul abruptly left the Thessalonian church, leaving them "orphaned" (see 1 Thess. 2:17) and has not yet returned to Thessalonica or, prior to this letter, even written them (3:1–6)—all this information could easily be used by opponents of the Thessalonian church to question the integrity of its founder.[14]

Our visit to you was not a failure (2:1). The NIV's translation of *kenē* as "failure" is better rendered here as "insincere." Paul, then, is defending the honesty of his motives during his past visit rather than the positive results of that visit.

Nor are we trying to trick you (2:3). The word "trick" (*dolos*) originally referred to catching fish by means of a bait and so developed the metaphorical meaning of "deceit, cunning, treachery."[15] Paul claims that he used no dishonest means to trick people into believing his preaching. The apostle's conduct, therefore, differs sharply from that of wandering philosopher-teachers, who employed various methods of deception to win followers and financial gain.[16]

We were gentle among you (2:7a). Instead of the word "gentle" (*ēpioi*) found in the NIV, more ancient and reliable manuscripts have the word "infants" (*nēpioi*), so that a better translation of this text reads: "We became *infants* among you."[17] This is the first of three striking family metaphors that Paul uses in this passage: "infants" (2:7a), "mother" (2:7b), and "father" (2:11). The purpose of this first metaphor of infants is to highlight the apostle's integrity. Unlike the wandering philosopher-teachers of that day, who were only interested in "pleas[ing] men" and who "used flattery" as a "mask to cover up greed" (2:4–5), Paul and his fellow missionaries acted as innocent as infants. Philo similarly speaks about the innocence of infants, claiming that "it is impossible for the greatest liar to invent a charge against them, as they are wholly innocent" (*Special Laws* 3.119).

Like a mother (2:7b). Instead of the common word for "mother" (*mētēr*), Paul employs a term with the specialized meaning of "wet nurse" (*trophos*), someone who suckles children. The use of wet nurses was widespread in the Greco-Roman world, and ancient writers typically portrayed the wet nurse as an important and beloved figure.[18] Since the original text refers to this woman nursing her *own* children, Paul has in view here the natural mother rather than the hired wet nurse. Yet he uses the unusual term *trophos* because this metaphor of a nursing mother underscores his sincere love for the Thessalonian Christians. A hired nurse competently cares for the children in her charge, but she cherishes her own children even more.

We loved you so much (2:8). The meaning of the rare verb used here (*homeiromai*) is illuminated by a fourth-century A.D. tombstone inscription (*CIG* 3.4000.7), where the term describes a father and mother's sad yearning for their deceased child. The word, therefore, expresses the deep affection that Paul has for the Thessalonian Christians, an affection like that between a parent and child.

We worked night and day (2:9). Although Paul does not say what kind of work he did, there are hints at his profession. He and his colleagues worked "with our own hands" (1 Cor. 4:12; cf. Acts 20:34), probably as tentmakers (Acts 18:3). Since tents were usually made with leather, it may be better to call Paul a "leather worker," one who not only made and repaired tents but a range of leather goods.[19] Paul likely learned this trade as part of his rabbinical training, since Jewish teachers were expected to support themselves by some form of labor.[20]

As a father (2:11). Paul likens himself to a father when he wants to emphasize the nurturing or instructional role he played in the lives of his converts.[21] The father in the Greco-Roman world was normally responsible for the education and training of his children.

The Jews, who . . . (2:14–16). The strong language that Paul uses in these verses to describe the Jews has led some to claim that this text is anti-Semitic and cannot have come from the hand of the apostle but is instead an addition inserted in the letter by a later writer.[22] Although the language is admittedly harsh, it stems from Paul's frustration with fellow Jews whose behavior has threatened the Gentile mission. The apostle does not have in view all Jews but only those who in some way were involved in the events mentioned in verses 15–16.[23] Furthermore, Paul speaks here somewhat hyperbolically as he also does elsewhere in his writings.[24]

The wrath of God has come upon them at last (2:16). There are a number of national disasters that the Jews suffered to which Paul may be referring: e.g., the famine in A.D. 46 (Acts 11:28), the banishment from Rome in A.D. 49 (Acts 18:2), persecutions under Tiberius Alexander.[25] It is also possible, however,

REFLECTIONS

NON-CHRISTIANS OFTEN DISMISS the claims of the gospel by pointing to the lack of integrity that many believers exemplify. They are especially quick to ridicule those disgraced TV evangelists who have preached the gospel only out of the selfish desire for human praise or financial gain. Believers today, therefore, must uphold the integrity of the gospel by following the example of Paul during his original visit to Thessalonica: He was as innocent as an infant (2:7b), as loving as a nursing mother (2:7c), and as nurturing as a father (2:11).

that the apostle is writing about an imminent judgment rather than a past one.[26]

Defense of Paul's Present Absence from Thessalonica (2:17–3:10)

The unbelieving citizens of Thessalonica (2:14) not only attacked the integrity of Paul with respect to his past visit to the city (2:1–16) but apparently also used the apostle's inability thus far to come back to the fledgling church to cast further doubts about the genuineness of his motives. One key concern of Paul in this section of the letter, therefore, is to reassure the Thessalonian Christians of his continued love and concern for them, despite his present failure to return for a second visit.

A second key concern focuses on the suffering that the Thessalonians are enduring for their commitment to Christ. Paul wants to encourage them to remain steadfast in their newfound faith even in the face of opposition. Although this second concern about persecution differs rather greatly from the first concern about Paul's separation from the Thessalonians, there is a link that logically connects these two topics together: Paul's original departure from Thessalonica and his inability to return were both the result of the same persecution that the believers in that city are currently experiencing.

Therefore, despite the differing themes that are addressed, 2:17–3:10 follows a logical line of argumentation. Paul begins with the first concern of his separation from the Thessalonians in 2:17–20. He then addresses the second concern of persecution in 3:1–5. The apostle concludes his argument by bringing the two concerns together in the good report about the Thessalonians given by the returning Timothy in 3:6–10.

We were torn away from you (2:17). The verb *aporphanizō* literally means "to be orphaned." The apostle thus depicts himself as a parent who has been orphaned from his children. This orphan metaphor conveys to the believers in Thessalonica Paul's feelings of deep anguish because of his separation from them.

Satan stopped us (2:18). The verb *enkoptō*, which literally means "to cut into," originally referred to the military practice of cutting up a road so as to make it impassable for a pursuing army.[27] Paul wants his readers to know that his present absence from them is not due to his personal choice but to the activity of Satan, who, in typical military fashion, has destroyed the apostle's path back to Thessalonica.

The crown in which we will glory (2:19). The crown that Paul refers to is not a royal tiara but a laurel wreath given to the victor in a Greek athletic contest. These crowns were woven out of palm or other branches, flowers, or certain plant

---

REFLECTIONS

PAUL STRESSES THAT PERSECUTION FOR ONE'S FAITH in Christ is a normal and expected feature of the Christian life (3:3b–4). There are many Christians in the world—brothers and sisters in such places as Laos, Saudi Arabia, Iraq, Sudan, Pakistan, Indonesia, and China (to mention only some)—who experience this truth every day in the form of church burnings or closings, harassment, fines, arrest, and imprisonment. Although believers in North America and elsewhere enjoy a certain measure of freedom and protection, they too ought to expect and be willing to be ridiculed and oppressed for their commitment to Christ.[A-2]

life.[28] Such crowns or wreaths would thus soon deteriorate—unlike the imperishable and unfading crown given to believers (1 Cor. 9:25; 1 Pet. 5:4). Paul encourages the Christians in Thessalonica by confidently claiming that they will be his victory wreath at the return of Christ.

We/I could stand it no longer (3:1, 5). Paul twice uses the uncommon verb *stegō*, which originally referred to keeping water out of a vessel, such as with a watertight house or a boat that doesn't leak.[29] The image that the apostle paints, therefore, is of his deep affection for the Thessalonians that he is no longer able to contain within himself and prevent from leaking out.

But Timothy . . . has brought good news about your faith and love (3:6). Timothy returns from Thessalonica with a good report that takes up the two concerns raised earlier in this passage. Paul's first concern about his separation from the Thessalonians (2:17–20) is answered with the news of the church's "love" for him: "that you always have pleasant memories of us and that you long to see us" (3:6). Paul's second concern about the persecution that his converts are enduring (3:1–5) is answered with the news of the church's "faith": that "in all our distress and persecution we were encouraged about you because of your faith . . . since you are standing firm in the Lord" (3:7–8).

◀ *left*

ATHLETE WITH WREATHS

A stone relief from Isthmia depicting a victorious athlete with his crowns.

▶ Who Went Where and What Did They Do?

A comparison of the movements of Paul and his coworkers described in 1 Thessalonians 3:1–10 with the account in Acts suggests that the following sequence of events likely took place:

Paul arrives in Athens (1 Thess. 3:1; see Acts 17:15–34), having left Silas and Timothy behind in Berea with instructions to rejoin him "as soon as possible" (Acts 17:15b).

After his two coworkers return to him in Athens, Paul sends Timothy back to Thessalonica in order to encourage the church that was being persecuted for its newfound faith (3:1–5).

Paul sends Silas somewhere in Macedonia (Acts 18:5), perhaps to the Philippian church, from which he received financial gifts to support the apostle and his coworkers in their preaching ministry (see Phil. 1:4; 4:10–20).

Silas and Timothy return to Paul (1 Thess. 3:6; see Acts 18:5), who by this time has left Athens to begin an eighteen-month ministry in Corinth (Acts 18:1–17).

Timothy gives an essentially good report about the Thessalonian church (3:6–10) but also informs Paul of several concerns, thereby prompting the apostle to write 1 Thessalonians.

Transitionary Prayers (3:11–13)

Paul moves from the first half of the letter body (2:1–3:10) to the second half (4:1–5:22) by means of two prayers (3:11–13).[30] The first prayer that God "may . . . clear the way for us to come to you" (3:11) looks back to Paul's concern in the previous verses about his separation from the Thessalonians (2:17–3:10). The second prayer looks ahead to three concerns that Paul is about to address: "so that you will be blameless and holy" (3:13) foreshadows the discussion of holiness in sexual conduct in 4:3–8; "make your love increase and overflow" (3:12) anticipates the discussion of brotherly love in 4:9–12; and "when our Lord Jesus comes" (3:13) prefigures the discussion of the return of Christ in 4:13–5:11.

Now may our God and Father himself and our Lord Jesus (3:11). The fact that the plural subjects of "God" and "Lord Jesus" occur with a singular form of the verb may suggest that Paul views these two as essentially a unity and so affirms the full deity of Jesus.[31] The close collocation of God and Jesus in the prayer indicates minimally that the apostle sees the two working together in unity; this undoubtedly has implications for the supreme position that Paul ascribes to the Son of God (1:10) alongside of the Father.[32]

Clear the way for us to come to you (3:11). This request looks back to metaphor in 2:18 concerning the military practice of cutting up a road so as to make it impassable for a pursuing army (see comments on 2:18). Paul's prayer, therefore, is that God the Father and Jesus will remove the obstacles that Satan has used to block the apostle's path back to the Thessalonian church.

How to Live in Order to Please God (4:1–12)

In the first half of the letter body (2:1–3:10) Paul has been concerned with defending his integrity and reestablishing the confidence of his readers. This renewed trust in the apostle (and thus also in the gospel he proclaims) is necessary not only to encourage the Thessalonian believers in the midst of their persecution but also to ensure that they will obey the moral instructions he will now give them in the second half of the letter body (4:1–5:22). The technical term for such ethical teaching is "paraenesis," from a Greek word meaning "exhortation, advice."[33] After opening the paraenetic section of 1 Thessalonians with a general appeal to increase in conduct that is pleasing to God (4:1–2), Paul addresses the specific issues of holiness in sexual conduct (4:3–8) and brotherly love within the church community (4:9–12).

▶ Sexual Conduct in the Greco-Roman World

The Greco-Roman world had a tolerant attitude toward sexual conduct, particularly sexual activity outside marriage. Marriages were not usually love matches, but family arrangements. Typically, men in their middle twenties were paired with young women barely in their teens whom they had never met. So it was expected that married men would have sexual relations with other women, such as prostitutes, female slaves, or mistresses. This explains why Demosthenes (384–322 B.C.) could state matter-of-factly: "Mistresses we keep for our pleasure, concubines for our day-to-day physical well-being, and wives to bear us legitimate children and to serve as trustworthy guardians over our households."[A-3] That attitudes had not changed at all some three centuries later is evident from the words of the Stoic philosopher Cato (95–46 B.C.), who praised those men who satisfied their sexual desires with a prostitute rather than another man's wife.[A-4]

A tolerant view of adultery and other sexual practices can also be seen from a variety of other sources. For example, funerary inscriptions reveal that concubinage was common. Prostitution was a business like any other, and profit from prostitutes working at brothels was an important source of revenue for many respectable citizens. Innkeepers and owners of cookshops frequently kept slave girls for the sexual entertainment of their customers. Adulterous activity was, in fact, so widespread that the emperor Augustus (63 B.C.–A.D. 14) established a new code of laws having to do with adultery and marriage—the "Julian Laws"—in a failed attempt to reform sexual practices. Within such a social context, it is not surprising that the Jewish Christian leaders of the Jerusalem church felt the need to include in their letter to Gentile Christians a warning "to abstain from sexual immorality" (see Acts 15:20, 29; 21:25). Paul issues the same warning to the Christians in Thessalonica (1 Thess. 4:3).

How to live in order to please God (4:1). The verb *peripateō* literally means "to walk" but has the metaphorical sense of "living one's life." It is not only one of Paul's favorite words to describe the Christian life (it occurs 32 times in his letters), it is also one of his more strategic terms as it is used to introduce themes that the apostle considered to be fundamental.[34] This metaphorical use of "walking" to describe moral conduct has its roots in Paul's Jewish background (approximately 200 of the 1547 occurrences of the Hebrew verb "to walk" in the Old Testament are metaphorical).

The metaphor also occurs in nonbiblical Greek (but with much less frequency and normally with a different verb, *poreuomai*) and thus would have been readily understood by Paul's readers.[35]

It is God's will that you should be sanctified (4:3a). The noun *hagiasmos*, which can be translated as "sanctification" or "holiness," is a key word in 4:3–8, occurring in various forms some four times. Holiness is an important Old Testament concept, which conveys the notion of "separation"—the need for God's covenant people to "come out" and be "distinct" from the surrounding peoples.[36] Holiness, therefore, is the boundary marker that separates God's people from all other nations. It is significant that Paul takes this standard of holiness, which had previously been the exclusive calling of Israel, and applies it here to the predominantly Gentile church in Thessalonica.[37]

Learn to control his own body (4:4). The noun *skeuos*, which literally means "vessel" or "household utensil," is used metaphorically here. One common interpretation takes *skeuos* as a metaphorical reference to "woman" or "wife," so that Paul is exhorting his readers "to take a wife" (RSV). A more likely interpretation views the noun as referring to one's own "body," so that the apostle commands each of his readers to "learn to control his own body" (NIV; NRSV; NEB; JB). It is also possible that *skeuos* refers more specifically to the male sex organ. The noun in secular Greek had such a euphemistic use. The strongly phallic character of the Cabirus and Dionysian cults, which were popular at Thessalonica, also supports this meaning.

Who gives you his Holy Spirit (4:8). Paul picks up the language of the Old Testament prophets about the gift of God's Spirit as a key blessing for the Jewish people in the eschatological age—language associated with the "new" or "everlasting" covenant—and applies it to the predominantly Gentile Christians in Thessalonica. This is evident in the apostle's description of God's giving his Holy Spirit "into you," an expression that echoes exactly the words of Ezekiel (see Ezek. 37:6, 14 [LXX]; see also 36:27).[38]

Taught by God (4:9). The unique expression "taught by God" (*theodidaktoi*) is further evidence that Paul is making use of the "new covenant" language of the prophets and applying it to the predominantly Gentile church of Thessalonica. The apostle here alludes to Isaiah's description of the messianic age as a time when God will live so intimately in and among his people through his Spirit that they will no longer have to

DIONYSUS

A Herm (statue) of Dionysus from the crypt of the Serapeion in Thessalonica.

▶ Dionysus and Sexual Symbolism

A statue of Dionysus was discovered in the temple of Serapis in Thessalonica. According to some mythical traditions, Dionysus suffered dismemberment. The legendary reconstitution of the god may have been ritually enacted by worshipers in the temple and would have affirmed the god's powers of renewal and regeneration. The sexual symbols and erotic activity associated with Dionysiac worship offer a possible background for the exhortations in 4:3–8 in general and for the meaning of *skeuos* in 4:6 in particular.[A-5]

be taught by human intermediaries, but will be "taught by God" (*didaktous theou*, Isa. 54:13; see also John 6:45, where Jesus quotes this same verse to show that "all will be taught by God" in the messianic age). Paul likely also has in mind Jeremiah's portrait of the new covenant as a period when God's people will not need others to teach them the law but will know it intimately, for God will write it on their hearts (Jer. 31:33–34).

Work with your hands . . . so that you will not be dependent on anybody (4:11b–12). The problem of idleness—Christians who refused to work—was an ongoing issue in the Thessalonian church. Paul first addressed this problem during the founding of the church (note the past tense in 4:11: "just as we told you"). He brings up the problem of idleness again in 1 Thessalonians, both here in 4:11–12 and later in 5:14 ("Warn those who are idle"). The problem apparently got

worse, thereby requiring Paul to address this matter yet again at greater length in 2 Thessalonians 3:6–15.

About Those Who Fall Asleep (4:13–18)

The Thessalonian church was confused over the fate of their fellow Christians who had died before Jesus' second coming. Unfortunately, it is not clear why the Thessalonians were "ignorant" (4:13) about this subject or what specific concern they had.[39] Paul's emphatic claim that living believers "will *certainly not precede* those who have fallen asleep" (4:15b) and that "the dead in Christ will rise *first*" (4:16b) before living believers suggests that the Thessalonian church worried that deceased believers would either miss out or be at some kind of disadvantage at Christ's return compared to those believers who are still alive on that day. After introducing the problem (4:13), Paul presents two arguments in response (an appeal in 4:14 to the church's confession about Christ's resurrection; an appeal in 4:15–17 to the "Lord's own word") before ending the discussion with a concluding exhortation (4:18).

Those who fall asleep (4:13). The use of "sleep" or "rest" as a euphemism for "death" is common, not only in biblical texts but in antiquity as well.[40] One should not find in this term, therefore, any support for the notion of "soul sleep," that is, that the soul exists in a nonconscious state of "sleeping" in the time between death and resurrection.

Grieve like the rest of men, who have no hope (4:13). Some Greek philosophers maintained that the soul was immortal and continued to exist after death. Certain

▶Tomb Inscriptions and the Afterlife

Archaeologists have discovered many tomb inscriptions in Thessalonica. They illustrate how little expectation for a life after death existed in the Greco-Roman world. Being together with one's spouse in the grave is the final expectation. Paul contrasts this hopelessness by claiming that believers will be reunited not only with each other but also with Christ.

The text of one tomb inscription from Thessalonica reads: "...for this woman had this surname, while she was still among the living. Because of her special disposition and good sense, her devoted husband created this tomb for her and also for himself, in order that later he would have a place to rest together with his dear wife, when he looks upon the end of life that has been spun out for him by the indissoluble threads of the Fates" (*CIG* 1973).[A-7]

mystery religions also attempted to assure their initiates of afterlife. Such ideas, however, were not well defined and appear not to have been held at a popular level. The much more common attitude toward death was the sense of complete hopelessness that is reflected in the concise statement of Theocritus: "Hopes are for the living; the dead have no hope."[41]

Jesus died and rose again (4:14). The phrase "Jesus died and rose again" may well be a pre-Pauline, creedal formula of the early church.[42] By appealing to confessional material of the early church concerning Christ's resurrection, Paul comforts the Thessalonian believers with an authoritative teaching that not merely he but they also, along with all other churches, believe.

The Lord's own word (4:15). It is not clear whether Paul is referring to (1) a saying of Jesus not preserved in the Gospels; (2) a paraphrasing of Jesus' apocalyptic teaching, such as is found in Mark 13 and Matthew 24; (3) a general summary of Jesus' teaching; or (4) a teaching revealed to Paul on the Damascus Road or elsewhere. The "Lord's own word" likely consists of the material in verses 16–17a, with verse 15 containing Paul's summary of this saying of Jesus. By appealing to the "Lord's own word," Paul further comforts the Thessalonian believers by showing that he is not merely giving his personal opinion but that his words are in agreement with the authoritative teaching of the Lord Jesus himself.

Will be caught up together with them in the clouds (4:17a). This verse contains the one explicit reference in the New Testament to the "rapture"—the sudden removal of believers from earth and their reunion with Jesus in the air at the Second Coming. The word "rapture" does not actually occur here but originates from the Latin translation in the Vulgate of the Greek verb *harpazō*. Elsewhere, this latter term refers to the violent action of being "taken by force" or "snatched away," usually to the benefit of the one being taken.[43]

To meet the Lord in the air (4:17b). The Greek word used here, *apantēsis*, which

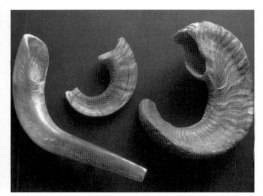

row, Irene writes: "But against such things [i.e., death], one can do nothing." She then ends her letter with words similar to that used by Paul in 4:18: "Therefore encourage each other." But whereas Irene appeals to the helplessness one has in the face of death, Paul holds before the Thessalonians the hope they have because of Jesus' resurrection (4:14) and Jesus' teaching (the "Lord's own word" in 4:15–17).

About Times and Dates (5:1–11)

Whereas 4:13–18 concerns the fate of *deceased* Christians at Jesus' return, 5:1–11 focuses on the fate of *living* Christians at the same eschatological event. The fact (1) that Paul two times reassures the believers in Thessalonica of what they already are ("sons of the light and sons of the day," 5:5; cf. v. 8), (2) that he reminds them that "God did not appoint us to suffer wrath" (5:9), and (3) that he exhorts them to "encourage one another and build each other up" (5:11), suggests that the Thessalonian Christians were not

◀ *left*

SHOFAR

The ceremonial Jewish trumpet made of a ram's horn.

lies behind the English translation "to meet," was a technical term in the ancient world. It referred to the meeting of a delegation of citizens from a city with an arriving dignitary in order to accord that visitor proper respect and honor by escorting him back to their city.[44] Such processions of leading citizens going out to welcome and accompany a visiting ruler or official back to the city were common in Hellenistic times.[45] The term *apantēsis* has this same sense in its two other New Testament occurrences: The wise virgins with their oil-filled lamps meet the bridegroom and escort him back to the banquet (Matt. 25:6); the Christians in Rome walk south to meet Paul on his prison journey and escort him back to the capital city (Acts 28:15). The picture that Paul presents, therefore, is of the church—consisting of both deceased (but now resurrected) and living Christians—meeting the descending Christ in the air and then escorting him back to earth.

Therefore encourage each other with these words (4:18). In a second-century A.D. letter (POxy 115) discovered in Egypt, a woman named Irene attempts to comfort grieving parents who have just suffered the loss of their son. After stating that she and her family have fulfilled the customary duties that express their sor-

REFLECTIONS

THE CONTRAST THAT PAUL MAKES IN 4:13 IS *NOT* that non-Christians grieve in the face of death whereas Christians do not express such sadness. Believers also grieve in the face of death. Such sorrow is natural, since death is not part of God's good created order but a painful consequence of the Fall. Death is not something that Christians happily embrace but an "enemy" (1 Cor. 15:26) that caused even the Lord Jesus to cry (John 11:35). Thus, tears in the face of death are not the sign of weak faith but of great love. But while Christians do grieve in the face of death just like non-Christians, there is an important difference: Christians grieve *with hope*. This hope is rooted in the knowledge that loved ones who have already passed away will in no way be at a disadvantage but will participate fully with living believers in glory of Christ's triumphal return.

merely curious about the timing of Christ's return but worried whether they were spiritually and morally worthy to meet the Lord on the day of his coming.[46]

About times and dates (5:1). Although the nouns translated as "times"(*chronōn*) and "dates" (*kairōn*) individually have distinguishable meanings, their tandem usage in the Septuagint (Dan. 2:21; 7:12; Wisd. Sol. 8:8) and the New Testament (Acts 1:7; 3:20–21) indicates that they together function as a conventional pair with a synonymous meaning. This stereotyped expression refers generally to the events of the end times and often is connected with the divine judgment that will take place then.

The day of the Lord (5:2). In the Old Testament the expression "the day of the Lord" often refers to the time of divine judgment for the enemies of God (e.g., Obad. 15) and the time of deliverance for the people of God (e.g., Joel 2:31–32; Zech. 14:1–21). This double aspect of judgment and deliverance is also found in Paul's references to "the day of the Lord," which he also terms "the day of our Lord Jesus [Christ]" (1 Cor. 1:8; 2 Cor. 1:14), "the day of [Jesus] Christ" (Phil. 1:6, 10; 2:16), or simply "the Day" or "this day" (1 Cor. 3:13; 1 Thess. 5:4; 2 Thess. 1:10). Since this judgment and deliverance will take place at the return of Christ, the expression "the day of the Lord" is another way of referring to the "coming" (*parousia*) of Jesus (1 Thess. 4:15).

Like a thief in the night (5:2). The metaphor of a thief in the night likely originates in the teaching of Jesus (Matt. 24:43; Luke 12:39), which was later picked up by not only Paul but other New Testament writers as well (see 2 Peter 3:10; Rev. 3:3; 16:15). The apostle uses this metaphor to emphasize both the unexpectedness of the Day's arrival and its threatening character as a time of judgment for those unprepared.

While people are saying, "Peace and safety" (5:3). Although the phrase "peace and safety" may look back to Old Testament prophetic warnings against false claims of peace on the eve of national destruction, it more likely has in view the contemporary political environment, namely, Roman imperial sloganeering.[47] *Pax et securitas* ("peace and safety") was a popular slogan of the imperial Roman propaganda machine, and the concept of "Roman peace" was vigorously promoted through various media: coins (see picture above), monuments, and official proclamations. Rome held out to all those who submitted to its rule the promise of peace and safety, virtually an offer of "salvation" from unrest and danger.[48] Paul, however, has a stern warning for all those who trust in the political power of Rome instead of in God: "Destruction will come on them suddenly, as labor pains on a pregnant woman, and they will [certainly][49] not escape" (1 Thess. 5:3).

Darkness/light, night/day (5:4–8). The metaphors of darkness and light as well as night and day occur often in the Old Testament, Jewish literature (1QS 3:13–4:26; 1QM 1:1, 3), and Paul's other letters (Rom. 1:21; 2:19; 3:11–13; 1 Cor. 4:5; 2 Cor. 4:6; 6:14; Eph. 4:18; 5:8–11; 6:12; Col. 1:13).[50] "Darkness" and "night" sym-

center ▶

"PEACE AND SAFETY"

A coin extolling the *Pax Augusti*, "the peace of Augustus."

bolize alienation from God and ignorance about the imminent arrival of the day of the Lord; conversely, "light" and "day" symbolize closeness to God and an awareness about the coming day of judgment.

Sons of the light (5:5). The formulation "sons of the light" appears in Luke 16:8 but is best known for its frequent occurrence in the Dead Sea Scrolls, where it refers to the members of the Qumran community, who were anticipating their eschatological battle against the "sons of darkness," that is, all those who did not belong to their fellowship. Similarly, the designation "sons of light" serves to make a sharp distinction between the Thessalonian believers, who are prepared for the day of the Lord, and those outside the Christian community, who are unaware of the impending divine judgment they will receive at Christ's return.

Putting on faith and love as a breastplate, and the hope of salvation as a helmet (5:8). The imagery of armor originates in Isaiah 59:17, where God is said to "put on righteousness as a breastplate, and the helmet of salvation." Paul uses this military image both here and elsewhere in his letters to describe a variety of virtues with which Christians should arm themselves in the spiritual battle against Satan and his evil hosts.[51] The three virtues that

the Thessalonians are exhorted to put on consist of the familiar triad of faith, love, and hope (see comments on 1:3).

For God did not appoint us to suffer wrath but to receive salvation (5:9). Paul comforts the Thessalonian believers by reminding them that their ultimate destiny on the day of the Lord rests not in their own work but in God's. This point was already made at the very beginning of the letter, when Paul states that God "has chosen you" (1:4), and it has been repeated a couple times thus far (2:12; 3:3). Here the apostle similarly claims that God has "appointed" or chosen these people of his not "to suffer wrath but to receive salvation."[52]

Final Exhortations (5:12–22)

At first glance, the exhortations in 5:12–22 appear to be something of a grab bag of diverse commands that have little connection with the Thessalonian church. A closer look, however, reveals a relatively clear structure through which Paul deals with four issues specifically connected to the situation in Thessalonica: esteeming congregational leaders (5:12–13); treating troubled congregational members (5:14–15); cultivating personal piety (5:16–18); and exercising spiritual gifts, especially prophecy (5:19–22).

▶ **"Peace and Safety" Provided by the Romans**

The Jewish historian, Josephus, records a decree from the citizens of Pergamum that praises the Romans for providing "peace [*asphaleia*] and safety [*eirēnē*]"—the same two words mentioned by Paul in 1 Thessalonians 5:3: "Decree of the people of Pergamum: 'In the presidency of Cratippus, on the first of the month Daisios, a decree of the magistrates. As the Romans in pursuance of the practices of their ancestors have accepted dangerous risks for the common safety [*asphaleia*] of all humankind and strive emulously to place their allies and friends in a state of happiness and lasting peace [*eirēnē*], the Jewish nation and their high priest Hyrcanus have sent as envoys to them....' "[A-8]

Those . . . who are over you in the Lord (5:12). The term *proïstamenoi* was used in secular Greek to refer to patrons or benefactors, that is, individuals who supported various clients or associations.[53] It may be, then, that Paul is referring here to wealthy individuals who, after being converted to Christianity, allowed their homes to be used as meeting places and provided financial and political support for the fledgling church. Such well-to-do people naturally became leaders, since the majority of the members belonged to the lower class and would not have the free time or education to work effectively in the congregation. One such patron of the Thessalonian church was Jason (Acts 17:5–9).

We urge you (5:14a). The verb *parakaleō* ("to urge, appeal") was part of an "appeal formula" commonly found in ancient letters to request that some action take place. This formula was used in official letters when kings and officials wanted to express a more friendly, less heavy-handed tone. Paul also uses the appeal formula in this nuanced manner, where his authority is not in question and he can make a request rather than a command in the confidence that his appeal will be obeyed.[54]

Warn those who are idle (5:14b). The first of three troubled groups in the Thessalonian congregation with whom Paul deals is "those who are idle" (*ataktoi*). This Greek word, used by the apostle four times in his two letters to describe this first group (the root *atakt-* occurs in 4:11; 2 Thess. 3:6, 7, 11), has two possible meanings.[55] One is derived from its use in military contexts to depict soldiers who would not keep step or follow commands—that is, those who were "obstinate" or "rebellious." The other stems from its use in the papyri of the Hellenistic period to describe students or workers who failed to do their work—that is, those who were "idle" or "lazy."[56]

The first meaning nicely captures the resistance of this group to their leaders (1 Thess. 5:12–14a), whereas the second meaning is supported by Paul's explicit commands to work found in both letters (4:11–12; 2 Thess. 3:6–15). It is best, therefore, to identify the first group here in 1 Thessalonians 5:14 as "rebellious idlers": members in the church who were not merely lazy but who obstinately refused to submit to the authority of their leaders and of the apostle. (For the cause of this group's problematic behavior, see "Why Did Some Thessalonian Christians Not Want to Work?" at 2 Thess. 3.)

Encourage the timid (5:14). The second troubled group addressed is the "timid" (*oligopsychoi*). This Greek word, which literally means having "little spirit/soul," occurs nowhere else in the New Testament and only rarely in other ancient writings so that it is difficult to deduce its precise meaning here. The usage of this word in the Septuagint signifies religious discouragement.[57] Paul, then, could be referring either to those who were shaken by the persecutions that the church had to endure (1 Thess. 2:14; 3:1–5) or to those who were anxious about various aspects of Christ's return (4:13–5:11).

Help the weak (5:14). The third troubled group with whom Paul deals is the "weak" (*asthenoi*). Although this Greek word can refer to physical weakness (i.e., those who are sick or ill), the larger context supports a reference to moral or spiritual weakness. Despite attempts to specify the weakness further (e.g., the refusal to eat certain foods [Rom. 14; 1 Cor. 8, 10], the struggle to live holy lives with respect to sexual conduct [1 Thess. 4:3–8], the anxiety surrounding "the times and dates" of the day of the Lord [5:1–11]),[58] there is not enough evidence to justify an exact identification.

Do not put out the Spirit's fire; do not treat prophecies with contempt. Test everything (5:19–22). The majority of the church's members—those who had "turned to God from idols" (1:9)—would have been all too familiar with various sorts of "ecstatic" activities practiced in the mystery religions and pagan cults. Some may have been leery of what appeared to be similar activities in the church and so attempted to limit the use of spiritual gifts such as prophecy.[59] But while Paul here affirms the work of the Spirit in general and prophecy in particular, he also seeks to regulate charismatic activity, calling on the Thessalonian believers to "test" everything that claims to be of the Spirit and "hold on to" only that which is found to be "good."

REFLECTIONS

THE DEEP MISTRUST AND DISDAIN in our modern culture toward authoritative structures has negatively impacted attitudes in the church toward those in leadership positions. Having rightly rejected a naïve trust in their pastor or other church leaders, many congregations have swung to the opposite extreme, treating those in a leadership position with a suspicion that borders on contempt. The church today, therefore, needs to both hear and heed Paul's exhortation to "respect" its leaders and "hold them in the highest regard in love because of their work" (5:12–13a).

Letter Closing (5:23–28)

Letters in the ancient world typically ended in brief fashion. Writers sometimes closed with final greetings, a health wish ("Take care of yourself in order that you may be well"), an autograph (some closing remarks written in the hand of the author rather than the secretary often employed to write the letter), a farewell wish (the Greek *errōso* literally means "Farewell" but has the colloquial sense of "Good-bye"), and the date. A first-century B.C. letter dealing with the matter of unirrigated land and the payment of taxes upon it, for example, ends: "Greet all your people. Athenarous and the rest of the children greet you. Take care of yourself in order that you may be well. Goodbye. Year 8, Epeiph" (POxy 1061).[60] Yet, the instances in which all—or even most—of these closing conventions occur simultaneously are rare.[61]

Although Paul's letter closings show that he was influenced by the epistolary practices of his day, they also reveal that the apostle was not limited to such practices. Paul cleverly adapts and expands the rather hackneyed epistolary conventions commonly found at the end of a letter such that his letter closings are truly unparalleled among extant letters of his day. In fact, the apostle carefully constructs his letter closings in such a skillful way that they relate directly to—sometimes, in fact, even summarize—the major concerns taken up in the bodies of their respective letters.[62]

May God himself (5:23–24). Instead of the simple and relatively fixed formula "May the God of peace be with you" (see Rom. 15:33; 2 Cor. 13:11; Phil. 4:9b), Paul in these verses has greatly expanded the peace benediction so that it echoes three major concerns addressed earlier in the letter: (1) The prayer for God to "sanctify you through and through" and for the Thessalonians to be "kept blameless" recalls the concern about proper conduct. (2) The reference to the "coming of our Lord Jesus Christ" echoes the concern about Christ's return. (3) The reassurance that "the one who calls you is faithful and he will do it" recalls the language of election and calling found in the letter (1 Thess. 1:4; 2:12; 4:7; 5:9)—language that comforts the Thessalonians in the midst of the persecution they are currently enduring.[63]

Greet all the brothers with a holy kiss (5:26). The practice of greeting others with a kiss, either when arriving or departing, occurs frequently in the Old Testament and the New Testament and so reflects a widespread custom in the ancient world.[64] The greeting kiss expressed not merely friendship but, more specifically, reconciliation and unity.[65] Paul's command to "greet all the brothers with a holy kiss," therefore, serves as a challenge to the Thessalonians to remove any hostility that may exist among them and to exhibit outwardly through the kiss greeting the unity they share as fellow members of the body of Christ.[66]

ANNOTATED BIBLIOGRAPHY

Best, Ernest. *A Commentary on the First and Second Epistles to the Thessalonians.* HNTC. New York: Harper & Row, 1972; reprint, Peabody, Mass.: Hendrickson, 1987.

A thorough treatment that still ranks as one of the best commentaries on the Thessalonian letters.

Gaventa, Beverly R. *First and Second Thessalonians.* Interpretation: A Bible Commentary for Teaching and Preaching. Louisville: John Knox, 1998.

A brief treatment that excels in its suggestions for application and preaching.

Holmes, Michael W. *1 & 2 Thessalonians.* NIVAC. Grand Rapids: Zondervan, 1998.

A judicious and readable exposition that applies the text in helpful and specific ways to contemporary culture and life.

Marshall, I. Howard. *1 and 2 Thessalonians.* NCBC. London: Marshall, Morgan & Scott, 1983.

A brief yet insightful commentary with an especially good and detailed discussion of introductory matters.

Wanamaker, Charles A. *Commentary on 1 & 2 Thessalonians.* NIGTC. Grand Rapids: Eerdmans, 1990.

An excellent full-length commentary on the Greek text that emphasizes rhetorical features of the letters.

Weima, Jeffrey A. D., and Stanley E. Porter. *An Annotated Bibliography of 1 & 2 Thessalonians.* NTTS 26. Leiden: Brill, 1998.

A helpful research tool that lists some 1200 works (the majority of which are annotated) that are germane for the interpretation of 1 and 2 Thessalonians.

CHAPTER NOTES

Main Text Notes

1. R. Riesner, *Paul's Early Period: Chronology, Mission Strategy, Theology* (Grand Rapids: Eerdmans, 1998), 341.
2. Cited by J. B. Lightfoot, *Biblical Essays* (London: Macmillan, 1893), 255.
3. See C. Edson, "Cults of Thessalonica (Macedonia III)," *HTR* 41 (1948): 153–204; K. P. Donfried, "The Cults of Thessalonica and the Thessalonian Correspondence," *NTS* 31 (1985): 336–56.
4. R. Jewett, *The Thessalonian Correspondence: Pauline Rhetoric and Millenarian Piety* (Philadelphia: Fortress, 1986), 126–32.
5. R. F. Hock, "The Workshop as a Social Setting for Paul's Missionary Preaching," *CBQ* 41 (1979): 438–50; A. J. Malherbe, *Paul and the Thessalonians* (Philadelphia: Fortress, 1987), 7–20.
6. 1 Thess. 2:2b, 14–15; 3:1–5; 2 Thess. 1:4–7; cf. Acts 17:5–7, 13; 2 Cor. 8:1–2.
7. J. L. White, *Light from Ancient Letters* (Philadelphia: Fortress, 1986), 39; P. CairZen I 59076.
8. For fuller treatments of the Pauline thanksgiving, see P. Schubert, *Form and Function of the Pauline Thanksgivings* (Berlin: Töpelman, 1939); P. T. O'Brien, *Introductory Thanksgivings in the Letters of Paul* (Leiden: Brill, 1977).
9. Rom. 15:18–19; 2 Cor. 12:12; see also Acts 14:3; 15:12.
10. See, e.g., Isocrates, *Demai* 4.11; Seneca, *Ep. Mor.* 6.5–6; 7.6–9; 11.9; Quintilian, *Inst. Orat.* 2.28; Philostratus, *Vit. Ap.* 1.19; 2 Macc. 6:2–28; *4 Macc.* 9:23. A good introduction to these texts is A. J. Malherbe, *Moral Exhortation: A Greco-Roman Sourcebook* (Philadelphia: Westminster, 1986).
11. 1 Thess. 2:2, 14–15; 3:1–5; 2 Thess. 1:4–7; cf. Acts 17:5–7; 2 Cor. 8:1–2.
12. J. Barclay, "Conflict in Thessalonica," *CBQ* 55 (1993): 512–30.
13. So Donfried, "Cults of Thessalonica," 336–56; Jewett, *Thessalonian Correspondence,* 126–32.
14. For a fuller exploration of the historical issues lying behind Paul's defense in 2:1–16, see J. A. D. Weima, "An Apology for the Apologetic

Function of 1 Thessalonians 2.1–12," *JSNT* 68 (1997): 73–99.

15. BAGD, 203. See also L. Morris, *The First and Second Epistles to the Thessalonians* (Grand Rapids: Eerdmans, 1991), 62.

16. On the typical conduct of traveling orators, see B. Winter, "The Entries and Ethics of Orators and Paul (1 Thessalonians 2:1–12)," *TnyBul* 44 (1993): 55–74, esp. 60–64.

17. So, e.g., G. Fee, "On Text and Commentary on 1 and 2 Thessalonians," ed. E. H. Lovering Jr, *SBL 1992 Seminar Papers* (Atlanta: Scholars, 1992), 174–79; S. Fowl, "A Metaphor in Distress: A Reading of *NEPIOI* in 1 Thessalonians 2.7," *NTS* 36 (1990): 469–73; B. R. Gaventa, "Apostles as Babes and Nurses in 1 Thessalonians 2:7," in *Faith and History: Essays in Honor of Paul W. Meyer*, ed. J. T. Carroll (Atlanta: Scholars, 1991), 194–98.

18. Gaventa, "Apostles as Babes and Nurses," 193–207.

19. W. Michaelis, "σκηνοποίος," *TDNT*, 7:393–94; P. W. Barnett, "Tentmaking," *DPL*, 925–27.

20. For a broader discussion of issues surrounding Paul's manual labor, see R. F. Hock, *The Social Context of Paul's Ministry: Tentmaking and Apostleship* (Philadelphia: Fortress, 1980); *Pirqe ʾAbot* 2:2; 4:7.

21. See also 1 Cor. 4:14–15; Phil. 2:22; Philem. 10.

22. So, e.g., B. A. Pearson, "1 Thessalonians 2.13–16: A Deutero-Pauline Interpolation," *HTR* 64 (1971): 79–94; D. Schmidt, "1 Thess. 2:13–16: Linguistic Evidence for an Interpolation," *JBL* 102 (1983): 269–79.

23. F. D. Gilliard, "The Problem of the Antisemitic Comma Between 1 Thessalonians 2.14 and 15," *NTS* 35 (1989): 481–502.

24. See C. J. Schlueter, *Filling up the Measure: Polemical Hyperbole in 1 Thessalonians 2.14–16* (Sheffield: JSOT, 1994).

25. Josephus, *Ant.* 20.102–22.

26. This sentence bristles with grammatical and interpretive difficulties that cannot be treated here because of space constraints. The reader is directed to the commentaries for a fuller discussion.

27. G. Stählin, "ἐγκοπή, ἐγκόπτω," *TDNT*, 3:855–56.

28. On crowns in the ancient world, see W. E. Raffety, "Crown," *ISBE*, 1:831–32.

29. G. H. Whitaker, "Love Springs No Leak," *Expositor* 8th ser. 21 (1921): 126ff.; W. Kasch, *TDNT*, 7:585–87.

30. The punctuation adopted by the NIV results in three prayers, whereas the original Greek has only two.

31. So, e.g., Morris, *Thessalonians*, 107–8.

32. I. H. Marshall, *1 and 2 Thessalonians* (Grand Rapids: Eerdmans, 1983), 100.

33. See further M. B. Thompson, "Teaching/Paraenesis," *DPL*, 922–23.

34. J. O. Hollow, *Peripateô as a Thematic Marker for Pauline Ethics* (San Francisco: Mellen, 1992).

35. H. Seesemann, "πατέω," *TDNT*, 5:940–45.

36. N. H. Snaith, *The Distinctive Ideas of the Old Testament* (New York: Schocken, 1944), 24–32; see Ex. 19:5–6; Lev. 20:23–26; Deut. 26:18–19.

37. On this key point, see further J. A. D. Weima, "'How You Must Walk to Please God': Holiness and Discipleship in 1 Thessalonians," in *Patterns of Discipleship in the New Testament*, ed. R. N. Longenecker (Grand Rapids: Eerdmans, 1996), 98–119.

38. Weima, "How You Must Walk," 110–12.

39. For an overview of the five major hypotheses, see Marshall, *Thessalonians*, 120–22; for a sixth, see C. A. Wanamaker, *Commentary on 1 & 2 Thessalonians* (Grand Rapids: Eerdmans, 1990), 166.

40. Gen. 47:30; Deut. 31:16; 1 Kings 2:10; Job 14:12–13; Ps. 13:3; Jer. 51:39–40; 2 Macc. 12:45; John 11:11–13; Acts 13:36; 1 Cor. 11:30; Homer, *Iliad* 11.241; Sophocles, *Electra* 509.

41. Theocritus, *Idyll* 4.42.

42. The primary reasons are threefold: (1) the phrase "we believe" is used elsewhere to introduce a creedal formula (see Rom. 10:9); (2) Paul employs the name "Jesus" alone instead of his expected practice of referring to "Christ"; (3) the verb "rose" (*anestē*) is a rare one in Paul's writings as he normally employs a different verb to describe the resurrection of Christ (he uses *egeirō* thirty-seven times, whereas *anistēmi* occurs only twice).

43. Acts 8:39; 23:10; 2 Cor. 12:2, 4; Rev. 12:5.

44. E. Peterson, "ἀπαντήσις," *TDNT*, 1:380–81. This widely held understanding of the word *apantēsis* has been challenged by M. Cosby, "Hellenistic Formal Reception and Paul's Use of *APANTESIS* in 1 Thessalonians 4:17," *BBR* 4 (1994): 15–34. For a rebuttal to Cosby, see R. H. Gundry, "A Brief Note on 'Hellenistic Formal Receptions' and Paul's Use of *APANTESIS* in 1 Thessalonians 4:17," *BBR* 6 (1996): 39–41.

45. BGU 2.362.7.17; Polybius, *History* 5.26.8; Josephus, *Ant.* 11.8.4; Cicero, *Atticus* 8.16.2; 16.11.6; Chrysostom, *Thessalonians: Homily* 8.62.44.

46. M. W. Holmes, *1 & 2 Thessalonians* (Grand Rapids: Zondervan, 1988), 165. So also Marshall, *Thessalonians*, 132.

47. In addition to the brief remarks of Donfried, "Cults of Thessalonica," 344, see especially, H. L. Hendrix, "Archaeology and Eschatology," in *The Future of Early Christianity: Essays in Honor of Helmut Koester*, ed. B. A. Pearson (Minneapolis: Fortress, 1991), 107–18; Jer. 6:14; 8:11; Ezek. 13:10–16; Mic. 3:5.

48. Holmes, *Thessalonians*, 167.

49. The NIV fails to translate the emphatic negation found in the original Greek.

50. E.g., Job 22:9–11; Ps. 27:1; 74:20; 82:5; 112:4; Prov. 4:18–19; Isa. 2:5; 9:2; 60:19–20; 1QS 1:9–10; 3:13, 24–25; 1QM 1:1, 3.

51. Rom. 13:12; 2 Cor. 6:7; Eph. 6:11–18.

52. On the important and complex concepts of "wrath" and "salvation" in Paul's letters, see G. Borchert, "Wrath, Destruction," *DPL*, 991–93, and L. Morris, "Salvation," *DPL*, 858–62.

53. LSJ, 1526.

54. In addition to here, see 1 Thess. 4:1, 10b; also Rom. 12:1–12; 15:30–32; 16:17; 1 Cor. 1:10; 4:16; 16:15–16.

55. See G. Delling, "ἄτακτος, ἀτακτέω," *TDNT*, 8:47–48; C. Spicq, "ἄτακτος, ἀτακτέω, ἀτάκτως," *TLNT*, 1:223–26.

56. G. Milligan, *St. Paul's Epistles to the Thessalonians* (London: Macmillan, 1908), 152–54 ("Note G. On *atakteô* and its cognates").

57. Ex. 6:9; Isa. 35:4; Sir. 7:10.

58. So, respectively, E. Best, *The First and Second Epistles to the Thessalonians* (London: Black, 1972), 231; G. Fee, *God's Empowering Presence* (Peabody, Mass.: Hendrickson, 1994), 57, n. 75; D. A. Black, "The Weak in Thessalonica: A Study in Pauline Lexicography," *JETS* 25 (1982): 307–21.

59. So, e.g., Best, *Thessalonians*, 239; Holmes, *Thessalonians*, 183–84. Donfried ("Cults of Thessalonica," 342) writes: "One should not overlook the obvious parallels between the following texts and the mystery cults . . . 1 Thess. 5.19–22 where Paul explicitly urges his hearers not 'to quench' the Spirit but 'to test' it. Quite clearly the Apostle does not wish the gift of the Spirit to be confused with the excesses of Dionysiac mysteries; for Paul the Spirit does not lead to 'Bacchic frenzies' but to joy precisely in the context of suffering."

60. White, *Light from Ancient Letters*, 107.

61. See J. A. D. Weima, *Neglected Endings: The Significance of the Pauline Letter Closings* (Sheffield: JSOT Press, 1994), 28–56.

62. Ibid., passim; see also J. A. D. Weima, "The Pauline Letter Closings: Analysis and Hermeneutical Significance," *BBR* 5 (1995): 177–98.

63. See the fuller discussion in Weima, *Neglected Endings*, 176–84.

64. For a listing of the relevant texts as well as a more detailed discussion of the kiss greeting, see G. Stählin, "φιλέω," *TDNT*, 9:119–46; S. Benko, "The Kiss," in *Pagan Rome and the Early Christians* (Bloomington, Ind.: Indiana Univ. Press, 1984), 79–102; W. Klassen, "The Sacred Kiss in the New Testament," *NTS* 39 (1993): 122–35.

65. See Gen. 33:4; 45:15; 2 Kings 14:33 (LXX); Luke 15:20.

66. See the fuller discussion in Weima, *Neglected Endings*, 111–14, 184–86; see also Rom. 16:16a; 1 Cor. 16:20b; 2 Cor. 13:12a.

Sidebar and Chart Notes

A-1. See further G. H. R. Horsley, "The Politarchs," *The Book of Acts in Its Graeco-Roman Setting*, eds. D. W. J. Gill and C. Gempf (Grand Rapids: Eerdmans, 1994), 419–31.

A-2. For an account of the suffering endured by Christians around the globe in the twentieth century, see James and Marti Hefley, *By Their Blood: Christian Martyrs of the Twentieth Century* (Grand Rapids: Baker, 1996); P. Marshall, *Their Blood Cries Out: The Untold Story of Persecution Against Christians in the Modern World* (Dallas: Word, 1997).

A-3. Demosthenes, *Orations* 59.122.

A-4. See also Horace, *Satire* 1.2.31–35.

A-5. Donfried, "Cults of Thessalonica," 337.

A-6. C. Colson, *The Body: Being Light in Darkness* (Dallas: Word, 1992), 46.

A-7. *Corpus Inscriptionum Graecarum*, ed. A. Boeckius (Hildescheim & New York: Georg Olms Verlag, 1977), 56.

A-8. Josephus, *Ant.* 14.10.22; trans. R. Marcus (LCL; Cambridge, Mass.: Harvard Univ. Press, 1933), 7.581.

2 THESSALONIANS

by Jeffrey A. D. Weima

Introduction

For comments on the city of Thessalonica and Paul's relationship with the church in that city, see the introduction to 1 Thessalonians.

Letter Opening and Thanksgiving (1:1–12)

Paul's letters always begin with the following fixed pattern: a listing of the sender(s), the recipients, a greeting, and then an extended thanksgiving to God for the faith and conduct of his readers. Although each of these features is typical of letters of that day, the apostle adapts and expands these conventions in a distinctly Christian way (see comments on 1 Thess. 1:1; 1:2–10).

Paul, Silas and Timothy (1:1). The inclusion of Silas and Timothy as cosenders, along with the frequent use of the plural "we" throughout the letter, might suggest that all three individuals mentioned in the letter opening functioned as the author of 2 Thessalonians. The use

CORINTH

Paul writes to the Thessalonians from Corinth.

> ## 2 Thessalonians
> ## IMPORTANT FACTS:
>
> - ■ **AUTHOR:** Paul (despite his mentioning Silas and Timothy as cosenders).
> - ■ **DATE:** A.D. 51 (Paul writes from Corinth).
> - ■ **PURPOSES:**
>   - To commend the church for enduring persecution.
>   - To correct false teaching about the "day of the Lord."
>   - To discipline those living in idleness.

of the first person "I" in the letter closing (3:17; see also 2:5), however, as well as evidence from his other letters (see comments on 1 Thess. 1:1), indicates that Paul is the real author of this letter. The name of the second person is actually "Silvanus," whom the writer of Acts calls "Silas."[1] "Silvanus" is Silas's Latin name, which he would have as a Roman citizen (16:37).

We ought always to thank God for you (1:3). The obligation of human beings to give thanks to God is a common theme in both Jewish and Christian writings of this time.[2] The Mishnah, for example, in the context of reminding Jews during the Passover of how the Lord redeemed them from Egypt, states: "Therefore, we are obligated to thank him who wrought all these wonders for our fathers and us."[3] The Christian letter known as *1 Clement* exhorts its readers: "We ought in every respect to give thanks to him" (38:4). Similarly, the *Epistle of Barnabas* states: "The good Lord revealed everything to us beforehand, in order that we might know him to whom we ought to give thanks and praise for everything" (7:1; see also 5:3). Thus, the phrase "we ought always to thank God" (so also 2:13) does not mean that Paul views thanksgiving as a duty rather than a joy. Instead, the apos-

tle is simply acknowledging, as do others of his day, the need for gratitude to be given to God, since he is responsible for the increased faith and love evident in the lives of the Thessalonian Christians.

All the persecutions and trials you are enduring (1:4). The suffering endured by the Thessalonian Christians started from the moment of their conversion (1 Thess. 1:6; 2:2; cf. Acts 17:5–7), continued during Paul's absence and the later visit of Timothy (1 Thess. 3:1–5), and had not ceased when 2 Thessalonians was written (2 Thess. 1:4–7). The kind of "persecutions" and "trials" that these believers experienced did not likely involve physical death or martyrdom,[4] since there is no evidence that the deaths in the church (1 Thess. 4:13–18) were a direct result of their faith. Instead, their suffering most likely consisted of social harassment—an experience that became all-too-common for Christians in the Greco-Roman world.

All this is evidence that God's judgment is right (1:5). The antecedent of "all this" is ambiguous[5] so that it is not clear what exactly Paul regards as "evidence" of God's just judgment. The traditional view sees "evidence" as looking back to "your perseverance and faith," so that it is the Thessalonian church's endurance of

▶ Social Harassment of Christians in the Greco-Roman World

Many sources, both within and without the New Testament, portray the resentment and offense felt by non-Christians when converts to Christianity refused to participate in normal social and cultic activities.[A-1] The exclusivity of the Christians' religion—their seemingly arrogant refusal to participate in or consider valid the worship of any god but their own—deeply wounded public sensibilities and even led to the charge that they were "atheists." Christians became easy targets of blame for earthquakes, floods, and agricultural failures, since these and other natural disasters were viewed as punishments from the gods, who felt slighted by this exclusive sect's failure to participate in cultic worship. Family members also felt a strong sense of betrayal over relatives who, on the basis of their newfound faith, broke ancestral traditions and showed an appalling lack of concern for their familial responsibilities.

oppression that shows God's just judgment.[6] A number of difficulties with this interpretation, however, has led to an alternative position: "Evidence" refers to the immediately preceding phrase ("persecutions and trials"), so that it is the sufferings of the church per se that constitute a sign of divine justice.[7] This interpretation is in keeping with a theology of suffering that can be found in Jewish literature of this period.[8] In these writings suffering is not viewed as a sign of God's rejection but somewhat paradoxically as a sign of God's acceptance insofar as he offers through it an opportunity for his elect to receive in this age the punishment for their few sins, thereby preserving the full measure of their reward in the age to come. At the same time suffering is also a sign of the absolute justice of God insofar as he insists on the punishment even of his elect.

God is just: He will pay back (1:6–7a). The principle of divine retribution, the *lex talionis* ("an eye for an eye, a tooth for a tooth"), is frequently associated in the Old Testament with the day of the Lord. Isaiah 66:6, for example, states: "Hear that uproar from the city, hear that noise from the temple! It is the sound of the LORD repaying his enemies all they deserve." That this principle also lies behind 1:6–7a is evident in the play on words that God will pay back "*trouble* to those who *trouble* you and give *relief* to you who are *troubled*." The *lex talionis* is rejected as a principle of human conduct (Matt. 5:38–48; Rom. 12:17), since one may easily act unjustly or out of vindictiveness. These dangers do not exist in divine conduct, however, since "God is just," and so this principle forms an essential aspect of any teaching about God's judgment.[9] It also provides an answer to the problem caused

by the prosperity of the wicked and the suffering of the righteous, by looking to the future judgment to redress the injustice of this present life.[10]

This will happen when the Lord Jesus is revealed from heaven (1:7b). The linking of the future return of Christ with the present suffering endured by the Thessalonian Christians suggests that Paul may have had in mind the concept of the "messianic woes." This was a widely held belief in the first century that the coming of the Messiah and/or the messianic age would be preceded by a period of intense suffering by God's people.[11] The notion of "messianic woes" may also explain the problem taken up in the next chapter. For if the Thessalonian believers viewed their suffering as part of the woes God's people would experience immediately prior to the return of Christ, they may have been more willing to believe the claim that "the day of the Lord has already come" (2:2).[12]

We constantly pray for you (1:11). Letter writers in the ancient world often included at the beginning (and sometimes also the end) a reference to the fact that they were praying for the physical health and well-being of their recipients. In a letter that can be dated precisely to 168 B.C. a woman writes to her absent husband: "Isias to Hephaistion: Greeting. If you are well and your other affairs turn out in a like fashion, it would be as I have been continually praying to the gods"(PLond 1:42).[13] Two centuries later a man named Sabinianus similarly begins a letter to his brother Apollinarius by greeting him and stating: "I myself make daily prayers regarding your welfare before the local gods that you may be preserved for a long time" (PMich 8:499).[14] Paul also opens his letter to the Thessalonian church by letting these Christians know that he constantly prays for them. The prayers of the apostle, however, are not directed to Dionysius, Serapis, Isis, Cabirus, and the other gods worshiped in Thessalonica but to "our God," who is identified in the letter opening as "our Father and the Lord Jesus Christ." The content of Paul's prayers does not deal with his recipients' physical health but with their spiritual well-being, namely, that they may be "worthy of his [God's] calling" and that "the name of our Lord Jesus may be glorified in you" (1:11–12).

The Day of the Lord (2:1–17)

Paul had taught the Thessalonian believers about "the day of the Lord"—the events surrounding the return of Christ—already at some length during his original ministry in their city (see comments on 2:5). Thus, when he wrote in his first letter about the unexpected arrival of this day and the judgment that would take place then (5:1–11), the apostle could legitimately state that he did not really need to write about such things, since the Thessalonian Christians were already sufficiently well-informed about this future event, so that it would not surprise them like a thief in the night. Sometime after receiving this letter, however, the church was confronted with the claim that the day of the Lord had already come—a claim that caused them a great deal of consternation.

Paul responds by first urging the church not to be alarmed by this false report (2 Thess. 2:1–2). He then explains why it is impossible for the day of the Lord to have already arrived: There must first occur certain clearly defined events, foremost of which involves the appear-

ance of the "man of lawlessness," who for the present time is being restrained (2:3–12). The apostle concludes his discussion with a thanksgiving (2:13–14), an exhortation (2:15), and a prayer (2:16), all of which are intended to comfort those shaken by the false report and to challenge the church instead to stand firm to the true teaching that he passed on to them.

Although the overview given above may sound relatively clear and simple, this passage has frustrated interpreters for centuries. For not only does Paul here make great use of apocalyptic imagery whose precise meaning is difficult to ascertain, the text also contains several grammatical irregularities and incompleted sentences. It is no exaggeration to claim that 2:1–17 is "probably the most obscure and difficult passage in the whole of the Pauline correspondence."[15]

Our being gathered to him (2:1). The immediate reference is to the comforting picture given in the previous letter of how all believers, both those who have already died and those who are still alive, will be gathered together to Jesus at his return (1 Thess. 4:16–17). This motif, however, goes back to the Old Testament hope in the gathering together of the scattered exiles to their own land on the day of the Lord and was taken over by Jesus and the early church to refer to the final gathering together of God's people with the Messiah.[16]

By some prophecy, report or letter (2:2a). Paul does not know for certain the means by which the false claim concerning the day of the Lord has been communicated. Thus, he lists three possibilities: a prophecy (the word used here literally is "spirit," but the NIV rightly sees this as a reference to a prophetic utterance), a report (lit., a "word," i.e., a nonecstatic spoken message), or a letter (either 1 Thessalonians or a forged letter attributed to the apostle). That Paul suspects a prophecy to be the most likely source is supported by two factors. First, Paul already anticipated in his first letter the need for the church to be more perceptive about "Spirit" utterances (1 Thess. 5:19–22). Second, this would explain why at the end of this passage the apostle exhorts the congregation to hold fast to what they have been previously taught by him "whether by word of mouth or by letter" (2 Thess. 2:15), but strikingly omits the first member of the triad in 2:2a "by some prophecy"—what Paul himself most likely believed to be the ultimate source of the false claim.[17]

The day of the Lord has already come (2:2b). The verb *enestēken* refers not to the imminence of the day of the Lord (KJV: "is at hand")[18] but rather to its actual presence (NIV: "has already come").[19] The Thessalonians did not likely view this day as a twenty-four period but as a complex period involving a number of events of which the return of Christ was just one part. They may have also viewed their own suffering as part of the "messianic woes," a period of severe distress before the appearance of the Messiah (see comments on 1:7b), and so been more willing to believe the claim that "the day of the Lord has already come."[20]

The man of lawlessness (2:3b–4). The man of lawlessness is typically identified with the Antichrist as well as the unnamed figure or figures who are expected to arise against Jesus prior to the time of his return.[21] The description of this figure here in 2 Thessalonians 2:3b–4 has striking similarities with a number

of Old Testament texts and events from the intertestamental period. For example, a number of the prophets describe pagan kings who made themselves out to be gods.[22] Or again, there are similarities with historical violations of the temple, such as when the Roman general Pompey in 63 B.C. entered the Most Holy Place and when the Roman emperor Caligula in A.D. 40 tried to set up a statue of himself there and so assert his claim to divinity.[23] The most probable situation, however, is that Paul is drawing from traditional material of early Christian eschatology that was based on the teachings of Jesus, who in turn incorporated the prophecy of Daniel in expounding his own views of the end times.[24]

I used to tell you these things (2:5). The imperfect tense of the verb (*elegon*) stresses the customary or repeated nature of the action: Paul had spoken often during his stay in Thessalonica about the man of lawlessness and his ultimate destruction at Christ's return.

What is holding him back / the one who now holds it back (2:6, 8). Paul states two times that the man of lawlessness and the rebellion associated with his appearance are currently being "held back"

THE JERUSALEM TEMPLE

A model of the temple and its courts.

center ▶

ANTIOCHUS
EPIPHANES

A coin with the
image of the noto-
rious Syrian ruler.

or "restrained." The apostle first refers to the *thing* (neuter) that is restraining (2:6) and then later describes the *one* (masculine) who is restraining (2:8). This complicates even further the already difficult task of identifying the "restrainer" (see "Who Is the Restrainer?").

The Lord Jesus will overthrow with the breath of his mouth (2:8). Paul describes the destruction of the man of lawlessness with imagery borrowed from Isaiah 11:4 (LXX), where the Prince from David's house "will strike the earth with the word of his mouth and with the breath of his lips he will destroy the wicked." Other biblical and intertestamental passages employ identical or similar idioms dealing with the force of the mouth or breath to consume the unrighteous.[25]

But we ought always to thank God for you (2:13). See comments on 2 Thessalonians 1:3.

From the beginning God chose you (2:13). There are compelling reasons to replace "from the beginning" with the alternate reading found in the NIV footnote "as his firstfruits" (so also NRSV, NAB).[26] The word "firstfruits" (*aparchē*) refers to the part of the harvest that was the earliest to ripen and that consequently reassured the farmer of the fuller share of the harvest yet to come. Paul, therefore, reassures the small, persecuted, and alarmed church of Thessalonica that God has chosen them as "firstfruits"—the first of many more who will surely join them in "shar[ing] in the glory of our Lord Jesus Christ" (2:14).

Prayer for Paul and the Thessalonians (3:1–5)

Paul begins to bring his second letter to a close (note "Finally" in 3:1) by first issuing some general exhortations about prayer (3:1–5) before going on to specific commands about the "idlers" (3:6–15). The apostle starts with a request for prayer for himself and his coworkers (3:1–2) but then shifts the focus to the Thessalonian Christians (3:3–4) and his prayer for them (3:5).

▶ Who Is the Restrainer?

A wide range of suggestions has been made concerning the identity of the "restrainer"—the thing and person that Paul refers to in both impersonal and personal terms (2:6, 8):[A-2]

1. The Roman Empire and the Emperor
2. The Principle of Law and Order and the Political Leaders
3. The Proclamation of the Gospel and the Proclaimer (Paul or other missionaries)
4. The Power of God and God Himself
5. The Presence of the Church and the Holy Spirit

6. The Force of Evil and Satan
7. The False Prophecy and the False Prophet
8. The Jewish State and James of Jerusalem

There is a wide consensus that the restraining influence is positive and beneficial, which eliminates proposals 6 and 7. None of the remaining options, however, is free from difficulties either. Many scholars, therefore, are driven to the conclusion reached long ago by Augustine, who said of this passage: "I frankly confess that the meaning of this completely escapes me."[A-3]

We have confidence in the Lord (3:4). Ancient letter writers, after requesting something of the recipient, sometimes express confidence in the recipient's willingness or ability to grant the request. The author of PMich 485, for example, states: "I am confident, however, that you will show no hesitation at all in the matter mentioned above." Another ancient letter concludes: "Although I am absent, yet I am confident that my affairs will be greatly promoted by Your Mightiness—in this confidence I have written to you" (SB 7656).[27] Such statements of confidence served to exert indirect pressure on the recipient to grant the request and so live up to the confidence that the writer has in him.[28] Paul also includes in his letters similar statements of confidence, although he "Christianizes" them by claiming that his confidence in his readers is ultimately rooted "in the Lord," who is here said to be "faithful" and to "strengthen and protect you from the evil one."[29] Yet there still remains indirect pressure on the Thessalonian Christians to live up to the confidence that the apostle has in them.

Disciplining Idlers (3:6–15)

The problem of some believers living in idleness was a longstanding one in the Thessalonian church. Paul first addressed this issue during his initial visit to Thessalonica, when he commanded his converts to work.[30] He dealt once again with the problem of idleness, albeit briefly, in his first letter (1 Thess. 4:11–12; 5:14a). But instead of getting better, the problem apparently got worse. Thus, for yet a third time and at much greater length, Paul addresses in 2 Thessalonians 3:6–15 the issue of living in idleness. He begins and ends his extended treatment of the matter with commands to avoid those who are idle (3:6, 14–15) and sandwiches between these commands appeals both to the example that he and his co-workers set (3:7–9) and to his explicit teachings about work (3:10–13).

Keep away from every brother who is idle. . . . Do not associate with him (3:6, 14). Paul commands the larger church community to discipline those who are idle through the practice of social

---

▶ Why Did Some Thessalonian Christians Not Want to Work?

Eschatological reason. The traditional explanation involves the Thessalonians' eschatological excitement over the imminent return of Christ. The belief that Jesus would return soon caused some believers to abandon ordinary earthly pursuits, such as working for a living, so that they could give full attention to spiritual preparation, eschatological discussion, and perhaps preaching. This group likely reasoned to themselves: "Since the end is near, work is a waste of time."[A-4]

Sociological reason. The challenging explanation looks for a sociological cause. A few appeal to the general disdain toward physical labor prevalent in the Greco-Roman world.[A-5] More, however, turn to the patron-client relationship that was popular in that day.[A-6] In this relationship, members of the lower class attached themselves to benefactors from among the upper class, from whom they then received sustenance and help in various matters in exchange for the obligation to reciprocate with expressions of gratitude and support. It is argued that Paul's converts included those of the urban poor who had formed client relationships with wealthy members in the Thessalonian church, but who exploited the generosity of their new Christian patrons.[A-7]

ostracism.[31] The verb "keep away from" (*stellesthai*) in 3:6 is a rather general term of withdrawal or avoidance, and so it is not clear to what degree the errant members are to be shunned. The verb "associate with" (*synanamignysthai*) is more specific and suggests that discipline minimally involved exclusion from the formal activities of the church, such as corporate worship and the meal that was typically a part of the Lord's Supper celebration (1 Cor. 5:11; 11:17–34).[32]

Idle (3:6, 7, 11). There is some debate whether the Greek root *atakt-* refers to the problem of "idleness" or "rebelliousness" (see comments on 1 Thess. 5:14).

How you ought to follow our example / to make ourselves a model for you to follow (3:7, 9). The notion of imitating some sort of moral exemplar was common in the ancient world, especially by teachers who exhorted their students to imitate them.[33] Paul also makes frequent use of this concept in his letters as he holds up not only himself as examples to be emulated. In 2 Thessalonians 3:7–9, the apostle reminds the Thessalonian church that he and his coworkers worked long ("night and day") and hard ("laboring and toiling") in order to not to become a financial burden to anyone, even though as leaders they were entitled to monetary support ("not because we do not have the right to such help").[34] Such conduct serves as a powerful model for the Thessalonian believers—both those who are idle and those who are still working—on the importance of self-sufficient labor.

We worked night and day (3:8). On the kind of labor done by Paul and his companions, see comments on 1 Thessalonians 2:9.

"If a man will not work, he shall not eat" (3:10). Although Paul's maxim here has no exact parallel, similar sayings can be found in Jewish and early Christian literature. Rabbi Abbahu, for example, is cited as stating: "If I do not work, I do not eat."[35] The Greek text makes clear that Paul is not speaking about the inability to work but rather the *refusal* to work (the text literally reads: "If someone does not *want* to work. . ."). While the church must continue to care for those who genuinely need help (3:13, "never tire of doing what is right"),[36] it must not tolerate those who are unwilling to work. The *Didache*, an early Christian manual of instruction, makes the same point in its teaching on how to deal with visitors "who come in the name of the Lord": "If the one who comes is merely passing through, assist him as much as you can. But he must not stay with you for more than two or, if necessary, three days. However, if he wishes to settle among you and is a craftsman, let him work for his living. But if he is not a craftsman, decide according to your own judgment how he shall live among you as a Christian, yet without being idle. But if he does

R E F L E C T I O N S

SOME TODAY ARE UNWILLING TO WORK, CONTENT rather to exploit the support provided by government welfare programs. Others, who are willing to work, view their labor only as a means to an end—that is, as the price they pay in order to obtain the pleasures of material wealth or weekend revelry (recall the popular acronym: T.G.I.F.—"Thank goodness it's Friday!"). The Scriptures teach, however, that work is a good creation gift instituted by God prior to the Fall (Gen. 2:15). Furthermore, Jesus is Lord over all areas of life—including the job site. Believers, therefore, ought to view their labor as one important way in which they serve Christ.

not wish to cooperate in this way [i.e., to work], then he is trading on Christ. Beware of such people."[37]

They are not busy; they are busybodies (3:11). The NIV nicely captures the word-play in Greek at work here. Instead of being busy with their work (*ergazomenous*), the idlers are busybodies (*periergazomenous*), who spend their free time becoming a nuisance, presumably by meddling into the affairs of others and causing unrest. This is the same problem that likely lies behind Paul's command in his first letter "to lead a quiet life, to mind your own business and to work with your hands."[38]

Yet do not regard him as an enemy, but warn him as a brother (3:15). The emperor Marcus Aurelius observes that if someone behaves rudely in the gymnasia, it is best simply to "avoid him, yet not as an enemy," and that the proper approach generally to such people is "to avoid them but not look askance or conceive hatred for them."[39] In a somewhat similar way, Paul exhorts the majority of the Thessalonian church to "keep away from" (3:6) and "not associate with" (3:14) anyone who is idle but at the same time to treat such a person "not as an enemy" but "as a brother." The goal of discipline, therefore, is not punitive but redemptive. Although exclusion from the community will cause idlers initially to "feel ashamed" (3:14), they will hopefully respond with repentance and restoration to full fellowship within the community.

Letter Closing (3:16–18)

Second Thessalonians has a relatively brief letter closing. Yet it contains three of the four epistolary conventions typically found in the Pauline letter closings: a peace benediction (3:16), greeting (3:17), and grace benediction (3:18).[40] On the closing conventions typically found in ancient letters and Paul's skillful adaptation and expansion of these conventions, see introduction to 1 Thessalonians 5:23–28.

I, Paul, write this greeting in my own hand (3:17). It was common in the ancient world to have the help of a secretary (the technical term is an *amanuensis*) in the writing of a letter.[41] These letters typically end with an "autograph"—some final remarks written by the sender in his or her own hand. Since the change of script would have been obvious to the reader of the letter, there was no reason to state explicitly that the author was now writing rather than the secretary. Yet a few such statements can be found. The sender of PGren 89, for example, states: "I wrote all in my own hand," and the letters of Cicero similarly contain a number of references to *mea manu* ("in my own hand").[42] Paul also closes five of his letters with the phrase "in my own hand," thereby indicating that he is now taking over from the secretary to write personally to his readers.[43] Since the apostle knew that his letters would be read in a public gathering, where it would not be possible to observe the obvious change in handwriting style, he needed to state explicitly that the closing material was written in his own hand. The function of the autograph here in 2 Thessalonians 3:17 is not to emphasize the authenticity of the letter (as many scholars assert) but its authority, especially for those "idlers" whom Paul anticipates will not obey the exhortations this letter contains (see 3:14a).[44]

CHAPTER NOTES

Main Text Notes

For full bibliography of some works, see notes in 1 Thessalonians.

1. See 1 Thess. 1:1; 2 Cor. 1:19; 1 Peter 5:12; Acts 15:22–40; 16:19–29; 17:4–15; 18:5.
2. R. D. Aus, "The Liturgical Background of the Necessity and Propriety of Giving Thanks According to 2 Thess. 1:3," *JBL* 92 (1973): 432–38. Reprinted in R. D. Aus, *Barabbas and Esther and Other Studies in the Judaic Illumination of Earliest Christianity* (Atlanta: Scholars, 1992), 193–200.
3. *m. Pesaḥ.* 10:5.
4. Contrast Donfried, "Cults of Thessalonica," 349–50, and a few others.
5. This phrase is not in the Greek text but is implied by the construction.
6. So, e.g., Best, *Thessalonians,* 254–56; Bruce, *Thessalonians,* 149; Marshall, *Thessalonians,* 172–73.
7. Although this interpretation has been advocated for some time already in several German and French commentaries, it has only more recently appeared in English-language works: see J. M. Bassler, "The Enigmatic Sign: 2 Thessalonians 1:5," *CBQ* 46 (1984): 496–510; Wanamaker, *Thessalonians,* 220–23; B. Gaventa, *First and Second Thessalonians* (Louisville: John Knox, 1998), 102–3.
8. 2 Macc. 6:12–16; *2 Bar.* 13:3–10; 48:48–50; 52:5–7; 78:5; *Pss. Sol.* 13:9–10.
9. Rom. 2:6–8; 12:19; 2 Cor. 5:10; Col. 3:25.
10. See further Best, *Thessalonians,* 256–57; Marshall, *Thessalonians,* 174–75.
11. E.g., 1QH 3:2–18; Mark 13; Rev. 8, 9, 11.
12. So R. D. Aus, "The Relevance of Isaiah 66.7 to Revelation 12 and 2 Thessalonians 1," *ZNW* 67 (1976): 252–68, esp. 263–64; Wanamaker, *Thessalonians,* 224.
13. White, *Light from Ancient Letters,* 65.
14. Ibid, 183.
15. W. Neil, *The Epistles of Paul to the Thessalonians* (London: Hodder and Stoughton, 1950), 155.
16. Isa. 43:4–7; 52:12; 56:8; Jer. 31:8; Joel 3:1–2; Zech 2:6; 2 Macc. 2:7; Matt. 23:37; Mark 13:27; Luke 13:34.
17. Fee, *God's Empowering Presence,* 71–75. A fuller exposition of Fee's position is found in his "Pneuma and Eschatology in 2 Thessalonians 2.1–2—A Proposal About 'Testing the Prophets' and the Purpose of 2 Thessalonians," in *Telling the Mysteries: Essays in New Testament Eschatology in Honor of Robert H. Gundry,* eds. T. E. Schmidt and M. Silva (Sheffield: JSOT Press, 1994), 196–215.
18. So A. M. G. Stephenson, "On the Meaning of *enestēken hē hēmera tou kyriou* in 2 Thessalonians 2, 2," in *StudEvan IV,* ed. F. L. Cross (Berlin: Akademie Verlag, 1968): 442–51; Bruce, *Thessalonians,* 165.

ANNOTATED BIBLIOGRAPHY

Best, Ernest. *A Commentary on the First and Second Epistles to the Thessalonians.* HNTC. New York: Harper & Row, 1972; reprint, Peabody, Mass.: Hendrickson, 1987.

A thorough treatment that still ranks as one of the best commentaries on the Thessalonian letters.

Gaventa, Beverly R. *First and Second Thessalonians.* Interpretation: A Bible Commentary for Teaching and Preaching. Louisville: John Knox, 1998.

A brief treatment that excels in its suggestions for application and preaching.

Holmes, Michael W. *1 & 2 Thessalonians.* NIVAC. Grand Rapids: Zondervan, 1998.

A judicious and readable exposition that applies the text in helpful and specific ways to contemporary culture and life.

Marshall, I. Howard. *1 and 2 Thessalonians.* NCBC. London: Marshall, Morgan & Scott, 1983.

A brief yet insightful commentary with an especially good and detailed discussion of introductory matters.

Wanamaker, Charles A. *Commentary on 1 & 2 Thessalonians.* NIGTC. Grand Rapids: Eerdmans, 1990.

An excellent full-length commentary on the Greek text that emphasizes rhetorical features of the letters.

Weima, Jeffrey A. D., and Stanley E. Porter. *An Annotated Bibliography of 1 & 2 Thessalonians.* NTTS 26. Leiden: Brill, 1998.

A helpful research tool that lists some 1200 works (the majority of which are annotated) that are germane for the interpretation of 1 and 2 Thessalonians.

19. So the vast majority of commentators; see, e.g., Best, *Thessalonians*, 279; E. J. Richard, *First and Second Thessalonians* (Collegeville, Minn.: Liturgical, 1995), 325.

20. Aus, "Relevance," 263–64; Wanamaker, *Thessalonians*, 240.

21. 1 John 2:18, 22; 4:3; 2 John 7; Matt. 24:5, 23–24; Mark 13:21–22; Luke 21:8; Rev. 13.

22. Isa. 14:13–14; Ezek. 28:2; Dan. 6:7.

23. *Pss. Sol.* 2; 17:11–14; Josephus, *Ant.* 14.4.4; Philo, *Embassy* 203–346; Josephus, *Ant.* 18.8.2–9.

24. Matt. 24; Mark 13; Dan. 7:25; 8:11; 9:26–27; 11:31, 36.

25. Ps. 32:6; 134:17; *1 Enoch* 14:2; 84:1; Job 4:9; Isa. 30:27–28; Rev. 19:15; *1 Enoch* 62:2; *4 Ezra* 13:10–11; *Pss. Sol.* 17:24, 35.

26. The difference in Greek between the two readings is only the addition or omission of a single letter. For a fuller discussion of the textual issues involved in this reading, see Fee, "On Text and Commentary," 179–80; idem, *God's Empowering Presence*, 77, n. 142; Holmes, *Thessalonians*, 252, n. 4.

27. Both letters are cited in S. N. Olson, "Pauline Expressions of Confidence in His Addressees," *CBQ* 47 (1985): 282–95.

28. Olson ("Pauline Expressions," 289) states: "The evidence of a variety of parallels suggest that such expressions [of confidence] are usually included to serve the persuasive purpose. Whatever the emotion behind the expression, the function is to undergird the letter's requests or admonitions by creating a sense of obligation through praise."

29. Gal. 5:10; 2 Thess. 3:4; Philem. 24; 2 Thess. 3:3.

30. 1 Thess. 4:11b; 2 Thess. 3:6, 10.

31. See also 1 Cor. 5:2, 5, 13; 2 Cor. 2:5–11; cf. Matt. 18:15–18.

32. For a more extended discussion, see J. T. South, *Disciplinary Practices in Pauline Texts* (Lewiston, N.Y.: Mellen, 1992).

33. See the texts cited above in note 9.

34. In addition to 2 Thess. 3:7, 9, see 1 Cor. 7:7–16; Gal. 4:12–20; Phil. 1:30; 4:9a; 1 Thess. 1:6; but others: God (Eph. 5:1); Christ (1 Cor. 11:1; Phil. 2:5–11; 1 Thess. 1:6); the churches of Judea (1 Thess. 2:14); Timothy (Phil. 2:19–24); Epaphroditus (Phil. 2:25–30).

35. *Gen. Rab.* 2.2 on Gen. 1:2.

36. See also Gal. 6:10; Eph. 4:28; 1 Tim. 5:3–8; Titus 3:14; as well as Paul's collection for the needy believers in Judea (Rom. 15:26–29; 1 Cor. 16:1–4; 2 Cor. 8–9; Gal. 2:10).

37. M. W. Holmes, ed., *The Apostolic Fathers*, trans. J. B. Lightfoot and J. R. Harmer (Grand Rapids: Baker, 1992), 265–66; *Did.* 12:2–5.

38. 1 Thess. 4:11; see also 1 Tim. 5:13.

39. This potential parallel with 2 Thess. 2:14 was first proposed by J. Moffatt, "2 Thessalonians iii. 14, 15," *ExpTim* 21 (1909–10): 328; Aurelius, *Meditationes* 6.20.

40. The only item missing is a hortatory section—some final commands or exhortations. On the various closing conventions found in Paul's letter closings, see Weima, *Neglected Endings*, 77–155.

41. See E. R. Richards, *The Secretary in the Letters of Paul* (Tübingen: Mohr-Siebeck, 1991); Weima, *Neglected Endings*, 45–50.

42. E.g., *Ad. Att.* 8.1; 13.28. See also Richards, *Secretary*, 173.

43. These five references, along with the personal comment of the secretary himself in Rom. 16:22 ("I, Tertius, who wrote down this letter, greet you in the Lord"), strongly suggest that Paul used an amanuensis in the writing of all his letters, even those in which he does not explicitly state that he is now writing "in my own hand" (see Weima, *Neglected Endings*, 118–26); 1 Cor. 16:21; Gal. 6:11; Col. 4:18a; 2 Thess. 3:17; Philem. 19.

44. So Marshall, *Thessalonians*, 232; Weima, *Neglected Endings*, 126–27.

Sidebar and Chart Notes

A-1. I am heavily indebted for the following to Barclay, "Conflict in Thessalonica," 513–16.

A-2. For an explanation and evaluation of these proposals, see Marshall, *Thessalonians*, 196–99; Wanamaker, *Thessalonians*, 250–52; L. Morris, "Man of Lawlessness and Restraining Power," *DPL*, 592–94.

A-3. Augustine, *City of God*, 20.19.

A-4. So, e.g., Best, *Thessalonians*, 175, 230, 331; Morris, *Thessalonians*, 130, 253.

A-5. So, e.g., Marshall, *Thessalonians*, 116, 223.

A-6. So, e.g., R. Russell, "The Idle in 2 Thess. 3:6–12: An Eschatological or Social Problem?" *NTS* 34 (1988): 105–19; B. Winter, "'If a Man Does Not Wish to Work. . .': A Cultural and Historical Setting for 2 Thessalonians 3:6–16," *TynBul* 40 (1989): 303–15.

A-7. There does not appear to be enough evidence available to determine with any high degree of certainty whether the eschatological or sociological reason is correct. For a discussion of the strengths and weaknesses of each position, see Weima, "'How You Must Walk,'" 113–15.

1 TIMOTHY

by S. M. Baugh

The Pastoral Epistles

First and Second Timothy and Titus have been termed the "Pastoral Letters" since the eighteenth century. Many scholars today think that these letters were written by a later follower of Paul and not by the apostle himself. Their reasons center on vocabulary and style, but recent research into the role of secretaries in ancient compositions has provided convincing explanation for the stylistic differences between the Pastorals and the other Pauline letters.

The tedious mechanics of writing, even among the well educated, was usually left to a secretary or even to a close friend, while the author concentrated on communicating the substance of his thought.[1] This is only natural, since polished oratory was the main goal of ancient higher education and the epitome of civilized life; written works were only secondary forms of communication, which were even then often designed to be read aloud in public (cf. Rev. 1:3).[2] The first-century Jewish author Josephus explicitly mentions

EPHESUS

The countryside surrounding the ancient city.

1 Timothy
IMPORTANT FACTS:

- ■ **AUTHOR:** The apostle Paul.
- ■ **DATE:** About A.D. 65 (after Paul's first Roman imprisonment).
- ■ **VENUES:** Paul is probably in Macedonia writing to Timothy at Ephesus.
- ■ **OCCASION:**
  - • To warn and inform Timothy about false teachers in the Ephesian area.
  - • To establish certain guidelines for church practices.
  - • To encourage Timothy in the conduct of his ministry.

secretaries who assisted him in his major compositions; two of his later works "are so different that one would hardly suppose them to be contemporary productions from the same pen."[3]

Furthermore, we should actually expect differences of style and content in the Pastorals from Paul's other letters. Paul wrote to his close associates, Timothy and Titus, who were fully versed in his teaching and practice, whereas letters like Romans or Colossians were written to churches who often needed extensive instruction from the apostle in more fundamental areas (cf. 1 Cor. 3:1–3). The Pastoral Letters naturally fit the picture of a senior missionary pastor writing to his associates on the kind of pastoral issues they can expect to face in their church planting ministry.[4]

Therefore, we can safely accept the Pauline authorship of the Pastorals. Even if a secretary helped Paul compose his letters, "the author assumed complete responsibility for the content and exercised this duty usually by checking, editing, or even correcting the draft."[5]

WESTERN ASIA MINOR

▼

The Occasion of First Timothy

All three Pastoral Letters present particular problems if we try to line them up with the chronology of Paul's life presented in Acts. While it appears to be possible to place the writing of 2 Timothy during Paul's custody in Caesarea (Acts 23–26), this creates more problems than it solves, since, for example, Demas had abandoned Paul in 2 Timothy 4:10, whereas he was with Paul after his transfer to Rome (Col. 4:14; Philem. 24). As a result, most scholars who accept Pauline authorship of the Pastorals understand a scenario like the one that follows.

The book of Acts ends with Paul in custody in Rome awaiting trial before Caesar. Paul had to wait over two years under house arrest in Rome for this trial to begin (Acts 28:30–31). The delay came because the Jewish authorities from Jerusalem had to appear personally at the trial in order to press charges and to make the case for the prosecution.

A law passed by the Roman senate in A.D. 61 discouraged anyone from making frivolous charges and from causing undue delay of legal process. The imperial authorities took stern measures against plaintiffs who did not appear in court to press their cases, so we must assume that there was pressure on the Sanhedrin in Jerusalem to send a delegation to Rome to prosecute Paul.[6] However, the mid–60s was a turbulent time in Jerusalem. The Jewish Sanhedrin was about to lose everything in the bloody insurrection of the Zealots, which broke out in A.D. 68 and ended in the decimation of Jerusalem and of its temple two years later—hence their delay in prosecuting Paul. It is conceivable that the problems in Jerusalem prevented the Jewish authorities from ever sending a prosecuting delegation to Rome. In such a case, the Romans may have released Paul, but with a stigma on his record.

After this first Roman imprisonment, Paul apparently spent more time ministering in Ephesus, where he left Timothy to carry on while he went to Macedonia (1 Tim. 1:3). Paul intended to return to Ephesus at some point (3:14; 4:13), but whether he did or not is unknown. First Timothy was probably written during the time Paul was in Macedonia.

During the same period after Paul's release from Rome, he had spent some time in Crete and left Titus there to carry on the work (Titus 1:5). Paul had made some inroads for the gospel while on his way to Rome (Acts 27), and it is reasonable to assume that he would return to further establish a church on this island and then leave behind a close associate like Titus to carry on the work. It was after this trip that Paul, while on his way to or already in Nicopolis in western Greece, wrote the letter to Titus.

Whether Paul actually arrived at Nicopolis is unknown; perhaps he had arrived and then returned to Asia Minor. It appears from hints in 2 Timothy (e.g., 2 Tim. 4:12–20) that Paul was arrested a second time in either Troas or elsewhere in Asia Minor and was again sent to Rome for trial. Perhaps the hostile Jewish elements in Asia Minor recorded in Acts instigated this second arrest. Second Timothy was apparently written during the time of this second Roman imprisonment. Paul now expects to be condemned to death (4:16–18). If his first Roman trial (i.e., where Acts ends) had concluded without a clear exoneration, the Roman authorities would have found a second arrest itself sufficient reason to condemn Paul.[7] He was a threat to public order, and as such they would have held him in chains "like a criminal" while awaiting trial (2:9). The Romans were obsessed with public order and were ready to punish any danger to the *pax Romana* with severe measures.

If this scenario is correct, the Pastoral Letters were Paul's final letters and fit into the end of his apostolic ministry. First Timothy would have been the first letter written, followed by Titus, then

At the beginnng of Curetes Street, two columns depict Hercules draped in a lion skin.

2 Timothy. Paul himself appears to be conscious of the impending end of his ministry, and he wants to securely ground the next generation in apostolic doctrine, practice, and pastoral insights, as well as to warn his associates of the threat of heresy and false teachers. This well accounts for the pastoral content of these letters and how they differ so much from Paul's more general letters to churches.

Timothy was prone to have been somewhat shy and abstemious in character (e.g., 1 Tim. 5:23). With Paul having just escaped Roman custody with his life, one can understand the uncertainties of ministry in the first century. As a result, Paul explains why he is writing 1 Timothy: "I am writing you these instructions so that, if I am delayed, you will know how people ought to conduct themselves in God's household" (1 Tim. 3:14–15). In other words, Timothy does not need a doctrinal handbook—he knew the gospel and the Scriptures well (2 Tim. 3:15)—

but he did need some practical advice on ecclesiastical matters and some encouragement to overcome his hesitancy because of his youth and relative inexperience (1 Tim. 4:12–16). That is precisely what Paul provides here. No one enjoys confrontation, and thus Paul also had to warn Timothy of the menace of heretical teaching in the church and how to confront it.

Salutation and Letter Opening (1:1–2)

Paul opens his letter to Timothy in much the same way as his other letters, yet with the distinctive focus on his apostolic appointment "by the command of God our Savior and of Christ Jesus our hope." Paul is not trying to magnify his ministry over against Timothy's but to assure his follower in the ministry that the "deposit" (2 Tim. 1:14) he is passing on to him is the genuine, divinely originated faith, not

▶ False Teachers in the Pastoral Letters

The precise tenets of the false teachers of whom Paul warns Timothy and Titus are difficult to determine. In part this is understandable, since they undoubtedly did not invite Paul to their meetings! They seem to be proto-Gnostic teachings (1 Tim. 6:20) colored by Jewish, pagan, and occult ideas and practices. And it is possible that Paul is warning against more than one group of false teachers, some of whom are from "the circumcision group" (Titus 1:10). Paul does provide us with a sketch of some of their main notions: devotion to myths, genealogies, and "godless chatter," a misguided and ill-informed focus on the law and "Jewish myths," ascetic practices, and teaching that the resurrection has already taken place.[A-1]

Paul further indicates that the false teachers

can also be spotted by a display of their evil motives, such as greed (1 Tim. 6:5; Titus 1:11). They can also be known by the evil things that accompanied and are produced by their teachings: controversies and factional strife (1 Tim. 1:4; 6:4–5), quarrels over words (6:4; 2 Tim. 2:14; Titus 3:9), and "foolish and stupid arguments" (2 Tim. 2:23), rather than "love, which comes from a pure heart and a good conscience and a sincere faith" (1 Tim. 1:5). The source of this gangrenous false teaching is ultimately the devil and his demons (4:1; 2 Tim. 2:26). Paul does give hope that this false teaching will not ultimately triumph against the truth of God: "But they will not get very far because, as in the case of those men, their folly will be clear to everyone" (2 Tim. 3:9).

the fabrications of the false teachers of whom he is about to warn him (see also Rom. 16:26; Titus 1:3).

Timothy my true son (1:2). Paul refers to Timothy as "my true son in the faith" (cf. 2 Tim. 2:1; Phil. 2:20, 22). The word "true" here can refer to a "natural" child. The first-century Alexandrian Jewish writer, Philo, for instance, uses this word to say that the Egyptian princess regarded Moses "as though her *natural* child."[8] The word can also refer to a "legitimate" versus an illegitimate child.[9] Here, Paul uses the term metaphorically: "my true son *in the faith.*" An interesting papyrus document uses this adjective "true" when it records the adoption of a nephew by a man: "that he might be your *true* son and firstborn as though born to you from your own blood."[10] Paul says, in effect, that Timothy is his heir in ministry and his representative to the church in Ephesus.

False Teachers (1:3–7)

Into Macedonia (1:3). It is not certain that Paul was still in Macedonia when he wrote this letter, but it is a reasonable possibility (cf. Titus 3:12). Macedonia, the homeland of Alexander the Great, was (and still is) a region to the north of Greece extending northwest to Illyricum (Rom. 15:19), north to the Balkan area, and east to Thrace. The capital of the Roman province of Macedonia was Thessalonica, and Berea—where Paul's ministry was so nobly received (Acts 17:10–13)—was the seat of its provincial assembly. An important overland road called the *Via Egnatia* ("Egnatian Road") ran from Asia Minor through the Macedonian cities of Philippi and Thessalonica on its way to the Adriatic Sea. Paul had first gone to Macedonia

as a result of a vision (16:9–10) and had an eventful time in the region, to say the least (16:11–17:15; 20:1–2).

Stay there in Ephesus (1:3). In Paul's day, Ephesus was fast becoming, in the grandiose language found on many of its later public documents, "the chief and greatest Mother-City ("metropolis") of Asia" (e.g., *Inschriften von Ephesos* [hereafter = *IvE*] 24) and "the largest emporium in Asia this side of the Taurus."[11] Paul had spent a considerable time evangelizing and teaching in Ephesus (Acts 18:19–20:1), and it was to become a chief center for the spread of early Christianity. In the early second century, Ignatius commented on the large size of the church there ("your multitudinousness").[12] According to tradition, the apostle John and Mary, Jesus' mother, made their home in Ephesus as well. Ephesus forms an important backdrop to 1 and 2 Timothy, and because it has been the subject of thorough archaeological investigation for the past century, evidence

REFLECTIONS

WHEN PAUL SAYS, "THE GOAL OF THIS COMMAND IS love," (1 Tim. 1:5) he is pointing to the instructions that Timothy is to command the opponents (cf. 2 Tim. 2:25–26). One can also more generally see that the outcome of all Christian instruction is love, which itself flows out of the great, spiritual benefits of the work of Christ: "a pure heart," which is a central requirement for seeing God (Matt. 5:8; cf. Ps. 24:4; 51:10; 2 Tim. 2:22); "a good conscience," which was brought into effect once and for all by the high priestly sacrifice of Christ (Heb. 9:14; 10:22; cf. 1 Tim. 1:19; 3:9; 4:2); and "a sincere faith," which is a faith "without hypocrisy" (contrast 1 Tim. 4:2). This lovely fruit of good teaching stands in stark contrast to the wrangling and division caused by the heretical teachers.

from this city will be brought in repeatedly throughout our commentary.

Paul sent Timothy to Ephesus in order to "command certain men not to teach false doctrines any longer" (1:3; cf. 6:3). This is not the last place in the Pastoral Letters where false teachers will be identified and warned against—it is a central theme of these letters.

Myths and endless genealogies (1:4). We are not quite sure what precise group engaged in such tiresome wrangling over "myths and endless genealogies." Was this a proto-Gnostic group? One feature of later Gnosticism was belief in a continuous emanation of being in discrete levels from a divine center like ripples on a pond. Some scholars think that these ranks of emanations could be called "genealogies." However, these might be "myths," but not "genealogies." Others point to the genealogies in the Old Testament and propose a Jewish group here. This seems more likely, given the syncretistic tendencies of the day. Paul possibly encountered a Jewish group who had amalgamated Hellenistic theosophical notions with biblical ideas.[13] Ignatius of Antioch, the early second-century Christian martyr and church leader, warned the church at Magnesia on Maeander (located about fifteen miles southeast of Ephesus) against "heterodoxies and ancient myths" connected with living "according to Judaism."[14]

"Myths and genealogies" were also a stock feature of the popular pagan literature of the day. The second-century B.C. historian Polybius contrasted his prosaic account of history with storytellers who dealt with "matters concerning genealogies and myths."[15] Earlier he had typified the target audience of this kind of literature: "The genealogical side appeals to those who are fond of a story, and the account of colonies, the foundation of cities, and their ties of kindred, such as we find, for instance, in Ephorus [ca. 405–330 B.C.], [it] attracts the curious and lovers of recondite lore."[16]

Teachers of the law (1:7). The opponents whom Timothy is to reprove want to be "teachers of the law." This is one word in Greek, *nomodidaskaloi* (lit., "law teachers"), and is only found elsewhere to refer to the Jewish scribes (Luke 5:17; accompanying the Pharisees) and a designation for Paul's teacher, Rabbi Gamaliel (Acts 5:34; cf. 22:3). Here the false teachers are concentrating on the law of Moses but do not understand the truth of the law despite their self-assurance. The Greek cities at the time revered certain "lawgivers" who were considered as founders of their civilization, much like the founding fathers of America. The most eminent was the sixth-century B.C. poet Solon, whose constitution and laws gave a distinctive direction to classical Athens.[17]

CHRYSIPPUS, A FAMOUS TEACHER

He was the successor of Cleanthes as the head of the Stoics (280–207 B.C.).

The Law's Proper Use (1:8–11)

In its prohibitive function, the law does not address the law-abiding but law-breakers. The list Paul gives of sample lawbreakers (1:9–10) seems generally comprehensible to us: rebels, murderers, and perjurers are punishable by modern laws. Yet our civil laws do not condemn all of the acts Paul lists here, like sin, adultery, or "perversion" (i.e., sodomy), nor did ancient civil laws; but they are a transgression of God's eternal covenant law (Isa. 24:5–6).

The ungodly and sinful, the unholy and irreligious (1:9). Ancient civil laws prohibited irreligion in various forms. One has only to read Acts 19:37 to see that blaspheming a state deity (in this case Artemis Ephesia) was a serious charge on a level with temple-robbing. Consider also that seditious impiety was one of the two capital charges successfully brought against Socrates by the Athenians, which led to his execution by suicide.[18]

Those who kill their fathers or mothers (1:9). Patricide and matricide are a singular horror for many peoples. In ancient Greek and Roman society, honor of one's parents was highly valued, so that, for example, even the unintentional murder of his father brought an indissoluble stain of guilt (Greek, *miasma*) on Oedipus, the subject of Greek tragic plays. Matricide was still a hot topic in Timothy's day, for in A.D. 59 the Emperor Nero had arranged for a shipwreck to get rid of his meddlesome mother, Agrippina—who was herself widely suspected of poisoning her husband, Emperor Claudius, to make room for Nero. The shipwreck plot failed, for Agrippina swam to safety, so Nero sent an assassin to do the job as she

was recovering from her narrow escape. In a (melodramatic) play written by an anonymous author after Nero's death, Agrippina appears as a vengeful ghost, saying in part: "Among the dead the memory still lives of my foul murder, the infamous offense for which my ghost still cries for vengeance."[19]

Slave traders (1:10). When Paul mentions "slave traders" among the list of gross lawbreakers, he is not mentioning an activity that was strictly illegal at the time—quite the contrary. Timothy could not have missed the prominent trade in slaves at Ephesus, which served as a wholesale market for slaves being sent from inland Asia Minor and other Eastern points of origin to the Roman West. Timothy would have seen the statue, possibly in the Ephesian marketplace, of C. Sallustius Crispus Passienus, Roman proconsul of Asia in A.D. 42/3, dedicated by "those who trade in the slave market" (*IvE* 3025). This and another similar Latin inscription from the time of the Emperor Trajan (*IvE* 646) indicate that the slave market was run by a Roman guild of slave traders. Hence, the slave trade itself was not illegal.

But how were these slaves acquired to begin with? The word for "slave trader" can also mean "kidnapper." The association of these two ideas is not coincidental, since there were five main sources for slaves in antiquity: captives in war, children of slaves, foundlings (children "exposed" [i.e., thrown out to die] by their parents and picked up by someone to be raised as their slaves), debt bondage, sale of oneself or one's children into slavery out of extreme poverty, and illegal kidnapping of free persons by brigands and pirates. The latter appear often in the literature of the period (e.g., the romantic novel by Xenophon of Ephesus, *Ephesiaca*). In real life, Paul often faced the threat of kidnapping during his missionary trips through inland Asia Minor (2 Cor. 11:26), especially during his trips through the narrow pass of the Taurus mountains (the "Cilician Gates") just west of Tarsus. This pass was a notorious place for ambush by bands of cutthroats.

The sound doctrine (1:10). Evil practices conflict with "sound doctrine." The word often rendered "sound" modifies "doctrine" or "words" in the Pastoral Letters. It comes from a word meaning "to be healthy" and contrasts with the gangrenous character of heresy. Christian doctrine brings spiritual health, and holiness of life is an integral outcome of Paul's gospel (1:11). Paul stresses that he was personally entrusted with this gospel in order to encourage his successor in the ministry by showing that the gospel he passes on to Timothy was of divine origin.[20]

Paul Was Shown Mercy (1:12–17)

Paul now focuses on the mercy of Christ Jesus on sinners, of whom Paul lists himself the premier example as a "blasphemer and a persecutor and a violent man" (1:13; cf. Acts 7:58–8:3; 9:1–2). In Paul's case, he was shown mercy not only because he acted in unbelief, but as a public demonstration of the tender mercies and grace of the Savior (1 Tim. 1:16).

A trustworthy saying (1:15). This "trustworthy saying" is the first of five occurrences of this kind of citation in the Pastoral Letters.[21] The saying here is brief and merely points to the purpose of Christ's incarnation: "to save sinners."[22]

To the King eternal (1:17). Paul closes this section with praise in a form I call an "ascription hymn" (though it may actually be a prayer, not a song). There are usually three elements to this format: specification of the recipient ("to the King eternal, immortal, invisible"), an "ascription" of certain blessed characteristics ("honor and glory"), and a closing with the solemn Jewish affirmation of the truth of the statement, "Amen." This type of format is also found, for instance, in the Book of Revelation in important places ascribing divine blessing both to God who sits on his heavenly throne and to the victorious Lamb.[23]

Instruction and Warning (1:18–20)

Fight the good fight (1:18). Comparing the Christian life with a contest or a fight is fairly common.[24] There is a parallel exhortation using the same key Greek words in *4 Maccabees*, an early first-century A.D. book. During a gruesome scene, one of seven Hebrew brothers under torture by King Antiochus IV ("Epiphanes"; reigned 175–64 B.C.) commends his brothers to follow his example of perseverance: "Fight the sacred and noble battle for religion" (*4 Macc.* 9:24).

Shipwrecked (1:19). Hymenaeus and Alexander, of whom only Hymenaeus is mentioned elsewhere (2 Tim. 2:17), and others are said to have "shipwrecked their faith." This image is powerful anywhere, but particularly at Ephesus, which was one of the most important seaports and shipping distribution points in the eastern Mediterranean. The shipwreck image was also vivid for Paul, of course, since "three times I was shipwrecked, I spent a night and a day in the open sea" (2 Cor.

11:25). With the small size of sailing craft in those days (see the box on 2 Tim. 4:21), lack of compass and other navigational aids, and the unpredictable storms at certain times of the year in the Mediterranean (late fall through early spring; cf. Acts 27:9), shipwrecks and drowning were all too common events for travelers by sea. Hence, shipwreck became a fairly common metaphor for tragedy or downfall in life: "A son born to the timocratic man at first emulates his father, and follows in his footsteps; and then sees him suddenly dashed, as a ship on a reef, against the state, and making complete wreckage of both his possessions and himself . . ." (Plato, *Republic* 553A–B; LCL trans.).

Instructions on Corporate Prayer (2:1–8)

First Timothy 2–3 concern the corporate life the church. This is a natural subject for Paul to address, given the late stage in his missionary career. He must have realized at this point that he had to make provision for the regular administration of the church after the apostolic period. The other Pastoral Letters demonstrate this same concern and account for some of the differences of style and content with Paul's other letters. The section before us begins and ends with an exhortation to regular prayer in the churches.

Prayers . . . for everyone (2:1). As Paul establishes church practice in this section and those that follow, it is notable that prayer forms the heart of the church's continuing ministry. By God's condescension and grace, he allows our "requests, prayers, intercession and thanksgiving" to have a role in his sovereign government of the world's affairs. A

typical interest of Paul as the apostle to the Gentiles (2:7; cf. Gal. 2:7–8) is that the church's prayers must be made for "everyone." In other words, prayer reaches out to all kinds of people. The word "everyone" in the NIV—*pantas anthrōpous* in Greek—can be better rendered "all kinds of people." In the plural, the Greek word for "all" (*pantes*) often refers inclusively to classes of people or of things—as it does later in this letter: "For the love of money is a root of *all kinds of* evil" (1 Tim. 6:10). There can be no discrimination whatsoever in our intercession and ministry.

For kings (2:2). Paul gives as examples of the sorts of people for whom we should pray "kings and all those in authority" (cf. Titus 3:1). There were only a few actual rulers with the title of "king" in Paul's day, though none in the territory surrounding Ephesus. The Romans had looked back to the expulsion of King Tarquinius Superbus some six centuries earlier by L. Junius Brutus as the founding of their republic. Hence, Roman emperors never dared take on the title "king," even when most sorely tempted—"Lord and god" perhaps (Suetonius, *Domitianus*, 13), but never "king." Yet the Greek-speaking people generically referred to high rulers, including the Roman emperors, as "kings," and the title

◀

NERO

He was the reigning "king" of the empire when Paul wrote this letter (A.D. 54–68).

came to correspond roughly to "sovereign" in English.[25]

And all those in authority (2:2). The people "in authority" in Ephesus at the time were both the Roman provincial governor and the local city officials, the latter of which included the Secretary of the People (Acts 19:35), city councilors, the market director, and others with official or semi-official powers. Paul asks the church to pray for Nero and other pagan leaders, in order that they might guarantee a stable society in which the church could prosper and "live peaceful and quiet lives in all godliness and holiness."

This is good and pleases God (2:3). Paul's statement about God's will in the next few verses needs to be interpreted carefully in light of what precedes and follows. In particular, Paul grounds prayer for all kinds of people in God's approval and good pleasure (2:3). This is an important qualification: If we are to be assured that God hears and answers our prayers, we must pray for the kinds of things he approves. Otherwise, he will not necessarily grant our requests. But for prayers such as those in 2:1–2, we can pray with full assurance of God's ready acceptance

and favorable response. Why? Why is God ready to hear requests and intercessions even on behalf of the likes of Nero? Paul addresses that question directly in 2:4–7 in the profoundest manner, so we must trace out his argument carefully next.

Wants all men to be saved (2:4). The "all men" whom God desires to be saved points us to his people derived from all the families of the earth. This is clear when we take 2:5–7 into view. Paul's argument can be paraphrased like this: If God is one, and there is only one Mediator with one way of redemption, and if God has chosen me to save *some* of the Gentile peoples in the scope of my apostolic mission, then we can legitimately conclude that God desires *any sort of person to be saved* regardless of ethnic origin. This was true in Old Testament times only on rare occasions, but now it is the norm by which the worldwide missionary effort of Christianity must be guided.

For there is one God (2:5). Paul rather abruptly invokes the oneness of God as substantiation for his understanding of God's will to save all kinds of people—not just Jews. The affirmation that there is only one God came naturally to Jews,

REFLECTIONS

THE CONCLUSION WE MUST DRAW from Paul's argument in 1 Timothy 2:1–8 is that any type of prejudice in the church's outreach, whether social, ethnic, racial, or otherwise, is inimical to the will of God. And we can and must pray for those still-unreached groups of peoples today with the same passion and assurance Paul had, whom God expressly desires us to reach with his gospel of grace and to call his people out "from every tribe and language and people and nation" (Rev. 5:9; cf. 7:9).

for whom the *shema* (Heb. "hear") of Deuteronomy 6:4 ("Hear, O Israel: The LORD our God, the LORD is one") acted as a banner and summary of their religion over against the polytheism of all of their neighbors (e.g., James 2:19). This same axiom is used by Paul elsewhere, as here, to establish that there is only one way of salvation for all people, not just the Jews, and that is the way of faith in the one Mediator, Jesus Christ.[26] (The argument of 1 Tim. 2:5, by the way, is far too subtle for a forger to reproduce and is one of the indelible marks of Paul's authorship of 1 Timothy.)

Who gave himself as a ransom (2:6). Christ is said to have offered himself as a "ransom" (or "redemption price") for all his people, not just those who are Jewish (cf. 1 John 2:2). It is the price paid to set us free (cf. Titus 2:14).[27]

The testimony given in its proper time (2:6). Testimony to what? To God's purpose to move redemption beyond the confines of Palestine in this age—some-

thing he had planned from the beginning (Gal. 3:8). Indeed, this is such a monumental point that Paul feels compelled to assure his friend that it is true in a most sober way: "I am telling the truth, I am not lying" (1 Tim. 2:7). One must read this passage in light of the worldwide unfolding of God's redemptive program. Now is the time. God has essentially issued a worldwide imperial edict: "In the past God overlooked such ignorance, *but now he commands all people everywhere to repent*" (Acts 17:30; emphasis added).

I was appointed a herald (2:7). Paul calls himself a "herald" of the true faith. Heralds were the most common medium of public communication in the days before newspapers. Timothy would have heard them often at Ephesus at funeral processions or any public meeting. A sacred

HERALD
Hermes, herald of Zeus, is here depicted on a column drum (325–300 B.C.) from the temple of Artemis at Ephesus.

herald (*hierokeryx* or just *keryx*) was also linked with various cults, including that of Artemis Ephesia. He led the formal rites and publicly recited the prayers.[28]

Lift up holy hands (2:8). Here Paul assumes that the church will adopt the Old Testament posture of supplication and of worship. "Hear my cry for mercy as I call to you for help, *as I lift up my hands* toward your Most Holy Place"; "*Lift up your hands* in the sanctuary and praise the LORD."[29]

Instructions on Church Order (2:9–15)

Paul continues his directions for the public ministry of the church. Here he focuses on women in the church. The historical background of this section of Scripture has often been misinterpreted, so we must proceed carefully with an eye fixed on the actual historical sources.[30]

Women to dress modestly (2:9). It was customary for women in ancient Greek cities to dress up in their very finest for public worship festivals. For instance, the historian Herodotus remarks that the Athenian women gathered in a temple precinct at the summons of a tyrant "in their best clothes as if they were off to a festival" (5.93). The romance novel by Xenophon of Ephesus opens with a great procession in honor of the patron goddess of Ephesus, Artemis Ephesia, at which all the young girls march in process in their very finest clothes, "for it was the custom at this festival to find husbands for the girls and wives for the young men."[31] Even the cult statues of goddesses were adorned in great finery at public festivals. At Ephesus, the statue of Artemis was dressed by young girls who

held an official title of "Adorner" (*kosmeteira*; e.g., *IvE* 2, 892, 983–84, 989).

In contrast to the prevailing practice, Paul instructs women (and, by implication, men as well) to focus their attention not on rich wardrobes, but on the inner beauty of Christian character. This instruction is not new or novel (e.g., 1 Peter 3:3–4); as Ignatius of Antioch puts it: Christians are a new Temple for God, appointed to be "shrine-bearers, Christ-bearers, sanctity-bearers, dressed up from head to toe in the commandments of Jesus Christ."[32]

Not with braided hair (2:9). In Paul's day, hairstyles were undergoing a radical change. Earlier in the Greek world, women's hairstyles were simple: The hair was pinned in the back and held up with a simple band or scarf. In public, respectable women would wear veils on the top of the head, which fell down the back to the shoulders and hid any elaborate hairdo. Only a shady woman or one

in mourning would appear in public with her hair untied and unveiled.[33] However, in the mid-first century, women throughout the empire were copying the elaborate braided and ornamented hairdos of the Roman empresses (many of whom were quite scandalous).[34]

A woman should learn in quietness. . . . I do not permit a woman to teach (2:11–12). These two verses are drawing an ever-increasing amount of comment today, but Paul's injunctions in 1 Timothy 2:11–12 require no special historical insights to understand.[35] He says that women are not called to serve in the office of teacher or of elder in the church. A crucial distinction to understand here is that between special and general office ministries. Ordained men are called to a special office by Christ (e.g., Rom. 10:15; Eph. 4:11), while nonordained men and all women in the church have a general office to serve the Lord in various capacities. If we did not have the chapter division between 1 Timothy 2:15 and 3:1 (which is a modern invention), this special office context of Paul's statements on women in 2:11–12 would be more obvious to us, since he

457

1 Timothy

▶ Was Ephesus a Feminist Culture?

There are abundant indicators in the historical remains of ancient Ephesus that it cannot be characterized as a feminist culture. Although its state deity was a goddess, many other states whose patriarchal character has never been questioned also worshiped goddesses (e.g., classical Athens worshiped Athena). The nature of a culture as feminist must be demonstrated through what we can know about its *institutions,* particularly its political, religious, social, and cultural institutions. So, for example, were the political figures of ancient Ephesus women or men?

The answer to this question is clearly that they were men like: Tib. Claudius Balbillus who had an Ephesian festival named after him (*IvE* 3041–42; the "Balbilleia"); the General, Prytanis, and Secretary of the People (Acts 19:35); Heraclides son of Heraclides son of Heraclides (a noble line) (*IvE* 14, 1387); L. Cusinius Velina the Overseer of Ephesus (the same word found in 1 Tim. 3:1) and Secretary of the People under Gaius and Claudius (*IvE* 659B, 660B, et al.); or the famous Asiarch Tib. Claudius Aristio, whom Pliny the Younger calls "the chief man (*princeps*) of the Ephesians" and whose political enemies forced him to appeal to Caesar as had Paul a few decades earlier.[A-2] These aristocratic men not only steered the ship of state and were at the pinnacle of Ephesian society and culture, they also filled and managed all the chief religious priesthoods and boards that ran the magnificent banking, agricultural, and fishing enterprise that was the temple of Artemis of Ephesus.

Ephesian women were indeed priestesses of Artemis and of other goddesses, but this was the norm in the Greco-Roman world, not a sign of feminism—or equally inaccurate, a sign of sacred prostitution.[A-3] Let us illustrate this point with but one example here.[A-4] An elaborate public funeral was established for the noble M. Antonius Albus (*IvE* 614C) and his wife Laevia Paula (*IvE* 614B) at Ephesus a few decades before Paul lived there. The inscription commemorating this lavish affair records that the funeral procession was accompanied by a herald who announced the following to all the spectators: "The Council and Citizenry hereby crowns Laevia Paula, daughter of Lucius, who led a modest and decorous life." The Greek word rendered "modest" here is the adjective form of a word found in 1 Timothy 2:9, "with decency and *propriety.*" Paul's contemporaries at Ephesus would have agreed that "propriety" or "modesty" was a female virtue, not radical feminism.[A-5]

proceeds directly to the requirements for male overseers of the church in 3:1–7.

Let us be clear that Paul is *not* forbidding women in 2:11–12 from teaching men in private out of their general office as believers (e.g., Acts 18:24–28), from discipling their children (cf. 2 Tim. 1:5; 3:15) and younger women in the church (Titus 2:3–4), or from participating in and giving leadership in hospitality (1 Tim. 5:10) or in other kinds of ministries and service to the Lord (e.g., Acts 9:36; Rom. 16:1–2). However, Paul clearly says as apostolic instruction (1 Tim. 2:7) that a woman should "learn in quietness and full submission . . . she must be silent" when it comes to the official teaching and ruling ministry of the church.

It has been asserted that Ephesus was such a haven for ancient feminism that Paul is only speaking about *Ephesian* women being in submission to male church officers here. However, this is not what he says *prima facie*. Paul's statements in these verses were meant to be taken as parallel with those addressed to men "everywhere" (2:8). It can be demonstrated that Ephesian culture was not driven by any kind of underlying feminist or egalitarian ideology, even though individual women or groups in antiquity may have expressed views along these lines from time to time (see accompanying box).

For Adam was formed first (2:13–15). Paul roots his instructions on male-female relations in the church in 2:9–12 squarely in the creation order. This effectively shows that his instructions have direct cross-cultural application.[36] Adam was created first, and similar to the rights given to the firstborn son in the Old Testament, who often held special rights

(e.g., Num. 3:2ff.; cf. *Bekhorot* 8), this gave Adam a certain official role and responsibility in the covenant family. Hence, it was *his* sin that brought death into the world, not Eve's (Rom. 5:12–21; 1 Cor. 15:21), even though Eve sinned first (1 Tim. 2:14; cf. Sir. 25:24), because Adam was the covenant head (cf. Hos. 6:7). And Adam's sin could only be reversed by Christ in his official role as "last Adam" (1 Cor. 15:45); indeed, Adam originally "was a pattern of the one to come" (Rom. 5:14). It is because of this structure that God has given the official role to teach and lead only to certain sons of Adam. Other believers hold what historically has been called the "general office of believer," with all of its own rights and responsibilities.[37]

Instructions on Church Office (3:1–13)

Overseer (3:1). The Greek term for "overseer" (*episkopos*) was used in secular Greek with a fairly broad range of meanings for someone who watched over someone else. This could be a tutor who watches over students, a soldier or a watchman who watches over a city, a guardian deity, or any kind of "guardian" (as 1 Peter 2:25). Paul uses *episkopos* here and in the parallel passage in Titus 1:6–9 as an alternative expression for an "elder" (*presbyteros*), which brings out the elder's role as a "guardian" of the welfare of the Christian churches under his care. This is clear from Paul's famous farewell speech to the elders of Ephesus, when he called these "elders" to meet him at Miletus (Acts 20:17) and said in part: "*Keep watch* over yourselves and all the flock of which the Holy Spirit has made you *overseers.* Be *shepherds* of the church of God, which he bought with his own blood"

(Acts 20:28; emphasis added). One can see from the highlighted words that an "overseer" was an elder in his role as a kind of guardian or watchman. As 1 Timothy 3:9 shows, the overseer was also to be a teacher of "deep truths of the faith."

The overseer must be above reproach (3:2). For the requirement of the elder to be the "husband of but one wife" (3:2; cf. 3:12; 5:9; Titus 1:6), see the comments on Titus 1:6. Paul insists on high moral standards for both the overseer (3:2–7) and the deacon (3:8–12) candidate. In the pagan world, such standards would only have a remote parallel with certain priesthoods in a city like Ephesus. For example, we read on extant Ephesian public inscriptions that certain priestesses served the state goddess, Artemis Ephesia, "with piety and decorum" (e.g., *IvE* 989A). And since Artemis was herself a virgin goddess (not a mother goddess, as some people think), it was required that her priests and priestesses themselves observe complete chastity while fulfilling their priestly term of office. This is evident on the following two examples, where "purely" refers to sexual purity (cf. Pausanias 8.13.1): "To Good Fortune. I, C. Scaptius Frontinus, *neopoios* [a temple overseer], City Counselor, along with my wife, Herennia Autronia, give thanks to you, Artemis, that I have completed a term as Essene *purely* and piously" (*IvE* 1578B; emphasis added); and, "The State Council and People honor Mindia Menandra, daughter of Gaius Mindius Amoenus, who completed her term as Priestess of the goddess *purely* and generously" (*IvE* 992A; emphasis added).

Beyond this, however, pagan priesthoods in the Greek world were often sold to the highest bidder and had no strin-gent moral requirements.[38] In Rome, the priesthoods were acquired through patronage connections (the Roman emperors held the highest priesthood with the title of *pontifex maximus* in the imperial period) and were usually held for life. As in the Greek world, priesthoods of Rome were usually reserved for the wealthy and well-born. Paul's statements about qualification for church office show a much different set of requirements. It is not wealth or nobility of birth that qualifies one to the Christian ministry, but a divine call (Rom. 10:14), as evidenced in part by a high moral character.

He must manage his own family well (3:4). Household management was the subject of a number of treatises in antiquity, including Xenophon's famous Socratic essay, the *Oeconomicus* (Greek for "household management"). In Xenophon's essay, the husband instructs his fourteen-year-old bride (the average age for marriage among Greek and Roman girls was fourteen to sixteen) on her vital role in managing the household resources, including the care and supervision of household slaves, while he

A MAN AND HIS FAMILY

A funerary stele from the Thessaloniki Museum.

supervised the gathering of produce from the farms. Because of the presence of slaves and freedmen in an average ancient household, management of sometimes large households could be demanding. An inscription from Philadelphia regulating a household cult evidences a large ancient household and its management (see accompanying box).

Deacons, likewise . . . (3:8–10, 12–13). The qualifications for deacons are similar to those for overseers. Both are to be self-controlled, free from avarice, monogamous, good managers of their households, and so forth. The primary difference seems to be that the overseer must be

"able to teach" (3:2), though both officers must have a firm grasp on Christian doctrine (3:9; cf. Titus 1:9). In both cases, the behavior of church office-holders must be above reproach for the sake of the church's health, the testimony of the church before the world, and their own consciences before the Lord.

In the same way, their wives . . . (3:11). Paul inserts the statement in 3:11 in the middle of his specification of deacon qualifications. The NIV translates: "In the same way, *[their] wives* are to be women worthy of respect. . ." (emphasis added; "their" is not in the Greek original). In the margin, however, the NIV translators pro-

---

▶ An Ancient Household Cult

We possess an inscription from Philadelphia in Lydia (Rev. 3:7–13) from the late second to early first century B.C., which regulated a household cult in a private household. Each household in antiquity typically had its own private cult in addition to members' participation in public or in other private cults. In this inscription, we find the head of the house managing the details of his household's behavior and cult practices. The text reads as follows (the word *oikos* is Greek for "household" or "house"):

> May Good Fortune Prevail. For health and common salvation and the finest reputation the ordinances given to Dionysius in his sleep were written up, giving access into his *oikos* to men and women, free people and slaves. . . . When coming into this *oikos* let men and women, free people and slaves, swear by all the gods neither to know nor make use wittingly of any deceit against a man or a woman, neither poison harmful to men nor harmful spells. They are not themselves to make use of a love potion, abortifacient, contraceptive, or any other thing fatal to children; nor are they to recommend it to,

nor connive at it with another. They are not to refrain in any respect from being well-intentioned towards this *oikos*. If anyone performs or plots any of these things, they are neither to put up with it nor keep silent, but expose it and defend themselves. Apart from his own wife, a man is not to have sexual relations with another married woman, whether free or slave, nor with a boy nor a virgin girl; nor shall he recommend it to another. . . . A free woman is to be chaste and shall not know the bed of, nor have sexual intercourse with, another man except her own husband. But if she does have such knowledge, such a woman is not chaste, but defiled and full of endemic pollution, and unworthy to reverence this god whose holy things these are that have been set up. She is not to be present at the sacrifices, nor to strike against (?) the purifications and cleansings (?), nor to see the mysteries being performed. But if she does any of these things from the time the ordinances have come on to this inscription, she shall have evil curses from the gods for disregarding these ordinances.[A-6]

vide an alternative: "deaconesses" for "their wives." The key word in the Greek text is *gynaikes* (where we get *gynecology*), which is the ordinary word for either "women" (e.g., 1 Tim. 5:2) or, in many contexts, "wives" (e.g., Eph. 5:22). The two renderings represent the two main interpretations of this verse.

The first view, represented in the NIV main text, takes the "women" here as "wives" of the deacons, since Paul's statement in 3:11 is imbedded in the midst of his discussion of male deacons' qualifications (e.g., *husband* of one wife). It does seem odd that the *wives* of a church officer must also have certain qualifications if they themselves do not serve in the office. And we must ask why *deacons'* wives have to be respectable, temperate, etc., but the wives of *overseers* go unmentioned. This leads to the second view.

The interpretation of 3:11 represented in the NIV margin translation ("deaconesses") takes the *gynaikes* here as female deacons alongside males. This would explain why Paul mentions them in the middle of his list of deacon quali-fications. The absence of a reference to "women" in the overseer section is now explicable (cf. 2:9–15). Paul is not legislating the qualifications for the wives of church officers in 3:11, but of female deacons. If this is so, why then didn't Paul simply clear up matters by saying *deaconesses* in 3:11 instead of the more ambiguous "women"? The answer is that Greek did not have a separate word for "deaconess" at that time. The same Greek word *diakonos* (from which we get "deacon" in English) was used to refer to either male or female "deacons" (accompanied by either the masculine or feminine article to express the gender of the noun when required). In other words, Paul had no real choice, so his use of "women" was as clear as anything to designate women deacons.

In either case, Paul specifies a high ethical standard for the women of 3:11, similar to the standards for overseers and deacons. The behavior code in 3:1–13 is not different from the ethical requirement for any Christian, but church officers should particularly exemplify these

▶**Deaconesses in Early Church History**

In A.D. 110, Pliny the Younger reported to the Emperor Trajan that he has examined Christians in his province of Bithynia (a Roman province north of Ephesus) to discover the nature of their presumed criminal activities and only found a harmless cult. He continues, "This made me decide it was all the more necessary to extract the truth by torture from two slave-women [*ancillae*], whom they call deaconesses [*ministrae*]."[A-7] We should note: (1) These women were slaves, and it was customary for Roman officials to interrogate slaves (but not others) under torture; (2) the women were called "deaconesses" by the Christians (Latin *ministrae* is the equivalent of Greek *diakonoi*). In other words, this seems to be an official title, not a generic reference to their being "servants" of some sort, since we already know them to have been "slaves" (*ancillae*). Hence, this suggests that the church had female deacons within forty or fifty years of the writing of 1 Timothy—perhaps women like Phoebe, "a servant [*diakonos*] of the church in Cenchrea" (Rom. 16:1).[A-8]

high qualities for the sake of "God's household" (3:15), even though they enjoy immunity from casual charges of wrongdoing (5:19).

Paul's Plans (3:14–16)

I hope to come to you soon (3:14). Paul hoped to visit Timothy and the church of Ephesus (and probably of surrounding cities) soon. Paul did not know when he would be able to make this proposed trip, and we do not know whether he actually made the trip. Subsequently, he was on trial in Rome at the writing of 2 Timothy, and we may suspect that Paul himself was unsure of his freedom of movement when he tells Timothy that he hopes to visit Ephesus soon.

The pillar and foundation of the truth (3:15). Paul had a high regard for the church since he calls it "the pillar and foundation of the truth." In this remarkable statement, he uses a building analogy, which would have spoken strongly to someone living in first-century Ephesus. This city was experiencing a remarkable building program, some of them of massive proportions. The temple of the city goddess, Artemis Ephesia, was the largest temple building in antiquity and one of the seven wonders of the ancient world. Its elaborately carved columns and foundation stones were of monumental size, which was particularly prized in a region that often suffered devastating earthquakes.

He appeared in a body (3:16). Paul appears to quote a brief summary of the truths of the gospel here, perhaps used to instruct people before their baptism. In many church services today the Apostles' or Nicene Creeds are recited regularly in worship services as testimony to the historic Christian faith. Paul could have been the author of this wonderful summary of the work of Christ, or he could

PILLAR AND FOUNDATION

The foundation of the temple of Apollo at Delphi.

REFLECTIONS

IN OUR PLURALISTIC AGE, THE universal church's role as the "pillar and foundation of the truth" is under direct and indirect assault, even from "church" people. Some refuse communion and membership with any church, or they carelessly roam from church to church without ever making any lasting commitment. In the scholarly realm, some evangelical theologians question whether faith in Christ is indeed required to enjoy eternal life, making church membership even more irrelevant and ultimately absurd. But God himself claims to be the patriarchal head of his "household" (3:15), and he takes this role seriously—so seriously that he gave his only Son to purchase his adopted family by his own blood. Not even hell itself and all of its devices will eventually overcome her and God's truth (Matt. 16:18; cf. 1 Tim. 4:1).

be passing on what had already become a traditional summary. In any case, in this verse one can see the historical work of Christ at the heart of Paul's gospel.

Warning about False Teaching (4:1–5)

Paul follows up his teaching on the qualifications of church officers in chapter 3 with specific warnings about false doctrine "in later times" (4:1), which Timothy himself will encounter since the whole era between the first and second coming of Christ is the "last hour" (1 John 2:18). Paul ends this chapter with some positive instructions for Timothy's public ministry (1 Tim. 4:6–16).

Things taught by demons (4:1). Paul is not concerned here with paganism per se, but with false teaching within the church. These false teachers have "abandoned the faith" they once embraced in order to follow demonic doctrines. The word "demon" (Gk. *daimonion*; plural *daimonia*) to ancient ears would not necessarily sound evil. Indeed, the pagan Greeks used to pour out a libation of wine to *Agathos Daemon* ("Good Demon"), who was, interestingly, represented in works of art by a snake. And Paul's original readers were accustomed to hearing about *daimonia* teaching and guiding people through oracles, prophecy, or in other ways. For instance, it was generally thought that the prophetic god Apollo used *daimonia* as agents for the oracles at Delphi on mainland Greece or at Didyma in Asia Minor. Socrates, the famous philosopher, claimed to be personally guided by such a *daimonion*, leading to ancient speculation on the identity of this being.[39] In contrast, Paul says that the Holy Spirit himself has *expressly* provided a warning against the teaching of *daimonia*, which are deceiving spirits (see also 1 John 4:1–3).

Whose consciences have been seared (4:2). Apostate teachers can wantonly betray their Lord because their "consciences have been seared as with a hot iron." This arresting analogy is clear in any culture, but it was particularly vivid in antiquity where penal branding took place. An inscription found in the vicinity of Ephesus threatens branding (possibly on the foot) as punishment for seditious bakers who had been instigating local riots (*IvE* 215). Closer to Paul's image, runaway slaves who were recaptured might have their foreheads branded by harsh masters (Apuleius, *Golden Ass* 9; 3 *Macc.* 2:29).[40]

They forbid people to marry and order them to abstain from certain foods (4:3). The apostle identifies asceticism as the particular subject that characterizes the teaching of liars. Paul was no gourmand objecting to the disapproval of delicacies. His argument strikes against the substitution of Christianity's true focal point of "love, which comes from a pure heart and a good conscience and a sincere faith" (1:5) with an empty ascetic exhibitionism (Col. 2:20–23). The rejection of monogamous marriage was not common among ancient peoples. Both the Greeks and Romans had high ideals of marriage, particularly for the purpose of childbearing and securing the family line.

For everything God created is good (4:4). Paul alludes to his rationale for holding foods and marriage in high esteem by referring to God's creation of these good things. After making the produce of sea and land God saw that it was "good" and later that all his creation, including the union of Adam with Eve, was "very good" (Gen. 1:20–21, 31). The ascetics do not sin against the gifts themselves, but against the Giver of every good and perfect gift (James 1:17) by contradicting and disbelieving his Word. Ambrosiaster, the name given to an unknown church father, wrote: "Why, then, do some people call that which God has blessed a sordid and contaminated work, unless because they themselves in some way raise their hands against God? For they would not criticize this [work], unless they had wicked ideas about God, the Maker of the work."[41] That God's good provisions in creation are not "to be rejected" but to be received with thanksgiving (1 Tim. 4:4) finds an interesting verbal parallel in Homer's *Iliad*, the closest thing to the Bible among the ancient Greeks: "The glorious gifts of the gods are never *to be rejected*."[42]

Training in Godliness (4:6–10)

The importance of the objective "truths of the faith and of the good teaching" must not be overlooked. (The word "teaching" or "doctrine" occurs four times in this chapter alone.) Timothy will be a "good minister" or servant of Christ if he conveys these things faithfully. But the reward for his faithfulness for himself and others is to be "brought up" on these things, or better, *nourished* by these things. Pure teaching of Christian doctrine, rather than being deadening for our spiritual life, is food for the soul.[43]

In stark contrast to the excellent doctrine stands the degrading myths of Timothy's contemporaries (cf. 1 Tim. 1:3–4). Rape, adultery, murder, lying, deceit, and trickery of every sort pervade the activities of the gods in ancient mythology. Many pagans thought that there might be an historical core to the myths, but that the poets and playwrights had added many embarrassing embellishments:[44] "The poets tell many lies" was a common ancient saying. Plato rather disdainfully rejected such myths from the educational program in his ideal republic.[45]

Physical training is of some value (4:8). "Physical training" would be familiar to Timothy. The Greek word for "training"

▶ Asceticism in Antiquity

Asceticism of various sorts was known in the New Testament world, though one must admit that its practitioners are found on the fringe of New Testament societies and their vital thought. Vegetarianism was taught by some Greek philosophical schools active in the first century, especially the Neopythagoreans and the Cynics. There were ascetic cult groups such as the followers of Cybele, who was served by emasculated priests. The latter, "a howling rabble" thumping drums and clashing cymbals, were suspected of being mere religious hucksters by some people.[A-9] Chaeremon the Stoic (one of Nero's tutors) is said by Porphyry to have described the ascetic lives of Egyptian temple priests who rejected various foods and practiced sexual abstinence (though not necessarily rejection of marriage itself). Likewise the Shrine of Heracles the Misogynist in Phocis required that annual priests had to remain chaste during their year of service. Plutarch comments: "For this reason they usually appoint as priests rather old men."[A-10] Josephus relates the Essene community's rejection of marriage because "it leads to domestic quarrels."[A-11] Some later heretical Christian groups like the Marcionites, Montanists, and Manichaeans taught asceticism in various forms.[A-12]

is *gymnasia* and is the source of our "gymnasium." There was no institution more characteristic of Hellenic culture than the gymnasium, where youths in schools were subjected to a rigorous course of athletics.[46] In earlier times, the gymnasium was essential for military training, since a city-state's army consisted of all male citizens. By NT times, a few noble Greeks might enter the Roman army, but most athletics in the gymnasium—aside from the numerous professional athletes and their guilds—had degenerated into the practice of "body sculpting." The Romans did not always go in for this, as Plutarch (a first-century Greek) explains:

> For the Romans used to be very suspicious of rubbing down with oil, and even today they believe that nothing has been so much to blame for the enslavement and effeminacy of the Greeks as their gymnasia and wrestling-schools, which engender much listless idleness and waste of time in their cities, as well as pederasty and the ruin of the bodies of the young men with regulated sleeping, walking, rhythmical movements, and strict diet; by these practices they have unconsciously lapsed from the practice of arms, and have become content to be termed nimble athletes and handsome wrestlers. (Plutarch, *Roman Questions*, 40; LCL translation)

The living God, who is the Savior (4:10). In first-century society, the word "savior" was familiar as the title of gods, emperors, provincial governors, and other patrons who provided certain *earthly benefactions* to communities or individuals in time of need. "Savior" was virtually synonymous with "benefactor." This can be easily substantiated, but an inscription from Ephesus illustrates this point by using the two words in parallel. The guild of silversmiths honored a provincial governor as "their own savior and benefactor in all things."[47]

One especially important example of "savior" relating to earthly benefactions comes from a recovered statue base inscription from Ephesus, which Timothy may have seen many times by the time he read this letter—recall that it was received at Ephesus (1:3). The statue was erected in honor of Julius Caesar in 48 B.C. after he had saved the province from financial ruin. The inscription reads: "The

GYMNASIUM
The remains of the gymnasium at Laodicea.

cities of Asia, along with the [citizen-bodies] and the nations, (honor) C. Julius C. f. Caesar, Pontifex Maximus, Emperor, and twice Consul, *the manifest god* (sprung) from Ares and Aphrodite, and *universal savior of human life*" (*IvE* 251; emphasis added). Both Caesar's divine honors and the "savior" title are of interest, for, in contrast, Paul says that we have set our hope in a *living God*—not this long-dead "manifest god"—and that our living God is the true benefactor of even these misguided pagans, "and especially of those who believe." In other words, Paul's statement in 4:10 has a polemical side effect in its original context.[48]

The Character of Timothy's Public Ministry (4:11–16)

Young pastors everywhere have taken encouragement from 4:11–12. In both the Roman and the Greek world, social and political leadership belonged to older men. The Latin word *senate* comes from *senex*, "old, senior." At Athens and other Hellenic cities like Ephesus, there was a

semiofficial body of elders, the *Gerousia* (from Gk., *geron*, "old man"), which played an important role in politics, religion, and society. Elders played a key role in the church also, and we read about "the elders" of Ephesus in Acts 20:17.[49]

In this ancient climate, one can appreciate Timothy's delicate position as a leader in the church. He is told to "*command* and teach these things," even to people who were senior to him in age. This might lead to pride, but the guard against this is found at the end of 4:12: The young pastor is to execute his office in an exemplary fashion with love and purity. To minister like this from the heart will naturally foster humility. A teacher is a *servant*.

The public reading of Scripture (4:13). Notice here how central the Word of God is to Timothy's ministry. He is to *devote* himself to its public reading, proclamation, and teaching. We take the Bible for granted today. In Timothy's day, even though books were widely available (2 Tim. 4:13), they were expensive, and not everyone could read. Thus the public reading and proclamation of the Word was especially vital for the health of the church. It was so important that God gave a special attestation of Timothy's ordination to this ministry "through a prophetic message" when the "body of elders" (Gk. *presbyteros*) laid their hands on him. This body was probably the Ephesian group whom Paul addressed in nearby Miletus (Acts 20:17). There were no religions in antiquity as "bookish" as Christianity except Judaism (e.g., Acts 15:21).

Be diligent in these matters (4:15). The young pastor is to be especially diligent and watchful both in his progress in sanctification and in his doctrine. Life and doctrine must never be separated in either the minister or in the church. They are the guarantee of perseverance in our holy faith, leading to salvation "both for yourself and your hearers."

Timothy's Ministry to Various Groups (5:1–2)

Paul instructs Timothy on his relations with others within the Christian community and, one would expect by implication, on how he should also deal with non-Christians. In 5:1–2, he summarizes Timothy's relations with both men and women, older and younger. This shows that the early Christians were drawn from a broad cross-section within their society, not from any one subgroup only (cf. 1 John 2:12–14).

Ministry to Widows (5:3–8)

Most of 1 Timothy 5 is taken up with how Timothy should administer and relate to widows. The obvious point is that there were enough widows in the early church in the Ephesus area for Timothy to be charged with this task, which could consume a substantial portion of the church's resources (cf. Acts 6:1–4).[50]

Those widows who are really in need (5:3). Widowhood could be a severe test in the Greco-Roman world, since women were usually not the direct heirs of their husband's wills. Rather, the widow had her dowry as well as any stipulation that the testator made for her care to his heirs (usually the male children of the marriage). If the son or sons did not care for their mother (or often, their stepmother), the woman could be in a dire condition if her dowry was not substantial (hence, Paul's stern statement in

5:8).[51] One Greek will from the mid-second century, for instance, leaves all the property to the son, but the use and income of the property went to the man's wife for the duration of her life (P.Oxy. 494). But this was not always the case, especially among the poor.

We should add that men outlived women in antiquity. Research has shown that the average life expectancy for women who survived childhood in the Hellenistic period was about thirty-six years and for men between forty-two and forty-five years. The difference is explained as the result of a high mortality rate of mothers during childbirth.[52]

The widow who lives for pleasure (5:6). Not all widows were obviously in desperate need. The wealthy widow could occupy her time in vain entertainments. For instance, read this reference in the younger Pliny regarding the later years of a socially prominent Roman matron:

> Ummidia Quadratilla is dead, having almost attained the age of seventy-nine and kept her powers unimpaired up to her last illness, along with a sound constitution and sturdy physique which are rare in a woman. . . . She kept a troupe of pantomime actors whom she treated with an indulgence unsuitable in a lady of her high position. . . . Once when she was asking me to supervise her grandson's education she told me that as a woman, with all a woman's idle hours to fill, she was in the habit of amusing herself playing draughts or watching her mimes.[53]

The Widow List (5:9–16)

Paul now turns his attention to the church's ministry to certain formally recognized widows. There was apparently a list kept by the church for the care of widows (cf. Acts 6:1 again), who were committed to staying single and providing certain services in return (care for children, hospitality, washing the feet of the saints, and other "good deeds"). These widows would pledge themselves to this arrangement for the duration of their life—hence Paul's restriction for younger widows to serve Christ in the church in this way (5:11–12). (Other-

GOSSIPING GIRLS

Terracotta statue of two gossiping women.

wise, Paul seems to contradict himself by criticizing younger widows for wanting to remarry in 5:11–12 and then telling them to remarry in 5:14.) In this way, these older saints who had no earthly family support were provided for in "God's household" (3:15), and they themselves could actively serve the saints in some way. The tasks they carried out may appear humble, but when carried out as a pledge to Christ (5:11) like the "widow's mite," they were undoubtedly a sweet savor to the Lord (cf. 5:24–25).

Instructions on Elders and Other Matters (5:17–25)

Paul now addresses particular treatment of the elders of the congregation. He had specified the qualifications for this office earlier, and now he gives some passing information about their office ("direct[ing] the affairs of the church" and especially "preaching and teaching") as well as some instructions about their financial support (implied in the "double honor," which is their due). Much has been written lately in scholarly literature about the social significance of honor and shame in Mediterranean societies of antiquity. This is particularly important for understanding the Corinthian correspondence, but we also see it here in Paul's reference to "double honors" for elders (cf. the fifth commandment: "*Honor* your father and your mother . . ."). See the accompanying box for an example of public honor at Ephesus.[54]

Ephesus and other Greek cities of the time had a body of elders, called the *Gerousia*, at the time (see above on 4:11–16). The elders of the church do not really correspond to this group in every way, but like the elders of the Jewish synagogue, they show the important gov-

R E F L E C T I O N S

PAUL, APPLYING THE FIFTH COMMANDMENT, SAYS that the one who neglects to care for his relatives "has denied the faith and is worse than an unbeliever" (5:8). This is strong language indeed, so we must carefully heed its message today, especially in our day of fragmented families. Divorce and widowhood plagued families in the first century; however, there were usually no governmental institutions to substitute for the family and short-circuit it as there are now. It was not unusual for a household in antiquity to include a widowed sister or aunt and the cousins.[A-13] And it was normal for elderly parents to join the household, for there were no rest homes or care centers in antiquity. Paul's instructions show just how vital the home is as a fundamental, divinely-ordained social institution.

ernmental role of older men in the social and religious life of the ancient communities. We cannot stress enough that religion, society, and politics were not separate spheres in antiquity as they are today. Hence the public priests, court officials, fathers of the clans, and city council members were normally one small group of older men in the city.

Use a little wine (5:23). This verse comes as a surprise to some people today because they are convinced that the Bible teaches total abstinence from alcoholic liquor. They may take the "wine" here to refer to grape juice, but that is not likely, since all wine used in antiquity was alcoholic. Without refrigeration or chemical preservatives, grape juice quickly turns to vinegar, whereas fermentation of wine was a form of preservation. Wine was alcoholic but not necessarily intoxicating, since the ancients regularly mixed their wine with varying parts of water.

The really surprising thing in 5:23 is that Paul advises Timothy to drink wine at *Ephesus.* The wine produced there was notoriously bad. The elder Pliny, who wrote a whole section of his *Natural History* (better thought of as a "Miscellany") on the different wines around in the mid-first century A.D., says: "As for the vintage of Mesogis, it has been found to cause headaches, and that of Ephesus has also proved to be unwholesome, because sea-water and boiled must [grape juice before it has fermented] are employed to season it."[55] Sea-water! It must have been wretched stuff, but Paul hopes that it will ward off Timothy's "frequent illnesses."

The sins of others trail behind them . . . good deeds are obvious (5:24–25). Paul ends this chapter with resumption of the thought from 5:22 about the sins of some, then concludes with the public character of good deeds. Life in the Mediterranean cities was (and is) a public life. With

---

▶ The Quest for Public Honors

One example of the demand for public honor in antiquity comes in the form of an inscribed letter from the Emperor Antoninus Pius to the Ephesian city fathers (Ephesus, A.D. 145). What is most remarkable about this letter is that the recipient had it inscribed in stone on a public building (which he financed) in order for all to see.

> Titus Aelius Hadrian Antoninus Pius . . . to the rulers, the council, and the people of the Ephesians, greetings. I did not learn about the generosity which Vedius Antoninus shows you from your letters but from his. Because, wishing to enlist my help for

the adornment of the public works which he promised you, he showed me how many and what magnificent buildings he is adding to the city. But you do not appreciate him properly [i.e., you have not given him enough public honors]. I, for my part, have granted him all that he requested. I appreciated that he hopes to make the city more august in a manner (looking) to the (future?), not following the fashion of many public figures who expend their generosity on spectacles, on distributions, and on prizes for the games (only) for the sake of immediate popularity (*IvE* 1491).

▶

EPHESUS

Terraced homes for
the wealthy citizens
of Ephesus. This has
been a key focus of
the archaeological
excavations.

cramped houses stacked one on top of another and with narrow, winding streets, people spent their lives openly before their neighbors. What was done in the home was soon known in the market-places, so that even good deeds that are not obvious "cannot be hidden."

Slaves' Obedience to Their Masters (6:1–2)

Galen, the second-century A.D. medical writer, estimated that one-third of the population of Pergamum in Asia Minor were slaves. Modern scholars usually believe that this figure may even be too low for cities like Ephesus, Athens, or Rome, so the issue of slavery was practical and important for Paul to address.

Ancient slavery was a variegated phenomenon. Private slaves could be found in great misery grinding flour in chains at a mill, or in relative prosperity working on their own in small businesses, hardly different in most respects from their free neighbors except that all of their profits

were at the disposal of their masters. Public slaves could be important government officials or menial attendants in the public baths. Slaves and freedmen (freed slaves) were everywhere, and few households did not have one or more maids and slave boys to do the household chores, cooking, and gardening. Essayists of the time expounded on the humanity of slaves and the essential equality of slave and free, but this sort of thing was an exercise in rhetoric or philosophy and had no practical effect on ancient slavery.[56]

Paul's instructions on the respectful attitude of slaves toward their masters

REFLECTIONS

PAUL WRITES THAT SLAVES MUST obey willingly as testimony to the power of the gospel. Today's Western societies do not have debt bondage or slavery. However by extension, Paul's instructions do apply to our relations with "all those in authority" over us (2:2).

comes against the backdrop of a standard theme in ancient comedies: the arrogant, back-talking slave. Over and over the Greek and Latin comic playwrights present slaves as mocking their masters behind their backs, talking back to them with barely disguised contempt when they could (often getting a cuffing for comic effect), and generally being villainous characters. Admittedly a large measure of this picture was simply the comedic portrait, but it no doubt contains an element of truth, especially when read in light of more direct historical sources.[57]

Godliness and Gain (6:3–10)

If anyone teaches false doctrines (6:3). In our day, good doctrine in a teacher often takes a back seat to charismatic stage presence. It is only natural, but such teachers sometimes lead people and churches to ruin. It was no different in the early centuries of the Christian church, as Paul indicates. Notice how he emphasizes "sound instruction," which can more literally be rendered "healthy" or "health-giving" instruction and which is contrasted with the "gangrenous" doctrine of heretics (2 Tim. 2:17). The evil doctrine of false teachers goes hand in glove with their evil and self-serving character.

Godliness with contentment is great gain (6:6). The avarice of the false teachers brings Paul to express some classic thoughts:

- "We brought nothing into the world, and we can take nothing out of it."

▶ Portrait of a False Teacher

Unfortunately, we can read about many quack teachers in the history of Christianity, but one of the more interesting is a fellow named Peregrinus of Parium in the region of Propontis (near the Hellespont). Peregrinus is interesting because a vivid portrait of this huckster was drawn in an essay by the second century A.D. humorist Lucian of Samosata (the Mark Twain or Garrison Keillor of antiquity). According to Lucian, Peregrinus had the following encounter in the church while running from the law:

It was then that he learned the wondrous lore of the Christians, by associating with their priests and scribes in Palestine. And—how else could it be?—in a trice he made them all look like children; for he was prophet, cult-leader, head of the synagogue, and everything, all by himself. He interpreted and explained some of their books and even composed many, and they revered him as a god, made use of him as a lawgiver, and set him down as a protector ("On the Death of Peregrinus" 11; LCL trans.).

Peregrinus was soon apprehended by the anti-Christian authorities—who were actually fairly tolerant in this period, so he must have made himself odious to them—and he was thrown into prison. The Christians both in Palestine and as far away as Asia Minor were said to have spared no expense helping Peregrinus in his imprisonment so that "he procured not a little revenue from it" and afterward lived "in unalloyed prosperity" off the church. Lucian thinks the Christians to be very gullible; he writes, "So if any charlatan and trickster, able to profit by occasions, comes among them, he quickly acquires sudden wealth by imposing upon simple folk" ("On the Death of Peregrinus" 13). In any case, Peregrinus soon apostatized from Christianity and became a Cynic philosopher. He made a sensational exit by immolating himself at the Olympic games in A.D. 165. Paul's warning against and characterization of false teachers finds clear points of contact with Peregrinus and many others afterward.

• "For the love of money is a root of all kinds of evil."

Root of all kinds of evil (6:10). No one in any society loves a grasping, avaricious individual. Such types were the brunt of frequent lampoons by the comic playwrights and essayists in antiquity. The student and successor of the philosopher Aristotle was a man named Theophrastus, who wrote a work called "Characters," or better, "Character Traits." Four of his thirty sketches center on character

flaws connected to money: "Sponging," "Pennypinching," "Lack of Generosity," and "Chiseling." The modern reader who reads these 2300-year-old portraits of defective characters will find many familiar themes and confirm Paul's statement about money being at the root of broken friendships, shattered marriages, a bad reputation, and all kinds of evil.

The Good Fight (6:11–16)

Fight the good fight of the faith (6:12). The background of the "good fight of the faith" is war. Wars were brewing on the horizon in Palestine at the time Paul wrote 1 Timothy, which eventually broke out in the Jewish revolt and all the horrible atrocities of which the Roman army was capable.[58] Otherwise, the Roman empire was relatively peaceful except on its faraway borders, where skirmishes with wandering barbarian tribes often took place. Timothy's fight is to be one "of the faith," which will confirm that his public confession of faith was genuine and thereby guarantee that he is indeed a holder of the

▶ "If We Have Food"

The staple foods in Asia Minor at the time of Timothy were bread, olive oil, fish (on the seacoasts), and wine. Sometimes one would enjoy meat after public sacrifices (usually oxen or pork) or a fowl. Some staples that the modern world takes for granted (e.g., potatoes, corn [maize], squash, and tomatoes) originated from the Americas and were not present in Europe until after Columbus. The ancients ate vegetables and fruits, but only in season, since food preservation was primitive though not entirely unknown. Meat and fish were usually salted (or stored in a jar of honey), otherwise meats especially had to be used right away because there was no refrigeration.

The wealthy, of course, ate sumptuously because they could afford it.[A-14] We possess an ancient Roman cookbook by a man named Apicius, which has happily been translated and edited by a man who was both a chef and a Latin scholar.[A-15] This cookbook contains some extravagant recipes like boiled ostrich, brains and bacon, and seafood minced with sea-onion, lovage, pepper, cumin, and laser root, as well as more mundane dishes like barley broth, wine sauces, and a sardine omelet. Most people in antiquity in the Mediterranean area, however, ate a basic diet of bread dipped in wine or oil and a dried fish now and then. Such a diet did not always lead to disease prevention and longevity.

eternal life he is to preach (6:12). It is a fight against evil, and its weapons are characterized by righteousness, godliness, love, and gentleness.[59]

God . . . the King of kings and Lord of lords (6:15). By ascribing to God the title "King of kings and Lord of lords" (titles ascribed to Christ in Rev. 17:14; 19:16), Paul uses language that was common in his day. The Roman emperors were technically not "kings," for the Romans were traditionally antiregal after they had overthrown the last of the old Tarquinian kings (see comments on 1 Tim. 2:2). But they were regularly given this title in the provinces, as we find in the Gospels (e.g., John 19:15), where local rulers like the Herods were styled "kings" (e.g., Matt. 14:9). But everyone in the Roman world knew what a king was, and now some of the Gentiles knew the "King of kings."

▶ Violence and Greek Athletics

It is commonly assumed that the brutal Roman gladiatorial games were practiced in Greece and Asia Minor in Paul's day, but I have my doubts that this is true. There is evidence for gladiatorial contests in Asia Minor in the second century A.D., but not in Paul's day fifty or sixty years earlier. There was no initial enthusiasm for these bloody affairs in the Greek world, and the Greeks had a long tradition of games of their own, which they were reluctant to give up or modify. In part this is because the Greek games were connected to religious rites. To change the contests in the games meant a virtual change of religion or even a possible violation of religious principles for the Greeks. For instance, to spill blood in contests before a sacrifice was sometimes thought to usurp the effectiveness of the attendant blood sacrifice and to offend the gods.

On the other hand, Greek athletics were sometimes brutal enough without gladiators. Boxing was regularly performed with leather straps bound across the athlete's hands to protect his knuckles. You can imagine that this gave no padding for the blows on the opponent. (Boxers sometimes used padded gloves in practice, however.) It was normal for boxers to receive grievous wounds, and the Greek Anthology (11.75) even contains a story about a boxer who was disinherited because he no longer resembled his portrait painted earlier in life; he could not prove his identity from the portrait because of his battered features. Even more dangerous than boxing was the Greek pankration event, which seems to resemble oriental martial arts or kick boxing because the boxers were allowed to use their feet to kick and to trip their opponent. Even without gladiators the Greek world of the first century certainly witnessed plenty of fighting.

God, who richly provides us with everything for our enjoyment (6:17). The expression "sinfully delicious" today dishonors God. If something is delicious, it is because God has made it so for our thankful enjoyment. We should give him thanks for this and for all of his other good gifts, because they are good. However, this does not mean that we should practice hedonism (a word derived from the Greek word for "pleasure"). The hedonists of Paul's day were the followers of Epicureus (cf. Acts 17:18), though gluttony and other idolatrous practices were commonplace enough among ancient peoples who had no philosophical pretensions.

What is falsely called knowledge (6:20). Paul concludes this letter with a final warning to hold fast to the gospel and to reject "godless chatter" and false teaching—"what is falsely called knowledge" and leads directly out of the church's doors. By referring to this teaching as so-called "knowledge," Paul may be referring to a trend that developed in later decades into a collection of heretical teachings now known as "Gnosticism" (from Gk. *gnōsis*, "knowledge"). This widespread movement was not connected with only one teacher, group, or location (though the main evidence for it comes from Egypt[60]). Gnosticism was to become a major threat to the orthodoxy of the Christian church.

REFLECTIONS

VARIOUS GROUPS IN THE EARLY CHURCH HAD A common denominator that is still a massive temptation today, namely, to focus on some *secret* or *special* knowledge available only to a select group in the church, which sets them above all the rest of the "common herd." Paul does not condemn the true knowledge of God or of the "sound instruction" (6:3) that he himself taught. But such secret, so-called knowledge is not only false knowledge of God, it is destructive to the unity of the faith and the bond of love that must typify the Christian community (e.g., 1 Cor. 8:1–3; Eph. 4:3).

Dibelius, Martin, and Hans Conzelmann. *The Pastoral Epistles.* Hermeneia. Philadelphia: Fortress, 1972.

This critical commentary relies on the typical reasons for rejecting Pauline authorship of the Pastorals, but helpfully gives detailed attention to the historical background and especially connections of the Pastoral Letters with the Hellenistic world.

Fee, Gordon D. *1 and 2 Timothy, Titus.* GNC. San Francisco: Harper & Row, 1984.

This is a concise commentary by a well-regarded NT and text-critical scholar in a popular format.

Guthrie, Donald. *The Pastoral Epistles: An Introduction and Commentary.* TNTC. Leicester and Grand Rapids: InterVarsity and Eerdmans, 1990 (rev. ed.).

A solid though brief commentary by a senior evangelical NT scholar.

Kelly, J. N. D. *A Commentary on the Pastoral Epistles.* TC. London: A. & C. Black, 1963; reprinted Grand Rapids: Baker, 1981.

This brief commentary sticks closely to the text and is marked by Kelly's characteristic sound judgment. Kelly is well versed in original sources and has produced a number of standard works in the later development of early Christianity, which add depth to his commentary.

Kidd, Reggie M. *Wealth and Beneficence in the Pastoral Epistles: A "Bourgeois" Form of Early Christianity?* Atlanta: Scholars, 1990.

This is the best of many such studies on the contemporary social and ethical background of the Pastoral Letters. Kidd surveys an extensive range of background material in this work.

Knight, George W. III. *Commentary on the Pastoral Epistles.* NIGTC. Grand Rapids and Carlisle: Eerdmans and Paternoster, 1992.

This detailed commentary on the Greek text of the Pastorals often gives illuminating historical insights as well as careful attention to the meaning of the grammar and language of the biblical text. The best technical commentary on the Pastorals in print today.

Lau, Andrew L. *Manifest in Flesh: The Epiphany Christology of the Pastoral Epistles.* WUNT 2/86. Tübingen: J. C. B. Mohr (Paul Siebeck), 1996.

This specialized study draws especially helpful connections between the epiphany material in the Pastorals with the OT and other Jewish literature.

Oden, Thomas C. *First and Second Timothy and Titus.* Interpretation. Louisville: John Knox, 1989.

Oden presents an elegant and sane defense of Pauline authorship in this topically arranged "commentary." There are a few rough spots regarding historical background of the biblical world (e.g., sacred prostitution at Ephesus, p. 95), but Oden augments his own helpful insights with a sprinkling of quotations of church fathers and Reformers, which gives the reader a wider view of the interpretation of the Pastoral Letters.

Young, Frances. *The Theology of the Pastoral Letters.* NTT. Cambridge: Cambridge Univ. Press, 1994.

This volume in a promising series spends considerable time trying to establish pseudonymous authorship of the Pastorals. Nevertheless, Young usefully reports on historical backgrounds of the Pastorals in places—for instance, on "teaching and learning in the ancient world" (pp. 79–84), though it seems mostly secondary and derivative.

CHAPTER NOTES

Main Text Notes

1. Cf. E. R. Richards, *The Secretary in the Letters of Paul* (WUNT 2.42; Tübingen: J. C. B. Mohr [Paul Siebeck], 1991). For indications of Paul's use of a secretary see 1 Cor. 16:21; Gal. 6:11; Col. 4:18; 2 Thess. 3:17; Philem. 19.

2. Isocrates stated the ancient view well: "The birthright of a liberal education is marked not by courage, wealth and similar distinctions, but most clearly of all by speech, the sign which presents the most reliable proof of education" (in M. Grant, ed., *Greek Literature: An Anthology* [London: Penguin, 1977], 225); see especially the classic: H. I. Marrou, *A History of Education in Antiquity* (New York: Sheed and Ward, 1956).

3. Josephus, *Ag. Ap.* 1.9 §50; H. St. J. Thackeray in his introduction to *Josephus* (LCL; Cambridge, Mass.: Harvard Univ. Press, 1926), 1:xiii.

4. For brief and helpful treatments on the authorship issue see E. E. Ellis, "Pastoral Letters," *DPL*, 658–66; D. A. Carson, Douglas J. Moo, and Leon Morris, *An Introduction to the New Testament* (Grand Rapids: Zondervan, 1992), 359–71; George W. Knight III, *The Pastoral Epistles: A Commentary on the Greek Text* (NIGTC; Grand Rapids and Carlisle: Eerdmans and Paternoster, 1992), 4–52.

5. Richards, *The Secretary in Paul's Letters*, 193; cf. 53–56.

6. The *SC Turpilianum*, Tacitus, *Ann.* 14.41; Harry W. Tajra, *The Trial of St. Paul* (WUNT 35; Tübingen: J. C. B. Mohr, 1989), 194.

7. See Tajra's remarks, *Trial of St. Paul*, 196.

8. Philo, *Moses* 1.15.

9. Philo, *Spec. Laws* 4.203.

10. P.Lips. 28; A.D. 381.

11. Strabo 14.1.24

12. Ignatius, *Ephesians* 1.3.

13. See H. Büchsel, "γενεαλογία," *TDNT*, 1:662–65.

14. *Magnesians* 8:1; cf. *Polycarp* 3:1; *Smyrnaeans* 6:2.

15. Polybius 9.2.1.

16. Polybius 9.1.1; LCL trans.

17. See Plutarch's *Solon* for an ancient biography.

18. Plato, *Apology*.

19. The play is ascribed to Seneca, but this is not accepted today. The quoted line is from E. F. Watling, trans., *Seneca: Four Tragedies and Octavia* (Baltimore: Penguin, 1966), 280.

20. See also Titus 1:3; cf. 1 Cor. 9:17; Gal. 2:7.

21. For a good discussion of these passages see George W. Knight, III, *The Faithful Sayings in the Pastoral Letters* (Nutley, N.J.: Presbyterian & Reformed, n.d.); see also 3:1; 4:9; 2 Tim. 2:11; Titus 3:8.

22. Cf. Matt. 9:13; Luke 5:32; 19:10; John 3:17; 12:46–47.

23. See also Ps. 115:1; Luke 2:14; Rom. 11:36; 16:27; Gal. 1:5; Eph. 3:21; Phil. 4:20; 2 Tim. 4:18; Heb. 13:21; 2 Peter 3:18; Jude 25; Rev. 1:6; 4:11; 5:12–13; 7:12.

24. E.g., 2 Cor. 10:4; Eph. 6:11–17; 1 Tim. 6:12; 2 Tim. 4:7.

25. E.g., Josephus, *J.W.* 3.8.3 §351.

26. Rom. 3:29–30; cf. Gal. 3:20; Eph. 4:5–6.

27. The standard work is Leon Morris, *The Apostolic Preaching of the Cross* (Grand Rapids: Eerdmans, 1955; now in subsequent editions).

28. E.g., *IvE* 687, 724, 1004, 1687.

29. Ps. 28:2; cf. Lam. 2:19; 3:41–42; Ps. 134:2; cf. 63:4; 119:48; emphasis added in each case.

30. For further reading see S. M. Baugh, "A Foreign World: Ephesus in the First Century," in *Women in the Church: A Fresh Analysis of 1 Timothy 2:9–15* (eds. A. Köstenberger, T. Schreiner, and H. S. Baldwin; Grand Rapids: Baker, 1995), 13–52.

31. *Ephesian Story* 1.2; see B. P. Reardon, ed., *Collected Ancient Greek Novels* (Berkeley: Univ. of California Press, 1989), 129.

32. Cf. Plutarch, "Advice to Bride and Groom" (*Moralia* 141E), for a similar commendation for a woman's adornment in her character rather than in her dress; Ignatius, *Ephesians* 9.2.

33. E.g., Shepherd of Hermas, *Similitudes* 9.9.5.

34. For more on this subject and sources see Baugh, "Foreign World," 47–48.

35. For a careful interpretation see esp. Thomas R. Schreiner, "An Interpretation of 1 Timothy 2:9–15: A Dialogue with Scholarship," *Women in the Church*, 105–54.

36. See also Jesus' teaching on divorce in Matt. 19:4–6; cf. 1 Cor. 11:8–9.

37. For more on this topic see especially E. P. Clowney, *The Church* (CCT; Downers Grove: InterVarsity, 1995).

38. So *IvE* 18C; cf. Hunt & Edgar, *Select Papyri*, LCL, vol. 2, nos. 353 and 425.

39. See Plutarch's first-century essay, "On the *Daemonion* of Socrates."

40. For runaways, see *New Docs 8* (1998): 1–46.

41. Ambrosiaster, *Quaestiones veteris et novi testamenti*, 125.5, trans. by David Hunter in Wimbush, ed., *Ascetic Behavior*, 103.

42. Homer, *Iliad* 3.65.

43. See also 2 Tim. 4:3; Titus 1:9; 2:1.

44. For one example, see Diodorus Siculus, 1.23.8.

45. Plato's *Republic* has a long discussion of the faults of the major poets like Homer and Hesiod, beginning in sec. 377.

46. See, e.g., the essay "On Gymnastics" by Philostratus (3d cent. A.D.), trans. in Rachel Sargent Robinson, *Sources for the History of Greek Athletics* (Chicago: Ares, 1981; reprint of 1955 edition), 212–32. Other texts in Robinson's book are also of interest; see also Waldo E. Sweet, *Sport and Recreation in Ancient Greek: A Sourcebook with Translations* (New York and Oxford: Oxford Univ. Press, 1987).

47. Dieter Knibbe and Bülent Iplikçioglu, "Neue Inschriften aus Ephesos IX," *JOAIW* 55 (1984) Hauptblatt: 130. Cf. F. W. Danker, *Benefactor: Epigraphic Study of a Graeco-Roman and New Testament Semantic Field* (St. Louis: Clayton, 1982).

48. See S. M. Baugh, "'Savior of All People: 1 Tim. 4:10 in Context," *WTJ* 54 (1992): 331–40.

49. E.g., see 4:14; Acts 15:6; James 5:14.

50. Cf. Bruce W. Winter, *Seek the Welfare of the City: Christians as Benefactors and Citizens* (Carlisle and Grand Rapids: Paternoster and Eerdmans, 1994), 62–78; see also *New Docs 8* (1998): 106–16 for treatment of this passage in light of background materials and for current bibliography.

51. For recent discussion and bibliography of women's dowries and inheritance particularly illumined by documents from Hellenistic Egypt see *New Docs 6* (1992): 1–18. Note, however, that one must always be cautious about universalizing Egyptian evidence to other parts of the ancient world.

52. See Sarah B. Pomeroy, *Families in Classical and Hellenistic Greece: Representations and Realities* (Oxford: Clarendon, 1997), 6–7.

53. Pliny, *Ep.* 7.24.

54. See also Danker, *Benefactor*; *New Docs 8* (1998): 114.

55. Pliny, *Nat. Hist.* 14.9.75.

56. E.g., Dio Chrysostom, *Orations* 14–15.

57. For sources on ancient slavery see Thomas Wiedemann, *Greek & Roman Slavery*. The *New Documents* series also contains a nice collection of sources and discussions on different aspects of ancient slavery scattered throughout its volumes; e.g., *New Docs 6* (1992): 48–81.

58. The classic detailed description of this war was written by the Jewish turncoat, Josephus: *J.W.* (*Bellum Judaicum*).

59. 1 Tim. 6:11; see also 1:18; 2 Tim. 4:7.

60. See James M. Robinson, ed., *The Nag Hammadi Library in English* (New York, et al.: Harper and Row, 1977).

Sidebar and Chart Notes

A-1. 1 Tim. 1:4; 4:7; 6:20; 2 Tim. 2:16; 4:4; Titus 3:9; 1 Tim. 1:7; Titus 3:9; Titus 1:14; 1 Tim. 4:3; 2 Tim. 2:18; cf. 1 Cor. 15:12.

A-2. Pliny, *Letters* 6.31; *IvE* 234–35 et al.; cf. Acts 19:31 for Asiarch.

A-3. See my "Cult Prostitution in New Testament Ephesus: A Reappraisal," *JETS* 42/3 (September 1999): 443–60.

A-4. For a more complete picture consult my "A Foreign World."

A-5. Cf., e.g., *New Docs 3* (1983): 8.

A-6. The translation here is that of S. C. Barton and G. H. R. Horsley, given in "A Hellenistic Cult Group and the New Testament Churches," *JAC* 24 (1981): 7–41 (p. 9); see also esp. Stanley K. Stowers, "A Cult From Philadelphia: Oikos Religion or Cultic Association?" in *The Early Church in Its Context* (eds. A. Malherbe, F. Norris, and J. Thompson; Leiden, Boston, and Cologne: E. J. Brill, 1998), 287–301.

A-7. Pliny, *Ep.* 10.96; LCL.

A-8. See A. N. Sherwin-White, *The Letters of Pliny: A Historical and Social Commentary* (Oxford: Clarendon, 1966), 708.

A-9. Ovid, *Fasti* 4.186; Apuleius, *Golden Ass* 8; Juvenal, *Satires* 6; Seneca, *Ep.* 108.

A-10. Plutarch, "Oracles at Delphi," *Moralia* 403F LCL).

A-11. Josephus, *Ant.* 1.18.5.

A-12. See Vincent Wimbush, ed., *Ascetic Behavior in Greco-Roman Antiquity: A Sourcebook* (Minneapolis: Fortress, 1990); J. K. Elliott, *The Apocryphal New Testament* (Oxford: Clarendon, 1993), for early texts that promote various forms of asceticism.

A-13. See ibid., also, W. K. Lacey, *The Family in Classical Greece* (Ithaca, N.Y.: Cornell Univ. Press, 1968).

A-14. See Naum Jasny, "The Breads of Ephesus and Their Prices," *AH* 21 (1947): 190–92.

A-15. Joseph Dommers Vehling, ed., *Apicius: Cookery and Dining in Imperial Rome* (Chicago: Walter M. Hill, 1936; Dover reprint ed. 1977).

2 TIMOTHY

by S. M. Baugh

Second Timothy is the second of the "Pastoral Letters." For a general introduction on the authorship of these letters, see the comments at the beginning of 1 Timothy.

The Occasion for Second Timothy

In the introduction to 1 Timothy, I sketched out a probable scenario for the events in Paul's life and the background of the three Pastoral Letters. In that scenario, 2 Timothy comes as the last letter written by Paul. He was in Rome again, imprisoned and awaiting trial the second time (see 4:12–20). Since he had left some belongings at Troas, it seems that Paul had been arrested there or in some other city in Asia Minor before being sent on to Rome for trial. There is a hint in *1 Clement* 5.7 (ca. A.D. 95; cf. the later Muratorian Canon) that Paul actually made it to the "limit of the west," that is, to Spain, as he had

REMAINS OF
LAODICEA IN
ASIA MINOR

◀

2 Timothy
IMPORTANT FACTS:

- **AUTHOR:** The apostle Paul.
- **DATE:** Perhaps A.D. 66–67 (during Paul's second Roman imprisonment?).
- **VENUES:** Paul is probably in Rome writing to Timothy in Asia Minor.
- **OCCASION:**
  - To convey his last thoughts and exhortations to Timothy in the face of probable martyrdom (4:6–8).
  - To warn against certain false teachers and apostate brothers.
  - To further encourage Timothy in the conduct of his ministry.

hoped (Rom. 15:24, 28). If true, he would have been released from this second Roman imprisonment, unless he had already gone to Spain between his two Roman imprisonments. The massive turbulence caused by the Jewish revolt and the concurrent Roman coups and brief civil war right around this time makes this conceivable if not certain. Nero's assassination in June of 68 inaugurated the "year of the four emperors": Galba (June 68 to January 69); Otho (January to March 69); Vitellius (April to December 69); and finally, Vespasian (December 69 to 79).

Paul is writing in anticipation of his condemnation and execution at Rome (4:6). He writes to Timothy to alert him

of his circumstances (2:9), to warn him of certain future dangers to the church and her doctrine (e.g., 4:3–4), and to ask Timothy and Mark to come to him and bring along certain items from Troas (4:9–13). Of all Paul's letters, this one is filled with poignant reflections by the apostle on his life's conclusion and the awareness that he must turn his ministry over to others.

Salutation and Letter Opening (1:1–2)

The letter opening and salutation here are much like those found in other letters of the time. The author first identifies

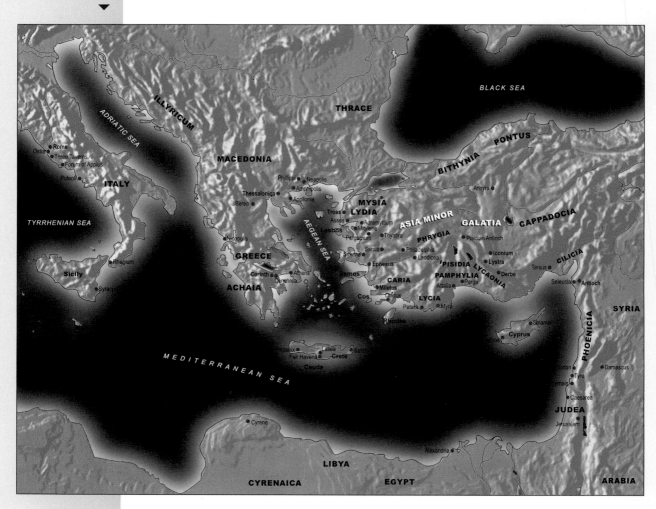

himself and then the recipient ("to Timothy, my dear son"), and he conveys his cordial respects. As often in Paul's letters, his identification includes his office, "an apostle of Christ Jesus", his divine appointment, "by the will of God", and a brief reminder of the focus of his apostolic ministry, "according to the promise of life that is in Christ Jesus." Paul is not magnifying himself, but assuring his young protégé that he is carrying on a divinely ordained ministry, even if Paul himself is soon to be martyred. Religious offices were regularly purchased in the Greek world (see accompanying box) or distributed by favor of patronage in Rome, but Paul received an appointment from God himself. This would be a striking contrast to a contemporary.

Grace, mercy and peace (1:2). Paul's greeting in 2 Timothy ends with an apostolic benediction in 1:2, "Grace, mercy and peace from God the Father and Christ Jesus our Lord." In most letters of the time, the standard opening ends with the word "greetings," or more effusive, "abundant greetings." For example, a second-century B.C. letter from Egypt begins: "Sarapion to his brothers Ptolemaeus and Apollonius *greetings*. If you are well, [it would be excellent]. I myself am well."[1] The standard word in Greek for "greetings" (*chairein*; see Acts 15:23; 23:26; James 1:1) sounds something like the Greek word for "grace" (*charis*), which suggests how the benediction came to be substituted in Christian letters.

Paul's Circumstances (1:3–18)

God, whom I serve, as my forefathers did (1:3). Paul does not usually refer to his "forefathers" as he does here. Yet he

---

▶ Sale of Religious Offices

The following letter illustrates the common practice of the sale of religious offices in the Hellenistic world as well as some of the elements of a Greek letter. This well-preserved letter happens to be an official petition, so it does not have any personal remarks. It is from an Egyptian named Pakebkis to a Roman public official. It reads:

Copy. To Tiberius Claudius Justus, administrator of the private account, from Pakebkis son of Marsisouchus, exempted priest of the famous temple of Soknebtunis also called Cronus and the most great associated gods, which is situated in the village of Tebtunis in the division of Polemon in the Arsinoite nome. I wish to purchase the office of prophet in the aforesaid temple, which has been offered for sale for a long time, on the understanding that I shall … [missing] … and carry the palm-branches and perform the

other functions of the office of prophet and receive in accordance with the orders the fifth part of all the revenue which falls to the temple, at the total price of 2200 drachmae instead of the 640 drachmae offered long ago by Marsisouchus son of Pakebkis, which sum I will pay, if my appointment is ratified, into the local public bank at the customary dates; and I and my descendants and successors shall have the permanent ownership and possession of this office forever with all the same privileges and rights, on payment (by each one) of 200 drachmae for admission. If therefore it seem good to you, my lord, you will ratify my appointment here in the city upon these terms and write to the strategus of the nome about this matter, in order that the due services of the gods who love you may be performed.[A-1]

clearly wants to bring up the issue of generational continuity in the service of God. He worships and serves God as had his Jewish ancestors. In 1:5 we see that Timothy also is continuing on in the faith of his grandmother and mother (see also 3:15). Perhaps the issue of continuity arises in Paul's mind because he knows that his life is drawing to a close, and he is therefore concerned that the next generation of ministers, like Timothy, must carry on his labors.

Continuity with one's ancestors in religion or in other areas of life was a key idea in the ancient Mediterranean world (cf. Acts 16:20–21). This is nowhere more apparent than in the noble Roman practice of making wax death masks (*imagines*) of one's parents.[2] In contrast, Paul would have no death mask made for him; however, he conveys a noble heritage of godly service at the command of the living God to Timothy, his "dear son" in the faith.[3]

In your grandmother Lois and in your mother Eunice (1:5). We have no other information about Timothy's grandmother, but of his mother we read this in Acts: "He [Paul] came to Derbe and then to Lystra, where a disciple named Timothy lived, whose mother was a Jewess and a believer, but whose father was a Greek" (Acts 16:1). Lystra was in the district of Lycaonia in the lower regions of the rough Galatian area in Asia Minor. It is notable that Lois had married a Greek. While this violated Old Testament law, it is not the only instance of the intermarriage of Jews with Greeks in Asia Minor. For example, in Acmonia in Phyrgia, a pagan priestess named Julia Severa had donated a large synagogue to the Jewish community in the Neronian period, probably at the instigation of her second husband, a Jew named Tyronius Rapo.[4]

The physical evidence for the large Jewish settlements in Asia Minor is remarkably scanty and probably indicates a thorough assimilation and accommodation of the Jews into their surrounding cultures, where they had lived for many centuries (Isa. 60:9; Obad. 20). Note as well that both the names Lois and Eunice are Greek, not Hebrew in origin, even though Lois at least was Jewish.

Immortality (1:10). Christ brought "life and immortality to light" (1:10). By saying these words without further elaboration, Paul shows just how thoroughly Jewish is the foundation of his thought. To a Greek of his day, "immortality" was the inherent property only of the gods

▶

JEWISH INSCRIPTION

The words were inscribed on a seat at the theater in Miletus: "the place of the Jews and the godfearers."

and of a few heroes and benefactors who were deified. Otherwise, "mortal" was a synonym for "human being." Some in the Greco-Roman world believed in transmigration of souls or reincarnation after death since it was introduced to the Greeks by Pythagoras in the sixth century B.C. There is, for instance, a famous and vivid passage in Virgil's *Aeneid* where Aeneas visits the underworld only to see the souls of the dead as they flit across the river to reinhabit bodies in the world above (*Aeneid* 6; late first century B.C.). In contrast, the Judeo-Christian worldview is expressed in Hebrews 9:27: "Man is destined to die once, and after that to face judgment."

Of this gospel (1:11). Paul was a herald, apostle, and teacher of the "gospel" (1:11). Christian usage has established this word with specialized meaning. Yet in Paul's day it was still used by his contemporaries to mean simply "good news" of some sort. It was used, for instance, to refer to a wedding announcement, a message about some happy event in the life of the emperor or of his family (e.g., his son passing into manhood), an imperial benefaction being granted to a city, the report of a military victory, or a message of other such glad tidings. The Greek word in 1:10 (*euangelion*) is the origin of our word "evangelist." Paul tells Timothy later in this book to fulfill his calling as an "evangelist" (4:5; cf. Acts 21:8; Eph. 4:11); that is, Timothy too was to be a messenger of the "good news" of the victory and benefactions of the King of kings, Jesus Christ, "who has destroyed death and has brought life and immortality to light through the gospel" (1:10).

I was appointed a herald (1:11). In the Greek world, a herald was more than just a town crier. Heralds made public announcements throughout a city to the citizen body like a crier, but they also acted as official messengers to other cities, carrying messages between governments. Furthermore, they assisted at public meetings, recited prayers at public sacrifices, and acted as emcees at public banquets. Paul has adapted the role of this common public figure to describe his own role as an official messenger from Christ (cf. 1 Tim. 2:7). By adding his credentials as "an apostle and a teacher," we see that his apostolic office gave him full authority from Christ to lay the foundation of the church and to instruct her in her growth in divine grace.

Everyone in the province of Asia has deserted me (1:15). Paul's exhortations to Timothy to stand firm in his ministry (1:13–14) takes on special urgency in light of the desertion from duty of "everyone in the province of Asia," particularly a certain Phygelus and Hermogenes (1:15). (Both names are Greek, but these men are otherwise unknown to us.) Paul must mean that the Christians from

WESTERN ASIA MINOR

▼

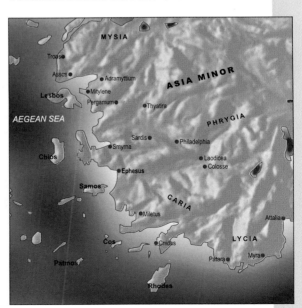

Asia Minor who were in Rome had abandoned him at his trial (cf. 4:16). Certainly other Christians in the region, like Onesiphorus (1:16) and Timothy himself who were in Asia at the time, had not forsaken him. But the desertion of many has obviously deeply grieved Paul.

Onesiphorus . . . often refreshed me (1:16). Paul contrasts the desertion of others with the faithful personal ministry of one Onesiphorus, who is also mentioned in 4:19 but nowhere else in the New Testament. "Onesiphorus" means "profit-bearer" (i.e., "profitable") in Greek and is a common name given to slaves. However, the fact that Onesiphorus has a "household" or family (1:16; 4:19) shows that he was probably a freedman, since slaves usually could not marry or have children of their own. Onesiphorus's freedman status is supported by the fact that he had the ability to travel to Rome on his own to hunt down Paul in order to minister to him. Many freedmen in the Roman empire had opportunities to acquire wealth and had the leisure to travel, so there is nothing unusual in this. In fact, some of the most powerful men in the Roman empire were the emperor's

freedmen and therefore of his "household" (cf. Phil. 4:22). It is notable that in the Christian community, there is absolutely no snobbery in relation to one's slave or freedman status, as there was in the world at the time.[5]

Exhortation to Faithfulness (2:1–7)

Paul continues his exhortations and warnings on false teachers to Timothy in chapter 2. The issue of false teachers has come up already in this letter as well as frequently in 1 Timothy, which should impress us not to think of the church in the apostolic age as dwelling in an idyllic golden age without trial and testing. The early church experienced the same kind of problems that plague the church today, but we also have the same resource today as then: protection given by our faithful Savior (e.g., 2:13).

Entrust to reliable men who will also be qualified to teach others (2:2). This statement shows that Paul does not envision the pastoral or teaching ministry to be the actions of one lone man, but of a plurality of leaders in the church.

A good soldier of Christ Jesus (2:3). When Paul tells Timothy to "endure hardship with us," the young pastor must act "like a good soldier" (2:3). It is the lot of all soldiers to put up with great hardships in the course of their duties, especially in wartime (cf. 4:5). We don't know exactly when 2 Timothy was composed, but it was around the time of a foiled plot to assassinate Nero in A.D. 65, led by Seneca and a tribune of a Praetorian cohort named Subrius Flavus. When asked by Nero why he broke his oath of loyalty (Latin *sacramentum*), Flavus

---

R E F L E C T I O N S

TIMOTHY, AS AN EVANGELIST—A MESSENGER OF the good news—was also to be a teacher of the "sound teaching" conveyed to him by Paul (1:13). Indeed, he was to *guard* this teaching as a "good deposit" entrusted to him (1:14). Guards were common in antiquity as now, and they tended to be rough characters. But Timothy was not to arm himself with sword or spear; rather, he was to guard his treasure through the Holy Spirit and to proclaim and teach his message "with faith and love in Christ Jesus." Christians, and especially Christian teachers, are not to take their cue from the world's ways, but from Christ's ways.

replied, "Because I detested you! I was as loyal as any of your soldiers as long as you deserved affection. I began detesting you when you murdered your mother and wife and became a charioteer, actor, and incendiary!"[6]

In addition, the year and a half from June of 68 to December of 69 was soon to witness the passing of the imperial crown from Nero to Galba to Otho to Vitellius and finally to Vespasian—all because of the loyalty or the treachery of the Roman troops under each man's command. Paul was speaking in general and theoretically about the dedication of a soldier to his commanding officer, but current events were witnessing just how important loyalty of soldiers toward their leaders could be. Timothy's self-denying service was to be to the Lord of lords and King of kings, who was first loyal to his subjects to the point of death on the cross.

As an athlete (2:5). The athlete shares features with the soldier: Both must endure hardship before gaining the victory (cf. 4:7). Yet here Paul invokes the fact that the athlete must compete "according to the rules" if he is to acquire the victory crown, implying that Timothy must acquire his "crown of righteousness" (4:8) by contesting according to the rules governing the servant of Christ. Many of the athletic contests in the Greek world had judges. For example, vase paintings of boxing matches often depict a judge supervising the match with a switch in his hand to enforce his rulings.

The hardworking farmer (2:6). Farming in the Western world today is performed by a small minority of the population. For example, the U. S. Census Bureau lists about 2 million full- and part-time farm operators out of a total population of over 270 million people (this figure does not list all farm laborers, just the "operators" or owners of farms); this is less than 1 percent. In antiquity, however—as well as in many parts of the world today—somewhere around 85 or 90 percent of the whole population was directly involved with growing or getting food as their primary occupation. Perhaps as little as 5 percent lived in ancient cities because a city requires surplus food production in the lands under its control to support the city-dwellers. In other words, Paul's analogy of the hardworking farmer would have been much more alive to his original readers than to many of us, because many of them were farmers or had farming experience.

The first to receive a share of the crops (2:6). At first sight, it may seem strange to say that a farmer should receive a share of

◀ *left*

ROMAN SOLDIER

A man modeling the typical dress of a Roman soldier at the Colosseum in Rome.

his own crops (2:6; cf. 1 Cor. 9:7). Were they not *his* crops? The answer is that they typically were not in Paul's day, since farms were often owned by absentee landlords. Ancient farmers were often like medieval serfs, who were tied to the lands they farmed but they did not own. Typically city residents, temples, or a city itself owned most of the outlying farm lands around a city.[7] It can be estimated from the placement of boundary markers that have been uncovered that the temple of Artemis of Ephesus owned as much as 77,000 acres of rich farm lands extending up to thirty miles outside the temple's precincts (which was itself about a mile outside of Ephesus). As just one example, here is a section out of the Greek novel from the period entitled *Daphnis and Chloe*, after the principal characters. The father of Chloe (the girl) approached Lamon, the father of Daphnis (the boy) to arrange a marriage between their children (although the usual custom was for the young man's father to approach the girl's). Both men worked small farmsteads with grain, grapes, and herds. Lamon responds:

> I'd be mad not to think it a great advantage to gain the friendship of your family, now that I'm an old man and need extra hands to get the work done. Besides, Chloe's a girl who's very much sought after, pretty and fresh and excellent in every way. But being a slave I can't make my own decisions about any member of my family. My master will have to be told of it and give his consent. So look here, let's put off the wedding until the autumn, for then he'll be here, according to reports that have been reaching us from town (3.31; Penguin trans.).

This small snippet illustrates many interesting features of ancient slave life

(e.g., the father cannot control his son's marriage), as well as the point at hand that a slave worked relatively independently on a small farm owned by someone else in a nearby city.

Christ and Paul's Chains (2:8–13)

This section begins with a brief statement about Jesus' resurrection and messianic identity in 2:8 ("raised from the dead, descended from David"), which summarizes Paul's gospel. This reference may have been part of a longer confession of faith such as found sketched out elsewhere in the New Testament and in the early church fathers. An example of the latter is this passage from Ignatius of Antioch in his letters to the Trallian church dated ca. A.D. 108: "Be deaf therefore when anyone speaks to you apart from Jesus Christ, who was of the family of David, and of Mary, who was truly born, both ate and drank, was truly persecuted under Pontius Pilate, was truly crucified and died in the sight of those in heaven and on earth and under the earth; who also was truly raised from the dead, when his Father raised him up."[8]

Chained like a criminal (2:9). Paul refers here to his own chains. He was in prison for the sake of Christ, the gospel, and the elect (2:10). From later statements (4:6, 16), Paul was obviously awaiting trial in Rome, probably before a Roman official of the Praetorian Guard.[9] Paul had evidently been arrested and sent to Rome from either Troas or from another city in Asia Minor (4:12, 20) rather than from Jerusalem and Caesarea, as in the book of Acts. He was thus awaiting trial after undergoing a preliminary examination by the Roman magistrate (4:16–19). Paul was in chains "like a criminal" (2:9). Not all prisoners were chained, and it shows in Paul's case that the Romans thought him to be dangerous or unreliable. Paul may have been held in a private home under guard or in one of the public prisons in Rome. The Romans and Greeks did not use prison as a form of punishment, but merely as a way to detain prisoners until trial. Afterward, various punishments such as fines, confiscation of property, banishment, enslavement, hard labor in the mines, or the death sentence were meted out. Paul expected the latter (4:6).

Here is a trustworthy saying (2:11). The lines of 2:11b–13 undoubtedly comprise the "trustworthy saying" (see comments on 1 Tim. 1:15).

Instructions to Timothy (2:14–26)

A workman who does not need to be ashamed (2:15). Paul exhorts Timothy to consider his task as a Christian minister and teacher as if he were a construction engineer "who correctly handles the word of truth" (2:15; cf. *1 Clement* 34.1). Paul uses a rare verb here for "correctly handles." The etymology comes from two words meaning "to cut something straight," and the verb is found with that meaning in the Greek translation of the OT referring to the setting out of a path or roadway in a straight direction (Prov. 3:6; 11:5). If the analogy Paul invokes refers to highway engineering and since the Roman roads back then—many of which are still in use today—are marvelous examples of careful and skillful work, we can understand that Timothy was to skillfully teach the word of God in an upright manner without deviating from the straight pathway into "quarreling about words" or "godless chatter" (2:14, 16).

Their teaching will spread like gangrene (2:17). In contrast with Timothy's "sound" (or "healthy") teaching (cf. 1 Tim. 1:10; 2 Tim. 1:13), the teaching of the ungodly "will spread like gangrene"

◀

ROMAN COLOSSEUM

The photo shows the area beneath the stadium floor.

(2 Tim. 2:17). In a world where antiseptics and sterilization were unknown, gangrene was a common malady. This was particularly so in antiquity where a medical consultant was as likely as anything to have his patient visit a hot springs, sleep in the temple of the god of healing (Asclepius), or pronounce a charm over an infection. Gangrene was often the result of such treatments.

Among them are Hymenaeus and Philetus (2:17). Paul names Hymenaeus and Philetus as two of the aberrant teachers of whom Timothy is to beware. Paul has already mentioned Hymenaeus, whom he had excommunicated (see 1 Tim. 1:20), but Philetus is otherwise unknown. However, he does mention their error: They claim that the general resurrection of the dead has already

REFLECTIONS

WHAT PAUL SAYS IN 2:18 AND OUR own observations today may discourage us about the debilitating effects of heresy on the church. But Paul does not stop with the negative. He encourages us in 2:19 by pointing to God's power and protection of the church. She is built on a solid foundation—Jesus Christ and his truth—by God himself, who has inscribed his seal on it. God owns and protects his church from all attacks external and internal, so that we can confidently sing the great hymn: "By schisms rent asunder, by heresies distressed. . . . The church shall never perish! Her dear Lord to defend, to guide, sustain, and cherish, is with her to the end" ("The Church's One Foundation," by Samuel S. Wesley).

occurred and thereby are destroying the faith of some (2 Tim. 2:18; cf. 1 Cor. 15). It is interesting to note that this particular heresy is making a comeback today by those who teach that the return of Christ and the general resurrection of the dead was fulfilled in A.D. 70.

Sealed with this inscription (2:19). The church of God is built on a solid foundation by God himself, who has inscribed his seal on it.[10] A seal was used in antiquity to prove the authenticity of something; in this case, God has inscribed his assurance to us that he knows his own and is secretly preserving them as well as issuing his command that all members of the visible church ("everyone who confesses the name of the Lord") must produce the good fruit of faith and turn away from evil. Inscriptions were found on all the solid marble and granite public buildings in antiquity, and the texts of these inscriptions comprise a major source for our understanding of life back then. Paul turns the commonplace sight of building inscriptions into a spiritual lesson.

Articles not only of gold and silver, but also of wood and clay (2:20). Paul refers to various kinds of "articles" or "vessels" found in a large household. Modern archaeologists have unearthed countless quantities of these objects—from delicate glass perfume jars to huge stone wine containers. The "ignoble" articles of 2:20 would include the rough clay chamber pots found in every household. There were public toilets in most of the larger cities—some with underground canals to carry away the waste—but chamber pots were still needed. The "noble" articles would include the fine table service dishes and ornamental painted ceramic jars. One common example of the latter that every Greek household contained was a special, beautifully painted amphora given to a bride at her wedding and then displayed prominently in the home thereafter.

Escape from the trap of the devil (2:26). Paul concludes his exhortations to Timothy in this chapter by telling him to "flee the evil desires of youth" and "foolish and stupid arguments" (2:22–23). Instead, he is to gently persuade and instruct his opponents, "in the hope that God will grant them repentance leading them to a knowledge of the truth" (2:25), and thus they will escape the "trap of the devil" (2:26). Trapping was a common form of hunting in antiquity. In early days, wild boar, lions, hare, and deer were trapped with nets, sometimes with the help of hounds. Birds too were trapped in nets or by applying sticky birdlime to branches where they congregated. This is a vivid image for the deadly effects of sin.

Warning of Last Days (3:1–9)

Throughout chapter 3, Paul warns Timothy about certain trends he will encounter in the last days. The New Testament writers were unanimously convinced that we live in the "last days," the "last times," the "last hour," and even "the end of the ages."[11] One of the features of the era between the first and second advents of Christ is the presence of great wickedness (2 Tim. 3:1–5) alongside the advance of the kingdom of Christ, who must rule in the midst of his enemies (Ps. 110:2). See also this statement in Jude: "In the last times there will be scoffers who will follow their own ungodly desires."[12]

The early church fathers understood the apostolic teaching on the last days and repeated it. For instance, Ignatius of Antioch (about A.D. 108) writes: "These are the last times. Therefore let us be modest, let us fear the long-suffering of God"; note also, "For in the last days the false prophets and the corrupters shall be multiplied."[13] The Qumran group in the desert of Judea had similar notions in some of their writings, though for them, the "final days" (1Q28a) were marked by physical warfare between the "sons of darkness" and the army of the "sons of light," that is, the sectarian group themselves (e.g., The War Scroll [1QM]), for they were "the last generation" (CD 1.12).[14] The Qumran group—whom one scholar called "fanatical separatists"—was eradicated by the Romans in about A.D. 68.

Having a form of godliness but denying its power (3:5). Today people outside of the Christian church usually do not put on a show of being *religious* and thereby adopt a "form of godliness" or "of piety." In our day, public demonstrations of piety are rare, but in antiquity, *everyone* (the Cynics and a very few others excepted) attended public religious functions. And piety in Greco-Roman religions was often measured by the size of one's donation to the public cults, so that honorific inscriptions from temple buildings often praised the person's "piety and generosity," which can be thought of together as "pious generosity." In other words, piety was commonly measured by external actions rather than by one's character. Hence, Paul says that false teachers may have the form of godliness, but the life-transforming power of true godliness begins with the fear of the Lord (Prov. 9:10) expressed as faith in Christ.

The kind who worm their way into homes (3:6). The typical large Greek home had a clear demarcation between the public areas of the house and the women's quarters (often on a second story). It was possible in a large household for a man to insinuate himself as a permanent guest under the patronage of the mistress of the house as a teacher or as a tutor for the children. Paul does not condemn the practice per se, but the morally corrupt hidden motives and practices that could result.

Just as Jannes and Jambres opposed Moses (3:8). These two names were assigned in Jewish sources to the Egyptian sorcerers who counterfeited the miracles of Moses in order to deceive Pharaoh (Ex. 7:11–22). While the names do not appear in the Old Testament text, Paul refers to them as commonly accepted figures with which many people were acquainted. For instance, we read this in the "Damascus Document" from Qumran: "For in ancient times there arose Moses and Aaron, by the hand of the prince of lights and Belial, with his cunning, raised up Jannes and his brother during the first deliverance of Israel" (CD 5.17–19). Even Pliny the Elder mentions Moses and Jannes in the same breath as well-known magicians from an earlier day.[15]

Paul's Example (3:10–17)

Persecutions, sufferings . . . in Antioch, Iconium and Lystra (3:11). The Antioch mentioned here is not the one in Syria, but the Pisidian Antioch in central Asia Minor. Pisidian Antioch was founded a few centuries earlier under the Seleucid kings and had grown in importance under Augustus. The nearby Pamphylian cities, Iconium and Lystra, were on the inland route east of Antioch, with Lystra being the hometown of Timothy. For the whole episode of persecution and Paul's experiences in these cities see Acts 13:14–

ANTIOCH AND LYSTRA

(left) One of the main streets in Pisidian Antioch.

(right) A view of the countryside from the site of ancient Derbe.

▼

14:23. In Lystra, Paul had been stoned by some Jews who had come from Antioch and Iconium and was left for dead (Acts 14:19), so it was a vivid memory to which he alludes in 2 Timothy 3:11.

From infancy you have known the holy Scriptures (3:15). Paul refers to Timothy's knowledge of the Scriptures "from infancy." This is remarkable testimony about the widespread access to the Old Testament in Asia Minor in this period. However, it is probable that Timothy's family did not own a whole Hebrew or Greek Old Testament. There were strict regulations for copying the Hebrew Old Testament (the "Torah"). A synagogue would usually have a special copy acquired at high expense. The standard Greek translation of the Old Testament of the day was the Septuagint (abbreviated LXX), which was presumably the version read and used outside of Palestine. Therefore, Timothy would probably have learned the Scriptures through public readings of the LXX in a synagogue in Lystra, for, as we read elsewhere: "Moses has been preached in every city from the earliest times and is read in the synagogues on every Sabbath" (Acts 15:21). Public reading was common in antiquity, where books were more expensive and rarer than today (cf. Col. 4:16; Rev. 1:3; see comments on 2 Tim. 4:13 for more on ancient books). There is a possibility that Timothy attended a private Torah school, though the student would normally have had to travel to a school in Jerusalem or Judea for this instruction (cf. Acts 22:3).

All Scripture is God-breathed (3:16). Second Timothy 3:16–17 have been foundational for our understanding of the nature of the divine inspiration of Scripture, especially the word rendered "God-breathed" (Gk. *theopneustos*). This word itself is rare, though not without analogies in the Greek language—for example, in Homer, the god Apollo "inbreathes" strength into Aeneas during battle with words of encouragement.[16] Compound words with "God" (or the names of various Greek deities) are common in Greek as adjectives and personal names (e.g., *theodidaktos*, meaning "God-taught"; the name Theophilus, meaning "God's friend" [cf. Luke 1:3; Acts 1:1]).

Book 5 of the *Sibylline Oracles* is probably the work of an Egyptian Jew (and others) between about A.D. 90 and 130. The word *theopneustos* appears in the *Oracles* to refer to man as "God-breathed" with the breath of life at creation (*Sib. Or.* 5.406; cf. Gen. 2:7). Paul clearly means something more special, however, since it is the *Scriptures* into which God pours his breath as one who speaks through them (cf. esp. Gal. 3:8, 22; 2 Peter 1:21). They are the very words of God.[17]

The religions of Greece and Rome in Paul's time were not dependent on written materials. There were sacred books containing oracular materials (e.g., the *Sibylline Oracles*), magic books with spells, incantations, charms, and so forth (cf. Acts 19:19), and other kinds of handbooks on practices such as augury (the interpretation of various omens). Moreover, the writing of the ancient poets like Homer or Hesiod were regarded as having particular authority in their myths about the gods, though at the same time there was a popular saying: "The poets tell many lies," especially about the gods.[18] In contrast, both Judaism and its offspring, Christianity, were and are religions that rely heavily on the inspired and authoritative Scriptures.

Charge to Faithful Service (4:1–5)

Paul gives Timothy a most solemn charge to carry out his full ministry of the Word based on the certain return of Christ, his kingdom, and the certain knowledge of opposition even within the church. Once again we see that the early church was threatened by serious apostasy and schismatic teaching, which Paul says will satisfy only the cravings of those who reject "sound teaching" in place of "myths" (4:3–4; cf. comments on 1 Tim. 4:6–7).

Do the work of an evangelist (4:5). Timothy is charged to be an "evangelist" or announcer of the glad tidings (see comments on 1:11). The term "evangelist" occurs only two other times in the New Testament: Ephesians 4:11, where it appears in a list of officers along with apostles, prophets, and pastors and teachers; and in Acts 21:8, where it describes Philip (see, e.g., 8:12, 40). There is no sense here that Timothy held a separate office from other pastors and teachers of the "presbytery" (1 Tim. 4:14). But Paul is charging him to focus on the Word of God in his ministry: "preach the Word . . . correct, rebuke and encourage. . . . Do the work of an evangelist" (2 Tim. 4:2, 5).

Paul's Final Reflections (4:6–18)

Poured out like a drink offering (4:6). Paul's "being poured out like a drink offering" is a metaphor of his coming departure from this life. Drink offerings or libations of wine were poured out as part of the Old Testament sacrificial service (Num. 4:7), but they were also a common part of Greek and Roman cult practice as an accompaniment of prayer. The farmer might pour a libation at the start of each

day, though the early Greek poet Hesiod gives this warning: "Never pour a libation of sparkling wine to Zeus after dawn with unwashed hands, nor to others of the deathless gods; else they do not hear your prayers but spit them back."[19] When embarking on a sea voyage, sailors would pour a bowl of wine into the sea with prayers for safety; on making landfall on foreign soil, Jason and the Argonauts poured a libation of honeyed wine on the earth to ask the gods and heroes of the place for a kind welcome.[20]

At other times, such as before a battle or another great venture, a special libation was poured out to accompany prayers for a successful outcome.[21] Libations also topped off a sacrifice, with the worshiper pouring wine or some other liquid on the altar after the burnt offering was mostly consumed. Finally, libations were also a standard part of any occasion where wine was drunk as a token of thanks to the gods. In Paul's case, he says that his life itself is a sacrificial prayer about to be poured out to the true God (cf. Phil. 2:17).

The crown of righteousness (4:8). There is no more common picture in the ancient Greek world of a successful athlete who was awarded a crown as his prize. For instance, a victor at the Olympic games

REFLECTIONS

PAUL, IN CONTRAST WITH THE PER- ishable military and athletic crowns of his day, was looking forward to receiving an imperishable "crown of righteousness." This crown is a free gift offered to all who have longed for the appearance of "the righteous Judge" (4:8).

was given a wreath of olive branches. But military victors were also given a crown. Pliny the Elder mentions several of the Roman military crown awards while discussing the *corona graminea*, "crown of grass"—also called the *corona obsidionalis*, "siege-crown"—as follows:

> No crown indeed has been a higher honour than the crown of grass among the rewards for glorious deeds given by the sovereign people, lords of the earth. Jewelled crowns, golden crowns, crowns for scaling enemy ramparts or walls, or for boarding men-of-war, the civic crown for saving the life of a citizen, the triumph crown—these were instituted later than this grass crown, and all differ from it greatly, in distinction as in character. . . . This same crown is called the siege crown when a whole camp has been relieved and saved from awful destruction.[22]

The Roman grass crown was, as its name suggests, a wreath plaited from ordinary grass, yet it was prized above all other military decorations. Pliny could find mention of only eight recipients over the span of several centuries.[23]

Demas . . . has deserted me (4:10). Paul names various people in 4:9–14: Demas (familiar form of Demetrius) was Paul's "fellow worker" (Philem. 24; cf. Col. 4:14), yet here he has abandoned Paul for Thessalonica, perhaps his hometown; Crescens (a Roman name) and Titus departed for other places, perhaps at Paul's request (cf. Titus 3:12). Luke is presumably the "beloved physician" (Col. 4:14, NRSV; cf. Philem. 24), who alone stayed with Paul in his hour of need. Mark is obviously John Mark, who had left prematurely during Paul's first mis-

sionary journey (Acts 12:25; 13:5, 13). It appears that Paul's former breach with Mark was now healed (Philem. 24; cf. 1 Peter 5:13). Tychicus was Paul's messenger for other letters and a fellow worker (Acts 20:4; Eph. 6:21; Col. 4:7). Carpus (Gk. word meaning "fruitful") and Alexander the metalworker are mentioned only here in the New Testament. Troas was a coastal city in northwest Asia Minor and was a natural point of departure for ships sailing for Rome.

When you come, bring the cloak (4:13). Paul asks Timothy to bring along a cloak he had left behind at Troas with a man named Carpus. This garment was a heavy tunic or overcoat worn over the normal outer garment in the cold winter months. The material was normally of a thick wool and was fairly valuable. Paul is evidently writing in late summer and wants Timothy to get his winter overcoat to him before the cold sets in (cf. 4:21).

And my scrolls (4:13). We know from ancient sources as well as from rich remains of papyrus documents that have survived in the dry sands of Egypt that the "scrolls" or "books" to which Paul refers were papyrus rolls, used for all kinds of writings. Papyrus was manufactured exclusively in Egypt in this period and jealously regulated by the Roman authorities, especially after a shortage of papyrus under Tiberius had caused alarm among the imperial bureaucrats.[24] The standard size scroll was sold in twenty sheet lengths. Longer works would require the copyist to glue more sheets onto the roll, though this could make the work unwieldy. Each sheet was four to nine inches wide, so that a standard scroll was roughly seven to fifteen feet long. Imagine trying to find a favorite passage at the end of a 15 foot

▶ The Library at Ephesus

One of the most notable features of the archaeological remains of ancient Ephesus is the Celsus library (built from A.D. 110 to 135). This beautiful edifice could house thousands of scrolls and books and was in a central part of town, where public lectures were conducted, perhaps even the vicinity of "the lecture hall of Tyrannus," where Paul had taught (Acts 19:9). Libraries and bookseller stalls were a common feature of big cities in antiquity and show that books were easily obtainable in antiquity.

long papyrus scroll. This problem encountered by early Christians trying to look things up in the New Testament documents is thought to have contributed to the rising popularity of the "codex" style of book, which we know today.[25]

What did Paul's scrolls contain? Copies of his own works? We do know that ancient authors—as do modern ones—normally kept copies of their works on hand. Or did Paul own a copy of the Gospel of John perhaps, with which his expressions show some remarkable similarity? Or were these Septuagint scrolls of the Old Testament? There is no way of knowing, of course, but it is tempting to speculate.

Especially the parchments (4:13). The word Paul uses for "parchments" is a Latin word (*membrana*) brought into Greek. Parchment was made from sheepskin or goatskin and provided a durable writing surface. Parchment required a special ink to adhere to it and it could be more expensive than papyrus, although it also allowed the advantage of being somewhat erasable when the ink from a previous work was scraped off the surface, producing a *palimpsest* or "redone" manuscript. If much erasing was anticipated, wax tablets were used, especially for school workbooks.

Some scholars believe that the word for "especially" in 4:13 is mistranslated. They prefer to read the Greek word as communicating clarifying information: "bring . . . my scrolls, *that is*, the parchments."[26] However, I am persuaded that "especially" in our versions is correct after examining all the New Testament and other ancient evidence adduced to support this rendering.

At my first defense (4:16). We cannot know the precise details of Paul's trial(s) in Rome; however, we know generally how such trials were conducted and we have the account of Paul's examinations in Judea under Felix and Festus in Acts 23–

25.²⁷ Paul mentions that he had been given a first defense, at which he undoubtedly took the occasion to preach Christ (2 Tim. 4:17) as he had in the defenses recorded in Acts (e.g., Acts 26). We do not know if Nero himself heard Paul's first defense or whether it was someone else. Early in his career, Nero left the mundane judicial and administrative details of his empire to his high advisors, including the popular Stoic teacher, Seneca.

I was delivered from the lion's mouth (4:17). Condemned criminals and many of the early Christian martyrs were often literally killed by lions or other beasts in the Roman amphitheaters. In this case, though, Paul is probably speaking metaphorically, since as a Roman citizen—even one from the provinces—he would not normally have been subjected to the amphitheater. Decapitation was the normal form of execution for a Roman citizen. Normally, only condemned slaves or *peregrini* (i.e., non-Roman inhabitants of the empire) died in the animal *venationes,* "hunts," testimony to the brutality possible under Roman rule.

Final Greetings (4:19–23)

Get here before winter (4:21). Paul wants Timothy to come to him before winter partly because he wants his winter overcoat (see comments on 4:13) and partly because winter travel at sea on small sailing ships was a dicey thing in antiquity (cf. Acts 27:9). The ships of the day were square-rigged, which made for slow sailing if the wind was on either beam (see accompanying box). It is

---

▶ Ships and Shipping

Ships of the period were constructed from edge-joined planks uniquely joined together, caulked with pitch, strengthened with interior frames, and finished off with an outer covering of lead sheathing. During storms, stout ropes were passed underneath the hull to strengthen it (Acts 27:17). The largest of the merchant ships could reach 180 feet long and 45 feet in beam, though most were smaller, some as small as a rowboat for local transport and fishing. The square sails on the larger ships allowed a typical speed of about four knots with the wind behind or on an aft quarter; however, if the wind came from a slight forward quarter the best they could do was to tack in a zigzag pattern or to wait for a change of wind direction. Some merchant galleys had oars manned by as many as 50 sailors during periods of calm or contrary winds. One or two large oars rigged to the aft sides of the ship acted as rudders when twisted on a pivot.

Pompey the Great had uprooted pirates from the eastern Mediterranean in a famous campaign in the previous century, so merchant ships in Paul's day plied the sea in relative safety and freedom and carried passengers on a space-available basis (Acts 21:2–3). Cargo holds were typically filled with grain, wine, or oil, as well as pottery, building stone, luxury items, and a wide variety of other goods (cf. Rev. 18:11–13), usually held in large earthenware jars. Investment in ships, cargoes, or single cruises was an important speculative financial opportunity in antiquity, sometimes yielding huge profits (cf. 18:17–18), or ending with disaster if the ship was wrecked.^A-2 Smaller vessels called "coasters" skimmed along the Mediterranean coastlines, trading from town to town along the way (Acts 21:1). Longer trips by bigger ships were made from the great seaports like Ephesus, Alexandria (cf. 27:6; 28:11), the Phoenician ports of Sidon and Tyre, and Puteoli near Naples (28:13).

estimated that these vessels could probably make an average speed of four or five knots over the course of a voyage, though much depended on the season, the winds, and the skill of the sailors.

Greet Priscilla and Aquila . . . (4:19). Paul ends this letter to Timothy with greetings to and from various people, which typify ancient letters, and with a report on the whereabouts of other colleagues (i.e., Priscilla, Aquila, Onesiphorus, Erastus, Trophimus, Eubulus, Pudens, Linus, and Claudia). Some of these people are known from elsewhere in the New Testament and some not, but we can see that Paul has not been entirely abandoned. The letter ends with the apostolic benediction: "The Lord be with your spirit. Grace be with you" (4:22).

ANNOTATED BIBLIOGRAPHY

Dibelius, Martin, and Hans Conzelmann. *The Pastoral Epistles.* Hermeneia. Philadelphia: Fortress, 1972.

This critical commentary relies on the typical reasons for rejecting Pauline authorship of the Pastorals, but helpfully gives detailed attention to the historical background and especially connections of the Pastoral Letters with the Hellenistic world.

Fee, Gordon D. *1 and 2 Timothy, Titus.* GNC. San Francisco: Harper & Row, 1984.

This is a concise commentary by a well-regarded NT and text-critical scholar in a popular format.

Guthrie, Donald. *The Pastoral Epistles: An Introduction and Commentary.* TNTC. Leicester and Grand Rapids: InterVarsity and Eerdmans, 1990 (rev. ed.).

A solid though brief commentary by a senior evangelical NT scholar.

Kelly, J. N. D. *A Commentary on the Pastoral Epistles.* TC. London: A. & C. Black, 1963; reprinted Grand Rapids: Baker, 1981.

This brief commentary sticks closely to the text and is marked by Kelly's characteristic sound judgment. Kelly is well versed in original sources and has produced a number of standard works in the later development of early Christianity, which add depth to his commentary.

Kidd, Reggie M. *Wealth and Beneficence in the Pastoral Epistles: A "Bourgeois" Form of Early Christianity?* Atlanta: Scholars, 1990.

This is the best of many such studies on the contemporary social and ethical background of the Pastoral Letters. Kidd surveys an extensive range of background material in this work.

Knight, George W. III. *Commentary on the Pastoral Epistles.* NIGTC. Grand Rapids and Carlisle: Eerdmans and Paternoster, 1992.

This detailed commentary on the Greek text of the Pastorals often gives illuminating historical insights as well as careful attention to the meaning of the grammar and language of the biblical text. The best technical commentary on the Pastorals in print today.

Lau, Andrew L. *Manifest in Flesh: The Epiphany Christology of the Pastoral Epistles.* WUNT 2/86. Tübingen: J. C. B. Mohr (Paul Siebeck), 1996.

This specialized study draws especially helpful connections between the epiphany material in the Pastorals with the OT and other Jewish literature.

Oden, Thomas C. *First and Second Timothy and Titus.* Interpretation. Louisville: John Knox, 1989.

Oden presents an elegant and sane defense of Pauline authorship in this topically arranged "commentary." There are a few rough spots regarding historical background of the biblical world (e.g., sacred prostitution at Ephesus, p. 95), but Oden augments his own helpful insights with a sprinkling of quotations of church fathers and Reformers, which gives the reader a wider view of the interpretation of the Pastoral Letters.

Young, Frances. *The Theology of the Pastoral Letters.* NTT. Cambridge: Cambridge Univ. Press, 1994.

This volume in a promising series spends considerable time trying to establish pseudonymous authorship of the Pastorals. Nevertheless, Young usefully reports on historical backgrounds of the Pastorals in places—for instance, on "teaching and learning in the ancient world" (pp. 79–84), though it seems mostly secondary and derivative.

Main Text Notes

1. P.Par. 43; LCL trans., emphasis added.
2. See Polybius 6.53.
3. Cf. 1 Cor. 4:17; Phil. 2:22.
4. See S. Applebaum, "The Legal Status of the Jewish Communities in the Diaspora," in *The Jewish People in the First Century* (eds. S. Safrai and M. Stern; Philadelphia: Fortress, 1976), 1.443.
5. For instance, there are several barbs hurled at imperial freedmen scattered throughout Juvenal's *Satires*.
6. Tacitus, *Ann.* 15:67; Penguin trans.
7. See *IvE* 3501–12; Dieter Knibbe et al., "Der Grundbesitz der ephesischen Artemis im Kaystrolstal," *ZPE* 33 (1979): 139–46.
8. Ignatius, *Trallians* 9.1–2.
9. See Acts 28:16 and discussion in A. N. Sherwin-White, *Roman Society and Roman Law in the New Testament* (Oxford: Oxford Univ. Press, 1963), 108–12; cf. Tajra, *Trial of St. Paul*.
10. Cf. Matt. 16:18; 1 Cor. 3:10–12; Eph. 2:20.
11. 2 Tim. 3:1; cf. Acts 2:17; Heb. 1:2; James 5:3; cf. Isa. 2:2; Hos. 3:5; 1 Peter 1:20; 1 John 2:18; Heb. 9:26.
12. Jude 18; cf. 2 Peter 3:3; 1 John 2:18.
13. Ignatius, *Ephesians* 11.1; *Didache* 16.3.
14. The Qumran materials can be found in: Florentino García Martínez, *The Dead Sea Scrolls Translated*, 2d ed. (New York, Cologne, and Grand Rapids: E. J. Brill and Eerdmans, 1996).
15. Pliny, *Nat. Hist.* 30.11.
16. Homer, *Iliad* 20.110.
17. The seminal work on Scripture and on the word *theopneustos* in 2 Tim. 3:16 is that of the old Princeton scholar, B. B. Warfield: *The Inspiration and Authority of the Bible* (Oxford: Oxford Univ. Press, 1927; repr. 1948 by Presbyterian and Reformed), esp. chap. 6.
18. E.g., Dio Chrysostom, *Or.* 18.3; Plato, *Republic* 376E–378E; Plutarch, *Moralia* 16A.
19. Hesiod, *Works and Days* 724–26.
20. Thucydides 6.32.1–2; *Argonautica* 2.1271–75.
21. E.g., *Iliad* 9.175f.; 16.225ff.
22. Pliny, *Nat. Hist.* 22.4.
23. Ibid., 22.5–7.
24. See Pliny (*Nat. Hist.* 13.68–89) for this crisis and for his survey of the papyrus manufacturing process.
25. See C. H. Roberts and T. C. Skeat, *The Birth of the Codex* (Oxford: Clarendon, 1983); Naphtali Lewis, *Papyrus in Classical Antiquity* (Oxford: Clarendon, 1974).
26. T. C. Skeat, "'Especially the Parchments': A Note on 2 Timothy IV.13," *JTS* 30 (1979): 173–77.
27. The principal works on this subject are: Tajra, *Trial of St. Paul*; Brian Rapske, *Paul in Roman Custody* (Grand Rapids: Eerdmans, 1994); though A. N. Sherwin-White's *Roman Society and Roman Law* is still very useful.

Sidebar and Chart Notes

A-1. P.Tebt. 294; LCL trans..
A-2. Cf. Shakespeare, *The Merchant of Venice*.

TITUS

by S. M. Baugh

The Occasion for Paul's Letter to Titus

I have already addressed briefly the issues of Pauline authorship and the probable background scenario for the composition of Titus (see the introduction to 1 Timothy). The letter to Titus was probably written between the time of Paul's first trial in Rome as narrated in Acts and a second Roman trial that forms the background to the writing of 2 Timothy. Paul's witness in Crete while on his way to Rome the first time (Acts 27) had formed an embryonic church, which he would naturally have wished to firmly establish upon his release. He had left Titus in Crete to carry on the work (Titus 1:5) while he himself set off for Nicopolis in western Greece. It was after this second, longer stay in Crete that Paul wrote the letter to Titus. Whether Paul wrote it from Nicopolis or while on his way there (or whether he arrived there at all) is unknown. But the main concerns of Paul in this letter show his concern that Titus be further equipped

CRETE

The harbor at Fair Havens.

▸ **Titus**
IMPORTANT FACTS:

- ■ **AUTHOR:** The apostle Paul.
- ■ **DATE:** ca. A.D. 66 (just before Paul's second Roman imprisonment?).
- ■ **VENUES:** Paul on his way to or in Nicopolis in Epirus (western Greece), writing to Titus on the island of Crete.
- ■ **OCCASION:**
  - • To give Titus specific and general instructions for his ministry in Crete.
  - • To remind Titus of Christian doctrines and ethical teachings.
  - • To warn against false teachers and apostate brothers.

for his ministry to the church on Crete and to give him various other personal instructions.

Paul intends to send either Artemas (otherwise unknown) or Tychicus to take over the work in Crete so that Titus can come to join him in Nicopolis before winter sets in.[1] As mentioned, Paul is either already in Nicopolis or about to go there.

There were several places named Nicopolis in the Greek world. The word means "Victory City" and was the name of cities founded by Alexander, Pompey, and Augustus to celebrate their military successes. This Nicopolis is the one on the western coast of Greece in the province of Epirus (about 200 miles west

and slightly north of Athens), founded by Augustus in 31–29 B.C. to celebrate his victory over Mark Antony. It was a Roman colony—meaning that it was originally a source of land grants for Augustus's veterans on their discharge. This city served as the regional economic and administrative capitol of the province of Epirus. Paul would naturally have gone there if he were going to Rome or returning from there.

Salutation and Letter Opening (1:1–4)

As often in Paul's letters, this letter's opening has a host of theological points to consider. It is as if Paul cannot wait to

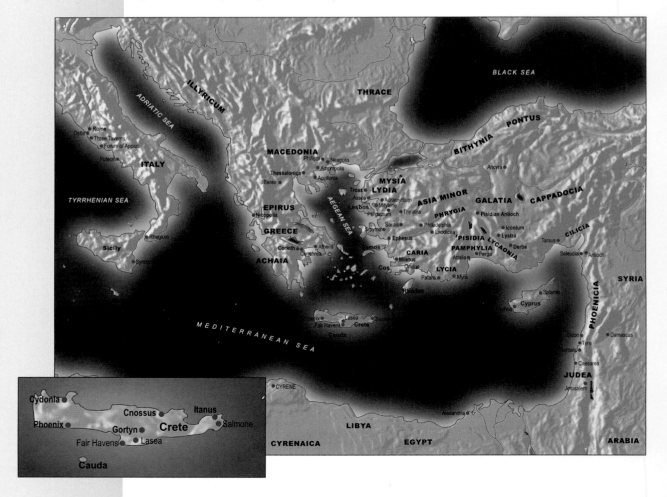

get to the body of the letter to glory in the gospel of Christ. Paul stresses his particular appointment to be an apostle—not to boast over against Titus, but, as in 1 Timothy 2:4–7, to show conclusively that God has by his appointment testified to his plan that even Gentiles (like Titus and the Cretans) are to be included in the covenant people of God (see comments on 1 Tim. 2:4–7).

God, who does not lie (1:2). When Paul says that God does not lie (1:2; cf. Heb. 6:18) and that he has promised eternal life to all who believe, Paul is speaking in light of two lying groups: (1) the Cretans, among whom Titus is working and who "are always liars" (Titus 1:12); and (2) the Greek/Cretan gods, who were ever lying and deceiving in the classical myths. There was never a greater lying trickster than Olympian Zeus, who always seemed to wrap himself in a fog in order to ravish some maiden out of sight from his wife, Hera, and then to lie about the deed. This caused some of the pagans embarrassment, which early Christian apologists exploited.[2]

To Titus, my true son (1:4). Titus, despite his Roman name, was a Greek who was an early companion of Paul in his missionary ventures (Gal. 2:1, 3). He is not mentioned in Acts, but Paul elsewhere speaks of him in the highest collegial terms (e.g., 2 Cor. 8:23). In addition to his work with Paul, Titus was now working on his own in Crete and would later go to Dalmatia (2 Tim. 4:10). He was called the first bishop of Crete in church tradition.

Titus's Task on Crete (1:5–16)

Husband of but one wife (1:6). When Paul tells Titus in 1:6 that the elder is to be the "husband of but one wife," he says something clear enough at first glance: Men who have more than one wife are excluded (cf. 1 Tim. 3:2, 12; also "wife of one husband" in 5:9). However, we run into a problem here because Greeks and Romans of the time did not practice polygamy; they were unambiguously monogamous. In consequence, we are left with only two options for understanding this statement about "husband of but one wife."

(1) The first option is that the man or wife involved must not be divorced and remarried. Divorce for the Greeks and Romans was fairly common, especially among the upper classes. Divorce could be initiated by either party (or even by the wife's father) and was usually the result of some failure to provide the basic requirements of the implicit contract, for instance, house and board or legitimate children. Read, for example, this statement in Dio Chrysostom (ca. A.D. 40–110), in a dialogue on slavery where one of his characters says: "Yes, I know that freeborn women often palm off other persons' children as their own on account of their childlessness, when they are unable to conceive children themselves, because each one wishes to keep her own husband and her home."[3] Clearly a Greek woman feared divorce for childlessness; raising up one or more heirs was considered vital to Greek and Roman families. A Greek man could also divorce his wife out of his obligation in order to marry a female heiress within his clan (an *epikleros*).[4]

(2) Paul perhaps means that a prospective elder should not have one or more concubines. This seems more likely to be Paul's meaning, for many Greeks and Romans of the time practiced concubinage. In the Greek world a Greek

man married around age thirty—in contrast, girls normally married around age fourteen—and it was taken for granted that before manhood "wild oats should be sown and done with. . . . Youth rates a certain indulgence."[5] This could occur with courtesans (*hetairai*) at the dinner parties (*symposia*) that a young man attended in a special room of Greek homes called the *andron* ("banquet hall," but more literally, "men's hall"). Furthermore, some men purchased courtesans as slaves and kept them as mistresses outside the home, while some married men had one or more concubines among the slave-girls in their households. "Don't many Athenian men have relations with their maidservants, some of them secretly, but others quite openly?"[6] Evidence for these practices is widespread.[7]

The same practices can be found among the Romans. Pliny the Younger, for example, reports on the murder of a Roman noble by a few of his slaves and mentions in a tellingly off-handed manner that the dead man's concubines raised a dreadful din on discovery of the dying man.[8] Neither the Greeks nor the

CRETE

The ruins at Knossos.

▼

Romans regarded these practices as adultery or polygamy. The Greeks conceived adultery as a sexual liaison of a free married woman with a man (married or not), but not of a man, married or not, with an unmarried woman.

Paul, as would any Jew, regards this common practice of concubinage the same as polygamy, since the sexual union is tantamount to a marital union (e.g., Gen. 2:24; 1 Cor. 6:16). Hence, he says that the overseer should be the "husband of but one wife," because union with a concubine or a prostitute constitutes another marital relation.

Cretans are always liars (1:12). The church fathers attributed the quotation on the Cretans in Titus 1:12 to Epimenides of Crete, a legendary figure from the seventh to sixth century B.C., whose works have all been lost. The line given here, "Cretans are always liars," does appear in the Hellenistic poet Callimachus, but he was not from Crete and thus not the "one of their own prophets," which Paul has in mind.[9] It was commonly understood in antiquity that the Cretans were a particularly cunning and self-serving lot, even by the Greeks who themselves deified sly tricksters like Odysseus (hero of Homer's *Odyssey* and many other tales). The Greek verb *kretizō*, "to Cretonize," meant "to double deal" and "to lie" all rolled into one (see also the accompanying box).

Instructions for Various Members of the Church (2:1–10)

Titus is told how to instruct various groups within the church: older men (2:2), older women (2:3), younger women (2:4–5; instructed by older women), and younger men (2:6). Then he mentions the instruction to be given to slaves (2:9–10). The instructions here focus on Christian character. Older men are to display a character that is "worthy of respect" (2:2). Older women are to live in such a way that they can instruct younger women to be godly homemakers (2:3–5), while younger men are to be "self-controlled" (2:6). Titus himself is to live out his own Christian integrity in order to silence any calumny that Christians merely spout high morals but live corrupt lives (2:7–8).

Older men to be . . . self-controlled (2:2). One recurring quality throughout 2:1–8 is the notion of "self-control." Paul wants older men, younger women, and younger men to demonstrate "self-control" (2:2, 5–6; cf. 1:8). In addition, he

---

▶ A Lying Cretan

The Hellenistic era historian Polybius (ca. 200–118 B.C.) records an episode that characterizes the attitude of the ancients toward Cretans. In 223/222 B.C. a royal viceroy of the Seleucid King Antiochus III named Achaeus had recovered lands for his king in Asia Minor from the Pergamene Empire, but he turned around and proclaimed himself king of these territories in 220 while Antiochus was away putting down rebels and fighting King Ptolemy of Egypt. Antiochus duly arrived on the scene and besieged Achaeus in Sardis, which was fairly impregnable.

Friends of Achaeus hatched a plot to get him out of Sardis from under Antiochus's nose and entrusted the affair to one of King Ptolemy's high officials named Bolis, who, Polybius tells us, was a Cretan and therefore "naturally astute" (8.16). Bolis arrived in Asia Minor and took counsel with his kinsman, Cambylus, who "discussed the matter from a thoroughly Cretan point of view," which meant that "they did not take into consideration either the rescue of the man in danger [Achaeus] or their loyalty to those who had charged them with the task, but only their personal security and advantage. Both of them, then, Cretans as they were, soon arrived at the same decision," which was to make off with the money given them to free Achaeus and to approach King Antiochus for more if they could turn Achaeus over to him (8.16).

Bolis, being a Cretan and therefore "ready to entertain every kind of suspicion regarding others" (8.20), came up with a cunning plan and secretly met with Achaeus to offer to smuggle him out of Sardis, while he really intended to nab Achaeus and turn him over to his enemy. Achaeus was ready to cooperate, though he introduced a few wrinkles of his own just in case there was some double-crossing. Polybius remarks: "Achaeus indeed was doing his best, but he did not consider that, as the saying is, he was trying to play the Cretan with a Cretan [lit. *kretizō*, "to Cretanize"]; for there was no probable precaution of this kind that Bolis had not minutely examined" (8.19). The sly and double-dealing Bolis succeeded and brought about the doom of Achaeus, showing just how futile it was to try "to Cretanize a Cretan."

uses a cognate verb when he says that older women, who display a high character, "can *train* the younger women" (2:4; emphasis added). There are other words for "train," "instruct," or "advise" in Greek, and the word used here is rare (occurring only here in the NT), so Paul wants us to see it as connected to the adjective "self-controlled" used in this section.

The words related to "self-control" in 2:1–6 are used often in ancient Greek and Roman discussions of ethics. The adjective form (Gk. *sōphrōn*) may also be rendered "prudent," as a quality of someone who displays thoughtful care in his or her conduct. It can also be rendered "chaste," particularly as it relates to the conduct of women; chastity and faithfulness in wives was a virtue especially prized by the ancient Greeks (and Romans). There are many examples, but the following tomb epigram will illustrate: "Praise the affection on the part of her husband, stranger, as you read of the wife of Stabulio, Cornelia Fortunata. She continued respectable, modest (*sōphrōn*), and left him sympathetic tears."[10]

To be busy at home (2:5). Interest in "family values" such as found in 2:3–5, was not rare in the first century. The emperor Augustus was so concerned about the lack of family interest among the Roman nobility (and thereby cutting off the lines of the old Roman families) that he passed a law penalizing Romans who did not marry or have legitimate children.[11] The historian Cassius Dio (born ca. A.D. 164) writes of an incident in the Forum when some Roman knights urged Augustus to repeal this law. Augustus had the unmarried and childless stand in one part of the assembly and the married and those with children stand in another. Seeing how few the latter were in number, Dio puts a long speech into Augustus's mouth about the duty of citizens to imitate the Romans of old, who were noble not only in military prowess

CRETE

The harbor at Phoenix.

but also in the size of their population, and to imitate even the gods themselves, who marry and beget children (36.2). He continues (in Dio's account):

You have done right, therefore, to imitate the gods and right to emulate your fathers, so that, just as they begot you, you also may bring others into the world; that, just as you consider them and name them ancestors, others also may regard you and address you in similar fashion; that the works which they nobly achieved and handed down to you with glory, you also may hand on to others; and that the possessions which they acquired and left to you, you also may leave to others sprung from your own loins. For is there anything better than a wife who is *chaste, domestic,* a good house-keeper, a rearer of children; one to gladden you in health, to tend you in sickness; to be your partner in good fortune, to console you in misfortune; to restrain the mad passion of youth and to temper the unseasonable harshness of old age? (36.3; LCL trans.; emphasis added).

The words rendered "chaste" and "domestic" in the original are the same as "self-controlled" and "busy at home" in Titus 2:5.

Slaves . . . not to talk back (2:9). Paul gives Titus instructions on what to teach slaves regarding their behavior toward their masters. These instructions recall those he has given elsewhere (e.g., Eph. 6:5–8; 1 Tim. 6:1–2). As mentioned in connection with 1 Timothy 6:1–2, perhaps more than one-third of the population of the cities of the time were slaves, and certainly more if you count freedmen. Paul wants slaves to act honestly

toward their masters and "not to talk back to them" (Titus 2:9). This latter instruction may seem unneeded to us, but to the ancients the insolent slave was a typical item of conversation portrayed in their literature and plays. For instance, in Menander's play *The Girl from Samos*, as is typical of many of his and of others' comic plays, the slaves are often insolent. In one scene a saucy cook and another slave appear when the second one bursts out: "For God's sake, Cook! I can't imagine why you bother to carry knives around with you. You're quite capable of slicing through everything with your tongue" (lines 282–84).[12] It is in light of this common portrayal of the insolence of slaves that Paul wants them to quietly obey their masters "so that in every way they will make the teaching about God our Savior attractive" (2:10).

The Gospel Summarized (2:11–15)

Our great God and Savior, Jesus Christ (2:13). The focus of Titus's teaching, Paul says, is to be the glorious work and future appearance of "our great God and Savior, Jesus Christ." The rendering of this latter

---

R E F L E C T I O N S

WE SHOULD READ THE WORD "REDEEM" IN 2:13 IN light of ancient slavery. To "redeem" someone in antiquity meant to purchase their freedom either from slavery or by way of ransom from pirates or kidnappers (who often sold their victims into slavery as well). It was no dead metaphor in Paul's day to say that Jesus Christ "gave himself for us to *redeem* us from all wickedness" (2:14; emphasis added). Here slavery to sin and captivity to its deathly consequences are portrayed as the chains that only our "great God and Savior" could break by giving himself over to death in our place.

phrase in the NIV makes it appear that Paul is calling Jesus Christ both God and Savior. This causes trouble for some commentators who believe that the New Testament writers do not ascribe divinity to Christ; hence, they prefer to read "the great God" and "our Savior, Jesus Christ" as independent from one another.[13] However, the original expression is perfectly clear in Greek; Paul is unambiguously giving Jesus Christ both titles here. It is significant that the Apostolic Fathers, the immediate heirs of the apostles, had no trouble ascribing deity to Christ in unequivocal fashion. For instance, Ignatius spoke of "our God, Jesus Christ" or of "the passion of my God" or of Christ as "from eternity with the Father."[14] The

church fathers were not infallible, of course, but neither were they simpletons to so misconstrue the New Testament's teaching on Christ if it does *not* teach his deity. Note too that the Roman procurator Pliny the Younger examined the practices of the early Christians and found, among other (harmless) practices, that they sang antiphonal hymns to Christ "as if to a god."[15]

Doing What Is Good (3:1–11)

Remind the people to be subject to rulers (3:1). Paul's instructions regarding submission to rulers and authorities (3:1)—all of whom were undoubtedly pagans at the time—shows that Chris-

---

▶ # The Gospel of the Deified Augustus's Birth

There survives a decree of the Roman governor of Asia from 9 B.C. and a corresponding decree of the provincial parliament (the Koinon of Asia) that changed the calendar of the cities of Asia Minor to start on the birthday of the deified Augustus. The texts of these decrees are pieced together primarily from inscriptions found near Priene [a city near Miletus] (OGIS 458). The decree of the Koinon of Asia is particularly interesting because it illustrates the Greek custom of calling the deified emperor a "god" (*theos*), because it uses the term *euangelion* ("good news" or "gospel") for the message of the emperor's birthday, and because it refers to the benefactions of the emperor as "salvation." The Koinon's decree follows in part. (Note that the sometimes awkward translation is due to the characteristic "Asiatic" rhetorical style, which even struck contemporaries as overly grandiloquent.)

> Caesar exceeded the hopes of [all] those who received [glad tidings] before us, not only surpassing those who had been [benefactors] before him, but not even [leaving any] hope [of

surpassing him] for those who are to come in the future; and (since) the beginning of glad tidings on his account for the world was the [birthday] of the god, and since Asia decreed in Smyrna, when the proconsul was Lucius Volcacius Tullus [ca. 30–28 B.C.] and the secretary was Pap[ion] from Dios Hieron, that the person who found the greatest honors for the god should have a crown, and Paulus Fabius Maximus the proconsul [ca. 10/9 B.C.], as benefactor of the province having been sent from that (god's) right hand and mind together with the other men through whom he bestowed benefits on the province, the size of which benefits no speech would be adequate to relate, has found something unknown until now to the Greeks for the honor of Augustus, that from Augustus' birthday should begin the time for life—for this reason, with good luck and for (our) salvation, it has been decreed by the Greeks in Asia that the New Year's first month shall begin for all the cities on the ninth day before the Kalends of

continued on next page . . .

REFLECTIONS

CHRISTIANS ARE TO INFLUENCE for good by doing good and being "peaceable and considerate... toward all men" (Titus 3:2). There are no groups whatsoever excluded here: rich, poor; powerful, powerless; men, women, children; black, white—all people are to be approached with equal consideration and respect. And Paul knows the secret of what makes this work: "true humility" (3:2), for it is arrogant pride that leads to inconsiderate and prejudicial behavior toward and slander of others. Paul wishes Titus to model this basic Christian humility for the Cretan church and for us.

tianity is not a social revolutionary religion. Its impact on society should always be profound and good. But it does not engage in revolutionary or bellicose tactics, since Christ's kingdom is not of this world (John 18:36).

God our Savior (3:4). Throughout 3:3–8, Paul uses the title "Savior" twice: once of God (3:4) and once of Christ (3:6); he also reiterates that God has "saved" us (3:5). The words, "Savior," "save," and "salvation" occur proportionally more often in the Pastoral Letters than in other New Testament books, so it was obviously on Paul's mind as he himself faced further imprisonment or was already in custody facing trial.[16] But the focus of most of the

... continued

October (September 23), which is the birthday of Augustus.[A-1]

It was a long-standing practice, especially among the Greeks in the East, to ascribe deity or quasi-divine status to mythical heroes, rulers, and others who provided some outstanding benefaction for them (as well as designating them as "savior"; see comments on 1 Tim. 4:10 and Titus 3:4–6). The Romans, on the other hand, were much slower to adopt deification of humans, and only then after they had made a careful linguistic distinction between *deus,* a "god" of the old pantheon, and *divus,* an officially "deified" human. It is a telling distinction of cultures to note the differences between the Greek East (especially Asia Minor) and Rome on this matter of deification of humans. The Greeks had no qualms whatsoever—they deified the emperors with great enthusiasm, ascribing them the title *theos,* "a god."[A-2] The Romans were much more level-headed, perhaps even cynical, about the whole affair. Deification of an emperor or of others was done by an official decree of the Roman Senate in the same way that a person's memory might be

obliterated through *damnatio memoriae* ("Condemnation of one's memory")—an official obliteration of the records of a person's existence.

Still, not all Romans were convinced that the Senate could actually deify someone. The Emperor Vespasian, on his deathbed, is said to have quipped as the end approached: "Oh dear! I must be turning into a god."[A-3] In addition, a bitingly satirical pamphlet thought to have been produced by Seneca right after Claudius's death, turned the "deification" (Gk. *apotheosis*) of Claudius into his "Pumpkinification" (Gk. *apocolocyntosis*)! Such are not the acts of people who take deification seriously.

For Paul the Jew, however, given all the strong emphasis on the oneness of God, which all Jews maintained over against their polytheistic neighbors, it comes as a profound revelation that he ascribes divine identity to Jesus Christ. A fully Trinitarian view is where Paul and the other NT writers clearly lead, as the church's best theologians throughout the centuries have always acknowledged. This is part of what Titus is to "teach ... encourage and rebuke with all authority" (Titus 2:15).

references to the salvation wrought by our Savior is different from what one normally finds in Greco-Roman antiquity, so we should look into this a little more fully.

Both gods and men were commonly called "saviors" in the Greek and Roman world (cf. comments on 1 Tim. 4:10). But the "salvation" referenced by the title "savior" and the "saving" they did to earn it were usually some benefaction or deliverance from danger in this life rather than a salvation from God's wrath and judgment as found in the Bible (e.g., Rom. 5:9; Heb. 9:27; see Apion's letter given in the box below). The Greek and Roman gods did not all act as judges, and the notion of a final judgment was not universally accepted in Greco-Roman religious conceptions. Many of the gods were known as "savior" gods and were given that title (e.g., Artemis Soteira, or "Savioress"), but Zeus in particular was given the title of "savior," and local varieties of Zeus were often known as Zeus Soter ("savior") or Zeus Soterios ("the Saving One").

Avoid foolish controversies (3:9). As he had similarly warned Timothy (see esp. comments on 1 Tim. 1:4), Paul now

---

▶ Savior Gods of the Pagan World

The following papyrus letter from the second century A.D. illustrates both the mention of a god who saved from shipwreck and other items found in ancient letters. The letter comes from an Egyptian who has just joined the Roman navy, writing back to his father on safe arrival at the Roman port of Misenum. (His given name is Apion, but the Romans have given him the new name, "Anthony the Great.") The god who was thought to save this fellow was the Egyptian god Serapis (also spelled "Sarapis"), the consort of Isis and often assimilated to another god, Osiris. The letter reads as follows:

> Apion to Epimachus, his father and lord, very many greetings. Before all else I pray for your health and that you may always be well and prosperous, together with my sister and her daughter and my brother. I thank the lord Serapis that when I was in danger at sea he straightway saved [Gk. *sōzō*] me. On arriving at Misenum I received from Caesar three gold pieces for traveling expenses. And it is well with me. Now I ask you, my lord and father, write me a letter, telling me first of your welfare [Gk. *sōtēria*], secondly of my brother's and sister's, and enabling me thirdly to make obeisance before your handwriting, because you

educated me well and I hope thereby to have quick advancement, if the gods so will. Give many salutations to Capiton and my brother and sister and Serenilla and my friends. I have sent you by Euctemon a portrait of myself. My name is Antonius Maximus, my company the Athenonica. I pray for your health. (B.G.U. 423; LCL trans.)

Men too were frequently called "saviors" in antiquity. Some men took the title on themselves; for example, a certain Milchos saved Nero's life during an assassination conspiracy and thereafter adopted the title "savior" as part of his name.[A-4] But more often the title "savior" was bestowed as a mark of honor by individuals or communities on someone who had done them some signal service. For instance, in an inscription originating from Metropolis, a village near Ephesus, the community declared Sextus Appuleius, proconsul of Asia in 23/22 B.C., as "their own savior" on an honorary statue (*IvE* 3435). Whether Appuleius had aided them in some time of distress or whether he had simply given them some desired privilege or other consideration to earn this title is unknown. In either case, the title denoted that he acted as a patron or benefactor for the community.

REFLECTIONS

NOTE IN THE PARAGRAPH TITUS
3:3–8 that we have the three Persons of the Trinity cooperating in the work of our salvation: the "kindness and love of God our Savior" is the Father (3:4); the Holy Spirit effects the "washing of rebirth and renewal" in our lives (3:5); and it is accomplished by the work of "Jesus Christ our Savior" (3:6). Christianity is a fully Trinitarian religion, focusing on the salvation worked out by all three members of the Trinity (see also Rom. 8:9–11; Heb. 9:14; 1 Peter 1:2 for similar Trinitarian passages). And this "salvation" is not only deliverance from evil in this life, but a gift to us to become heirs of eternal life (Titus 3:7).

warns Titus to avoid "foolish controversies" because they are "unprofitable and useless" (Titus 3:9). People who turn such nonessential issues into the center of our faith are merely being divisive and should be shunned (3:10–11). Note that "genealogies" and "quarrels about the law" point to issues that are not at the center of Christianity's interests.

Final Remarks (3:12–15)

Zenas the lawyer (3:13). Zenas is otherwise unknown. The job title "lawyer" (Gk. *nomikos*) is somewhat analogous to a lawyer of today. A "lawyer" in the Jewish world was a "scribe" who was an expert in the Mosaic law and functioned as a teacher among the Jews (e.g., Matt. 22:35; Luke 10:25 for the same Greek word used of the scribes). In the Roman world, a "lawyer" would often have been an imperial Roman jurist attached to the staff of the emperor or to the staff of a

provincial governor. The most famous Roman jurist is Justinian, whose collections and digest of Roman law in the sixth century A.D. form a major source of our knowledge of earlier Roman jurisprudence. Zenas was probably a Roman jurist in some capacity rather than what we would think of today as a trial lawyer.

Apollos (3:13). Apollos is a colleague of Zenas and is undoubtedly the Alexandrian Jew known from Acts 18–19 and from 1 Corinthians. That he was still active at this later date shows just how sketchy is our knowledge of the exact movements of the apostles and their associates in the earliest church period.

Grace be with you all (3:15). As we find with most letters in antiquity, Paul ends this letter with greetings from others and from himself to Titus and the church in Crete (see the letter of Apion given in a box above). He puts the finishing touches on his greetings with the benediction: "Grace be with you all," showing with the plural reference here that he expects others to profit from the reading of this letter besides Titus himself.

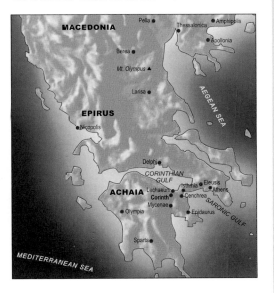

GREECE
Nicopolis was on the western side of Greece in the territory of Epirus.

ANNOTATED BIBLIOGRAPHY

Dibelius, Martin, and Hans Conzelmann. *The Pastoral Epistles*. Hermeneia. Philadelphia: Fortress, 1972.

This critical commentary relies on the typical reasons for rejecting Pauline authorship of the Pastorals, but helpfully gives detailed attention to the historical background and especially connections of the Pastoral Letters with the Hellenistic world.

Fee, Gordon D. *1 and 2 Timothy, Titus*. GNC. San Francisco: Harper & Row, 1984.

This is a concise commentary by a well-regarded NT and text-critical scholar in a popular format.

Guthrie, Donald. *The Pastoral Epistles: An Introduction and Commentary*. TNTC. Leicester and Grand Rapids: InterVarsity and Eerdmans, 1990 (rev. ed.).

A solid though brief commentary by a senior evangelical NT scholar.

Kelly, J. N. D. *A Commentary on the Pastoral Epistles*. TC. London: A. & C. Black, 1963; reprinted Grand Rapids: Baker, 1981.

This brief commentary sticks closely to the text and is marked by Kelly's characteristic sound judgment. Kelly is well versed in original sources and has produced a number of standard works in the later development of early Christianity, which add depth to his commentary.

Kidd, Reggie M. *Wealth and Beneficence in the Pastoral Epistles: A "Bourgeois" Form of Early Christianity?* Atlanta: Scholars, 1990.

This is the best of many such studies on the contemporary social and ethical background of the Pastoral Letters. Kidd surveys an extensive range of background material in this work.

Knight, George W. III. *Commentary on the Pastoral Epistles*. NIGTC. Grand Rapids and Carlisle: Eerdmans and Paternoster, 1992.

This detailed commentary on the Greek text of the Pastorals often gives illuminating historical insights as well as careful attention to the meaning of the grammar and language of the biblical text. The best technical commentary on the Pastorals in print today.

Lau, Andrew L. *Manifest in Flesh: The Epiphany Christology of the Pastoral Epistles*. WUNT 2/86. Tübingen: J. C. B. Mohr (Paul Siebeck), 1996.

This specialized study draws especially helpful connections between the epiphany material in the Pastorals with the OT and other Jewish literature.

Oden, Thomas C. *First and Second Timothy and Titus*. Interpretation. Louisville: John Knox, 1989.

Oden presents an elegant and sane defense of Pauline authorship in this topically arranged "commentary." There are a few rough spots regarding historical background of the biblical world (e.g., sacred prostitution at Ephesus, p. 95), but Oden augments his own helpful insights with a sprinkling of quotations of church fathers and Reformers, which gives the reader a wider view of the interpretation of the Pastoral Letters.

Young, Frances. *The Theology of the Pastoral Letters*. NTT. Cambridge: Cambridge Univ. Press, 1994.

This volume in a promising series spends considerable time trying to establish pseudonymous authorship of the Pastorals. Nevertheless, Young usefully reports on historical backgrounds of the Pastorals in places—for instance, on "teaching and learning in the ancient world" (pp. 79–84), though it seems mostly secondary and derivative.

Main Text Notes

1. See Acts 20:4; Eph. 6:21; Col. 4:7; 2 Tim. 4:12; Titus 3:12.
2. For instance, Clement of Alexandria's *Exhortation to the Greeks*, 1–2.
3. Dio Chrysostom, *Orations* 15.8.
4. Cf. Lacy, *Family*, 108–9.
5. Juvenal, *Satires* 8.
6. Dio Chrysostom, *Orations* 15.5.
7. See Demosthenes' speech *Against Neaira*. For an important recent study related to this issue see Jennifer A. Glancy, "Obstacles to Slaves' Participation in the Corinthian Church," *JBL* 117 (1998): 481–501.
8. Pliny, *Ep.* 3.14.
9. Callimachus, *Hymn to Zeus* 8.
10. The text and translation are from *New Docs* 4 (1987): 151–52; cf. *New Docs* 6 (1992): 18–22 for more on this topic and recent bibliography.
11. The *ius trium liberorum*. See Pliny, *Ep.* 10.2; cf. 2.13; Tacitus, *Ann.* 15.19.
12. Many other examples from Greek and Roman comedy could be adduced. The slave Sceparnio is a good instance from the Roman comic play *The Rope* (*Rudens*) by Plautus (ca. 211 B.C.).
13. E.g., Martin Dibelius and Hans Conzelmann, *The Pastoral Epistles* (Hermeneia; Philadelphia: Fortress, 1972), 143.
14. *Romans* 3.3; *Polycarp* 8.3; cf. *Smyrnaeans* 1.1 (and one ms. at 10.1); *Romans* 6.3; *Magnesians* 6.1; cf. John 1:1.
15. Pliny, *Ep.* 10.96.
16. See W. Foerster, "σῴζω," *TDNT*, 7:965–1024.

Sidebar and Chart Notes

A-1. Translation by Robert K. Sherk, *Rome and the Greek East to the Death of Augustus* (Cambridge: Cambridge Univ. Press, 1984), 125–26.
A-2. See S. R. F. Price, *Rituals and Power: The Roman Imperial Cult in Asia Minor* (Cambridge: Cambridge Univ. Press, 1984).
A-3. Suetonius, *Vespasian* 23.
A-4. Tacitus, *Ann.* 15.71.3.

PHILEMON

by S. M. Baugh

The Setting of Philemon

Philemon is the briefest of Paul's letters, consisting of only twenty-five verses. It is unlike Paul's other correspondence in that it is a private letter to an individual and to a house church. The closest equivalent is the letter to Titus, though even that has more general instructions for the benefit of others. There is no real objection to the genuineness of Pauline authorship, and the letter itself has been accepted as canonical from the earliest period, although it was not often cited in early Christian literature. The private nature of the subject matter makes the lack of citation of Philemon understandable.

A few scholars believe that Archippus (v. 2) was the addressee and owner of Onesimus, but this has not seemed likely to most. Philemon, by being addressed first in verse 1, is evidently the addressee and owner of Onesimus, and it was in his house that the church met (v. 2). An early tradition held that Apphia was the wife of Philemon and that Archippus was their son. This is a natural reading of verse 2,

COLOSSE
The unexcavated tel.

> ▶ **Philemon**
> # IMPORTANT FACTS:
>
> - ■ **AUTHOR:** The apostle Paul.
> - ■ **DATE:** About A.D. 60/61 (during Paul's first Roman imprisonment).
> - ■ **VENUES:** Paul is probably in prison in Rome writing to Philemon at Colosse.
> - ■ **OCCASION:**
>   - To reconcile Philemon with his slave, Onesimus.
>   - To tell of Paul's news to his fellow workers and to the church in Philemon's house.

but it cannot be substantiated beyond this. Because of connections between Philemon and the situation and people mentioned in Paul's letter to the Colossians, it is possible that Philemon was a resident of Colosse and that both Philemon and Colossians were written at roughly the same time. Because of this, commentaries on Philemon are often included with ones on the book of Colossians.[1]

The Occasion of Philemon

Paul was in prison when he wrote to Philemon (vv. 1 and 9); however, he hoped to be released and to stay with Philemon in the near future (see comments on v. 22). The occasion for this letter was the return of the slave Onesimus to his master; this is obvious enough in the letter. However, how the slave Onesimus of Colosse fell in with Paul in custody in Rome—halfway across the Mediterranean—is a problem. Some have proposed that Onesimus was sent to Paul by Philemon, then he somehow got into trouble with his master and needed restoring. But the letter seems more likely to suggest that Onesimus is a runaway slave. But if Onesimus were a runaway, why would he link up with Paul? It appears from verse 10 that Onesimus was not a

COLOSSE AND EPHESUS

Colosse was about 100 miles due east of Ephesus.

▼

Christian when he first met Paul. But how could Onesimus come across Paul when he was in custody? Was Onesimus captured by the Roman authorities as a runaway? If that were the case, how could he, a prisoner, link up with Paul who was also in custody? All these issues have led most scholars to say that "somehow" Onesimus came into contact with Paul in Rome.

A recent suggestion, however, provides a compelling solution to the problem of Onesimus's contact with Paul.[2] Onesimus did not just run away from Philemon, but he ran away *to Paul* in order to secure Paul's aid in restoring him to his master's good graces for some reason. When a slave fell into his master's extreme disfavor, it could go very badly for him. In such cases, the slave had nothing but dismal prospects. In some cases they ran to one of their master's friends to beg his intercession (see comments below for examples). This scenario well explains how Onesimus could have met up with Paul: He sought him out. It also explains why Paul writes to secure Philemon's reconciliation with Onesimus and why Paul, not the Roman authorities, was sending Onesimus back to Philemon if he were a runaway. This will be the background assumed in my comments below.

Salutation and Letter Opening (1–3)

Paul does not open this letter with the usual identification of his apostolic office and summary of some aspects of the gospel. Instead, we have a brief identification of Paul as "a prisoner of Christ Jesus" (v. 1; cf. v. 9; i.e., a prisoner *for the sake of* Christ) and of "Timothy our brother," who was with Paul at this time. Next comes the identification of the recipients of the letter (v. 2) and a bene-

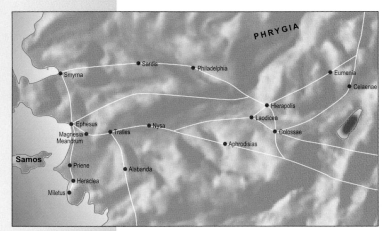

diction in the name of God the Father and of Jesus Christ (v. 3).

The letter is addressed to Philemon, "our dear friend and fellow worker" (v. 1; cf. v. 24 for other "fellow workers"). Paul and Philemon had developed a close association earlier, possibly while Paul was ministering in Ephesus (Acts 19). According to Colossians 4:9, Onesimus was from Colosse, so presumably his master Philemon was as well. Colosse lay about a hundred miles inland from Ephesus, connected by a route that went up the Maeander River valley and then passed through Laodicea to Colosse.

To Apphia our sister, to Archippus our fellow soldier (2). Early tradition and some today hold that Apphia was the wife of Philemon (known only from v. 2), which is possible but not certain. Some also believe that Archippus (Gk. "Commander of the horse") was the son of Philemon and Apphia, which is also possible. At the close of his instructions to the Colossian church, Paul writes: "Tell Archippus: 'See to it that you complete the work you have received in the Lord'" (Col. 4:17). It is possible that Archippus was ministering in Colosse and was for this reason Paul's "fellow soldier." If he were Philemon's son, it serves as further confirmation that this family and the church in their house were in Colosse.

And to the church that meets in your home (2). Paul also addresses the church meeting in Philemon's home (cf. Rom. 16:5; Col. 4:15). It is only natural that the church would need a place of meeting, and the home of a benefactor with its typical open inner courtyard would have supplied a suitable location.[3] Sometimes gatherings in these courtyards were made more pleasant through the erection of large and richly worked awnings covering the whole area—the sort of awnings that Paul himself may have dealt with in his capacity as a "tentmaker."[4]

Commendation of Philemon (4–7)

Your love has given me great joy and encouragement (7). Philemon has been active in sharing his faith by demonstrations of love for and service to his fellow Christians (vv. 5–7). Paul's praise for Philemon's service here is not forced flattery, but a sincere expression of his appreciation for the man's worthy service to Christ. This section of the letter shows that Paul is not domineering or demanding in his relations to Philemon, but truly considers him a friend worthy of his respect and admiration as a Christian brother who is also serving the Lord.

Intercession for Onesimus (8–22)

In Christ I could be bold and order you to do what you ought to do (8). To modern readers, this line may seem overbold, perhaps even threatening. However, to the ancient reader, this shows the complex interactions at work here. Paul may be "in chains" (v. 13) and Philemon may be his "dear friend" (v. 1)—perhaps even a wealthy and important friend—but Paul the apostle is his superior in the

SLAVE DOCUMENT

A first-century papyrus document recording the purchase of two slaves.

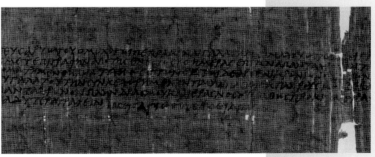

Lord. Paul does not bludgeon Philemon with this fact—one does not do that—but he does make it clear that what he is offering Philemon is the opportunity to obey him in this matter without losing face. Philemon's "obedience" (v. 21) to Paul can take the form of a spontaneous favor (v. 14), where he can "do even more than I ask" (v. 21).

Paul—an old man and now also a prisoner of Christ Jesus (9). As in verse 1, Paul says that he is "a prisoner of Christ Jesus." It was for the sake of Christ that he was "in chains for the gospel" (v. 13; cf. v. 23). Similarly, the early second-century Christian bishop Ignatius of Antioch went to Rome for his martyrdom "in bondage in Christ Jesus," chained between a rough troop of soldiers.[5] Paul's Roman imprisonment was a rough, frustrating period for him, though not entirely unfruitful for the gospel since Onesimus "became my son while I was in chains" (v. 10; cf. Acts 28). Paul made converts to Christ even in custody awaiting his trial.[6]

▶ Patronage in the Roman World

The letters of the younger Pliny are particularly helpful in showing patronage at work in the Roman world. Every day, a Roman noble would attend to the morning visit of his "clients," in whose troubles and concerns he would intercede. If a man wished to find a husband for his daughter, his patron would recommend and arrange a suitable match.[A-1] He might also supply the girl with a proper dowry.[A-2] If a man wished to rise in station and enter the rank (*ordo*) of the "knights" (*equites*), his patron would supply the requisite funds.[A-3] A patron would intercede in land purchase.[A-4] A highly placed patron could even ask for grant of civil, religious, or military offices for his "friends" or other benefits, such as grant of citizenship for his clients, which included his freedmen.[A-5] This system was a code of honor and debt under the name of "friendship" (Latin, *amicitia*): "For, according to the code of friendship, the one who takes the initiative puts the other in his debt and owes no more until he is repaid."[A-6] A patron was not optional in such a world: "No one can make a start, however outstanding his abilities, if he lacks scope and opportunity *and a patron to support him.*"[A-7] And patronage was not confined to the interaction of individuals. Whole towns and villages were under the patronage of certain nobles, whose citizens could count on favors and assistance provided they showed the proper honors to their "godfather."[A-8]

Paul's subtle maneuvers with Philemon in verses 8–22 are only understood against the background of the ancient patronage system, which worked on many different levels of Greco-Roman society (see comments in the accompanying box).[A-9] As the owner and head of his household, Philemon was in every way the patron of Onesimus. For Paul to meddle in this family relationship—for slaves were members of the family—took utmost delicacy and a twofold claim. (1) Paul must either be Philemon's superior and patron or, if they were roughly equals, Philemon must owe him a debt of friendship, which Paul could claim as needing repayment in the matter at hand. This is the reason why Paul subtly suggests that Philemon owes him, as it were, even his very self (v. 19). Eternal life is a debt of great importance indeed! (2) Paul must establish that he has some claim of patronage on the slave Onesimus. It was the duty of a patron to pay the debts of members of his household, yet Paul intercedes for Onesimus directly, when he says: "If he has done you any wrong or owes you anything, charge it to me. . . . I will pay it back" (vv. 18–19). This is unmistakably the act of a patron, and it makes Paul's intercession for Onesimus all the more effective; yet would not have given offense to Philemon, who perfectly understood and accepted Paul's points.

▶ **Manumission and Paul**

Ancient slavery strikes the modern reader as a cruel institution. Indeed, it sometimes could be very cruel. Why then did not Paul speak out against it, or why did he not simply order Philemon to manumit Onesimus instead of sending him back? The answer involves knowing first that manumission of a slave often did not change his situation much. He simply became a freedman, though he might still remain in the same situation within his former master's household—only his legal status having changed. The Greco-Roman world was very much *family-oriented*, and for a slave to be manumitted and sent out of the household would actually be potentially greatly disadvantageous. Without a family, he would have no immediate social, legal, or occupational connections. Nevertheless, F. F. Bruce was correct to say that the letter to Philemon "brings us into an atmosphere in which the institution [of slavery] could only wilt and die."[A-10] And in the letter of Philemon, Paul applied what he preached: in Christ there is neither slave nor free (Gal. 3:28).

My son Onesimus (10). "Onesimus" means "profitable or "beneficial" in Greek and is a common slave name. Paul comes close to punning on this name in verse 11, saying that though Onesimus was formerly "useless" to Philemon, now he was "useful" (Gk. *euchrēston*).[7] Paul does carry on the pun, however, when he says that he wishes Philemon to accede to his wishes, in order that "I may have some *benefit* from you" (v. 20; emphasis added). The Greek verb form for "to have benefit" used in verse 20 is etymologically related to the name "Onesimus."

Paul mentioned Onesimus in Colossians 4:9 as "our faithful and dear brother, who is one of you"; thus we assume that Onesimus—and therefore Philemon—lived in Colosse. Where Onesimus came from originally is impossible to tell. He could have been a "house-born" slave, born to one of Philemon's slaves and therefore an indentured member of the household. Or he could have been purchased from outside the household, a foundling infant raised into slavery perhaps.[8]

As I noted in the introduction, it seems most likely that Onesimus intentionally ran away from Philemon and ran *to* Paul in order to seek his intercession on his behalf with Philemon over some quarrel between the master and slave. This letter is Paul's intercession. We know of other such cases (see accompanying box for one). A master vexed with a slave might put him to death in extreme cases (though this meant a significant loss of property, for a slave was regarded as property).[9] More commonly, the slave would be beaten, demoted to menial jobs, or sent away to hard labor on the family farm, in a mill, or in some other brutally arduous occupation. Faced with such a prospect, Onesimus, who undoubtedly knew of Philemon's high regard for Paul, fled to him and found him in Rome. But in the course of events, Onesimus became a Christian (v. 10), and therefore Paul was sending Onesimus back to Philemon (v. 12) as his brother in Christ (v. 16) as well as a beloved helper to Paul, who served in Philemon's absence at his side (vv. 12–13, 16).

I, Paul, am writing this with my own hand (19). Paul adds a concluding note in his own hand in other letters.[10] Paul probably dictated his letters, but perhaps he subscribed his own greetings as an authentication of the letter. Philemon, on the other hand, was probably wholly written by Paul.[11]

Prepare a guest room for me (22). The way Paul asks Philemon to "prepare" a room for him (v. 22) means something more like, "hold a room in readiness for me." Paul did not know when he would be released, and he asks Philemon to be prepared for some distant eventuality.

Closing and Greetings (23–25)

Paul closes his letter with the greetings of his companions: Epaphras, Mark, Aristarchus, Demas, and Luke. These men were his "fellow workers," as was Philemon himself (v. 1). The letter concludes with an apostolic blessing in the name of the Lord Jesus Christ.

▶ Intercession for a Slave

Cassius Dio provides an instructive description of a man's intercession with his friend on behalf of a slave. The intercessor is the Emperor Augustus and the slave owner is the famously cruel Vedius Pollio, who kept a pool filled with man-eating eels into which he would throw errant slaves. Dio describes the incident like this:

> Once, when he [Vedius Pollio] was entertaining Augustus, his cup-bearer broke a crystal goblet. Thereupon Pollio, paying no attention to his guest, ordered the slave to be thrown to the eels. The boy fell on his knees before Augustus and implored his protection, and the emperor at first tried to persuade Pollio not to commit so appalling an action. When Pollio paid no heed, Augustus said, "Bring all your other drinking vessels like this one, or any others of value that you possess for me to use." When these were brought, he ordered them to be smashed. Pollio was naturally vexed at the sight; but since he could no longer be angry about the one goblet in view of the multitude of others that had been destroyed, and could not punish his servant for an act which Augustus had repeated, he restrained himself and said nothing.[A-11]

ANNOTATED BIBLIOGRAPHY

Bruce, F. F. *The Epistles to the Colossians, to Philemon, and to the Ephesians.* NICNT. Grand Rapids: Eerdmans, 1984.

    Bruce had a wide knowledge of the ancient world and applies it in all his commentaries with great benefit and soundness.

Lightfoot, J. B. *Saint Paul's Epistles to the Colossians and to Philemon.* London and New York: Macmillan, 1890.

    Even though it is dated, Lightfoot's commentary is still profitable, full of rich insights into the ancient world and into biblical and early patristic texts.

O'Brien, Peter T. *Colossians, Philemon.* WBC. Waco: Word, 1982.

    O'Brien's works are always scholarly and reliable. His comments on Philemon are no exception.

Wright, N. T. *The Epistles of Paul to the Colossians and to Philemon.* TNTC. Grand Rapids: Eerdmans, 1986.

    This commentary series always provides useful material. Wright's comments are brief but helpful.

Main Text Notes

1. For general introduction see D. A. Carson, Douglas J. Moo and Leon Morris, *An Introduction to the New Testament* (Grand Rapids: Zondervan, 1992), 387–90.

2. The original suggestion is that of Peter Lampe, "Keine 'Sklavenflucht' des Onesimus," *ZNW* 76 (1985): 135–37; summarized and expanded in B. M. Rapske, "The Prisoner Paul in the Eyes of Onesimus," *NTS* 37 (1991): 187–203 and S. Scott Bartchy, "Philemon, Epistle To," *ABD*, 5:305–9; cf. *New Docs* 8 (1998): 1–46.

3. Cf. Robert J. Banks, *Paul's Idea of Community: The Early House Churches in Their Cultural Setting* (Peabody, Mass.: Hendrikson, 1994); Bradley Blue, "Acts and the House Church," in *The Book of Acts in Its Graeco-Roman Setting* (D. W. J. Gill and C. Gempf, eds.; Grand Rapids and Carlisle: Eerdmans and Paternoster, 1994), 119–222.

4. See Peter Lampe, "Paulus—Zeltmacher," *BZ* 31 (1987): 256–61; Steven M. Baugh, "Paul and Ephesus: The Apostle Among His Contemporaries" (Ph.D. diss.; Irvine, Calif.: Univ. of California, 1990), 101–19.

5. Ignatius, *Romans* 1.1. 5.1; cf. *Philadelphians* 5.1–2.

6. See the full treatment of Brian Rapske, *The Book of Acts and Paul in Roman Custody* (Grand Rapids and Carlisle: Eerdmans and Paternoster, 1994); cf. Harry W. Tajra, *The Trial of St. Paul* (WUNT 35; Tübingen: J. C. B. Mohr, 1989).

7. Cf. Plato, *Republic* 411A; Shepherd of Hermas, *Vision* 3.6.7; *Mandata* 5.6.6 for other contrasts between useful and useless.

8. "Foundlings" were infants rejected by their parents at birth and left somewhere to die, who were then picked up and raised by someone else. Often foundlings became the slaves of their finders, who might make a business of finding and raising children into slavery (as we know from extant papyrus nursing contracts from Egypt). For a handy collection of documents see Thomas Wiedemann, *Greek and Roman Slavery* (Baltimore and London: Johns Hopkins Univ. Press, 1981).

9. Cf. Martin Hengel, *Crucifixion* (Philadelphia: Fortress, 1977), 51–63 for crucifixion as *servile supplicium*, "the slaves' punishment."

10. 1 Cor. 16:21; Gal. 6:11; Col. 4:18.

11. Cf. E. R. Richards, *The Secretary in the Letters of Paul* (WUNT 2/42; Tübingen: J. C. B. Mohr [Paul Siebeck], 1991).

Sidebar and Chart Notes

A-1. Pliny, *Ep.* 1.13.

A-2. Ibid., 2.4; 6.32.

A-3. Ibid., 1.19.

A-4. Ibid., 1.24.

A-5. Ibid., 2.9, 13; 3.2, 8; 4.4, 17; 6.25; 10.12; cf. 10.13; 10.6–7, 10–11.

A-6. Ibid., 7.31.

A-7. Cf. A. N. Sherwin-White, *The Letters of Pliny: A Historical and Social Commentary* (Oxford: Clarendon, 1966), ad loc; Pliny, *Ep.* 6.23 (emphasis added).

A-8. E.g., Pliny, *Ep.* 3.4; 4.1.

A-9. Cf. Richard P. Saller, *Personal Patronage under the Early Empire* (Cambridge: Cambridge Univ. Press, 1982).

A-10. F. F. Bruce, *Paul: Apostle of the Heart Set Free* (Exeter and Grand Rapids: Paternoster and Eerdmans, 1977), 401.

A-11. Cassius Dio, *Roman History* 54.23, Penguin trans.

CREDITS FOR PHOTOS AND MAPS